Crossroads of the Conflict
Defining Hours for the Blue and Gray

A Guide to the Monuments of Gettysburg

By
Donald W. McLaughlin

Outskirts Press, Inc.
Denver, Colorado

Crossroads of the Conflict
Defining Hours for the Blue and Gray: A Guide to the Monuments of Gettysburg
All Rights Reserved.
Copyright © 1986 Donald W. McLaughlin
First Printing: June 2008
V1.0

Cover photo: by Judith McLaughlin
Cover design: by Rick Nadeau

Outskirts Press, Inc.
http://www.outskirtspress.com

Outskirts Press and the "OP" logo are trademarks belonging to Outskirts Press, Inc.

For information address, Delanson Publishing, PO Box 304, Delanson, NY 12053

ISBN: 978-1-4327-2287-6

PRINTED IN THE UNITED STATES OF AMERICA

*I dedicate this book to
the love of my life, my wife,
Shirley ("Mickey")
who trekked through the woods, fields, and marshes
with me to document the history of the
Battle of Gettysburg*

*and to all the persons who
gave their lives for our country*

TABLE OF CONTENTS

TABLE OF CONTENTS (continued)

Comments and Acknowledgements

This book is a heartfelt family effort that will place our husband, father and grandfather in our hearts permanently and recognize his contribution to the greatest battle of the Civil War. This book is a culmination of work by many individuals who saw it through to completion. First of course was Donald W. McLaughlin our father and grandfather. He completed the research, fieldwork and writing of this book. He passed away in 2000 leaving his much-loved wife of 52 years Shirley, "Mickey" or "Mike", as her friends, and family know her. He also left seven adult children, Mary Grace, Judith, James Robert, Stephen, Kathleen, Jon Patrick and Kevin and his grandchildren.

Our Dad was an inspirational man to all of us. We spent the vacations of our youth traveling around locating the history of the areas in which we lived. As a family of nine we followed the railroads and the battlefields of the Northeast, which were his passion. Mom, of course, was always by his side trudging through the forest, swamps and fields looking for anything from railroad spikes to Revolutionary War bullets or Civil War canon balls. She was the devoted wife and follower of Dad's dreams and is one of the main reasons we have published this book, so that she will have a copy for her memories.

Over the years we all visited our parents in Gettysburg. During these family moments, Dad's maps and charts would mysteriously appear about the battle and we would have a history lesson. After a lecture about the Battlefield, we would all climb into his 10-passenger van and drive the Park's beautiful fields. Dad would describe the battle to us as we toured the roads and pathways of the Park.

Gettysburg is unlike any place on earth. It is a place of serenity with a spirituality that is mysteriously inexplicably tied to the soil, trees, fences and fields. It has a panoramic landscape that takes you over and calls to you even when you are not there. It is a place you must go back to because you feel or sense the lost and lonely souls of the Civil War dead. The purity of the light, contrasted with the darkness, of that battle changes you forever as you drive through its consecrated, hallowed roadways and paths. It is an area that our Dad missed from the moment he retired and kept close to his heart from that time forward. It is a place that lives within us because he recounted its story so often.

This book was a joint effort, but Mary ("B") our oldest sister was the true spirit behind the book. She kept the dream alive for the past 10 years ensuring that the book was scanned, typed and formatted in the proper manner. She spent endless months and years' making sure the book was of the quality that Dad would expect. Without her, Dad's words written on an old typewriter and his hand-drawn maps on onionskin paper would not be available for print. Kathleen, the reader and historian for the project, knew Dad's work and admired it. She also knew, along with her children Stephen, Jenny, Scott and Matt, the Battlefield from her frequent trips to Pennsylvania when the children were young. Kath and the kids toured the Battlefield each and every visit to Gettysburg with "Pop-Pop". Scotty could recite the story of Little Round Top and the Slaughter Pen from the time he was 4 or 5 years old, with Jenny chiming in to correct him as needed. Scott, Matt and Stephen serve in the military today and remember their Grandfather with such fondness and love, he would be so proud if them. Stephen, our brother, along with his son Stevie, has made numerous trips to Gettysburg to photograph, walk the battlefield and meet the guides who are still there and remember our Dad. He prepared photos and information for "B" to synthesize into the book. He has been the loudest supporter, the *"nuisance"* who kept the fires burning within each of us, insisting that this book be published. Jim, the eldest son, has encouraged and pushed to see the book in print and has helped with the technical part of "things" with computers, website design, etc. Patrick was the first to recommend that we self-publish this work and remained supportive and encouraging as we proceeded. Patrick's children, Jacob, Isaac and Bethany along with Stevie have never met their grandfather but have heard of him in family legends from all of us. Kevin our brother is the Sgt., the soldier, and he has memorialized our father in his devote and unswerving dedication to this country in his role as a member of the US military for nearly 20 years. He is the one who walked the fields with Dad as a 19-20 year old when he lived in Gettysburg, just before he enlisted. He is a veteran of the Gulf War, Bosnia and the Iraq War and we salute him. Finally I am Judith; I have inherited my father's deep love of history and writing. He encouraged me in my own pursuits. My children, Erin the oldest grandchild who, of the grandchildren had "Grapaw" the longest in her life, Ryan and Briana who loved and admired their "Pee Paw", all remember the Battlefield best of all with their four cousins. The cousins knew every nook and cranny of its 6,000 acres and taught my children all they knew. Finally, I must thank my husband Dan who encouraged and supported each endeavor as we proceeded through this publishing process.

We are grateful to be able to publish this book about a Battle that so touched our Dad's life. Not everyone can say that they became the history they loved, but our Dad did by moving to Gettysburg. He knew the hills, valleys and fields integrally as if they were old friends. He was able to make history come alive for us as children and then again as adults. That story telling continues with our children today. From these early experiences many of us are devote, amateur historians in various fields of study. He passed along his passion and his intense love of history, literature and travel to his children and grandchildren

Additionally, we would like to thank Rick Nadeau for his technical graphic abilities and his supportive and on-going friendship in this process. Without his graphic skills we would not have been able to publish this book. Elayne Ryba is "B"'s friend and cheerleader and Grace Salerno who was instrumental with her proofing and fixing of the original scanned documents. We thank Eric Campbell, Gettysburg Battlefield Park Ranger and all the Battlefield guides who knew our Dad during his time in Gettysburg. We would like to thank the late John Andrews, Supervisor of the Battlefield Guides, during Dad's tenure as a guide, for his encouragement and support of Dad's work and Col. John C. Slaughter, Medical Corps United States Army (retired) for his support and enthusiasm for getting the Book published. We would like to thank our Mom for her encouragement and love. And our Dad, we miss him.

Respectfully,

Judith McLaughlin
November 2007

FORWARD

The monuments, markers and tablets on the Battlefield of Gettysburg were erected by the men who fought there; by the States they came from; by the United States Government; the Gettysburg Battlefield Memorial Association; Veterans; other patriotic organizations; and by individuals interested in the battle and its participants.

The inscriptions on these memorials relate the gist (but not the whole story) of what happened at Gettysburg between June 30th and July 4th, 1863, in this decisive battle of the American Civil War. In 1867, a group of survivors of the 1st Minnesota Infantry Regiment, gathered in the Gettysburg Military Cemetery and dedicated a monument to the memory of their comrades who had fallen in the Battle of Gettysburg four years before. It was the first monument erected on the Gettysburg Battlefield. One hundred eighteen years later on October 25, 1985, a monument was dedicated to the memory of the 26th North Carolina Infantry Regiment, in the west end of Reynolds Woods where they had fought the Iron Brigade of the Army Of The Potomac. Between these two dates more than 1300 monuments, markers, tablets and other memorials have been erected on the Gettysburg Battlefield.

The purpose of this compilation is to put on paper the inscriptions on these structures, which describe what happened at Gettysburg in 1863, so that they can be used for research, reference or just plain interesting reading for anyone interested in the Battle of Gettysburg. However, many of the monument inscriptions include more than Gettysburg information-such as the unit's entire Civil War history or its total casualties for the entire war or the list of battles in which it fought, etc. This book does not include that type of information; it includes only that part of the monument's inscription, which pertains to the Battle Of Gettysburg.

A large number of maps and an index have been included so that any structure, which is listed in the text, can be located on the battlefield. The index refers the reader to the page where the monument and its inscription are listed. A masthead map on that page shows the monument's location on the battlefield. Also, more than 50 full-page maps are included, each covering a larger area than the "masthead" maps. All maps have been hand drawn by D.W. McLaughlin and are not to scale — they show the approximate location of monuments on the battlefield and their relationship to one another.

D.W. McLaughlin
October 1998

Crossroads of the Conflict
Defining Hours for the Blue and Gray

A Guide to the Monuments of Gettysburg

Introduction

The story of the Gettysburg Battlefield is depicted on over 1,300 monuments/markers and 400 cannons that have been placed on the Battlefield throughout the past 140 years. The Gettysburg National Military Park currently encompasses 6,000 acres and is the site of one of the most visited battlefields in the United States. It is located in south central Pennsylvania, 50 miles northwest of Baltimore, Maryland. The Battle of Gettysburg was the largest and northernmost battle fought during the Civil War. It was waged in the first three days of July 1863. This Battle was a critical turning point, *or the crossroads,* in the Civil War, which determined the future of the United States of America. The Battle successfully ended the invasion of the North by the Confederate Army, led by General Robert E. Lee. The Battle of Gettysburg was the bloodiest single battle of the Civil War, resulting in the death, wounding or capture of 51,000 soldiers.

Crossroads of the Conflict: The Defining Hours for the Blue and Gray, offers the reader important information about the Battlefield that is not contained in a single volume prior to the release of this work. This book provides the factual recordings of the inscriptions on the monuments of the Battlefield at Gettysburg. These are the monuments that stand as a symbol to American's struggle to survive as a nation. Through this book the words on the monuments come to life as a lasting memorial to those who died during this conflict.

Crossroads of the Conflict is unique. It is a chronological study of the monuments in the order in which the events took place as the battle progressed. This book can be used to provide the reader with a hands-on reference while touring the Battlefield by bus, car or on foot. It also serves to offer the reader an historical account of the significance of each monument, brigade marker and flank marker (left and right) on the battlegrounds. In addition, the author has included numerous hand-drawn maps throughout the book to assist the reader in understanding how the Battle, itself, unfolded.

The author, Donald W. McLaughlin, often with his wife, Shirley, painstakingly walked the Battlefield recording and documenting the strategic maneuvers of the troops throughout the 3 days of the battles. Through his comprehensive research McLaughlin offers unusual information based on his field exploration. He also notes many of the hourly changes of troops as the battle progressed.

From his home base in upstate New York, the author traveled regularly to the Gettysburg Battlefield. For a number of years he visited and chronicled the Battlefield and eventually decided to relocate to Gettysburg. McLaughlin was enamored with the battlefield and spent hours each day walking the fields, forests and hills searching for monuments that hadn't been seen in decades. Often finding monuments that were not recorded, he meticulously researched and documented his discoveries, noting them in extensive journals. Ultimately he was determined to locate and document every marker and monument on the battlefield. The Battle took place on over 20,000 acres and included skirmishes within the rural town of Gettysburg. McLaughlin has thoroughly recorded and researched every known, and many unknown, markers of the battle in the 6,000 acres of the current Park.

This work, based on nearly 10 years of research, provides McLaughlin's journals and recordings to the public. The book was used by McLaughlin to provide distinctive tours of the Battlefield in his years as a Licensed Battlefield Guide from 1983 until his retirement in 1997. This book will now be available in print for the public. What now exists is a record of Gettysburg monuments, unlike any other, for future generations to benefit from and enjoy.

GENERAL INFORMATION

Bronze tablets mounted on large granite blocks or marble bases, describe the part played in the Battle of Gettysburg by each Army, Corps, Division and Brigade (both Union and Confederate), and each Confederate Artillery Battalion. These tablets were erected by the Gettysburg Battlefield Memorial Association in the early 1900's.

Inscriptions on monuments describe the part played by most Union Regiments and Artillery Batteries, and by three Confederate Regiments These regimental or battery monuments were, for the most part, paid for by the home states of the regiments or batteries and were erected beginning in the 1880's. Since United States Regular Army Regiments and Artillery Batteries had no home state, the Federal Government erected a bronze tablet for each Regular Regiment or Battery, similar in appearance to those described above. These tablets were erected after the turn of the (twentieth) century.

Black iron tablets describe the part played by all Confederate Artillery Batteries. On the battlefield, this type of tablet is also used to describe a 2nd position of a Confederate Brigade or Union Artillery Battery. Off the battlefield, **black iron itinerary tablets**, often many miles away, describe the movements of the Armies as they maneuvered toward the battlefield and away from it.

Most of these tablets and monuments are visible from the 30 miles of road in Gettysburg National Military Park.

The **bronze tablets** and most of the **iron tablets** have a standard design. The unit is identified at the top of the tablet, the commander's name is listed and its movements during the battle are described in chronological order. In most cases the information on the tablet concludes with the unit's casualties at the bottom of the tablet. In this book, the inscription has been copied without change excepting that the unit's name stands out on the left margin of the page for clearer identification.

Inscriptions on monuments usually describe a regiment's movements chronologically, but unlike the tablets they had no standard design. The monuments are of many shapes and sizes and the inscriptions frequently were adapted to fit the shape of the monuments. Hence, some inscriptions are in a circle or diamond or other shape. The dates may be in the middle of the inscription. The commander's name and the regiment's casualties may or may not be listed. In this book, the inscriptions are made consistant in format with those of the tablets by straight typing across the page. The unit is identified in the left margin, and the commander's name, if not on the monument, is added at the top of the text. If an artillery battery monument does not list the number and type (types) of guns, this information is added after the commander's name. Casualties, if not listed, are added at the end of the text. No change is made in the inscription other than these.

No interpretation of the inscription is made.

If casualty figures are listed in or with the monument inscription, those same figures are included in this text. If, however, the monument inscription does not include casualties, the figures which are added to the text are those of Colonel W. F. Fox from his study of casualties as listed on pages 139-156 (Union) and Pages 176-187 (Confederate) in Volume 1 of the 3 Volume *New York At Gettysburg*. These figures are identified in this text by (NY@Gbg) which follows the casualty figures.

Some inscriptions have little or no punctuation as they appear on the monument or tablet. In some cases this makes the message very difficult to understand. Therefore, an occasional comma or semi-colon has been added in an attempt to make the inscription more understandable.

Any wording in parenthesis in combination with the word "Note:" is wording which is not on the monument. It has been added to call attention to something pertaining to the unit which would not other wise be apparent in the inscription. Example (Note: Refer to Page 142 for this regiment's other monument.)

IDENTIFICATION OF COMBAT UNITS

The following information describes how this book has been written:

INFANTRY REGIMENTS

On page 1 in this book, notice the initials in the left margin

149ᵗʰ Pa
2-3-1*
This identifies the 149th Pennsylvania Volunteer Infantry Regiment of the 2nd Brigade of the 3rd Division of the 1st Corps of the Union Army of The Potomac. This is how the data appears on the monument but, by abbreviating it in the left margin, it stands out for easier identification. To the right of the abbreviation on page 1 is the regiment's name "1st Regiment Bucktail Brigade". (Not all regiments have names but this one does.) On the next line is the commander's name. Note that Lieutenant Colonel Dwight was replaced by Captain Glenn. Col. Dwight was wounded and Capt. Glenn was the senior surviving officer of the regiment. The next lines describe the movements of the 149th PA during the three days of the battle. The last lines list the 149th PA's casualties during the three days as they are listed on the monument. If the casualty figures had been followed by the symbol (NY@Gbg) as in the case of the 19th Indiana on page 4, that would mean that the casualties were not listed on the monument but, rather had been obtained from *New York At Gettysburg* as explained on page iv.

A regular Army Regiment would have a bronze tablet instead of a monument and would be identified as in the margin to the left. The initials identify the 7th United States Regular Army Infantry Regiment of the 2nd Brigade of the 2nd Division of the 5th Corps.

ARTILLERY BATTERIES

The equivalent of the regiment in the Artillery is the Battery. On Page 5 notice the abbreviation in the left margin:

Battery B
1ˢᵗ Pa*
1ˢᵗ Corps
Artillery
 Brigade
Again, note the commander's name. There were four- 3 inch rifle guns in the battery. It fought at this location on July 1st only, but the asterisk tells you to check the index for the battery's other position or positions. The index lists Battery B-1st Pa under "Pennsylvania" or it is cross indexed under "Army of the Potomac, Battery Markers" for Pages 5, 64 and 116. Regular Army Batteries are identified as shown to the left. Refer to page 1 for example.

CAVALRY REGIMENTS

Cavalry Regiments are identified on their monuments like Infantry Regiments excepting that many of the inscriptions reverse the "Brigade-Division-Corps" arrangement and instead list it as "Corps-Division-Brigade". On page 6, for example, the

8ᵗʰ NY
Cavalry
C-1-1

is identified in the left margin as "C-1-1" meaning it is listed on the monument as "Cavalry Corps, 1st Division, 1st Brigade. Other than this difference, the Cavalry regimental monument inscriptions are typed in this book in the same format as are the Infantry monument inscriptions.

BRIGADES

Refer to Page 2:

2-3-1
in the left margin identifies the 2nd Brigade of the 3rd Division of the 1st Corps, which the men preferred to call "The Bucktail Brigade". This is not a monument but is a bronze tablet mounted on a marble base as described on Page D. The Brigade was composed of three Pennsylvania Regiments, the 143rd, 149th and 150th. Note that Col. Stone who was wounded, was replaced by Col. Wister of the 150th Pa Infantry, who was senior Regimental

Commander (note Col. Wister's name as commander of the 150th Pa at the bottom of Page 2. When he moved up to take command of the Brigade, he was replaced by his 2nd in command, Lt. Col. Huidekoper, who was later wounded and replaced by Capt. Widdis who was probably the senior Company Commander.) Looking back up at Col. Wister, note that when he was wounded he was replaced as Brigade Commander by Col. Dana of the 143rd Pa (bottom of Page 9) who was next in seniority of the three regimental commanders in the Brigade. As further evidence of the terrible battle this Brigade was engaged in on the afternoon of July lst, 1863, note the 853 total casualties of the 1315 men in the Brigade.

Union Brigade tablets are mounted on square marble bases.

CONFEDERATE BRIGADES

On Page 4:

Hill's Corps shows in the left margin where General Archer's Brigade is listed. The format is the same as for a Union Brigade,
Heth's excepting that Confederate units were identified by their commander's name. Hence, General Archer's Brigade
Division of General Heth's Division of Gen. Hill's Corps is listed in the margin of page 4 as Hill's Corps, Heth's Divi-
Archer's sion, Archer's Brigade.
Brigade

Confederate Brigade Tablets are mounted on round marble bases.

DIVISIONS

Page 19 shows:

3rd Divisions are on bronze tablets mounted on large granite blocks. As they are listed on page 7. Note that the 3rd
Division Division of the 1st Corps lists the 1st, 2nd and 3rd Brigades and that Col. Stone's 2nd Brigade which was
1st Corps previously mentioned under "Brigades" is listed here as part of the 3rd Division. Confederate Divisions are
listed by the commander's name (see Rodes' Division, Ewell's Corps on page 19).

CORPS

Page 8A lists:

1st Corps in the left margin. At the Battle of Gettysburg there were seven Union Infantry Corps and one Union Cavalry
Army of the Corps. The Infantry Corps were the 1st, 2nd, 3rd, 5th, 6th, 11th and 12th and they are listed on bronze tablets
Potomac mounted on large granite blocks as are the three Confederate Corps tablets. For example, page 17 lists General
Ewell's 2nd Confederate Corps.

ARMIES

Bronze Tablets on large granite blocks list the organizations of the two armies. General Meade's Army of the Potomac is listed on Page 87. General Lee's Army of Northern Virginia is listed on page 227.

ABBREVIATIONS

Adv.	Advance		Gen.	General
ANV.	Army Of Northern Virginia		Gbg.	Gettysburg
A Of P	Army Of The Potomac			
Arty.	Artillery		HQ	Headquarters
Ave.	Avenue			
			Ind.	Indiana
			Inf.	Infantry
Bn.	Battalion			
Bat. or Btry.	Battery		K	Killed
Brig.	Brigade			
B.G. or Brig. Gen.	Brigadier General		Lieut. Gen. or Lt. Gen.	Lieutenant General
			LF	Left Flank
Cap.	Captured		Lt.	Light or Lieutenant
Capt.	Captain			
Cas.	Casualties		M	Missing
C or Cav.	Cavalry		Maj.	Major
Cem.	Cemetary		M.G. or Maj. Gen.	Major General
Chmbg.	Chambersburg		Mon.	Monument
Col.	Colonel		MW	Mortally Wounded
Con. or Confed.	Confederate			
Comp.	Company		Natl.	National
Cos	Companies			
			Pos.	Position
Div.	Division		Reg.	Regular
			Regt.	Regiment
Embg.	Emmitsburg		Sgt.	Sergeant
			RF	Right Flank
			Rd.	Road
			RR	Railroad
			Tot.	Total
			W.	Wounded

CONFED 2ND CORPS

Newville Road

Carlisle Road

Heidlersburg Road

CONFED 3RD CORPS

1st Shot Fired

UNION 11TH CORPS

Rock Creek

Knoxlyn Road

Herr's Ridge Rd

Mummasburg Road

UNION 1ST CORPS

RR Under Construction

Chambersburg Pike

York Pike

Hanover Road

Gettysburg

Washington Ave

East Confederate Ave

Emmitsburg Rd

Taneytown Road

Cemetery Ridge

Baltimore Pike

Culp's Hill

Not To Scale

Battle of Gettysburg

1st Day-July 1, 1863

The fighting began northwest of Gettysburg early in the morning when the Confederate 3rd Corps fought the Union 1st Corps along the Chambersburg Pike. The fighting spread northward after midday, when the Confederate 2nd Corps attacked the Union 11th Corps from the Newville and Heidlersburg Roads. The fighting of July 1st ended in the evening after the two Confederate Corps had driven the two Union Corps through Gettysburg to East Cemetery Hill, Culp's Hill and Cemetary Ridge.

This compilation of monument inscriptions begins with the marker where the first shot was fired, northwest of Gettysburg (see upper left of this map and upper left of the map on Page 1). The inscription of the "First Shot Fired" marker is on Page 1.

THE SYMBOLS LISTED BELOW ARE USED TO IDENTIFY THE MONUMENTS, MARKERS, TABLETS, STATUES, ETC. WHICH ARE DRAWN ON THE MAPS IN THESE PAGES

SYMBOL	TYPE	REPRESENTING	DESCRIPTION
	Bronze Tablet	Army of The Potomac, Union Corps or Division or Brigade, Regular Army Regiment, Regular Army Artillery Battery, Volunteer Artillery Brigade.	Brigade Tablet Mounted on Square Marble base. All other Tablets are on large vertical Granite Blocks.
	Bronze Tablet	Army of Northern Virginia, Confederate Corps or Division or Brigade or Artillery Battalion	Brigade Tablet and Artillery Battalion Tablet Mounted on Round Marble base. All other Tablets are Mounted on large vertical Granite blocks.
	Iron Tablet	Union Army Battery (other than Regular Army)	Mounted on Black Iron Shaft.
	Iron Tablet	Confederate Artillery Battery	Mounted on Black Iron Shaft.
	Iron Tablet	Confederate Brigade Advanced Position	Mounted on Black Iron Shaft.
	Regimental or Battery Monument	Principal Position of Volunteer Regiment or Volunteer Artillery Battery	Usually Granite or Marble in a Great Variety of Shapes and Sizes.
	Regimental Marker	Other than Principal Position of Regiment or Battery	Usually a Square Granite Marker or tablet or may be another monument.
	Flank Marker or Company Marker	Left and/or Right Flank of Regiment or Battery or Position of a Coppany.	Usually a Small Square or Rectangular Granite Marker.
	Army Or Corps Headquarters	Site of Headquarters of Army Commander or Corps Commander or Chief of Artillery	Cannon Barrel Mounted Vertically on Stone, Granite or Marble Base.
	State Monument	Monument Erected by Union or Confederate State.	
	Statue	Standing or Equestrian	Bronze Sculpture
	Building	House, Barn or other Structure	Identified by Owner's Name.
	Miscellaneous Marker	Marker or Inscription of a type not listed above	Granite or Metal Marker.

*Asterisk   Used whenever a Division or Brigade or Regiment or Battery has more than one Monument or Marker.   Check the Index for other Monument or Marker.

~ Gettysburg Battlefield Monuments, Locations & Inscriptions ~

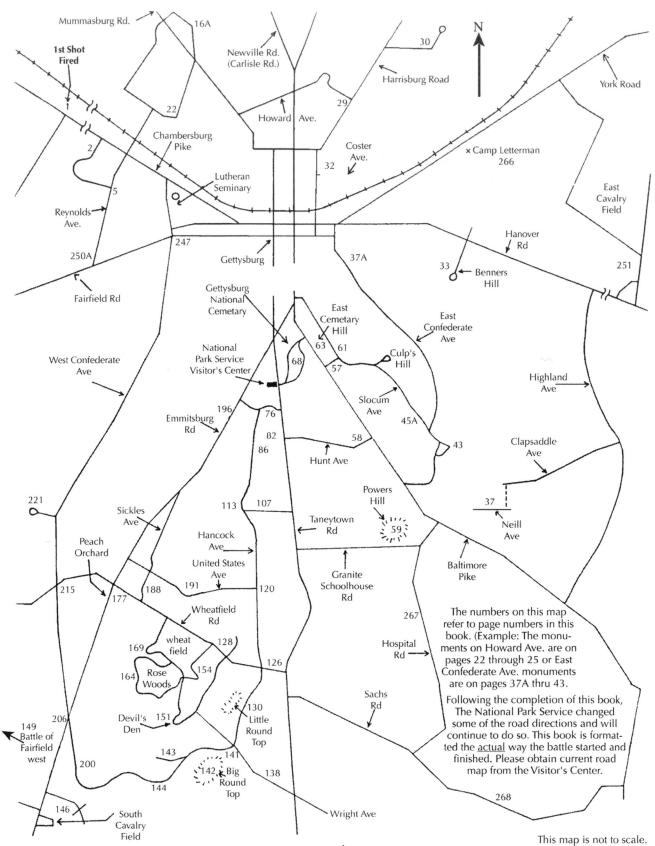

Mummasburg Rd.
16A

1st Shot Fired

Newville Rd. (Carlisle Rd.)

30

Harrisburg Road

N

York Road

22

Howard Ave.

29

2

Chambersburg Pike

Coster Ave.

32

× Camp Letterman
266

East Cavalry Field

5

Lutheran Seminary

Reynolds Ave.

247

Gettysburg

37A

Hanover Rd

251

250A

Fairfield Rd

33

Benners Hill

Gettysburg National Cemetary

East Cemetary Hill

East Confederate Ave

63 61

West Confederate Ave

National Park Service Visitor's Center

68

57

Culp's Hill

Highland Ave

196

76

Slocum Ave

45A

Emmitsburg Rd

82

58

43

Clapsaddle Ave

86

Hunt Ave

221

113

107

Powers Hill

37

Neill Ave

Sickles Ave

Taneytown Rd

59

Peach Orchard

Hancock Ave

United States Ave

120

Granite Schoolhouse Rd

Baltimore Pike

215

177

188

191

Wheatfield Rd

128

126

267

Hospital Rd

169

wheat field

The numbers on this map refer to page numbers in this book. (Example: The monuments on Howard Ave. are on pages 22 through 25 or East Confederate Ave. monuments are on pages 37A thru 43.

164

Rose Woods

154

149 Battle of Fairfield west

206

Devil's Den

151

130 Little Round Top

Sachs Rd

200

143

141

142 Big Round Top

138

Following the completion of this book, The National Park Service changed some of the road directions and will continue to do so. This book is formatted the <u>actual</u> way the battle started and finished. Please obtain current road map from the Visitor's Center.

144

146

South Cavalry Field

Wright Ave

268

xvi

This map is not to scale.

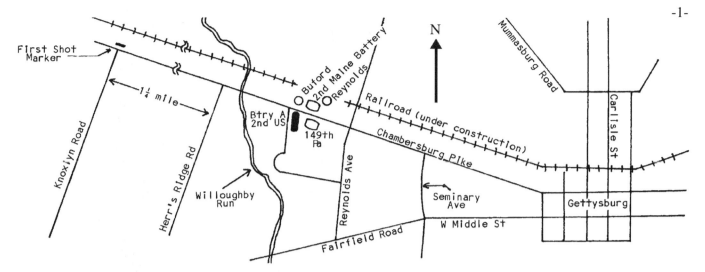

1st Shot   First Shot Gettysburg, July 1, 1863, 7:30 AM.
Marker   Fired By Capt. Jones with Sergeant Shafer's carbine,
                 Company E, 8th Illinois Cavalry.
Erected   Erected 1886 By Capt. Jones, Lt. Riddler and Sergeant Shafer.

Buford's   In memory of Major General John Buford, Commanding 1st Division Cavalry Corps, Army of The Potomac,
Statue   who with the first inspiration of a Cavalry Officer selected this battlefield July 1, 1863. From this crest was fired
                 the opening gun of the battle, one of four cannon at the base of this memorial.

Engraved   The four cannon guarding the base of this statue belong to Horse Battery A-2nd US Artillery. This piece was the
Plate on   opening gun of the battle fired from this spot under the personal direction of General Buford, July 1, 1863. Serial
1st Gun   Number 233PIC°1862.
Fired

2nd Maine   Capt. James A. Hall
Lt. Battery* Six 3 inch rifles
1st Corps   <u>7-1</u>: Casualties: killed 2; wounded 18; Total 20
Artillery
Brigade

Reynold's   Major General John F. Reynolds
Statue   Cadet USMA 7/1/1837, Brevet 2nd Lt. 3rd US Arty 7/1/41, 2nd Lt. 10/32/41, 1st Lt. 6/18/46, Capt. 3/3/55, Lt.
                 Col. 14th Inf. 5/14/61, Col. 5th Inf. 6/1/63, Brig. Gen. USV 8/20/61, Maj. Gen. 11/29/62, Brevet Capt. USA
                 9/23/46 for gallant and meritorious conduct at Monterey, Mex.; Maj. 2/3/47 for gallant and meritorious conduct
                 at Buene Vista, Mex.

149th PA   1st Regiment Bucktail Brigade
2-3-1*   Lt. Col. Walton Dwight, Capt. James Glenn
          <u>7-1</u>: Regiment held this position from 11:30 AM until 1st Corps retired, resisting several assaults of the enemy,
              making two successful charges to the RR cut and changing front to rear under fire.
          <u>7-2</u>: Moved to support of the left, remained on picket all night.
          <u>7-3</u>: Moved to left center where its other monument stands.
          Casualties: killed or mortally wounded 66; wounded 159; captured or missing 111; total 336 of 450 carried into
          action.

*see index

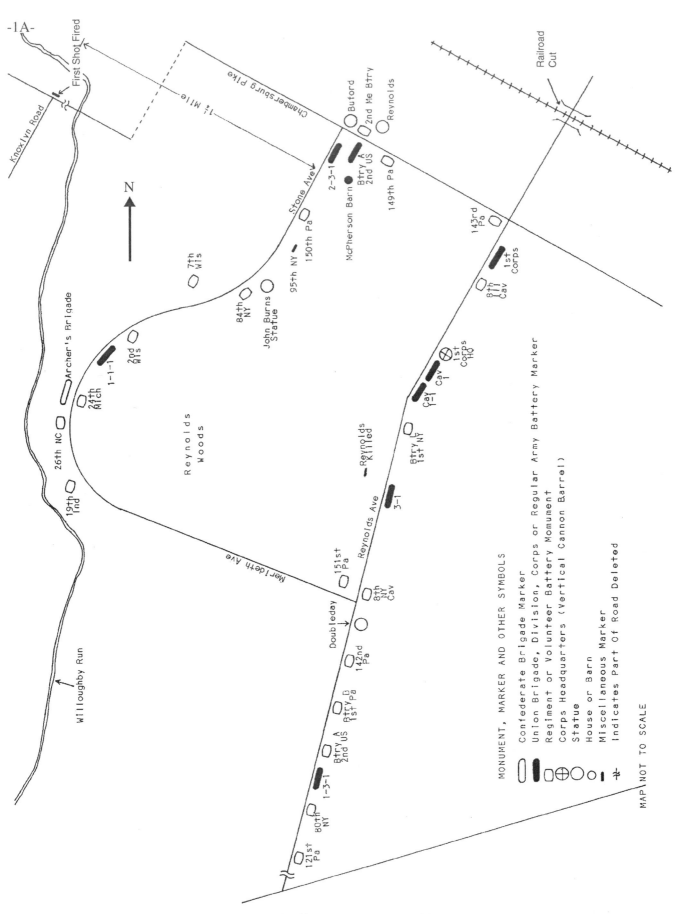

-1A-

First Shot Fired

Knoxlvn Road

Chambersburg Pike

1¼ Mile

Railroad Cut

Buford

2nd Me Btry

Reynolds

2-3-1

Btry A 2nd US

McPherson Barn

149th Pa

143rd Pa

1st Corps

8th Cav

N

7th Wis

84th NY

John Burns Statue

95th NY

150th Pa

Stones Ave

Archer's Brigade

1-1-1

2nd Wis

24th Mich

26th NC

19th Ind

Reynolds Woods

Reynolds Killed

1st Corps HQ

Cav 1

1-1 Cav

Btry 1st NY

3-1

Willoughby Run

Meridith Ave

Reynolds Ave

151st Pa

8th NY Cav

Doubleday

142nd Pa

Btry D 1st Pa

Btry A 2nd US

1-3-1

80th NY

121st Pa

MONUMENT, MARKER AND OTHER SYMBOLS

Confederate Brigade Marker

Union Brigade, Division, Corps or Regular Army Battery Marker

Regiment or Volunteer Battery Monument

Corps Headquarters (Vertical Cannon Barrel)

Statue

House or Barn

Miscellaneous Marker

Indicates Part Of Road Deleted

MAP NOT TO SCALE

~ Gettysburg Battlefield Monuments, Locations & Inscriptions ~

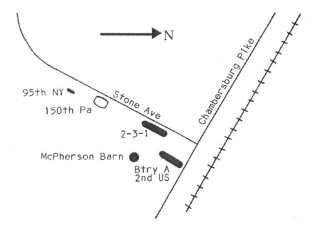

Cavalry	Lt. John H. Calef
Corps	Six 3 inch Rifles
2ⁿᵈ Brigade	6-30: Arrived in evening from Emmitsburg and took position on Chambersburg Pike.
Horse	7-1: Advanced with the cavalry, went into position with right action on right of the road and left section on left
Artillery	and center section with Col. William Gamble's Brigade on the right of the Fairfield Road. The first gun of
Battery A	the battle was fired from the right section and the positions held under a severe fire until the 1st Corps
2ⁿᵈ US*	arrived about 10 AM. The Battery was then relieved by Capt. J. A. Hall's 2nd Maine Battery and after being

Cavalry
Corps
2ⁿᵈ Brigade
Horse
Artillery
Battery A
2ⁿᵈ US*

Lt. John H. Calef
Six 3 inch Rifles
6-30: Arrived in evening from Emmitsburg and took position on Chambersburg Pike.
7-1: Advanced with the cavalry, went into position with right action on right of the road and left section on left and center section with Col. William Gamble's Brigade on the right of the Fairfield Road. The first gun of the battle was fired from the right section and the positions held under a severe fire until the 1st Corps arrived about 10 AM. The Battery was then relieved by Capt. J. A. Hall's 2nd Maine Battery and after being supplied with ammunition, returned about 3 PM but under a front and enfilading fire, it retired to a line in front of Cemetary Ridge and bivouacked for the night near the 3rd Corps.
7-2: In the morning, marched with 1st Brigade of Major General John Buford's Division to Taneytown en route to Westminster.
Casualties: 12 men wounded; 13 horses killed

2-3-1
The Bucktail Brigade
Col. Roy Stone, Col. Langhorne Wister, Col. E. L. Dana-143rd, 149th, 150th Pennsylvania Infantry
7-1: Arrived and went into position at the McPherson buildings between Reynolds Woods and the RR Cut and was subjected to a heavy front and enfilading artillery fire from the right. Repulsed repeated attacks of Brig. Gen. Daniel's, Brigade Major Gen. Rodes' Division from the right as well as front attacks, until pressed on both flanks and in front by superior numbers, it retired to Seminary Ridge and held temporary breastworks there until the Corps, before overwhelming numbers, retired to Cemetary Hill, when the Brigade with the Division took position at the left of the cemetery on and near the Taneytown Road.
7-2: Late in the afternoon moved to the left and took position previously occupied by the 1st Division 2nd Corps.
7-3: Remained in the same position under heavy artillery fire in the afternoon
Casualties: Killed 109, Wounded 465, Missing 279; Total 853; Present 1315

150ᵗʰ PA*
2-3-1
2nd Regiment Bucktail Brigade
Col. Langhorne Wister, Lt. Col. Henry S. Huidekoper, Capt. C. C. Widdis
7-1. The Regiment held this position from 11:30 AM to 3:30 PM. This monument marks the most advanced line facing west occupied by the Regiment. Repeated changes of front were made to meet assaults from the north and west and the right wing charged to the RR Cut. In retiring, it made several stands and engaged the enemy.
7-2: In the evening moved to support the left and held position on the Emmitsburg Road.
7-3: In the morning moved to the left center and remained until the close of the battle.
Casualties: 53 killed and mortally wounded, 134 wounded; 77 missing; total 264 of 397 present.

95ᵗʰ NY*
2-1-1
Col. George H. Biddle, Maj. Edward Pye
95th NY Infantry, July 1st, 1863, 10 AM

*see index

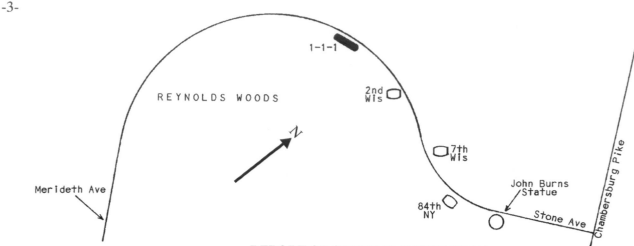

REPORT OF GENERAL DOUBLEDAY

John
Burns
Statue

My thanks are specially due to a citizen of Gettysburg, who although over 70 years of age, shouldered his musket and offered his services to Col. Wister's 150th Pennsylvania Volunteers. Col. Wister advised him to fight in the woods as there was more shelter there but he preferred to join our line of skirmishers in the open field. When the troops retired, he fought with the Iron brigade. He was wounded in three places.

84th NY*   14th New York State Militia (14th Brooklyn)
2-1-1   Col. Edward B. Fowler

    7-1: Here in the forenoon the regiment opened fire on Hill's Corps. Afterward charged successfully on Davis' Brigade at the RR Cut to the right and rear of this position as indicated by a monument there. Later had a running fight through Gettysburg to Culp's Hill.

    7-2: Repulsed the advance of Johnson's Division at night, then moved to the right to reinforce the 12th Corps as reported on a tablet on a boulder to the right of the hill.

    Casualties: killed 13, wounded 105, missing 99; total 217

7th Wis.*   Col. William W. Robinson, Maj. Mark Finnicum
1-1-1   7-1: This monument marks one of the advanced positions of the Regiment in battle. It went into action with 370 men and lost 194.

    7-2: Position of this Regiment indicated by stone marker on Culp's Hill.

    7-3: Same as July 2nd.

    Casualties: Killed 39; Wounded 103; Missing 52; 194 total; 370 present

2nd Wis.*   Col. Lucius Fairchild, Maj. George H. Otis
1-1-1   7-1: position held.

    7-2: position on Culp's Hill.

    7-3: Same as July 2nd.

    Casualties: Killed 26; Wounded 155; Missing 52; Total 233; Effective Strength 302

1-1-1   The Iron Brigade
    Brig. Gen. Solomon Meredith, Col. William W. Robinson
    19th Indiana, 24th Mich., 2nd, 6th, 7th Wis. Infantry

    7-1: Arrived at 10 AM, went into position and charged Brig. Gen. Archer's brigade in Reynolds Woods. Forced the Confederate line across Willoughby Run, capturing General Archer and many prisoners. 19th Ind, 24th Mich., 2nd and 7th Wis. retired and formed line in Reynolds Woods, 6th Wis. having gone to support of 2nd Brigade against Brig. Gen. Davis' Brigade Maj. Gen. Heth's Division. At 4 PM, being outflanked and hard pressed, the Brigade retired under heavy fire of infantry and artillery to Seminary Ridge and then to Cemetary Hill and to the north slope of Culp's Hill and entrenched.

    7-2: Repulsed without loss a sharp attack at night. About sunset, the 6th Wis. went to support of 3rd Brigade 2nd Division 12th Corps and assisted in repelling attacks during the night.

    7-3: Repulsed a sharp attack in the morning without loss.

    Casualties: Killed 171; Wounded 920; Missing 262; Total 1353; Present 1883

*see index

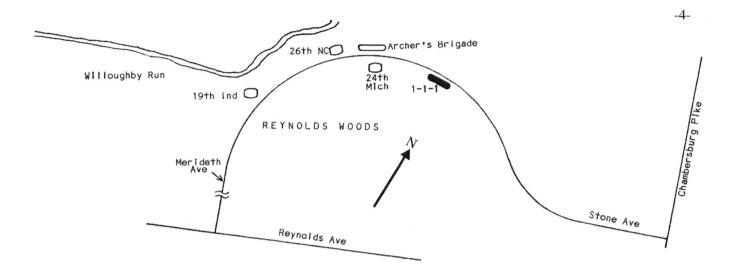

24ᵗʰ Mich   Col. Henry A. Morrow, Capt. Albert M. Edwards
1-1-1   <u>7-1</u>:   Arriving upon the field to the south of these woods in the forenoon, this Regiment with others of the Brigade (2nd and 7th Wis. and 19th Ind.) charged across the stream in front to the crest beyond, assisting in the capture of a large portion of Archer's Tennessee Brigade. It was then withdrawn to this position where it fought until the line was outflanked and forced back.
       <u>7-2&3</u>:   On Culp's Hill.
       Casualties: Killed 89, Wounded 218, missing 56; Total 363

Hill's   Brigadier General James Archer
Corps   5th Battalion & 13th Ala., 1st, 7th, 14th Tennessee Infantry
Heth's   <u>7-1</u>:   The Brigade moved from Cashtown early in the morning toward Gettysburg. After a march of six miles,
Division   came in view of the Union forces. The Brigade was deployed on the west bank of Willoughby Run and
Archer's   about 10 AM advanced. Encountered 1st Division 1st Brigade 1st Corps beyond the Run. The firing contin-
Brigade*   ued for a short time when a large force appearing on the right flank and opening a cross fire, the position became untenable. The Brigade was forced back across the Run but advanced with the Division later in the day. The advance in the morning reached this position.
       <u>7-2</u>:   Not engaged.
       <u>7-3</u>:   Formed part of the column of Longstreet's Assault.
       <u>7-4</u>:   Brigade took up the line of march during the night to Hagerstown.
       Casualties: Killed 16; Wounded 144; Missing 517; Total 677 (NY@Gbg)

19ᵗʰ Indiana   Col. Samuel J. Williams
1-1-1   <u>7-1</u>:   position held.
       Casualties: Killed 27; Wounded 133; Missing 50; Total 210 (NY@Gbg)

26ᵗʰ N.C.   (Note: See next page.)

TWENTY SIXTH
NORTH CAROLINA REGIMENT

Pettigrew's Brigade   Heth's Division
Army Of Northern Virginia

Henry King Burgwyn, Jr.
Colonel

John Thomas Jones   John Randolph Lane
Major   Lieutenant Colonel

Pettigrew's Brigade moved toward Gettysburg early on the morning of July 1, and shortly after noon deployed in line of battle on the ridge 600 yards west of here. The 26th North Carolina stood on the Brigade's left flank, facing these woods and the 24th Michigan of Meredith's Iron Brigade. The order to advance was made about 2:30 PM. On nearby Willoughby Run the Regiment received a galling fire from the opposite bank. By Major Jones' account the "fighting was terrible" with the forces "pouring volleys into each other at a distance not greater than twenty paces". After about an hour the Regiment had incurred heavy losses: Colonel Burgwyn had been mortally wounded and Lieutenant Colonel Lane injured. The attack continued until the Union troops, fell back through the streets of Gettysburg and took up positions south of the town.

On July 9th, Brigadier General James Johnston Pettigrew wrote that the Regiment had "covered itself with glory...it fell to the lot of the 26th to charge one of the strongest positions possible... with a gallantry unsurpassed". Addressing his remarks to Zebulon Baird Vance, who had served as Colonel of the 26th until his election as Governor in August 1862, Pettigrew concluded that "your old comrades did honor to your association with them and to the State they represented".

Erected By The State Of North Carolina
1985

(Note: On October 5th, 1985, in his dedication speech, Warren W. Hassler, Jr.,
Professor of History, Pennsylvania State University, listed the casualties of the 26th
North Carolina in its fight with the Iron Brigade at 708 of 800 present.)

NY@GBG   Killed 86, Wounded 502, Missing No Report

Engaged	843	"Regimental Strengths at Gettysburg"
Killed & M W	172	
Wounded & Missing	443	"Confederate Death Roster"
Missing	72	
Total Casualties	687	

$$\frac{687}{843} = .81 \text{ or } 81\% \text{ Casualties}$$

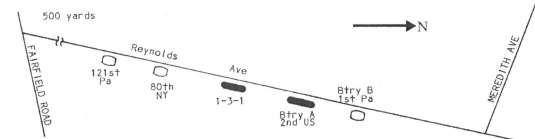

121st PA*
1-3-1
Colonel Chapman Biddle, Major Alexander Biddle
7-1: Occupied this position, the extreme left of the Union line.
7-2&3: On Cemetary Ridge.

Casualties: Killed & Died of Wounds 20, Wounded 98, Missing 61; Total 179
Present at Gettysburg: 11 Officers & 295 Men

80th NY*
1-3-1
20th New York Militia; The Ulster Guard
Colonel Thomas B. Gates
7-1: Held substantially this position from about 12 Noon to 4 PM.
7-2: On Cemetary Hill in support of 3rd Corps.
7-3: In front line of battle resisting Pickett's attack.
Casualties: Killed 35, Wounded 111, Missing 24; Total 170 - Number Engaged: 375

1-3-1
Brig. Gen. Thomas A. Rowley, Col. Chapman Biddle
80th NY, 121st, 142nd, 151st Pa. Infantry
7-1: Arrived and went into position about 11:30 AM left of Reynolds Woods. The 151st Pa having been sent to reinforce 2nd Brig on right of Reynolds Woods, the remaining regiments with Btry B-1st Pa formed line facing west and held this position until near 4 PM, when being pressed with superior numbers in front and outflanked on the left, the Brigade retired to Seminary Ridge. On the withdrawal of the Corps, the Brigade retired to Cemetary Hill and formed on the left along Taneytown Road and remained there until Noon of July 2nd.
7-2: Between 5 and 6 PM the Brigade was moved to the left centre from which 1st Div 2nd Corps had been taken to support 3rd Corps.
7-3: Remained in the same position and assisted in repelling Longstreet's Assault in the afternoon, taking many prisoners. At 6 PM withdrew to former position on Taneytown Road.
Casualties: Killed 111, Wounded 557, Missing 230; Total 898

Battery A
2nd US*
Cavalry
Corps
2nd Brigade
Horse
Artillery
Lt. John H. Calef
Six 3 Inch Rifles
6-30: Arrived in the evening from Emmitsburg and took position on the Chambersburg Pike.
7-1: Advanced with the 1st Div. Cav. Corps, the right and left sections on the Chambersburg Pike, the centre section under Sgt. Charles Pergel posted here with the 1st Brig 1st Div Cav Corps and assisted in repulsing an attack of the Confederate infantry. This section having been withdrawn, joined the battery in the rear and again advanced with left and relieved Btry B-1st Maine Arty on Chambersburg Pike in the afternoon, but was soon compelled by a front and enfilading fire to retire. Rejoined the battery in position with the Cavalry on the left in front of Cemetary Ridge and remained during the night.
Casualties: Wounded 12 men; 13 Horses Killed.

Battery B
1st PA*
1st Corps
Artillery
Brigade
Capt. James H. Cooper
Four 3 Inch Rifles
7-1: The Battery arrived here about noon and engaged Confederate Artillery on Herr's Ridge. About 1:30 PM moved to rear. Changed front, engaged Carter's Artillery and shelled Rodes' Infantry on Oak Hill. About 3 PM moved to the woods in front of the Theological Seminary and resisted the final attack of Scales, Perrin's and other brigades.
Casualties: Killed 3, Wounded 9; Total 12

*see index

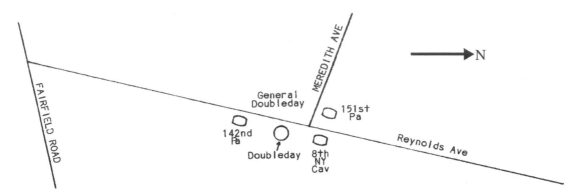

142nd PA
1-3-1
Col. Robert P. Cummins, Lt. Col. Alfred B. McCalmont

7-1: Marched from near Emmitsburg reaching the field via Willoughby Run. Formed line facing northward. Occupied this position; changed it to support artillery. Reformed here and engaged a brigade composed of the 11th, 26th, 47th and 52nd North Carolina Infantry. In the afternoon outflanked and retired firing to a position near the Seminary. Here engaged a brigade composed of the 1st, 12th, 13th and 14th South Carolina Infantry. After a gallant fight, again outflanked and retired to Cemetary Hill.

7-2: In position at Cemetary Hill.

7-3: Moved a half mile to the left and exposed to the artillery fire of the enemy.

Casualties: Killed 31, Wounded 110, Missing 70; Total 211

Doubleday's
Statue

Abner Doubleday, Major General, USV
1819 - 1893
Commanded 1st Corps At Gettysburg, July 1st, 1863

Cadet USMA 9/1/1838, Brevet 2nd Lt. 3rd US Arty 7/1/42, 2nd Lt 1st Arty 2/24/45,1st Lt 3/3/47,Capt 3/3/55, Maj 17th Inf 5/14/61, Lt Col 17th Inf, 9/20/63, Col 35th Inf 9/15/67, Unassigned 3/15/69, Assigned to 24th Inf 9/15/70, Retired 12/11/73.

Brig. Gen. USV 2/3/62, Maj. Gen. 11/29/62 Commanding 2nd Brig. 1st Div. 3rd Corps (McDowell's) at Manassas (1862), 1st Div 1st Corps at South Mountain, Antietam and Fredericksburg and 3rd Div 1st Corps at Chancellorsville. Brevetted Lt. Col. USA 9/17/62 for gallant and meritorious services at the Battle of Antietam, Md, Col USA 7/2/63 for gallant and meritorious services at the Battle of Gettysburg, Pa. Brevetted Brig. Gen. and Maj. Gen. USA 3/13/65 for gallant and meritorious services during the war.

151st PA
1-3-1
Lt. Col. George F. McFarland, Capt. Walter L. Owens, Col. Harrison Allen

7-1: Fought here and in the grove west of the Theological Seminary.

7-2: In reserve on Cemetary Hill.

7-3: In position on left centre and assisted in repulsing the charge of the enemy in the afternoon.

Casualties: Killed & Mortally Wounded 81, Wounded 181, Missing 75; Total 337. Present at Gettysburg: 467.

8th NY
Cavalry
C-1-1
Lt. Col. William L. Markell

7-1: Pickets of this Regiment were attacked about 5 AM by the advance skirmishers of Heth's Confederate Division. The Regiment engaged the enemy west of Seminary Ridge, with the Brigade stubbornly contesting the ground against great odds until about 10:30 AM when it was relieved by the advance regiments of the 1st Corps. On reforming line, the Regiment took an advanced position on Hagerstown Rd. Late in the day delayed enemy's advance by attacking his right flank, thereby aiding the infantry in withdrawing to Cemetary Hill. In the evening, encamped on left flank.

7-2: Buford's Division retired toward Westminster.

Casualties: Killed 3, Wounded 10, Missing 21; Total 34

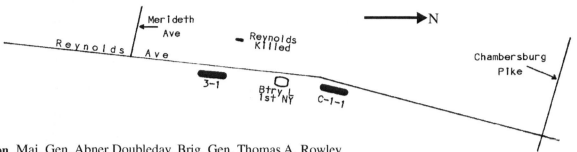

3rd Division Maj. Gen. Abner Doubleday, Brig. Gen. Thomas A. Rowley
1st Corps
    1st Brigade   Brig. Gen. Thomas A. Rowley, Col. Chapman Biddle
    2nd Brigade   Col. Roy Stone, Col. Langhorne Wister, Col. E. L. Dana
    3rd Brigade   Brig. Gen. George Stannard, Col. Francis Randall
    <u>7-1</u>: Arrived about 11 AM. 1st Brigade took position in field on left of Reynold's Woods, 2nd Brigade on Chambersburg Pike relieving 2nd Brigade 1st Division. These Brigades were actively engaged from 2 to 4 PM and retired with the Corps and took position south of the cemetary fronting Emmitsburg Road. 3rd Brigade joined at dusk.
    <u>7-2</u>: At sunset sent to support of 3rd Corps on its right on Emmitsburg Road and captured 80 prisoners and recaptured 4 guns.
    <u>7-3</u>: In position on left of 2nd Division 2nd Corps. Assisted in repulsing Longstreet's Assault, capturing many prisoners and three stand of colors.
    Casualties: 265 Killed, Wounded 1297, Missing 541; Total 2103.

Reynolds   Maj. Gen. John F. Reynolds Commanding Left Wing, 1st, 3rd and 11th Corps, Army of The Potomac.
Killed   Erected By The State Of Pennsylvania, July 1886.

Battery L   Company E, 1st New York Light Attached
1st NY*   Capt. Gilbert H. Reynolds, Lt. Geaoge Breck
1st Corps   <u>7-1</u>: Near Chambersburg Pike.
Artillery   <u>7-2</u>: Engaged with enemy from position on Cemetary Hill.
Brigade   <u>7-3</u>: Engaged with enemy from position on Cemetary Hill.
    Casualties: Killed 1, Wounded 15, Missing 1; Total 17 (NY@Gbg)

C-1-1   Col. William Gamble
Cavalry   8th, 12th Illinois (4 Companies), 3rd Ind (3 Companies), 8th NY Cav.
Corps   <u>6-30</u>: Started early for Gettysburg and encountered two Mississippi regiments and a section of artillery and
1st Division   after a short skirmish, proceeded to Gettysburg, when a detachment of Maj. Gen. Heth's Division about
1st Brigade   to enter Gettysburg, withdrew toward Cashtown leaving pickets 4 1/2 miles from Gettysburg.
    <u>7-1</u>: Between 8 and 9 AM the Confederates advanced in force from Cashtown. The Brigade was dismounted and with Battery A-2nd US, held its position for more than two hours against infantry and artillery in superior numbers and until M. G. Reynolds arrived with 1st Division 1st Corps, after which the Brigade was engaged on the left of the infantry. On retiring to Cemetary Hill, the Brigade took position on the left in front of Little Round Top.
    <u>7-2</u>: Relieved by 3rd Corps and marched to Taneytown enroute to Westminster.
    Casualties: Killed 13, Wounded 58, Missing 28; Total 99

*see index

Cavalry   Brig. Gen. John Buford
  Corps   1st Brigade   Col. William Gamble
1st Division 2nd Brigade   Col. Thomas Devin

Reserve Brigade Brig. Gen. Wesley Merritt

6-29: Engaged in picketing, scouting and patrolling westerly and northerly to Hagerstown. Finding no Confederate force, General Buford with the 1st and 2nd Brigades recrossed the mountain and camped near Fairfield.

6-30: Arrived at Gettysburg at 11 AM, as a detatchment of Heth's Confederate Division was about to enter, but it withdrew on the approach of the two Brigades of the Division. General Buford deployed his cavalry along the ridge between the Mummasburg and Fairfield Roads with pickets well advanced.

7-1: Was attacked between 8 and 9 AM by Heth's Division and Pegram's Artillery Battalion, which were held in check until arrival of the 1st Corps. The 2nd Brigade picketed the approaches from the north and retarded the advance of Ewell's Corps until the 11th Corps arrived. About 4 PM, retreated to Cemetary Hill and formed on left of town and bivouacked for the night in front of Little Round Top, extending pickets early to Fairfield.

7-2: Started in the morning for Westminster to guard Army trains.

7-3: The Reserve Brigade Cavalry Corps arrived about noon on the Emmitsburg Road and engaged for four hours the Confederate right.

Casualties: Killed 28, Wounded 116, Missing 274; Total 418

1st Corps
Head-
quarters

Army of The Potomac
1st Corps Headquarters
Major General Abner Doubleday

July 1, 1863

Located 230 Yards Southeast
From Here, Near The Pike

8th Illinois Major John L. Beveridge
  Cavalry   7-1: First line of battle occupied until relieved by 1st Corps. One squadron picketed ridge east of Marsh Creek
  C-1-1   and supported by another squadron, met enemy's right advance. Lt. Jones, Company E, fired first shot as the enemy crossed Marsh Creek bridge. On reforming line, Regiment took an advanced position on Hagerstown Road. Late in the day, delayed enemy's advance by attacking his right flank, thereby aiding the infantry in withdrawing to Cemetary Hill. In the evening, encamped on left flank.

7-2: Buford's Division retired toward Westminster.

Casualties: Killed 1, Wounded 5, Missing 1; Total 7 (NY@Gbg)

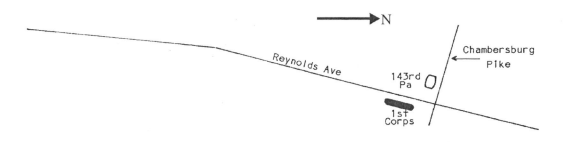

1st Corps   Maj. Gen. John F. Reynolds, Maj. Gen. Abner Doubleday, Maj. Gen. J. Newton
Army of   1st Division   Brig. Gen. James S. Wadsworth
the   2nd Division Brig. Gen. John C. Robinson
Potomac   3rd Division   Maj. Gen. Abner Doubleday, Brig. Gen. Thomas A. Rowley

    <u>7-1</u>: Arrived Gettysburg between 10 AM and 12 Noon. Relieved Buford's Division and became engaged with Archer's and Davis's Brigades, Heth's Division, Hill's Corps. General Reynolds fell mortally wounded about 10:15 AM. The Confederates, having been reinforced from Hill's and Ewell's Corps, made a vigorous attack at 2 PM with superior numbers along the entire line. At 4 PM the Corps retired and took positions on Cemetary Ridge and Culp's Hill.

    <u>7-2&3</u>: Wadsworth's Division occupied the north part of Culp's Hill, connected with the 12th Corps on the right and Robinson's and Rowley's Divisions on Cemetary Ridge, with detatchments elsewhere.

    Casualties: Killed 666, Wounded 3231, Missing 2162; Total 6059

143rd PA*   Col. Edmund L. Dana, Lt. Col. John D. Musser
2-3-1

    <u>7-1</u>: This monument marks the right of first position facing north and 2nd position facing west which the Regiment held from 11:30 AM till the 1st Corps fell back to last position on Seminary Ridge, right resting on the Railroad Cut.

    <u>7-2</u>: Regiment was in line on left centre.

    <u>7-3</u>: Assisted in repulsing the final charge of the enemy.

    Casualties: Killed 21, Wounded 141, Missing 91; Total 253 (NY@Gbg).

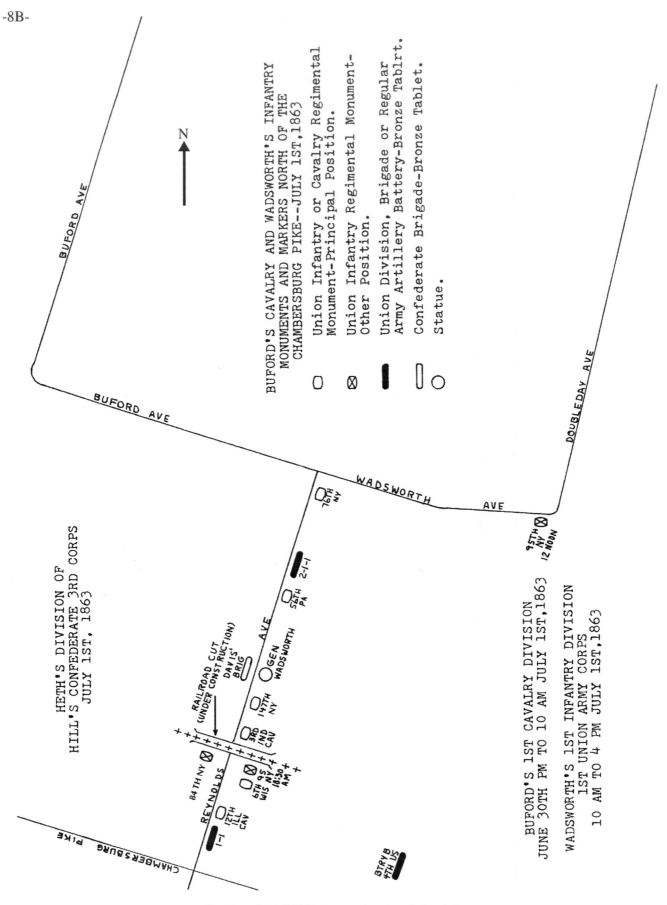

N

BUFORD'S CAVALRY AND WADSWORTH'S INFANTRY
MONUMENTS AND MARKERS NORTH OF THE
CHAMBERSBURG PIKE--JULY 1ST,1863

Union Infantry or Cavalry Regimental
Monument-Principal Position.

Union Infantry Regimental Monument-
Other Position.

Union Division, Brigade or Regular
Army Artillery Battery-Bronze Tablrt.

Confederate Brigade-Bronze Tablet.

Statue.

HETH'S DIVISION OF
HILL'S CONFEDERATE 3RD CORPS
JULY 1ST, 1863

BUFORD'S 1ST CAVALRY DIVISION
JUNE 30TH PM TO 10 AM JULY 1ST,1863

WADSWORTH'S 1ST INFANTRY DIVISION
1ST UNION ARMY CORPS
10 AM TO 4 PM JULY 1ST,1863

~ Gettysburg Battlefield Monuments, Locations & Inscriptions ~

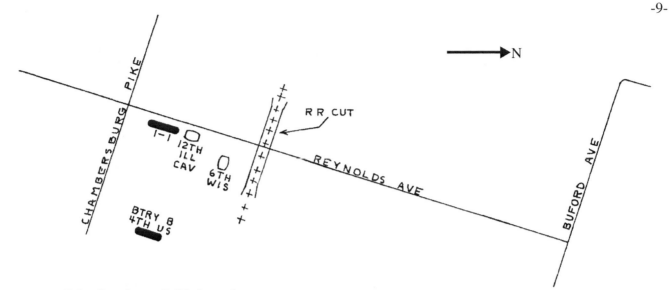

1st Division Brig. Gen. James S. Wadsworth
1st Corps   1st Brigade   Brig. Gen. Solomon Meredith
         2nd Brigade   Brig. Gen. Lysander Cutler
         7-1: Arrived at 10 AM, the first Union Infantry on the field. Formed across Chambersburg Pike, relieving 1st Division, Cavalry Corps and was immediately attacked by Archer's and Davis' Brigades, Heth's Division which were repulsed with heavy losses. At 2 PM, both sides having been heavily reinforced, the fighting was renewed with great energy, the two Brigades fighting separately where most needed. At 4 PM, the Confederates having advanced in superior numbers and enveloping both flanks, the Division retired by order of the General commanding to Cemetary Hill and went into position on the north side of Culp's Hill.
         7-2&3: Entrenched on Culp's Hill and repulsed attacks made in the evening of the 2nd and morning of the 3rd.
         Casualties: 299K + 1229W + 627M = 2155 Total

12th Illinois Col. George H. Chapman
  Cavalary* 7-1: First line of battle held until relieved by 1st Corps. One Squadron picketing east of Marsh Creek met
  C-1-1   enemy's left advance. The Regiment retired to the ridge on the left rear with the Brigade. Fought dismounted, repulsing attacks of the enemy. Covered the withdrawal of line to Cemetary Hill and in the evening took position on left flank of the Army.
         7-2: Division retired toward Winchester.
         Casualties: 4K + 10W + 6M = 20 Total (NY@Gbg)

Battery B Lt. James Stewart
  4th US* 6 Napoleans
  1st Corps 7-1: In position about 200 yards south of the Lutheran Seminary until 3 PM when ordered to support 2nd
  Artillery   Division, 1st Corps and took position on Seminary Ridge, half of Battery in command of Lt. James Davidson
  Brigade   between Chambersburg Pike and the RR Cut. The other half north of the Cut in the corner of the woods, was actively engaged. The Battery afterward retired with the troops to Cemetary Hill. Went into position on Baltimore Pike opposite Evergreen Cemetary commanding the approach from the town. Two guns on the Pike, two in the field, two having been disabled.
         Casualties: 2K + 31W + 3M = 36 Total

6th Wis.* Lt. Col. Rufus R. Dawes
  1-1-1 7-1: In the charge made on the RR Cut, the 2nd Mississippi Regiment of officers, men and battle flag surrendered to the 6th Wisconsin.
         7-2&3: The Regiment lay on Culp's Hill on the evening of the 2nd. It moved to the support of Greene's Brigade and assisted to repulse Johnson's Division.
         Casualties: 30K + 116W + 22M = 168 Total

*see index

~ Gettysburg Battlefield Monuments, Locations & Inscriptions ~

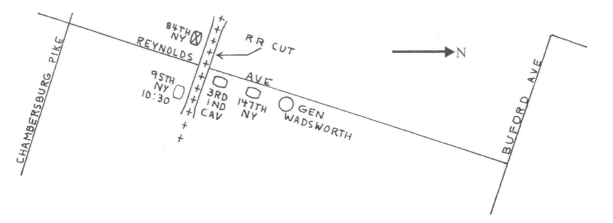

95ᵗʰ NY*   Col. George H. Biddle, Maj. Edward Pye
2-1-1   7-1:   This Regiment south of the McPherson House, engaged the enemy at 10 AM. At 10:30 AM changed front, advanced to this position with the 84th NY and 6th Wis, repulsed and captured a large part of Davis' Mississippi Brigade in the RR Cut. At noon, held position on Oak Hill, indicated by marker. Being out-flanked, moved to right of Seminary supporting Battery B-4th US. Retired from that position to Culp's Hill where it remained during July 2nd and 3rd.
Casualties: 7K + 62W + 46M = 115 Total

84ᵗʰ NY*   14th NY State Militia (14th Brooklyn) Col. Edward Fowler
2-1-1   7-1:   First engaged the enemy between the McPherson House and Reynolds Grove. Subsequently moved to this place and engaged Davis' Brigade. Remained at RR Cut at Seminary Ridge until final retreat. Had a running fight through Gettysburg to Culp's Hill. On this spot at 10:30 AM, this Regiment participated in the repulse of Davis' Brigade and the capture of a large portion of that command.
7-2&3:   On the evening of July 2nd and again in the morning of July 3rd went to the aid of Greene's Brigade and was heavily engaged.
Casualties: 217 of 355 by the War Department record.

3ʳᵈ Indiana   (6 Companies) Col. George H. Chapman
Cavalary   (Note: Col. Chapman also commanded the 12th Illinois Cavalry - see previous page)
C-1-1   7-1:   Position held here.
Casualties: 6K + 21W + 5M = 32 Total (NY@Gbg)

147ᵗʰ NY*   Lt. Col. Francis Miller, Major George Harney
2-1-1   7-1:   Position 10 AM.
Casualties: 76 K + 146 W + 79 M = 301 Total of 380 Present

Wadsworth   Brevet Maj. Gen. James Samuel Wadsworth USV 1807-1864.
Statue   In command of the 1st Division, 1st Corps at the Battle of Gettysburg, July 1, 2 and 3, 1863.
Volunteer Aide-de-Camp with rank of Major on personal staff of Brig. Gen. Irvin McDowell at Battle of Manassas 7/21/1861.
Brig. Gen. USV 8/23/61 and from 8/27/61 to 3/12/62 in command of a brigade of new regiments in McDowell's Division, Army of the Potomac. Military Governor of District of Columbia 3/17 to 11/19/62. Commanded 1st Division, 1st Corps 12/23 to 12/26/62; 1st Corps 12/26 to 1/4/63; 1st Division, 1st Corps 2/4 to 2/27/63; 1st Corps 2/27 to 3/6/63 and 1st Division 1st Corps from 3/9 to 3/22; 3/25 to 5/17; 5/27 to 7/15/63. Assigned 10/9/63 to special duty inspection of colored troops to 9/18/63. Detailed 1/9/64 on Court Of Inquiry. Ordered 3/15/64 to report to Gen. Meade. In command of 4th Division, 5th Corps 3/27 to 4/11/64; 4/13/64 until mortally wounded 5/6/64 in the Battle of the Wilderness, Va. Died 5/8/64.
Appointed Brevet Maj. Gen. USV to rank from 5/6/64 for gallant conduct at the Battles of Gettysburg and the Wilderness.

*see index

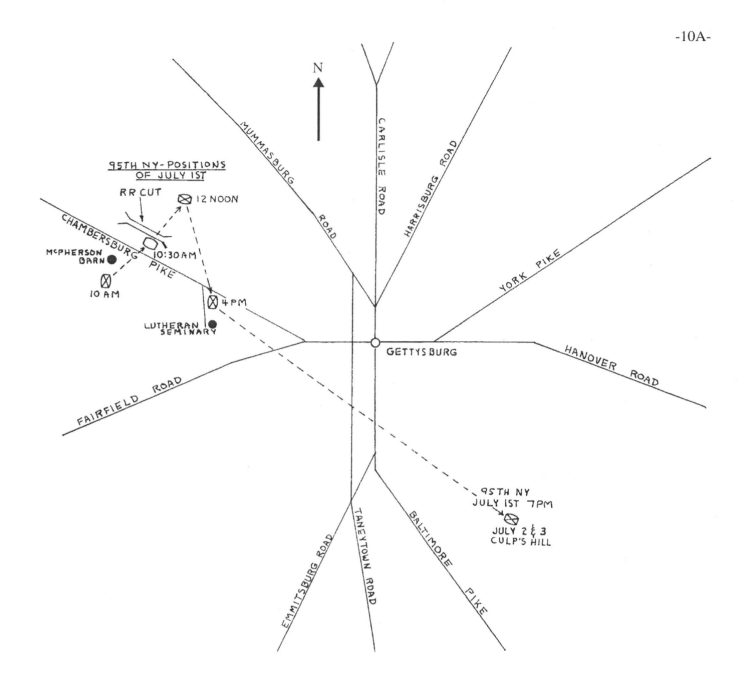

(Note: Some of the regiments of the Army Of The Potomac erected more than one marker on the Gettysburg Battlefield to indicate different positions at which they fought. For example, the 95th New York Infantry Regiment (2nd Brigade, 1st Division, 1st Corps) was in action at several points in the first day's battle northwest of Gettysburg. They erected markers at four of those points, each showing the time of day. When the 1st Corps retired to Cemetary Hill in the evening, the 95th NY moved over to Culp's Hill and joined with the 12th Corps in defending that hill in the battles of July 2nd and 3rd. They erected one marker there. It is thus possible to trace their movements to some extent. Most regiments have one marker, several have two and a few regiments have three or four. The 95th New York has five as shown on the map.)

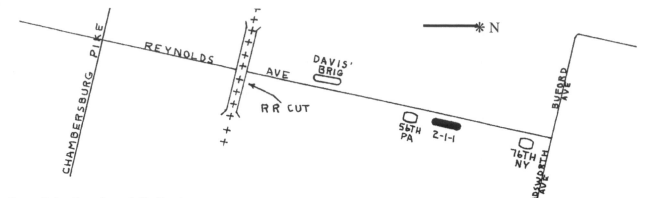

Hill's Corps Brig. Gen. Joseph R. Davis
Heth's 2nd, 11th, 42nd Mississippi and 55th North Carolina
Division 7-1: Formed west of Herr's Tavern, crossed Willoughby Run about 10 AM, advanced in line and soon encoun-
Davis tered artillery supported by 2nd Brigade, 1st Division, 1st Corps. The engagement was stubborn. The
Brigade* advance was made to the RR Cut. After a short interval the attack was renewed at the Cut and the Brigade
was forced back, losing many killed and wounded. A large force advancing on the right and rear opening
a heavy flank fire, the order was given to retire. About 3 PM the Brigade again moved forward with the
Division and reached the suburbs of the town. The Brigade in the advance in the morning, reached the RR
Cut.
7-2: Not engaged.
7-3: Formed part of the column of Longstreet's Assault.
7-4: Took up the march to Hagerstown during the night.
Casualties: 180K + 717W (Note: Casualties are not listed on the marker. These are from NY@G and do not
include the missing.)

56th PA Col. J. W. Hofman
(9 Cos) 7-1: The Regiment here delivered the opening fire of the infantry in the Battle of Gettysburg in the forenoon.
2-1-1 7-2: Occupied position on Culp's Hill as indicated by stone markers.
Casualties: 17K + 58W + 55M = 130 of 252

2-1-1 Brig. Gen. Lysander Cutler
7th Indiana, 76th, 84th, 95th, 147th NY, 56th (9 Cos) Pa. Infantry
7-1: Arrived 9:45 AM and took position on right of Reynolds Woods. 76th and 147th NY and 56th Pa, north of
RR Cut were fiercely attacked by Davis' Brigade, Maj. Gen. Heth's Division but the 84th and 95th NY
assisted by the 6th Wis. made a charge to the Cut, to which Davis' Brigade attempted to retreat, and
captured many prisoners and two stand of colors. The Brigade held its 1st position until 2 PM when it was
relieved by 2nd Brigade, 3rd Division and went into position on Oak Ridge on the left of the 2nd Division,
and assisted in the capture of a large part of Iverson's Brigade. Remained under a heavy fire until 4 PM
when it retired by order of the General Commanding to Cemetery Hill and took position on Culp's Hill.
The 7th Ind joined on Culp's Hill.
7-2: At night the 84th and 147th NY went to the support of 3rd Brigade, 2nd Division, 12th Corps and was
actively engaged, remaining through the night.
7-3: Repulsed an attack in the morning and remained in position until the close of the battle.
Casualties: 128K + 509W + 365M = 1002 Total

76th NY* Major Andrew J. Grover, Capt. John E. Cook
2-1-1 7-1: Fire opened here at 10 AM. Second stand at RR Cut.
7-2&3: Third stand at Culp's Hill.

Casualties: 32K + 132W + 7OM = 234 Total of 348 engaged

*see index

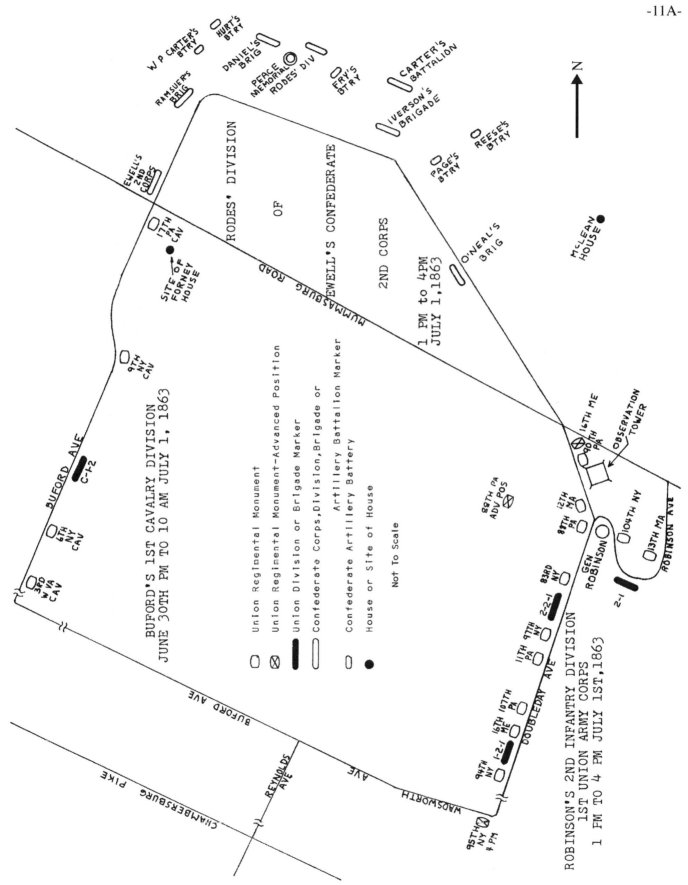

~ Gettysburg Battlefield Monuments, Locations & Inscriptions ~

95th NY*
2-1-1
7-1: 3rd position on Oak Hill at noon
Casualties: (Note: See Index for other positions).

94th NY
1-2-1
Col. Adrian R. Root, Maj. Samuel A. Moffett
Casualties: 12K + 58W + 175M = 245 Total (NY@Gbg)

1-2-1
Brig. Gen. Gabriel R. Paul, Col. Samuel H. Leonard, Col. Adrian R. Root, Col. Richard Coulter, Col. Peter Lyle.
16th Maine, 13th Mass, 94th, 104th NY, 107th Pa Infantry.
7-1: Arrived about noon and went into position near the Seminary and threw up breastworks. About 2:30 PM moved to the right of Corps in support of 2nd Brigade. Repulsed repeated attacks and was engaged until 4 PM, then retired to Seminary Ridge and constructed breastworks. The 11th Pa was transferred from the 2nd Brigade.
7-2: About noon relieved by 3rd Division, 2nd Corps and went to rear in support of batteries on Cemetary Hill. At sunset moved to the left to support the 3rd Corps and returned to Cemetary Hill.
7-3: At 9 AM went to support of 12th Corps and at 3 PM to the left and took position on right of 2nd Corps in support of a battery and there remained until the close of the battle.
Casualties: 51K + 357W + 633M-1041 Total

16th ME*
1-2-1
Col. Charles W. Tilden, Maj. Archibald D. Leavitt
7-1: Fought here from 10 AM to 4 PM when the Division was forced to retire by command of Gen. Robinson to Col. Tilden. The Regiment was moved to the right near the Mummasburg Road as indicated by a marker there with orders "to hold the position at any cost".
7-2: In position with Division on Cemetary Hill.
7-3: In position with Division on Cemetary Hill.
Casualties: 11K + 62W + 159M = 232 of 275 strength of Regiment

107th PA.*
1-2-1
Lt. Col. James MacThomson, Capt. Emanuel D. Roath
7-1: Regiment fought here from 1 PM until the Corps retired, then took position on the left of Cemetary Hill.
7-2: Moved to the left to support 2nd Corps in the evening. After repulse of the enemy, returned to former position.
7-3: Moved several times to reinforce different parts of the line.
Casualties: 11K + 56W + 98M = 165 Total (NY@Gbg)

11th PA.
2-2-1
Col. Richard Coulter, Capt. Benj. F. Haines, Capt. John B. Overmeyer
7-1: Casualties: 13K + 62W + 57M = 132 of 292 Present

97th NY
2-2-1
Capt. Charles Wheelock, Maj. Charles Northrup
7-1: Held enemy in check here from 12:30 PM to 3 PM. During this time, charged across the field to the west assisting in capturing Iverson's Brigade and securing the flag of the 20th No Carolina.
Casualties: 12K + 36W + 78M = 126 Total

*see index

~ Gettysburg Battlefield Monuments, Locations & Inscriptions ~

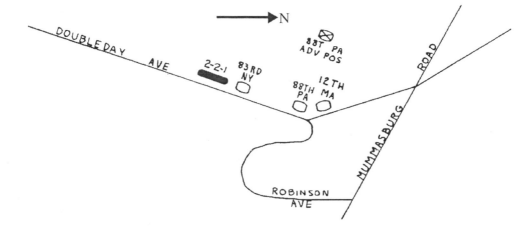

2-2-1   Brig. Gen. Henry Baxter
12th Mass, 83rd, 97th NY, 88th, 90th Pa. Infantry
7-1:   Arrived about noon, took position on right of Corps on Mummasburg Road with 2nd Brigade, 1st Division on left. Repulsed an attack of Col. O'Neal's Brigade, then changed front and with the assistance of 2nd Brigade, 1st Division captured 1000 prisoners and three stand of colors of Iverson's Brigade. Afterward, relieved by 1st Brigade and retired to the RR Cut to support Battery B-4th US. At 4 PM retired to Cemetary Hill and constructed breastworks. The 11th Pa was transferred to the 1st Brigade.
7-2:   About 10 AM relieved by 2nd Brigade, 2nd Division, 2nd Corps and placed in reserve. At 4 PM supported a battery of the 11th Corps.
7-3:   Moved to rear of cemetary early in the morning in support of 12th Corps. At 2 PM formed on right and rear of 2nd Corps and there remained until close of the battle.
Casualties: 40K + 258W + 350M =648 Total

83rd NY   9th NY Militia, Lt. Col. Joseph A. Moesch
2-2-1   7-1:   Engaged on this ground from 1 to 3 PM. Assisted in the capture of Iverson's Brigade.
7-2&3: At Zeigler's Grove on Cemetary Hill. Supported 11th, 12th and 2nd Corps Batteries.
Casualties: 6K +18W + 58M = 82 Total (NY@Gbg)

88th PA*   Maj. Benezet F. Foust, Capt. Henry Whiteside
2-2-1   7-1:   About noon, the Regiment was in line along the Mummasburg Rd. about 200 yards southeast of this monument. Later it changed direction and formed here, charged forward and captured two battle flags and a number of prisoners. At 4 PM, the Division was overpowered and forced through town.
7-2:   The Regiment was in position facing the Emmitsburg Road.
7-3:   At Zeigler's Grove as indicated by markers.
Casualties: 7K + 52W + 51M = 110 of 296 engaged.

88th PA*   7-1:   The Regiment charged to this point capturing two battle flags and a number of prisoners.
Advanced   (Note: This marker is approximately 50 yards west of 88th PA monument described above.)
Marker

12th Mass.   The Webster Regiment. Col. James J. Bates, Lt. Col. David Allen, Sr.
2-2-1   7-1:   Position held.
Casualties: 5K + 52W + 62M = 119 Total (NY@Gbg)

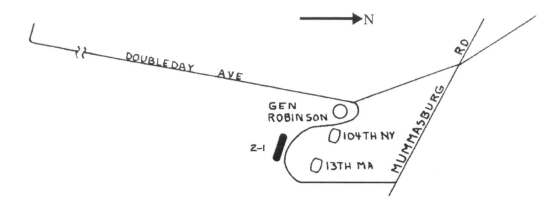

Robinson   John Cleveland Robinson, Brevet Major General, USA; 1817-1897
Statute   Commanded 2nd Division, 1st Army Corps at Gettysburg, July 1-3, 1863.
                 Cadet USMA 7/1/1835, 2nd Lt. 5th US Inf. 10/27/39, 1st Lt. 6/18/46, Capt 8/12/50, Maj. 2nd Inf. 2/20/62, Col.
                 43rd Inf. 7/28/66, Ret 5/6/69. Col. 1st Mich. 9/1/61, Honorably Discharged 4/25/62, Brig. Gen. USV
                 4/28/62, Honorably Mustered out of Volunteer Service 9/1/66. Commanding 1st Brigade, 3rd Division, 3rd
                 Corps in Peninsula Campaign 1862, Manassas 1862 and Fredericksburg; 2nd Division, 1st Corps at
                 Chancellorsville, Gettysburg and Mine Run Campaign; 2nd Division, 5th Corps at the Wilderness and
                 Spotsylvania.
                 Awarded Medal of Honor under resolution of Congress 3/28/1894 for most distinguished gallantry at the Battle
                 of Laurel Hill, Va 5/16/64 where he was severely wounded.
                 Breveted Lt. Col. USA 7/1/63 for gallant and meritorious services at the Battle of Gettysburg, Col. 5/5/64 for
                 gallant and meritorious services at the Battle of the Wilderness, Va, Brig. Gen. for gallant and meritorious
                 services at the Battle of Spotsylvania, Va, Maj. Gen. 3/16/65 for gallant and meritorious services in the field
                 during the War, Maj. Gen. USV 6/27/64 for gallant and meritorious services during the War.

104th NY   Col. Gilbert C. Prey
1-2-1   7-1: Casualties: 11K + 91W + 92M = 194 Total

2nd Division Brig. Gen. John C. Robinson
1st Corps   1st Brigade   Brig. Gen. Gabriel R. Paul, Col. S. H. Leonard, Col. Adrian R. Rook, Col. Peter Lyle,
                         Col. R. Coulter
                     2nd Brigade Brig. Gen. Henry Baxter
                 7-1: Arrived Seminary about noon. Hotly engaged on right and right center from about 2 PM to 4PM, when on
                       the advance of Rodes' Division against the front and flanks, the Division by order of the General Com-
                       manding, retired with the Corps through Gettysburg to Cemetary Hill. Went into position on the left,
                       parallel to the Emmitsburg Road.
                 7-2: Relieved about noon by 3rd Division, 2nd Corps, placed in reserve and thereafter sent to support of 3rd,
                       11th and 2nd Corps at different times and places.
                 7-3: At daylight moved to the support of batteries on Cemetary Hill. At 9AM sent to support of 12th Corps. At
                       3 PM, took position on right of 2nd Corps and remained until close of the battle.
                 Casualties: Killed 91; Wounded 616, Missing 983; Total 1690

13th Mass   Col. Samuel H. Leonard, Lt. Col. N. Walter Batchelder
1-2-1   7-1: Position held.
                 Casualties: 7K + 77W + 101M = 185 Total

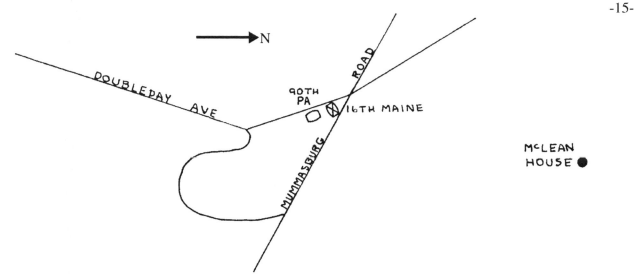

90th PA*
2-2-1
Col. Peter Lyle, Maj. Alfred J. Sellers, Col. Peter Lyle
7-1: Here fought the 90th Pa on the afternoon of July 1,1863.
Casualties: 11 Killed, 44 Wounded, 39 Missing; Total 94 Engaged 203

16th Maine*
1-2-1
Col. Charles W. Tilden, Maj. Archibald D. Leavitt
7-1: Position held at 4 o'clock PM by the 16th Maine Inf. While the rest of the Division was retiring, the Regiment having moved from the position at the left where its monument stands, under orders to hold this position at any cost. It lost on this field 11 Killed, 62 Wounded, 159 Missing; 232 Total of 275 engaged.

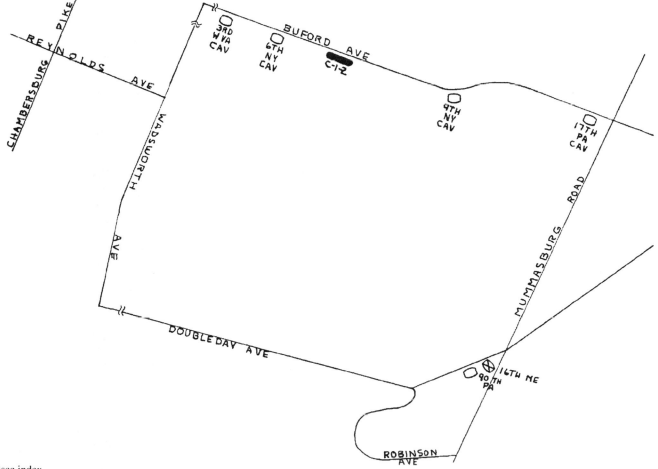

*see index

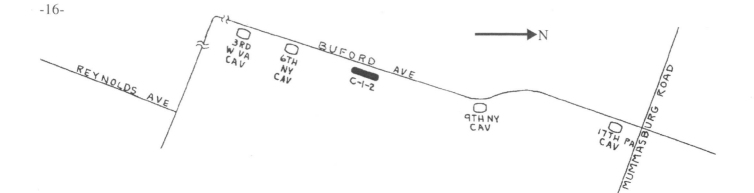

3rd W Va
Cavalry
C-1-2

(Two Companies) Capt. Seymour B. Conger

7-1: Position held.

Casualties: 4 Missing (NY@Gbg)

6th NY
Cavalry
C-1-2

Maj. William E. Beardsley

6-30: Arrived Gettysburg

7-1: Skirmished dismounted on this line until arrival of 1st Corps, and the rest of the day on the right of the York Road, then returned to Cemetary Hill, one squadron being among the last Union troops in Gettysburg that day. Bivouacked in Peach Orchard that night.

7-2: Engaged enemy skirmishers until relieved by troops of the 3rd Corps, then moved to Taneytown.

7-3: Moved to Winchester, then moved with Buford's Division in pursuit of the enemy.

7-8: Engaged enemy at Boonsboro, Md., holding that position.

Casualties: 1 Killed, 5 Wounded, 16 Missing: Total 22

C-1-2
Cavalry
1st Division
2nd Brigade

Thomas C. Devin

6th, 9th, NY, 17th Pa, 3rd W Va (2 Cos)

6-30: Started early for Gettysburg and encountered two Mississippi Regiments and a section of artillery and after a short skirmish proceeded to Gettysburg, arriving there as a detachment of Maj. Gen. Heth's Division was about to enter town, but it withdrew toward Cashtown, leaving pickets 4 and 1/2 miles from Gettysburg.

7-1: Between 8 and 9 AM, the Confederates advanced in force from Cashtown. The Brigade dismounted and with Battery A-2nd US held its position for more than two hours against infantry and artillery in superior numbers until the arrival of the 11th Corps and then held the approach by the York Pike. Later ordered to the Emmitsburg Road and formed line with right flank resting on the town. Bivouacked in front of Little Round Top.

7-2: Relieved by 3rd Corps. Marched to Taneytown enroute to Westminster.

Casualties: 2 Killed, 3 Wounded, 23 Missing: Total 28

9th NY
Cavalry
C-1-2

Col. William Sackett

7-1: Position at 8 AM. Picket on Chambersburg Pike fired on at 5:00 AM.

Casualties: 2 Killed, 2 Wounded, 7 Missing: Total 11

17th PA
Cavalry
C-1-2

Col. Josiah H. Kellogg

7-1: Regiment held this position from 5 AM until arrival of 1st Corps. The Brigade then moved to the right covering the roads to Carlisle and Harrisburg and holding the enemy in check until relieved by troops of the 11th Corps. It then took position on the right flank of the infantry and later aided in covering the retreat of the 11th Corps to Cemetary Hill. It went into position with the Division on the left of the Army.

Casualties: 4 missing total (NY@Gbg)

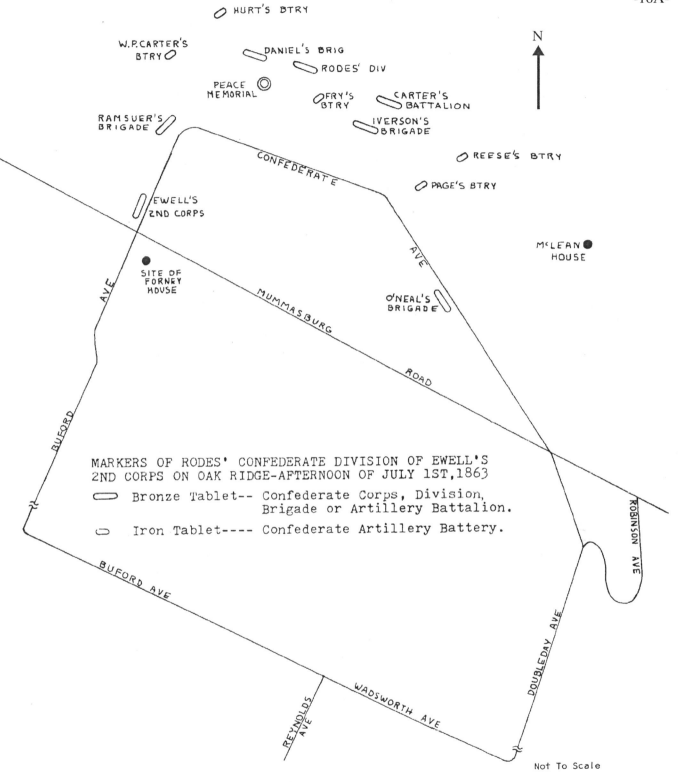

MARKERS OF RODES' CONFEDERATE DIVISION OF EWELL'S
2ND CORPS ON OAK RIDGE-AFTERNOON OF JULY 1ST,1863

⬭ Bronze Tablet-- Confederate Corps, Division,
              Brigade or Artillery Battalion.

⬭ Iron Tablet---- Confederate Artillery Battery.

Not To Scale

"In Memory of Martin L. Wade, this land located north of the village of Heidlersburg, Adams County, Pennsylvania, and occupied by Confederate troops under the command of Major General Robert E. Rodes, immediately prior to the Battle of Gettysburg, is being dedicated to the Township of Tyrone by the State of Alabama to be used for public purposes. This land was given to the State of Alabama in the Last Will and Testament of Martin L.Wade, dated June 20, 1966".

Note: The bronze tablet on which the above quotation is inscribed is fastened to a rock about 200 to 300 yards north of the junction of Heidlersburg Road and Route 234. The rock is on the west side of Heidlersburg Road.

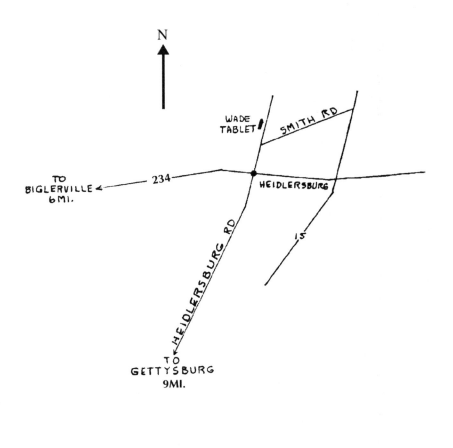

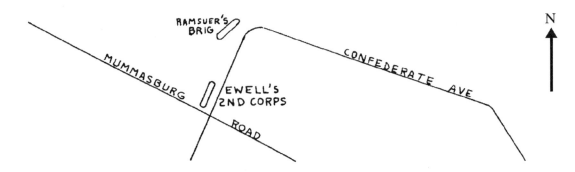

Ewell's
2nd Corps

Army of Northern Virginia

2nd Army Corps   Lt. Gen. Richard S. Ewell
Early's Division   Maj. Gen. Jubal A. Early
Johnson's Division   Maj. Gen. Edward Johnson
Rodes' Division   Maj. Gen. Robert E. Rodes
Artillery Reserve   Col. J. Thompson Brown 8 Batteries

7-1: The Corps occupied the left of the Confederate line and reached the field in the following order: Rodes' Division by Newville Road about noon, and deploying along Oak Ridge soon became engaged. Early's Division on the Harrisburg Pike about 1 PM and united with Rodes' left in an attack on 1st and 11th Corps Union troops and drove them through the town to Cemetary Hill. The two Divisions occupied the town.
Johnson's Division reached the field about nightfall and not engaged. Late in the night moved along the railroad and took position on the left of the Corps northeast of town.

7-2: In the early morning, Johnson's Division was ordered to take possession of a wooded hill on the left. Skirmishers were advanced and a desultry fire kept up until 4 PM when the artillery from Benner's Hill opened. The firing continued for two hours; the batteries were withdrawn. The Division, about dusk, was advanced to the assault in connection with Early's Division on the right. The battle continued until after dark. A partial success was made by a portion of each division but not being supported on the right, was withdrawn to the former positions.

7-3: Early in the morning an attack was made by Johnson's Division, having been reinforced by three brigades from the Corps. Two other assaults were made but failed. Early's Division was withdrawn and occupied its former position in the town and was not again engaged. Rodes' Division held a position west of the town and not engaged.

Casualties: 809 Killed, 3823 Wounded, 1305 Missing; Total 5937

Ewell's
Corps
Rodes'
Division
Ramseur's
Brigade

Brig. Gen. Stephen Dodson Ramseur

2nd, 4th, 14th, 30th North Carolina Infantry

7-1: Soon after Iverson's and O'Neal's Brigades had each suffered the repulse of three regiments with heavy losses, Ramseur's Brigade moved from its position here and vigorously assailed the right wing of the Union forces. The 14th and 30th Regiments with O'Neal's 3rd Alabama, turned the flank of the Union forces while the 2nd Regiment together with Dole's Brigade and a part of O'Neal's, struck them in the rear. A struggle ensued in which both sides suffered severely and the conflict here only ended with the retreat of the Union Corps from Seminary Ridge. In that retreat, the Brigade made active pursuit and captured many prisoners.

7-2: Skirmishing on the southern borders of the town.

7-3: In sunken road southwest of town.

7-4: In line on Seminary Ridge. Began the march to Hagerstown.

Present 1090, 23 Killed, 129 Wounded, 44 Missing; Total 196.

THE SYMBOLS LISTED BELOW ARE USED TO IDENTIFY THE MONUMENTS, MARKERS, TABLETS, STATUES, ETC. WHICH ARE DRAWN ON THE MAPS IN THESE PAGES

SYMBOL	TYPE	REPRESENTING	DESCRIPTION
	Bronze Tablet	Army of The Potomac, Union Corps or Division or Brigade, Regular Army Regiment, Regular Army Artillery Battery, Volunteer Artillery Brigade.	Brigade Tablet Mounted on Square Marble base. All other Tablets are on large vertical Granite Blocks.
	Bronze Tablet	Army of Northern Virginia, Confederate Corps or Division or Brigade of Artillery Battalion	Brigade Tablet and Artillery Battalion Tablet Mounted on Round Marble base. All other Tablets are Mounted on large vertical Granite blocks.
	Iron Tablet	Union Army Battery (other than Regular Army)	Mounted on Black Iron Shaft.
	Iron Tablet	Confederate Artillery Battery	Mounted on Black Iron Shaft.
	Iron Tablet	Confederate Brigade Advanced Position	Mounted on Black Iron Shaft.
	Regimental or Battery Monument	Principal Position of Volunteer Regiment or Volunteer Artillery Battery	Usually Granite or Marble in a Great Variety of Shapes and Sizes.
	Regimental Marker	Other than Principal Position of Regiment or Battery	Usually a Square Granite Marker or tablet or may be another monument.
	Flank Marker or Company Marker	Left and/or Right Flank of Regiment or Battery or Position of a Company.	Usually a Small Square or Rectangular Granite Marker.
	Army Or Corps Headquarters	Site of Headquarters of Army Commander or Corps Commander or Chief of Artillery	Cannon Barrel Mounted Vertically on Stone, Granite or Marble Base.
	State Monument	Monument Erected by Union or Confederate State.	
	Statue	Standing or Equestrian	Bronze Sculpture
	Building	House, Barn or other Structure	Identified by Owner's Name.
	Miscellaneous Marker	Marker or Inscription of a type not listed above	Granite or Metal Marker.
*Asterisk		Used whenever a Division or Brigade or Regiment or Battery has more than one Monument or Marker.	Check the Index for other Monument or Marker.

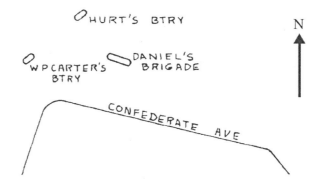

Ewell's Corps Rodes' Division T. Carter's Battalion W. Carter's Battery	The King William Artillery. Capt. W. P. Carter
	2 - 10 Pounder Parrotts, 2 Napoleans

Ewell's Corps Rodes' Division T. Carter's Battalion W. Carter's Battery

The King William Artillery. Capt. W. P. Carter

2 - 10 Pounder Parrotts, 2 Napoleans

7-1: Soon after arriving here, opened an enfilading fire on the Union forces near the Chambersburg Pike, causing some to seek shelter in the railroad cuts. Their guns replied slowly but not without inflicting some losses on the Battery in its exposed position. Later in the day, it moved to the foot of this ridge to aid Dole's Brigade in repelling the 11th Corps and rendered effective service. When the fight ended by withdrawal of the 1st Corps, it pursued the Union forces to the edge of town.

7-2: In position, not engaged.

7-3: The Parrott guns were on Seminary Ridge near the RR Cut, participated in the cannonade before Pickett's Charge.

Casualties: 4 Killed, 7 Wounded, Total 11. Ammunition expended 572 Rounds.

Hill's Corps Artillery Reserve McIntosh's Battalion Hurt's Battery*

Hardaway (Alabama) Artillery. Capt. W. B. Hurt

2 Whitworths, 2 - 3 Inch Rifles

7-1: The Whitworths in position to right of Chambersburg Pike near the position of Pegram's Battalion. Opened fire slowly and effectively, shelling the woods occupied by the Union troops to the right of the town.

7-2: The Battery in position on Seminary Ridge south of Hagerstown Road exposed to heavy Union sharp-shooter fire and artillery.

7-3: The Whitworths were moved to this position and fired with great effect; the 3 inch rifles remaining on Seminary Ridge south of the Hagerstown Road.

7-4: Withdrew in evening to Marsh Creek on the Emmitsburg Road.

Losses not reported in detail.

Ewell's Corps Rodes' Division Daniel's Brigade*

Brig. Gen. Junius Daniel

32nd, 43rd, 45th, 53rd and 2nd Battalion North Carolina Infantry.

7-1: Brigade formed to right of Division and its line extended from Forney Field to the RR Cut near the McPherson barn. The Regiments did not at first move together nor attack the same troops. The 43rd and 53rd Regiments aided by O'Neal's 3rd Alabama and Iverson's 12th North Carolina attacked the Union line in the Sheads and Forney Woods. The 45th Regiment and 2nd Battalion fought the 2nd Brigade, 3rd Division, 1st Corps near the RR Cuts and being joined by the 32nd Regiment and other troops, compelled retreat. The Brigade was reunited and lost heavily in the struggle which dislodged the Union forces from Seminary Ridge.

7-2: On Seminary Ridge all day. After nightfall moved into town.

7-3: Marched before daylight to Culp's Hill to aid Johnson's Division.

7-4: Occupied Seminary Ridge and at night began the march to Hagerstown.

Present 2100. 165 Killed, 635 Wounded, 116 Missing; Total 916

*see index

~ Gettysburg Battlefield Monuments, Locations & Inscriptions ~

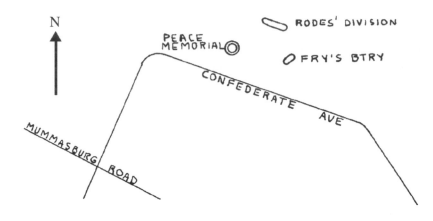

Ewell's	Major General Robert E. Rodes
Corps	Daniel's Brigade Brig. Gen. Junius Daniel
Rodes'	Dole's Brigade Brig. Gen. George Doles
Division*	Iverson's Brigade Brig. Gen. Alfred Iverson
	Ramseur's Brigade Brig. Gen. S. D. Ramseur
	O'Neal's Brigade Col. E. A. O'Neal
	Artillery Battalion, 4 Batteries, Lt. Col. Thomas H. Carter

7-1: Advancing by the Newville Road, occupied Oak Hill about noon. The line formed and advanced in the following order:

Doles' Brigade deployed in the valley north of town and left of the Division and was opposed by the 11th Corps.

O'Neal's Brigade advanced on ridge and meeting a portion of 1st Union Corps was driven back with heavy losses.

Iverson's Brigade was also driven back with heavy losses after advancing against the Union 1st Corps.

Daniel's Brigade was ordered to the support of Iverson but became separated by a change of direction. Moved to the railroad on the right where Heth's Division was engaged.

Ramseur's Division was held in reserve.

After a severe conflict the Union troops retired.

7-2: The Division occupied ground near and west of the town and was not engaged.

7-3: The Brigades of Daniel and O'Neal were ordered to report to Gen. Johnson on the left early in the morning and joined in the attack on Culp's Hill. The remainder of the Division held the position of the day before and at night retired to Seminary Ridge.

Casualties: 421 Killed, 1728 Wounded, 704 Missing; Total 2853

Ewell's	The Orange (Virginia) Artillery. Capt. C. W. Fry
Corps	2 - 10 Pounder Parrotts, 2 - 3 Inch Rifles
Rodes'	
Division	
Carter's	
Battalion	
Fry's	
Battery*	

7-1: Opened fire soon after arriving here upon the Union troops near the Chambersburg Pike to which their artillery replied with a heavy fire which caused some loss. Soon afterward the Union forces extended their line northward to the Mummasburg Road and this Battery, by its enfilading fire, aided our infantry in the severe conflict which ended with the withdrawal of the 1st Corps from Seminary Ridge.

7-2: In position but not engaged

7-3: All guns on Seminary Ridge near the RR Cut and took part in the cannonade preceeding Longstreet's Assault.

7-4: After nightfall, began the march to Hagerstown.

Losses not reported in detail. Ammunition expended 882 Rounds

Peace	PEACE ETERNAL IN A NATION UNITED
Memorial	

(Note: Dedicated on July 3, 1938 during the last reunion of the Blue and the Gray, by President Franklin D Roosevelt and a Northern and Southern Veteran of the Civil War.)

*see index

PEACE ETERNAL IN A NATION UNITED

UNITED STATES COMMISSION
Harry H. Woodring
Hugh L. White
Joseph F. Guffey
Harry L. Haines
Mervin Jones

CONTRIBUTING STATES
Pennsylvania

New York	Wisconsin
Indiana	Tennessee
Virginia	Illinois

PENNSYLVANIA
STATE COMMISSION
John S. Rice, Chairman
Willis D. Hall
Henry W. A. Hanson
Frederick B. Kerr
Victor C. Mather
William S. McLear, Jr.
Gerald P. O'Neill
William A. Schnader
Edward C. Shannon
Paul L. Roy, Executive Secretary

(East Side Of Tower)

WITH FIRMNESS

IN THE RIGHTS

AS GOD GIVES US

TO SEE THE RIGHT

Lincoln

(West Side Of Tower)

AN ENDURING LIGHT

TO GUIDE US

IN UNITY

AND FELLOWSHIP

(Tablet In Rear Of Memorial)

—ETERNAL LIGHT—
Dedicated By
Franklin D. Roosevelt
During The Observance Of The
75th Anniversary Of The
Battle of Gettysburg
July 3, 1938

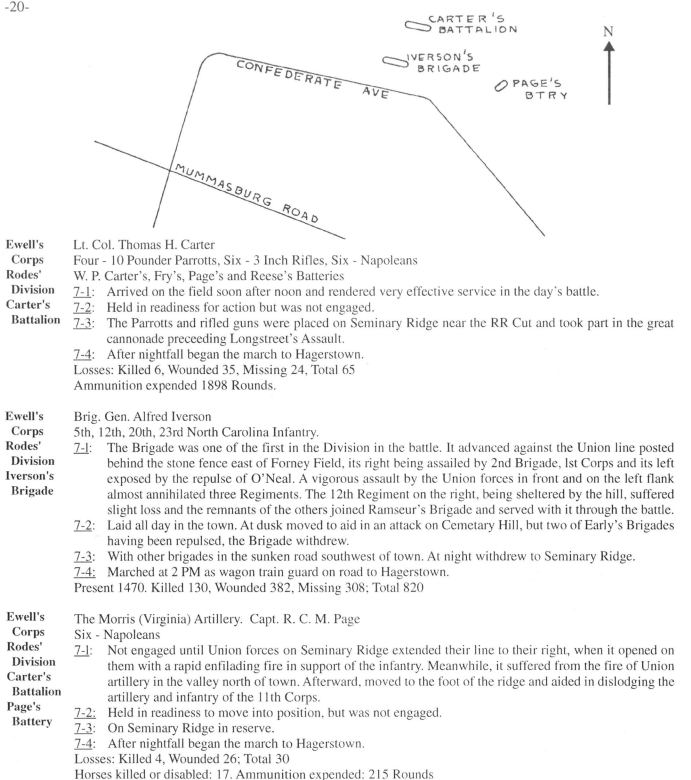

Ewell's Corps Rodes' Division Carter's Battalion

Lt. Col. Thomas H. Carter
Four - 10 Pounder Parrotts, Six - 3 Inch Rifles, Six - Napoleans
W. P. Carter's, Fry's, Page's and Reese's Batteries

7-1: Arrived on the field soon after noon and rendered very effective service in the day's battle.

7-2: Held in readiness for action but was not engaged.

7-3: The Parrotts and rifled guns were placed on Seminary Ridge near the RR Cut and took part in the great cannonade preceeding Longstreet's Assault.

7-4: After nightfall began the march to Hagerstown.

Losses: Killed 6, Wounded 35, Missing 24, Total 65
Ammunition expended 1898 Rounds.

Ewell's Corps Rodes' Division Iverson's Brigade

Brig. Gen. Alfred Iverson
5th, 12th, 20th, 23rd North Carolina Infantry.

7-1: The Brigade was one of the first in the Division in the battle. It advanced against the Union line posted behind the stone fence east of Forney Field, its right being assailed by 2nd Brigade, 1st Corps and its left exposed by the repulse of O'Neal. A vigorous assault by the Union forces in front and on the left flank almost annihilated three Regiments. The 12th Regiment on the right, being sheltered by the hill, suffered slight loss and the remnants of the others joined Ramseur's Brigade and served with it through the battle.

7-2: Laid all day in the town. At dusk moved to aid in an attack on Cemetary Hill, but two of Early's Brigades having been repulsed, the Brigade withdrew.

7-3: With other brigades in the sunken road southwest of town. At night withdrew to Seminary Ridge.

7-4: Marched at 2 PM as wagon train guard on road to Hagerstown.

Present 1470. Killed 130, Wounded 382, Missing 308; Total 820

Ewell's Corps Rodes' Division Carter's Battalion Page's Battery

The Morris (Virginia) Artillery. Capt. R. C. M. Page
Six - Napoleans

7-1: Not engaged until Union forces on Seminary Ridge extended their line to their right, when it opened on them with a rapid enfilading fire in support of the infantry. Meanwhile, it suffered from the fire of Union artillery in the valley north of town. Afterward, moved to the foot of the ridge and aided in dislodging the artillery and infantry of the 11th Corps.

7-2: Held in readiness to move into position, but was not engaged.

7-3: On Seminary Ridge in reserve.

7-4: After nightfall began the march to Hagerstown.

Losses: Killed 4, Wounded 26; Total 30
Horses killed or disabled: 17. Ammunition expended: 215 Rounds

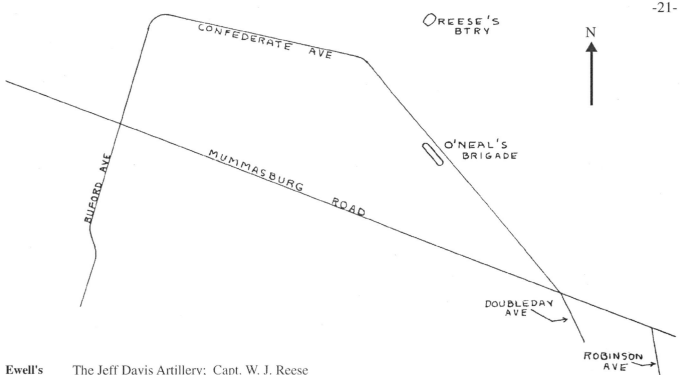

Ewell's **Corps** **Rodes'** **Division** **Carter's** **Battalion** **Reese's** **Battery**	The Jeff Davis Artillery; Capt. W. J. Reese Four 3 Inch Rifles 7-1: Was placed in position here in support of Doles' Brigade against two Divisions of the 11th Corps massing on his front and left flank. It rendered effective service not only in protecting Doles' left flank but also aided in dislodging infantry and artillery from their position. 7-2: Remained in reserve. 7-3: In position on Seminary Ridge near the RR Cut and took part in the cannonade preceding Longstreet's Assault. 7-4: After nightfall began the march to Hagerstown. Losses not reported. Ammunition expended: 229 Rounds

Ewell's **Corps** **Rodes'** **Division** **O'Neal's** **Brigade***	Col. E. A. O'Neal 3rd, 5th, 6th, 12th, 26th Alabama Infantry 7-1: Soon after arriving at this position, three Regiments attacked the Union flank, the 5th Regiment being ordered to guard the wide interval between the Brigade and Doles' Brigade in the valley on the left, and the 3rd Regiment joining Daniel's Brigade, and afterward Ramseur's Brigade. The three Regiments were repulsed with heavy losses, but the entire Brigade took part in the general attack soon made by the Confederates which finally dislodged the Union forces from Seminary Ridge. 7-2: The Brigade in position all day in or near the town but not engaged. 7-3: The 5th Regiment laid in the southern borders of the town firing upon the Union Artillery with their long range rifles. The other Regiments moved to Culp's Hill to reinforce Johnson's Div. 7-4: Moved to Seminary Ridge. At night began the march to Hagerstown. Present 1794. Killed 73, Wounded 430, Missing 193; Total 696.

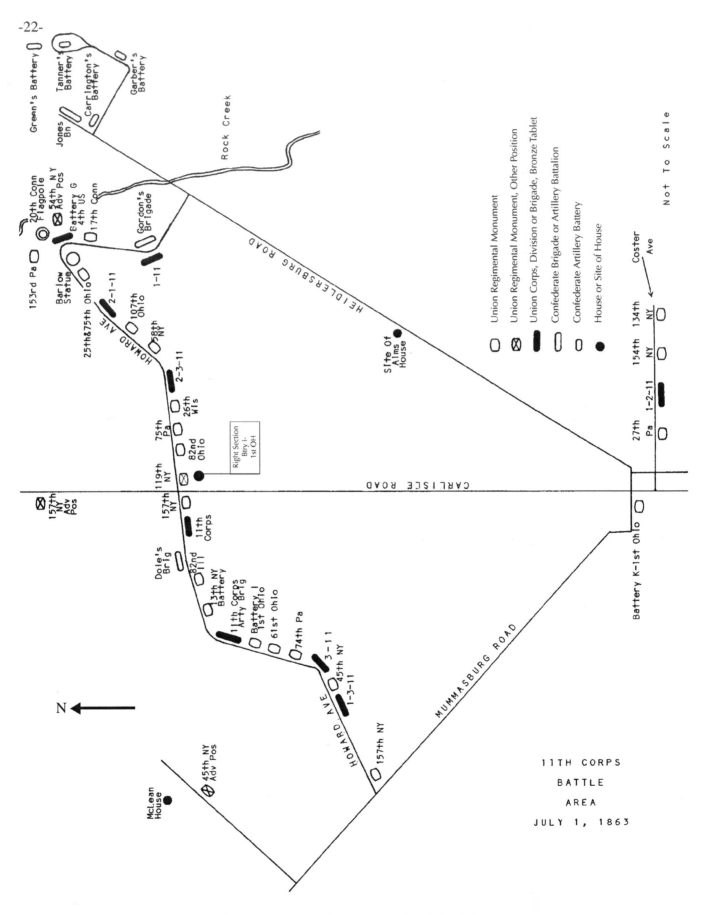

Green's Battery
Tanner's Battery
Carrington's Battery
Garber's Battery
Jones Bn

Rock Creek

20th Conn Flagpole
54th NY Adv Pos
Battery G 4th US
17th Conn
Gordon's Brigade
153rd Pa
Barlow Statue
2-1-11
107th Ohio
1-11
25th&75th Ohio
58th NY
HOWARD AVE
2-3-11
26th Wis
75th Pa
82nd Ohio
Right Section Btry I- 1st OH
119th NY
157th NY
157th NY Adv Pos

HEIDLERSBURG ROAD

Site Of Alms House

CARLISLE ROAD

Union Regimental Monument
Union Regimental Monument, Other Position
Union Corps, Division or Brigade, Bronze Tablet
Confederate Brigade or Artillery Battalion
Confederate Artillery Battery
House or Site of House

Not To Scale

Coster Ave
154th NY
134th NY
27th Pa
1-2-11

Battery K-1st Ohio

11th Corps
Dole's Brig
82nd 111
13th NY Battery
11th Corps Arty Brig
Battery I 1st Ohio
61st Ohio
74th Pa
3-11
45th NY
1-3-11

MUMMASBURG ROAD

HOWARD AVE

157th NY

N

45th NY Adv Pos
McLean House

11TH CORPS
BATTLE
AREA
JULY 1, 1863

~ Gettysburg Battlefield Monuments, Locations & Inscriptions ~

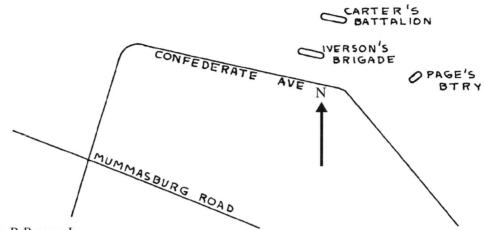

157ᵗʰ NY*
1-3-11
Col. Phillip P. Brown, Jr.
7-1: Lost here 10 officers, 291 men.

1-3-11
Brig. Gen. Alexander Schimmelfennig, Col. George von Amsberg, 82nd, 111th, 45th, 157th NY, 61st Ohio, 74th PA Infantry.

7-1: Arrived about 1 PM and advanced to connect with the right of the 1st Corps on Oak Hill but was met by a heavy artillery and musket fire. After being engaged between two and three hours and pressed closely upon the front and flanks by superior numbers, the Brigade was compelled to retire with the Corps through town to Cemetary Hill. The streets and alleys of the town became congested with the mass of infantry and artillery and many were captured. The Brigade formed and took position on Cemetary Hill between the 1st and 2nd Divisions of the Corps.

7-2: At 4 PM, the Brigade was subject to a heavy artillery fire converging on Cemetary Hill. At dark a sudden attack was made on the right and the Brigade was sent to the support of Brig. Gen. Ames and returned after midnight except the 74th Pa which remained under Gen. Ames.

7-3: Skirmishing but not engaged.

Casualties: 751 Killed, Wounded and Missing.

45ᵗʰ NY*
1-3-11
Col. George von Amsberg, Lt. Col. Adolphus Bobke

7-1: Went into action 11:30 AM by deploying four companies as skirmishers about 100 yards to rear of this position, then advanced, supported by the other six companies, about 540 yards under terrific artillery and sharpshooter fire to a point indicated by a marker in front. Regiment assisted in repelling a charge on the flank of the 1st Corps to the left, capturing many prisoners. Covered retrograde movement into town, fighting through the streets. A portion of the Regiment was cut off and took shelter in houses and yards on Chambersburg Street, holding enemy at bay until 5:30 PM when they surrendered after destroying their arms. Those captured refused parole hoping to encumber the enemy, believing the Union Army would capture the crippled foe and thereby effect their release. Sadly disappointed, they suffered indescribable misery in Andersonville and other prisons, neglected, often maltreated and finally, believing themselves forgotten and forsaken, many died martyrs and joined their more fortunate comrades who fell gloriously on this field.

7-2: Remnant of Regiment exposed to heavy artillery fire on Cemetary Hill. In the evening moved hastily to Culp's Hill and assisted in repulsing an attack on Greene's Brigade of the 12th Corps.

7-3: Again exposed to artillery and sharpshooter fire whereupon Sergent Link with volunteers dislodged the enemy sharpshooters in the edge of the town, nearly all of the attacking party being killed or wounded in the effort.

Casualties: 11 Killed, 35 Wounded, 178 Missing; Total 224 of 375.

45ᵗʰ NY*
Advanced position about 540 yards in advance of principal monument.

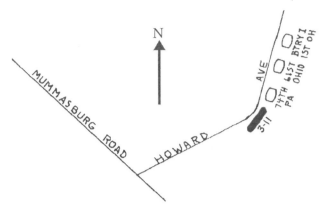

3rd Division Maj. Gen. Carl Schurz, Brig. Gen. Alexander Schimmelfennig
11th Corps 1st Brigade   Brig. Gen. Alexander Schimmelfennig, Col. Geo.V. Amsberg
             2nd Brigade   Col. Walter Kryzanowski

             <u>7-1</u>:   Arrived about noon. Advanced to connect with the right of the 1st Corps, with the 1st Division on the right, but was repulsed with a strong artillery and infantry fire from Rodes' Division of Ewell's Corps. Engaged until past 4 PM and then retreated through the town to Cemetary Hill, bringing up the rear of the Corps, and took position behind stone walls with 1st Division on right and 2nd Division on left; skirmishers in houses 300 to 500 yards in front.

             <u>7-2</u>:   In position in two lines behind stone walls of the Cemetary. At 7PM, the 1st Brigade was sent to the support of the 1st Division. One Regiment remained there. Four Regiments went further to the right and assisted in repelling a 9 PM attack made through the woods on the 1st Corps. Between 8 and 9 PM, an attack on East Cemetery Hill was made by Hays' Louisiana Brigade and a detatchment from the 2nd Brigade was hastened to the point of attack and after a short but vigorous hand-to-hand conflict, the attack was repulsed.

             <u>7-3</u>:   Not engaged except skirmishing

             <u>7-4</u>:   Detachments from the Division entered town and captured over 300 Confederates left on the retreat of their forces.

             Casualties: 133 Killed, 684 Wounded, 659 Missing; Total 1476

74th PA*   Col. Adolph von Hartung, Lt. Col. Alexander von Mitzel, Capt. Gustave Schleiter, Capt. Henry Krauseneck
1-3-11   <u>7-1</u>:   Fought here from 2 PM until the Corps fell back.
             <u>7-2</u>:   In line with Division in front of Cemetery Hill.
             Casualties: 10 Killed, 40 Wounded, 60 Missing; Total 110

61st Ohio*   Col. Stephen J. McGroarty
1-3-11   <u>7-1</u>:   Deployed as a skirmish line in advance of Brigade and moved toward Oak Hill where it supported Dilger's Battery-one section, and engaged the enemy. Withdrew with the Corps to Cemetary Hill.
             <u>7-2</u>:   To assistance of 12th Corps on Culp's Hill.
             Casualties: 6 Killed, 36 Wounded, 12 Missing; Total 54 of 309 engaged

Battery I   Capt. Hubert Dilger
1st Ohio*   Six Napoleans
11th Corps   <u>7-1</u>:   Marched Emmitsburg to Gettysburg. At once upon arriving, it advanced rapidly to the Carlisle Road, and
   Artillery   having taken position near this spot, immediately engaged the enemy. Reinforced by Wheeler's Battery,
   Brigade   advanced twice from this position. Retired with 11th Corps but was halted and again engaged the enemy before crossing the bridge into town. During the remainder of the battle, the Battery held the extreme right of Maj. Osborn's line on Cemetery Hill.
             Casualties: 13 Wounded Total

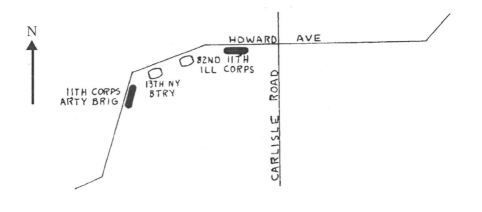

11th Corps Artillery Brigade   Maj. Thomas W. Osborn

1st NY Battery I	Six	3 Inch Rifles	Capt. Michael Weidrich
13th NY Battery	Four	3 Inch Rifles	Lt. William Wheeler
1st Ohio Battery I	Six	12 Pounders	Capt. Hubert Dilger
1st Ohio Battery K	Four	12 Pounders	Capt. Lewis Heckman
4th US Battery G	Six	12 Pounders	Lt. Bayard Wilkeson, Lt. Eugene A. Bancroft

7-1: Arrived with Corps. All engaged except New York Battery. Artillery retired and took position on Cemetary Hill west of Baltimore Pike.

7-2: Brigade reinforced in morning by five batteries from the Artillery Reserve.

7-3: At 1 PM the Confederates opened a terrific fire, enfilading from the right, followed by an infantry charge on which artillery of this command was concentrated with great effect.

Casualties: 7 Killed, 53 Wounded, 9 Missing; Total 69. 98 horses killed

82nd Illinois 1-3-1   Lt. Col. Edward S. Salomon

7-1: First line of battle. Retreated to Cemetery Hill.

7-2: Participated in repulse of Ewell's Corps.

Casualties: 112 Killed, Wounded and Missing.

13th NY Battery 11th Corps Artillery Brigade   Lt. William Wheeler
Four 12 Pounders
Casualties: 8 Wounded, 3 Missing; Total 11

11th Corps   Major General Oliver O. Howard
1st Division   Brig. Gen. Francis Barlow
2nd Division Brig. Gen. Adolph von Steinwehr
3rd Division   Maj. Gen. Carl Schurz

7-1: Schurz Division arrived 10:30 AM, was formed northwest of town. Barlow's Division was formed on Schurz' right. Steinwehr's Division was placed on Cemetary Hill. The line in front was attacked by brigades of Rodes' and Early's Divisions. About 4 PM the Corps was forced to retire to Cemetary Hill and formed on each side of the Baltimore Pike.

7-2: Corps remained in same position until about 4 PM when the Confederate Artillery opened fire from Benner's Hill and Seminary Ridge but was silenced by the artillery under Col. Wainright and Maj. Osborn. At 8 PM Hays Louisiana Brigade and Hoke's North Carolina Brigade attacked positions on East Cemetery Hill but were repulsed.

7-3: At 1 PM the Confederate artillery within range opened fire on this position which was followed by an unsuccessful charge on the 2nd Corps position.

Casualties: 369 Killed, 1922 Wounded, 1510 Missing; 3801 Total

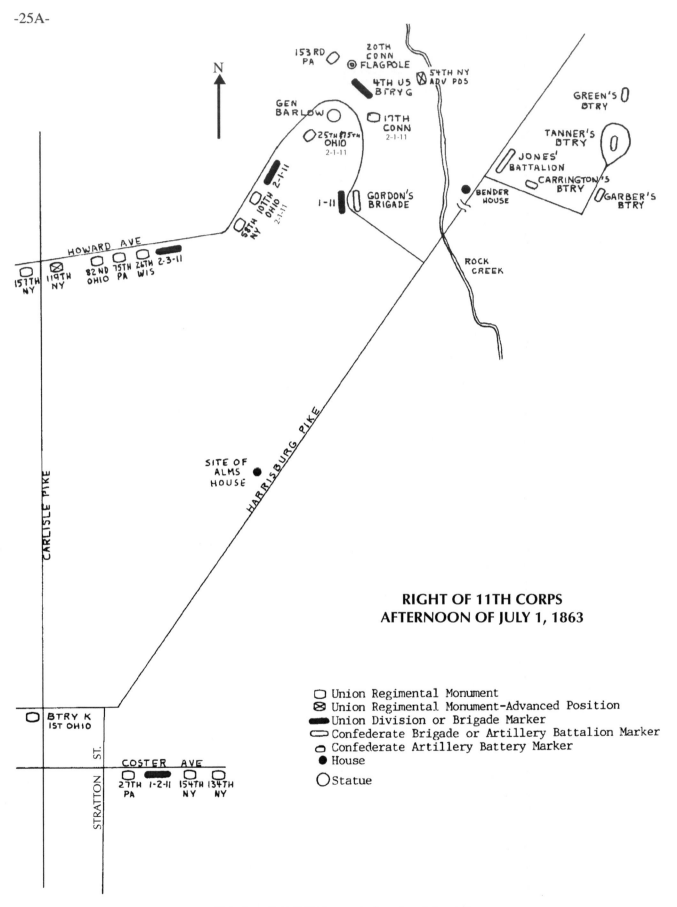

N

153RD PA

20TH CONN FLAGPOLE

54TH NY ADV POS

4TH US BTRY G

GEN BARLOW

17TH CONN 2-1-11

25TH 75TH OHIO 2-1-11

GREEN'S BTRY

TANNER'S BTRY

JONES' BATTALION

CARRINGTON'S BTRY

GARBER'S BTRY

BENDER HOUSE

110TH OHIO 2-1-11

56TH NY

1-11

GORDON'S BRIGADE

ROCK CREEK

HOWARD AVE

157TH NY

119TH NY

82ND OHIO

75TH PA

26TH WIS

2-3-11

CARLISLE PIKE

SITE OF ALMS HOUSE

HARRISBURG PIKE

RIGHT OF 11TH CORPS
AFTERNOON OF JULY 1, 1863

◻ Union Regimental Monument
⊗ Union Regimental Monument-Advanced Position
▬ Union Division or Brigade Marker
⬭ Confederate Brigade or Artillery Battalion Marker
⬯ Confederate Artillery Battery Marker
● House

◯ Statue

BTRY K 1ST OHIO

STRATTON ST.

COSTER AVE

27TH PA

1-2-11

154TH NY

134TH NY

~ Gettysburg Battlefield Monuments, Locations & Inscriptions ~

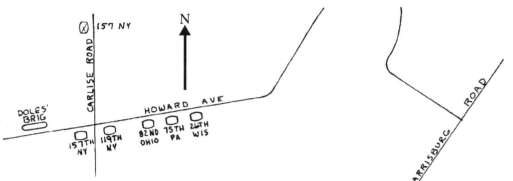

Ewell's	Brig. Gen. George Doles
Corps	4th, 12th, 21st, 44th Georgia Infantry
Rodes'	7-1: About 1 PM the Brigade formed line in the fields east of Oak Hill and skirmished with Union 2nd Brigade,
Division	1st Division, Cavalry and aided Gordon's Brigade in dislodging the Union forces from Barlow Hill and
Doles'	their line from thence to the Heidlersburg Road. Then joined Ramseur and others in their attack upon the
Brigade	rear of the 1st Corps which after a long struggle was compelled to retire from Seminary Ridge. The

Ewell's Corps Rodes' Division Doles' Brigade

Brig. Gen. George Doles

4th, 12th, 21st, 44th Georgia Infantry

7-1: About 1 PM the Brigade formed line in the fields east of Oak Hill and skirmished with Union 2nd Brigade, 1st Division, Cavalry and aided Gordon's Brigade in dislodging the Union forces from Barlow Hill and their line from thence to the Heidlersburg Road. Then joined Ramseur and others in their attack upon the rear of the 1st Corps which after a long struggle was compelled to retire from Seminary Ridge. The Brigade took many prisoners from the 1st and 11th Corps which it pursued to the southern borders of the town.

7-2: Lay all day in the town on West Middle Street. After dark moved out to aid in contemplated attack on Cemetary Hill.

7-3: In line with other brigades in the sunken road southwest of town.

7-4: On Seminary Ridge all day. At night began march to Hagerstown.

Casualties: 86 Killed, 124 Wounded, 31 Missing; Total 241 of 1369

157th NY*
1-3-11

Col. Phillip P. Brown, Jr.

7-1: 300 yards in advance is marker.

Casualties 27 Killed, 166 Wounded, 114 Missing; Total 307

Rt. Section Battery 1 1st Ohio* 11th Corps Artillery Brigade

Capt. Hubert Dilger

2 - Napoleans, 2 guns were posted 100 yds in rear of this tablet.

119th NY*
2-3-11

Col. John T. Lockman, Lt. Col. Edward F. Lloyd

Casualties: 11 Killed, 70 Wounded, 59 Missing; Total 140 of 300 taken into action.

82nd Ohio*
2-3-11

Col. James S. Robinson, Lt. Col. David Thomson

7-1: Arrived from Emmitsburg at noon. Moved rapidly to the support of Dilger's Battery near the Carlisle Road. At 3 PM changed front to the right and advanced to a position 125 yards in front of this monument, where exposed both front and flank to a severe fire it engaged the enemy then approaching from York. After an obstinate struggle, the Regiment being outflanked on both sides withdrew to Cemetary Hill where it remained until close of the battle.

7-2&3: Held position at stone wall near the cemetary as shown by a monument there.

Casualties: 18 Killed, 85 Wounded, 78 Missing; Total 181 of 258 engaged

75th PA*
2-3-11

Col. Francis Mahler, Maj. August Ledig

7-1: Fought on this position from 2 PM until the Corps retired.

7-2&3: At stone wall near cemetary.

Casualties: 111 of 219

26th Wis
2-3-11

Lt. Col. Hans Boebel, Capt. John W. Fuche

7-1: This position.

7-2&3: On Cemetary Hill.

Casualties: 46 Killed, 134 Wounded, 37 Missing; Total 217 of 516 effective strength.

*see index

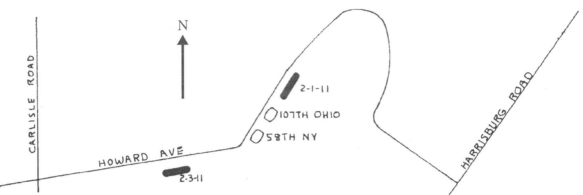

2-3-11   Col. Walter Krzyzanowski

58th, 119th NY, 82nd Ohio, 75th Pa, 26th Wis. Infantry

7-1:   Arrived about 1 PM. Marched through the town to the front. Took position on the line of the Corps on the right of the 1st Brigade and was engaged with Brig. Gen. Doles' Brigade, Maj. Gen. Rodes' Division and other forces for more than two hours. About 4 PM the Corps having been flanked and forced back by superior numbers, it retreated thru the town to Cemetary Hill and took position behind stone walls. Skirmishers were actively engaged in houses 300 to 500 feet in front.

7-2:   In the same position until between 8 and 9 PM when a fierce attack was made on East Cemetery Hill by Brig. Gen .Hays' Brigade and Battery I-1st NY was momentarily captured but the 58th and 119th NY were hastened to its support and assisted in repelling the attack.

7-3:   Not engaged beyond skirmishing but was subjected to a heavy artillery fire.

7-4:   119th NY and 26th Wis made a reconnaissance, going about two miles to the east of town and capturing many stragglers.

Casualties: 75 Killed, 388 Wounded, 206 Missing; Total 669

58ᵗʰ NY
2-3-11   Lt. Col. August Otto, Capt. Emil Koenig

7-1:   Two companies of the Regiment held this position until ordered to Cemetary Hill, where they were joined by the other companies.

7-2&3: After Pickett's Charge skirmished into Gettysburg.

Casualties: 2 Killed, 15 Wounded, 3 Missing; Total 20

107ᵗʰ Ohio*   Col. Seraphim Meyer, Capt. John M. Ludz
2-1-11

7-1:   Left Emmitsburg at 8 AM and reached Gettysburg at 1 PM. Engaged the enemy with the Brigade, losing heavily. Subsequently fell back to East Cemetary Hill.

7-2:   In the evening formed in front of Weidrich's Battery. Participated in repulsing the attack of Hays' Louisiana Brigade. Captured the colors of the 8th Louisiana Tigers.

7-3:   Remained on East Cemetary Hill exposed to fire of sharpshooters and artillery.

7-4:   Made a sortie through the town.

Casualties: 23 Killed, 111 Wounded, 77 Missing; Total 211 of 480

2-1-11   Brig. Gen. Adelbert Ames, Col. Andrew L. Harris

17th Conn, 25th, 75th, 107th Ohio Infantry.

7-1:   Arrived about noon and advanced along the Harrisburg Road. Four companies of the 17th Conn. advanced as skirmishers across Rock Creek to the Bender House. The rest of the Brigade, taking position on Barlow Knoll at the left of the 1st Brigade, was hotly engaged until 4 PM when being enfiladed by artillery and superior numbers, the Brigade with the Division was forced to retire and retreated through the town to Cemetary Hill to a position along the stone wall at right angles to the Baltimore Pike facing the town.

7-2:   Remained under a hot sharpshooters fire from the houses in thetown until sunset, when Brig. Gen. Hays' Brigade charged, penetrating a line left open by the removal of the 17th Conn. to the right shortly before, and reaching the batteries on the hill, where after a hand to hand conflict, the attack was repulsed with heavy loss, including the colors of the 8th Louisiana captured by the 107th Ohio.

7-3:   No other engagement.

Casualties: 68 Killed, 366 Wounded, 344 Missing; Total 778

*see index

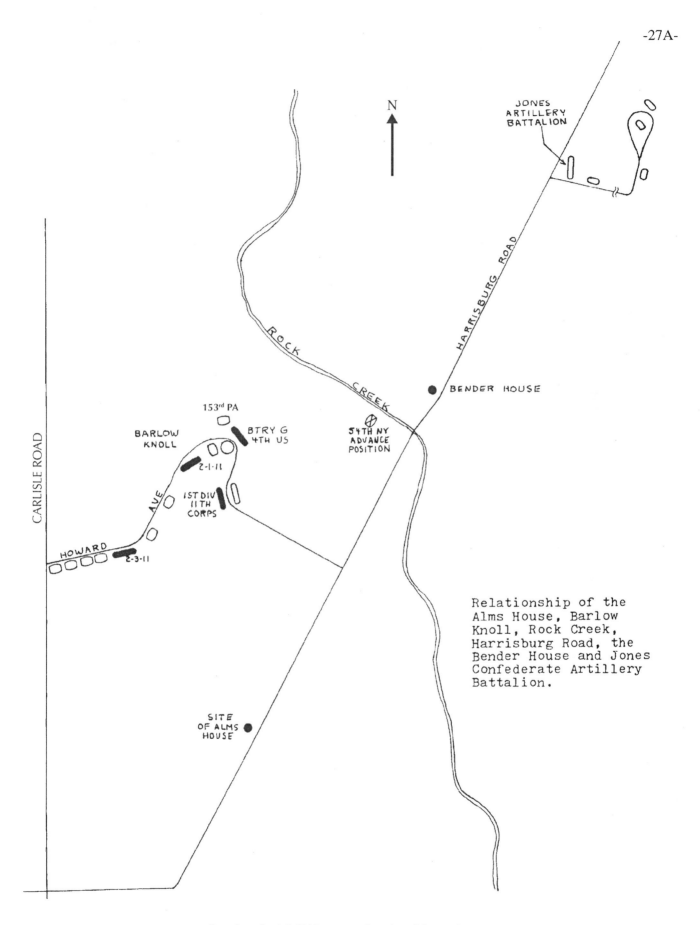

N

JONES
ARTILLERY
BATTALION

HARRISBURG ROAD

ROCK CREEK

BENDER HOUSE

153rd PA

BARLOW
KNOLL

BTRY G
4TH US

54TH NY
ADVANCE
POSITION

2-1-11

1ST DIV
11TH
CORPS

CARLISLE ROAD

AVE

HOWARD

2-3-11

SITE
OF ALMS
HOUSE

Relationship of the
Alms House, Barlow
Knoll, Rock Creek,
Harrisburg Road, the
Bender House and Jones
Confederate Artillery
Battalion.

~ Gettysburg Battlefield Monuments, Locations & Inscriptions ~

THE SYMBOLS LISTED BELOW ARE USED TO IDENTIFY
THE MONUMENTS, MARKERS, TABLETS, STATUES, ETC.
WHICH ARE DRAWN ON THE MAPS IN THESE PAGES

SYMBOL	TYPE	REPRESENTING	DESCRIPTION
	Bronze Tablet	Army of The Potomac, Union Corps or Division or Brigade, Regular Army Regiment, Regular Army Artillery Battery, Volunteer Artillery Brigade.	Brigade Tablet Mounted on Square Marble base. All other Tablets are on large vertical Granite Blocks.
	Bronze Tablet	Army of Northern Virginia, Confederate Corps or Division or Brigade or Artillery Battalion	Brigade Tablet and Artillery Battalion Tablet Mounted on Round Marble base. All other Tablets are Mounted on large vertical Granite blocks.
	Iron Tablet	Union Army Battery (other than Regular Army)	Mounted on Black Iron Shaft.
	Iron Tablet	Confederate Artillery Battery	Mounted on Black Iron Shaft.
	Iron Tablet	Confederate Brigade Advanced Position	Mounted on Black Iron Shaft.
	Regimental or Battery Monument	Principal Position of Volunteer Regiment or Volunteer Artillery Battery	Usually Granite or Marble in a Great Variety of Shapes and Sizes.
	Regimental Marker	Other than Principal Position of Regiment or Battery	Usually a Square Granite Marker or tablet or may be another monument.
	Flank Marker or Company Marker	Left and/or Right Flank of Regiment or Battery or Position of a Company.	Usually a Small Square or Rectangular Granite Marker.
	Army Or Corps Headquarters	Site of Headquarters of Army Commander or Corps Commander or Chief of Artillery	Cannon Barrel Mounted Vertically on Stone, Granite or Marble base.
	State Monument	Monument Erected by Union or Confederate State.	
	Statue	Standing or Equestrian	Bronze Sculpture
	Building	House, Barn or other Structure	Identified by Owner's Name.
	Miscellaneous Marker	Marker or Inscription of a type not listed above	Granite or Metal Marker.

*Asterisk   Used whenever a Division or Brigade or Regiment or Battery has more than one Monument or Marker.   Check the Index for other Monument or Marker.

~ Gettysburg Battlefield Monuments, Locations & Inscriptions ~

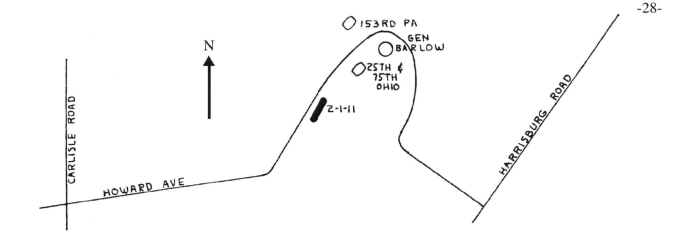

25th & 75th Ohio* 25th Ohio: Lt. Col. Jeremiah Williams, Capt. Nathaniel J. Manning, Lt. William Mahoney, Lt. Israel White
75th Ohio: Col. Andrew L. Harris, Capt. George B. Fox

2-1-11

7-1: Arriving at Gettysburg from Emmitsburg, advanced beyond the own and under a heavy cannonade took position here supporting Battery G-4th US Artillery.

7-2: Held an advanced line on East Cemetary Hill.

7-3: Early in the morning led the advance into town.

Casualties: 25th Ohio-16 Killed, 96 Wounded, 71 Missing; Total 183 of 220 Present
75th Ohio-38 Killed, 62 Wounded, 86 Missing; Total 186 of 269 Present

Barlow Statue Francis Channing Barlow, Major General US Volunteers 1834-1896. In command of 1st Division, 11th Corps at Gettysburg July 1, 1863. Private 12th NY Militia 4/19/1861, 1st Lt. 5/2/61, Honorably Mustered out 8/5/61, Lt. Col. 61st NY Inf 11/9/61, Col. 4/14/62, Brig. Gen. USV 9/19 62, Maj. Gen. 5/26/65, Resigned 11/16/65. Commanding 61st NY Inf at Yorktown and Fair Oaks in the Seven Days Battle; 61st and 64th at Antietam; 2nd Brig., 2nd Div., Howard's Corps at Chancellorsville; 1st Div., Howard's Corps at Gettysburg; 1st Div., Hancock's Corps at the Wilderness, Spotsylvania, Cold Harbor and Petersburg and 2nd Div., Hancock's Corps at Appomattox. Wounded severely at Antietam and Gettysburg.

Breveted Maj. Gen. Volunteers 8/1/64 for highly meritorious and distinguished conduct throughout the campaign and particularly for gallant and meritorious conduct while leading his Division in an assault on the enemy's works at Spotsylvania 5/12/64.

153rd PA* Maj. John F. Frueauff

1-1-11

7-1: The Regiment held this position in the afternoon until the Corps was outflanked and it retired, when it took position along the lane at the front of East Cemetary Hill.

7-2: Assisted in repulsing the enemy's assault in the evening.

7-3: Remained until close of the battle.

Casualties: Killed and Died of Wounds 41, Wounded 124, Missing 46; Total 211 of 569 Carried into action.

*see index

~ Gettysburg Battlefield Monuments, Locations & Inscriptions ~

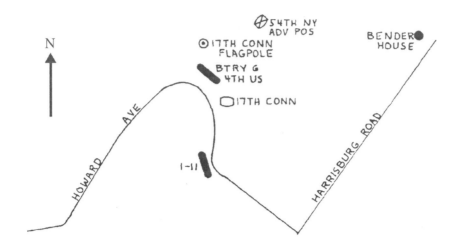

17th Conn.   Erected by the 17th Connecticut Volunteer Association.
  Flagpole

54th NY*   Maj. Stephen Kovacs
1-1-11   A detail of 45 men from this Regiment occupied this position.
Advanced   Casualties: 7 Killed, 47 Wounded, 48 Missing; Total 102 (NY@Gbg)
  Position

Battery G*   Lt. Bayard Wilkeson, Lt. Eugene A. Bancroft
4th US   Six 12 Pounders
11th Corps   7-1:   Arrived at Gettysburg about 11 AM. Advanced and took position two sections on Barlow Knoll, the left
Artillery   section detached near the Alms House. Engaged Confederate infantry and artillery on the right and the
Brigade   left. Lt. Wilkeson fell early, mortally wounded and the command evolved on Lt. Bancroft. The sections
                 were compelled to change positions several times. Retired about 4 PM, one section relieving a section of
                 Battery I-1st Ohio on Baltimore Street and covering the retreat. Took position on Cemetary Hill about 5
                 PM.
        7-2:   Moved to rear of Cemetary facing Baltimore Pike. In action at the cemetary from 4:30 PM until 7 PM.
        7-3:   About 2 PM two sections were engaged in the cemetary until the repulse of the Confederates.
        Casualties: Killed 2, Wounded 11, Missing 4; Total 17; 31 horses killed. Ammunition expended:1400 rounds.

17th Conn   Lt. Col. Douglas Fowler, Maj. Allan G. Brady
2-1-11   7-1:   In memory of their gallant comrades who fell here and on is battlefield on the 2nd and 3rd days of July
                 1863.
        Casualties: Killed 20, Wounded 81, Missing 96; Total 197 (NY@Gbg)

1st Division   Brig. Gen. Francis Barlow, Brig. Gen. Adelbert Ames
11th Corps   1st Brigade   Col. Leopold von Gilsa
        2nd Brigade   Brig. Gen. Adelbert Ames, Col. Andrew L. Harris
        7-1:   Arrived about 10:30 AM. Went into position on a hill about a mile north of Gettysburg, the left extending
                 southwest, connecting with 3rd Division. Attacked by Doles' and Gordon's Brigades under enfilading fire
                 from Jones' Artillery Battalion. Hoke's and Hays' Brigades of Early's Division moved across Rock Creek
                 upon the right and rear and compelled a retreat through the town to Cemetary Hill, and the Division took
                 position on East Cemetary Hill at its base, 1st Division, 1st Corps on the right and 3rd Division, 11th Corps
                 on the left.
        7-2:   Attacked at 8 PM by Hays' and Hoke's Brigades. Repulsed at 9:30 PM with the aid of 2nd Brigade, 3rd
                 Division, 1st Corps.
        7-3:   At 1 PM heavy cannonade opened and continued with considerable effect for an hour and a half, followed
                 by a charge on the 2nd Corps on the left, which was repulsed with great loss.
        Casualties: Killed 122, Wounded 677, Missing 507; Total 1306

*see index

~ Gettysburg Battlefield Monuments, Locations & Inscriptions ~

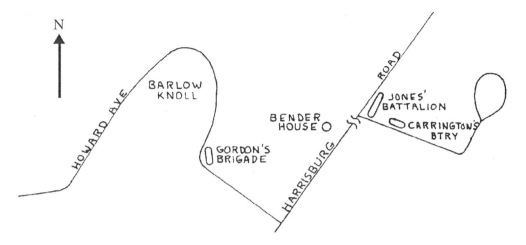

Ewell's	Brig. Gen. John B. Gordon
Corps	13th, 26th, 31st, 38th, 60th, 61st Georgia Infantry
Early's	7-1: Arrived on the field from Harrisburg Road in early afternoon and formed line on north side of Rock
Division	Creek. About 3 PM moved across the Creek to the support of Rodes' left, which was attacked from
Gordon's	Barlow Knoll. Charged the Union forces upon this hill and after a most obstinate resistance, succeeded in
Brigade*	breaking the line. The Brigade was afterward moved to the support of Smith's Brigade on the York Road.

Brig. Gen. John B. Gordon

13th, 26th, 31st, 38th, 60th, 61st Georgia Infantry

7-1: Arrived on the field from Harrisburg Road in early afternoon and formed line on north side of Rock Creek. About 3 PM moved across the Creek to the support of Rodes' left, which was attacked from Barlow Knoll. Charged the Union forces upon this hill and after a most obstinate resistance, succeeded in breaking the line. The Brigade was afterward moved to the support of Smith's Brigade on the York Road. Captured a large number of prisoners during the day.

7-2: Moved to the railroad in support of Hays' and Avery's Brigades in their attack on Cemetary Ridge.

7-3: Not engaged.

7-4: At 2 PM the Brigade was withdrawn and moved to the Cashtown Road.

Casualties: Killed 71, Wounded 270, Missing 39; Total 380

Ewell's Corps / Early's Division / Jones' Battalion

Lt. Col. H. P. Jones

2 - 10 Pounder Parrotts, Six 3 Inch Rifles, Eight Napoleons.

Carrington's, Tanner's, Green's, Garber's Batteries

7-1: Arrived on the field with Early's Division about 2:45 PM. Moved into battery 400 yards east of this position. Opened an effective enfilading fire from 12 guns on the 11th Corps and a flank fire on infantry retiring from Seminary Ridge. Ceased firing as the Confederate infantry advanced.

7-2&3: Remained in same position. Not actively engaged.

Casualties: 2 Killed, 6 Wounded; Total 8. (NY@Gbg)

Ewell's Corps / Early's Division / Jones' Battalion / Carrington's Battery

Capt. James McD Carrington. The Charlottesville (Virginia) Artillery

Four - Napoleons

7-1: Arrived on the field with Early's Division in the afternoon. Brigade was ordered to cross Rock Creek and move in the rear of Gordon's Brigade, then advancing. Went into battery on a street in suburbs of the town and remained until near dark when ordered to a position near the railroad.

7-2&3: Remained near the railroad, not engaged.

7-4: Moved in the rear of Early's Division.

Casualties not reported.

*see index

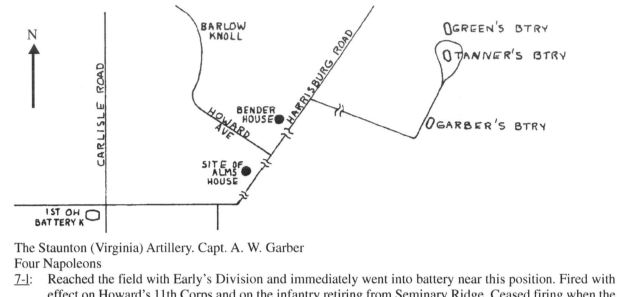

Ewell's	The Staunton (Virginia) Artillery. Capt. A. W. Garber
Corps	Four Napoleons
Early's	7-1: Reached the field with Early's Division and immediately went into battery near this position. Fired with
Division	effect on Howard's 11th Corps and on the infantry retiring from Seminary Ridge. Ceased firing when the
Jones'	Confederate infantry advanced.
Battalion	7-2&3: Occupied the same position, not engaged.
Garber's	Casualties: 1 Wounded; Total. Ammunition expended: 106 Rounds.
Battery	

Ewell's
Corps
Early's
Division
Jones'
Battalion
Tanner's
Battery

The Courtney (Virginia) Artillery. Capt W. A. Tanner

Four 3 Inch Rifles

7-1: Arrived on the field with Early's Division. Moved into battery on the north side of Rock Creek. Opened an effective fire on Union infantry on south side of Creek. Ceased firing as the Confederate infantry advanced.

7-2: Took position of the day before. Remained until 3 PM. Ordered to report on the York Road and remained until the morning of July 3rd. Not engaged.

7-3: Moved nearer the town and remained until night. Ordered to the Wagon Park to move with train to the rear.

Casualties not reported. Ammunition expended: 595 Rounds.

The Louisiana Guard Artillery. Capt C .A. Green

Ewell's
Corps
Early's
Division
Jones'
Battalion
Green's
Battery*

Two 10 Pounder Parrotts; Two 3 Inch Rifles

7-1: Arrived on the field with Early's Division. Placed to the right of Tanner's Battery on the north side of Rock Creek and opened fire on Union troops on south side of Creek. Continued firing with effect until Confederate infantry was in position and advancing.

7-2: Occupied position of the previous day. Before sunset was ordered to General Hampton at Hunterstown with the section of Parrott guns. Engaged Battery M-2nd US. Fell back a mile, remained for the night.

7-3: Moved forward with the cavalry about 2 PM. Guns opened on a column of advancing cavalry. Received a severe fire and ordered to be withdrawn. Again engaged in the afternoon.

Casualties: 2 Killed, 5 Wounded. Ammunition expended: 161 Rounds.

Capt. Lewis Heckman

1st Ohio
Battery K
11th Corps
Artillery
Brigade

Four 12 Pounders

7-1: Arrived about noon. This Battery, Capt. Lewis Heckman Commanding, went into position here in reserve. When the 11th Corps began to retire, it engaged the enemy with great gallantry. After severe losses it was withdrawn.

Casualties: Killed 2, Wounded 11, Missing 2; Total 15

*see index

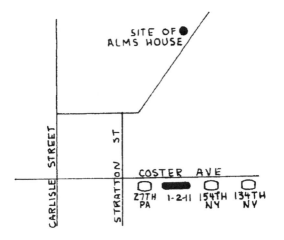

27ᵗʰ PA*   Lt. Col. Lorenz Cantador
1-2-11   <u>7-1</u>:   Casualties: 6 Killed, 29 Wounded , 76 Missing; Total 111

1-2-11   Col. Charles R. Coster
            134th, 154th NY, 27th, 73rd Pa Infantry
            <u>7-1</u>:   Arrived about 2 PM and went into position on Cemetary Hill supporting Battery 1-1st NY, skirmishers occupying a church and nearby house. Advanced about 3:30 PM through the town and faced to the right and intercepted the advance of Brig. Gen. Hays' and Brig. Gen. Hoke's Brigades, Maj. Gen. Early's Division, then moving toward town in rear of 1st Division, 11th Corps and held them from the line of retreat of that Division to Cemetary Hill. Retired to East Cemetary Hill about 4:30 PM and resumed former position right of 2nd Brigade with 3rd Division on right.
            <u>7-2</u>:   In same position during the day under fire of artillery and sharpshooters. At 8 PM Brig. Gen. Hays' Brigade charged the position and was repulsed with heavy loss. The 27th Pa bore a conspicuous part in repelling this attack. Battery 1-1st NY was temporarily captured but was immediately recovered.
            <u>7-3</u>:   Not actively engaged.
            Casualties: Killed 56, Wounded 228, Missing 313; Total 597

154ᵗʰ NY   Lt. Col. Daniel B. Allen
1-2-11   <u>7-1</u>:   1 Killed, 21 Wounded, 178 Missing; 200 Total
            <u>7-2&3</u>: Occupied position on East Cemetary Hill.

134ᵗʰ NY*   Lt. Col. Allen H. Jackson
1-2-11   <u>7-1</u>:   The Regiment was thrown forward to check the rapid advance of Early's Division, Ewell's Corps and protect Barlow's Division that was being hard pressed. The Confederate line of battle outflanking the Brigade in overwhelming numbers, the 134th Regiment occupying the extreme right of the Union line was crushed by the impact and the flank and rear firing of that desperate charge. This tablet marks the position where its casualties were greatest of any battle in which it was ever engaged.
            <u>7-2&3</u>: The Regimental monument on East Cemetary Hill is on the ground occupied.
            Losses at Gettysburg: 252

73ʳᵈ PA*   (Note: See Page 65 for position of this Regiment.)
1-2-11

*see index

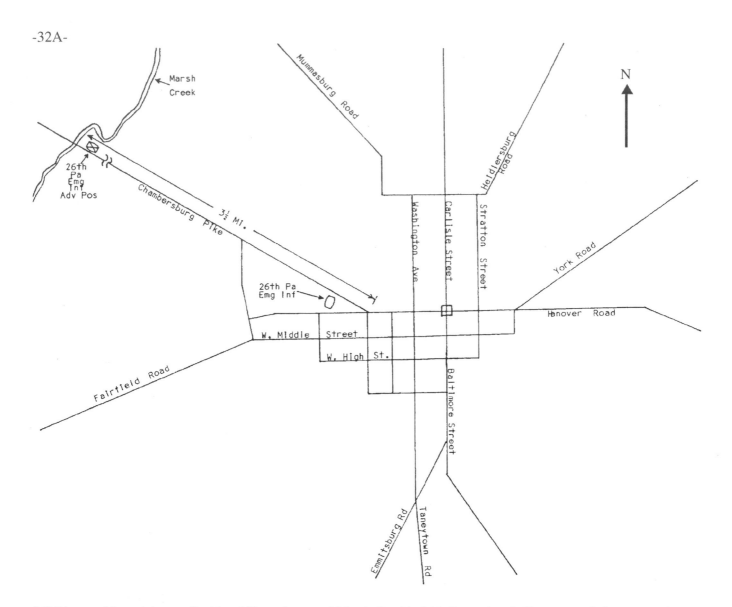

26th PA Emergency Infantry   (Note: Advance Position 200 yards east of Marsh Creek). 26th Pennsylvania Emergency Infantry met the advance of Early's Division, C.S.A. on the morning of June 26, 1863.

26th PA Emergency Infantry Department of the Susque-hanna   26th Pa. Emergency Infantry organized at Harrisburg and volunteered for the emergency. Mustered into United States Service June 22, 1863. Company A recruited from Pennsylvania College and Gettysburg. Total enrollment 743. Captured and missing in the Gettysburg Campaign, 176 officers and men. The first Union Regiment to engage the Confederates at Gettysburg after delaying their advance one day.

    <u>6-25</u>: Reached Gettysburg in advance of the Army of the Potomac.

    <u>6-26</u>: In the morning marched out the Chambersburg Pike and met the rebel column at Marsh Creek and forced by overwhelming numbers to withdraw. In the afternoon on the Hunterstown Road, had a severe engagement with the rebel cavalry, inflicting upon them some loss.

    <u>6-28</u>: Reached Harrisburg having marched 60 consecutive hours.

    <u>6-30</u>: Advanced from Harrisburg after the rebels in retreat.

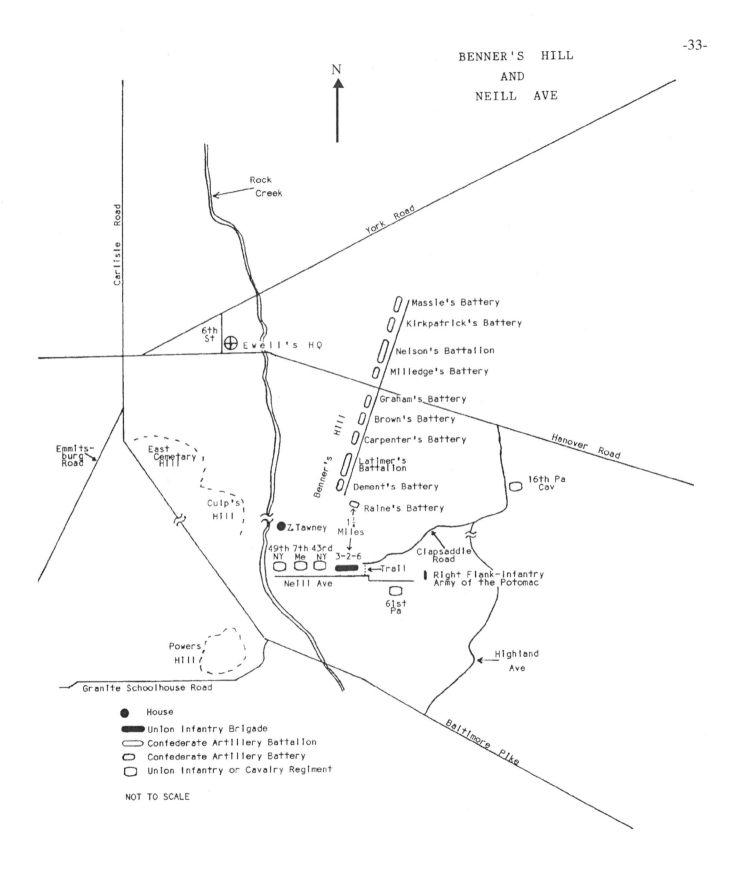

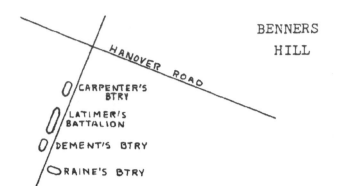

Ewell's Corps Johnson's Division Latimer's Battalion Raine's Battery

The Lee (Virginia) Battery. Capt. C. I. Raine

Two - 20 Pounder Parrotts; One - 10 Pounder Parrott; One - 3 Inch Rifle.

7-2: The 10 Pounder Parrott and 3-Inch Rifle took position here about 4 PM and were engaged in the severe cannonade that lasted over two hours. They also aided in supporting the attack of Johnson's Division on Culp's Hill and did not retire until dark. The 20 Pounder Parrotts took an active part in the cannonade from their position some distance in rear of the other guns.

7-3: The 20 Pounder Parrotts were actively engaged in the great cannonade.

7-4: Withdrew from the field.

Losses: Wounded 8. Horses Killed 3

Ewell's Corps Johnson's Division Latimer's Battalion Dement's Battery

The 1st Maryland Battery. Capt. William F. Dement

Four- Napoleons

7-2: In position here about 4 PM and took part in the cannonade against Union batteries on East Cemetary Hill and Culp's Hill which continued over two hours. When the Battalion was withdrawn two guns of the Battery were left here to aid in repelling any attack. Soon afterward opened fire in support of Johnson's infantry on Culp's Hill which drew from Union guns a heavy response by which Major Latimer was mortally wounded.

7-3: Remained in reserve.

7-4: Withdrew from the field with the Battalion.

Losses: Killed 1, Wounded 4. Horses Killed 9

Ewell's Corps Johnson's Division Latimer's Battalion

Major J. W. Latimer, Capt. C. I. Raine

Two - 20 Pounder Parrotts; Five - 10 Pounder Parrotts; Three - 3 Inch Rifles; Six - Napoleons.

7-1: After dark crossed Rock Creek and camped on this ridge.

7-2: At 4 PM the Battalion, except the 20 Pounder Parrotts, took position here and was engaged more than two hours in a heavy cannonade with Union artillery on Cemetary Hill, Stevens Knoll and Culp's Hill. Ammunition exhausted and losses severe, the guns were withdrawn except four to cover the advance of Johnson's infantry against Culp's Hill. In the renewed firing, Major Latimer was mortally wounded. In the cannonade, the 20 Pounder Parrotts in position one half mile north, took an active part.

7-3: The 20 Pounder Parrotts took part in the great cannonade while the other batteries were in reserve.

Losses: Killed 10, Wounded 49. Horses Killed 30

Ewell's Corps Johnson's Division Latimer's Battalion Carpenter's Battery

The Alleghany (Virginia) Artillery. Capt. J. C. Carpenter

Two - Napoleons; Two - 3 Inch Rifles

7-2: The Battery took a prominent part in the cannonade against the Union artillery on East Cemetary Hill and other points, which began about 4 PM and continued over two hours. Some of the Union guns on the left enfiladed the Battalion and caused the Battery to suffer severely, and having exhausted its ammunition, it was ordered to withdraw.

Losses: Killed 5, Wounded 24. Horses Killed 9

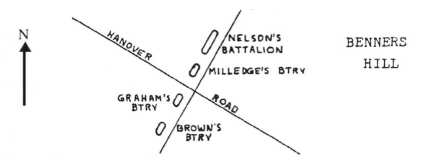

Ewell's
Corps
Johnson's
Division
Latimer's
Battalion
Brown's
Battery

The Chesapeake (Maryland) Artillery. Capt William D. Brown

7-2: Took position here about 4 PM and was engaged for two hours in a severe conflict with the Union batteries on Cemetary Hill and Stevens Knoll. Capt. Brown being severely wounded, one of his guns disabled and his ammunition exhausted, the Battery was withdrawn by order of General Johnson.

7-:3: Remained in reserve and not engaged.

7-4: Withdrew from the field with the Battalion

Losses: Killed 4, Wounded12. Horses killed 9

Ewell's
Corps
Artillery
Reserve
Dance's
Battalion
Graham's
Battery

The Rockbridge (Virginia) Artillery. Capt. A. Graham

Four - 20 Pounder Parrotts

7-1: The Battery arrived too late to participate in the engagement of the day. It was ordered to report to Lt. Col. H. P. Jones, Commanding Artillery, Early's Division and moved into position on the left to the south and east of the town.

7-2: Remained in position on the left firing occassionally.

7-3: Remained in position during the day and rejoined the Battalion during the night. Took up the line of march to Hagerstown.

Ammunition expended: 439 Rounds. Losses not reported in detail.

Ewell's
Corps
Artillery
Reserve
Nelson's
Battalion
Milledge's
Battery

Georgia Artillery. Capt. John Milledge

The Battery arrived too late to participate in the engagement of 7/1.

7-2: Took position on Seminary Ridge one quarter mile north of the Chambersburg Pike. About 11 AM moved to the rear of Pennsylvania College and remained until night when the Battery returned to the position of the morning.

7-3: Ordered to the extreme left of the Confederate line to find a position to withdraw the fire from the Confederate infantry. Opened fire about noon, firing about 20 to 25 rounds.

7-4: Took position west of town and at midnight moved on the march to Hagerstown.

Ammunition expended: 48 Rounds.

Ewell's
Corps
Artillery
Reserve
Nelson's
Battalion

Lt. Col. William Nelson

Patrick's, Massie's and Milledge's Batteries

7-1: The Battalion arrived on the field too late to participate in the engagement of the day. Was ordered to report to Chief of Artillery, Rodes' Division.

7-2: Took position on Seminary Ridge one quarter mile north of the Chambersburg Pike. About 11 AM moved to rear of Pennsylvania College and remained until night when returned to position of the morning.

7-3: Ordered to extreme left of Confederate line to find a position to withdraw fire from Confederate infantry. Opened fire about 12 Noon, firing about 25 rounds. About midnight moved with Johnson's Division to Seminary Ridge.

7-4: Was ordered to take position on ridge west of town. At night took up the march to Hagerstown.

Ammunition expended: 48 Rounds. Casualties not reported.

Ewell's Amhearst (Virginia) Artillery. Capt T. J. Kirkpatrick
Corps One - 3 Inch Rifle, Three - Napoleans.
Artillery 7-1: The Battery arrived on the field too late to participate in the engagement of the day.
Reserve 7-2: Took position on Seminary Hill one quarter mile north of the Chambersburg Pike. About 11 AM moved to
Nelson's   rear of Pennsylvania College and remained until night when the Battery returned to the position of the
Battalion   morning.
Kirkpatrick's 7-3: Ordered to the extreme left of the Confederate line. At midnight moved with Johnson's Division to Semi-
Battery   nary Ridge.
        7-4: Took position on the ridge west of town and at midnight took up the march to Hagerstown.

Ewell's The Fluvanna (Virginia) Artillery. Capt J. L. Massie
Corps 7-1: The Battery arrived on the field too late to participate in the engagement of the day.
Artillery 7-2: Took position on Seminary Ridge one quarter mile north of the Chambersburg Pike. About 11 AM moved
Reserve   to the rear of Pennsylvania College and remained until night when the Battery returned to the position of
Nelson's   the morning.
Battalion 7-3: Ordered to extreme left of Confederate line. At midnight moved with Johnson's Division to Seminary
Massie's   Ridge.
Battery 7-4: Took position on the ridge west of town and at midnight moved on the march to Hagerstown.

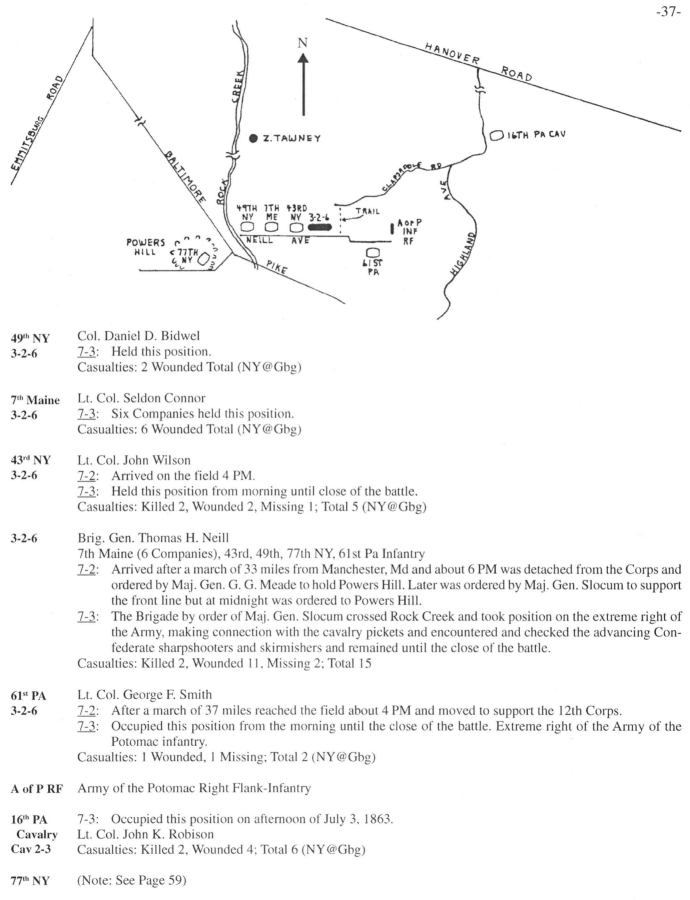

49th NY
3-2-6
Col. Daniel D. Bidwel
7-3: Held this position.
Casualties: 2 Wounded Total (NY@Gbg)

7th Maine
3-2-6
Lt. Col. Seldon Connor
7-3: Six Companies held this position.
Casualties: 6 Wounded Total (NY@Gbg)

43rd NY
3-2-6
Lt. Col. John Wilson
7-2: Arrived on the field 4 PM.
7-3: Held this position from morning until close of the battle.
Casualties: Killed 2, Wounded 2, Missing 1; Total 5 (NY@Gbg)

3-2-6
Brig. Gen. Thomas H. Neill
7th Maine (6 Companies), 43rd, 49th, 77th NY, 61st Pa Infantry
7-2: Arrived after a march of 33 miles from Manchester, Md and about 6 PM was detached from the Corps and ordered by Maj. Gen. G. G. Meade to hold Powers Hill. Later was ordered by Maj. Gen. Slocum to support the front line but at midnight was ordered to Powers Hill.
7-3: The Brigade by order of Maj. Gen. Slocum crossed Rock Creek and took position on the extreme right of the Army, making connection with the cavalry pickets and encountered and checked the advancing Confederate sharpshooters and skirmishers and remained until the close of the battle.
Casualties: Killed 2, Wounded 11, Missing 2; Total 15

61st PA
3-2-6
Lt. Col. George F. Smith
7-2: After a march of 37 miles reached the field about 4 PM and moved to support the 12th Corps.
7-3: Occupied this position from the morning until the close of the battle. Extreme right of the Army of the Potomac infantry.
Casualties: 1 Wounded, 1 Missing; Total 2 (NY@Gbg)

A of P RF
Army of the Potomac Right Flank-Infantry

16th PA
Cavalry
Cav 2-3
7-3: Occupied this position on afternoon of July 3, 1863.
Lt. Col. John K. Robison
Casualties: Killed 2, Wounded 4; Total 6 (NY@Gbg)

77th NY
(Note: See Page 59)

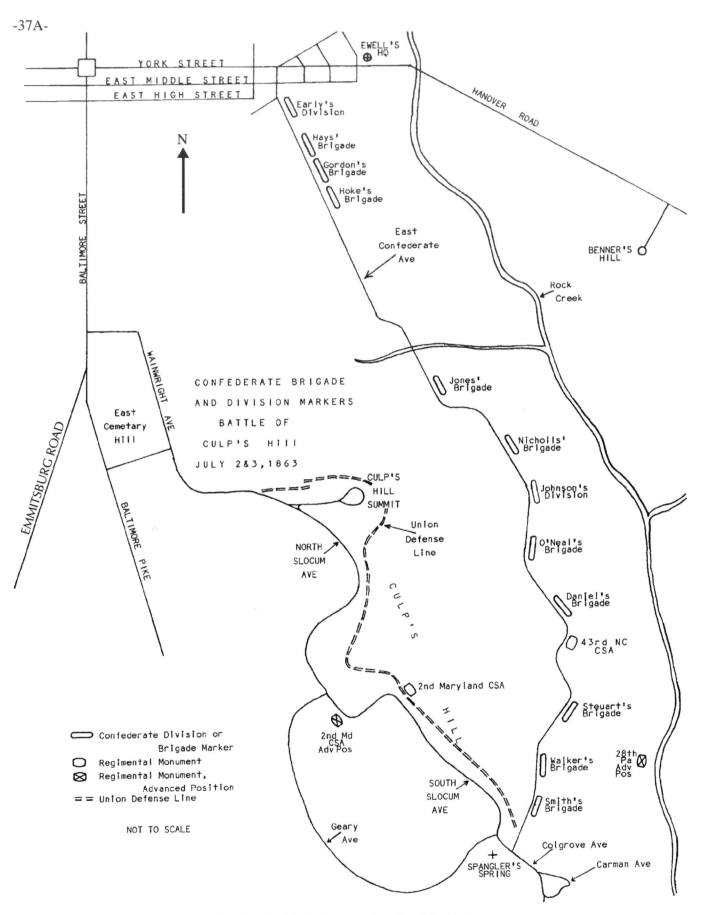

~ *Gettysburg Battlefield Monuments, Locations & Inscriptions* ~

THE SYMBOLS LISTED BELOW ARE USED TO IDENTIFY
THE MONUMENTS, MARKERS, TABLETS, STATUES, ETC.
WHICH ARE DRAWN ON THE MAPS IN THESE PAGES

SYMBOL	TYPE	REPRESENTING	DESCRIPTION
	Bronze Tablet	Army of The Potomac, Union Corps or Division or Brigade, Regular Army Regiment, Regular Army Artillery Battery, Volunteer Artillery Brigade.	Brigade Tablet Mounted on Square Marble base. All other Tablets are on large vertical Granite Blocks.
	Bronze Tablet	Army of Northern Virginia, Confederate Corps or Division or Brigade or Artillery Battalion	Brigade Tablet and Artillery Battalion Tablet Mounted on Round Marble base. All other Tablets are Mounted on large vertical Granite blocks.
	Iron Tablet	Union Army Battery (other than Regular Army)	Mounted on Black Iron Shaft.
	Iron Tablet	Confederate Artillery Battery	Mounted on Black Iron Shaft.
	Iron Tablet	Confederate Brigade Advanced Position	Mounted on Black Iron Shaft.
	Regimental or Battery Monument	Principal Position of Volunteer Regiment or Volunteer Artillery Battery	Usually Granite or Marble in a Great Variety of Shapes and Sizes.
	Regimental Marker	Other than Principal Position of Regiment or Battery	Usually a Square Granite Marker or tablet or may be another monument.
	Flank Marker or Company Marker	Left and/or Right Flank of Regiment or Battery or Position of a Coppany.	Usually a Small Square or Rectangular Granite Marker.
	Army Or Corps Headquarters	Site of Headquarters of Army Commander or Corps Commander or Chief of Artillery	Cannon Barrel Mounted Vertically on Stone, Granite or Marble Base.
	State Monument	Monument Erected by Union or Confederate State.	Bronze Sculpture
	Statue	Standing or Equestrian	Identified by Owner's Name.
	Building	House, Barn or other Structure	Granite or Metal Marker.
	Miscellaneous Marker	Marker or Inscription of a type not listed above	Check the Index for other Monument or Marker.

*Asterisk   Used whenever a Division or Brigade or Regiment or Battery has more than one Monument or Marker.

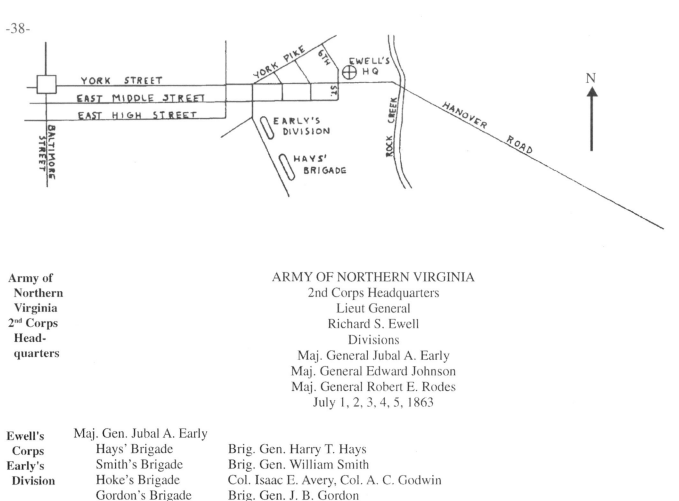

Army of Northern Virginia 2nd Corps Head- quarters

ARMY OF NORTHERN VIRGINIA
2nd Corps Headquarters
Lieut General
Richard S. Ewell
Divisions
Maj. General Jubal A. Early
Maj. General Edward Johnson
Maj. General Robert E. Rodes
July 1, 2, 3, 4, 5, 1863

Ewell's Corps Early's Division

Maj. Gen. Jubal A. Early
    Hays' Brigade   Brig. Gen. Harry T. Hays
    Smith's Brigade   Brig. Gen. William Smith
    Hoke's Brigade   Col. Isaac E. Avery, Col. A. C. Godwin
    Gordon's Brigade   Brig. Gen. J. B. Gordon
    Artillery Battalion 4 Batteries Lt. Col. H. P. Jones

7-1: The Division arrived about noon within two miles of Gettysburg. Formed line across road north of Rock Creek. Gordon's brigade ordered to support of a brigade in Rodes' Division, engaged with a division of the 11th Corps which had advanced to a wooded hill in front of town. The remainder of the Division was ordered forward as Gordon's Brigade was engaged. After a short and severe contest, the Union forces were forced through town losing many prisoners. Later in the day, Gordon's Brigade was ordered to the York Pike in support of Smith's Brigade. Hays' and Hoke's Brigades occupied the town.

7-2: In early morning, Hays' and Hoke's Brigades took position to front and left of town. Gordon's Brigade, in reserve, moved to rear of these Brigades. Smith's Brigade remained on York Road. The Division was held in this position until nearly dusk, when Hays' and Hoke's Brigades advanced on Cemetary Hill. The Brigades reached the crest of the hill but not being supported on the right, were forced to retire. Gordon's Brigade advanced to support the attack.

7-3: At daylight, Smith's Brigade was ordered to support Johnson's Division on the left. Hays' and Hoke's Brigades formed line in town, holding the position of the previous day. Gordon's Brigade held the line of the day before. The Division was not further engaged.

7-4: In the morning the Division was withdrawn to the Cashtown Road west of town.

Casualties: Killed 156, Wounded 806, Missing 226; Total 1188

Ewell's Corps Early's Division Hay's Brigade

Brig. Gen. Harry T. Hays
5th, 6th, 7th, 8th, 9th Louisiana Infantry
7-1: Advanced at 3 PM with Hoke's Brigade. Flanked 11th Corps. Aided in taking two guns. Pursued retreating Union troops into town, capturing many prisoners and late in the evening halted on East High Street.

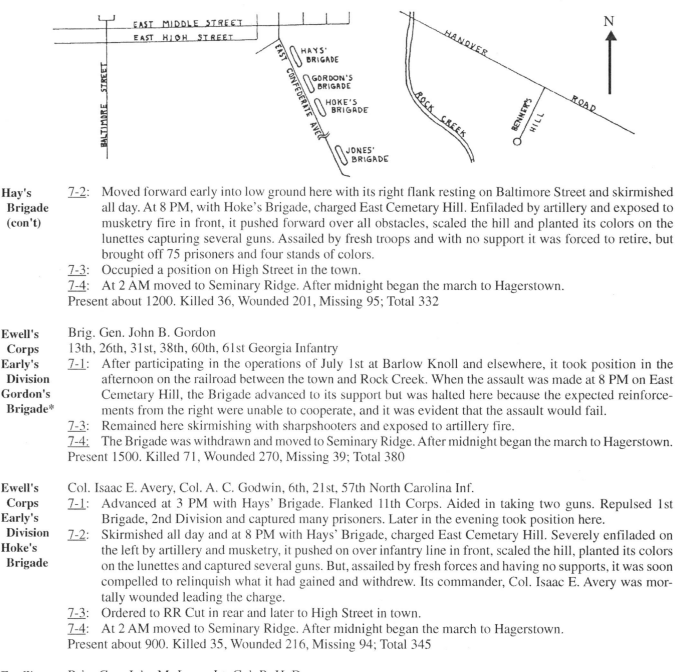

Hay's Brigade (con't)

7-2: Moved forward early into low ground here with its right flank resting on Baltimore Street and skirmished all day. At 8 PM, with Hoke's Brigade, charged East Cemetery Hill. Enfiladed by artillery and exposed to musketry fire in front, it pushed forward over all obstacles, scaled the hill and planted its colors on the lunettes capturing several guns. Assailed by fresh troops and with no support it was forced to retire, but brought off 75 prisoners and four stands of colors.

7-3: Occupied a position on High Street in the town.

7-4: At 2 AM moved to Seminary Ridge. After midnight began the march to Hagerstown.

Present about 1200. Killed 36, Wounded 201, Missing 95; Total 332

Ewell's Corps Early's Division Gordon's Brigade*

Brig. Gen. John B. Gordon
13th, 26th, 31st, 38th, 60th, 61st Georgia Infantry

7-1: After participating in the operations of July 1st at Barlow Knoll and elsewhere, it took position in the afternoon on the railroad between the town and Rock Creek. When the assault was made at 8 PM on East Cemetery Hill, the Brigade advanced to its support but was halted here because the expected reinforcements from the right were unable to cooperate, and it was evident that the assault would fail.

7-3: Remained here skirmishing with sharpshooters and exposed to artillery fire.

7-4: The Brigade was withdrawn and moved to Seminary Ridge. After midnight began the march to Hagerstown.

Present 1500. Killed 71, Wounded 270, Missing 39; Total 380

Ewell's Corps Early's Division Hoke's Brigade

Col. Isaac E. Avery, Col. A. C. Godwin, 6th, 21st, 57th North Carolina Inf.

7-1: Advanced at 3 PM with Hays' Brigade. Flanked 11th Corps. Aided in taking two guns. Repulsed 1st Brigade, 2nd Division and captured many prisoners. Later in the evening took position here.

7-2: Skirmished all day and at 8 PM with Hays' Brigade, charged East Cemetery Hill. Severely enfiladed on the left by artillery and musketry, it pushed on over infantry line in front, scaled the hill, planted its colors on the lunettes and captured several guns. But, assailed by fresh forces and having no supports, it was soon compelled to relinquish what it had gained and withdrew. Its commander, Col. Isaac E. Avery was mortally wounded leading the charge.

7-3: Ordered to RR Cut in rear and later to High Street in town.

7-4: At 2 AM moved to Seminary Ridge. After midnight began the march to Hagerstown.

Present about 900. Killed 35, Wounded 216, Missing 94; Total 345

Ewell's Corps Johnson's Division Jones' Brigade

Brig. Gen. John M. Jones, Lt. Col. R. H. Duncan
21st, 25th, 42nd, 44th, 48th, 50th Virginia Infantry

7-1: Arrived near nightfall and took position east of Rock Creek and north of Hanover Road with pickets advanced to the front.

7-2: About 4 PM moved forward to support artillery on Benners Hill. Crossed Rock Creek at 6 PM and assailed the Union forces on the summit of Culp's Hill, charging up the steep northern slope nearly to the Union breastworks and continuing the struggle until dark.

7-3: In line near here all day, sometimes skirmishing heavily. About midnight moved with the Division and Corps to Seminary Ridge northwest of town.

7-4: Occupied Seminary Ridge. About 10 PM began the march to Hagerstown.

Present 1600. 58 Killed, 302 Wounded, 61 Missing; Total 421

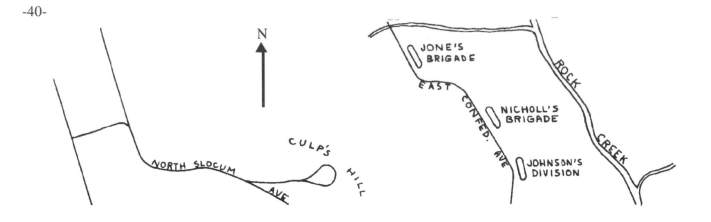

Ewell's Corps Johnson's Division Nicholl's Brigade	Col. J. M. Williams

1st, 2nd, 10th, 14th, 15th Louisiana Infantry

7-1: Arrived near nightfall and took position east of Rock Greek, north of Hanover Road and on right of Division.

7-2: About 6 PM changing to left of Jones' Brigade, crossed the Creek, attacked Union forces on Culp's Hill, drove in their outposts, and reached and held a line about 100 yards from their breastworks, against which a steady fire was maintained for hours and some vigorous but unsuccessful assaults were made.

7-3: At dawn the Brigade reopened the fire and continued for many hours, then retired to the line near the Creek, whence about midnight it moved with the Division and Corps to Seminary Ridge.

7-4: Occupied Seminary Ridge. About 10 PM began the march to Hagerstown.

Present about 1100. Killed 43, Wounded 309, Missing 36; Total 388

Ewell's Corps Johnson's Division — Maj. Gen. Edward Johnson

Steuart's Brigade	Brig. Gen. George H. Steuart
Stonewall Brigade	Brig. Gen. James A. Walker
Nicholl's Brigade	Col. J. M. Williams
Jones' Brigade	Brig. Gen. John M. Jones, Lt. Col. R. H. Duncan
Artillery Battalion	4 Batteries Maj. J. W. Latimer, Capt. C. L. Raine

7-1: The Division arrived on the field too late to participate in engagement of the day. Moved to the northeast of town during the night to take possession of a wooded hill that commanded Cemetary Ridge.

7-2: Early in the morning, skirmishers advanced and a desultry fire kept up. The artillery posted on hill in rear of line and opened fire about 4 PM. The infantry advanced to assault at dusk up the steep hill. Steuart's Brigade captured a line of works on the left. Firing continued at close range during the night.

7-3: The assault was renewed in the early morning. An attempt was made by the Union forces to retake the works occupied the night before, and was repulsed. The Division, being reinforced by four brigades, two other assaults were made and repulsed. Retired at 10:30 AM to former position of July 2nd, which was held until 10 PM when the Division was withdrawn to the ridge northwest of town.

7-4: The Division took up the line of march during the day.

Casualties: Killed 229, Wounded 1269, Missing 375; Total 1873

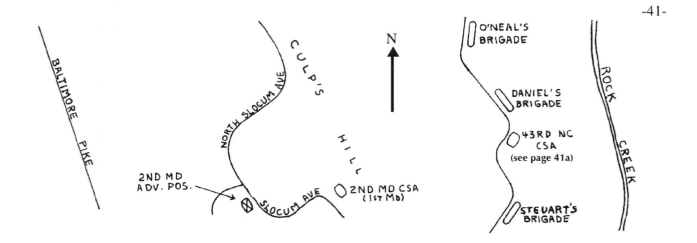

Ewell's Corps
Rhode's Division
O'Neal's Brigade*

Col. E. A. O'Neal
3rd, 5th, 6th, 12th, 26th Alabama Infantry

7-3: After taking part in the battles of the 1st and 2nd days elsewhere on the field, the Brigade leaving the 5th Regiment on guard, marched at 2 AM from its position in town to Culp's Hill to reinforce Johnson's Division. Arrived at daybreak and was soon under fire but not actively engaged until 8 AM, when it advanced against the breastworks on the eastern slope of the main summit of the hill, gaining there a position near the Union works and holding it under a terrific fire for three hours, until withdrawn by Gen'l Johnson with his entire line to the base of the hill near the Creek. From thense it moved during the night to Seminary Ridge west of town and rejoined Rodes' Division.

7-4: Occupied Seminary Ridge. Late at night it began the march to Hagerstown.

Present 2100. Killed 73, Wounded 430, Missing 193; Total 696

Ewell's Corps
Rhode's Division
Daniel's Brigade*

Brig. Gen. Junius Daniel
32nd, 43rd, 45th, 53rd Regiments and 2nd Battalion North Car Inf.

7-3: After taking part in the battles of the 1st and 2nd days elsewhere on the field, the Brigade marched about 1:30 AM from its position in the town to Culp's Hill to reinforce Johnson's Division. Arriving about 4 AM, it fought at different points wherever ordered through the long and fierce conflict, its main position being in the ravine between the two summits of Culp's Hill. At the close of the struggle near noon, it was withdrawn by Gen. Johnson with the rest of his line to the base of the hill from whense it moved during the night to Seminary Ridge west of town and there rejoined Rodes' Division.

7-4: Occupied Seminary Ridge. Late at night began the march to Hagerstown.

Present 2100. Killed 165, Wounded 635, Missing 116; Total 916

Ewell's Corps
Johnson's Division
Steuart's Brigade

Brig. Gen. George H. Steuart
1st Md. Bn., 1st, 3rd North Carolina, 10th, 23rd, 37th Virginia Inf.

7-1: Arrived about nightfall and took position near Hanover Road about a mile east of Rock Creek with left at edge of woods.

7-2: Crossing Rock Creek about 6 PM, the 3rd NC and 1st Md attacked the lesser summit of Culp's Hill. Reinforced later by other regiments, the Union breastworks thinly manned at some points, were occupied to the southern base of the main summit, but only after a vigorous and desperate conflict.

7-3: The Union troops reinforced, renewed the conflict at dawn and it raged fiercely until 11 AM, when this Brigade and the entire line fell back to the base of the hill and from thence moved about midnight to Seminary Ridge northwest of the town.

7-4: Occupied Seminary Ridge. About 10 PM began march to Hagerstown.

Present about 1700. Killed 83, Wounded 409, Missing, 190; Total 682

*see index

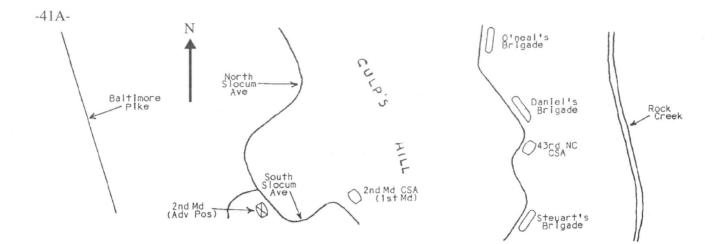

43rd NORTH CAROLINA REGIMENT

Daniel's Brigade   Rode's Division
Ewell's Corps
Army of Northern Virginia

Thomas Stephen Kenan, Colonel

William Gaston Lewis
Lieutenant

Walter Jones Boggan
Colonel Major

As they approached the field of battle on the morning of July 1, the 43rd North Carolina, along with the rest of Daniel's Brigade, heard the distant booming of cannon. Early in the afternoon the Regiment moved to the right and onto open ground where they were met by a steady fire. Their steady progress was checked by the deep railroad cut, but subsequent assaults were successful in breaking the Union line. Having suffered heavily, the regiment rested for the night west of town. The next morning the 43rd supported a battery just north of the Seminary. Shelling from guns on the nearby heights inflicted some losses. Toward evening the Regiment took up a position on the southern edge of town.

Before daybreak on July 3, the 43rd moved to the extreme left of the Confederate line to take part in the assault on Culp's Hill. Passing this point and advancing under heavy fire, they occupied the earthworks abandoned by Union troops. Attempting to push beyond the works, the Regiment was exposed to a most severe fire of cannister, shrapnel, and shell at short range. During the attack Colonel Kenan was wounded and taken from the field and command passed to Lieutenant Colonel Lewis. The Regiment retired to this point and remained exposed and under fire until ordered to recross Rock Creek in the early evening.

"ALL THAT MEN COULD DO, WAS DONE NOBLY"

Erected By The State of North Carolina

1988

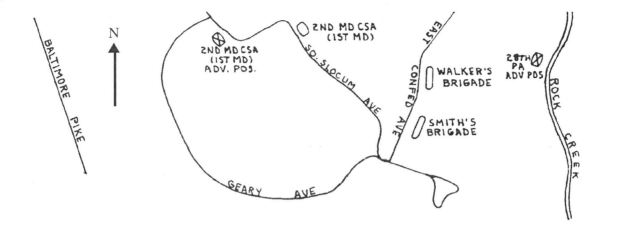

28th PA*	Capt. John Flynn
1-2-12	7-2: The Regiment took position here about 8 AM. Deployed as skirmishers and was engaged with the enemy
(advance	during the day. Remained until 7 PM when it was ordered to rejoin the 1st Brigade.
position)	Casualties: Killed 3, Wounded 23, 2 Missing; Total 28.

Ewell's	Brig. Gen. James A. Walker
Corps	2nd, 4th, 5th, 27th, 33rd Virginia Infantry.
Johnson's	7-1: Arrived near nightfall and took position east of Rock Creek near Hanover Road at border of woods on left
Division	of Division.
Walker's	7-2: Guarded Division all day on its flank from Union forces in woods nearby, skirmishing with them sharply
Brigade	at times and finally driving them away. After dark, crossed Rock Creek and rejoined the Division which
(Stonewell	had crossed about 6 PM and occupied part of the Union breastworks.
Brigade)	7-3: Took part in the unsuccessful struggle lasting from daybreak until near noon and then retired to the foot of
	the hill and from thence, about midnight, moved with the Division and Corps to Seminary Ridge.
	7-4: Occupied Seminary Ridge. About 10 PM began the march to Hagerstown.
	Present 1450. Killed 35, Wounded 208, Missing 87; Total 330

Ewell's	Brig. Gen. William Smith
Corps	31st, 49th, 52nd Virginia Infantry
Early's	7-3: The Brigade, having been detached two days guarding York Pike and other roads against the reported
Division	approach of Union cavalry, was ordered to Culp's Hill to reinforce Johnson's Division. Arriving early, it
Smith's	formed line along this stone wall, receiving and returning fire of infantry and sharpshooters in the woods
Brigade	opposite and being also subjected to heavy fire of artillery. It repulsed the charge of the 2nd Mass and 27th
	Ind Regiments against this line and held its ground until the Union forces regained their works on the hill.
	It then moved to a position further up the Creek and during the night marched to Seminary Ridge, where
	it rejoined Early's Division.
	7-4: Occupied Seminary Ridge. After midnight began the march to Hagerstown.
	Present 800. Killed 12, Wounded 113, Missing 17; Total 142

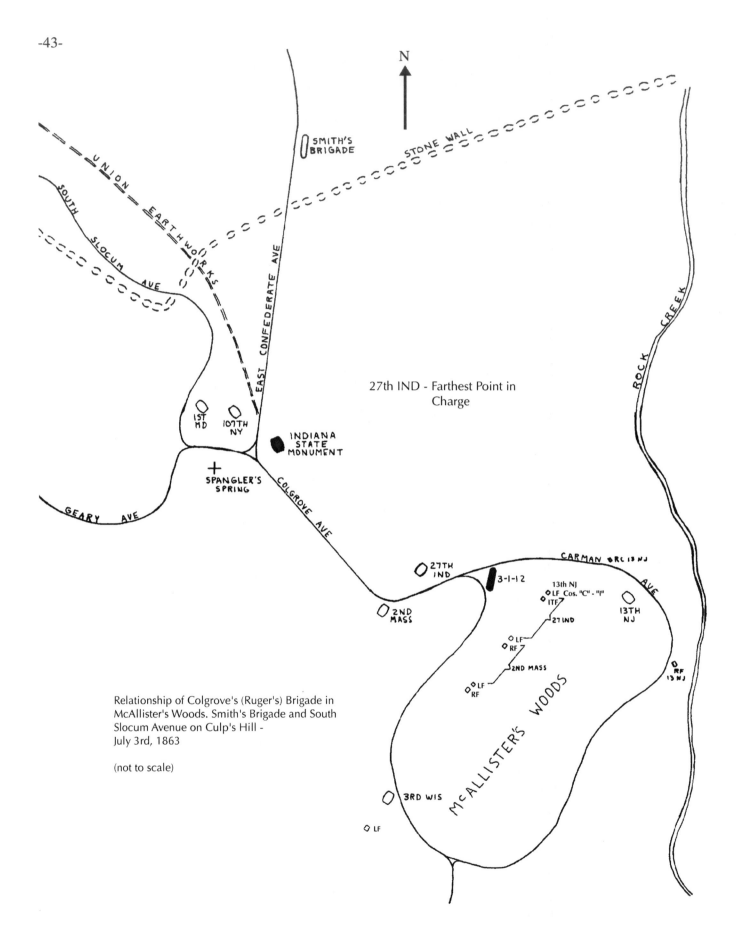

N

SMITH'S BRIGADE

STONE WALL

UNION EARTHWORKS

SOUTH SLOCUM AVE

EAST CONFEDERATE AVE

ROCK CREEK

27th IND - Farthest Point in Charge

1ST MD

107TH NY

INDIANA STATE MONUMENT

SPANGLER'S SPRING

COLGROVE AVE

GEARY AVE

CARMAN BRC 13 NJ

27TH IND

3-1-12

13th NJ

LF Cos. "C" - "I"

ITF

13TH NJ

2ND MASS

27 IND

LF
RF

RF
13 NJ

2ND MASS

LF
RF

Relationship of Colgrove's (Ruger's) Brigade in McAllister's Woods. Smith's Brigade and South Slocum Avenue on Culp's Hill - July 3rd, 1863

(not to scale)

McALLISTER'S WOODS

3RD WIS

LF

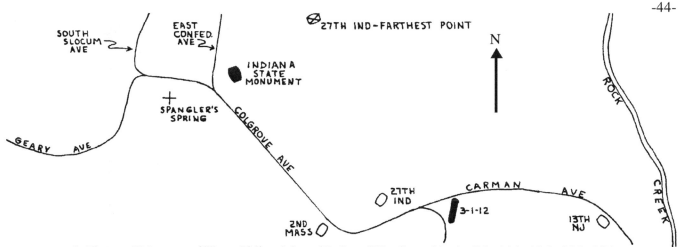

Indiana State Monument	In Honored Memory of Those Valiant Men of Indiana Who Served in the 7th, 14th, 19th, 20th, 27th (Cos I & K), 1st Indiana Cavalry (Cos A, B, C, D, E, F), 3rd Indiana Cavalry.

Indiana units engaged Confederate forces at Gettysburg and sustained some of the first casualties among the Union ranks. In this battle to preserve the Union, 552 men from Indiana were casualties to that cause. Dedicated to Those Hoosiers Who so Nobly Advanced Freedom on this Great Battlefield.

27th Ind*   Lt. Col. John R. Fesler
3-1-12
     7-3:   This monument marks the ground over which the left wing of the 27th Indiana advanced in a charge made by the Regiment in the morning.
     Casualties: 110 Killed and Wounded, 1 Missing; Total 111 of 339 engaged

27th Ind*
Farthest Point
     7-3:   This marks the farthest gained by the 27th Indiana Regiment in its charge at 6 AM on July 3,1863 on the works at the base of the hill behind this tablet. Four color bearers were killed and four were wounded.

2nd Mass   Lt. Col. Charles R. Mudge, Capt. Thomas R. Robeson, Lt. Henry V. D. Stone, Capt. Thomas B. Fox
3-1-1
     7-3:   From the hill behind this monument, the 2nd Massachusetts Infantry made an assault upon the Confederate troops in the works at the base of Culp's Hill opposite. The Regiment carried to the charge 22 officers and 294 enlisted men. It lost 4 officers and 41 enlisted men killed and mortally wounded and 6 officers and 84 enlisted men wounded.
     To Perpetuate the Honored Memories of that Hour The Survivors of the Regiment Have Raised this Stone - 1879

3-1-12   Brig. Gen. Thomas H. Ruger, Col. Silas Colgrove
     27th Ind, 2nd Mass, 13th NJ, 107th NY, 3rd Wis. Infantry
     7-1:   Arrived with the Division and bivouacked for the night east of Rock Creek.
     7-2:   After sharp skirmishing in front, crossed Rock Creek and went into position with the left on Culp's Hill, the right in McAllister's Woods, a swale in between. Breastworks were constructed at sunset. Went to support of the left of the Army and returned and found the works on the left of the swale occupied by Confederates. Those on the right were unoccupied and immediately repossessed.
     7-3:   2nd Mass and 27th Ind in the morning charged across the open swale to get possession of a stone wall and woods on the left but were repulsed with great loss, the 27th Ind falling back in a direct line, the 2nd Mass toward the left. A Confederate countercharge was made across the swale but receiving a front and enfilading fire, it was quickly repulsed and the Confederate force left the works and retired across Rock Creek.
     7-4:   The Brigade with a battery and three regiments of the 1st Brigade made a reconnaissance in front and around and through the town, the Confederate forces having withdrawn to Seminary Hill.
     Casualties: Killed 49, Wounded 225, Missing 5; Total 279

*see index

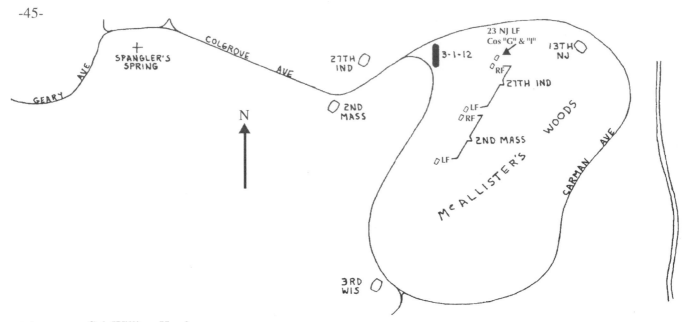

3rd Wis   Col. William Hawley
3-1-12
       7-1:   This Regiment went into position on this part of the line on the evening of July 1st.
       7-2:   In the evening moved to the left to reinforce the 3rd Corps. Returned to this position the same night.
       7-3,4,5: Remained in this position until morning of July 5th.
       Casualties: Killed 2, Wounded 8; Total 10.

13th NJ*   Col. Ezra A. Carman
3-1-12
       7-1:   Reached this battlefield at 5 PM July 1st and with the Brigade went into position on the north side of
              Wolf's Hill. During the night occupied a position in support of Btry M-1st NY Artillery.
       7-2:   In morning held position near Culp's Hill. In afternoon marched to relief of 3rd Corps near Round Top.
              At night returned to right of the Army.
       7-3:   Occupied position marked by this monument, supporting 2nd Mass and 27th Ind in their charge on
              Confederate flank. In evening moved to extreme right to support of Gregg's Cavalry.
       Casualties: Killed 2, Wounded 19; Total 21

13th NJ*   Companies G and I Left Flank.

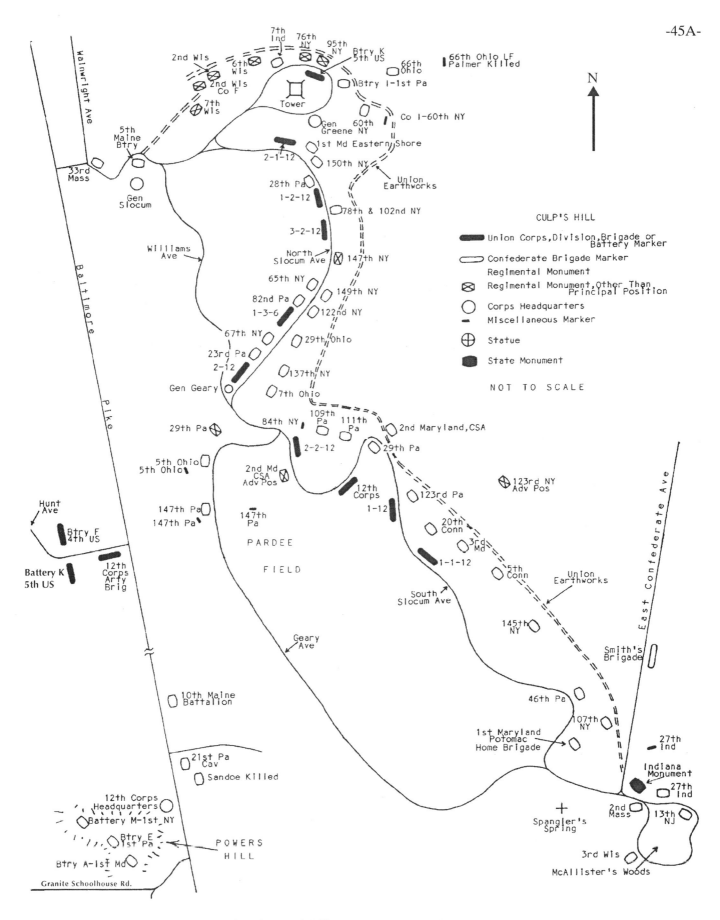

N

CULP'S HILL

▬ Union Corps,Division,Brigade or
　　　　Battery Marker
▭ Confederate Brigade Marker
　　Regimental Monument
⊗ Regimental Monument,Other Than
　　　　Principal Position
○ Corps Headquarters
- Miscellaneous Marker
⊕ Statue
▮ State Monument

NOT TO SCALE

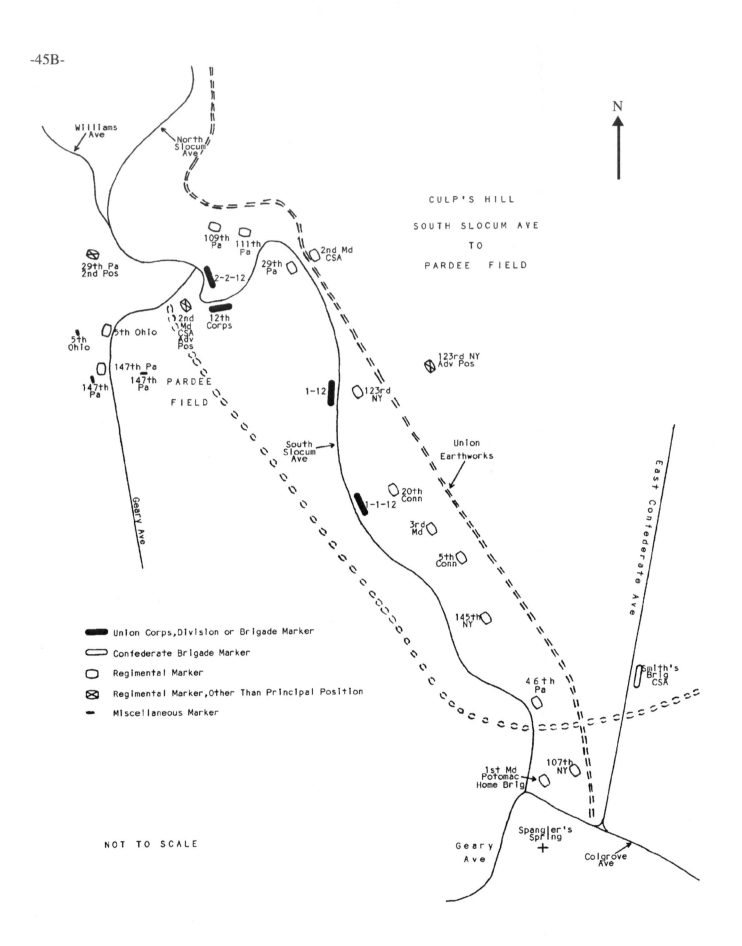

N

Williams Ave

North Slocum Ave

CULP'S HILL

SOUTH SLOCUM AVE

TO

PARDEE FIELD

109th Pa

111th Pa

2nd Md CSA

29th Pa 2nd Pos

2-2-12

29th Pa

2nd Md CSA Adv Pos

12th Corps

5th Ohio

5th Ohio

147th Pa

147th Pa

147th Pa

PARDEE FIELD

123rd NY Adv Pos

1-12

123rd NY

South Slocum Ave

Union Earthworks

Geary Ave

20th Conn

1-1-12

3rd Md

5th Conn

145th NY

East Confederate Ave

Smith's Brig CSA

46th Pa

107th NY

1st Md Potomac Home Brig

Spangler's Spring

Geary Ave

Colgrove Ave

■ Union Corps,Division or Brigade Marker

▭ Confederate Brigade Marker

◯ Regimental Marker

⊗ Regimental Marker,Other Than Principal Position

▬ Miscellaneous Marker

NOT TO SCALE

~ *Gettysburg Battlefield Monuments, Locations & Inscriptions* ~

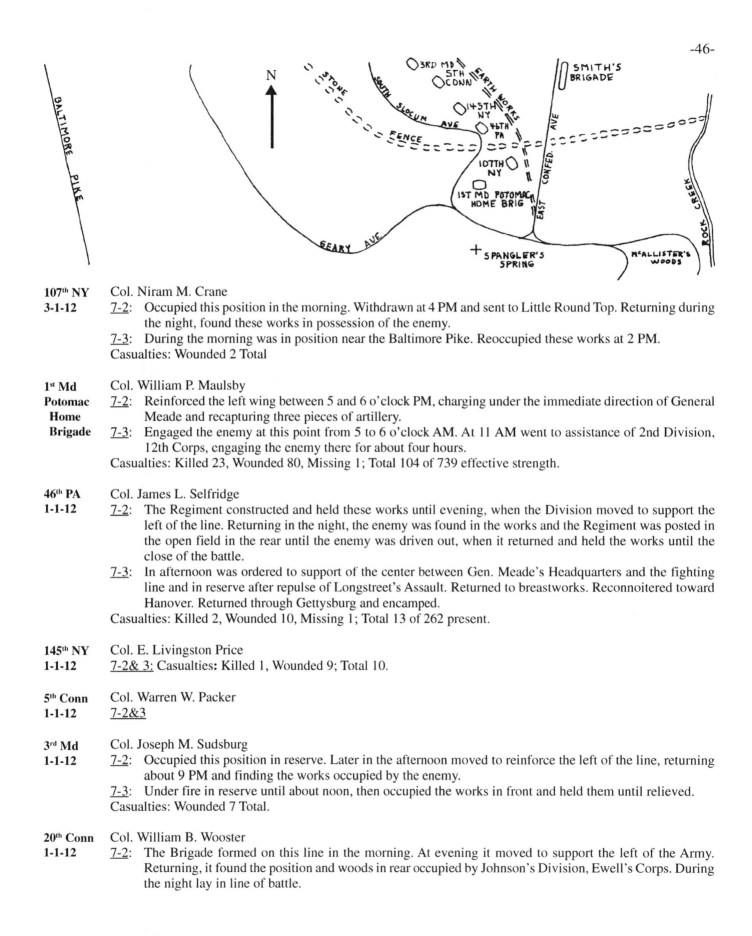

107ᵗʰ NY
3-1-12
Col. Niram M. Crane
<u>7-2</u>: Occupied this position in the morning. Withdrawn at 4 PM and sent to Little Round Top. Returning during the night, found these works in possession of the enemy.
<u>7-3</u>: During the morning was in position near the Baltimore Pike. Reoccupied these works at 2 PM.
Casualties: Wounded 2 Total

1ˢᵗ Md
Potomac
Home
Brigade
Col. William P. Maulsby
<u>7-2</u>: Reinforced the left wing between 5 and 6 o'clock PM, charging under the immediate direction of General Meade and recapturing three pieces of artillery.
<u>7-3</u>: Engaged the enemy at this point from 5 to 6 o'clock AM. At 11 AM went to assistance of 2nd Division, 12th Corps, engaging the enemy there for about four hours.
Casualties: Killed 23, Wounded 80, Missing 1; Total 104 of 739 effective strength.

46ᵗʰ PA
1-1-12
Col. James L. Selfridge
<u>7-2</u>: The Regiment constructed and held these works until evening, when the Division moved to support the left of the line. Returning in the night, the enemy was found in the works and the Regiment was posted in the open field in the rear until the enemy was driven out, when it returned and held the works until the close of the battle.
<u>7-3</u>: In afternoon was ordered to support of the center between Gen. Meade's Headquarters and the fighting line and in reserve after repulse of Longstreet's Assault. Returned to breastworks. Reconnoitered toward Hanover. Returned through Gettysburg and encamped.
Casualties: Killed 2, Wounded 10, Missing 1; Total 13 of 262 present.

145ᵗʰ NY
1-1-12
Col. E. Livingston Price
<u>7-2 & 3:</u> Casualties: Killed 1, Wounded 9; Total 10.

5ᵗʰ Conn
1-1-12
Col. Warren W. Packer
<u>7-2&3</u>

3ʳᵈ Md
1-1-12
Col. Joseph M. Sudsburg
<u>7-2</u>: Occupied this position in reserve. Later in the afternoon moved to reinforce the left of the line, returning about 9 PM and finding the works occupied by the enemy.
<u>7-3</u>: Under fire in reserve until about noon, then occupied the works in front and held them until relieved.
Casualties: Wounded 7 Total.

20ᵗʰ Conn
1-1-12
Col. William B. Wooster
<u>7-2</u>: The Brigade formed on this line in the morning. At evening it moved to support the left of the Army. Returning, it found the position and woods in rear occupied by Johnson's Division, Ewell's Corps. During the night lay in line of battle.

THE SYMBOLS LISTED BELOW ARE USED TO IDENTIFY
THE MONUMENTS, MARKERS, TABLETS, STATUES, ETC.
WHICH ARE DRAWN ON THE MAPS IN THESE PAGES

SYMBOL	TYPE	REPRESENTING	DESCRIPTION
	Bronze Tablet	Army of The Potomac, Union Corps or Division or Brigade, Regular Army Regiment, Regular Army Artillery Battery, Volunteer Artillery Brigade.	Brigade Tablet Mounted on Square Marble base. All other Tablets are on large vertical Granite Blocks.
	Bronze Tablet	Army of Northern Virginia, Confederate Corps or Division or Brigade or Artillery Battalion	Brigade Tablet and Artillery Battalion Tablet Mounted on Round Marble base. All other Tablets are Mounted on large vertical Granite blocks.
	Iron Tablet	Union Army Battery (other than Regular Army)	Mounted on Black Iron Shaft.
	Iron Tablet	Confederate Artillery Battery	Mounted on Black Iron Shaft.
	Iron Tablet	Confederate Brigade Advanced Position	Mounted on Black Iron Shaft.
	Regimental or Battery Monument	Principal Position of Volunteer Regiment or Volunteer Artillery Battery	Usually Granite or Marble in a Great Variety of Shapes and Sizes.
	Regimental Marker	Other than Principal Position of Regiment or Battery	Usually a Square Granite Marker or tablet or may be another monument.
	Flank Marker or Company Marker	Left and/or Right Flank of Regiment or Battery or Position of a Coppany.	Usually a Small Square or Rectangular Granite Marker.
	Army Or Corps Headquarters	Site of Headquarters of Army Commander or Corps Commander or Chief of Artillery	Cannon Barrel Mounted Vertically on Stone, Granite or Marble Base.
	State Monument	Monument Erected by Union or Confederate State.	
	Statue	Standing or Equestrian	Bronze Sculpture
	Building	House, Barn or other Structure	Identified by Owner's Name.
	Miscellaneous Marker	Marker or Inscription of a type not listed above	Granite or Metal Marker.

*Asterisk   Used whenever a Division or Brigade or Regiment or Battery has more than one Monument or Marker.   Check the Index for other Monument or Marker.

~ Gettysburg Battlefield Monuments, Locations & Inscriptions ~

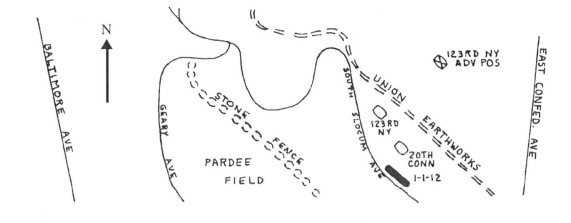

20th Conn   <u>7-3</u>:   At dawn advanced under cover of artillery and fought five hours, driving the enemy and reoccupying the
(con't)   works. Was relieved by the 123rd NY. In the afternoon moved to support the 2nd Corps against Longstreet's
            Assault. This Regiment went from Virginia with the 12th Army Corps to the Army of the Cumberland and
            marched with General Sherman to the sea.
         Casualties: Killed and Wounded 28.

1-1-12   Col. Archibald L. McDougall
         5th, 20th Conn, 3rd Md, 123rd, 145th NY, 46th Pa Infantry
         <u>7-1</u>:   Marched from Littlestown and when two miles from Gettysburg, advanced on Wolf's Hill, then occupied
            by a Confederate force. Retired and bivouacked until morning.
         <u>7-2</u>:   Crossed Rock Creek in the morning and formed in two lines on Culp's Hill to the right of 2nd Division, the
            rear line being behind a stone wall, the front line 40 yards in front where breastworks were immediately
            constructed. Late in the day went to support of 3rd Corps line and after dark returned and found the works
            and woods in rear in possession of Johnson's Division.
         <u>7-3</u>:   At daybreak, the Brigade with the artillery and infantry, the Corps attacked Johnson's Division which had
            been reinforced from Rodes' and Early's Divisions, and at 10 AM recaptured the works after a fierce
            contest. In the afternoon was sent to the support of the 2nd Corps.
         Casualties: Killed 12, Wounded 60, Missing 8; Total 80.

123rd NY*   The Washington County Regiment
1-1-12   Lt. Col. James C. Rogers, Capt. Adolphus H. Tanner
         <u>7-1</u>:   Marched from Littlestown. Formed line of battle on Wolf's Hill. Bivouacked near the Baltimore Pike.
         <u>7-2</u>:   Advanced to this line and built a heavy breastworks of logs. At about 6 PM moved to support the left near
            Little Round Top. Returning in the night found works in possession of the enemy, as no troops were left to
            occupy them.
         <u>7-3</u>:   At about 11 AM made a charge and recovered these works. About 4 PM moved to support line then
            repelling Pickett's Charge. A little later had a sharp skirmish in front of this line. At night repelled an attack
            with heavy loss to the enemy.
         <u>7-4</u>:   Made reconaissance around Wolf's Hill and through Gettysburg over the Hanover Road.
         Casualties: Killed 3, Wounded 10, Missing 1; Total 14 (NY@Gbg)

123rd NY*   The skirmishers of the 123rd NY reached this point on the afternoon of July 3, 1863.
Advanced
Position

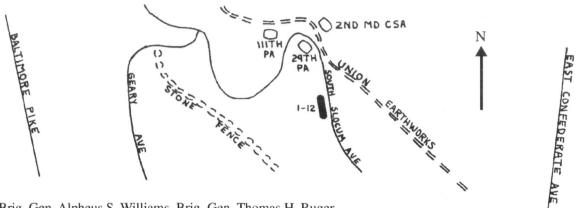

1st Division Brig. Gen. Alpheus S. Williams, Brig. Gen. Thomas H. Ruger
12th Corps 1st Brigade   Col. Archibald L. McDougall
2nd Brigade   Brig. Gen. Henry H. Lockwood
3rd Brigade   Brig. Gen. Thomas H. Ruger, Col. Silas Colgrove

7-1: Approaching Rock Creek on the Baltimore Pike, the Division moved on a crossroad to occupy Wolf's Hill but retired at sunset and took position east of Rock Creek for the night. 1st and 6th Corps having been included in Gen Slocum's command, Gen Williams assumed command of the Corps, Gen. Ruger of the 1st Division, and Col. S. Colgrove of the 3rd Brigade.

7-2: Brig. Gen. Lockwood's Brigade joined the Corps early in the morning, not having been assigned to a division was subject to the direct orders of the Corps Commander, assigned on July 5th to the 1st Division. The Division at 8 AM crossed Rock Creek and formed on the right of 2nd Division, its left on Culp's Hill, the right in McAllister's Woods. Breastworks were constructed along the line. Late in the day the Division moved to support 3rd Corps and Johnson's Confederate Division advanced and occupied the vacant works.

7-3: At daylight attacked the Confederate infantry and was hotly engaged with charges and countercharges at different points until 10:30 AM when the Confederate forces retired.

7-4: Early in the morning, General Slocum with a detatchment of infantry and a battery, made a reconaissance in front to Gettysburg without opposition.

Casualties: Killed 96, Wounded 406, Missing 31; Total 533

29th PA* Col. William Richards, Jr.
2-2-12

7-2: Position of the Regiment at 7 PM. The Brigade was withdrawn and on returning during the night, found the enemy in these works. The Regiment took position in rear of this line with its right as indicated by the tablet erected to the left and rear, and from there a charge of the enemy at daybreak was repulsed.

7-3: A charge of the enemy at daybreak was repulsed. After a contest of over seven hours in which the Regiment participated, it reoccupied and held the works until the close of the battle.

Casualties: Killed 15, Wounded 43, Missing 8; Total 146 of 485

**2nd Md
CSA*
Steuart's
Brigade** Formerly 1st Maryland CSA
Lt. Col. James R. Herbert

7-2: Advancing from Rock Creek about 7 PM, occupied the line of works at this point and held its position until next morning.

7-3: In the morning, the Battalion moving by the left flank,formed at right angles with, and inside, the works and charged under a fire in front, flank, and rear to a stone planted 100 yards west from this monument.

Casualties: Killed 52, Wounded 140; Total 192 of 400 Strength.

**111th PA
2-2-12** Lt. Col. Thomas M. Walker, Col. George A. Cobham, Jr., Lt. Col. Charles Randall

7-2: The Regiment built these works. In the evening it was withdrawn with the Brigade and returning during the night, found the enemy in the works.

7-3: Assisted in repulsing a charge of the enemy at daylight and after seven and one-half hours of continuous fighting in which it participated, regained the works and held them until the close of the battle.

Casualties: Killed 5, Wounded 18; Total 23 of 259 carried into action.

*see index

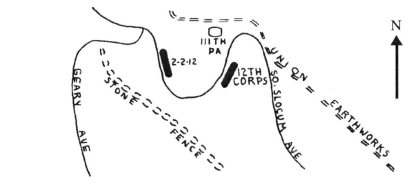

12th Corps Maj. Gen. Henry W. Slocum, Brig. Gen. Alpheus S. Williams
1st Division   Brig. Gen. Alpheus S. Williams, Brig. Gen. Thomas H. Ruger.
2nd Division   Brig. Gen. John W. Geary
7-1: Marched from near Littlestown to Two Taverns. In the afternoon, hearing the 1st and 11th Corps were engaged near Gettysburg, the Corps advanced on the Baltimore Pike; Williams' Division to a position east of Rock Creek, Geary's Division to the left of the Union line extending to the summit of Little Round Top.
7-2: In the morning the Corps took position on the right of 1st Corps on a line extending from the top of Culp's Hill, southeasterly across the low meadow into McAllister's Woods. Later in the day, the Corps, except Greene's Brigade, was withdrawn to support the left of the Army. Johnson's Confederate Division at night advanced under cover of darkness and took possession of the works on the Corps line on the right of Greene's Brigade. About midnight the Corps returned and finding Johnson's Division in possession of their works, formed a line in front of that Division.
7-3: Before 1 AM, the artillery of the Corps and Rigby's Maryland Battery from Reserve Artillery, in all 26 guns, were so placed as to command the line occupied by Johnson's Division and at daylight opened fire, under cover of which the infantry was advanced and attacked the Confederate position, and after a contest lasting seven hours, recaptured the works. Many prisoners and over 5000 small arms were captured. In the afternoon the Corps was in readiness to move.
7-4: General Slocum in the morning, advanced with a detatchment of Ruger's Division and a battery and found that the Confederates in front had retired.
Casualties: Killed 204, Wounded 812, Missing 66; Total 1082.

2-2-12 Col. George A. Cobham, Jr, Brig. Gen. Thomas Kane, Col. George A. Cobham, Jr,
29th, 109th, 111th Pa Infantry
7-1: Arrived late in afternoon and took position in support of a section of Battery K-5th US on the left of the Baltimore Pike.
7-2: In the morning took position on Culp's Hill connecting with the right of 3rd Brigade and constructed breastworks. Near sunset, moved out on Baltimore Pike and returned at dusk and found the breastworks in possession of Major General Johnson's Division. Entered the woods in rear of 3rd Brigade and took position perpendicular to, and nearly at right angles, with it.
7-3: At 3:30 AM the artillery opened fire over the Brigade and Maj. Gen. Johnson's Division advanced and attacked in force, exposing its line in front and enfilading fire from infantry and to a destructive fire for seven hours with great loss. Brig. Gen. Steuart's Brigade was immediately in front. No further firing except by skirmishers and sharpshooters.
Casualties: Killed 23, Wounded 66, Missing 9; Total 98.

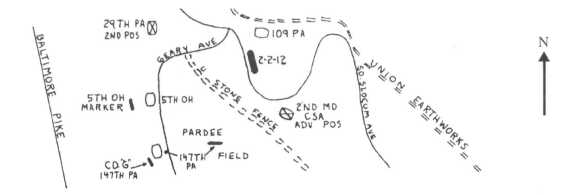

2nd Md. CSA* Advanced Position

"Point reached by 1st Maryland Battalion, CSA, July 3, 1863."

147th PA* 1-2-12

Lt. Col. Ario Pardee

7-1: On the night of July 1st, this Regiment lay on the northern slope of Little Round Top, holding the extreme left of the Union Army.

7-2: At 6 AM, moved to Culp's Hill where it was held in reserve until evening; then marched toward the left with the Brigade.

7-3: Returned at about 3 AM and occupied this position.

Casualties: Killed 6, Wounded 14; Total 20 of 298 present.

147th PA* Co. G

July 3, 1863

(Note: This is a small granite marker a few feet behind the above.)

147th PA*

(Note: Marker on boulder in Pardee Field.)

7-3: At 5 AM, the 147th Pa Volunteers, Lt. Col. Ario Pardee, Jr. was ordered to charge and carry the stone wall occupied by the enemy. This they did in handsome style, their firing causing heavy loss to the enemy who then abandoned the entire line of the stone wall. Report of Brig. Gen. John W Geary, Commanding 2nd Division, 12th Corps.

5th Ohio* 1-2-12

Col. John H. Patrick

7-1: Moved over to line north of Little Round Top.

7-2: Moved to Culp's Hill and at evening moved as far as Rock Creek to reinforce the left. Returned to Culp's Hill at night.

7-3: In the morning was engaged, where this monument stands, until 11 AM in repulsing the enemy and retaking the Union works.

Casualties: Killed 2, Wounded 16; Total 18 of 315 present for duty.

5th Ohio*

(Note: A 5th Ohio marker is fastened to a boulder about 50 feet behind the 5th Ohio monument.)

29th PA* 2-2-12 2nd Position

Capt. Wilber F. Stevens, Capt. Edward Hayes

7-1: Wolf's Hill

7-2: (Note: See Page 48)

7-3: Note: This position)

109th PA* 2-2-12

Capt. Frederick L. Gimber

7-1: The Regiment arrived within two miles of Gettysburg about 5 PM and took position on the left of the Baltimore Pike.

7-2: It moved here and built these works. In the evening it was withdrawn with the Brigade, and returning in the night, found the works in the possession of the enemy, when it formed at right angles to this line behind a ledge of rocks to the left and rear of this position as designated by a marker.

*see index

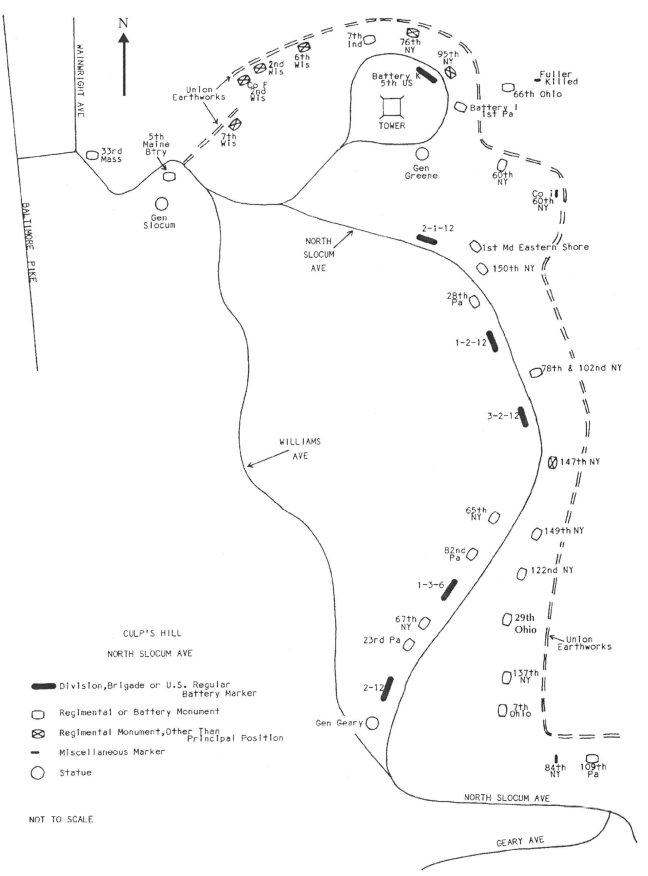

N

WAINWRIGHT AVE

7th Ind

76th NY

95th NY

Fuller Killed

2nd Wis

6th Wis

Battery K 5th US

66th Ohio

Union Earthworks

Co F 2nd Wis

TOWER

Battery I 1st Pa

33rd Mass

5th Maine Btry

7th Wis

Gen Greene

60th NY

BALTIMORE PIKE

Gen Slocum

Co i 60th NY

NORTH SLOCUM AVE

2-1-12

1st Md Eastern Shore

150th NY

28th Pa

1-2-12

78th & 102nd NY

3-2-12

WILLIAMS AVE

147th NY

65th NY

149th NY

82nd Pa

122nd NY

1-3-6

29th Ohio

Union Earthworks

67th NY

23rd Pa

137th NY

CULP'S HILL

NORTH SLOCUM AVE

2-12

7th Ohio

Gen Geary

Division, Brigade or U.S. Regular Battery Marker

Regimental or Battery Monument

Regimental Monument, Other Than Principal Position

Miscellaneous Marker

Statue

84th NY

109th Pa

NOT TO SCALE

NORTH SLOCUM AVE

GEARY AVE

~ Gettysburg Battlefield Monuments, Locations & Inscriptions ~

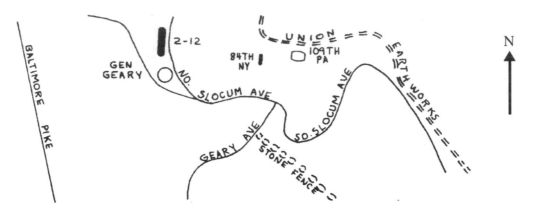

109th PA*   <u>7-3</u>:   After severe fighting in the morning, this line was recaptured and held until the close of the battle.
(con't)   Casualties: Killed 3, Wounded 6, Missing 1; Total 10 of 149.

84th NY*   Col. Edward B. Fowler
(14th   <u>7-1</u>:   In the first day of the battle this Regiment was heavily engaged with the 1st Corps at the Railroad tracks
Brooklyn)   beyond the Seminary as indicated by a monument there.
2-1-1   <u>7-2</u>:   Here at about 9 PM, the Regiment, while moving from its position to the left of this to reinforce Greene's
              Brigade, unexpectedly encountered the advance of Johnson's Division of Ewell's Corps which had crossed
              the abandoned works and was advancing toward the Baltimore Pike. By opening fire on them, the Regi-
              ment caused them to halt while the 12th Corps returned and drove them back.
        <u>7-3</u>:   At daylight the Regiment rejoined the Brigade, but soon afterward moved again to the right to reinforce
              the 12th Corps and fought in the trenches and laid in reserve until the repulse of the enemy.
        Casualties: Killed 13, Wounded 105, Missing 99; Total 217 (NY@Gbg)

Geary's   John White Geary, Capt. 2nd Pa Inf 12-21-1846; Lt Col 1-7-47; Col 11-3-47. Honorably mustered out
Statue   7-21-48. Col. 28th Pa Inf 6-28-61; Discharged for promotion 5-15-62: Brig. Gen. USV 4-25-62; Honorably
        mustered out 1-15-66. Brevetted Maj. Gen. USV 1-12-65 "For fitness to command and promptness to
        execute". Born 12-30-1819 at Mount Pleasant, Pa. Died 2-8-73 at Harrisburg.

2nd Division Brig. Gen. John W. Geary
12th Corps   1st Brigade   Col. Charles Candy
        2nd Brigade   Col. George A. Cobham, Jr., Brig. Gen. Thomas L. Kane
        3rd Brigade   Brig. Gen. George S. Greene
        <u>7-1</u>:   Arrived on the Baltimore Pike and went into position about 5 PM, the 1st and 3rd Brigades on the line
              from Cemetary Ridge to Little Round Top, 2nd Brigade on the left of the Baltimore Pike.
        <u>7-2</u>:   In the morning the 1st and 3rd Brigades took position on the right of the 1st Corps on Culp's Hill connect-
              ing with the 1st Division on the right. Breastworks were thrown up along the entire front. At 7 PM, the 1st
              and 3rd Brigades on the Baltimore Pike moved off intending to support the 3rd Corps. Brig. Gen. Greene
              extended the 3rd Brigade over the line of the 2nd Brigade, refusing his right. Being reinforced by about
              750 men from the left, he held his position against attacks of Johnson's Confederate Division.
        <u>7-3</u>:   At 3:30 AM an attack by infantry and artillery was made on Johnson's Division and after a contest of 7
              hours, the Confederates were driven from their position, losing heavily in Killed, Wounded and Prisoners;
              also 3 battle flags and over 5000 small arms.
        Casualties: Killed 108, Wounded 397, Missing 35; Total 540

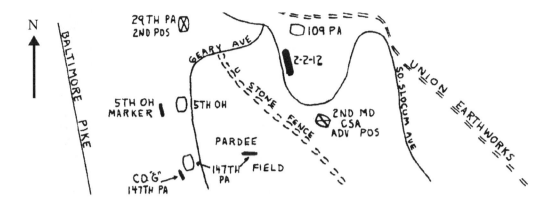

7th Ohio   Col. William R. Creighton
1-2-12   7-1:   Arrived near Little Round Top in the evening.
              7-2:   Held positions on Culp's Hill from morning until 6 PM, then moved with the Brigade to support the left. Returned at midnight to Culp's Hill and remained there until the close of the battle.
              Casualties: Killed 1; Wounded 17, Total 18

137th NY   Col. David Ireland
3-2-12   7-2:   Held this position until retreat of the rebel army.
              Casualties: Killed 40, Wounded 87, Missing 10; Total 137

29th Ohio   Capt. Edward Hayes
1-2-12   7-2&3: Occupied several positions in this vicinity both in the entrenchments and in reserve.
              Casualties: Killed 7, Wounded 31; Total 38.

23rd PA   Birney's Zouaves, Lt. Col. John F. Glenn
1-3-6   7-1:   About 9 PM marched from Manchester, Md.
              7-2:   Ordered to Culp's Hill where it remained until ordered to support of left center. Placed in rear of this position at 9:30 AM and subsequently, five companies advanced into the breastworks. During the heavy cannonade it moved with the Brigade to support the left center.
              7-4:   Started in pursuit of Lee.
              Casualties: Killed 1, Wounded 13; Total 14

67th NY   Col. Nelson Cross
1-3-6   7-3:   Held this position, then moved double-quick to left center to resist Confederate charge upon Union batteries.
              Casualties: Missing 1 Total

1-3-6   Brig. Gen. Alexander Shaler
              65th, 67th, 122nd NY, 23rd, 82nd Pa Infantry.
              7-2:   Arrived about 2 PM from Manchester, Md and late in the day moved to northeast slope of Little Round Top and held in reserve, bivouacking for the night near the Taneytown Road in rear of 2nd Brigade.
              7-3:   Ordered to the left and at 8 AM to the right to the support of the 2nd Division-12th Corps. Took position in woods on Culp's Hill beyond which action was proceeding and was engaged under command of Brig. Gen. J. W. Geary from 9 until 11 AM, when the original line of the 12th Corps was regained. At 3 PM the 6th Corps returned and under a terrific fire of artillery was ordered by Maj. Gen. Meade to remain in rear of 3rd Corps and to report to Maj. Gen. Newton. At 7 PM moved one half mile to right in reserve and remained during the night. Rejoined the Division the next morning.
              Casualties: 15 Killed, 56 Wounded, 3 Missing; Total 74.

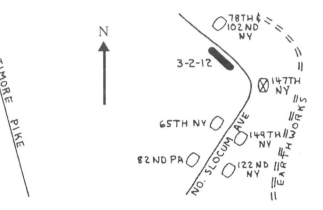

122nd NY   Col. Silas Titus
1-2-12   <u>7-3</u>:   Assisted in repulsing the attack on the morning of July 3rd.
          Casualties: Killed 10, Wounded 34; 44 Total

149th PA   Col. Henry A. Barnum, Lt. Col. Charles B. Randall
3-2-12   <u>7-1</u>:   At 5 PM, occupied position near Little Round Top.
          <u>7-2&3</u>: At 4 AM, moved here, built these works and defended them.
          Casualties: Killed 6, Wounded 46, Missing 3; Total 55

82nd PA   Col. Isaac C. Bassett
1-3-6   <u>7-3</u>:   Marched from near Little Round Top and occupied the works in front at 4:30 AM, relieving other troops.
          Casualties: Wounded 6 Total.

65th NY   Col. Joseph E. Hamblin
1-3-6   <u>7-2</u>:   Arrived on the field at 2 PM.
          <u>7-3</u>:   At daylight moved from the base of Little Round Top to Culp's Hill. Held this position until 3 PM, then
              moved to the left center.
          Casualties: Killed 4, Wounded 5; Total 9

147th NY*   (Note: No inscription on this monument.)
2-2-1
3-2-12   Brig. Gen. George S. Greene
          60th, 78th, 102nd, 137th, 149th NY Infantry
          <u>7-1</u>:   Arrived about 5 PM and took position on the left of the 1st Corps on Cemetery Ridge.
          <u>7-2</u>:   At 6 AM took position on Culp's Hill on the right of the 1st Corps with 2nd Brigade on right. Breastworks
              were constructed. At 6:30 PM the 1st and 2nd Brigades were ordered to follow the 1st Division to support
              the left of the Army, leaving this Brigade to occupy the entire Corps line. The 137th NY was moved into
              the position of the 2nd Brigade when the line was attacked by Maj. Gen. Johnson's Division which made
              four distinct charges. And at 8 PM occupied the works that the 1st Division had vacated but were success-
              fully repulsed from the line held by this Brigade, the 137th NY having changed front to face the enemy.
              The Brigade was reinforced by about 750 men from the 1st and 11th Corps.
          <u>7-3</u>:   At daylight, Maj. Gen. Johnson, having been reinforced, advanced and a fierce engagement ensued for
              seven hours, when after suffering heavy losses, he was forced back from the entire line.
          Casualties: Killed 67, Wounded 212, Missing 24; Total 303

78th and   Lt. Col. Herbert Hammerstein (78th NY)
102nd NY   Col. James C. Lane, Capt. Lewis R. Stegman (102nd NY)
3-2-12   <u>7-2&3</u>: This ground occupied during the battle by the 78th and 102nd NY, skirmishers out in front.
          Casualties: Killed 10, Wounded 38, Missing 11; Total 59

*see index

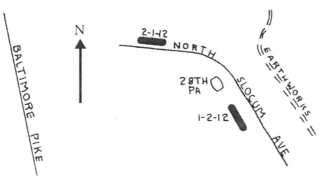

1-2-12   Col. Charles Candy

5th, 7th, 29th Ohio, 28th, 147th Pa Infantry

7-1:   Arrived at 5 PM and took position on left of 3rd Brigade between the 1st Corps and the Round Tops. The 5th Ohio and 147th Pa occupied Little Round Top during the night as skirmishers.

7-2:   Moved to Culp's Hill in the morning and took position as a reserve in rear of the 3rd Brigade. At 7 PM moved to the rear on Baltimore Pike across Rock Creek. Returned at midnight and formed on the right of 3rd Brigade perpendicular to its line.

7-3:   At daylight the artillery opened on the Confederate line. The 147th Pa advanced and captured a stone wall. The other regiments were in reserve and at intervals relieved the regiments of the 2nd and 3rd Brigades. The 66th Ohio advanced beyond the breastworks and poured an enfilading fire on the Confederates occupying the works on the right. At 10:30 AM Johnson's forces were forced from the works. Skirmishing continued all day.

Casualties: Killed 18, Wounded 119, Missing 2; Total 139

28th PA
1-2-12   Capt. John Flynn

7-1:   Arrived at 5 PM, went into position north of Little Round Top.

7-2:   At 6:30 AM moved to Culp's Hill where the Regiment was advanced to Rock Creek to support skirmish line. At dark retired and moved with the Brigade.

7-3:   Returned at 3 AM. At 8 AM relieved troops in breastworks. Was relieved in turn and again advanced and occupied the works from 4 PM to 10 PM.

Casualties: Killed 6, Wounded 20, Missing 2; Total 28 of 303.

2-1-12   Brig. Gen. Henry H. Lockwood

1st Md. Potomac Home Brigade, 1st Md Eastern Shore, 150th NY

7-2:   1st Potomac Home Brigade and 150th NY arrived at 8 AM and went into position between Rock Creek and Baltimore Pike on the right of the Division, Brig. Gen. Lockwood receiving orders direct from the General Commanding Corps. Late in the day the Brigade went with the Division to support 3rd Corps line and advanced over the ground from which the 3rd Corps had previously been forced. The 150th NY drew off three abandoned guns of the 9th Mass Battery and returned at midnight.

7-3:   Took part in the recapture of the works in which Maj. Gen. Johnson's Division took possession of during the abscence of the Division the previous night. At 8 AM the 1st Md Eastern Shore arrived and joined the Brigade. Ordered in the afternoon to the 2nd Corps line near the cemetery to render support where needed. The Brigade was not assigned to the Division until July 5th.

Casualties: Killed 35, Wounded 121, Missing 18; Total 174.

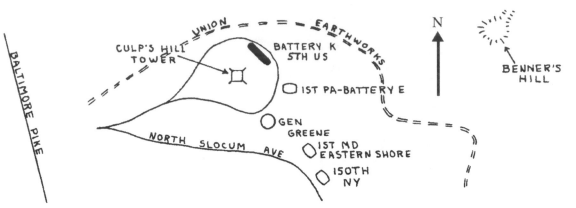

1st Md
Eastern
Shore
2-1-12

Col. James Wallace

Maryland's Tribute To Her Loyal Sons

<u>7-3</u>:   Five companies held the works in front of this stone in the morning, relieving other troops and remaining until noon when they were relieved. The remainder of the Regiment were in position during the same time about 300 yards to the right.

Casualties: Killed 5, Wounded 18, Missing 2; Total 25

150th NY*
2-1-12

Dutchess County Regiment. Col. John H. Ketcham

<u>7-2&3</u>:   The Regiment defended these works on July 3rd from 6:30 to 9:30 AM and from 10AM to 12 noon and captured 200 prisoners.

Casualties: Killed 7, Wounded 23, Missing 15; Total 45 (NY@ Gbg)

Battery K*
5th US
12th Corps
Artillery
Brigade

Lt. David H. Kinsey

Four - 12 Pounders

<u>7-1</u>:   Marched to within a mile and a half of Gettysburg.

<u>7-2</u>:   At daybreak, took position to command a gap between the 1st and 12th Corps. At 5 PM, one section was placed on the summit of Culp's Hill and assisted in silencing Confederate batteries on Benner's Hill. At 6 PM rejoined the Battery at the foot of Power's Hill.

<u>7-3</u>:   At 1 AM, was posted with Lt. S. T. Rugg's Battery F-4th US Artillery on the south side of the Baltimore Pike opposite the center of the line of the 12th Corps. At 4:30 AM, opened fire on the Confederates in possession of the line vacated by the 12th Corps the previous night. Firing continued at intervals until after 10 AM when the Confederates were driven out. Remained in the same position exposed to the severe shelling which came over the Cemetery Hill in the afternoon.

Casualties: Wounded 5 Total.

Battery E*
Ind. PA Lt

Knap's Independent Battery

Greene's
Statue

Brig. Gen. George S. Greene

This monument commemerates the services of Gen. Greene and of the New York troops under his command comprising the 60th, 78th, 102nd, 137th, 149th Regiments of Infantry forming the 3rd Brigade, Geary's Division of Slocum's 12th Corps and the 45th, 84th, 147th, 157th Regiments sent to his support during the night of July 2-3, when assisted by 6th Wisconsin, 82nd Illinois, 61st Ohio these troops held the flank of the Army against the attacks of a greatly superior force.

Cadet USMA 6/24/1819, 2nd Lt. US Artillery 7/1/23, 1st Lt. 5/1/29, Resigned 6/30/36. Col. 60th NY Inf 1/18/62, Brig. Gen. USV 4/28/62, Commanded 3rd Brig-2nd Div. Banks' Corps at the Battle of Cedar Mountain, 8/9/62, 2nd Div. Mansfield's Corps at Antietam, 9/17/62, 3rd Brig, 2nd Div Slocum's Corps at Chancellorsville 5/1 to 3/63, at Gettysburg, 7/1, 2, 3/63 and at Wauhatchie,Tennessee, 10/28/63 where he was severely wounded. Returned to field duty March 1865, joining Sherman's Army in North Carolina. In action at Kingston 3/10/65 and in command of Provisional Division until Sherman's Army disbanded.

Breveted Major General United States Volunteers 3/30/65. Honorably Discharged, 4/30/66.

*see index

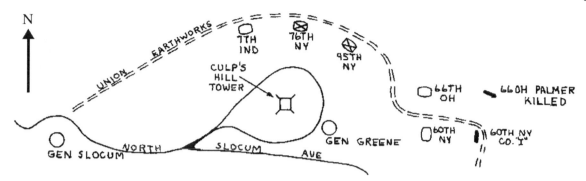

7th Ind   Col. Ira C. Grover
2-2-1   7-1,2,3: (Note: No inscription)

76th NY*   Maj. Andrew J. Grover, Capt. John E. Cook
2-1-1   7-2&3: (Note: No inscription)

95th NY*   Col. George H. Biddle, Maj. Edward Pye
2-1-1   7-2&3: (Note: No inscription)

66th Ohio*   7-1: Arrived in position just north of Little Round Top 5 PM.
1-2-12   7-2: In morning moved to Culp's Hill and entrenched.
    Lt. Col. Eugene Powell
    7-3: At daybreak advanced over the Union breastworks and with the right here and left at tablet below,
        opened an enfilading fire on the enemy.

66th Ohio*   7-3: Here Major J. C. Palmer fell mortally wounded.
Palmer   (Note: This is the "tablet" referred to above.)
Killed   66th Ohio Casualties: Killed 11, Wounded 41; Total 52

60th NY*   Casualties: Killed 11, Wounded 41; Total 52
3-2-12   Col. Abel Godard
60th NY*   7-2&3: Capt. Jesse Jones
Co I

Slocum   Major General Henry Warner Slocum, US Volunteers; 1826 - 1894
Statue   In command of the right wing of the Army of the Potomac at the Battle of Gettysburg, July 1,2,3, 1863.
    "Stay And Fight It Out"—General Slocum at the Council of War, July 2, 1863. Erected by the State of New
    York, 1902.
    Cadet USMA 7/1/1848; 2nd Lt. 1st Artillery 7/1/52; 1st Lt. 3/3/55. Resigned 10/31/56. Col. 27th NY Inf, 5/21/
    61. Severely wounded, Bull Run 7/21/61. Brig. Gen. of Volunteers, 8 /9/61. Assigned to command of 2nd Bri-
    gade, Franklin's Division, Army of the Potomac, 9/4/61, and to command of 1st Division, 6th Corps, 5/18/62.
    Temporarily commanded the Right Wing of the Army of the Potomac consisting of the 5th, 11th and 12th Corps,
    4/28-30/63. In command of the Right Wing of the Union Army composed of the 5th and 12th Corps at Gettysburg,
    7/l,2,3/63. Relinquished command of the 12th Corps, 4/18/64, and on 4/27/64, assumed command of the Mili-
    tary District of Vicksburg, which he held till 8/14/64. Assumed command of the 20th Corps and of the Left Wing
    of Sherman's Army, known as the Army of Georgia, 10/11/64. Assigned in orders dated 6/27/65 to the command
    of the Department of the Mississippi, headquartered at Vicksburg, which he held until 9/18/65 and on 9/28/1865,
    General Slocum resigned from the Army and was Honorably Discharged. Army, known as the Army of Georgia,
    10/11/64. Assigned in orders dated 6/27/65 to the command of the Deptartment of the Mississippi, headquar-
    tered at Vicksburg, which he held until 9/18/65 and on 9/28/1865, General Slocum resigned from the Army and
    was Honorably Discharged.

*see index

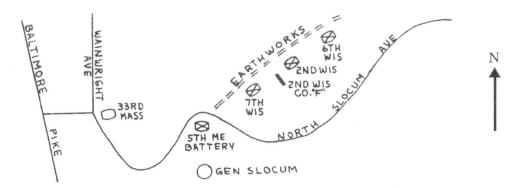

5th Maine Light Battery* **1st Corps Artillery Brigade**	Capt. Greenleaf T. Stevens, Lt. Edward N. Whittier Six - 12 Pounders 7-1: Engaged north of Seminary. Also engaged here. 7-2: "In assault on East Cemetary Hill in the evening, the enemy, Hays' and Hoke's Brigades, exposed their left flanks to Steven's Battery which poured a terrible fire of double cannister into their ranks." (Note: The above quotation is described as being from General Doubleday's battle report.) 7-3: Engaged here. Casualties: Killed 3, Wounded 13, Missing 6; Total 22
7th Wis* **1-1-1**	(Note: No inscription)
2nd Wis* **Co F**	(Note: No inscription)
2nd Wis* **1-1-1**	(Note: No inscription)
6th Wis* **1-1-1**	(Note: No inscription)
33rd Mass **2-2-11**	7-2: Detatched from 2nd Brigade, 2nd Division, llth Corps. After supporting batteries in action on Cemetary Hill, while in position in a line extending westward from this spot, withstood and assisted in repelling a charge of the enemy infantry in its front. Casualties: Killed 8, Wounded 36; Total 44 Col. Adin B. Underwood

*see index

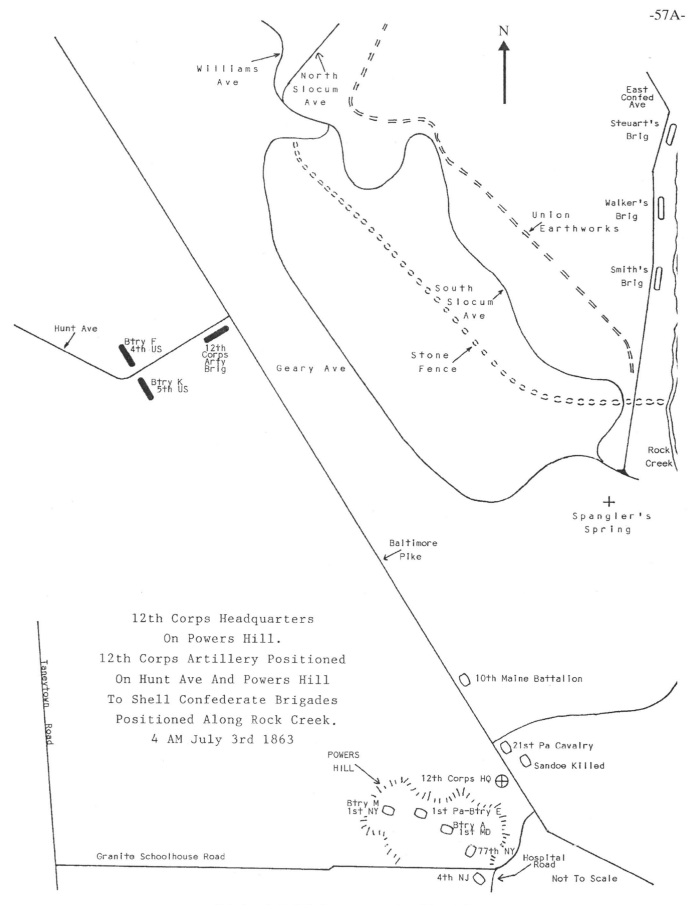

N

Williams Ave

North Slocum Ave

East Confed Ave

Steuart's Brig

Walker's Brig

Union Earthworks

Smith's Brig

Hunt Ave

Btry F 4th US

12th Corps Arty Brig

Btry K 5th US

Geary Ave

South Slocum Ave

Stone Fence

Rock Creek

Spangler's Spring

Baltimore Pike

12th Corps Headquarters
On Powers Hill.
12th Corps Artillery Positioned
On Hunt Ave And Powers Hill
To Shell Confederate Brigades
Positioned Along Rock Creek.
4 AM July 3rd 1863

Taneytown Road

10th Maine Battalion

21st Pa Cavalry

Sandoe Killed

POWERS HILL

12th Corps HQ

Btry M 1st NY

1st Pa-Btry E

Btry A 1st MD

77th NY

Granite Schoolhouse Road

4th NJ

Hospital Road

Not To Scale

~ Gettysburg Battlefield Monuments, Locations & Inscriptions ~

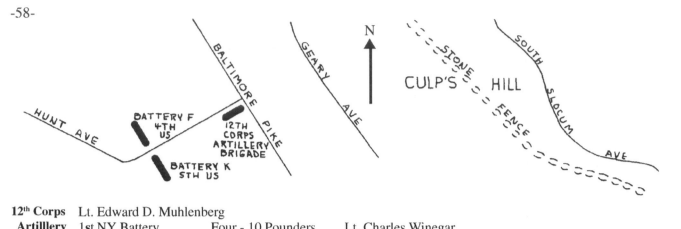

12th Corps	Lt. Edward D. Muhlenberg		
Artilllery	1st NY Battery	Four - 10 Pounders	Lt. Charles Winegar
Brigade	Penna Battery E	Six - 10 Pounders	Lt. Charles Atwell
	Battery F - 4th US	Six - 10 Pounders	Lt. Sylvanus Rugg
	Battery K - 5th US	Four - 10 Pounders	Lt. David Kinzie

7-1: About noon, two batteries moved from Two Taverns with 1st Division toward the Hanover Road to within a mile and a half of Gettysburg. The other two batteries moved with 2nd Division and encamped for the night the same distance from town.

7-2: In the afternoon, three guns of Penna Battery E and two of Battery K-5th US were placed on the summit of Culp's Hill and were engaged at once with Confederate Artillery. At night Penna Battery E and Battery M-1st NY were placed on Powers and McAllister's Hills, Battery F-4th US and Battery K-5th US at the base of Powers Hill.

7-3: Battery F-4th US and Battery K-5th US in rear of the centre of the Corps, Penna. Battery E and Battery A-Md (Six 3-Inch Rifles from the Artillery Reserve) on Powers Hill, all commanding the valley of Rock Creek. At daylight, the artillery (26 guns) opened on the position occupied by Major General Johnson's Confederate Division and fired for 15 minutes, then ceased to allow the infantry to advance. Began firing again at 5:30 AM and continued at intervals until 10:30 AM, when the Confederates were forced from their position among the entire line.

Casualties: 9 men wounded, 3 mortally.

Battery F Lt. Sylvanus T. Rugg
4th US Six - 12 Pounders
12th Corps 7-1: Approached Gettysburg on the Baltimore Pike to Two Taverns and took position to counteract any move-
Artilllery ments of the Confederates from towards Hanover. At noon ,marched to one and one half miles of Gettysburg.
Brigade 7-2: Took position so as to command a gap between the 1st and 12th Corps.

7-3: At 1 AM, posted opposite the center of the line of the 12th Corps and at 4:30 opened fire on the Confederates, who had taken possession of a portion of the 12th Corps line the preceeding night. Continued firing until after 10 AM when the Confederates were driven from the line. In the afternoon, the Battery was exposed to a severe shelling which passed over Cemetary Hill.

Casualties: Wounded 1 Man Total.

Battery K* Lt. David H. Kinzie
5th US Four - 12 Pounders
12th Corps 7-1: Marched to within a mile and a half of Gettysburg.
Artilllery 7-2: At daybreak, took position to command a gap between the 1st and 12th Corps. At 5 PM one section was
Brigade placed on the summit of Culp's Hill and assisted in silencing Confederate batteries on Benner's Hill. At 6 PM rejoined the Battery at the foot of Powers Hill.

7-3: At 1 AM, posted with Battery F-4th US Artillery on the south side of Baltimore Pike, opposite the centre of the line of the 12th Corps. At 4:30 AM, opened fire on the Confederates in possession of the line vacated by the 12th Corps the preceeding night. Firing continued at intervals until after 10 AM when the Confederates were driven out. In the same position exposed to shelling which came over Cemetary Hill in the afternoon.

Casualties: Wounded 5 Total.

*see index

10th Maine Provost Guard, 12th Corps Headquarters
Battalion Capt. John D. Beardsley

12th Corps Army Of The Potomac, 12th Corps Headquarters
Major General Henry W. Slocum, July 1, 2, 3, 4, 1863.

77th NY The Bemis Heights Battalion. Lt. Col. Winsor B. French
3-2-6 July 3, 1863

Md Lt Capt. James H. Rigby
Battery A Six - 3 Inch Rifles
1st Vol 7-2: Occupied this position. Engaged a battery of the enemy.
Brigade 7-3: In the morning, shelled the woods in front for nearly three hours, driving out the enemy.
Artillery (Note: Casualties not mentioned.)
Reserve

Ind PA Lt* Lt. Charles A. Atwill (Note: Knap's Battery)
Battery E Six - 10 Pounder Parrotts
12th Corps 7-2: At 3:30 AM, one gun was placed on Culp's Hill in the position marked by a monument and was joined by
Artillery   two others at 5 PM, when the three guns engaged the enemy's batteries on Benner's Hill. These guns were
Brigade   withdrawn when the infantry was ordered to the left and the battery went into position where it remained
        until the close of the battle.
Casualties: Three Wounded of 139 Present.

1st NY Lt. Charles E. Winegar
Battery M Four - 10 Pounder Parrotts
12th Corps 7-2&3: Held this position
Artillery (Note: Casualties not mentioned.)
Brigade

*see index

~ Gettysburg Battlefield Monuments, Locations & Inscriptions ~

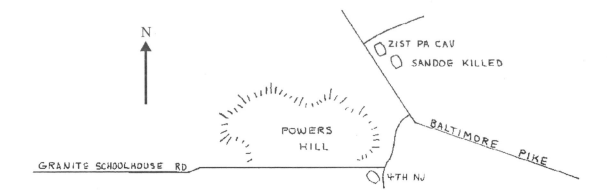

21ˢᵗ PA*   6-26: Near this spot fell Private George W. Sandoe, an advance scout of a company of volunteer cavalry, after-
Cavalry   wards Company B, 21st Pennsylvania Cavalry; the first Union soldier killed at Gettysburg.

Sandoe   Erected To The Memory Of The 21st Pennsylvania Cavalry (182nd Regiment) By The Regimental
Killed   Association and Friends. Dedicated October 4, 1884.
                6-26: Near this spot fell Private George W. Sandoe of Captain Robert Bell's Independent Cavalry Company of
                        Adams County. He was the first soldier killed on the battlefield of Gettysburg.

4ᵗʰ NJ   7-2&3: 4th NJ Vols
6ᵗʰ Corps   Train Guard
                July 2-3, 1863

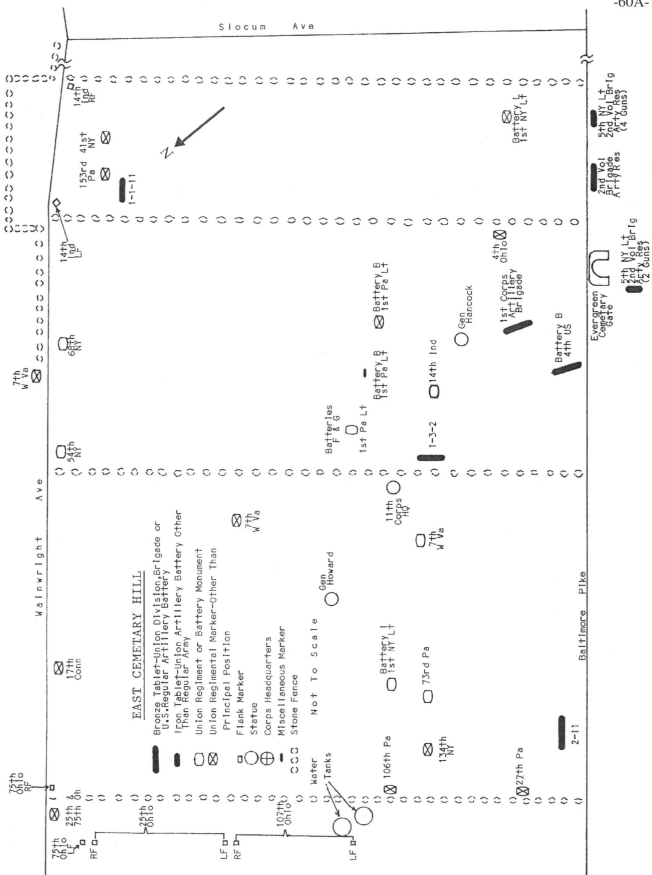

Slocum Ave

N

14th Ind RF

41st NY

153rd Pa

1-1-11

14th Ind LF

Battery 1st NY Lt

5th NY Lt 2nd Vol Brig Arty Res (4 Guns)

2nd Vol Brigade Arty Res

7th W Va

68th NY

4th Ohio

1st Corps Artillery Brigade

Battery B 1st Pa Lt

Gen Hancock

Battery B 4th US

5th NY Lt 2nd Vol Brig Arty Res (2 Guns)

Evergreen Cemetary Gate

54th NY

Batteries F & G 1st Pa Lt

Battery B 1st Pa Lt

14th Ind

1-3-2

11th Corps HQs

7th W Va

7th W Va

17th Conn

EAST CEMETARY HILL

Bronze Tablet–Union Division,Brigade or U.S.Regular Artillery Battery

Iron Tablet–Union Artillery Battery Other Than Regular Army

Union Regiment or Battery Monument

Union Regimental Marker–Other Than

Principal Position

Flank Marker

Statue

Corps Headquarters

Miscellaneous Marker

Stone Fence

Water Tanks

Not To Scale

Gen Howard

Battery I 1st NY Lt

73rd Pa

106th Pa

134th NY

27th Pa

2-11

75th Ohio RF

25th & 75th Oh

25th Ohio

107th Ohio

75th Ohio LF

RF

LF

RF

LF

Wainwright Ave

Baltimore Pike

~ Gettysburg Battlefield Monuments, Locations & Inscriptions ~

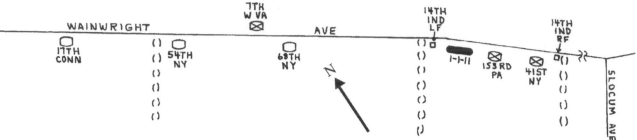

14th Indiana*   <u>7-2</u>:   Right Flank of 14th Indiana from 8 PM to close of battle. 4th Ohio on right.
1-3-2

41st NY   Lt. Col. Detleo von Einseidel. The Dekalb Regiment.
1-1-11   July 2nd and 3rd.
           Casualties: Killed 15, Wounded 58, Missing 2; Total 75.

153rd PA*   Major John F. Frueauff
1-1-11   Casualties: Killed 23, Wounded 142, Missing 46; Total 211 (NY@Gbg)

14th Indiana*   <u>7-2</u>:   Left Flank of the 14th Indiana from 8 PM to close of battle. 7th Virginia on the left.
1-3-2
1-1-11   Col. Leopold von Gilsa
           41st, 54th (54th NY was advanced to west bank of Rock Creek; see page 25A), 68th NY, 153rd Pa Infantry
           (153rd NY now is on page 25A on Barbor Knoll).
        <u>7-1</u>:   The Brigade, except 41st NY, having been temporarily left at Gettysburg, arrived at noon and took position one mile north of town on left of Harrisburg Road and right of Rock Creek, 2nd Brigade on right, 3rd Division on left. Advanced over a knoll into woods in front and encountered Brig. Gen. Gordon's Brigade and was attacked by Brig. Gen. Doles' Brigade, Maj. Gen. Rodes' Division and subjected to a severe enfilading artillery fire from Lt. Col. Jones' Battalion on a knoll east of Rock Creek, and forced back to the Alms House, where being outflanked, this Brigade fell back with the Corps to Cemetary Hill and took position behind a stone wall on the right of the Corps. The 41st NY rejoined the Brigade during the night.
        <u>7-2</u>:   Remained in position all day engaged as skirmishers. An attack in the evening on Cemetary Hill on the left was repulsed with the aid of 1st Brigade, 3rd Division, 2nd Corps.
        <u>7-3</u>:   Under artillery fire for an hour and a half, but not engaged.
        Casualties: Killed 54, Wounded 310, Missing 163; Total 527

68th NY   Col. Gotthilf Bourry
1-1-11   <u>7-1</u>:   This Regiment participated in the first day of the battle.
        <u>7-2&3</u>:   The Regiment held this position
        Casualties: Killed 8, Wounded 63, Missing 67; Total 138

7th West
Virginia*   <u>7-3</u>:   (Note: This marker on north side of Wainwright Ave. has no inscription.)
1-3-2

54th NY   Major Stephen Kovacs
1-1-11   <u>7-1</u>:   Skirmishing on extreme right near Rock Creek.
        <u>7-2</u>:   At sunset, severe fighting in this position.
        <u>7-3</u>:   Held same position.
        Casualties: Killed 7, Wounded 47, Missing 48; Total 102

17th Conn   Lt. Col. Douglas Fowler
2-1-11   <u>7-1</u>:   After a fierce engagement with Early's Division at Barlow Knoll, as marked by a monument there, this Regiment formed in line of battle on East Cemetery Hill.
        <u>7-2</u>:   In the evening, took position here and was engaged in repulsing the desperate assault of Hays' and Hoke's Brigades.
        Casualties: Killed 20, Wounded 81, Missing 96; Total 197 (NY@Gbg)

*see index

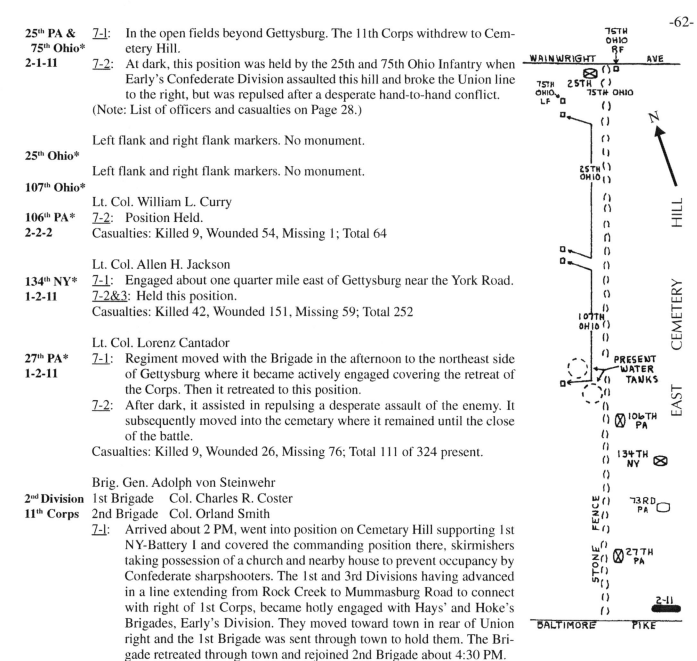

25ᵗʰ PA &
75ᵗʰ Ohio*
2-1-11

7-1: In the open fields beyond Gettysburg. The 11th Corps withdrew to Cemetery Hill.

7-2: At dark, this position was held by the 25th and 75th Ohio Infantry when Early's Confederate Division assaulted this hill and broke the Union line to the right, but was repulsed after a desperate hand-to-hand conflict.
(Note: List of officers and casualties on Page 28.)

Left flank and right flank markers. No monument.

25ᵗʰ Ohio*

Left flank and right flank markers. No monument.

107ᵗʰ Ohio*

Lt. Col. William L. Curry

106ᵗʰ PA*
2-2-2

7-2: Position Held.
Casualties: Killed 9, Wounded 54, Missing 1; Total 64

Lt. Col. Allen H. Jackson

134ᵗʰ NY*
1-2-11

7-1: Engaged about one quarter mile east of Gettysburg near the York Road.
7-2&3: Held this position.
Casualties: Killed 42, Wounded 151, Missing 59; Total 252

Lt. Col. Lorenz Cantador

27ᵗʰ PA*
1-2-11

7-1: Regiment moved with the Brigade in the afternoon to the northeast side of Gettysburg where it became actively engaged covering the retreat of the Corps. Then it retreated to this position.

7-2: After dark, it assisted in repulsing a desperate assault of the enemy. It subsequently moved into the cemetary where it remained until the close of the battle.
Casualties: Killed 9, Wounded 26, Missing 76; Total 111 of 324 present.

Brig. Gen. Adolph von Steinwehr

2ⁿᵈ Division
11ᵗʰ Corps

1st Brigade   Col. Charles R. Coster
2nd Brigade   Col. Orland Smith

7-1: Arrived about 2 PM, went into position on Cemetary Hill supporting 1st NY-Battery 1 and covered the commanding position there, skirmishers taking possession of a church and nearby house to prevent occupancy by Confederate sharpshooters. The 1st and 3rd Divisions having advanced in a line extending from Rock Creek to Mummasburg Road to connect with right of 1st Corps, became hotly engaged with Hays' and Hoke's Brigades, Early's Division. They moved toward town in rear of Union right and the 1st Brigade was sent through town to hold them. The Brigade retreated through town and rejoined 2nd Brigade about 4:30 PM.

7-3: Not engaged but subject to fire of sharpshooters and artillery.
Casualties: Killed 107, Wounded 507, Missing 332; Total 946.

Capt. Daniel F. Kelley

73ʳᵈ PA
1-2-11

7-1: Arrived on Cemetery Hill at 2 PM and at a later hour moved into the town near the square to cover the retreat of the Corps.

7-2: In the morning took position in the cemetery. At dusk, moved hastily to this position and in a severe contest assisted in repulsing a desperate assault on these batteries.

7-3: Returned to its former position in the cemetery and assisted in repulsing the enemy's final assault.
Casualties: Killed 7, Wounded 27; Total 34 (NY@Gbg)

*see index

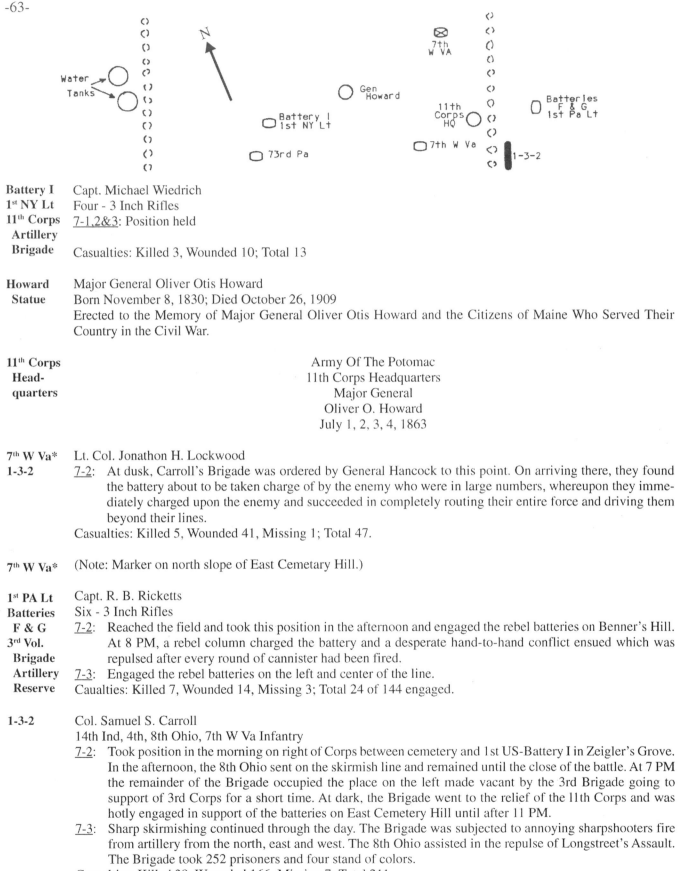

Battery I
1st NY Lt   Capt. Michael Wiedrich
11th Corps   Four - 3 Inch Rifles
Artillery   7-1,2&3: Position held
Brigade

Casualties: Killed 3, Wounded 10; Total 13

Howard   Major General Oliver Otis Howard
Statue   Born November 8, 1830; Died October 26, 1909
                  Erected to the Memory of Major General Oliver Otis Howard and the Citizens of Maine Who Served Their
                  Country in the Civil War.

11th Corps   Army Of The Potomac
Head-   11th Corps Headquarters
quarters   Major General
                                               Oliver O. Howard
                                              July 1, 2, 3, 4, 1863

7th W Va*   Lt. Col. Jonathon H. Lockwood
1-3-2   7-2: At dusk, Carroll's Brigade was ordered by General Hancock to this point. On arriving there, they found
                        the battery about to be taken charge of by the enemy who were in large numbers, whereupon they imme-
                        diately charged upon the enemy and succeeded in completely routing their entire force and driving them
                        beyond their lines.
                  Casualties: Killed 5, Wounded 41, Missing 1; Total 47.

7th W Va*   (Note: Marker on north slope of East Cemetary Hill.)

1st PA Lt   Capt. R. B. Ricketts
Batteries   Six - 3 Inch Rifles
F & G   7-2: Reached the field and took this position in the afternoon and engaged the rebel batteries on Benner's Hill.
3rd Vol.   At 8 PM, a rebel column charged the battery and a desperate hand-to-hand conflict ensued which was
Brigade   repulsed after every round of cannister had been fired.
Artillery   7-3: Engaged the rebel batteries on the left and center of the line.
Reserve   Caualties: Killed 7, Wounded 14, Missing 3; Total 24 of 144 engaged.

1-3-2   Col. Samuel S. Carroll
                  14th Ind, 4th, 8th Ohio, 7th W Va Infantry
                  7-2: Took position in the morning on right of Corps between cemetery and 1st US-Battery I in Zeigler's Grove.
                        In the afternoon, the 8th Ohio sent on the skirmish line and remained until the close of the battle. At 7 PM
                        the remainder of the Brigade occupied the place on the left made vacant by the 3rd Brigade going to
                        support of 3rd Corps for a short time. At dark, the Brigade went to the relief of the 11th Corps and was
                        hotly engaged in support of the batteries on East Cemetery Hill until after 11 PM.
                  7-3: Sharp skirmishing continued through the day. The Brigade was subjected to annoying sharpshooters fire
                        from artillery from the north, east and west. The 8th Ohio assisted in the repulse of Longstreet's Assault.
                        The Brigade took 252 prisoners and four stand of colors.
                  Casualties: Killed 38, Wounded 166, Missing 7; Total 211

*see index

~ Gettysburg Battlefield Monuments, Locations & Inscriptions ~

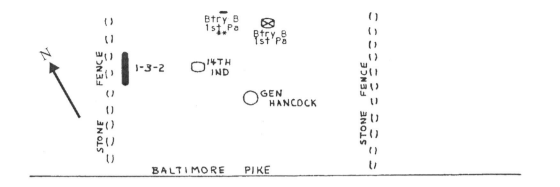

14th Indiana* Col. John Coons

1-3-2   7-2: In the evening a determined effort was made by Hays' and Hoke's Brigades of Early's Division to carry East Cemetery Hill by storm. The Union troops supporting the batteries occupying this ground were overwhelmed and forced to retire. Weidrich's Battery was captured and two of Rickett's guns were spiked. Carroll's Brigade, then in position southwest of the cemetery, was moved to the rescue. Advancing in double quick time from the cemetery and across the Baltimore Pike, the men went in with a cheer. The 14th Ind. met the enemy among the guns on this ground where a hand-to-hand struggle ensued, resulting in driving the enemy from the hill. Then took a position along the stone fence at the bottom of the hill southeast from this point facing the east, the right and left flanks being designated by stone markers there placed, which position was held until the end of the battle.
Casualties: Killed 6, Wounded 25, Total 31 (NY@Gbg)

1st PA Lt   Capt. James H. Cooper
Battery B**   Four - 3 Inch Rifles
1st Corps   7-1: Arrived at noon. Took position and was engaged between Hagerstown Road and Chambersburg Pike near
Artillery   Willoughby Run. Changed position to the right and swept Oak Hill with its fire. Withdrew to the Lutheran
Brigade   Seminary where it fought until after 4 PM. Retired to this position.
(possibly   7-2: Remained in this position until close of heavy artillery contest with enemy's batteries on Benner's Hill
Cooper's   during afternoon engagement, when relieved by Rickett's Battery.
Battery)   7-3: Was engaged on left center during the final attack and repulse of the enemy.
Casualties: Killed 3, Wounded 9; Total 12; 1050 rounds expended

Hancock   Major General Winfield Scott Hancock, United States Army, Born Feb. 14, 1824, Died Feb. 9, 1886.
Statue   Cadet USMA 7/1/1840, Brevet 2nd Lt. 6th US Infantry, 2nd Lt. 6/18/46, Regimental Quartermaster 7/30/48 to 10/1 49, Regimental Adjutant 10/1/49 to 11/55, 1st Lt. 1/27/53 to 6/5/60, Vacated Commission 6/5/50, Capt. and Assistant Quartermaster USA 11/7/55, Maj. and Quartermaster 11/30/63, Vacated Commission 8/12/64, Brig. Gen. USA 8/12/64 for gallant and distinguished services in the battles of the Wilderness, Spotsylvania and Cold Harbor and in all the operations of the Army in Virginia under Lt. Gen. Grant. Maj. Gen. 7/26/66, Brig. Gen. USV 9/23/61, Maj. Gen. 11/29/ 62, Vacated Commission 7/26/66. Breveted 1st Lt. USA 8/20/47 for gallant and meritorious conduct in the Battles of Conreras and Cherubusco, Mexico, Maj. Gen. 3/13/65 for gallant and meritorious services in the Battle of Spotsylvania, Virginia.
The Senate and House of Representatives of the United States of America in Congress assembled resolve (joint resolution approved 4/21/66), that in addition to the thanks heretofore voted by joint resolution approved 1/28/ 64 to *** and the officers and soldiers of the Army of the Potomac for the skill and heroic valor which at Gettysburg repulsed, defeated and drove back, broken and dispirited, the veteran army of the rebellion, the gratitude of the American people, and the thanks of their representatives in Congress, are likewise due and are hereby tendered to Major General Winfield Scott Hancock for his gallant, meritorious and conspicuous share in that great and decisive victory.

    **   Battery B-1st Pa Light Artillery (Cooper's Battery) erected a granite marker on East
         Cemetery Hill, date not sure but possibly 1879. The inscription is illegible. The larger
         monument nearby to the southeast was erected by the same Battery in 1889.
    *** this is not clear on the monument.
*see index

~ Gettysburg Battlefield Monuments, Locations & Inscriptions ~

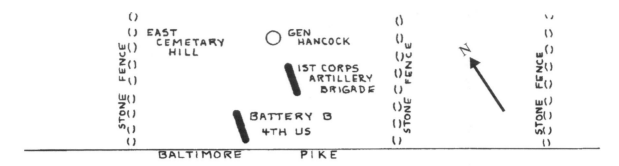

Battery B* Lt. James Stewart
4th US Six - 12 Pounders
1st Corps <u>7-2&3</u>: Remained in this position.
Artillery Casualties: Killed 2, Wounded 31, Missing 3; Total 36
Brigade

1st Corps	Col. Charles S. Wainwright		
Artillery	Maine 2nd Battery B	Six - 3 Inch Rifles	Capt. James A. Hall
Brigade	Maine 5th Battery E	Six - 12 Pounders	Capt. Greenleaf T. Stevens, Lt. Edward N. Whittier
	1st NY Battery L	Four - 3 Inch Rifles	Capt. Gilbert H. Reynolds
	1st Pa Battery B	Four - 3 Inch Rifles	Capt. James H. Cooper
	4th US Battery B	Four - 12 Pounders	Lt. James Stewart

<u>7-1</u>: Arrived between 10 and 11 AM. Battery B-2nd Maine in advance relieved Battery A-2nd US on Chambersburg Pike and became hotly engaged with artillery in front and infantry on right, but was compelled to retire from the ridge. About 2 PM, the Confederates, having opened with artillery from Oak Hill on right, the batteries in advance were compelled to withdraw and take position on ridge in rear and on both sides of Reynolds' Woods, but again being flanked and enfiladed by Confederate infantry and artillery, the Union forces were withdrawn to Seminary Ridge and at 4 PM retired through the town to Cemetery Hill. On reaching Cemetery Hill, the artillery was immediately put in position for defense.

<u>7-2</u>: Not engaged until 4 PM when the Confederates opened on the position with four - 20 Pounders and six - 10 Pounder Parrotts, but were compelled to withdraw. Battery B-1st Pa relieved by Batteries F & G 1st Pa. At dusk the position on East Cemetery Hill was attacked by Brig. Gen. Hays' and Brig. Gen. Hoke's Brigades. They fought through Battery I-1st NY into Batteries F & G-1st Pa, spiking one gun. The cannoniers stood to their guns and with handspikes, rammers and stones and the aid of the infantry that was hurried to their defense, the attack was repulsed between 8 and 9 PM.

<u>7-3</u>: No serious engagement.
Casualties: Killed 9, Wounded 86, Missing 11; Total 106

*see index

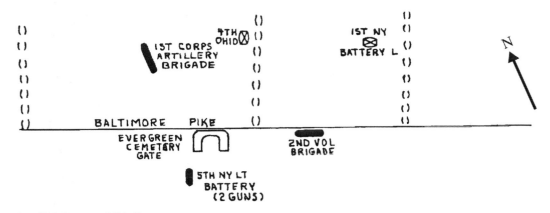

4th Ohio*   Lt. Col. Leonard W. Carpenter

1-3-2   <u>7-2</u>: In the evening, Carroll's Brigade was sent from its position with the 2nd Corps to reinforce this portion of the line, and this monument marks the position where, as part of that Brigade, the 4th Ohio Infantry at that time participated in repelling an attack by the enemy.

Casualties: Killed 7, Wounded 17; Missing 5; Total 29

1st NY Lt   Battery E serving with Battery L*

Battery L*   Lt. George Breck

1st Corps   Four - 3 Inch Rifles

    Artillery   <u>7-2&3</u>: These works were built and held by Battery L against assaults of infantry and artillery.

    Brigade   "This monument is committed to the care of a dear country we were proud to serve".

Casualties: Killed 1, Wounded 15, Missing 1; Total 17

5th NY Lt*   Capt. Elijah D. Taft

2nd Vol   Six - 20 Pounder Parrotts

    Brigade   <u>7-2</u>: Arrived and halted in park about 10 AM. Moved to the Evergreen Cemetery at 3:30 PM and engaged from

    Artillery   4 PM until dark. Two guns posted in the Cemetery firing westerly, four guns south of, and facing Balti-

    Reserve   more Pike and firing on a Confederate battery on Benner's Hill.

    (2 guns)   <u>7-3</u>: Engaged at intervals in same position until 4 PM; when relieved by three of the guns on Baltimore Pike.

Casualties: (Note: See other position on next page.)

2nd Vol   Capt. Elijah D. Taft

    Brigade   1st Conn Heavy-Battery B   Capt. Alvord P. Brooker   Not engaged

    Artillery   1st Conn Heavy-Battery M   Capt. F. A. Scott   Not engaged

    Reserve   2nd Conn Battery   Capt. John W. Sterling

    <u>7-2</u>: Reinforced 3rd Corps line and late in the day retired and formed line under Lt. Col. F McGilvery on left of 2nd Corps.

        5th NY Battery   Capt. Elijah D. Taft

    <u>7-2&3</u>: Engaged on Cemetery Hill.

Casualties: Killed 1, Wounded 5, Missing 2; Total 8

*see index

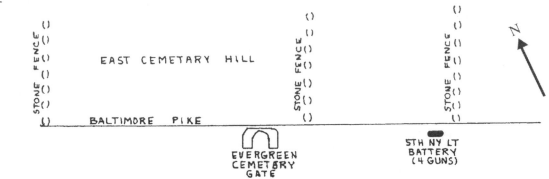

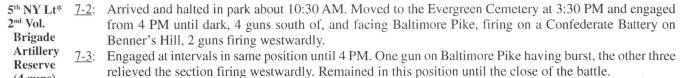

5th NY Lt*
2nd Vol.
Brigade
Artillery
Reserve
(4 guns)

7-2: Arrived and halted in park about 10:30 AM. Moved to the Evergreen Cemetery at 3:30 PM and engaged from 4 PM until dark, 4 guns south of, and facing Baltimore Pike, firing on a Confederate Battery on Benner's Hill, 2 guns firing westwardly.

7-3: Engaged at intervals in same position until 4 PM. One gun on Baltimore Pike having burst, the other three relieved the section firing westwardly. Remained in this position until the close of the battle.

Casualties: Killed 1, Wounded 2; Total 3; 1114 rounds fired

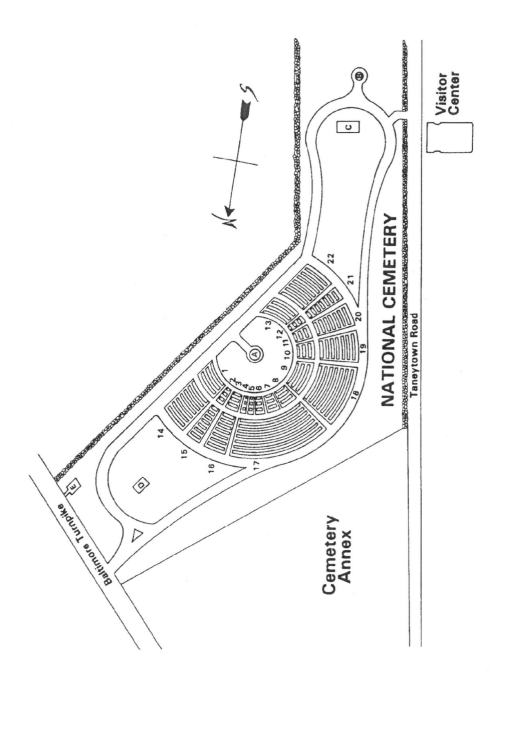

GRAVES

1. Unknown
2. Illinois
3. West Virginia
4. Delaware
5. Rhode Island
6. New Hampshire
7. Vermont
8. New Jersey
9. Wisconsin
10. Connecticut
11. Minnesota
12. Maryland
13. U.S. Regulars
14. Unknown
15. Maine
16. Michigan
17. New York
18. Pennsylvania
19. Massachusetts
20. Ohio
21. Indiana
22. Unknown

MONUMENTS

A. Soldiers' National Monument
  —Site of Gettysburg Address
B. Monument to Lincoln's Gettysburg Address
C. Speaker's Rostrum
D. New York State Monument
E. Rest Rooms

~ Gettysburg Battlefield Monuments, Locations & Inscriptions ~

GETTYSBURG NATIONAL MILITARY CEMETARY

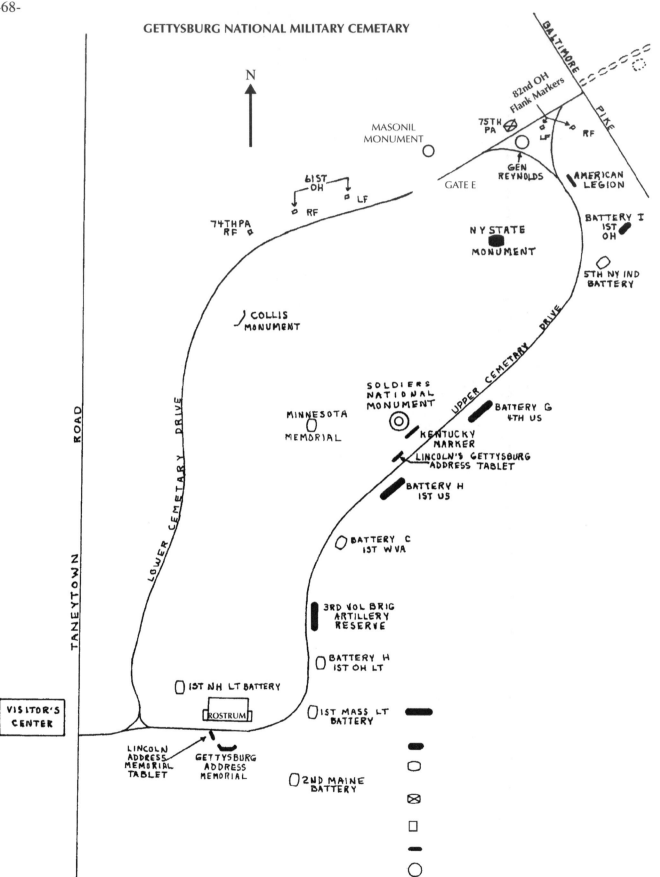

~ Gettysburg Battlefield Monuments, Locations & Inscriptions ~

THE SYMBOLS LISTED BELOW ARE USED TO IDENTIFY THE MONUMENTS, MARKERS, TABLETS, STATUES, ETC. WHICH ARE DRAWN ON THE MAPS IN THESE PAGES

SYMBOL	TYPE	REPRESENTING	DESCRIPTION
	Bronze Tablet	Army of The Potomac, Union Corps or Division or Brigade, Regular Army Regiment, Regular Army Artillery Battery, Volunteer Artillery Brigade.	Brigade Tablet Mounted on Square Marble base. All other Tablets are on large vertical Granite Blocks.
	Bronze Tablet	Army of Northern Virginia, Confederate Corps or Division or Brigade of Artillery Battalion	Brigade Tablet and Artillery Battalion Tablet Mounted on Round Marble base. All other Tablets are Mounted on large vertical Granite blocks.
	Iron Tablet	Union Army Battery (other than Regular Army)	Mounted on Black Iron Shaft.
	Iron Tablet	Confederate Artillery Battery	Mounted on Black Iron Shaft.
	Iron Tablet	Confederate Brigade Advanced Position	Mounted on Black Iron Shaft.
	Regimental or Battery Monument	Principal Position of Volunteer Regiment or Volunteer Artillery Battery	Usually Granite or Marble in a Great Variety of Shapes and Sizes.
	Regimental Marker or Battery	Other than Principal Position of Regiment tablet or may be another monument.	Usually a Square Granite Marker or
	Flank Marker or Company Marker	Left and/or Right Flank of Regiment or Battery or Position of a Coppany.	Usually a Small Square or Rectangular Granite Marker.
	Army Or Corps Headquarters	Site of Headquarters of Army Commander or Corps Commander or Chief of Artillery	Cannon Barrel Mounted Vertically on Stone, Granite or Marble Base.
	State Monument	Monument Erected by Union or Confederate State.	
	Statue	Standing or Equestrian	Bronze Sculpture
	Building	House, Barn or other Structure	Identified by Owner's Name.
	Miscellaneous Marker	Marker or Inscription of a type not listed above	Granite or Metal Marker.
	*Asterisk	Used whenever a Division or Brigade or Regiment or Battery has more than one Monument or Marker.	Check the Index for other Monument or Marker.

~ Gettysburg Battlefield Monuments, Locations & Inscriptions ~

Gettysburg National Military Park, Gettysburg, Pa.
by Frederick Tilberg
National Park Service Historical Handbook Series No. 9
Washington, D.C. 1954 (Revised 1962)

July	1863	Pennsylvania's Governor Curtain visits the battlefield; appoints Attorney David Wills his special agent.
Aug	1863	Wills purchased acreage on Cemetery Hill. Engaged William Saunders (Landscape Gardener) to lay out ground in "State Lots". Each of the Union States made contributions for landscaping. Transfer of Union dead to Cemetery begins.
Nov	1863	President Lincoln's Gettysburg Address.
Mar	1864	Commonwealth of Pennsylvania incorporates the Cemetery.
Feb	1864	Interment of last Union dead of the battle.
	1864	Appropriations from the States enclosed the Cemetery with a stone wall, iron fence, gateways, headstones for graves, and a Keeper's Lodge.

3500 Union dead reentered in the new Cemetery.

3706 Total of Civil War Veterans in the Cemetery.

1664 of 3500 are unknown (685 in State Lots, 979 in Unknown Lots). Board of Commissioners responsible for care of Cemetery was composed of representatives from all 18 Union States.

	1868	Pennsylvania Legislature authorizes Board of Commissioners to recommend transfer of the Cemetery to the Federal Government.
May	1872	Secretary of War accepted Title to Cemetery from Commonwealth of Pennsylvania.
July	1869	Soldier's National Monument dedicated.
Feb	1895	Congress passes Act which establishes Gettysburg National Military Park. Gettysburg battlefield Memorial Association transfers battlefield to the Federal Government.
Jan	1912	Lincoln Address Memorial erected by the Park Commission near the west gate of the Cemetery
	1933	Gettysburg National Military Park transferred from the War Department to the Department of the Interior to be administered by the National Park Service.

The Confederate dead who had been buried on the battlefield during and after the battle, were transferred to Southern Cemeteries in 1870-1873 by the Confederate Ladies Memorial Associations of Richmond, Raleigh, Charleston and Savannah. Their work was directed by Dr. Rufus B. Weaver, Professor of Applied Anatomy at Hahnemann Medical College, Philadelphia, Pa. The following data is from Dr. Weaver's report.

3320 Confederate dead shipped from Gettysburg to the following places:
2935 to Richmond, Virginia
137 to Raleigh, North Carolina
74 to Charleston, South Carolina
101 to Savannah, Georgia
73 to individual burial places

Source of Confederate dead information: *Gettysburg Times Visitor's* Supplement 1962, Page 60

*   Data from "Gettysburg National Military Park, Gettysburg, PA." by Frederick Tilberg-National Park Service Historical Handbook Series, No. 9 Washington, D.C. 1954 (Revised 1962) except references to Dr. Weaver.
** Gettysburg Times, Visitor's Supplement; 1962, Page 60

(Note: The above information is not listed on any monument or marker in the Gettysburg National Military Park. It is included here, not because it was a part of the Battle of Gettysburg, but rather because it was a direct result of that battle and therefore is closely related to events described on the Battlefield monuments.)

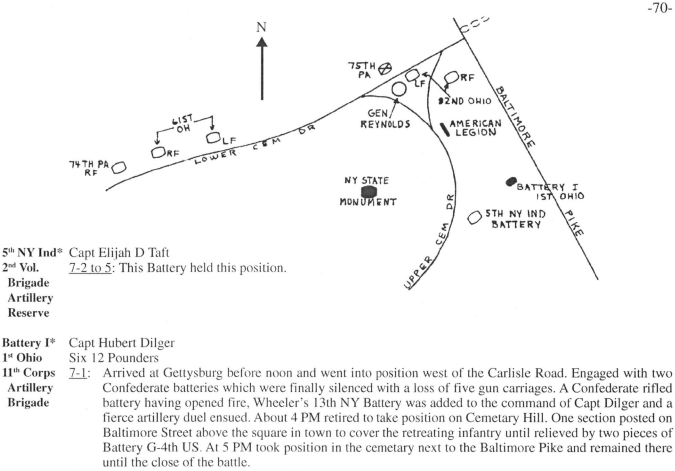

5th NY Ind*   Capt Elijah D Taft
2nd Vol.   <u>7-2 to 5</u>: This Battery held this position.
  Brigade
  Artillery
  Reserve

Battery I*   Capt Hubert Dilger
1st Ohio   Six 12 Pounders
11th Corps   <u>7-1</u>:   Arrived at Gettysburg before noon and went into position west of the Carlisle Road. Engaged with two
  Artillery   Confederate batteries which were finally silenced with a loss of five gun carriages. A Confederate rifled
  Brigade   battery having opened fire, Wheeler's 13th NY Battery was added to the command of Capt Dilger and a
                  fierce artillery duel ensued. About 4 PM retired to take position on Cemetary Hill. One section posted on
                  Baltimore Street above the square in town to cover the retreating infantry until relieved by two pieces of
                  Battery G-4th US. At 5 PM took position in the cemetary next to the Baltimore Pike and remained there
                  until the close of the battle.
           Casualties: Wounded 13 Total. One gun disabled.

American   The American Legion Prays For Peace
Legion   —but Peace With Honor
Tablet   We Pray That Mankind Will Accept As A Basis
                              for This Peace The Trinity Of
                     Religious, Political and Social Freedom Won In
                              The American Revolution
                              Preserved In The Civil War
                    Protected In The Spanish American War And
               Defended In The Great Wars And In The Korean Conflict

                              Dedicated By The-American Legion
                              This Eleventh Day Of November, 1955

82nd Ohio*   Left Flank and Right Flank Markers (No Monument Here)
2-3-11

75th PA*   In Memory Of Our Comrades.
2-3-11

61st Ohio*   Left Flank and Right Flank Markers (No Monument Here)
1-3-11

74th PA*   Right Flank Marker (No Monument Here)
1-3-11

Reynolds   Major General John F. Reynolds, USA
  Statue   Killed at Gettysburg July 1 MDCCCLX111.
                  TO HIS MEMORY BY THE 1ST ARMY CORPS.
                  Born at Lancaster, Pa, Sept XX1, MDCCCXX.

*see index

New York State Monument To The Officers And Soldiers Of The State Of New York Who Fell In The Battle Of Gettysburg July 1, 2, 3, 1863. Many Of Whom Are Here Buried.
This Monument Is Erected By A Grateful Commonwealth.

Official Returns Of Casualties In The New York Commands:
Killed   82 Officers,   912 Enlisted Men
Wounded   306 Officers,   3763 Enlisted Men
Captured Or Missing 69 Officers,   1685 Enlisted Men

GROUPS OF OFFICERS PORTRAYED ON BRONZE RELIEFS

FRONT (SOUTH)
Maj. Gen. D. E. Sickles of NY Wounded
Brig. Gen. J. B. Carr of NY
Brig. Gen. J. H. H. Ward of NY
Bvt. Maj. Gen. S. K. Zook of NY Killed
Brig. Gen. C. K. Graham of NY Wounded
Brig. Gen. R. B Ayres of NY
Brig. Gen. S. H. Weed of NY Killed
Brig. Gen. H. E. Tremain of NY

OBVERSE (NORTH)
Maj. Gen. H. W. Slocum of NY
Maj. Gen. A. Pleasanton of DC
Brig. Gen. J. S. Wadsworth of NY
Brig. Gen. G. S. Greene of NY
Brig. Gen. H. J. Hunt of Ohio
Brig. Gen. J. J. Bartlett of NY
Brig. Gen. D. A. Russell of NY
Brig. Gen. A. Shaler of NY
Col. H. A. Barnum of NY

RIGHT (EAST)
Maj. Gen. J. F. Reynolds of PA Killed
Maj. Gen. A. Doubleday of NY Wounded
Brig. Gen. A. von Steinwehr of NY
Brig. Gen. J. C. Robinson of NY
Brig. Gen. F. C. Barlow of NY Wounded
Col. F. C. Devin of NY

LEFT (WEST)
Maj. Gen. W. S. Hancock of PA Wounded
Maj. Gen. D. Butterfield NY Wounded
Maj. Gen. G. K. Warren of NY Wounded
Brig. Gen. J. J. Kilpatrick of NY
Gen. A. S. Webb of NY Wounded

Collis Memorial Bvt. Maj. Gen. H. T. Collis, USV
Col. 114th Regiment Pennsylvania Volunteer Infantry-Collis' Zouaves
Born February 4, 1838 Died May 11, 1902.
Erected By The Survivors Of His Regiment And His Friends.

Battery G* 4th US 11th Corps Artillery Brigade Lt. Eugene Bancroft
Six 12 Pounders
7-1: Arrived Gettysburg about 11 AM. Advanced and took positions two sections on Barlow's Knoll, the left section detached near The Alms House. Engaged Confederate infantry and artillery on right and left. Lt. Wilkeson fell early mortally wounded and the command evolved on Lt. Bancroft. The sections were compelled to change positions several times. Retired about 4 PM, one section relieving a section of Battery I-1st Ohio on Baltimore Street in covering the retreat. About 5 PM took position on Cemetary Hill.
7-2: Moved to rear of cemetery facing Baltimore Pike. In action at the cemetary from 4:30 until 7:30 PM.
7-3: About 2 PM, two sections were engaged in the cemetary until the repulse of the Confederates.
Casualties: Killed 2, Wounded 11; Total 17. 31 Horses Killed. Ammunition Expended 1400 rounds.

*see index

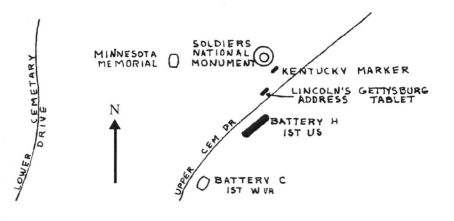

Minnesota   1 st Minnesota Volunteers.
Monument* "All Time Is The Millenium Of Their Glory"
The surviving members of the 1st Minnesota Regiment Infantry, to the memory of their late associates who "died on the field of honor" at Gettysburg, July 1863.

"These dead shall not have died in vain."
"It is rather for us to be here dedicated to the great task remaining before us - that from these honored dead we take increased devotion to that cause to which they gave the last full measure devotion - that we here highly resolve that these dead shall not have died in vain, that this nation, under God, shall have a new birth of freedom and that government of the people, by the people, for the people, shall not perish from the earth."

Lincoln
Nov. 19, 1863

Abraham Lincoln delivered his Gettysburg Address on this spot November 19, 1863, when the Soldier's National Cemetary was dedicated. This monument, a memorial to the soldiers who fell here, was the first one erected on the battlefield. The corner statues represent War, History, Peace and Plenty, with the Genius of Liberty surmounting the column.

Dedicated July 1, 1869
Architect: J. G. Batterson
Sculptor: Randolph Rogers

Kentucky honors her son, Abraham Lincoln who delivered his immortal address at the site now marked by the Soldier's Monument.
(Note: The Gettysburg Address, cast in bronze, is on this marker)

Battery H   Lt. Chandler P. Eaken
1ˢᵗ US   Six 12 Pounders
1ˢᵗ Regular   7-2:   In position facing Emmitsburg Road on Cemetary Hill. Lt. Eaken was severely wounded after his guns
   Brigade   went into battery and the command evolved on Lt. Phillip D. Mason.
   Artillery   Casualties: Killed 1, Wounded 8, Missing 1; Total 10.
   Reserve

Battery C   Capt. Wallace Hill
1ˢᵗ W Va.   Four 10 Pounder Parrotts
3ʳᵈ Vol.   Commemorating Valor 1st West Virginia Artillery
   Brigade   Casualties: Killed 2, Wounded 2; Total 4.
   Artillery
   Reserve

*see index

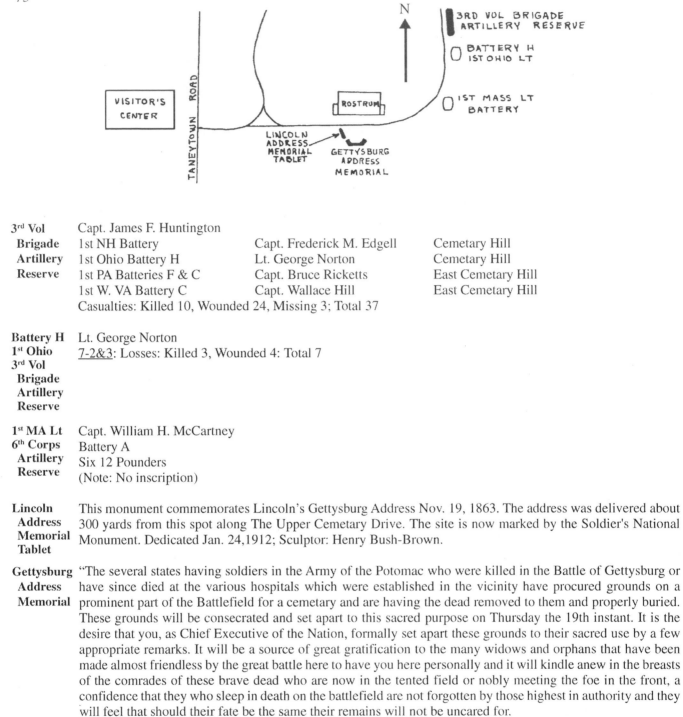

3rd Vol Brigade Artillery Reserve	Capt. James F. Huntington		
	1st NH Battery	Capt. Frederick M. Edgell	Cemetary Hill
	1st Ohio Battery H	Lt. George Norton	Cemetary Hill
	1st PA Batteries F & C	Capt. Bruce Ricketts	East Cemetary Hill
	1st W. VA Battery C	Capt. Wallace Hill	East Cemetary Hill

Casualties: Killed 10, Wounded 24, Missing 3; Total 37

Battery H 1st Ohio 3rd Vol Brigade Artillery Reserve
Lt. George Norton
7-2&3: Losses: Killed 3, Wounded 4: Total 7

1st MA Lt 6th Corps Artillery Reserve
Capt. William H. McCartney
Battery A
Six 12 Pounders
(Note: No inscription)

Lincoln Address Memorial Tablet
This monument commemorates Lincoln's Gettysburg Address Nov. 19, 1863. The address was delivered about 300 yards from this spot along The Upper Cemetary Drive. The site is now marked by the Soldier's National Monument. Dedicated Jan. 24,1912; Sculptor: Henry Bush-Brown.

Gettysburg Address Memorial
"The several states having soldiers in the Army of the Potomac who were killed in the Battle of Gettysburg or have since died at the various hospitals which were established in the vicinity have procured grounds on a prominent part of the Battlefield for a cemetery and are having the dead removed to them and properly buried. These grounds will be consecrated and set apart to this sacred purpose on Thursday the 19th instant. It is the desire that you, as Chief Executive of the Nation, formally set apart these grounds to their sacred use by a few appropriate remarks. It will be a source of great gratification to the many widows and orphans that have been made almost friendless by the great battle here to have you here personally and it will kindle anew in the breasts of the comrades of these brave dead who are now in the tented field or nobly meeting the foe in the front, a confidence that they who sleep in death on the battlefield are not forgotten by those highest in authority and they will feel that should their fate be the same their remains will not be uncared for.

From a letter to Abraham Lincoln, President of the United States, who on November 19, 1863 near this place delivered the address at the dedication of the cemetery.
(Note: Bronze Tablet on right of memorial has Gettysburg Address.)

Erected in compliance with Act of 53rd Congress 3rd Session, Introduced by Major General Daniel E Sickles, Representative from 10th District of New York to establish a Military Park at Gettysburg, Pennsylvania. Approved by the President February 11, 1895.

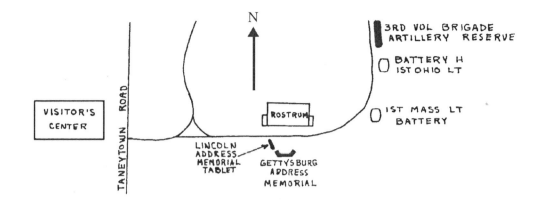

2nd Maine Battery* 1st Corps Artillery Brigade

Capt. James A. Hall
(Note: No Inscription)

1st NH Lt. 3rd Vol Brigade Artillery Reserve

Capt. Frederick M. Edgell
Six 3 Inch Rifles.
(Note: No Inscription)

*see index

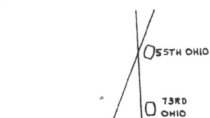

(Note: Position of Col,. Orland Smith's 2nd Brigl. 2nd Div., 11th Corps east of Cemetary North of Visitor Center.)

55th Ohio Col. Charles B. Gambee
2-2-11 <u>7-1</u>: Arrived 2:20 PM. In this position, which it held through the battle with severe loss. Its skirmishers drove back those of the enemy and seized a barn, between the lines, where 12 of its men were surrounded and captured by the enemy's main line.
Casualties: Killed 6, Wounded 31, Missing 12; Total 49

73rd Ohio Lt. Col. Richard Long
2-2-11 <u>7-1,2&3</u>:
Casualties: Killed 21, Mortally Wounded 19, Wounded 104, Missing 1; Total 145 of 338.

2-2-11 Col. Orland Smith
33rd Mass, 136th NY, 55th and 73rd Ohio Infantry
<u>7-1</u>: Arrived at 2 PM and went into position on Cemetary Hill in line behind stone walls along Emmitsburg and Taneytown Roads facing northwest and supporting Battery I-1st NY, 33rd Mass was detatched during the battle and placed under command of Brig. Gen. A. Ames. The 136th NY was on the exteme left onf the Corps connecting on its right with the 55th and 73rd Ohio.
<u>7-2</u>: Shapshooting kept up all day by Union troops from stone walls and by the Confederates in houses in the town with considerable loss.
<u>7-3</u>: Sharp skirmishing continued with artillery firing from Confederate batteries east of town.
Casualties: Killed 51, Wounded 278, Missing 19; Total 348

136th NY Col. James Wood, Jr.
2-2-11 Casualties: Killed 17, Wounded 89, Missing 3; Total 109

33rd Mass*

*see index

~ Gettysburg Battlefield Monuments, Locations & Inscriptions ~

THE SYMBOLS LISTED BELOW ARE USED TO IDENTIFY THE MONUMENTS, MARKERS, TABLETS, STATUES, ETC. WHICH ARE DRAWN ON THE MAPS IN THESE PAGES

SYMBOL	TYPE	REPRESENTING	DESCRIPTION
	Bronze Tablet	Army of The Potomac, Union Corps or Division or Brigade, Regular Army Regiment, Regular Army Artillery Battery, Volunteer Artillery Brigade.	Brigade Tablet Mounted on Square Marble base. All other Tablets are on large vertical Granite Blocks.
	Bronze Tablet	Army of Northern Virginia, Confederate Corps or Division or Brigade or Artillery Battalion	Brigade Tablet and Artillery Battalion Tablet Mounted on Round Marble base. All other Tablets are Mounted on large vertical Granite blocks.
	Iron Tablet	Union Army Battery (other than Regular Army)	Mounted on Black Iron Shaft.
	Iron Tablet	Confederate Artillery Battery	Mounted on Black Iron Shaft.
	Iron Tablet	Confederate Brigade Advanced Position	Mounted on Black Iron Shaft.
	Regimental or Battery Monument	Principal Position of Volunteer Regiment or Volunteer Artillery Battery	Usually Granite or Marble in a Great Variety of Shapes and Sizes.
	Regimental Marker	Other than Principal Position of Regiment or Battery	Usually a Square Granite Marker or tablet or may be another monument.
	Flank Marker or Company Marker	Left and/or Right Flank of Regiment or Battery or Position of a Company.	Usually a Small Square or Rectangular Granite Marker.
	Army Or Corps Headquarters	Site of Headquarters of Army Commander or Corps Commander or Chief of Artillery	Cannon Barrel Mounted Vertically on Stone, Granite or Marble Base.
	State Monument	Monument Erected by Union or Confederate State.	
	Statue	Standing or Equestrian	Bronze Sculpture
	Building	House, Barn or other Structure	Identified by Owner's Name.
	Miscellaneous Marker	Marker or Inscription of a type not listed above	Granite or Metal Marker.

*Asterisk — Used whenever a Division or Brigade or Regiment or Battery has more than one Monument or Marker.

Check the Index for other Monument or Marker.

~ Gettysburg Battlefield Monuments, Locations & Inscriptions ~

In the late afternoon of July 1, 1863, Gen. Meade and his staff left Taneytown for Gettysburg. They arrived about 12:00 midnight (about 6 hours.

The Corps Commanders of The Army of The Potomac, reported to General Meade on the situation

General Meade established his headquarters at the Leister House, Mrs. Leister leaving the battlefield to find safer quarters. See page 76 for the Leister House location.

Also see the monument which was erected in Frederick, MD in 1930, during the Civil War Centennial.

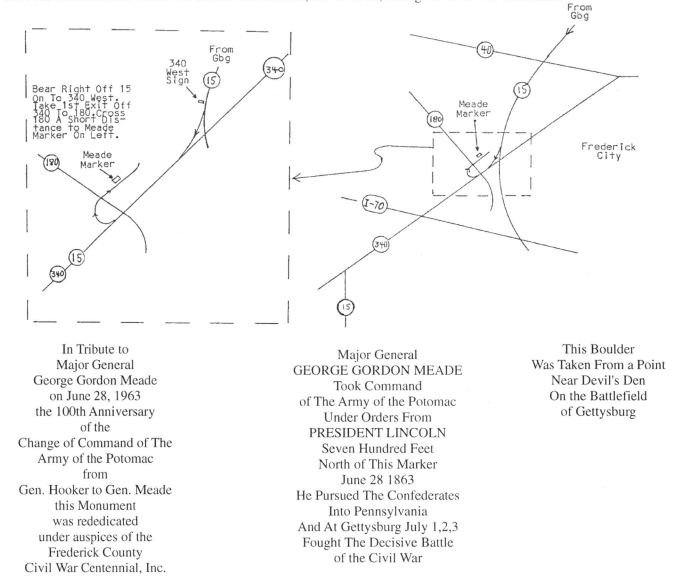

In Tribute to
Major General
George Gordon Meade
on June 28, 1963
the 100th Anniversary
of the
Change of Command of The
Army of the Potomac
from
Gen. Hooker to Gen. Meade
this Monument
was rededicated
under auspices of the
Frederick County
Civil War Centennial, Inc.

Major General
GEORGE GORDON MEADE
Took Command
of The Army of the Potomac
Under Orders From
PRESIDENT LINCOLN
Seven Hundred Feet
North of This Marker
June 28 1863
He Pursued The Confederates
Into Pennsylvania
And At Gettysburg July 1,2,3
Fought The Decisive Battle
of the Civil War

Marked by
The Pennsylvania
Historical Commission
1930

This Boulder
Was Taken From a Point
Near Devil's Den
On the Battlefield
of Gettysburg

(west face)

(south face)

(east face)

~ Gettysburg Battlefield Monuments, Locations & Inscriptions ~

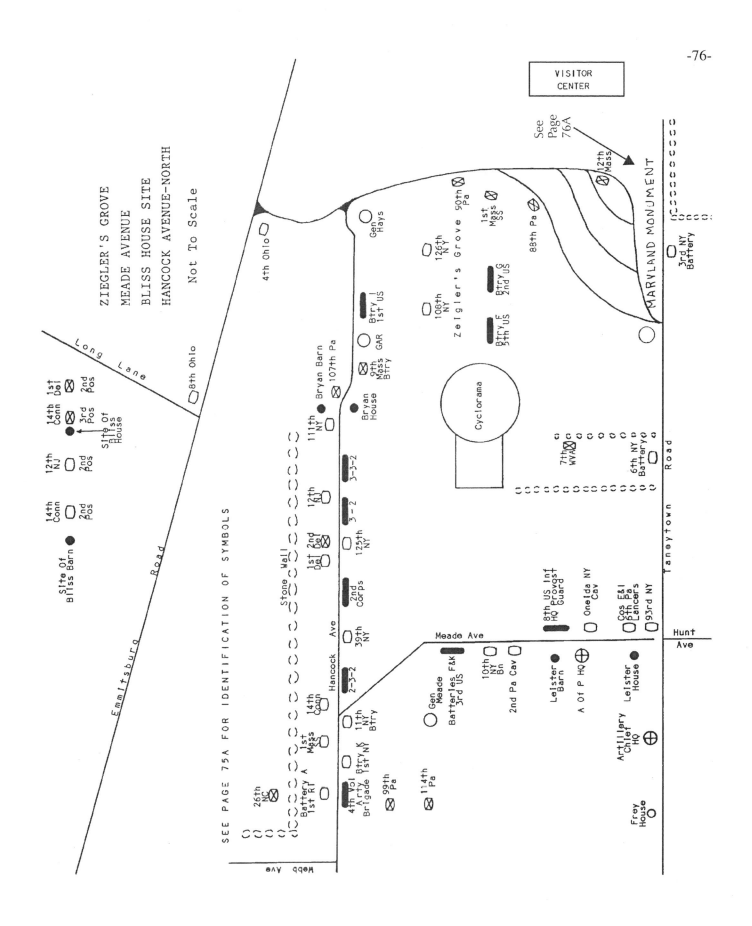

VISITOR CENTER

ZIEGLER'S GROVE
MEADE AVENUE
BLISS HOUSE SITE
HANCOCK AVENUE-NORTH

Not To Scale

See Page 76A

12th Mass

MARYLAND MONUMENT

3rd NY Battery

Long Lane

4th Ohio

Gen Hays

Zeigler's Grove 90th Pa

1st Mass SS

88th Pa

8th Ohio

126th NY

Btry G 2nd US

Site Of Bliss House

Btry I 1st US

108th NY

Btry F 5th US

14th Conn 1st Del 2nd Pos 3rd Pos

Bryan Barn 107th Pa

9th Mass Btry GAR

12th NJ 2nd Pos

111th NY

Bryan House

Cyclorama

14th Conn 2nd Pos

Emmitsburg Road

Stone Wall

3-3-2

7th WVA

6th NY Battery

Site Of Bliss Barn

SEE PAGE 75A FOR IDENTIFICATION OF SYMBOLS

12th NJ

3-2

1st Del 2nd Del

125th NY

Hancock Ave

2nd Corps

8th US Inf HQ Provost Guard

Oneida NY Cav

Cos E&I 6th Pa Lancers

93rd NY

Taneytown Road

39th NY

Meade Ave

Hunt Ave

14th Conn

2-3-2

Gen Meade

Batteries F&K 3rd US

10th NY Bn

2nd Pa Cav

Leister Barn

A of P HQ

Leister House

1st Mass

11th NY Btry

Artillery Chief HQ

Battery A 1st RI

Btry N 1st N

4th Vol Arty Brigade

99th Pa

114th Pa

Frey House

26th NC

Webb Ave

~ Gettysburg Battlefield Monuments, Locations & Inscriptions ~

Maryland's Monument

Final Tribute
More than 3000 Marylanders served on both sides of the conflict at the Battle of Gettysburg. They could be found in all branches of the Army from the rank of "private" to "Major General" and on all parts of the battlefield, brother against brother would be their legacy, particularly on the slopes of Culp's Hill.
This symbolized the aftermath of the battle and the war.
Brothers again Marylanders all. The State of Maryland proudly honors its sons, who fought at Gettysburg in defense of the causes they held so dear.

Participating Maryland Commands

Union	Confederate
1st Eastern Shore Infantry	2nd Infantry
1st Potomac Home Brigade Infantry	1st Cavalry
4th Infantry	1st Artillery
1st Cavalry	2nd Artillery Baltimore
Co A, Parnell Legion Cavalry	Light
Battery A, 1st Artillery	4th Artillery, Chesapeake

*see index

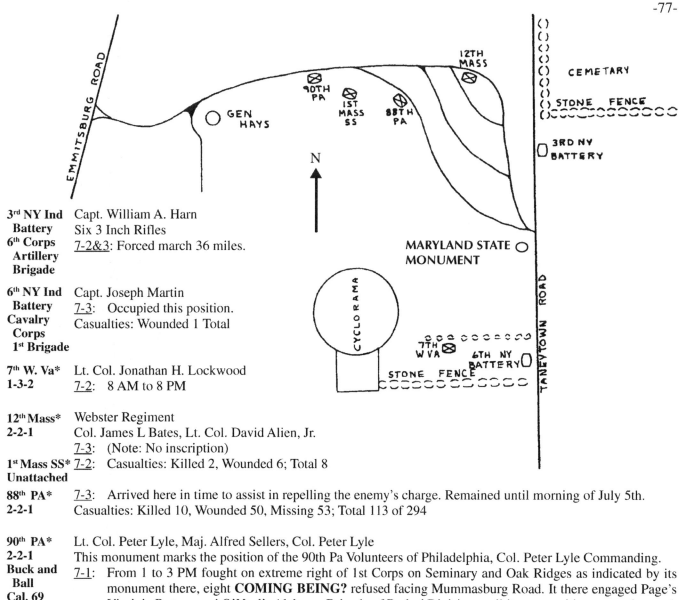

3rd NY Ind Battery Capt. William A. Harn
6th Corps Six 3 Inch Rifles
Artillery Brigade 7-2&3: Forced march 36 miles.

6th NY Ind Battery Capt. Joseph Martin
Cavalry Corps 7-3: Occupied this position.
1st Brigade Casualties: Wounded 1 Total

7th W. Va* Lt. Col. Jonathan H. Lockwood
1-3-2 7-2: 8 AM to 8 PM

12th Mass* Webster Regiment
2-2-1 Col. James L Bates, Lt. Col. David Alien, Jr.
7-3: (Note: No inscription)
1st Mass SS* 7-2: Casualties: Killed 2, Wounded 6; Total 8
Unattached

88th PA* 7-3: Arrived here in time to assist in repelling the enemy's charge. Remained until morning of July 5th.
2-2-1 Casualties: Killed 10, Wounded 50, Missing 53; Total 113 of 294

90th PA* Lt. Col. Peter Lyle, Maj. Alfred Sellers, Col. Peter Lyle
2-2-1 This monument marks the position of the 90th Pa Volunteers of Philadelphia, Col. Peter Lyle Commanding.
Buck and Ball Cal. 69 7-1: From 1 to 3 PM fought on extreme right of 1st Corps on Seminary and Oak Ridges as indicated by its monument there, eight **COMING BEING?** refused facing Mummasburg Road. It there engaged Page's Virginia Battery and O'Neal's Alabama Brigade of Rodes' Division until its ammunition was exhausted. Three Regiments of Iverson's Brigade were captured on our Brigade's front.
7-2: Occupied Cemetary Hill and in the evening moved to the left of 2nd Corps, returning during the evening to this position.
Casualties: Killed 11, Wounded 44, Missing 39; Total 94 of 208

Hays Statue Cadet USMA 7/1/1840, Brev. 2nd Lt. 4th US Inf. 7/1/44, 2nd Lt. 8th Inf. 6/18/46, Resigned 4/12/48. Capt. 16th Inf. 5/14/1861, Major 12th PA Inf. 4/25/61, Honorably Mustered out 8/5/61. Col. 63rd Pa Inf. 10/9/61 Brig. Gen. USV 9/29/62, Brevet 1st Lt. USA 5/9/46 "For gallant conduct in the Battle of Palo Alto and Resaca De La Palma, Texas". Major 6/30/62 "For gallant and meritorious service at the Battles of Fair Oaks, Peach Orchard and Glendale, Va.". Col. 7/2/63 "For gallant and meritorious service at the Battle of Gettysburg, Pa". For gallant and meritorious service at the Battle of Malvern Hill, Va.". Brevetted Maj. Gen. USV 5/5/64 "For gallant and distinguished conduct at the Battles of the Peninsula, Gettysburg and Wilderness." Born 7/8/1819 at Franklin, Pa; Killed at the Battle of the Wilderness.

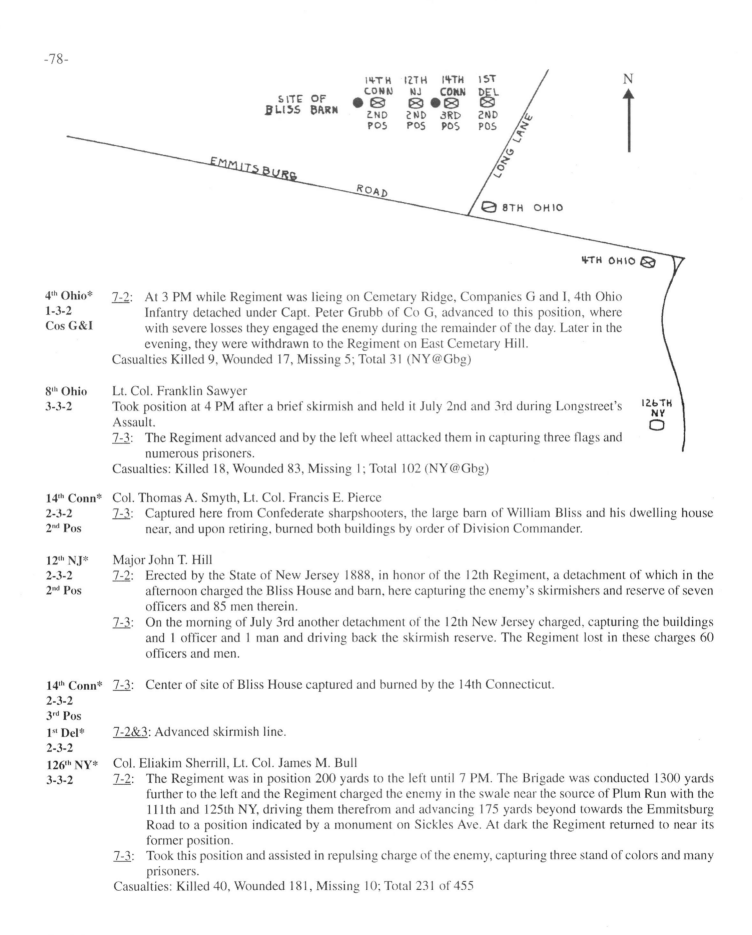

4th Ohio*
1-3-2
Cos G&I

7-2: At 3 PM while Regiment was lieing on Cemetary Ridge, Companies G and I, 4th Ohio Infantry detached under Capt. Peter Grubb of Co G, advanced to this position, where with severe losses they engaged the enemy during the remainder of the day. Later in the evening, they were withdrawn to the Regiment on East Cemetary Hill.
Casualties Killed 9, Wounded 17, Missing 5; Total 31 (NY@Gbg)

8th Ohio
3-3-2

Lt. Col. Franklin Sawyer
Took position at 4 PM after a brief skirmish and held it July 2nd and 3rd during Longstreet's Assault.
7-3: The Regiment advanced and by the left wheel attacked them in capturing three flags and numerous prisoners.
Casualties: Killed 18, Wounded 83, Missing 1; Total 102 (NY@Gbg)

14th Conn*
2-3-2
2nd Pos

Col. Thomas A. Smyth, Lt. Col. Francis E. Pierce
7-3: Captured here from Confederate sharpshooters, the large barn of William Bliss and his dwelling house near, and upon retiring, burned both buildings by order of Division Commander.

12th NJ*
2-3-2
2nd Pos

Major John T. Hill
7-2: Erected by the State of New Jersey 1888, in honor of the 12th Regiment, a detachment of which in the afternoon charged the Bliss House and barn, here capturing the enemy's skirmishers and reserve of seven officers and 85 men therein.
7-3: On the morning of July 3rd another detachment of the 12th New Jersey charged, capturing the buildings and 1 officer and 1 man and driving back the skirmish reserve. The Regiment lost in these charges 60 officers and men.

14th Conn*
2-3-2
3rd Pos

7-3: Center of site of Bliss House captured and burned by the 14th Connecticut.

1st Del*
2-3-2

7-2&3: Advanced skirmish line.

126th NY*
3-3-2

Col. Eliakim Sherrill, Lt. Col. James M. Bull
7-2: The Regiment was in position 200 yards to the left until 7 PM. The Brigade was conducted 1300 yards further to the left and the Regiment charged the enemy in the swale near the source of Plum Run with the 111th and 125th NY, driving them therefrom and advancing 175 yards beyond towards the Emmitsburg Road to a position indicated by a monument on Sickles Ave. At dark the Regiment returned to near its former position.
7-3: Took this position and assisted in repulsing charge of the enemy, capturing three stand of colors and many prisoners.
Casualties: Killed 40, Wounded 181, Missing 10; Total 231 of 455

*see index

Battery G
2ⁿᵈ US
6ᵗʰ Corps
Artillery
Brigade

Lt. John H. Butler
Six 12 Pounders
7-2: Arrived in the afternoon with the Corps and held in reserve.
7-3: Brought up to Zeigler's Grove in rear of 3rd Division, 2nd Corps on the repulse of Longstreet's Assault.

Battery F
5ᵗʰ US
6ᵗʰ Corps
Artillery
Brigade

Lt. Leonard Martin
Six 10 Pounder Parrotts
7-2: Arrived in the afternoon with the Corps and held in reserve.
7-3: Brought up to Zeigler's Grove in rear of 3rd Division, 2nd Corps on the repulse of Longstreet's Assault.

108ᵗʰ NY
2-3-2

Lt. Col. Francis E. Pierce
7-2: Occupied this position.
7-3: Supporting Battery I-1st US Artillery during artillery duel in the afternoon. Sustained a terrific fire without being able to return a shot. During the charge of the enemy, the left of the Confederate line lapped its front and came within 50 yards of it before breaking.
Casualties: Killed 16, Wounded 86; Total 102 of 200.

Battery I
1ˢᵗ US
2ⁿᵈ Corps
Artillery
Brigade

Lt. George A. Woodruff, Lt. Tully McCrea.
7-2: Arrived and took position in Zeigler's Grove on the left of Evergreen Cemetary.
7-3: Actively engaged in assisting in repelling Longstreet's Assault. Lt. Woodruff mortally wounded on July 3rd and the command evolved on Lt. McCrea.
Casualties: Killed 1, Wounded 24; Total 25

G A R
Memorial

Senior Vice-Commander of the Grand Army of the Republic Albert Woolson of Duluth, Minnesota, The Last Survivor.
Dedicated September 12, 1956 by National Auxiliary To Sons Of Union Veterans Of The Civil War 1861-1865.

9ᵗʰ Mass
Battery*
3ʳᵈ Position

Capt. John Bigelow, Lt. Richard S. Milton
Two guns, Lt. Milton commanding.
7-3&4: Only officer and guns effective after engagement in Trostle Field.
Casualties: Killed 8, Wounded 18, Missing 2; Total 28.

107ᵗʰ PA*
1-2-1

Lt. Col. James MacThomson, Capt. Emanuel D. Roath
7-1: Went into action with 255 officers and men.
7-2: Occupied this position.
Casualties: Lost during the three days in killed, wounded and missing —165 officers and men.

*see index

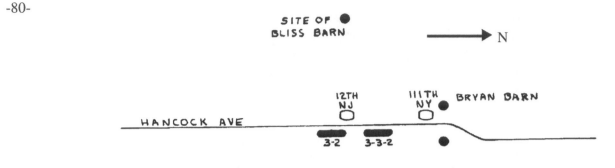

111ᵗʰ NY Col. Clinton D. MacDougal, Lt. Col. Isaac M. Lusk, Capt. Aaron P. Seeley
3-3-2 <u>7-2</u>: Arrived early morning, took position near Zeigler's Grove. Went to relief of 3rd Corps in afternoon. Took this position that evening and held it until close of battle.
Casualties: Killed 58, Wounded 177, Missing 14; Total 249. Number engaged (eight companies): 390.

3-3-2* Col. George L. Willard, Col. Eliakim Sherrill, Lt. Col. James M. Bull.
<u>7-2</u>: Took position in morning along Cemetery Ridge at right of the angle. Near sunset, went to the left to support 3rd Corps. Charged Brigadier General Barksdale's Brigade in the wooded swale at the head of Plum Run forcing it back and capturing many prisoners. The 39th NY recaptured Battery I-5th US from the 21st Mississippi. Col. Willard was killed and General Barksdale mortally wounded. At dark the Brigade returned and was held in reserve.
<u>7-3</u>: Engaged on the skirmish line with much loss. At 3 PM, after a terrific cannonade of two hours, the Brigade was moved up to the line of the 2nd Brigade and assisted in repulsing Longstreet's Assault in which Col. Sherrill was mortally wounded. A large detail from the Brigade under Capt. Armstrong of the 125th NY and the 8th Ohio on the skirmish line, withdrew to the right and poured in a deadly fire upon the left of the assaulting lines and then charging, captured prisoners and flags.
Casualties: Killed 139, Wounded 542, Missing 33; Total 714
39th (4 Companies), 111th, 125th, 126th NY Infantry

12ᵗʰ NJ* Major John T. Hill
2-3-2 "Buck and Ball-Cal. 69"
In Memory of the Men of the 12th New Jersey Volunteers Who Fell Opon This Field July 2 and 3, 1863, And Who Elsewhere Died Under The Flag, This Monument Is Dedicated By Their Surviving Comrades As An Example to Future Generations.
<u>7-2&3</u>: Two charges were made by this Regiment on the Bliss Barn.
Casualties: Killed 22, Wounded 84, Missing 9; Total 115

3-2 Brigadier General Alexander Hays
3ʳᵈ Division 1st Brigade Col. S. S. Carroll
2ⁿᵈ Corps 2nd Brigade Col. Thomas A. Smyth, Lt. Col. Francis Pierce
3rd Brigade Col. George L. Willard, Col. Eliakim Sherrill, Lt. Col. James M. Bull
<u>7-2</u>: About 8 AM, took position on Cemetery Ridge, relieving 2nd Division, 1st Corps, and at noon advanced to the stone wall in front. Late in the day, the 3rd Brigade went to the support of 3rd Corps on the left and became engaged with Barksdale's Mississippi Brigade, capturing many prisoners. At dark, Col. Carroll, with the 4th Ohio, 7th W. Va., and 14th Indiana of the 1st Brigade, went to the support the 11th Corps on East Cemetery Hill and remained there until the close of the battle.
<u>7-3</u>: The Bliss Barn in front, occupied by sharpshooters, was burned by order of General Hays. At 1 PM, a heavy artillery fire from the Confederate line was concentrated on the positions of the 2nd and 3rd Divisions of the Corps for two hours, followed by a charge of more than 15,000 infantry, which was repulsed with loss, the Division capturing about 1,500 prisoners and 15 stand of colors. The muskets found on the field after the charge numbered about 3,500.
<u>7-4</u>: Sharp skirmishing in front all day.
Casualties: Killed 238, Wounded 987, Missing 66; Total 1291.

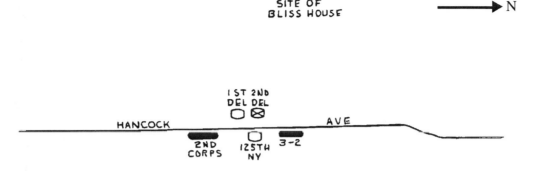

125ᵗʰ NY*
3-3-2
Col. George Lamb Willard, Colonel 125th NY Infantry, Major 19th Infantry, Brevet Colonel US Army. Born July 15, 1827, Killed in Action July 2, 1863, while in command of his brigade at the place marked by a granite monument 1070 yards to the left.

> 7-2: Regiment in line at the stone wall until 7PM when the Brigade went to the support of the 3rd Corps. Charged and drove back Barksdale's Mississippi Brigade. Returned at 8:30 PM.

> 7-3: Regiment in front on line of stone wall west side of Hancock Avenue at time of Longstreet's Assault.

Casualties: Killed 26, Wounded 104, Missing 9; Total 139 of 500

2ⁿᵈ Del*
4-1-2
Col. William P. Baily
Skirmish line 2nd Regiment Delaware Volunteer Infantry, July 3, 1863.
Casualties: Killed 11, Wounded 61, Missing 12; Total 84 (NY@Gbg)

1ˢᵗ Del*
2-3-2
Lt. Col. Edward P. Harris, Capt. Thomas B. Hizer, Lt. William Smith, Lt. John Dent
7-2&3: Position held by the 1st Regiment Delaware Volunteer Infantry.
Erected By The State Of Delaware To Commemorate The Gallantry Of Her Sons. AD 1885
Casualties: Killed 10, Wounded 54, Missing 13; Total 77 (NY@Gbg)

2ⁿᵈ Corps
Major General Winfield S. Hancock
1st Division   Brig. Gen. John C. Caldwell
2nd Division   Brig. Gen. John Gibbon, Brig. Gen. William Harrow
3rd Division   Brig. Gen. Alex Hays
Artillery Brigade   Capt. John Hazard

> 7-2: Arrived between 6 and 8 AM on Taneytown Road and went into position on Cemetery Hill on right of 5th Corps and at the left of the cemetery, relieving a part of the 1st Corps; Caldwell's Division on the left, Gibbon in the center, Hays on the right of line from Cemetery Hill to Round Top. Between 5 and 6 PM, Caldwell's Division was sent to the support of the 3rd Corps and was engaged until sunset, then retired to its first position.

> 7-3: At 1 PM, the Confederate artillery opened a heavy fire all along the line of Hill's Corps and the left of Longstreet's Corps for two hours when an assault under the command of General Longstreet was made by a force of about 15000, which was repulsed with great loss in Killed, Wounded and Prisoners.

Casualties: Killed 797, Wounded 3194, Missing 379; Total 4369

*see index

~ Gettysburg Battlefield Monuments, Locations & Inscriptions ~

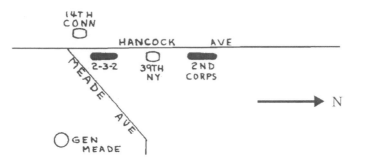

39th NY*
3-3-2
(4 Cos)

Major Hugo Hildebrand
The Garibaldi Guards
7-2: This Regiment at about 7PM, being ordered to support General Sickles' line, charged and drove the enemy, recapturing the guns and equipment of Battery I-5th US Artillery. A stone tablet marks the place where this incident occurred.
7-3: This Regiment, composed of four companies, held this position.
Casualties: Killed 15, Wounded 80; Total 95

2-3-2

Col. Thomas A. Smyth, Lt. Col. Francis E. Pierce
14th Conn, 1st Del, 12th NJ, 108th NY Infantry
7-2: Took position early in morning along a stone fence on Cemetery Ridge at the left of Zeigler's Grove, supporting Battery I-1st US on the right. Sharp skirmishing during the day and artillery firing at intervals in the afternoon. At night the line of the Brigade was extended to the angle to cover the portion previously occupied by the 3rd Brigade.
7-3: In the afternoon, the Bliss Barn, having been occupied by the Confederate sharpshooters, the 14th Conn, by order of Brig. Gen. Hays, recaptured and burned the barn. At 1 PM, a terrific cannonade was opened in front which continued for two hours, followed by a charge of the Divisions of Maj. Gen. Pickett, Brig. Gen. Pettigrew, and Maj. Gen. Pender which was repulsed by the Brigade, reinforced by the 3rd Brigade. More than 1200 prisoners and 9 stand of colors were captured by the Brigade.
7-4: Brigade remained in position until the close of the battle with sharp skirmishing during the day.
Casualties: Killed 61, Wounded 279, Missing 26; Total 366

14th Conn*
2-3-2

Major Theodore G. Ellis
7-1: Reached vicinity of Gettysburg in the evening.
7-2: Held this position.
7-3: The Regiment took part in the repulse of Longstreet's Grand Charge, capturing in their immediate front more than 200 prisoners and five battle flags. On the 3rd, captured from the enemy sharpshooters, the Bliss buildings in their far front and held them until ordered to burn them.
7-4: Held this position.
Casualties: 10 Killed, 52 Wounded, 4 Missing; Total 66. (NY@Gbg)

**Meade's
Statue**

Major General George Gordon Meade
United States Army
Commander of The Army Of The Potomac
Born December 31, 1815   Died November 6, 1872
Cadet USMA 9/l/1831, Brevet 2nd Lt. 3rd US Artillery 7/1/35, 2nd Lt. 12/31/35; Resigned and Honorably Discharged l0/26/36, 2nd Lt. Topographical Engineers 5/18/42; 1st Lt. 8/4/51; Capt 5/19/56, "For 14 years Continuous Service", Major 718/52 (Merged into Corps of Engineers 3/3/63.) Vacated Commission 7/3/63, Brig. Gen. USA 7/3/63; Maj. Gen. 8/16/64; Breveted 1st Lt. USA 9/3/46 "For gallant conduct in the several conflicts at Monterrey, Mexico." Brig. Gen. USV 8/31/6l; Maj. Gen. 11/29/62; Vacated Commission in Volunteer Service 12/6/64. The Senate and the House of Representatives in Congress assembled resolved (in joint resolution approved January 28, 1864) "That the gratitude of the American people and the thanks of their representatives in Congress are due, and are hereby tendered **to Major General George G. Meade** and the officers of that Army (Army Of The Potomac) for the skill and heroic valor which, at Gettysburg, repulsed, defeated and drove back, broken and dispirited beyond the Rappahannock the veteran army of the rebellion."

*see index

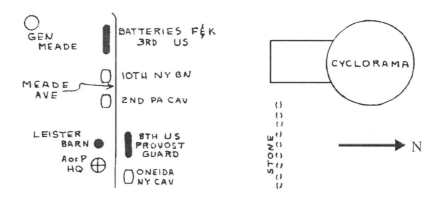

Batteries	Lt. John J. Turnbull
F&K	Six - 12 Pounders
3rd US*	7-1: Took position on crest of hill near Gen. Meade's Headquarters.
1st Regular	7-2: Moved to position on right of log house on Emmitsburg Road on the line held by Gen. Humphreys' 2nd
Brigade	Division, 3rd Corps and became immediately engaged, but was compelled to retire with loss of 45 horses
Artillery	killed and four guns captured, which were soon recaptureed.
Reserve	7-3. Went into position on crest of hill at left of Evergreen Cemetery near Army Headquarters and remained
	until close of battle.
	Casualties: Killed 9, Wounded 4, Missing 1; Total 14

2nd PA	Col. R. Butler Price, Provost Guard, Army Headquarters
Cavalary	7-3: Held this position until close of day when it conducted 3,000 prisoners to Westminster, Md. Detatchments
Provost	served on other parts of the field during the battle.
Guard	

10th NY	Major George F. Hopper
Battalion	National Zouaves
2-3-2	7-3: Held this position with 8 officers and 90 enlisted men as Provost Guard, Hays' Division during Plckett's
	Charge.
	Casualties: Killed 2, Wounded 4; Total 6

8th US	Capt. Edward W. Reed
(8 Cos)	7-2: Arrived in morning and engaged in Provost Duty until close of battle.
Provost	
Guard	
Army HQ	

Oneida NY	7-2&3: General Meade's Escort and Headquarters Orderlies and Couriers.
Ind Cav	
Army HQ	

*see index

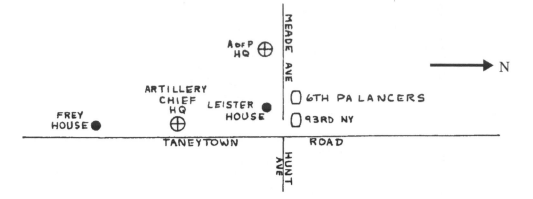

6th PA   On duty as an escort to Major General George G. Meade.

Lancers*   <u>7-3</u>: The main body of this Regiment was actually engaged on the extreme left of the Army on the Emmitsburg

(Cos E&I)   Pike, where a monument has been erected commemorating their services. Four companies were specially

Cav-1-Res   detailed by General Meade for hazardous duty in rear of Lee's Army.

93rd NY   Capt John S. Crocker

<u>7-2&3</u>: Headquarters Guard - Army Headquarters

General Meade's Head-quarters

HEADQUARTERS

OF

MAJOR GENERAL

GEORGE G. MEADE

COMMANDING

ARMY OF THE POTOMAC

Artillery Head-quarters

Headquarters of Brig. General Henry J. Hunt, Chief of Artillery
ARMY OF THE POTOTMAC

JULY 2, 3, 4, 5

1863

*see index

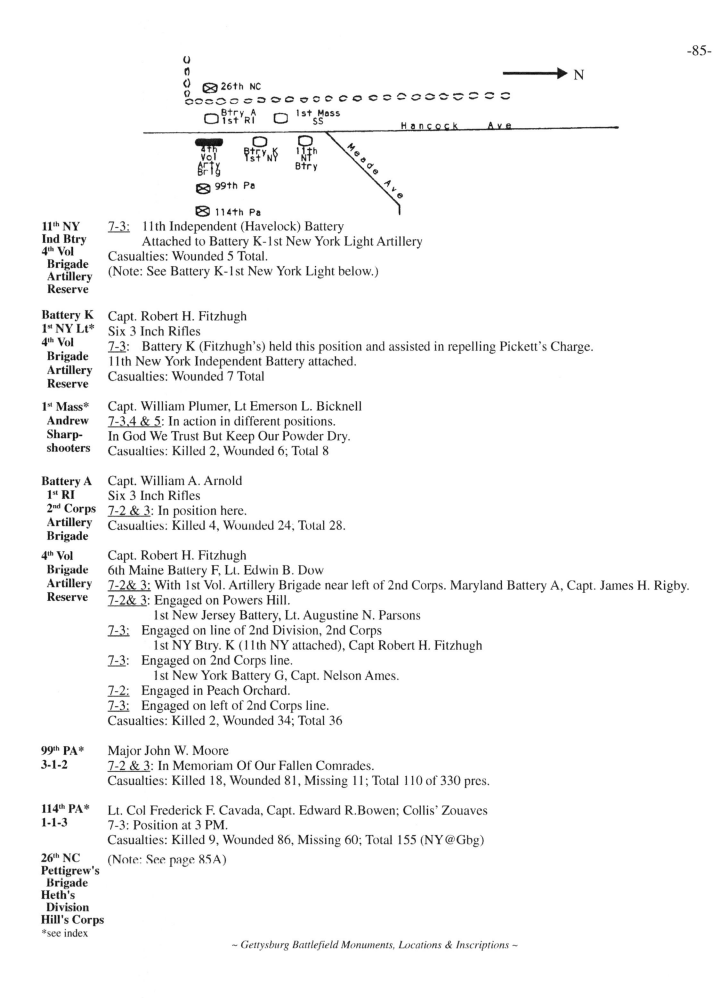

11th NY
Ind Btry
4th Vol
Brigade
Artillery
Reserve

<u>7-3:</u>   11th Independent (Havelock) Battery
        Attached to Battery K-1st New York Light Artillery
Casualties: Wounded 5 Total.
(Note: See Battery K-1st New York Light below.)

Battery K
1st NY Lt*
4th Vol
Brigade
Artillery
Reserve

Capt. Robert H. Fitzhugh
Six 3 Inch Rifles
<u>7-3:</u>   Battery K (Fitzhugh's) held this position and assisted in repelling Pickett's Charge.
11th New York Independent Battery attached.
Casualties: Wounded 7 Total

1st Mass*
Andrew
Sharp-
shooters

Capt. William Plumer, Lt Emerson L. Bicknell
<u>7-3,4 & 5:</u> In action in different positions.
In God We Trust But Keep Our Powder Dry.
Casualties: Killed 2, Wounded 6; Total 8

Battery A
1st RI
2nd Corps
Artillery
Brigade

Capt. William A. Arnold
Six 3 Inch Rifles
<u>7-2 & 3:</u> In position here.
Casualties: Killed 4, Wounded 24, Total 28.

4th Vol
Brigade
Artillery
Reserve

Capt. Robert H. Fitzhugh
6th Maine Battery F, Lt. Edwin B. Dow
<u>7-2& 3:</u> With 1st Vol. Artillery Brigade near left of 2nd Corps. Maryland Battery A, Capt. James H. Rigby.
<u>7-2& 3:</u> Engaged on Powers Hill.
        1st New Jersey Battery, Lt. Augustine N. Parsons
<u>7-3:</u>   Engaged on line of 2nd Division, 2nd Corps
        1st NY Btry. K (11th NY attached), Capt Robert H. Fitzhugh
<u>7-3:</u>   Engaged on 2nd Corps line.
        1st New York Battery G, Capt. Nelson Ames.
<u>7-2:</u>   Engaged in Peach Orchard.
<u>7-3:</u>   Engaged on left of 2nd Corps line.
Casualties: Killed 2, Wounded 34; Total 36

99th PA*
3-1-2

Major John W. Moore
<u>7-2 & 3:</u> In Memoriam Of Our Fallen Comrades.
Casualties: Killed 18, Wounded 81, Missing 11; Total 110 of 330 pres.

114th PA*
1-1-3

Lt. Col Frederick F. Cavada, Capt. Edward R.Bowen; Collis' Zouaves
7-3: Position at 3 PM.
Casualties: Killed 9, Wounded 86, Missing 60; Total 155 (NY@Gbg)

26th NC
Pettigrew's
Brigade
Heth's
Division
Hill's Corps
*see index

(Note: See page 85A)

TWENTY SIXTH

NORTH CAROLINA REGIMENT

PETTIGREW'S BRIGADE HETH'S DIVISION

HILL'S CORPS

ARMY OF NORTHERN VIRGINIA

Although nearly destroyed during its successful attack against Meredeth's Iron Brigade on July 1st, the Twenty Sixth North Carolina Regiment joined in the Pickett-Pettigrew charge on the afternoon of July 3. Advancing under solid shot, spherical case, cannister, and musketry, the Regiment charged to within ten paces of the stone wall in their front.

The scene was described by an artilleryman of a Rhode Island Battery:...As a regiment of Pettigrew's Brigade (The Twenty Sixth North Carolina) was charging. and had almost reached the wall just in front of us, Sgt. M. C. Olney cried out '...Fire that gun! Pull! Pull!'. The No. 4 obeyed orders and the gap made in that North Carolina Regiment was simply terrible. Under this galling fire, the Twenty Sixth North Carolina was compelled to retire with the Brigade from this point to Seminary Ridge.

"The Men Of The Twenty Sixth Regiment Would
Dress On Their Colors In Spite Of The World"

Erected By The State Of North Carolina
1986
(Near The High Water Mark)

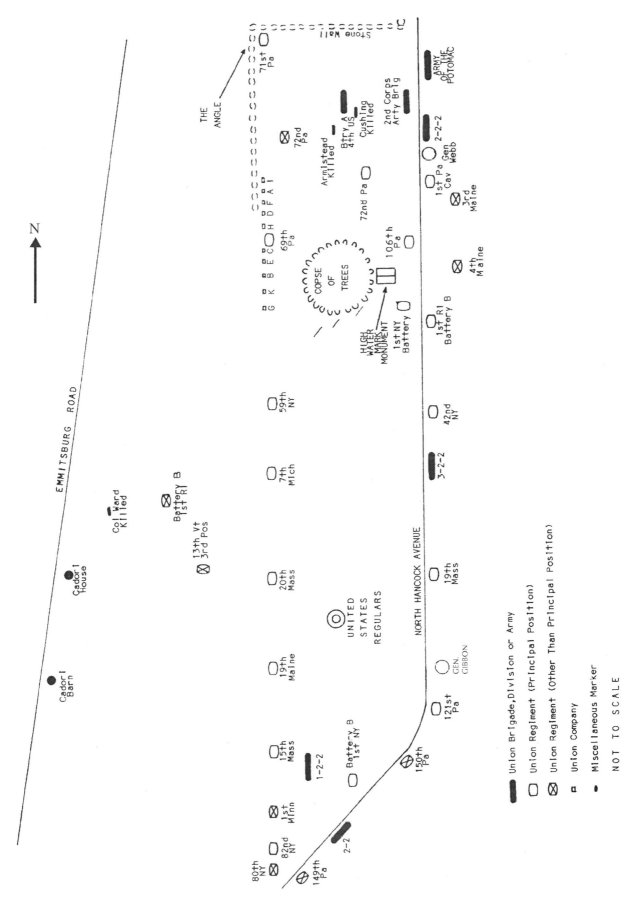

~ Gettysburg Battlefield Monuments, Locations & Inscriptions ~

THE SYMBOLS LISTED BELOW ARE USED TO IDENTIFY
THE MONUMENTS, MARKERS, TABLETS, STATUES, ETC.
WHICH ARE DRAWN ON THE MAPS IN THESE PAGES

SYMBOL	TYPE	REPRESENTING	DESCRIPTION
	Bronze Tablet	Army of The Potomac, Union Corps or Division or Brigade, Regular Army Regiment, Regular Army Artillery Battery, Volunteer Artillery Brigade.	Brigade Tablet Mounted on Square Marble base. All other Tablets are on large vertical Granite Blocks.
	Bronze Tablet	Army of Northern Virginia, Confederate Corps or Division or Brigade or Artillery Battalion	Brigade Tablet and Artillery Battalion Tablet Mounted on Round Marble base. All other Tablets are Mounted on large vertical Granite blocks.
	Iron Tablet	Union Army Battery (other than Regular Army)	Mounted on Black Iron Shaft.
	Iron Tablet	Confederate Artillery Battery	Mounted on Black Iron Shaft.
	Iron Tablet	Confederate Brigade Advanced Position	Mounted on Black Iron Shaft.
	Regimental or Battery Monument	Principal Position of Volunteer Regiment or Volunteer Artillery Battery	Usually Granite or Marble in a Great Variety of Shapes and Sizes.
	Regimental Marker	Other than Principal Position of Regiment or Battery	Usually a Square Granite Marker or tablet or may be another monument.
	Flank Marker or Company Marker	Left and/or Right Flank of Regiment or Battery or Position of a Company.	Usually a Small Square or Rectangular Granite Marker.
	Army Or Corps Headquarters	Site of Headquarters of Army Commander or Corps Commander or Chief of Artillery	Cannon Barrel Mounted Vertically on Stone, Granite or Marble Base.
	State Monument	Monument Erected by Union or Confederate State.	
	Statue	Standing or Equestrian	Bronze Sculpture
	Building	House, Barn or other Structure	Identified by Owner's Name.
	Miscellaneous Marker	Marker or Inscription of a type not listed above	Granite or Metal Marker.

*Asterisk   Used whenever a Division or Brigade or Regiment or Battery has more than one Monument or Marker.   Check the Index for other Monument or Marker.

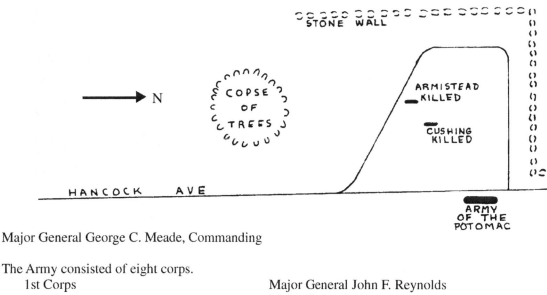

Army of the Potomac	Major General George C. Meade, Commanding

The Army consisted of eight corps.

1st Corps	Major General John F. Reynolds
	Major General Abner Doubleday
	Major General John Newton
2nd Corps	Major General Winfield S. Hancock
	Brigadier General John Gibbon
3rd Corps	Major General Daniel B. Sickles
	Major General David B. Birney
5th Corps	Major General George Sykes
6th Corps	Major General John Sedgwick
11th Corp	Major General Oliver O. Howard
12th Corps	Major General Henry W. Slocum
	Brigadier General Alpheus S. Williams
Cavalry Corps	Major General Alfred Pleasanton
Artillery Reserve Brigade	Brigade General Robert O. Tyler

7-1: The 1st and 11th Corps arrived and were engaged north and west of Gettysburg and fell back to Cemetary Hill in rear of the town. The 12th Corps and a large part of the 3rd Corps arrived at close of the day.

7-2: The remainder of the 3rd Corps and the 5th and 2nd Corps arrived in the morning, the 6th Corps in the afternoon. The 3rd Corps having advanced, was attacked by Longstreet's Confederate Corps and Anderson's Division of Hill's Corps. The 5th Corps and the 1st Division of the 2nd Corps going to the support of the 3rd Corps, an engagement ensued until nightfall, when the Union forces had been driven from their advanced position and the Confederates repulsed.

7-3: The 12th Corps having by order vacated a large part of its line on Culp's Hill on the night of July 2nd and Johnson's Division of Ewell's Corps having occupied the works, the 12th Corps in the morning attacked and regained the lines it had previously vacated. Hill's Corps and Pickett's Division of Longstreet's Corps in the afternoon attacked the line of the 2nd Corps and were repulsed with great loss. Stuart's Confederate Cavalry in the afternoon attacked the 2nd Cavalry Division and the 2nd Brigade of the 3rd Cavalry Division and was repulsed.

(Note: No casualties are listed on this tablet.)

Armistead Killed

Brigadier General Lewis A. Armistead, CSA, fell here July 3, 1363

Cushing Killed

Erected In Honor Of Lt. A. H. Cushing and His 4th US-Battery A By Col. R. Penn Smith And His 71st Pennsylvania Volunteer Regiment.

~ Gettysburg Battlefield Monuments, Locations & Inscriptions ~

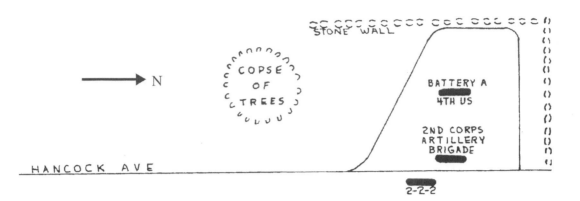

Battery A	Lt. Alonzo H. Cushing and Sargeant Frederick Fuger
4th US	Six - 3 Inch Rifles.

2nd Corps Artillery Brigade

7-2: Arrived and took position wlth the Brigade of Brig. Gen. A. S. Webb, 2nd Division, 2nd Corps and took part in the artillery engagements during the day.

7-3: Engaged in the repulse of Longstreet's Assault and lost all its officers killed or wounded, all the guns but one, and all its horses but three were disabled. Lt. Cushing was killed while firing the last shot from the last effective gun. After the repulse of Longstreet's Assault, the Battery was withdrawn.

Casualties: Killed 6, Wounded 32; Total 38.

2nd Corps Artillery Brigade

Capt. John G. Hazard

1st NY-Battery B	4 - 10 Pounders	Lt. Albert S. Sheldon, Capt. James M. Rorty, Lt. Robert E. Rogers
1st RI-Battery A	6 - 3 Inch Rifles	Capt. William A. Arnold
1st RI-Battery B	4 - 12 Pounders	Lt. Frederick Brown, Lt. Wm. S. Perrin
1st US-Battery I	6 - 12 Pounders	Lt. Geo. A. Woodruff, Lt. Tulley McCrea
4th US-Battery A	6 - 3 Inch Rifles	Lt. Alonzo H. Cushing, Sgt. Fred Fuger

7-1: Marched from Uniontown, MD at 2 PM. Went into position at 11 PM on the Taneytown Road three miles from Gettysburg.

7-2: Moved with the Corps at daylight and went into position on battle line in order from right to left as mentioned. The batteries were engaged toward night with some loss.

7-3: Engaged with the Confederate artillery in front at 8AM and along the whole line at 1 PM, and assisted in repulsing Longstreet's Assault in the afternoon.

Casualties: Killed 27, Wounded 119, Missing 3; Total 149

2-2-2

Brig. Gen. Alexander S. Webb.

69th, 71st, 72nd, 106th Pa Infantry

7-2: The 69th Pa took position along the advance line of the stone wall at the left of the angle, the other Regiments of the Brigade in the rear at the ridge. During the day, two companies of the 71st and two of the 106th were sharply engaged on the skirmish line. About sunset, Brig. Gen. Wright's Brigade charged across the Emmitsburg Road to the Union line past the guns of Battery B-1st RI but were soon repulsed with the loss of many prisoners, and forced back beyond the Emmitsburg Road. All the guns were temporarily lost but were retaken. At night, the 71st and 106th Pa, except two companies on the skirmish line, were sent to the support of the 11th Corps on East Cemetary Hill; the 71st returned at midnight, the 106th remained there.

7-3: At 3 PM, after heavy cannonading for two hours, Major General Pickett's Division of about 5000 men charged the line held by this and the 3rd Brigade, breaking through the line at the angle. Reinforcements coming up quickly, the charge was repulsed with great loss. Nearly 1000 prisoners and six battle flags were reported captured by the Brigade.

Casualties: Killed 114, Wounded 338, Missing 39; Total 491

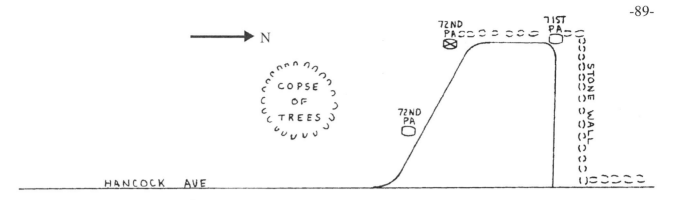

71st PA
2-2-3   Col. R. Penn Smith

This Regiment was organized April 29, 1861, being the first three-year regiment to complete its organization. It was enlisted in Philadelphia by Senator E. D. Baker by special authority from the War Department to be credited to the State of California and was known as the "California Regiment".

After the death of Col. E. D. Baker at Ball's Bluff October 21, 1861, it was claimed by its native state and became the 71st Pennsylvania.

7-2:   To the left of this point, the 71st Pa assisted in repulsing the furious attack of Wright's Georgia Brigade.

7-3:   During the terrific cannonade the Regiment occupied a position 60 yards in the rear of this spot. A number of the men voluntarily helped to work Cushing's disabled battery. As the enemy emerged from Seminary Ridge, the Regiment was ordered forward, the left wing to this point, the right to the wall in the rear. When Picket's Division rushed upon the left wing in overwhelming numbers, it fell back into line with the right, thus bringing the whole Regiment into action with the additional use of a large number of loaded muskets gathered from the battlefield of the previous day. The Regiment captured a number of prisoners and three flags.

Casualties: Killed 21, Wounded 58, Missing 19; Total 98 of 331 carried into action.

72nd PA*
2-2-3   Col. DeWitt C. Baxter, Lt. Col. Theodore Hesser

7-2&3: The ground of the last assault, The Philadelphia Brigade, Brig. Gen. Alexander S. Webb held this angle. Casualties in the battle 495

72nd PA*
2-2-2   The 72nd Pa Volunteers "Philadelphia Fire Zouaves", Col. DeWitt C. Baxter lost 10 officers and 182 men of 473 present for duty. The Regiment erects this tribute to the memory of fallen comrades.

2nd Position 7-2:   The Regiment reached this angle at 1 AM; took position in rear of this monument; supported Cushing's Battery A-4th US Artillery. At 6 PM, assisted in repulsing an attack of the enemy and in making a counter-charge, driving them beyond the Emmitsburg Road, capturing 250 prisoners.

7-3:   The Regiment assisted in repulsing the charge of the enemy on the angle at 3 PM and in capturing many standards and prisoners. During the cannonade which proceeded the charge, The Regiment was in line 60 yards to the left and rear of this monument. When the Rebels forced the troops from the first line, the 72nd fought its way to the front and occupied the wall.

Present at Gettysburg 458. Killed and Mortally Wounded 62, Wounded 133, Missing 2; Total of Killed, Wounded and Missing 197.

*see index

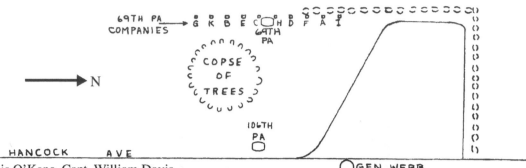

69ᵗʰ PA
2-2-2

Col. Dennis O'Kane, Capt. William Davis

7-2: This position was held by the 69th Philadelphia Volunteers. Late in the afternoon, this Regiment assisted in repulsing a desperate attack made by Wright's Georgia Brigade.

7-3: About 1 o'clock PM, the line was subjected to an artillery fire from nearly 150 guns lasting over one hour, after which Pickett's Division charged this position, was repulsed and nearly annihilated, the contest on the left and center of this Regiment, for a time being hand-to-hand. Of the regimental commanders attacking, but one remained unhurt. General Garnett was killed and General Kemper desperately wounded, and General Armistead, after crossing the stone wall above the right of this command, two companies of which changed front to oppose him, fell mortally wounded. A number of Confederate flags were picked up on this front after the battle.

On this spot fell our commander, Col. Dennis O'Kane. His true glory was either victory or death. At the moment of achieving the former, he fell victim to the latter. While rallying the right to repulse Armistead, the Lt. Col. Martin Tschauny, was killed. He was also wounded on the previous day, but refused to leave the field. The Major and the Adjutant were also wounded.

Erected by the surviving members and their friends in the Commonwealth of Pennsylvania.
Out of an aggregate strength of 258, the Regiment suffered a loss of 137.

106ᵗʰ PA*
2-2-2

Lt. Col. William L. Curry

7-2: In the evening, the Regiment assisted in repulsing a charge of the enemy on this line and made a counter-charge to the Emmitsburg Road, in which three guns of Battery B-1st RI were recovered and at the Cadori House, captured 250 prisoners. In the evening the Regiment moved to East Cemetary Hill to reinforce the 11th Corps.

7-3: Remained on East Cemetary Hill as indicated by monument. Companies A and B continued here and assisted in repulsing the final assault of the enemy in the afternoon.

Casualties: Killed 12, Wounded 51, 1 Missing; Total 64 of 335 present.

Webb
Statue

Alexander Stuart Webb, Brevet Major General. USA, 1835-1911.
Commanded 69th, 71st, 72nd and 106th Pa Infantry (Philadelphia Brigade) which resisted Longstreet's Assault of July 3, 1863.
Cadet USMA, 7/1/1851, Brevet 2nd Lt. 4th US Artillery, 7/1/55, 2nd Lt. 2nd Artillery, 10/20/55,
1st Lt., 4/28/61, Capt. 11th Infantry, 5/14/61, Lt. Col. 44th Infantry, 7/28/66, 5th Infantry, 3/15/69.
Honorably Discharged at his own request, 12/5/70.
Major 1st RI Light Artillery, 9/14/61, Lt. Col. and Assistant Inspector General (by assignment) 8/20/62 to 7/28/63.
Brig. Gen. USV, 6/23/63, Honorably Mustered Out of Volunteer Service, 1/15/66. In command of 2nd Division, 2nd Corps Rapidan Campaign and 1st Brigade, 2nd Division, 2nd Corps in the Wilderness. Severely wounded at Spotsylvania, 5/12/64. Chief of Staff Army of the Potomac, 1/11/65 to 6/28/65.
Assistant Inspector General - Division of the Atlantic, 7/1/65 to 2/28/66.
Awarded Congressional Medal of Honor for distinguished personal gallantry at the Battle of Gettysburg where he was wounded. Brevetted Major USA "For gallant and meritorious services at the Battle of Bristoe Station, VA.; Col. 5/12/64 "For gallant and meritorious services at the Battle of Spotsylvania; " Brig. Gen. 3/13/65 "For gallant and meritorious services in the campaign terminating with the insurgent army under Robert E. Lee." Major General 3/13/65 "For gallant and meritorious services during the war." Brevetted Maj. Gen., USV 8/1/64 "For gallant and distinguished conduct at the Battle of Gettysburg, PA, Brustoe Station, the Wilderness and Spotsylvania, VA."

*see index

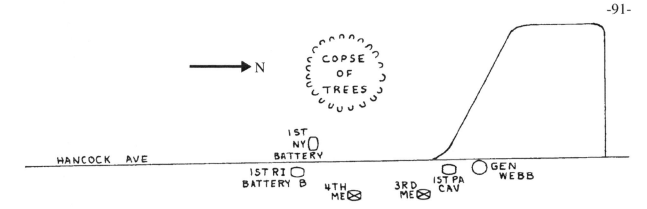

1st PA   Col. John P. Taylor

Cavalary   7-3: At the opening of the artillery fire on the afternoon of July 3rd, the Regiment was in line to the left and

C-2-1   rear of this position with orders from General Meade to "Charge the assault column should it succeed in breaking the infantry line in front."

          Casualties: None of 418 present.

3rd Maine*   Col. Moses B. Lakeman

2-1-3   7-2: Engaged in the Peach Orchard.

          7-3: In support.

          Casualties: Killed 18, Wounded 59, Missing 45; Total 122

4th Maine*   Col. Elijah Walker, Capt. Edwin Libby

2-1-3   7-2: Engaged at Devil's Den. Col. Elijah Walker in command wounded.

          7-3: In support here. Capt. Edwin Libby in command.

          Casualties: Killed 11, Wounded 59, Missing 74; Total 144 (NY@Gbg)

1st RI Lt   Lt. Fred Brown

Battery B   Brown's Battery B, 1st Rhode Island Light Artillery.

2nd Corps   Four - 12 Pounders

Artillery   Casualties: Killed 7, Wounded 19; 2 Missing; Total 28 (NY@Gbg)

Brigade

1st NY   Capt. Andrew Cowan

Battery   7-3: During the cannonade preceding Longstreet's Assault, the Battery was engaged a short distance farther

6th Corps   to the left, but by order of General Webb, it moved at a gallop to this position which Battery B-1st RI

Artillery   had occupied. Skirmishing had just commenced. The Confederate lines were advancing and continued

Brigade   their charge in the most splendid manner up to our position. The artillery fire was continuous and did much execution. Our last charge, double cannister, was fired within 10 yards of their guns.

          7-5: The Battery was relieved in the morning and returned to the 6th Corps.

          Casualties: Killed 4, Wounded 8; Total 12.

*see index

THE HIGH WATER MARK MONUMENT AT THE COPSE OF TREES

COMMANDS HONORED

In recognition of the patriotism and gallantry displayed
by their respective troops who met or assisted to repulse

LONGSTREET'S ASSAULT

The following States have contributed to erect this tablet:
Maine, New Hampshire, Vermont, Massachusetts, Rhode Island,
Connecticut, New York, New Jersey, Delaware, Pennsylvania,
West Virginia, Ohio, Michigan and Minnesota.

INFANTRY COMMANDS WHICH MET LONGSTREET'S ASSAULT

SECOND CORPS (HANCOCK'S), SECOND DIVISION (GIBBON'S)

The First Brigade (Harrow's) was composed of the
19th Me, 15th Mass, 1st Minn. and 82nd NY Regiments
Second Brigade (Webb's); 69th, 71st, 72nd and 106th Pa
Third Brigade (Hall's); 19th & 20th Mass, 42nd & 59th NY and 7th Mich.

UNITED STATES SHARPSHOOTERS

1st Regiment; Cos. A, B, D, H, NY; C, I, K, Mich.; E, NH; F, VT; G, WIS.
2nd Regiment; Cos A, MINN.; B, MICH.; C, Pa; D, ME; E, H, VT; F, G, NH.

THIRD DIVISION (HAYS) First Brigade (Carroll's) 8th Ohio.
2nd Brigade (Smyth), 14th Conn., 2nd Del, 12th NJ, 108 & 10th NY Bn.
Third Brigade (Willard's), 39th, 111th, 125th & 126th NY

FIRST ARMY CORPS (NEWTON'S) THIRD DIVISION (DOUBLEDAY'S)

First Brigade (Rowley's), 80th NY & 151st Pa
Third Brigade (Stannard's), 13th, 14th & 16th VT.

Assisted by the Artillery, the 1st Pa Cavalry
and Companies D & K, 6th NY Cavalry

INFANTRY COMMANDS IN LONGSTREET'S CHARGING COLUMN'S

HETH'S DIVISION
ARCHER'S TENNESSEE BRIGADE

13th Ala, 5th Ala Bn, 1st, 7th, 14th Regiments

DAVIS'S MISSISSIPPI BRIGADE

2nd, 11th, 42nd Miss & 55th NC Regiments

PETTIGREW'S NORTH CAROLINA BRIGADE

11th, 26th, 44th & 52nd North Carolina Regiments

BROCKENBROUGH'S VIRGINIA BRIGADE

40th, 47th, 55th Virginia Regts., 22nd Virginia Bn.

PICKETT'S DIVISION

KEMPER'S VIRGINIA BRIGADE
1st, 3rd, 7th, 11th, 24th Va. Regts.
GARNETT'S VIRGINIA BRIGADE
8th, 18th, 19th, 28th, 56th Va. Regts.
ARMISTEAD'S VIRGINIA BRIGADE
9th, 14th, 38th, 53rd, 57th Va. Regts.

PENDER'S DIVISION

LANE'S NORTH CAROLINA BRIGADE
7th, 18th, 28th, 33rd & 37th Regts.
SCALES' BRIGADE
13th, 16th, 22nd, 34th, 38th Regts.

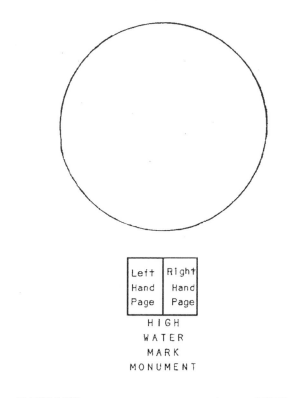

N

Left Hand Page | Right Hand Page

HIGH
WATER
MARK
MONUMENT

HANCOCK   AVENUE

GETTYSBURG BATTLEFIELD MEMORIAL ASSOCIATION
Organized April 30, 1984

Directors 1895

Gov. Daniel H. Hastings	Col. Chas. H. Buehler	Calvin Hamilton	J. Lawrence Schick
John B. Batchelder	Bvt. MG Geo. S. Greene	Capt. H. W. McKnight	John M. Vanderslice
Col. George E. Briggs	Lt. C. E. Goldsborough	MG Daniel E. Sickles	Bvt. MG Lewis Wagner
Bvt. MG Joseph B. Carr	Bvt. Maj. Chill W. Hazard	MG Henry W. Slocum	Bvt. MG Alex S. Webb
MG S.W. Crawford	Jacob A. Kitzmiller	Capt. Frank D. Sloat	Bvt. Lt. Col. Charles Young
BG Lucius W. Fairchild	John C. Linehan	Samuel McC. Swope	Bvt. Lt. Col. John P. Nicholson
Bvt. MG D. McM. Gregg	Capt. Edward McPherson	Col. Wheelock C. Veazey	

HIGH WATER MARK OF THE REBELLION

REPULSE OF
LONGSTREET'S ASSAULT

LONGSTREET'S ASSAULT
WAS REPULSED BY
Webb's, Hall's and Harrow's Brigades of
GIBBON'S DIVISION, SECOND ARMY CORPS

Smyth's and Willard's Brigades and
Portions of Carroll's Brigade of
HAYS' DIVISION, SECOND ARMY CORPS
and the First Massachusetts Sharpshooters
(unattached)

Portions of Rowley's and Stannard's Brigades of
DOUBLEDAY'S DIVISION, FIRST ARMY CORPS

HAZARD'S 2ND CORPS ARTILLERY BRIGADE
Consisting of
Woodruff's, Arnold's, Cushing's, Brown's and Rorty's Batteries

And on the Left by
Cowan's, Fitzhugh's, Parson's, Wheeler's, Thomas's,
Daniel's & Sterling's Batteries and

McGILVERY'S ARTILLERY BRIGADE
Consisting of
Thompson's, Phillip's, Hart's, Cooper's, Dowe's and Ames'
Batteries

and by Hazlitt's Battery on Little Round Top

and Supported by
DOUBLEDAY'S DIVISION, FIRST ARMY CORPS
Which was in Position
on the Immediate Left of the Troops Assaulted

THE THIRD ARMY CORPS
Moved Up to Within Supporting Distance on the Left and

ROBINSON'S DIVISION OF THE FIRST ARMY CORPS
Moved into Position to Support the Right

(Note: The above inscription takes up the entire right hand page of the bronze replica of an open book which is
mounted on the base of the High Water Mark Monument at the Copse of Trees. See Page 95 for the left hand page.)

HIGH WATER MARK OF THE REBELLION

This Copse of Trees was the Landmark
Toward Which Longstreet's Assault was Directed
JULY 3, 1863

The Assaulting Column
Was Composed Of

Kemper's, Garnett's and Armistead's Brigades of
PICKETT'S DIVISION
Archer's, Davis's, Pettigrew's and Brockenbrough's Brigades of
HETH'S DIVISION
And Scales's and Lane's Brigades of
PENDER'S DIVISION
Supported on the Right by Wilcox's and Perry's Brigades of
ANDERSON'S DIVISION
on the Left by Thomas's and McGowan's Brigades of
PENDER'S DIVISION
and in the Rear by Wright's, Posey's and Mahone's Brigades of
ANDERSON'S DIVISION
and Assisted by the Following Artillery
CABELL'S BATTALION
Consisting of
Manly's, Fraser's, McCarthy's and Carlton's Batteries
ALEXANDER'S BATTALION
Woolfolk's, Jordan's, Gilbert's, Moody's, Parker's and Taylor's Batteries
ESHLEMAN'S BATTALION
Squire's, Richardson's, Miller's and Norcom's Batteries
DEARING'S BATTALION
Stribling's, Caskie's, Macon's and Blount's Batteries
CUTTS' BATTALION
Ross's, Patterson's and Wingfield's Batteries
POAGUE'S BATTALION
Wyatt's, Graham's, Ward's and Brooke's Batteries
PEGRAM'S BATTALION
McGraw's, Zimmerman's, Brander's, Marye's and Crenshaw's Batteries
McINTOSH'S BATTALION
Rice's, Hurt's, Wallace's and Johnson's Batteries
CARTER'S BATTALION
Reese's, Carter's, Page's and Fry's Batteries
BROWN'S BATTALION
Watson's, Smith's, Cunningham's and Griffin's Batteries

DESIGNED AND ERECTED UNDER THE DIRECTION
OF JOHN B. BATCHELDER

CAST BY THE HENRY-BONNARD
BRONZE CO., NEW YORK 1891

(Note: The above inscription takes up the entire left hand page of the bronze replica of an open book which is mounted on the base of the High Water Mark Monument at the Copse of Trees. See Page 94 for the right hand page.)

THE SYMBOLS LISTED BELOW ARE USED TO IDENTIFY THE MONUMENTS, MARKERS, TABLETS, STATUES, ETC. WHICH ARE DRAWN ON THE MAPS IN THESE PAGES

SYMBOL	TYPE	REPRESENTING	DESCRIPTION
	Bronze Tablet	Army of The Potomac, Union Corps or Division or Brigade, Regular Army Regiment, Regular Army Artillery Battery, Volunteer Artillery Brigade.	Brigade Tablet Mounted on Square Marble base. All other Tablets are on large vertical Granite Blocks.
	Bronze Tablet	Army of Northern Virginia, Confederate Corps or Division or Brigade or Artillery Battalion	Brigade Tablet and Artillery Battalion Tablet Mounted on Round Marble base. All other Tablets are Mounted on large vertical Granite blocks.
	Iron Tablet	Union Army Battery (other than Regular Army)	Mounted on Black Iron Shaft.
	Iron Tablet	Confederate Artillery Battery	Mounted on Black Iron Shaft.
	Iron Tablet	Confederate Brigade Advanced Position	Mounted on Black Iron Shaft.
	Regimental or Battery Monument	Principal Position of Volunteer Regiment or Volunteer Artillery Battery	Usually Granite or Marble in a Great Variety of Shapes and Sizes.
	Regimental Marker	Other than Principal Position of Regiment or Battery	Usually a Square Granite Marker or tablet or may be another monument.
	Flank Marker or Company Marker	Left and/or Right Flank of Regiment or Battery or Position of a Company.	Usually a Small Square or Rectangular Granite Marker.
	Army Or Corps Headquarters	Site of Headquarters of Army Commander or Corps Commander or Chief of Artillery	Cannon Barrel Mounted Vertically on Stone, Granite or Marble Base.
	State Monument	Monument Erected by Union or Confederate State.	
	Statue	Standing or Equestrian	Bronze Sculpture
	Building	House, Barn or other Structure	Identified by Owner's Name.
	Miscellaneous Marker	Marker or Inscription of a type not listed above	Granite or Metal Marker.
*	Asterisk	Used whenever a Division or Brigade or Regiment or Battery has more than one Monument or Marker.	Check the Index for other Monument or Marker.

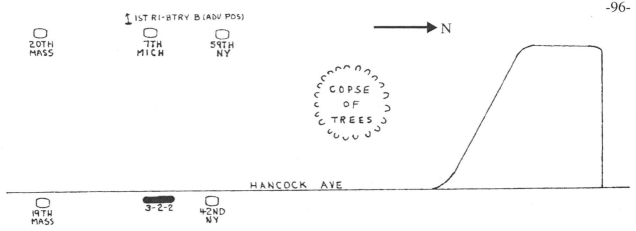

3-2-2   Col. Norman J. Hall
             19th, 20th Mass, 7th Mich, 42nd, 59th NY Infantry
             <u>7-2</u>: Took position on line at left of 2nd Brigade and the Copse of Trees. The 19th Mass and 42nd NY late in the day advanced to support 2nd Division, 3rd Corps but retired on 2nd Division being forced back. The Brigade was attacked by Brig. Gen. Wright's Georgia Brigade which overran Battery B-lst RI, then in advance, but was repulsed with a heavy loss and forced beyond the Emmitsburg Road.
             <u>7-3</u>: Remained in position. At 3PM, Longstreet's Assault was made after a cannonade of two hours. The Brigade and 2nd Brigade received the charge of Major General Pickett' s Division, which was repulsed with great loss in killed, wounded, prisoners and flags. In this engagement the 1st Brigade and the other troops were rushed to the support of the two Brigades engaged and contributed to the victory. The Brigade remained in this position until the close of battle.
             Casualties: Killed 81, Wounded 282, Missing 14; Total 377

42nd NY   The Tammany Regiment, Capt. James E. Mallon
3-2-2   <u>7-2</u>: Went to support of 3rd Corps about 5 PM.
             <u>7-3</u>: Held this position and assisted in repulse of Pickett's Division.
             Casualties: 15 Killed, 55 Wounded, 4 Missing; Total 74.

19th MA   Col. Arthur F. Devereaux
3-2-2   <u>7-3</u>: The l9th Regiment Massachusetts Volunteer Infantry of the 3rd Brigade, 2nd Division, 2nd Army Corps stood here in the afternoon of July 3, 1863.
             Casualties: Killed 9, Wounded 61, Missing7; Total 77

59th NY   Lt. Col. Max Thoman, Capt. William McFadden
3-2-2   <u>7-2&3</u>: Four companies of this Regiment held this position where Max A. Thoman, Lt. Col. in command fell mortally wounded.
             Casualties: Killed 6, Wounded 28; Total 34 (NY@Gbg)

7th Mich   Lt. Col. Amos E. Steel, Jr., Maj. Sylvanus W. Curtis
3-2-2   The Regiment held this position during the engagement of July 2 and 3.
             <u>7-2</u>: In evening changed front to the left, meeting and aiding in driving back the enemy.
             <u>7-2</u>: Assisted in repulsing Pickett's Charge, changing front to the right and assaulting the advancing force in flank.
             Casaulties: Killed 21, Wounded 44; Total 65 of 165 Present for duty.

20th Ma   Col. Paul J. Revere, Lt. Col. George N. Macy, Capt. Henery L. Abbott
3-2-2   This monument marks the position occupied by the 20th Massachusetts Infantry in line of battle, July 2nd and 3rd until advanced to the front of the Copse of Trees on its immediate right to assist in repelling the charge of Longstreet's Corps.
             Casaulties: Killed 30, Wounded 94, Missing 3; Total 127

1st RI   Battery B, 1st Rhode Island
Battery B

UNITED STATES REGULARS MONUMENT

Front Side
(East)

ERECTED BY THE CONGRESS

to commemorate the services
of that portion of the

ARMY OF THE POTOMAC
composed of
Cavalry Artillery Infantry and Engineers
of the Regular Army of the United States
In the Gettysburg Campaign June-July 1863

Rear Side
(West)

UNITED STATES ARMY

The Artillery Consisting of 26 Batteries Was Distributed Over The Field
Among The Several Army Corps And Placed In Position Where Their
Services Were Most Needed

Brig. General Henry J. Hunt   Chief of Artillery

Four Regiments of Cavalry under Brig. General Wesley Merritt Took
Position On The Right Flank Of The Confederate Line Of Battle

Eleven Regiments of Infantry Were On The Field Ten With The Second Division
Fifth Corps And One At Headquarters Army of The Potomac

Battalion of U.S. Engineers
Capt. George H. Mendell, Commanding

Casualties Killed 12 Officers & 159 Enlisted Men Killed
Wounded 62 Officers & 861 Enlisted Men
Missing 6 Officers and 275 Enlisted Men

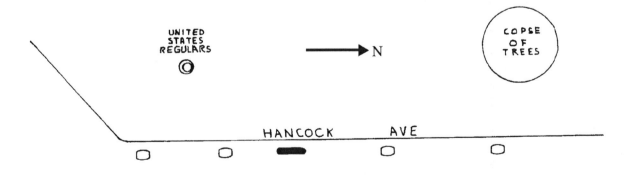

~ Gettysburg Battlefield Monuments, Locations & Inscriptions ~

UNITED STATES REGULARS MONUMENT (con't)

Right Side
(North)

UNITED STATES ARTILLERY

Batteries	E & G	1st Regiment	Captain Alanson M. Randall
Battery	H	1st Regiment	Lieut. Chandler P. Eakin
Battery	I	1st Regiment	Lieut. George A. Woodruff
Battery	K	1st Regiment	Captain William M. Graham
Battery	A	2nd Regiment	Lieut. John H. Calef
Batteries	B & L	2nd Regiment	Lieut. Edward Heaton
Battery	D	2nd Regiment	Lieut. Edward B. Williston
Battery	G	2nd Regiment	Lieut. John H. Butler
Battery	M	2nd Regiment	Lieut. A. C. M. Pennington, Jr.
Battery	C	3rd Regiment	Lieut. William D. Fuller
Batteries	F & K	3rd Regiment	Lieut. John C. Turnbull
Battery	A	4th Regiment	Lieut. Alonzo H. Cushing
Battery	B	4th Regiment	Lieut. James Stewart
Battery	C	4th Regiment	Lieut. Evan Thomas
Battery	E	4th Regiment	Lieut. Samuel S. Elder
Battery	F	4th Regiment	Lieut. Sylvanus T. Rugg
Battery	G	4th Regiment	Lieut. Bayard Wilkeson, Lieut. Eugene A. Bancroft
Battery	K	4th Regiment	Lieut. Francis W. Seeley, Lieut. Robert James
Battery	C	5th Regiment	Lieut. Guilian V. Weir
Battery	D	5th Regiment	Lieut. Charles E. Hazlett, Lieut. B. F. Rittenhouse
Battery	F	5th Regiment	Lieut. Leonard Martin
Battery	I	5th Regiment	Lieut. Malbone F Watson, Lieut. C. C. McConnell
Battery	K	5th Regiment	Lieut. David H. Kinzie

continued on page 99

UNITED STATES REGULARS MONUMENT (con't)

Left Side
(South)

UNITED STATES CAVALRY

Reserve Brigade Brig. General Wesley Merritt

1st Regiment	Captain Richard S. C. Lord, Commanding
2nd Regiment	Captain Theophilus F. Rodenbough, Commanding
3rd Regiment	Captain Julius W. Mason, Commanding
6th Regiment	Major Samuel S. Starr, Lieut. Lewis H. Carpenter
	Lieut. Nicholas Nolan, Captain Ira W. Claflin, Commanding

UNITED STATES INFANTRY

Fifth Army Corps Second Division
Brig. General Romeyn B. Ayres, Commanding

1st Brigade Colonel Hannibal Day

3rd Regiment	Captain Henry W. Freedley, Capt. Richard G. Lay, Commanding
4th Regiment	Captain Julius Adams Jr., Commanding
6th Regiment	Captain Levi C. Bootes, Commanding
12th Regiment	Captain Thomas S. Dunn, Commanding
14th Regiment	Major Grotius R. Giddings, Commanding

2nd Brigade Colonel Sidney Burbank

2nd Regiment	Major Arthur T. Lee, Commanding
7th Regiment	Captain David P. Hancock, Commanding
10th Regiment	Captain William Clinton, Commanding
11th Regiment	Major DeLancey Floyd Jones, Commanding
17th Regiment	Lieut. Col. J. Durell Greene, Commanding
8th Regiment	Captain W. H. Read, at Army of the Potomac Headquarters

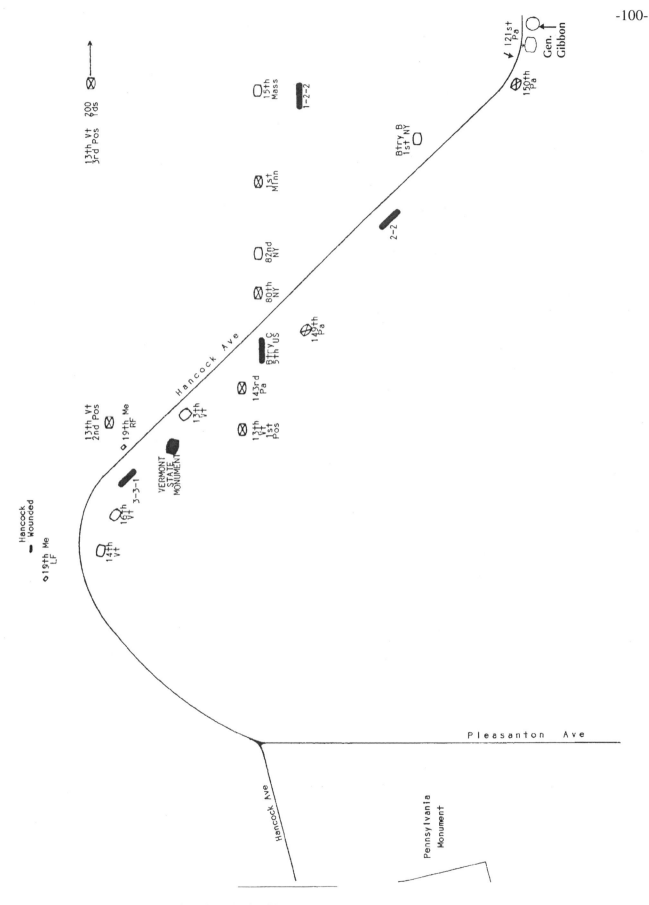

~ Gettysburg Battlefield Monuments, Locations & Inscriptions ~

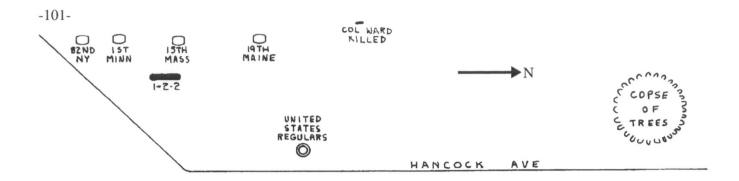

1-2-2   Brig. Gen. William Harrow, Col. Francis Heath
19th Maine, 15th Mass, 1st Minn, 82nd NY Infantry
Early in the morning took position in the rear of 2nd and 3rd Brigades. 15th Mass and 82nd NY were advanced to the Emmitsburg Road on the right of Cadori House to support 3rd Corps. The other two Regiments were moved to the left on a line with the 3rd Brigade. The 3rd Corps having been forced back, the advanced 15th Mass and 82nd NY were compelled to retire to the main line by Brig. Gen. Wright's Brigade which captured several pieces of artillery but supports coming quickly to the Union line, they forced the Confederates back across Emmitsburg Road with heavy loss and retook the captured artillery. Col. Ward, 15th Mass. and Col. Huston, 82nd NY were mortally wounded.

> 7-3:   At 1 PM a terrific cannonade was opened along the Confederate line in front which continued for about two hours, followed by a charge of over 15,000 infantry, its right striking 2nd and 3rd Brigades. This Brigade moved at once to the right and assisted the other two Brigades in repelling the assault and capturing a large number of prisoners and several flags.

Casualties: Killed 147 Wounded 573, Missing 48; total 768.

19th Maine*   Col. Francis Heath, Lt. Col. Henry W. Cunningham
1-2-2
> 7-2:   In the evening this Regiment, at a position on the left of Battery G-5th US, helped to repel the enemy that had driven in Humphrey's Division, taking 1 battle flag and recapturing four guns.
> 7-3:   After engaging the enemy's advance from this position, it moved to the right to the support of the 2nd Brigade and joined in the final charge and repulse of Pickett's Command.

Casualties: Killed 65, Wounded 137, Missing 4; Total 206 Of 405

15th Mass*   Col. George H. Ward, Lt. Col. George C. Joslin
1-2-2
> 7-3: Position held
Casualties: Killed 23, Wounded 97, Missing 28; Total 148.
> 7-2:   George H. Ward, Commanding 15th Regiment Massachusetts Volunteers here fell mortally wounded. His comrades and fellow citizens of Worcester raised this memorial of his valor and patriotism.

1st Minn*   Col. William Colville Jr., Capt. Nathan S. Messick, Captain Henry C. Coates
1-2-2
> 7-3:   The survivors of the Regiment aided here in repelling Pickett's charge and ran hence to the aid of Webb's Brigade, taking a conspicuous part in the countercharge which successfully ended the conflict, losing there 17 additional killed and wounded and capturing a Confederate flag. There Captains Nathan Messick and William Farrell successfully commanding the Regiment, were killed. Total killed and wounded in the battle 232 of 330 engaged.

82nd NY   Lt. Col. James Huston, Capt. John Darrow
1-2-2
> 7-2:   In the evening moved to the Emmitsburg Road to protect flank of 3rd Corps. Fought here until outflanked. Returning to this line, the Regiment reformed under a galling fire, then advanced, driving the enemy before them. Regained their former position, capturing the colors of the 48th Georgia. Among the killed was Colonel Huston, commanding the Regiment.
> 7-3:   At the time of the enemy's assault in the afternoon, the Regiment moved to the right toard the Copse of Trees and assisted in repulsing the enemy, capturing the falgs of the 1st and 7th Virginia Regiments.

Casualities: Killed 45, Wounded 132, Missing 15; Total 192

*see index

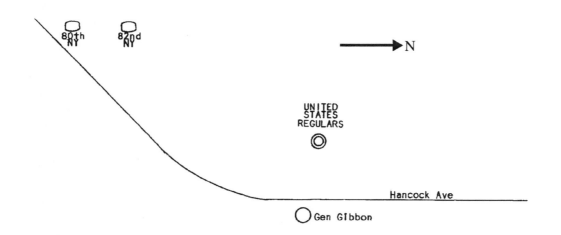

80th NY*   Col. Theodore B. Gates
1-3-1   7-3: From a position south of this point, the New York State Militia delivered a most destructive fire into the
                     attacking Southerners right flank. As the enemy infantry moved obliquely to the left, the New York Regi-
                     ment advanced north along the line, firing as they moved to the right. Occupying a new position near the
                     Copse of Trees, the Ulster Guard fought to repel Longstreet's Assault, finally charging a group of Confed-
                     erates, driving them from the shelter of the slashing. Capt. Ambrose M. Baldwin was mortally wounded in
                     the final action near the Copse of Trees. Major W. A. Van Rensselaer was wounded near the slashing.
               Casualties: Killed 35, Wounded 111, Missing 324; Total 170 (NY@Gbg.)

General   **JOHN GIBBON**
Gibbon   Brigadier General
                                                   July 2-3, 1863

At Gettysburg commanded 2nd Division, 2nd Corps on July 3, 1863, serving with "conspicuous gallantry and
distinction" in the repulse of Longstreet's Assault, until he was wounded and carried from the battlefields.

At the beginning of the Civil War, John Gibbon was a Captain in the 4th Artillery serving in the Utah Territory.
Assigned as Chief of Artillery in McDowwell's Division, he participated in the advance on Fredericksburg
during the Peninsula Campaign. He was promoted to Brigadier General, May 2, 1862, thereafter taking command of the Iron Brigade which participated in the Battles of Second Bull Run South Mountain and Antietam. In
November, 1862 he became commander of the 2nd Division, 1st Corps. He was wounded in the left arm and
shoulder at the Battle of Gettysburg. In charge of draft depots in Cleveland and Philadelphia until March 1864,
he returned to 2nd Division, 2nd Corps participating in the Battle of The Wilderness, SPotsylvania, Cold Harbor
and the investment to Petersberg. Gibbon was promoted to Major General effective June 2, 1864. He was in
temporary command of the 18th Corps before being placed in command of the 24th Corps, Army of James in
January 1865. General Gibbon was in charge of the surrender of the Army of Northern Virginia at Appomattox,
April 1865.
                     "He has a Keen Eye, and is Bold as a Lion..."

                                                  GIBBON
                                                  1827-1896
John Gibbon was born April 20, 1827 in the Holmseburg section of Philadelphia, Pa. At the age of 10 he moved
with his family to North Carolina where he remained until he entered the United States Military Academy at
West Point. Gibbon graduated from the Academy in 1847, 20th in a class of 38 becoming an artillery officer. He
served in the Mexican War fighting in Mexico City and Toluca. After serving in the Seminole War he spent five
years as an instructor then quartermaster at the Military Academy. Gibbon authored *The Artillerist Manual*,
which was published by the War Department in 1860. After the Civil War he was appointed Colonel of the 36th
Infantry and then in 1869 the 7th U.S. Infantry. Commanding several posts in the west, much of Gibbon's duties
were against the Indians. His troops took part in the 1876 campaign in which Custer was defeated at the Little

*see index

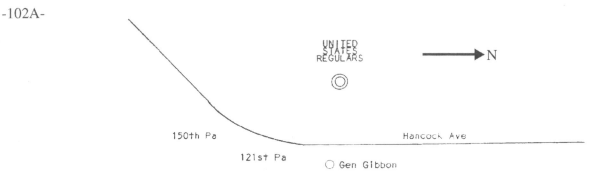

General Gibbon (con't)   Big Horn. Gibbon's troops arrived on the field in time to rescue the survivors and bury the dead. In 1877 he took part in the campaign against the Nez Perces during which he was seriously wounded. On July 10, 1885, Gibbon was promoted to Brigadier General in the Regular Army. He transferred to the Department of Columbia in 1885, then served in the Department of the Pacific until his retirement. General Gibbon retired in 1891, thereafter residing in Baltimore, Maryland. He served as Commander-in-Chief of the Military Order Of The Loyal Legion Of The United States 1895-1896. General Gibbon died on February 6, 1896 and is buried in Arlington National Cemetery.

121st PA*
1-3-1
Major Alexander Biddle, Col. Chapman Biddle
7-1: Extreme left of Union line facing west First Day.
7-2&3: Occupied Cemetary Ridge.
Erected By The Survivors Of This Regiment In Memory of Their Fallen Comrades
Casualties: Killed 12, Wounded 106, Missing 61; Total 179 of 265.

150th PA*
2-3-1
Col. Langhorne Wister, Lt. Col. H. S. Huidekoper, Capt. C. C. Widdis
7-1: This Regiment fought near the Chambersburg Pike beyond the town where its monument stands, losing 264 of 397 engaged.
7-2: In the evening skirmished to the Emmitsburg Road in front of this position, recovering two guns. Remained on the skirmish line until morning.
7-3: Held this position under fire until the close of the battle.
(Note: See other monument inscription for details of casualties.)

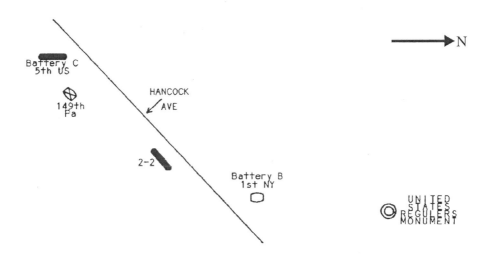

Battery B*
1st NY Lt.
2nd Corps
Artillery
Brigade

Lt. Albert S. Sheldon, Capt James McK Rorty, Lt. Robert E. Rogers
Four 10 Pounder Parrotts
<u>7-3</u>:   Position held in the afternoon.
Casualties: Killed 10, Wounded 16; Total 26

2-2
2nd Division
2nd Corps

Brig. Gen. John Gibbon, Brig. Gen. William Harrow
   1st Brigade   Brig. Gen. William Harrow, Col. Francis Heath
   2nd Brigade   Brig. Gen. Alexander S. Webb
   3rd Brigade   Brig. Gen. Norman J. Hall
One Company of Massachusetts Sharpshooters
<u>7-2</u>:   Arrived between 6 and 7 AM and went into position between Cemetary Hill and Round Top, 3rd Division
          on right and 1st Division on left; 2nd Brigade constituting the right, 3rd Brigade on the left and 1st Brigade
          in reserve. Sharp skirmishing continued through the day and artillery fire at intervals until near sunset,
          when the 3rd Corps having been driven back. Wright's Georgia Brigade furiously attacked the Division
          and was repulsed with loss including many prisoners, the 12th Corps coming to the support of the left.
<u>7-3</u>:   Artillery firing until 9 AM, sharp skirmishing during the day. At 1 PM the Confederates concentrated fire
          of over 100 guns on the 2nd and 3rd Divisions and after two hours of uninterrupted firing, a force of over
          15,000 infantry charged and was repulsed with great loss of life, prisoners and flags. The Division re-
          mained in position with no further engagement than skirmish firing.
Casualties: Killed 344, Wounded 1202, Missing 10l: Total 1647

149th PA*
2-3-1

Lt. Col. Walter Dwight, Capt. James Glenn
July 3, 1863
Casualties: Killed 53, Wounded 172, Missing 111; Total 336

Battery C
5th US
1st Regular
Brigade
Artillery
Reserve

Lt. Gulian V. Weir
<u>7-2</u>:   Arrived at Gettysburg from near Taneytown and in the afternoon was ordered to the front and by direction
          of Major General W. S. Hancock, took position 500 yards further to the front and by order of Brig. Gen.
          John Gibbon opened fire on the Confederates on the left front. The Confederates advanced to within a few
          yards, no infantry opposing. Three of the guns were captured by the Confederates and drawn off to the
          Emmitsburg Road but were recaptured by the 13th Vermont and another regiment.
<u>7-3</u>:   In the rear of the line until Longstreet's Assault was made when the Battery was moved up to Brig. Gen.
          Webb's line and opned with cannister at short range on the advancing Confederates. At 6:30 PM, returned
          to the Artillery Reserve.
Casualties: Killed 2, Wounded 14; Total 16

*see index

~ Gettysburg Battlefield Monuments, Locations & Inscriptions ~

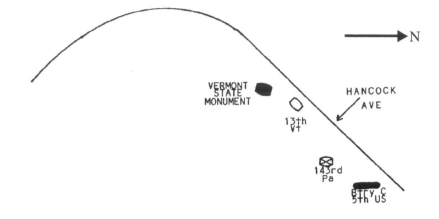

Battery B*
1st NY Lt.
2nd Corps
  Artillery
  Brigade

Col. Edmund L Dana, Lt. Col. John D. Musser

7-2&3: Held this position and assisted in the repulse of the enemy on the 3rd. Lost here 16 Killed and Wounded.

7-1: Monument erected on the First Day's Field near Reynold's Grove where the Regiment lost 145 Killed & Wounded and 21 Missing out of 465 present for duty.

13th
Vermont*
3-3-1

ON THIS FIELD THE RIGHT REGIMENT OF STANNARD'S VERMONT BRIGADE
3rd Brigade, 3rd Division, 1st Corps

Col. Francis V. Randall, Maj. Joseph J. Boynton, Lt. Col. William D. Munson

7-2: Five Companies under Lt. Col. Munson supported the batteries on Cemetary Hill. Near evening, the other five Companies, commanded by Col. Francis V. Randall, charged to the Rogers House on the Emmitsburg Rd, captured 83 prisoners and recapturing four guns after which they took position here and were soon joined by the five Companies from Cemetary Hill.

7-3: In the morning 100 men advanced 45 yards under the fire of sharpshooters and placed a line of rail. When the Confederate column crossed the Emmitsburg Rd, the Regiment advanced to the rail breastworks and opened fire as the Confederates obliqued to their left. The Regiment changed front forward on 1st Company, advanced 200 yards attacking Confederate right flank, throwing it into confusion and capturing 243 prisoners.

The statue on the 13th Vermont monument represents Lt. Stephen F. Brown, Company K, who arrived on the field without a sword but seizing a camp hatchet, carried it in the battle until he captured a sword from a Confederate officer. Persevering and determined like him were all of the men of this Regiment of Green Mountain Boys. Prior to the Gettysburg campaign, the Vermont Brigade was chiefly picketing a line between Centerville and Occouquan, Virginia. 48 hours after the Army passed pursuing the enemy to this field, the Regiment was ordered to join the 1st Corps. Haste was so urgent that an order forbade leaving the ranks for water and after forced marches with all the attendant privations incident thereto, and lack of rations by reason of the Commissary Train being diverted, it arrived on the battlefield July 1st.

Casualties: Killed 22, Wounded 80; Total 102 of 402 engaged.

*see index

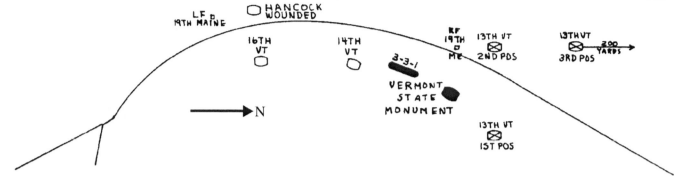

13th Vermont 3-3-1 1st Position   F. V. Randall, Colonel, Right of Stannard's Brigade
1st Position, 3rd Day, 2nd Position 45 yards in front

13th Vermont 3-3-1 2nd Position   13th Vermont, Right of Stannard's Brigade
2nd Position, 3rd Day
Next 200 yards to right.

13th Vermont 3-3-1 3rd Position   F. V. Randall, Colonel, Right of Stannard's Brigade
3rd Position, 3rd Day.
Struck Pickett's Flank here.
(Note: See page 86 map for 3rd position in front of 20th Mass.)

3-3-1   Brig. Gen. George J. Stannard, Col. Francis V. Randall
12th, 13th, 14th, 15th, 16th Vermont Infantry.
(12th and 15th Regiments were guarding Trains.)
7-1: Arrived at dusk took position on right of 3rd Corps.
7-2: Joined the Corps and went into position at the left of the cemetary. Just before dusk a detachment advanced to the Emmitsburg Road and captured about 80 prisoners and recovered four abandoned Union guns.
7-3: In position on left or 2nd Division, 2nd Corps at the time of Longstreet's Assault. The 13th and 16th advanced against Pickett's Division, changed front forward and attacked its right, throwing it into confusion and capturing many prisoners. The 16th and part of the 14th then went to the left and attacked the advancing Brigades of Brig. Gen. Wilcox and Perry (Lang) and captured three flags and many prisoners .
Casualties: Killed 45, Wounded 274, Missing 32: Total 351

16th Vermont 3-3-1   Col. Wheelock G. Veazey
7-2: Participated near this point in action of July 2nd. Picketed this line that night. Held same as skirmishers until attacked by Pickett's Division on July 3rd.
7-3: Rallied here and assaulted his flank to the right 400 yards, then changed front to the left, charged left flank of Wilcox and Perry's Brigades at this point. Captured many prisoners and two strands of colors. The point to which the above inscription refers is south 58 degrees, west 1000 feet from this monument and near the northerly end of the Cadori thicket.
Casualties: Killed 16, Wounded 102, Missing 1; Total 119

14th Vermont 3-3-1   Col. William T. Nichols
19 Killed and 76 Wounded

19th Maine 1-2-2   7-2: Left and right flank markers.

Hancock Wounded   July 2nd, 1863

*see index

West Side
(front)

VERMONT STATE MONUMENT

VERMONT IN HONOR OF HER SONS WHO FOUGHT HERE

North Side

FIRST VERMONT BRIGADE

Second, Third, Fourth, Fifth and Sixth Regiments
Brigadier General L. A. Grant, Commanding Second Brigade Second Division Sixth Corps

7-1: The Brigade reached the field near Little Round Top in the afternoon by a forced march of 32 miles and soon after was assigned to the left Union flank, where it held a line from the summit of Round Top to the Taneytown Road until the close of the battle.

East Side

SECOND VERMONT BRIGADE

Twelfth, Thirteenth, Fourteenth, Fifteenth and Sixteenth Regiments
Brigadier General George J. Stannard, Commanding
Third Brigade Third Division First Corps

7-1: The Brigade arrived on Cemetary Hill, The 12th and 15th Regiments were detached guarding the Corps trains.

7-2: About sunset, the 13th, 14th and 16th moved to this part of the field, retook Battery C-5th US and re-established the Union line.

7-3: These Regiments held the front line in advance of this spot in the crisis of the day. The 13th and 16th changed front and advancing 200 yards to the right, assaulted the flank of Pickett's Division. The 16th then moved back 400 yards to the left and charged the flank of Wilcox's and Perry's Brigades. The 14th supported these charges. The Brigade captured three flags and many prisoners.

South Side

FIRST VERMONT CAVALRY

Lieutenant Colonel Addison W. Preston, Commanding
First Brigade Third Division Cavalry Corps

6-30: This Regiment fought Stuart's Cavalry at Hanover.

7-2: Opposed Hampton's Cavalry at Hunterstown.

7-3: Charged through the 1st Texas Infantry and upon the line of Law's Brigade at the foot of Round top.

VERMONT SHARPSHOOTERS

Company F, 1st US Sharpshooters; Companies E&H, 2nd US Sharpshooters
Second Brigade First Division Third Corps

7-2: Company F aided in checking the advance of Wilcox's Brigade west of Seminary Ridge. Companies E&H resisted Law's Brigade west of Devil's Den and upon the Round Tops.

7-3: The three Companies took part in the repulse of Pickett's Charge.

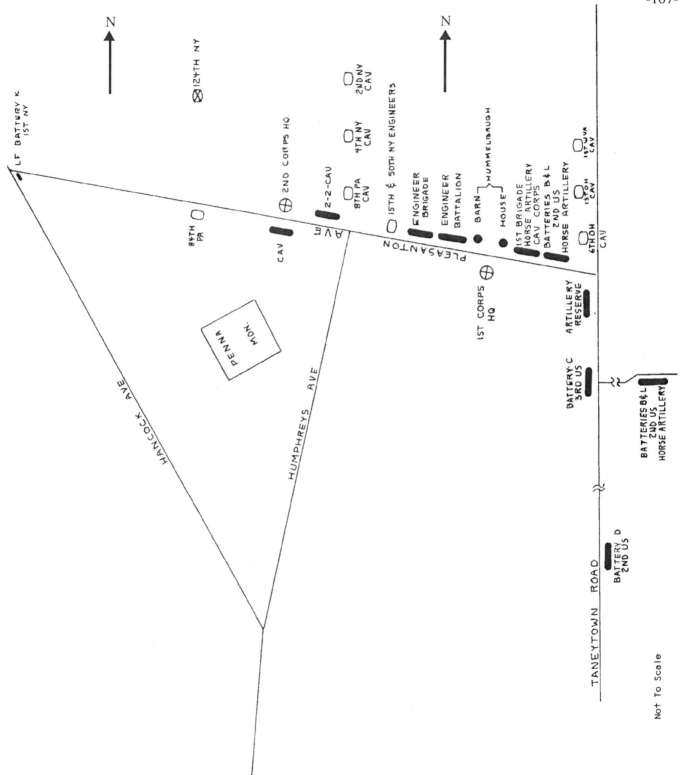

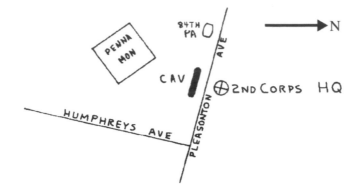

13th Vermont 3-3-1 2nd Position	Lt. Col. Hilton Opp

13th **Vermont** **3-3-1** **2nd Position** — Lt. Col. Hilton Opp

7-1: The Regiment was on duty guarding the Division wagon trains. Moved with the column from Taneytown to Emmitsburg and on the opening of the battle was ordered with the train to Westminster, Md.

7-2: It arrived at 7 AM and picketed the roads near the wagon parks until the close of the battle.

Cavalary Corps — Maj. Gen. Alfred E. Pleasanton

1st Division	Brig. Gen. John Buford
2nd Division	Brig. Gen. David McM Gregg
3rd Division	Brig. Gen. Judson Kilpatrick
Headquarters Guard	Co C 1st Ohio Capt. Samuel
Horse Artillery	1st Brigade Capt. James M. Robertson
2nd Brigade	Capt. John C. Tidball

6-29: Buford's Division advanced and extended its lines to left as far as Hagerstown to discover Confederate forces, if any, on left of the Army. Gregg's Division moved to right of the Army to Westminster, covering the country toward York and Carlisle by reconnaissance and patrols. Kilpatrick's Division advanced to Hanover

6-30: Gamble's and Devin's Brigades, Buford's Division, advanced to Gettysburg. Kilpatrick's Division encountered Stuart's Cavalry at Hanover. Two Brigades of Gregg's Division were ordered to Gettysburg. Huey's 3rd Brigade was left at Westminster.

7-1: Gamble's and Devin's Brigades encountered Heth's Division Hill's Corps on 2nd ridge west of Gettysburg. When 1st and 11th Corps retreated to Cemetary Hill, the Cavalry took position first on the left connecting with the town and later further to the left in front of Little Round Top.

7-2: On the arrival of the 3rd Corps, to Westminster, Kilpatrick's Division marched toward Gettysburg and was ordered to the right and was attacked at Hunterstown by a detachment of Stuart's Command which was repulsed.

7-3: Merrit's Brigade arrived and skirmished with the Confederate right while the 6th US advanced to Fairfield and became engaged. Kilpatrick with Farnsworth's Brigade took position on left of battle line and made a charge in the afternoon on the Confederate right but was repulsed with loss including Gen. Farnsworth killed. Gregg's Division on the right was attacked by Stuart's Cavalry in the afternoon but with the aid of Custer's Brigade of Kilpatrick's Division, the attack was repulsed.

Casualties: Killed 91, Wounded 354, Missing 407; Total 852

2nd Corps — Army of the Potomac, 2nd Corps Headquarters
Major General Winfield S. Hancock, July 1, 2, 3, 4, 1863

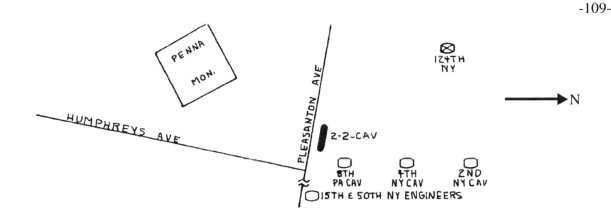

124th NY*   Col. A. Van Horne Ellis, Lt. Col. Francis M. Cummins
2-1-3   7-3:   Occupied this position during Pickett's Charge
              Casualties Killed 28, Wounded 57, Missing 57; Total 90

Cav-2-2   Col. Pennock Huey
              2nd, 4th NY, 6th Ohio, 8th Pa Cavalry
              6-30: Participated in the Gettysburg Campaign with the Division until it arrived at Hanover Jct., Pa, ordered the
                   Brigade to Manchester, Md. and all the roads were held by pickets until the afternoon of the 3rd.
              7-3:   Orders were received to go via Westminster to Emmitsburg to take possession of that place.
              7-4:   Moved to Westminster and received supplies and marched to Emmitsburg, arriving at noon. Pursuant to
                   orders, the Brigade joined 3rd Division, Cavalry Corps.

8th PA   Capt. William A. Corrie
 Cavalry   This Regiment, detached with the 2nd Corps, covered the rear of the Army on the march from Virginia. At
Cav-2-2   Frederick, rejoined the Cavalry Corps and with Gregg's Division moved in the advance to Gettysburg.
              7-1:   Moved hastily to Manchester to protect trains.
              7-4:   Joined in pursuit of the enemy, participating in the attack at Monterrey Pass and in the many other Cavalry
                   engagements until the enemy retreated into Virginia.

4th NY   Lt. Col. Augustus Pruyn
 Cavalry   6-30: This Regiment participated in the Gettysburg Campaign until reaching Hanover Jct., when with the Bri-
Cav-2-2   gade it was detached and moved to Manchester, where it picketed the surrounding country until July 3rd
                   when it proceeded to Westminster.
              7-4:   Joined Kilpatrick's Division in pursuit of the enemy, and with it participated at Monterey Pass that night,
                   and in the many other Cavalry engagements until the enemy recrossed the Potomac.

2nd NY   Lt. Col. Otto Harhaus
Cavalry   6-30: This Regiment was engaged in the battles and skirmishes of the Cavalry Corps until the Brigade reached
Cav-2-2   Hanover Jct. June 30th, when it was moved hastily to Manchester to guard trains against rumored move-
                   ments of the enemy, and picketed the surrounding country.
              7-4:   Joined 3rd Division in pursuit of the enemy and participated in the Cavalry engagements until the enemy
                   retreated to Virginia.

15th and 50th Headquarters, Army of the Potomac
NY
Engineers

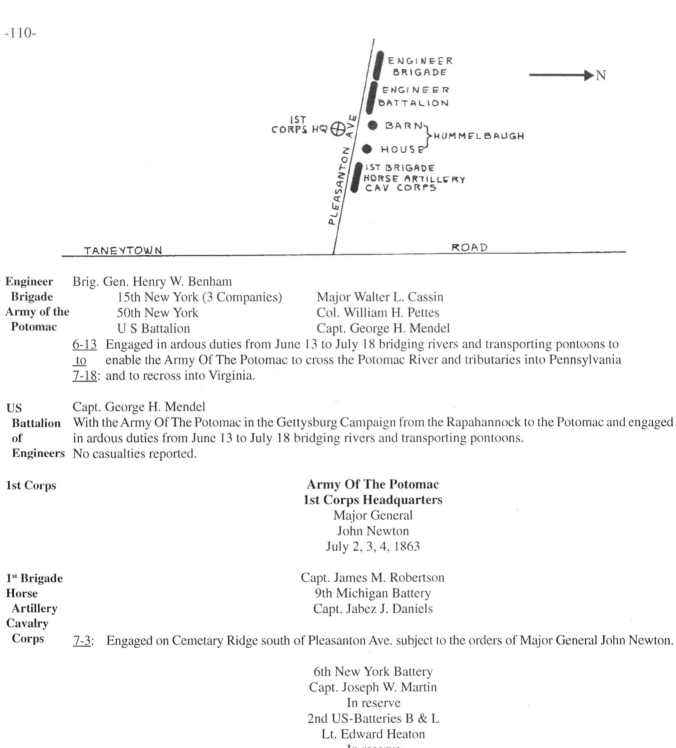

Engineer Brigade Army of the Potomac Brig. Gen. Henry W. Benham
        15th New York (3 Companies)   Major Walter L. Cassin
        50th New York   Col. William H. Pettes
        U S Battalion   Capt. George H. Mendel

6-13 to 7-18: Engaged in ardous duties from June 13 to July 18 bridging rivers and transporting pontoons to enable the Army Of The Potomac to cross the Potomac River and tributaries into Pennsylvania and to recross into Virginia.

US Battalion of Engineers Capt. George H. Mendel
With the Army Of The Potomac in the Gettysburg Campaign from the Rapahannock to the Potomac and engaged in ardous duties from June 13 to July 18 bridging rivers and transporting pontoons. No casualties reported.

1st Corps

**Army Of The Potomac
1st Corps Headquarters**
Major General
John Newton
July 2, 3, 4, 1863

1st Brigade Horse Artillery Cavalry Corps

Capt. James M. Robertson
9th Michigan Battery
Capt. Jabez J. Daniels

7-3: Engaged on Cemetary Ridge south of Pleasanton Ave. subject to the orders of Major General John Newton.

6th New York Battery
Capt. Joseph W. Martin
In reserve
2nd US-Batteries B & L
Lt. Edward Heaton
In reserve
2nd Us-Battery M
Lt. A. C. M. Pennington

7-3: With the Cavalry on the right.

4th US-Battery E
Lt. Samuel S. Elder

7-3: With 1st Brigade, 3rd Division on the left.
Casualties: Killed 2, Wounded 6; Total 8

~ Gettysburg Battlefield Monuments, Locations & Inscriptions ~

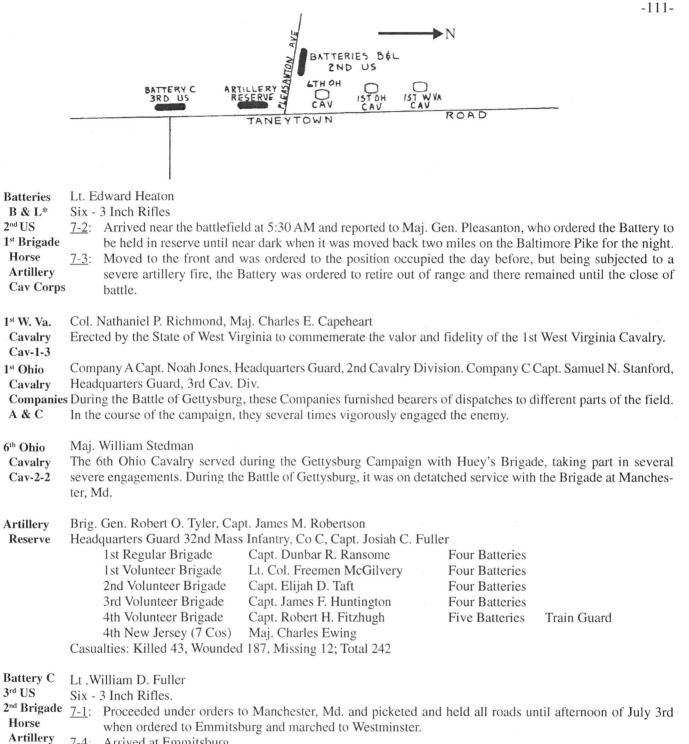

Batteries	Lt. Edward Heaton
B & L*	Six - 3 Inch Rifles
2nd US	7-2: Arrived near the battlefield at 5:30 AM and reported to Maj. Gen. Pleasanton, who ordered the Battery to
1st Brigade	be held in reserve until near dark when it was moved back two miles on the Baltimore Pike for the night.
Horse	7-3: Moved to the front and was ordered to the position occupied the day before, but being subjected to a
Artillery	severe artillery fire, the Battery was ordered to retire out of range and there remained until the close of
Cav Corps	battle.

1st W. Va.	Col. Nathaniel P. Richmond, Maj. Charles E. Capeheart
Cavalry	Erected by the State of West Virginia to commemorate the valor and fidelity of the 1st West Virginia Cavalry.
Cav-1-3	

1st Ohio	Company A Capt. Noah Jones, Headquarters Guard, 2nd Cavalry Division. Company C Capt. Samuel N. Stanford,
Cavalry	Headquarters Guard, 3rd Cav. Div.
Companies	During the Battle of Gettysburg, these Companies furnished bearers of dispatches to different parts of the field.
A & C	In the course of the campaign, they several times vigorously engaged the enemy.

6th Ohio	Maj. William Stedman
Cavalry	The 6th Ohio Cavalry served during the Gettysburg Campaign with Huey's Brigade, taking part in several
Cav-2-2	severe engagements. During the Battle of Gettysburg, it was on detached service with the Brigade at Manchester, Md.

Artillery — Brig. Gen. Robert O. Tyler, Capt. James M. Robertson
Reserve — Headquarters Guard 32nd Mass Infantry, Co C, Capt. Josiah C. Fuller

1st Regular Brigade	Capt. Dunbar R. Ransome	Four Batteries
1st Volunteer Brigade	Lt. Col. Freemen McGilvery	Four Batteries
2nd Volunteer Brigade	Capt. Elijah D. Taft	Four Batteries
3rd Volunteer Brigade	Capt. James F. Huntington	Four Batteries
4th Volunteer Brigade	Capt. Robert H. Fitzhugh	Five Batteries	Train Guard
4th New Jersey (7 Cos)	Maj. Charles Ewing	

Casualties: Killed 43, Wounded 187, Missing 12; Total 242

Battery C	Lt .William D. Fuller
3rd US	Six - 3 Inch Rifles.
2nd Brigade	7-1: Proceeded under orders to Manchester, Md. and picketed and held all roads until afternoon of July 3rd
Horse	when ordered to Emmitsburg and marched to Westminster.
Artillery	7-4: Arrived at Emmitsburg.
Cav Corps	Not engaged.

*see index

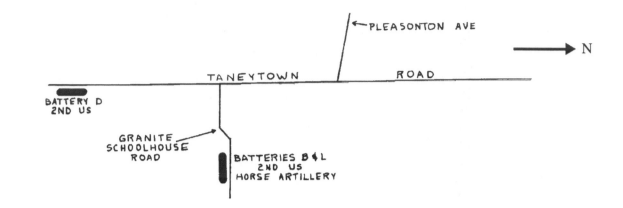

Battery D Lt. Edward P. Williston
2nd US Four - 12 Pounders
6th Corps <u>7-2</u>: Arrived with Corps and took position and remained on Taneytown Road.
  Artillery Not engaged.
  Brigade

Batteries Lt. Edward Heaton
  B & L* Arrived at 5:30 AM. In reserve during the day and at night withdrew two miles to the Baltimore Pike.
2nd US <u>7-3</u>: Advanced to former position in the morning and ordered to the reserve artillery and for a time exposed to
1st Brigade severe fire. In the evening was withdrawn to the position of the previous night.
  Horse
  Artillery
  Cav Corps

*see index

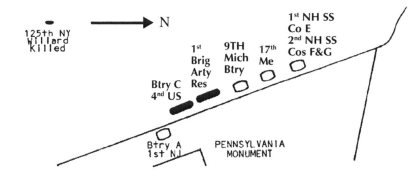

Battery K
1ˢᵗ NY Lt*

Left Flank of Battery K-1st New York Light Artillery.

New Hamp.
Sharp-
shooters

<u>7-3</u>: New Hampshire; Cos E-1st Regiment, F & G-2nd Regiment; Berdan's U S Sharpshooters. 2nd Brigade, 1st Division, 3rd Corps.

17ᵗʰ Me*
3-1-3

Lt. Col. Charles B. Merrill
<u>7-2</u>: This Regiment fought in the Wheatfield as shown by the monument there, losing 120 men.
<u>7-3</u>: Position of the 17th Maine Infantry, July 3, 1863.
Losses: Killed 2, Wounded 10.

9ᵗʰ Mich.
Battery
1ˢᵗ Brig.
Horse
Artillery
Cav Corps

Capt. Jabez J. Daniels
<u>7-3</u>: This monument marks the position held by the 9th Michigan Battery from 12:30 PM until 7:00 AM the following day.
322 rounds of shot, shell and cannister expended. 23 horses killed
Casualties: Killed 1, Wounded 4; Total 5.

1ˢᵗ Regular
Brigade
Artillery
Reserve

Capt. Dunbar R. Ransom
1st US Battery H, Lt. Chandler P. Eakin, Lt. Phillip E. Mason.
<u>7-2&3</u>: Engaged on Cemetary Hill.
  3rd US Batteries F & K   Lt. John C. Turnbull
<u>7-2</u>: Engaged on Emmitsburg Road on right of the Smith House.
<u>7-3</u>: On and near Cemetary Ridge.
  4th US Battery C   Lt. Evan Thomas
<u>7-2&3</u>: Engaged on Cemetary Ridge on left of 2nd Corps.
  5th US Battery C   Lt. Gulian V. Weir
<u>7-2&3</u>: Engaged on Cemetary Ridge and in front and on left of 2nd Corps.
Casualties: Killed 13, Wounded 53, Missing 2; Total 68

Battery C
4ᵗʰ US
1ˢᵗ Reg
Brigade
Artillery
Reserve

Lt. Evan Thomas
Six - 12 Pounders.
<u>7-2</u>: Arrived and took position on crest of hill near General Meade's Headquarters on left of 2nd Corps and was actively engaged in repelling attack of Confederates.
<u>7-3</u>: In position near left of 2nd Corps line.
Casualties: Killed 1, Wounded 17; Total 18.

Battery A
1ˢᵗ NJ Lt
4ᵗʰ Vol
Brigade
Artillery
Reserve

Hexamer's New Jersey Battery, Lt. Augustin N. Parsons
Six - 12 Pounders
<u>7-3</u>: From its position in reserve southwest of Power's Hill, galloped into action at 3 PM. Fired 120 rounds of shrapnel at Pickett's Column and 80 shells at a battery in left front. Position in action 45 yards east of this stone.
Casualties: Killed 2, Wounded 7; Total 9

125ᵗʰ NY*
3- 3-2

Col. C. L. Willard, 125th New York Infantry was killed at this spot on the evening of July 2nd, 1863, while leading in a charge the 3rd Brigade, 3rd Division, 2nd Corps.
Erected by the survivors of the 125th New York Infantry—1888.

*see index

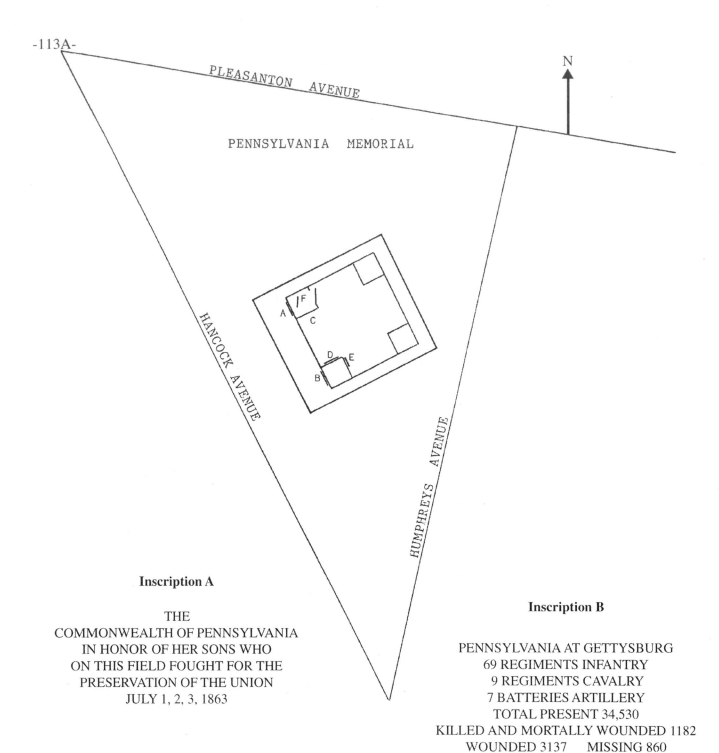

PLEASANTON AVENUE

PENNSYLVANIA MEMORIAL

N

HANCOCK AVENUE

HUMPHREYS AVENUE

A F
C
D E
B

Inscription A

THE
COMMONWEALTH OF PENNSYLVANIA
IN HONOR OF HER SONS WHO
ON THIS FIELD FOUGHT FOR THE
PRESERVATION OF THE UNION
JULY 1, 2, 3, 1863

Inscription B

PENNSYLVANIA AT GETTYSBURG
69 REGIMENTS INFANTRY
9 REGIMENTS CAVALRY
7 BATTERIES ARTILLERY
TOTAL PRESENT 34,530
KILLED AND MORTALLY WOUNDED 1182
WOUNDED 3137   MISSING 860

Inscription C

MEMORIAL TO THE SOLDIERS OF PENNSYLVANIA WHO FOUGHT
AT GETTYSBURG JULY 1863, ERECTED UNDER AUTHORITY
OF ACTS OF THE GENERAL ASSEMBLY OF PENNSYLVANIA
APPROVED JUNE 13, 1907, FEBRUARY 11, 1909, BY
EDWIN S. STUART
GOVERNOR OF THE COMMONWEALTH

~ Gettysburg Battlefield Monuments, Locations & Inscriptions ~

INSCRIPTION C (CONTINUED)

The Commissioners Charged With The Selection Of The Design For The Memorial
And The Construction Of It, And Who Undertook The Collection Of The Names
And Figures And Other Data Thereon, Which, Necessarily, Are Approximate, Were
St.Clair A. Mulholland   Henry S. Huidekoper   John P. Taylor
Charles F. McKenna   Edward L. Whittelsey
George P. Morgan   Charles E. Quail   Edward A. Irvin
Henry H. Cumings   Jacob C. Stineman

Inscription D

To The Loyal Women
Who Through Four Years Of War, Endured
Suffering And Bereavement,
This Tablet Is Dedicated
In Grateful Recognition Of Their Patriotism
By The Men Of Pennsylvania
Who Served In The Army And Navy Of The United
States During The War Of The Rebellion.

Inscription E

Pennsylvania Soldiers Of The Army Of The Potomac
Who Participated In The Battle Of Gettysburg
2133 Officers Of Whom 73 Were Killed Or Mortally Wounded
32,114 Enlisted Men Of Whom 1139 Were Killed Or Mortally Wounded
Total Engaged Or On Duty 34,247 - Total Killed Or Mortally Wounded 1212
-Revision of figures on the granite outside-
There were required in the construction of the Pennsylvania Memorial:
1252 tons of cut granite - 740 tons of sand - 366 tons of cement
1240 tons of broken stone - 50 tons of steel - 22 tons of bronze
Total 3840 tons

Inscription F

Memorial erected in 1910
Dedicated September 27, 1910
W. Liance Cotrell Architect
Samuel A. Murray Sculpter
Harrison Granite Co. Contractors

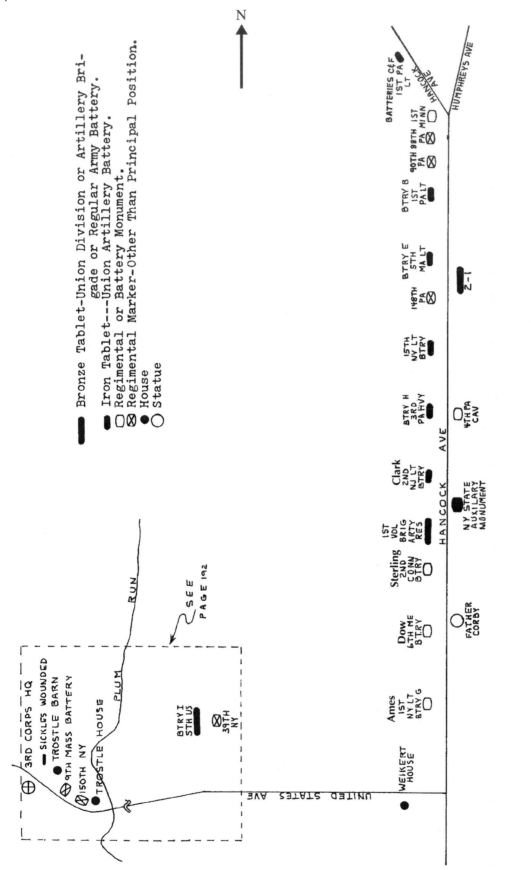

Hancock Ave South Of The Pennsylvania Monument

Not To Scale

~ Gettysburg Battlefield Monuments, Locations & Inscriptions ~

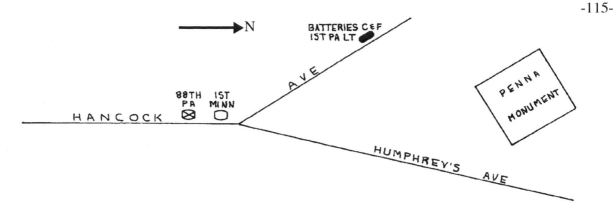

Batteries	Hampton's Battery, Capt. James Thomson
C & F*	Five 3 Inch Rifles.
PA Ind Lt.	<u>7-3</u>: Position occupied July 3, 1863.
1st Vol.	On this field 7 men fell and 11 were wounded.
Brigade	This tablet erected to their memory by the surviving members of the Battery, July 3, 1885.
Artillery	Casualties: Killed 2, Wounded 23, Missing 3; Total 28 (NY@Gbg)
Reserve	

1st Minn*

2-2-1

Col. William Colville

<u>7-2</u>: On the afternoon of July 2nd, Sickles' 3rd Corps having advanced from this line to the Emmitsburg Road, eight companies of the 1st Minnesota numbering 262 men were sent to this place to support a battery. Upon Sickles' repulse, as his men were passing here in confused retreat, two Confederate Brigades in pursuit were crossing the swale. To gain time to bring up reserves and save this position, General Hancock in person ordered the eight companies to charge the rapidly advancing enemy. The order was instantly repeated by Col. William Colville, and the charge was instantly made down the slope at full speed through the concentrated fire of the two brigades, breaking with the bayonet the enemy's front line as it was crossing the small brook in the low ground there. The remnant of the eight companies, nearly surrounded by the enemy, held its entire force at bay for a considerable time and till it retired on the approach of the reserves. The charge successfully accomplished its object. It saved this position and probably the battle-field. The loss of the eight companies in the charge was 215 killed and wounded, more than 83%. 47 men were still in line and no man missing. In self-sacrificing desperate valor this charge has no parallel in any war. Among the severely wounded were Col. William Colville, Lt. Col. Charles P. Adams and Maj. Mark W. Downie. Among the killed Capt. Joseph Perriam, Capt. Lewis Muller and Lt. Waldo Ferrar.

<u>7-3</u>: The Regiment participated in the repulse of Pickett's Charge, losing 17 more men killed and wounded.

88th PA*

2-2-1

Maj. Benezet F. Foust, Capt. Henry Whiteside

<u>7-2</u>: Held this position from the evening of July 2nd, 1863 until the morning of July 3rd. The principal Monument is erected on Oak Ridge, the scene of the first day's battle. Erected by the survivors August 27, 1883.

*see index

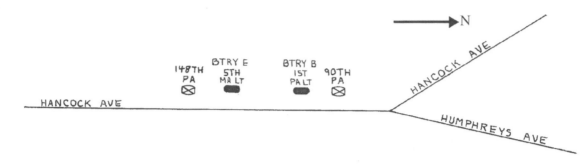

90ᵗʰ PA*
2-2-1

Col. Peter Lyle, Maj. Alfred J. Sellers, Col. Peter Lyle

7-1: Heavily engaged on Oak Ridge and Mummasburg Road, where the granite tree monument stands. On retirement of the Corps, it was formed in line of battle on Cemetary Hill supporting a battery.

7-2: On the evening of July 2nd was ordered to this position and deployed as skirmishers, advancing beyond the Emmitsburg Road. The Confederate General Barksdale, who had fallen mortally wounded in the attack upon the 3rd Corps was found upon the field and carried to the rear by men of this Regiment. After dark the Regiment returned to Cemetary Hill.

7-3: Moved to the east or rear of Cemetary Hill in support of the 12th Corps engaged on Culp's Hill; then to the support of batteries on the brow of the hill, and soon after, at the time of the assault upon the 2nd Corps, the Regiment changed position on the double quick and joined their line of battle at Zeigler's Grove as indicated by the Eagle Monument there.

Casualties: Killed 8, Wounded 45, Missing 40; Total 93.

Battery B*
1ˢᵗ PA Lt
1ˢᵗ Corps
Artillery
Brigade

Capt. James H. Cooper

Four - 3 Inch Rifles

7-3: Moved to this position from East Cemetary Hill at 3 PM during a heavy cannonade and opened fire on a Confederate battery in front. In half an hour, a line of Confederate infantry approached over the hill about 1000 yards distant. The Battery, in connection with the batteries in line, fired case shot until the Confederates reached cannister range, a few charges of which compelled their retreat.

Casualties: Killed 3, Wounded 9; Total 12.

Battery E*
5ᵗʰ MA Lt
1ˢᵗ Vol
Brigade
Artillery
Reserve

10th New York Battery attached. Capt. Charles A. Phillips

Six - 3 Inch Rifles

7-2: Withdrew at 5 PM from the field near the Peach Orchard and went into battery here.

7-3: About 1:30 PM, by order of Brig. Gen. Hunt, fired on the Confederate batteries but did little damage. Opened an enfilading fire soon after on Longstreet's advancing line of infantry and assisted in repulsing the assault. A charge was made within the range of the battery immediately afterward by the Florida Brigade and at the same time a Confederate battery opened on the left front, which at once received the concentrated fire of the batteries of the Brigade, driving the cannoneers from their guns which they abandoned.

7-4: Remained in this position until afternoon.

Casualties: Killed 2, Wounded 14; Total 16.

148ᵗʰ PA*
1-1-2

Lt. Col. Robert McFarlane

148th Regiment Pennsylvania Infantry, 1st Brigade, 1st Division, 2nd Corps

7-3: Occupied this position July 3, 1863.

Casualties: Killed 19, Wounded 101, Missing 5: Total 125

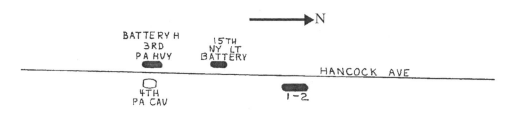

1-2   Brig. Gen. John G. Caldwell
1st Division 1st Brigade   Col. Edward E. Cross, Col. H. B. McKeen
2nd Corps   2nd Brigade   Col. Patrick Kelly
              3rd Brigade   Brig. Gen. Samuel K. Zook, Lt. Col. John Fraser
              4th Brigade   Col. J. R. Brooke
              7-2: Arrived about 7 AM and went into position on right of 3rd Corps on the line between the Cemetary and
                    Round Top, the 2nd Division on the right. Between 5 and 6 PM went to the Wheatfield, subject to the
                    orders of General Sykes in support of 3rd Corps line, the line previously occupied by 3rd Brigade, 1st
                    Division, 3rd Corps. Was engaged with Anderson's Brigade, Hood's Division until sunset with heavy
                    losses including Col. Cross and Gen. Zook killed early in the engagement. Returned to former position in
                    2nd Corps line.
              7-3: The Division formed in single line, threw up breastworks and remained in position until close of battle.
              Casualties: Killed 187, Wounded 880, Missing 208; Total 1275

15th NY Lt*   Capt. Patrick Hart
  Battery   Four - 12 Pounders
1st Vol   7-2: Engaged in the Peach Orchard. Retired about dark and reported to Brig. Gen. R. O. Tyler, Artillery Re-
  Brigade   serve.
  Artillery   7-3: Ordered early to the front and took position in the battalion on the left of Battery E-5th Massachusetts.
  Reserve   Directed by Gen. Hancock to open on the Confederate batteries with solid shot and shell. Upon the
                    advance of the Confederate infantry, fired shell and shrapnel and cannister when the line was within 500
                    yards. A second line advancing was met with double cannister which dispersed it. The fire of the Battery
                    was then directed against the artillery on the Confederate right and several caissons and limbers were
                    exploded by the shells.
              7-4: Remained in this position until noon.
              Casualties: Killed 3, Wounded 13; Total 16

Battery H*   Capt. William D. Rank
3rd PA Hvy   Two - 3 Inch Rifles
C-2-1   7-2: Marched with the 2nd Cavalry Division and went into position on the Hanover Road three miles from
                    Gettysburg.
              7-3: In position here in the early morning and was engaged in the afternoon assisting in the repulse of Longstreet's
                    Assault.
              Casualties: 1 man missing.

4th PA   Lt. Col. William E. Doster
 Cavalry   7-2: Detached on the morning of July 2nd from the Brigade at junction of White Run and Baltimore Pike.
 C-2-3   Ordered to report to Headquarters, Army Of The Potomac. Supported a battery temporarily, near this
                    position. On picket at night.
              7-3: Returned late in the afternoon to 2nd Cavalry Division.
              Casualties: 1 Killed Total.

*see index

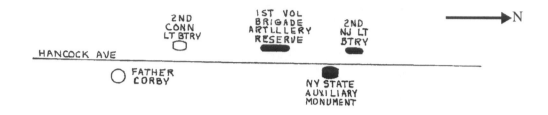

1ˢᵗᵈ NJ Lt Battery B* 3ʳᵈ Corps Artillery Brigade (2ⁿᵈ NJ Battery)

Capt. A. Judson Clark, Lt. Robert Sims
Six - 10 Pounder Parrotts
7-2: Engaged in the action in a field near the Peach Orchard. Retired to the rear for want of support.
7-3: In line here with the Artillery Brigade during the heavy cannonading and the charge and repulse of Longstreet's Assault but was not engaged.
Casualties: Killed 1, Wounded 16, Missing 3; Total 20

New York Auxiliary Monument

The State Of New York In Recognition Of The Services Rendered By Those Corps, Division and Brigade Commanders At Gettysburg Not Elsewhere Honored On This Field.
(Note: Listed on the monument are the names of 41 Brigade, Division, and Corps Commanders. In addition, the inscription on the monument mentions that eight Commanders are honored by Bronze Statues elsewhere on this field. There is also a list of names of eight Cavalry organization Commanders, nineteen Artillery Commanders Two Engineer Regiment Commanders and ninety-nine Infantry Regiment Commanders.)

1ˢᵗ Vol. Brigade* Artillery Reserve

Lt. Col. Freeman McGilvery
5th Massachusetts Battery (10th NY attached)
Capt. C. A. Phillips
7-2: Engaged on 3rd Corps line on Wheatfield Road.
     9th Massachusetts Battery
     Capt. John Bigelow, Lt. R. S. Milton
7-2: Engaged on 3rd Corps line on Wheatfield Road.
7-3: In Zeigler's Grove.
     15th New York Battery
     Capt. Patrick Hart
7-2: Engaged on 3rd Corps line on Wheatfield Road.
7-3: On 2nd Corps line on the Wheatfield Road.
     Pennsylvania Batteries C&F
     Capt. James Thompson
7-2: Engaged in the Peach Orchard.
7-3: On line with Battery K-4th US and Hart's Battery on left.
Casualties: Killed 17, Wounded 71, Missing 5; Total 93.

2ⁿᵈ Conn. Lt 2ⁿᵈ Vol. Brigade Artillery Reserve

Capt. John W. Sterling.
Four - James 3.67 Inch Rifles
7-3: Position July 3, 1863.
Casualties: Wounded 3, Missing 2; Total 5

Father Corby's Statue

To The Memory Of Father William Corby, CSC, Chaplin 88th Regiment, New York Infantry; 2nd Brigade, 1st Division, 2nd Corps, The Irish Brigade, July 2, 1863.
This memorial depicts Father Corby, a chaplain of the Irish Brigade, giving general absolution and blessing before battle at Gettysburg, July 2, 1863.
President — University of Notre Dame 1866-72, 1877-81.

*see index

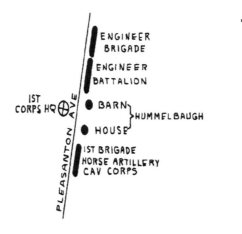

1ˢᵗ NY Lt* **Battery G** **4ᵗʰ Vol** **Brigade** **Artillery** **Reserve**	Capt. Nelson Ames. Six - 12 Pounders Battery G (Ames), 1st New York Light Artillery July 3, 1863 Casualties: Wounded 7 Total.
6ᵗʰ Me Lt **Battery** **4ᵗʰ Vol** **Brigade** **Artillery** **Reserve**	Lt. Edwin B. Dow Four - 12 Pounders Dow's 6th Maine Battery Casualties: Wounded 13 Total
39ᵗʰ NY	(Note: See Page 188A and 192)

39ᵗʰ NY   (Note: See Page 188A and 192)

Battery I **5ᵗʰ US**	"	"	"	"	"
150ᵗʰ NY	"	"	"	"	191
9ᵗʰ Mass **Battery**	"	"	"	"	"
Sickles **Wounded**	"	"	"	"	"
3ʳᵈ Corps **Head-** **quarters**	"	"	"	"	"

*see index

THE SYMBOLS LISTED BELOW ARE USED TO IDENTIFY
THE MONUMENTS, MARKERS, TABLETS, STATUES, ETC.
WHICH ARE DRAWN ON THE MAPS IN THESE PAGES

SYMBOL	TYPE	REPRESENTING	DESCRIPTION
	Bronze Tablet	Army of The Potomac, Union Corps or Division or Brigade, Regular Army Regiment, Regular Army Artillery Battery, Volunteer Artillery Brigade.	Brigade Tablet Mounted on Square Marble base. All other Tablets are on large vertical Granite Blocks.
	Bronze Tablet	Army of Northern Virginia, Confederate Corps or Division or Brigade or Artillery Battalion	Brigade Tablet and Artillery Battalion Tablet Mounted on Round Marble base. All other Tablets are Mounted on large vertical Granite blocks.
	Iron Tablet	Union Army Battery (other than Regular Army)	Mounted on Black Iron Shaft.
	Iron Tablet	Confederate Artillery Battery	Mounted on Black Iron Shaft.
	Iron Tablet	Confederate Brigade Advanced Position	Mounted on Black Iron Shaft.
	Regimental or Battery Monument	Principal Position of Volunteer Regiment or Volunteer Artillery Battery	Usually Granite or Marble in a Great Variety of Shapes and Sizes.
	Regimental Marker	Other than Principal Position of Regiment or Battery	Usually a Square Granite Marker or tablet or may be another monument.
	Flank Marker or Company Marker	Left and/or Right Flank of Regiment or Battery or Position of a Coppany.	Usually a Small Square or Rectangular Granite Marker.
	Army Or Corps Headquarters	Site of Headquarters of Army Commander or Corps Commander or Chief of Artillery	Cannon Barrel Mounted Vertically on Stone, Granite or Marble Base.
	State Monument	Monument Erected by Union or Confederate State.	
	Statue	Standing or Equestrian	Bronze Sculpture
	Building	House, Barn or other Structure	Identified by Owner's Name.
	Miscellaneous Marker	Marker or Inscription of a type not listed above	Granite or Metal Marker.
*Asterisk		Used whenever a Division or Brigade or Regiment or Battery has more than one Monument or Marker.	Check the Index for other Monument or Marker.

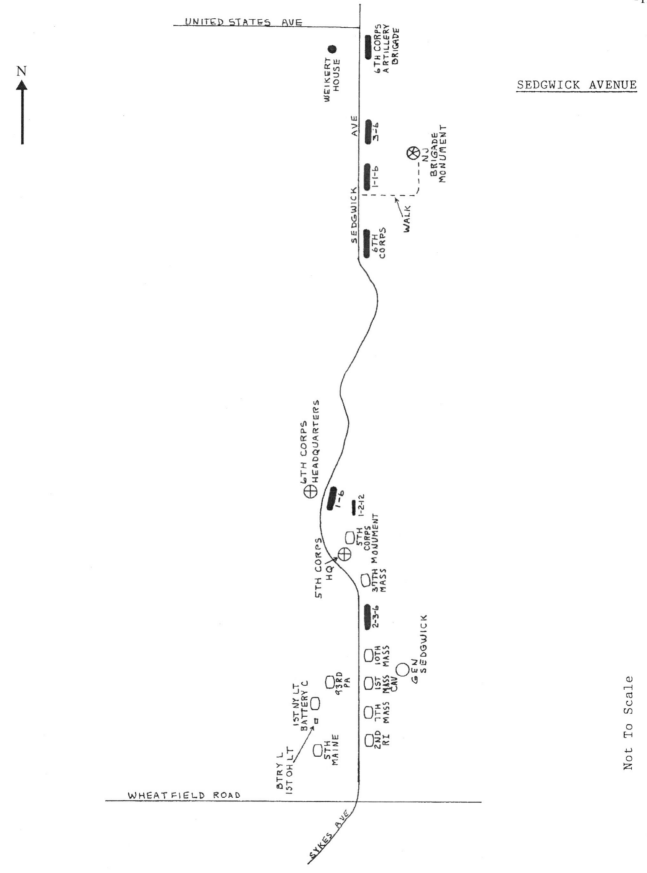

SEDGWICK AVENUE

Not To Scale

~ Gettysburg Battlefield Monuments, Locations & Inscriptions ~

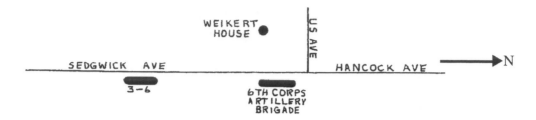

6th Corps Artillery Brigade	Col. Charles A Tompkins	
Mass 1st Battery A		Six - 12 Pounders
	Capt. William A. McCartney	
New York 1st Battery		Six - 3 Inch Rifles
	Capt. Andrew Cowan	
New York 3rd Battery		Six - 10 Pounder Parrotts
	Capt. William A. Harn	
1st Rhode Island Battery C		Six - 3 Inch Rifles
	Capt. Richard Waterman	
1st Rhode Island Battery G		Six - 10 Pounder Parrotts
	Capt. George W. Adams	
2nd US Battery D		Six - 2 Pounders
	Lt. Edward B. Williston	
2nd US Battery G		Six - 12 Pounders
	Lt. John H. Butler	
5th US Battery F		Six - 10 Pounder Parrotts
	Lt. Leonard Martin	

7-2: Arrived in the afternoon and evening from Manchester, Md. and the artillery was placed under orders of Brig. Gen. H. J. Hunt, Chief of Artillery of the Army.

7-3: The Batteries were placed in reserve on different portions of the field so as to be available, but with the exception of 1st New York Battery were not engaged.

Casualties: Killed 4, Wounded 8; Total 12

3-6
3rd Division
6th Corps

Major General John Newton, Brig. Gen. Frank Wheaton
1st Brigade   Brig. Gen. Alex Shaler
2nd Brigade   Col. Henry L. Eustis
3rd Brigade   Col. David J. Nevin
Artillery Brigade   Col. Charles H. Tompkins

7-2: Arrived about 2 PM and late in the day marched toward the north slope of Little Round Top.
3rd Brigade with 2nd Brigade, 1st Division went into action at sunset on the right of 1st Brigade, 3rd Division, 5th Corps on the northwest slope of Little Round Top and the combined force drove the advancing Confederates back down the slope across Plum Run Marsh and a hundred yards up the slope beyond. 1st and 2nd Brigades were in reserve on the northeast slope of Little Round Top.

7-3: 1st Brigade was ordered to the left, and at 8 AM to the support of 2nd Division 12th Corps on the right. 2nd Brigade was sent to the right center to report to Gen. Newton. The 3rd Brigade remained under the command of Gen. Bartlett supporting 1st Brigade 3rd Division, 5th Corps in the vicinity of the Wheatfield.

Casualties: Killed 20, Wounded 148, Missing 28; Total 196

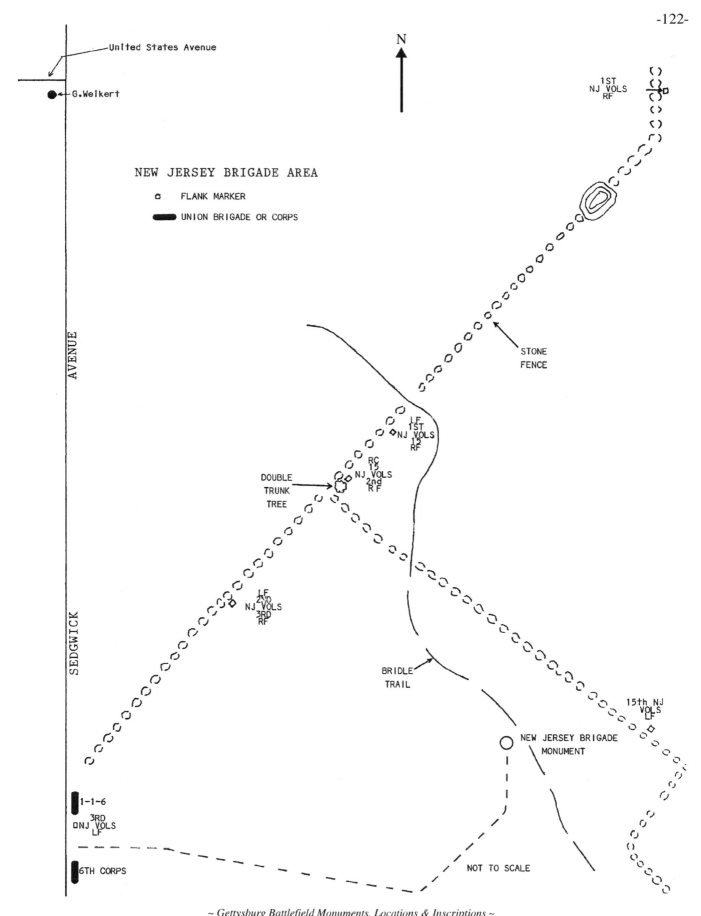

N

United States Avenue

G.Weikert

1ST
NJ VOLS
RF

NEW JERSEY BRIGADE AREA

☐ FLANK MARKER

▬▬▬ UNION BRIGADE OR CORPS

STONE
FENCE

AVENUE

LF
1ST
NJ VOLS
15
RF

RC
15
NJ VOLS
2nd
RF

DOUBLE
TRUNK
TREE

SEDGWICK

LF
2ND
NJ VOLS
3RD
RF

BRIDLE
TRAIL

15th NJ
VOLS
LF

NEW JERSEY BRIGADE
MONUMENT

1-1-6

3RD
NJ VOLS
LF

6TH CORPS

NOT TO SCALE

~ Gettysburg Battlefield Monuments, Locations & Inscriptions ~

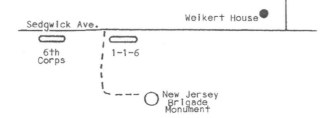

1-1-6   Brig. Gen. Alfred T. A. Torbert

1st, 2nd, 3rd, 15th New Jersey Infantry

7-2:   Arrived about 4 PM from Manchester, Md., a distance by the route taken of about 35 miles. Having halted an hour only, after sunset moved to the east slope of north side of Little Round Top and arriving there at dark was held in reserve until morning.

7-3:   Moved to a position SE of Weikert House. Remained until close of battle. Not engaged except on the skirmish line.

Casualties: Wounded 11 Total

New Jersey   First Brigade New Jersey Volunteers
Brigade   Brig. Gen. Alfred T. A. Torbert
Monument 1st, 2nd, 3rd, 4th, and 15th Regiments Infantry

1st Brig. 1st Div. 6th Corps

7-2:   In reserve.

7-3&4: Detached from the Corps, held this position.

Erected By The State Of New Jersey, A. D. 1888, In Testimony Of The Patriotism, Courage And Patient Endurance Of Her Volunteer Soldiers.

"Kearny's New Jersey Brigade"
Fought in all the important battles of the Army Of The Potomac
From May, 1861 To The End Of The War At Appomattox Court House, 1865
Total Strength 13,805 Including 10th, 23rd and 40th Regiments, New Jersey Volunteers, Which Were Attached To The Brigade.

This Site Rededicated July 1, 1963
Civil War Centennial Commission
State Of New Jersey
Richard J. Hughes, Governor

6th Corps   Maj. Gen. John Sedgwick

July 2, 3, 4, 5, 1863

        1st Division   Brig. Gen. Horatio G. Wright
        2nd Division   Brig. Gen. Albion P. Howe
        3rd Division   Maj. Gen. John Newton, Brig. Gen. Frank Wheaton
        Artillery Brigade   Col. Charles H. Tompkins

The Corps, being in reserve, its operations were mostly by brigades independent of each other and on different positions of the field.

7-2:   Arrived in the afternoon after a march of over 30 miles. Nevin's Brigade, Wheaton's Division and Bartlett's Brigade, Wright's Division went into action about sunset on the left center between the divisions of the Fifth Corps and assisted in repulsing the Confederate assault. Russell's and Torbert's Brigades, Wright's Division were held in reserve. Neill's Brigade, Howe's Division was sent to the right of the line. Grant's Brigade was sent to the extreme left of the line east of Little Round Top. Shaler's Brigade, Wheaton's Division was held in reserve near the left centre.

7-3:   The Brigades of the Corps were put into position where needed at different points on the line from right to left until the close of the battle.

Casualties: Killed 27, Wounded 185, Missing 30; Total 242

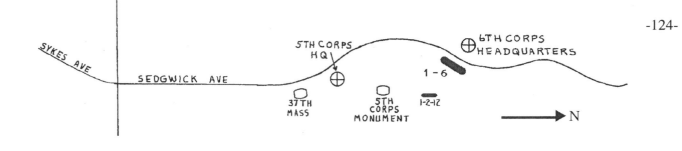

	Army Of The Potomac
6th Corps Headquarters	6th Corps Headquarters Major General John Sedgwick July 2, 3, 4, 5, 1863

1-6   Brig. Gen. Horatio G. Wright
1st Division   1st Brigade   Brig. Gen. Alfred T. A. Torbert
6th Corps   2nd Brigade   Brig. Gen. Joseph J. Bartlett
         3rd Brigade   Brig. Gen. David A. Russell

7-2:   Arrived about 4 PM and 6 PM. The 2nd Brigade with the 3rd Division moved into position. 1st and 3rd Brigades were massed and held in reserve.

7-3:   1st Brigade placed in line in left center subject to the orders of General Newton commanding 1st Corps on the right. 3rd Brigade was sent to the extreme left to General Wright in command there. At 5 PM General Wright with his troops moved to the support of 5th Corps then threatened. The Brigades of the Division then remained in same position during the day and succeeding night.

7-4:   The 3rd Brigade moved to the left of 5th Corps and occupied the slope of Little Round Top.

Casualties: Killed 1, Wounded 17; Total 18

1-2-12*   Col. Charles Candy
       5th Ohio Infantry   Col. J. H. Patrick
       7th Ohio Infantry   Col. W. R. Creighton
       29th Ohio Infantry   Capt. W. F. Stevens, Capt. Edward Hayes
       66th Ohio Infantry   Lt. Col. E. Powell
       28th Pa Infantry   Capt. John Flynn
       147th Pa Infantry   Lt. Col. Ario Pardee, Jr

7-1:   About 5 PM, took position along the ridge in rear of this tablet. The 5th Ohio and 147th Pa occupied Little Round Top at dusk on picket duty.

7-2:   Early in the morning, Brigade moved to Culp's Hill.

	Army Of The Potomac
5th Corps Headquarters	5th Corps Headquarters Major General George Sykes July 2, 3, 4, 1863

5th Corps Headquarters Monument   5th Corps Headquarters

Arrived on the field from Hanover via Bonaughtown at 5 PM, July 2, 1863. Headquarters, July 2, 3, 4, 1863.

37th Mass   Col. Oliver Edwards
2-3-6   7-2:   Second Brigade, 3rd Division, 6th Corps, July 2, 1863

Casualties: Killed 2, Wounded 26, Missing 19; Total 47

*see index

~ Gettysburg Battlefield Monuments, Locations & Inscriptions ~

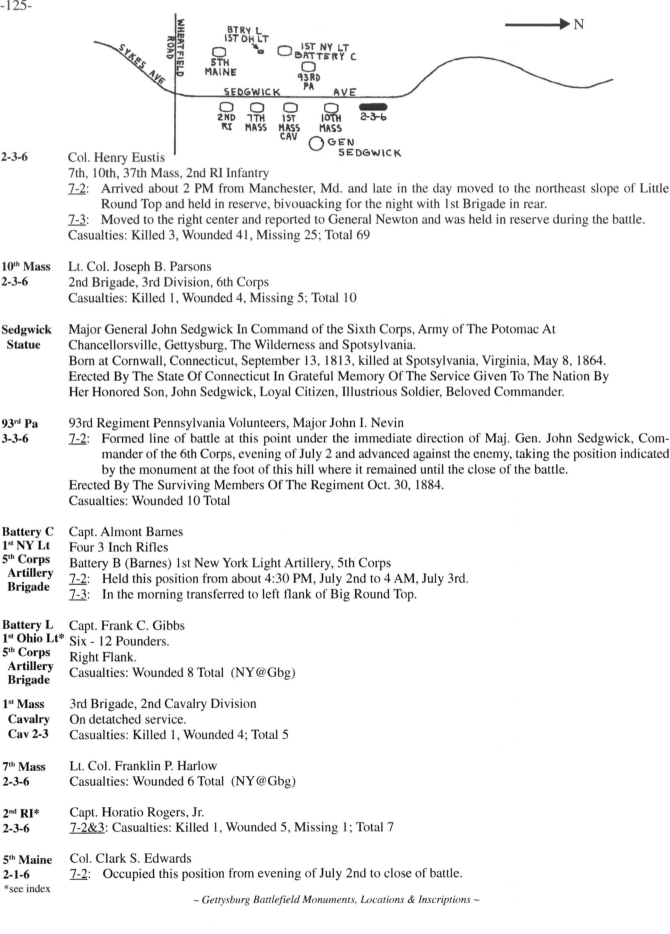

2-3-6   Col. Henry Eustis
7th, 10th, 37th Mass, 2nd RI Infantry
<u>7-2</u>: Arrived about 2 PM from Manchester, Md. and late in the day moved to the northeast slope of Little
   Round Top and held in reserve, bivouacking for the night with 1st Brigade in rear.
<u>7-3</u>: Moved to the right center and reported to General Newton and was held in reserve during the battle.
Casualties: Killed 3, Wounded 41, Missing 25; Total 69

10th Mass   Lt. Col. Joseph B. Parsons
2-3-6   2nd Brigade, 3rd Division, 6th Corps
Casualties: Killed 1, Wounded 4, Missing 5; Total 10

Sedgwick   Major General John Sedgwick In Command of the Sixth Corps, Army of The Potomac At
Statue   Chancellorsville, Gettysburg, The Wilderness and Spotsylvania.
Born at Cornwall, Connecticut, September 13, 1813, killed at Spotsylvania, Virginia, May 8, 1864.
Erected By The State Of Connecticut In Grateful Memory Of The Service Given To The Nation By
Her Honored Son, John Sedgwick, Loyal Citizen, Illustrious Soldier, Beloved Commander.

93rd Pa   93rd Regiment Pennsylvania Volunteers, Major John I. Nevin
3-3-6   <u>7-2</u>: Formed line of battle at this point under the immediate direction of Maj. Gen. John Sedgwick, Commander of the 6th Corps, evening of July 2 and advanced against the enemy, taking the position indicated
   by the monument at the foot of this hill where it remained until the close of the battle.
Erected By The Surviving Members Of The Regiment Oct. 30, 1884.
Casualties: Wounded 10 Total

Battery C   Capt. Almont Barnes
1st NY Lt   Four 3 Inch Rifles
5th Corps   Battery B (Barnes) 1st New York Light Artillery, 5th Corps
Artillery   <u>7-2</u>: Held this position from about 4:30 PM, July 2nd to 4 AM, July 3rd.
Brigade   <u>7-3</u>: In the morning transferred to left flank of Big Round Top.

Battery L   Capt. Frank C. Gibbs
1st Ohio Lt*   Six - 12 Pounders.
5th Corps   Right Flank.
Artillery   Casualties: Wounded 8 Total (NY@Gbg)
Brigade

1st Mass   3rd Brigade, 2nd Cavalry Division
Cavalry   On detatched service.
Cav 2-3   Casualties: Killed 1, Wounded 4; Total 5

7th Mass   Lt. Col. Franklin P. Harlow
2-3-6   Casualties: Wounded 6 Total (NY@Gbg)

2nd RI*   Capt. Horatio Rogers, Jr.
2-3-6   <u>7-2&3</u>: Casualties: Killed 1, Wounded 5, Missing 1; Total 7

5th Maine   Col. Clark S. Edwards
2-1-6   <u>7-2</u>: Occupied this position from evening of July 2nd to close of battle.
*see index

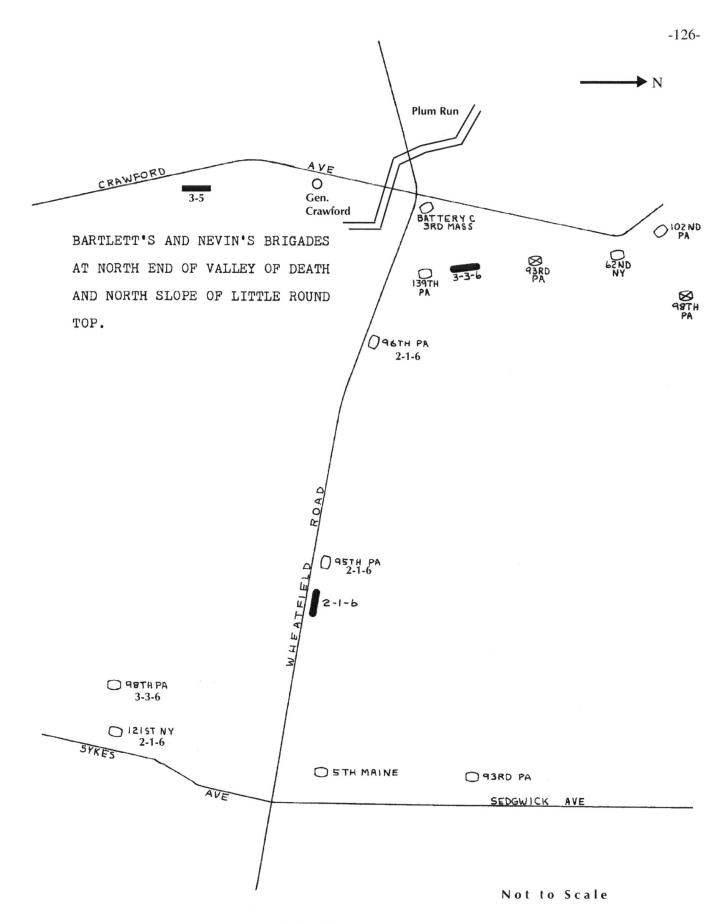

N

Plum Run

CRAWFORD AVE

3-5

Gen. Crawford

BATTERY C
3RD MASS

102ND PA

BARTLETT'S AND NEVIN'S BRIGADES
AT NORTH END OF VALLEY OF DEATH
AND NORTH SLOPE OF LITTLE ROUND
TOP.

139TH PA

3-3-6

93RD PA

62ND NY

98TH PA

96TH PA
2-1-6

WHEATFIELD ROAD

95TH PA
2-1-6

2-1-6

98TH PA
3-3-6

121ST NY
2-1-6

SYKES

AVE

5TH MAINE

93RD PA

SEDGWICK AVE

Not to Scale

~ Gettysburg Battlefield Monuments, Locations & Inscriptions ~

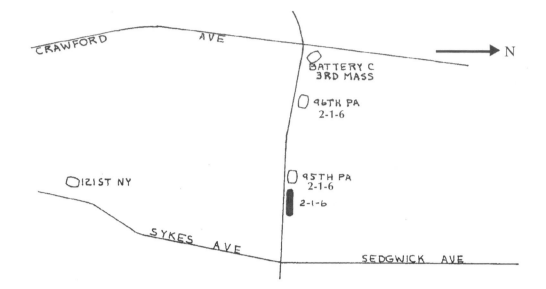

2-1-6   Brig. Gen. Joseph Bartlett
5th Maine, 121st New York, 95th, 96th Pennsylvania Infantry.
7-2: The Brigade arrived late in the day and was formed in two lines to support 5th Corps, of which the troops in front were giving ground. The 3rd Brigade, 3rd Division was formed on the left and then advanced to the front. Remained in the same position during the night. The 121st NY was detatched from the Brigade on its arrival and supported Battery L-1st Ohio until the close of the battle.
7-3: 3rd Brigade 3rd Division was assigned to Brig. Gen. Bartlett's Command which was in an advanced position. Late in the day, the 3rd Brigade 3rd Division in a second line, at an interval of 200 yards supported 1st Brigade 3rd Division 5th Corps in an advance through the Wheatfield and the woods on the south, but soon after being engaged, the 3rd Brigade 3rd Division advanced to the front and the combined forces captured about 200 prisoners from Brig. Gen. Benning's Brigade and the colors of the 15th Georgia. At dark the Brigade was recalled to a line a few hundred yards in advance of the original position.
Casualties: Killed 1, Wounded 4; Total 5

95th PA   Lt. Col. Edward Carroll
2-1-6   The Gosline Zouaves
7-2: Occupied this position in reserve from evening of July 2nd to morning of July 3rd, 1863.
Casualties: Killed 1, Wounded 1; Total 2

96th PA   Major William H. Lessig
2-1-6   7-2: Position of the 96th Regiment Pennsylvania Volunteers, 2nd Brigade, 1st Division, 6th Army Corps from 5 PM of the 2nd until the morning of the 5th of July, 1863.
Casualties: Wounded 1 Total

Battery C   Lt. Aaron F. Walcott
3rd Ma Lt   Six - 12 Pounders.
5th Corps   7-2: 3rd Massachusetts Battery, 5th Corps Artillery, July 2, 1863.
Artillery   Casualties: Wounded 6 Total
Brigade

121st NY   (Note: See Page 131)
2-1-6

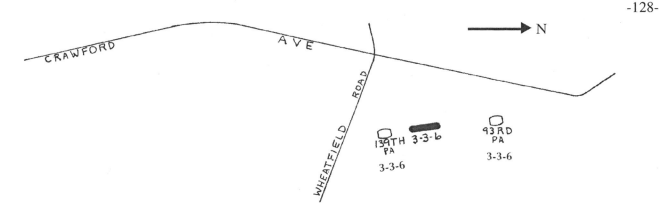

139ᵗʰ PA *   Col. Frederick H. Collier, Lt. Col. William H. Moody
3-3-6
           <u>7-1</u>:   Left Manchester, Md. at 9 PM.
           <u>7-2</u>:   Arrived at Rock Creek at 2 PM. Towards evening, the Brigade moved rapidly to the front to support the Union left, this Regiment deploying to the right of Little Round Top and advanced with 1st Brigade Pennsylvania Reserves, driving the enemy into the Wheatfield. Retired to and held this position.
           <u>7-3</u>:   In the evening the Regiment moved with the Pennsylvania Reserves and advanced about 900 yards to the position indicated by a Greek Cross tablet and assisted in forcing the enemy back. Subsequently returned to this position.
           Casualties: Killed 4, Wounded 16; Total 20 of 511 present.

3-3-6   Brig. Gen. Frank Wheaton, Col. David J. Nevin
           62nd NY, 93rd, 98th, 102nd, 139th Pa Infantry
           <u>7-2</u>:   Arrived about 2 PM and late in the day moved to the north slope of Little Round Top. On the advance of Brig. Gen. Wofford's Brigade and others, forcing 1st and 2nd Brigades 2nd Division 5th Corps across Plum Run and up the west base of Little Round Top, this Brigade with the 1st Brigade 3rd Division 5th Corps on its left countercharged, forcing the Confederates down the hill and across Plum Run and marsh and 100 yards up the slope beyond, and remained during the night, having recaptured two Napalean guns.
           <u>7-3</u>:   Assigned to the command of Brig. Gen. Bartlett in the morning and remained in the advanced position of the previous night. Late in the day supported 1st Brigade 3rd Division 5th Corps at an interval of 200 yards in an advance through the Wheatfield and the woods on the south, encountering a detachment of Brig. Gen. Benning's Brigade, and the combined forces captured about 200 prisoners of that Brigade and the colors of the 15th Georgia. At dark, the line was recalled to a position of a few hundred yards in advance of the original line. The Brigade sustained some loss in this movement. One Napalean and three caissons belonging to the 9th Massachusetts Battery were recaptured.
           Casualties: Killed 2, Wounded 51; Total 53

93ʳᵈ PA *   Major John I. Nevin
3-3-6
           <u>7-2</u>:   After charging with the Brigade from the right of Little Round Top in the evening, and assisting in the repulse of the enemy and in the capture of a number of prisoners, the Regiment retired to and held this position until the close of the battle.
           Casualties: Killed 1, Wounded 9; Total 10

*see index

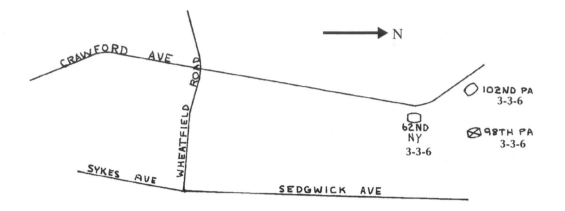

62ⁿᵈ NY   Lt. Col. Theodore B. Hamilton
3-3-6   The Anderson Zouaves
           July 2nd, 1863, 7:15 PM
           On the site of this monument, the Regiment under command of Lt. Col. T. B. Hamilton charged the enemy and recaptured two guns.
           Casualties: Killed 1, Wounded 11; Total 12 (NY@Gbg)

102ⁿᵈ PA   Col. John W. Patterson
3-3-6   The Regiment was detailed at Manchester, Md. to guard trains to Westminster. At the latter place, a detatchment of three officers and 100 men was sent to Gettysburg with the supply train.
           <u>7-3</u>: On its arrival the morning of the 3rd, it was posted on this line. The rest of the Regiment picketed the roads leading from Westminster to Gettysburg until the close of the battle.

98ᵗʰ PA* Major John B. Kohler
3-3-6   <u>7-2</u>: The Regiment was the advance of the 6th Corps in its march from Manchester, Md. to the battlefield and occupied this position from the evening of July 2nd until the close of the battle.
           Casualties: Wounded 11 Total (NY@Gbg)

*see index

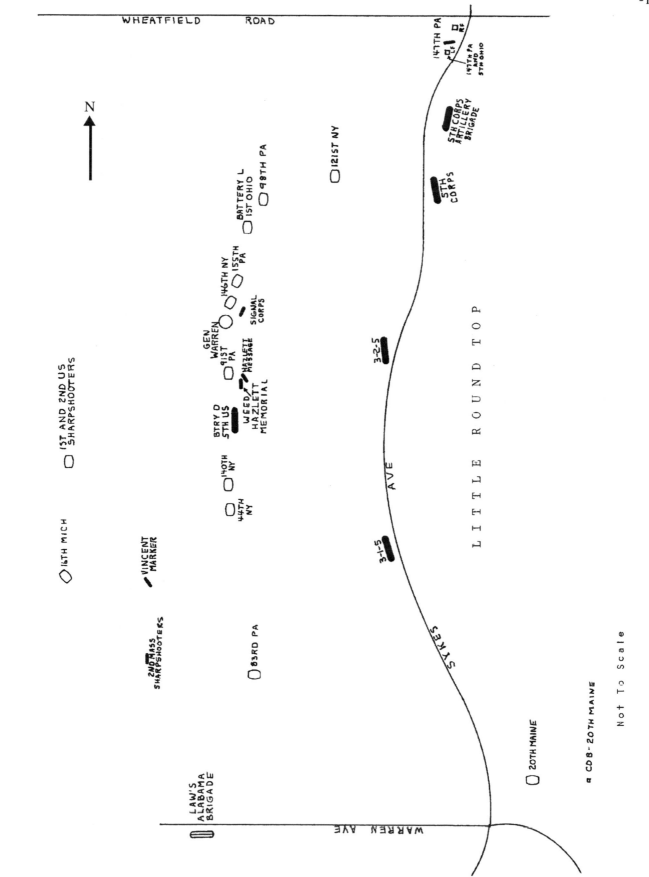

~ Gettysburg Battlefield Monuments, Locations & Inscriptions ~

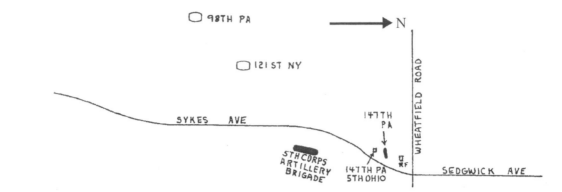

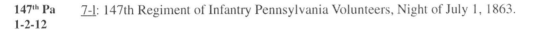

147ᵗʰ Pa
1-2-12

7-1: 147th Regiment of Infantry Pennsylvania Volunteers, Night of July 1, 1863.

147ᵗʰ Pa
5ᵗʰ Ohio
Flank
Marker

147th Pa. (Note: This inscription is on west side of marker.)
5th Ohio (Note: This inscription is on south side of marker.)

5ᵗʰ Corps
Artillery
Brigade

Capt. Augustus P. Martin

	Mass 3rd	Battery C	Six 12 Pounders

Lt. Aaron F. Walcott

	1st New York	Battery C	Four 3 Inch Rifles

Capt. Almont Barnes

	1st Ohio	Battery L	Six 12 Pounders

Capt. Frank C. Gibbs

	5th US	Battery D	Six 10 Pounder Parrotts

Lt. Charles E. Hazlett,
Lt. Benjamin A. Rittenhouse

	5th US	Battery I	Four 3 Inch Rifles

Lt. Malbone F. Watson

7-2: Arrived on the field on the left between 5 and 6 PM. Battery D-5th US, Battery C-3rd Mass and Battery I-5th US in rear of 1st Division and Battery L-1st Ohio and Battery C-1st NY in rear of 2nd Division. Battery D-5th US was placed on the summit of Little Round Top and Battery C-3rd Mass and Battery I-5th US were engaged further to the right in rear of 3rd Corps until dark. Battery L-1st Ohio was placed on the north slope and at the base of Little Round Top.

7-3: Battery D-5th US remained on Little Round Top. Battery 1 - 5th US being unserviceable, was sent from the field. The position of Battery L-1st Ohio remained nearly the same. At 3 AM, Battery C-1st NY and Battery C-3rd Mass moved to the extreme left and not engaged.

Casualties: Killed 8, Wounded 33, Missing 2; Total 43.

121ˢᵗ NY
2-1-6

Col. Emery Upton
7-2&3: Held this position from evening of July 2nd, 1863 until close of battle.
Casualties: Wounded 2 Total (NY@Gbg)

98ᵗʰ Pa*
3-3-6

Major John B. Kohler. TO OUR FALLEN COMRADES.
7-2,3&4: Leading the Corps in the march from Manchester, Md. Arrived here about 5 PM, immediately charged to the Wheatfield and woods to the left. About dark rejoined the Brigade north of the road where other monument stands.
Casualties: Wounded 11 Total. (NY@Gbg)

*see index

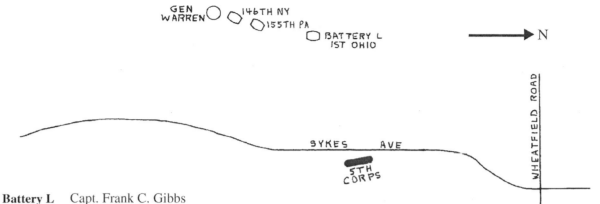

Battery L **1ˢᵗ Ohio*** **5ᵗʰ Corps** **Artillery** **Brigade**	Capt. Frank C. Gibbs Six - 12 Pounders 7-2: Arriving on the field at 8 AM went into position under a brisk skirmish fire on the extreme right on Wolf Hill. Afterwards moved to north slope of Little Round Top and there became hotly engaged with Longstreet's Corps, then trying to turn the left. 7-3: Held same position. Casualties: Wounded 2 Total.

5ᵗʰ Corps Major General George Sykes

    1st Division   Brig. Gen. James Barnes

    2nd Division   Brig. Gen. Romeyn B. Ayres

    3rd Division   Brig. Gen. Samuel W. Crawford

    Artillery Brigade   Capt. Augustus P. Martin

7-2: Arrived early in the morning and went into position on the right of the 12th Corps. Later crossed Rock Creek via Baltimore Pike and was massed in the field until late in the afternoon. Moved to the left between 4 and 5 PM, Barnes' and Ayres' Divisions taking possession of Little Round Top and reinforcing the 3rd Corps line, Crawford's Division in reserve. All of the Brigades of the Corps except Fisher's were engaged at intervals until night.

7-3: Barnes' Division except Tilton's Brigade, north of Little Round Top with Wright's Division, 6th Corps on the right, left and rear. Ayres' and Crawford's Divisions and Tilton's Brigade on the Round Tops. These positions were held during the day.

7-4: In same positions, except reconnissance from each Division were made in front during the day.

Casualties: Killed 365, Wounded 1611, Missing 211; Total 2187.

155ᵗʰ PA
3-2-5 Lt. Col. John H. Cain

7-2,3 & 4: Position occupied July 2nd, 3rd and 4th, 1863.

Casualties: Killed 6, Wounded 13; Total 19 (NY@Gbg)

146ᵗʰ NY
3-2-5 5th Oneida, Colonels Garrard, Jenkins and Grindlay

7-2&3: From this position General Meade observed the battle for a time on July 3rd.

Casualties: Killed 4, Wounded 24; Total 28.

Warren
Statue 7-2: Led to this spot by his military sagacity on July 2nd, 1863 Governeur Kemble Warren, then Chief Engineer of the Army of the Potomac, detected General Hood's flanking movement and by promptly assuming the responsibility of ordering troops to this place, saved the key of the Union position.

Promoted for gallant services from the command of a regiment in 1861, through successive grades to the command of the 2nd Army Corps in 1863 and permanently assigned to that of the 5th Army Corps in 1864, Major General Warren needs no eulogy. His name is enshrined in the hearts of his countrymen. This statue is erected under the auspices of the Veteran's Organization of his old Regiment, the 5th New York Volunteers, Duryee Zouaves in memory of their beloved commander.

Dedicated August 8, 1888.

*see index

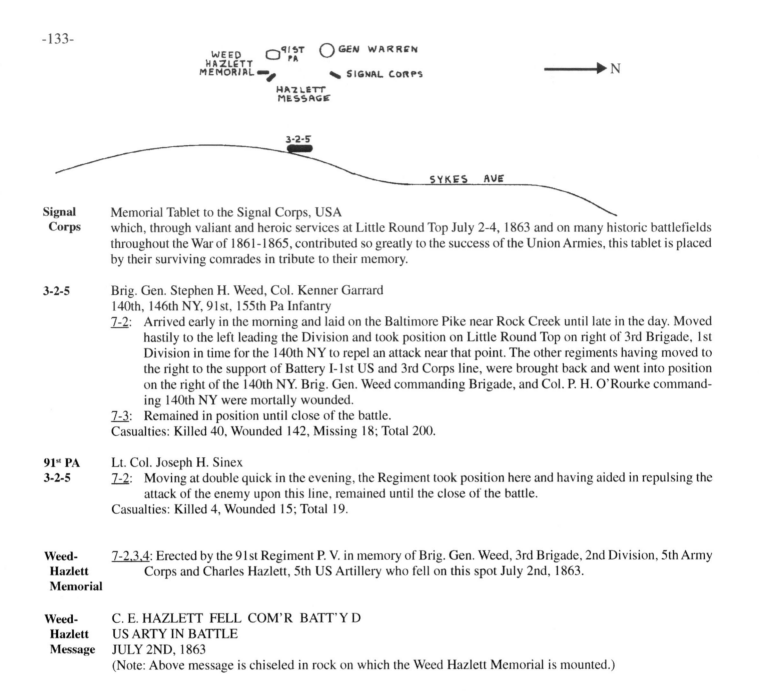

Signal Corps Memorial Tablet to the Signal Corps, USA
which, through valiant and heroic services at Little Round Top July 2-4, 1863 and on many historic battlefields throughout the War of 1861-1865, contributed so greatly to the success of the Union Armies, this tablet is placed by their surviving comrades in tribute to their memory.

3-2-5 Brig. Gen. Stephen H. Weed, Col. Kenner Garrard
140th, 146th NY, 91st, 155th Pa Infantry
<u>7-2</u>: Arrived early in the morning and laid on the Baltimore Pike near Rock Creek until late in the day. Moved hastily to the left leading the Division and took position on Little Round Top on right of 3rd Brigade, 1st Division in time for the 140th NY to repel an attack near that point. The other regiments having moved to the right to the support of Battery I-1st US and 3rd Corps line, were brought back and went into position on the right of the 140th NY. Brig. Gen. Weed commanding Brigade, and Col. P. H. O'Rourke commanding 140th NY were mortally wounded.
<u>7-3</u>: Remained in position until close of the battle.
Casualties: Killed 40, Wounded 142, Missing 18; Total 200.

91ˢᵗ PA
3-2-5 Lt. Col. Joseph H. Sinex
<u>7-2</u>: Moving at double quick in the evening, the Regiment took position here and having aided in repulsing the attack of the enemy upon this line, remained until the close of the battle.
Casualties: Killed 4, Wounded 15; Total 19.

Weed-Hazlett Memorial <u>7-2,3,4</u>: Erected by the 91st Regiment P. V. in memory of Brig. Gen. Weed, 3rd Brigade, 2nd Division, 5th Army Corps and Charles Hazlett, 5th US Artillery who fell on this spot July 2nd, 1863.

Weed-Hazlett Message C. E. HAZLETT FELL COM'R BATT'Y D
US ARTY IN BATTLE
JULY 2ND, 1863
(Note: Above message is chiseled in rock on which the Weed Hazlett Memorial is mounted.)

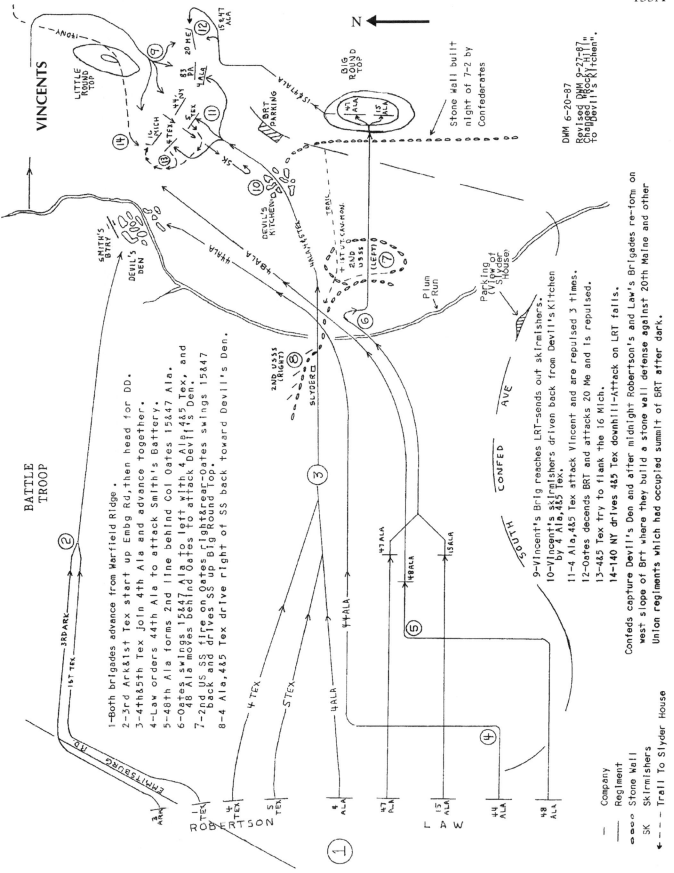

VINCENTS

BATTLE TROOP

N

Stone Wall built night of 7-2 by Confederates

DWM 6-20-87
Revised DWM 9-27-87.
Changed "Rocky Hill"
to "Devil's Kitchen".

1—Both brigades advance from Warfield Ridge.

2—3rd Ark&1st Tex start up Embg Rd,then head for DD.

3—4th&5th Tex join 4th Ala and advance together.

4—Law orders 44th Ala to attack Smith's Battery.

5—48th Ala forms 2nd line behind Col Oates 15&47 Ala.

6—Oates swings 15&47 Ala to left with 4 Ala,4&5 Tex, and 48 Ala moves behind Oates to attack Devil's Den.

7—2nd US SS fire on Oates right&rear-Oates swings 15&47 back and drives SS up Big Round Top.

8—4 Ala,4&5 Tex drive right of SS back toward Devil's Den.

9—Vincent's Brig reaches LRT-sends out skirmishers.

10—Vincent's skirmishers driven back from Devil's Kitchen by 4 Ala,4&5 Tex.

11—4 Ala,4&5 Tex attack Vincent and are repulsed 3 times.

12—Oates descends BRT and attacks 20 Me and is repulsed.

13—4&5 Tex try to flank the 16 Mich.

14—140 NY drives 4&5 Tex downhill-Attack on LRT falls.

Confeds capture Devil's Den and after midnight Robertson's and Law's Brigades re-form on west slope of Brt where they build a stone wall defense against 20th Maine and other Union regiments which had occupied summit of BRT after dark.

_ Company
| Regiment
000 Stone Wall
SK Skirmishers
- - - Trail To Slyder House

~ Gettysburg Battlefield Monuments, Locations & Inscriptions ~

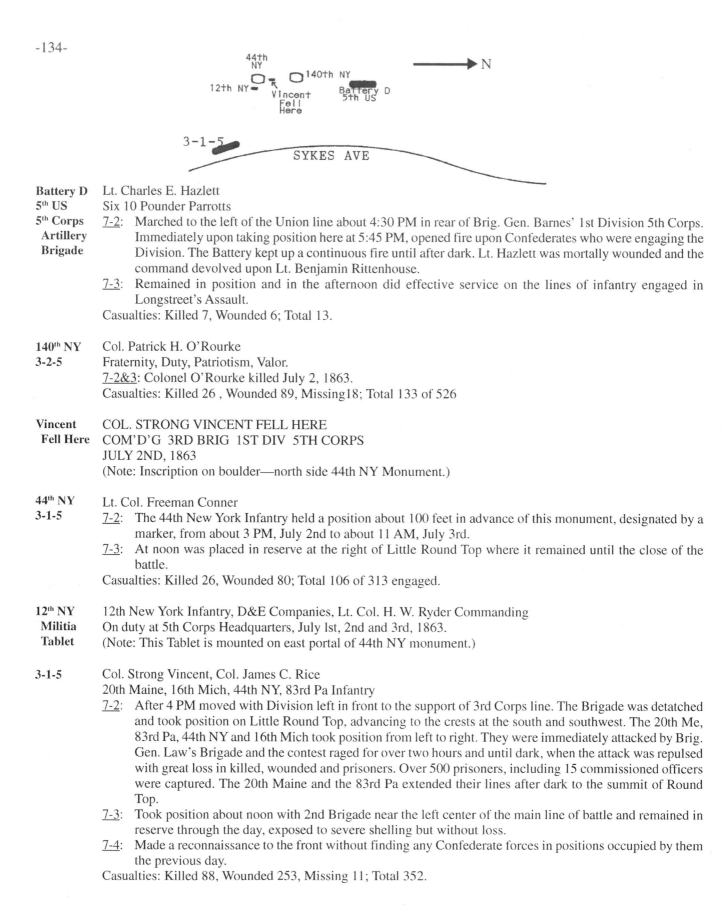

Battery D
5th US
5th Corps Artillery Brigade

Lt. Charles E. Hazlett

Six 10 Pounder Parrotts

7-2: Marched to the left of the Union line about 4:30 PM in rear of Brig. Gen. Barnes' 1st Division 5th Corps. Immediately upon taking position here at 5:45 PM, opened fire upon Confederates who were engaging the Division. The Battery kept up a continuous fire until after dark. Lt. Hazlett was mortally wounded and the command devolved upon Lt. Benjamin Rittenhouse.

7-3: Remained in position and in the afternoon did effective service on the lines of infantry engaged in Longstreet's Assault.

Casualties: Killed 7, Wounded 6; Total 13.

140th NY
3-2-5

Col. Patrick H. O'Rourke

Fraternity, Duty, Patriotism, Valor.

7-2&3: Colonel O'Rourke killed July 2, 1863.

Casualties: Killed 26 , Wounded 89, Missing18; Total 133 of 526

Vincent Fell Here

COL. STRONG VINCENT FELL HERE

COM'D'G 3RD BRIG 1ST DIV 5TH CORPS

JULY 2ND, 1863

(Note: Inscription on boulder—north side 44th NY Monument.)

44th NY
3-1-5

Lt. Col. Freeman Conner

7-2: The 44th New York Infantry held a position about 100 feet in advance of this monument, designated by a marker, from about 3 PM, July 2nd to about 11 AM, July 3rd.

7-3: At noon was placed in reserve at the right of Little Round Top where it remained until the close of the battle.

Casualties: Killed 26, Wounded 80; Total 106 of 313 engaged.

12th NY
Militia
Tablet

12th New York Infantry, D&E Companies, Lt. Col. H. W. Ryder Commanding

On duty at 5th Corps Headquarters, July 1st, 2nd and 3rd, 1863.

(Note: This Tablet is mounted on east portal of 44th NY monument.)

3-1-5

Col. Strong Vincent, Col. James C. Rice

20th Maine, 16th Mich, 44th NY, 83rd Pa Infantry

7-2: After 4 PM moved with Division left in front to the support of 3rd Corps line. The Brigade was detached and took position on Little Round Top, advancing to the crests at the south and southwest. The 20th Me, 83rd Pa, 44th NY and 16th Mich took position from left to right. They were immediately attacked by Brig. Gen. Law's Brigade and the contest raged for over two hours and until dark, when the attack was repulsed with great loss in killed, wounded and prisoners. Over 500 prisoners, including 15 commissioned officers were captured. The 20th Maine and the 83rd Pa extended their lines after dark to the summit of Round Top.

7-3: Took position about noon with 2nd Brigade near the left center of the main line of battle and remained in reserve through the day, exposed to severe shelling but without loss.

7-4: Made a reconnaissance to the front without finding any Confederate forces in positions occupied by them the previous day.

Casualties: Killed 88, Wounded 253, Missing 11; Total 352.

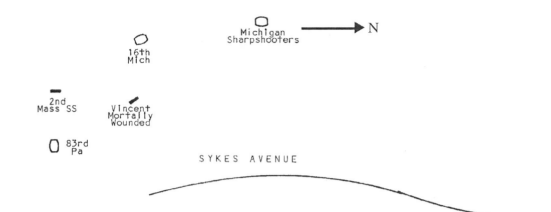

Vincent Mortally Wounded

General Strong Vincent
3rd Brigade First Division 5th Corps
Wounded July 2, Died July 7, 1863.

Michigan Sharp-shooters 2-1-3

Company C 1st Regiment US Sharpshooters
Fought on this field July 2nd near Sherfy House; here July 3rd.
Wounded 1 officer, 5 men, Missing 1 man; Total 7.

Company I 1st Regiment US Sharpshooters
Fought upon this field July 2nd near Pitzer's Run; here July 3rd.
1 officer Killed, 1 officer, 3 men wounded; Total 5

Company K 1st Regiment US Sharpshooters
Fought upon this field July 2nd near Sherfy House; here July 3rd.
4 men wounded.

Company B 2nd Regiment US Sharpshooters
Fought upon this field July 2nd near Slyder House on extreme left, afterwards at this point;
July 3rd on Cemetary Ridge near centre of line.
4 men wounded.

Erected By The State Of Michigan To Her Martyrs And
Heroes Who Fought In Defense Of Liberty And Union.

16th Mich 3-1-5

Lt. Col. Norval E. Welsh
7-2: The Regiment held this position during the afternoon and night and assisted in defeating the desperate attempts of the enemy to capture Little Round Top.
Casualties: Killed 23, Wounded 34, Missing 3; Total 60 of 356

2nd Mass Sharp-shooters* 1-1-5

July 3, 1863
1st Brigade 1st Division 5th Corps
Attached to the 22nd Massachusetts Infantry

83rd PA 3-1-5

Capt. Orpheus S. Woodward
7-2: The Brigade was hurried to Little Round Top about 5 PM, this Regiment taking position in front of this monument and repulsed several desperate charges of the enemy, after which this Regiment assisted in driving the enemy beyond, and in taking possession of Big Round Top.
7-3: On the morning of the 3rd, rejoined the Brigade on the left centre.
Casualties: Killed 10, Wounded 45; Total 55 of 308 present.

*see index

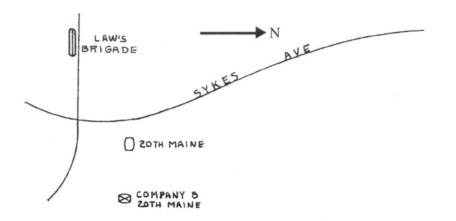

20th Maine Col. Joshua L. Chamberlain
3-1-5   <u>7-2</u>: Here the 20th Maine Regiment, Col. Joshua L. Chamberlain, Commanding, forming the extreme left of the National line of battle, on the 2nd Day of July, 1863, repulsed the attack of the extreme right of Longstreet's Corps and charged in turn, capturing 308 prisoners. The Regiment lost 38 killed or mortally wounded and 93 wounded out of 353 engaged. This monument, erected by the survivors of the Regiment AD 1886, marks very near the spot where the colors stood.
Names Of The Officers And Men Of The 20th Maine Volunteers Who Were Killed Or Died Of Wounds Received In The Action: (Note: The names of 38 officers and men of Companies A, C, D, G, F, H, I and K are listed on the monument.)

Company B Position of Co. B, 20th Me. Vols. Capt. Walter G. Morrill. Detatched as skirmishers attacking enemy's right
20th Maine flank afternoon of July 2, 1863.
3-1-5

Longstreet's Brig. Gen. Evander M. Law, Col. James L. Sheffield
  Corps   4th, l5th, 44th, 47th, 48th Alabama Infantry
Hood's   <u>7-2</u>: Arrived on the field about 4 PM and advanced against the Union positions. The 4th, 15th and 47th Regi-
 Division   ments attacked Little Round Top and continued the assault until dark. The 44th and 48th assisted in captur-
Law's   ing the Devil's Den and three guns of Smith's New York Battery.
 Brigade Casualties: Killed 74, Wounded 276, Missing 146; Total 496 (NY@Gbg)

THE SYMBOLS LISTED BELOW ARE USED TO IDENTIFY
THE MONUMENTS, MARKERS, TABLETS, STATUES, ETC.
WHICH ARE DRAWN ON THE MAPS IN THESE PAGES

SYMBOL	TYPE	REPRESENTING	DESCRIPTION
●	Bronze Tablet	Army of The Potomac, Union Corps or Division or Brigade, Regular Army Regiment, Regular Army Artillery Battery, Volunteer Artillery Brigade.	Brigade Tablet Mounted on Square Marble base. All other Tablets are on large vertical Granite Blocks.
○	Bronze Tablet	Army of Northern Virginia, Confederate Corps or Division or Brigade or Artillery Battalion	Brigade Tablet and Artillery Battalion Tablet Mounted on Round Marble base. All other Tablets are Mounted on large vertical Granite blocks.
●	Iron Tablet	Union Army Battery (other than Regular Army)	Mounted on Black Iron Shaft.
○	Iron Tablet	Confederate Artillery Battery	Mounted on Black Iron Shaft.
▯	Iron Tablet	Confederate Brigade Advanced Position	Mounted on Black Iron Shaft.
▢	Regimental or Battery Monument	Principal Position of Volunteer Regiment or Volunteer Artillery Battery	Usually Granite or Marble in a Great Variety of Shapes and Sizes.
⊗	Regimental Marker	Other than Principal Position of Regiment or Battery	Usually a Square Granite Marker or tablet or may be another monument.
▫	Flank Marker or Company Marker	Left and/or Right Flank of Regiment or Battery or Position of a Company.	Usually a Small Square or Rectangular Granite Marker.
⊕	Army Or Corps Headquarters	Site of Headquarters of Army Commander or Corps Commander or Chief of Artillery	Cannon Barrel Mounted Vertically on Stone, Granite or Marble Base.
◆	State Monument	Monument Erected by Union or Confederate State.	
○	Statue	Standing or Equestrian	Bronze Sculpture
●	Building	House, Barn or other Structure	Identified by Owner's Name.
▪	Miscellaneous Marker	Marker or Inscription of a type not listed above	Granite or Metal Marker.

*Asterisk   Used whenever a Division or Brigade or Regiment or Battery has more than one Monument or Marker.   Check the Index for other Monument or Marker.

~ Gettysburg Battlefield Monuments, Locations & Inscriptions ~

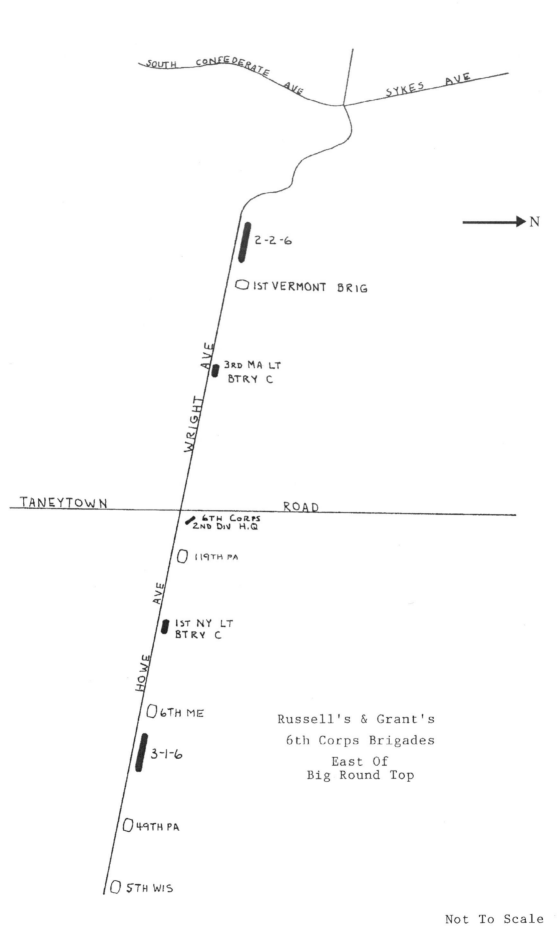

South Confederate Ave

Sykes Ave

N

2-2-6

1st Vermont Brig

Wright Ave

3rd MA Lt Btry C

Taneytown Road

6th Corps 2nd Div H.Q

119th PA

Howe Ave

1st NY Lt Btry C

6th ME

3-1-6

49th PA

5th Wis

Russell's & Grant's
6th Corps Brigades
East Of
Big Round Top

Not To Scale

~ Gettysburg Battlefield Monuments, Locations & Inscriptions ~

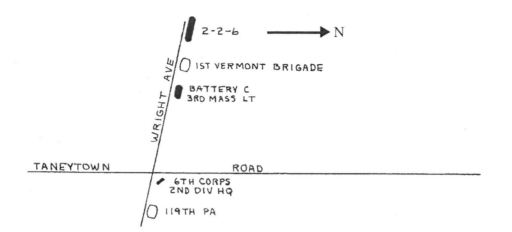

2-2-6   Col. Lewis A. Grant
2nd, 3rd, 4th, 5th, 6th Vermont Infantry
7-2:   Arrived about 5 PM after a march of 33 miles from Manchester, Md. Moved to the left later, and at dark, to the extreme left with one regiment, the 5th Vermont on picket.
7-3:   The Brigade advanced a short distance and took position with its right on the east slope of Round Top, its left on the Taneytown Road and remained until the close of the battle under no fire except that from artillery.
Casualties: Wounded 1 Total. (NY@Gbg)

1st Vermont   2nd, 3rd, 4th, 5th and 6th Regiments
Brigade   Reaching this field by a forced march of 32 miles in the evening of July 2nd, the Brigade took position on the left Union flank, near this point in anticipation of an attack by the enemy and held the same July 3rd and 4th.

Battery C*   Lt. A. F. Walcott
3rd Mass   Six 12 Pounders.
Light   7-3:   At 3 AM, moved to and occupied this position until the close of the battle.
5th Corps   Casualties: Wounded 6 Total. (NY@Gbg)
Artillery
Brigade

2nd Division   Brig. Gen. Albion Howe
6th Corps   2nd Brigade   Col. Lewis A. Grant
Head-   3rd Brigade   Brig. Gen. Thomas H. Neill
quarters   7-2:   Division left Manchester, Md. at 1 AM and reached Gettysburg at 5 PM, marching 33 miles. 2nd Brigade was moved to the left center and finally to the extreme left. 3rd Brigade was placed in position on Powers Hill.
7-3:   2nd Brigade remained on the extreme left of the line. 3rd Brigade moved to the extreme right to connect with the Union Cavalry.
The Brigades remained in these positions until the close of the battle.
Casualties: Killed 2, Wounded 12, Missing 2; Total 16 (NY@Gbg)

119th PA*   Col. Peter Ellmaker
3-1-6   7-2:   Formed line afternoon of July 2nd in rear of ridge to right of Little Round Top.
7-3:   Morning of the 3rd moved to this position. Afternoon marched to rear of left centre, thence to face of Round Top.
Casualties: Wounded 12 Total (NY@Gbg)

*see index

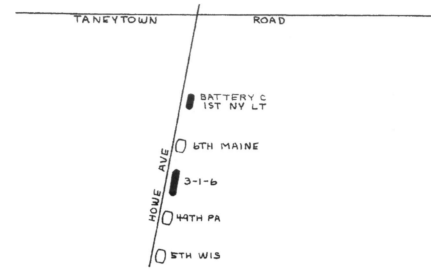

Battery C	Capt. Almont Barnes
1st NY Lt	Four 3 Inch Rifles
5th Corps	7-3: At 3 AM moved to and occupied this position until the close of the battle.
Artillery	Casualties: Killed 4, Wounded 8; Total 12 (NY@Gbg)
Brigade	

6th Maine   Col. Hiram Burnham
3-1-6   7-3: Held this position. In afternoon moved to support of centre, then to Big Round Top.

3-1-6   Brig. Gen. David A. Russell
6th Maine, 49th (4 Cos), 119th Pa, 5th Wis Infantry
7-2: Arrived about 4 PM from Manchester, Md. and moved to the east slope of the northern side of Little Round Top, arriving at dark and held in reserve until morning.
7-3: Moved to the extreme left and on the east slope of Round Top and remained until late in the afternoon, then went into position in the left centre in support of 5th Corps. Not engaged.
7-4: Moved to the left of 5th Corps and occupied the slope of Round Top.
Casualties: Wounded 2 Total.

49th PA   Lt. Col. Thomas M. Hulings
3-1-6   7-2: This Regiment made a continuous march from Manchester, Md. arriving on the field the afternoon of July 2nd.
7-3: Occupied this position in reserve from the morning of the 3rd until the enemy's assault in the afternoon when it moved to support the centre, thence to Round Top.

5th Wis   Col. T. S. Allen
3-1-6   7-3: This Regiment moved from centre to this spot early July 3rd, 1863, to resist threatened attack on this flank. Moved hastily back in the afternoon to assist in repelling attack on the centre, and later took position on the crest of Big Round Top.

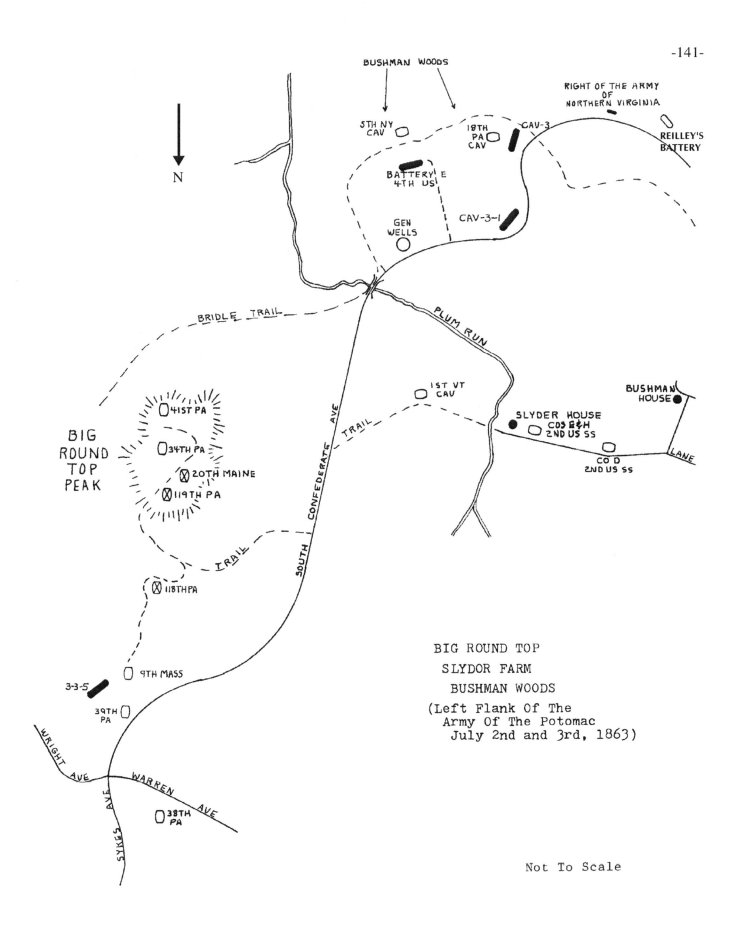

BIG ROUND TOP
SLYDOR FARM
BUSHMAN WOODS

(Left Flank Of The
Army Of The Potomac
July 2nd and 3rd, 1863)

Not To Scale

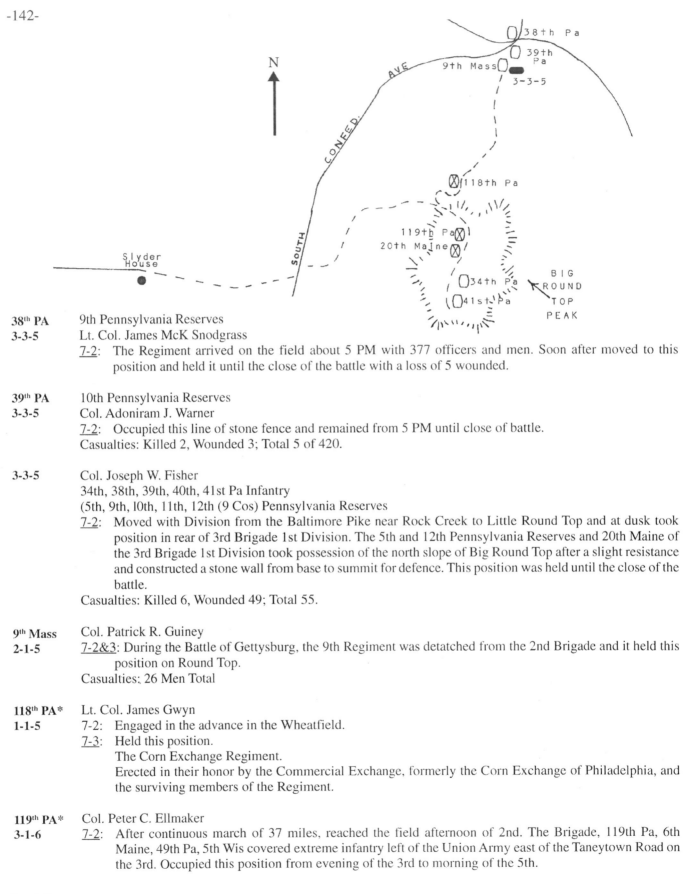

38th PA
3-3-5
9th Pennsylvania Reserves
Lt. Col. James McK Snodgrass
7-2: The Regiment arrived on the field about 5 PM with 377 officers and men. Soon after moved to this position and held it until the close of the battle with a loss of 5 wounded.

39th PA
3-3-5
10th Pennsylvania Reserves
Col. Adoniram J. Warner
7-2: Occupied this line of stone fence and remained from 5 PM until close of battle.
Casualties: Killed 2, Wounded 3; Total 5 of 420.

3-3-5
Col. Joseph W. Fisher
34th, 38th, 39th, 40th, 41st Pa Infantry
(5th, 9th, 10th, 11th, 12th (9 Cos) Pennsylvania Reserves)
7-2: Moved with Division from the Baltimore Pike near Rock Creek to Little Round Top and at dusk took position in rear of 3rd Brigade 1st Division. The 5th and 12th Pennsylvania Reserves and 20th Maine of the 3rd Brigade 1st Division took possession of the north slope of Big Round Top after a slight resistance and constructed a stone wall from base to summit for defence. This position was held until the close of the battle.
Casualties: Killed 6, Wounded 49; Total 55.

9th Mass
2-1-5
Col. Patrick R. Guiney
7-2&3: During the Battle of Gettysburg, the 9th Regiment was detatched from the 2nd Brigade and it held this position on Round Top.
Casualties: 26 Men Total

118th PA*
1-1-5
Lt. Col. James Gwyn
7-2: Engaged in the advance in the Wheatfield.
7-3: Held this position.
The Corn Exchange Regiment.
Erected in their honor by the Commercial Exchange, formerly the Corn Exchange of Philadelphia, and the surviving members of the Regiment.

119th PA*
3-1-6
Col. Peter C. Ellmaker
7-2: After continuous march of 37 miles, reached the field afternoon of 2nd. The Brigade, 119th Pa, 6th Maine, 49th Pa, 5th Wis covered extreme infantry left of the Union Army east of the Taneytown Road on the 3rd. Occupied this position from evening of the 3rd to morning of the 5th.

*see index

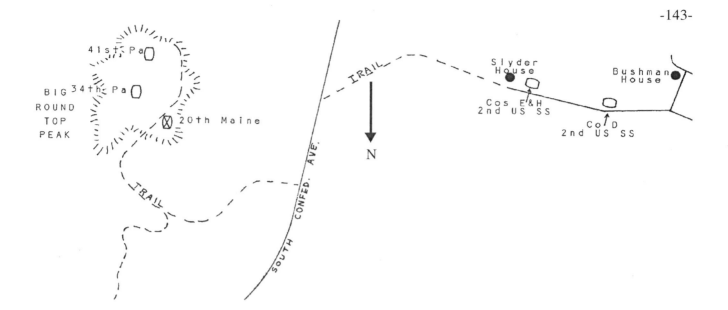

20ᵗʰ Maine* Col. Joshua Chamberlain
3-1-5   <u>7-2</u>: The 20th Maine Regiment captured and held this position on the evening of July 2nd, 1863, pursuing the enemy from its front on the line marked by the monument below. The Regiment lost in the battle 130 killed and wounded out of 358 engaged. This monument marks the extreme left of the Union line during the battle of the 3rd day.

34ᵗʰ PA   5th Pennsylvania Reserves
3-3-5   Lt. Col. George Dare
               <u>7-2</u>: Occupied this position on the evening of July 2nd and held it to the close of the battle.
               Casualties: 2 Wounded Total (NY@Gbg) Present at Gettysburg 24 Officers and 310 men.

41ˢᵗ PA   12th Pennsylvania Reserves
3-3-5   Col. Martin D. Hardin
               <u>7-2</u>: Occupied this position on the evening of July 2nd and held it until the close of the battle.
               Present at Gettysburg 26 officers and 294 men. Casualties: 1 Killed, 1 Wounded; Total 2.

1ˢᵗ Vermont Lt. Col. Addison W. Preston
 Cavalry   <u>6-30</u>: In the Gettysburg Campaign this Regiment fought Stuart's Cavalry at Hanover, Pa.
 Cav 1-1   <u>7-2</u>: Fought Stuart at Hunterstown.
               <u>7-3</u>: Fought on this field led by Brig. Gen. Elon J. Farnsworth, who fell near this spot. Charged through 1st Texas Infantry and to the line of Law's Brigade, receiving the fire of five Confederate regiments and two batteries and losing 67 men.

Cos E & H <u>7-1</u>: Arrived on field at 6 PM
2nd US   <u>7-2</u>: Met the onset of Longstreet's Corps near this point and helped to check its advance upon Round Top.
 Sharp-   <u>7-3</u>: Reinforced the front lines in the repulse of Pickett's Assault.
 shooters <u>7-4</u>: Skirmished all day along the Emmitsburg Road.
2-1-3   Casualties: Wounded 9, Missing 6; Total 15 of 48.

Co. D   <u>7-2</u>: 2nd US Sharpshooters, Maine Volunteers, Company D.
2ⁿᵈ US   Casualties: Killed 1, Wounded 5, Missing 5; Total 11.
 Sharp-
 shooters

*see index

~ Gettysburg Battlefield Monuments, Locations & Inscriptions ~

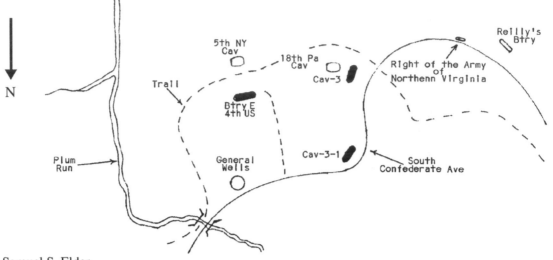

Battery E	Lt. Samuel S. Elder
4th US	Four 3 Inch Rifles
2nd Brigade	7-3: Arrived on the field and took position a hill southwest of Little Round Top and engaged under Brig. Gen.
Horse	E. J. Farnsworth in the afternoon against the Confederate right.
Artillery	Casualties: Killed 1 Total.

5th NY 6-30: This Regiment met and repulsed the portion of Lee's Cavalry under the personal command of
Cavalry Gen. J. E. B. Stuart in the streets of Hanover, a hand-to-hand fight capturing Lt. Col. Paine and 75 men
Cav-3-1 with a loss of 26 men killed and wounded.

7-2: This Regiment attacked Gen. Stuart's Cavalry at Hunterstown and afterwards made a flank movement to this position.

7-3: This Regiment under command of Major John Hammond here supported Battery E-4th US Horse Artillery. Lt. S. S. Elder, losing 6 men.

Wells
Statue

WILLIAM WELLS
Brevet Major General, U.S. Vols.
1837-1892
1st Lieut., Co. C, 1st Vermont Cavalry, Nov 18, '61
Major Dec. 30, 1862
Colonel July 2, 1864
Brevet Brigadier General, U.S. Vols., Feb 22, 1865
Brevet Major General, U.S. Vols. "for gallant and
meritorious services" March 13, 1865
Brigadier General, U.S. Vols. May 19, 1865
Honorably Mustered Out Jan. 15, 1866
Once Wounded And Once A Prisoner
Awarded Medal Of Honor for "most distinguished
gallantry at Gettysburg July 3, 1863"
Commander Of Sheridan's Cavalry Corps

At 5 PM, July 3, 1863 the 2nd Battalion, 1st Vermont Cavalry led by Major William Wells, General Farnsworth commanding the Brigade riding by his side, crossed Plum Run near this point, charging over stone walls amid rocks and through woods till they encountered five regiments of Law's Confederate Brigade, near the spot where the Regimental Monument stands.

The 1st Battalion and part of the 3rd, Lt. Col. A. W. Preston Commanding, were ordered to the support of the 2nd. Moved northerly to the Slidor House, turned into the lane and struck Law's Brigade in the flank. The onset was terrific, sabers and bayonets, revolvers and muskets being freely used. After a struggle, the hill was carried by the 1st Vermont and the prisoners captured sent to the rear.

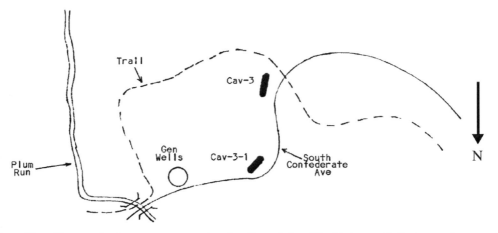

Wells
Statue
(con't)

The three Battalions united soon came under the fire of the 4th Alabama Infantry and presently of the 9th Georgia Infantry, which answered a summons to surrender by a destructive musketry, those unhurt escaping mostly to the south.

This memorial signalizes the valor of the officers and men of the 1st Vermont Cavalry who here paid to the nation the uttermost tribute of devotion.

Cav-3-1

Brig. Gen. Elon J. Farnsworth, Col. Nathaniel P. Richmond

5th NY, 18th Pa, 1st Vt, 1st W. Va. (10 Cos) Cavalry

6-30: Arriving at Hanover about noon and was attacked by Maj. Gen. Stuart's Cavalry and Horse Artillery which first encountered the 18th Pa in the rear of the column. Later the Brigade was engaged and Maj. Gen. Stuart having been forced from the town, retired with the loss of a battle flag and over 70 men.

7-1&2: Not engaged.

7-3: Moved to the left to attack the Confederate right and rear arriving about 1 PM, and became engaged with Confederate skirmishers being supported at 3 PM by the Reserve Cavalry Brigade on the left. At 5:30 PM the 18th Pa, 1st Vt and 1st W Va charged the Confederate left through the woods and among stone fences held by superior forces of infantry and artillery, but were repulsed with heavy loss including Brig. Gen. Farnsworth killed.

Casualties: Killed 21, Wounded 34, Missing 43; Total 98.

Cav-3
Cavalry
Corps
3rd Division

Brig. Gen. Judson Kilpatrick

1st Brigade   Brig. Gen. Elon J. Farnsworth, Col. Nathaniel Richmond

2nd Brigade   Brig. Gen. George A. Custer

6-30: The 1st Brigade was attacked by Stuart's Cavalry at Hanover and was repulsed.

7-1: Marched to Berlin to intercept Stuart without success.

7-2: Arrived on the field of Gettysburg at 2 PM. Moved over the road from Gettysburg to Abbottstown and was attacked at sundown near Hunterstown by Stuart's Cavalry which was driven from the field after an engagement of two hours.

7-3: Moved to attack the Confederate right and rear. The 2nd Brigade reported to General Gregg and was engaged on the extreme right. General Farnsworth arrived on the extreme left at 1 PM and became engaged with the Confederate skirmishers and was supported by the Reserve Brigade on his left. About 5:30 PM, the 1st and Reserve Brigades advanced, General Farnsworth with the 1st W Va and 18th Pa through the woods and across stone walls occupied by superior forces of Confederate infantry and artillery and was repulsed with heavy loss and General Farnsworth killed.

7-4: Moved to Emmitsburg.

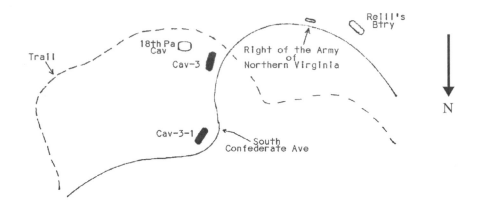

18th PA
Cavalry
Cav-3-1

Lt. Col. William P. Brinton

<u>6-30</u>: Regiment participated in cavalry fight at Hunterstown.

<u>7-2:</u> Hunterstown.

<u>7-3:</u> Occupied this position and in the afternoon charged with the Brigade upon the enemy's infantry behind the stone wall to the north of this position on the outer edge of the woods.

Casualties: Killed 2, Wounded 4, Missing 8; Total 14.

Army of
Northern
Virginia

RIGHT OF THE ARMY OF NORTHERN VIRGINIA

Reilly's
Battery*

(Note: See Page 201 for Reilly's Battery).

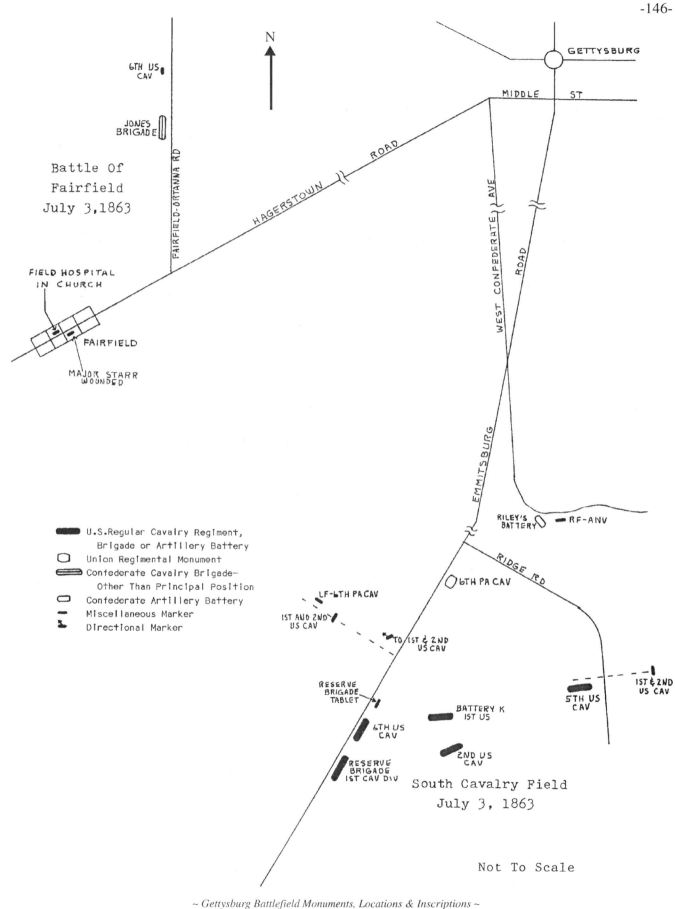

N

Battle Of Fairfield July 3,1863

6TH US CAV

JONES BRIGADE

FAIRFIELD-ORTANNA RD

HAGERSTOWN ROAD

FIELD HOSPITAL IN CHURCH

FAIRFIELD

MAJOR STARR WOUNDED

GETTYSBURG

MIDDLE ST

WEST CONFEDERATE AVE

EMMITSBURG ROAD

RILEY'S BATTERY — RF-ANV

RIDGE RD

U.S.Regular Cavalry Regiment, Brigade or Artillery Battery
Union Regimental Monument
Confederate Cavalry Brigade- Other Than Principal Position
Confederate Artillery Battery
Miscellaneous Marker
Directional Marker

LF-6TH PA CAV

6TH PA CAV

1ST AND 2ND US CAV

TO 1ST & 2ND US CAV

1ST & 2ND US CAV

RESERVE BRIGADE TABLET

BATTERY K 1ST US

5TH US CAV

6TH US CAV

2ND US CAV

RESERVE BRIGADE 1ST CAV DIV

South Cavalry Field July 3, 1863

Not To Scale

~ Gettysburg Battlefield Monuments, Locations & Inscriptions ~

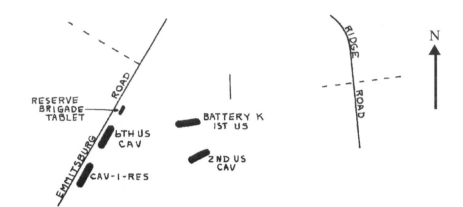

Reserve	Brig. Gen. Wesley Merritt
Brigade	6th Pa, 1st, 2nd, 5th, 6th United States Cavalry
1st Division	7-1: Engaged in picketing and patrolling the roads through the mountains, detatchments scouting the country
Cavalary	about Hagerstown, Cavetown and other points.
Corps	7-2: Marched to Emmitsburg, Md.

7-3: At noon marched four miles on the road to Gettysburg. Met Confederate detatchments and for more than a mile, drove them from stone fences, barricades and other positions, being engaged four hours, and until the operations were brought to a close by a heavy rain. The 6th US under Major S. S. Starr was detatched and marched to Fairfield to intercept a Confederate wagon train supposed to be in that vicinity but encountered a superior force and was compelled to fall back with heavy loss.

Casualties: Killed 28, Wounded 116, Missing 274; Total 418

6th US	Major Samuel S. Starr
Cavalry*	7-3: Moved at 12 PM with the Brigade from Emmitsburg to attack the Confederate right and rear but was
Cav-1-Res	detatched from the Brigade to intercept a Confederate wagon train supposed to be near Fairfield or Millerstown. Engaged a superior force of the Confederate Cavalry near Millerstown and withdrew after heavy loss.

Casualties: Killed 6, Wounded 28, Missing 208; Total 242

Reserve	<div align="center">Position Of The Reserve Brigade First Division Cavalry Corps 1st, 2nd, 5th, 6th US Cavalry And Battery K—1st US Artillery</div>
Brigade	
Tablet	

2nd US	Capt. Theodore F. Rodenbaugh
Cavalry	7-2: Moved with the Brigade at 12 PM under Brig. Gen. Wesley Merritt from Emmitsburg and attacked the
Cav-1-Res	Confederate right and rear and was engaged for four hours until the action was brought to a close by a heavy rain.

Caualties: Killed 3, Wounded 7, Missing 7; Total 17

Battery K	Capt. William M. Graham
1st US	7-3: Arrived on the field and took position on the left with cavalry and engaged during the attack of Brigadier
2nd Brigade	General E. J. Farnsworth and Brigadier General Wesley Merritt's Brigades on the Confederate right.
Horse	Casualties: Killed 2, Wounded 1; Total 3
Artillery	
Cavalry	
Corps	

*see index

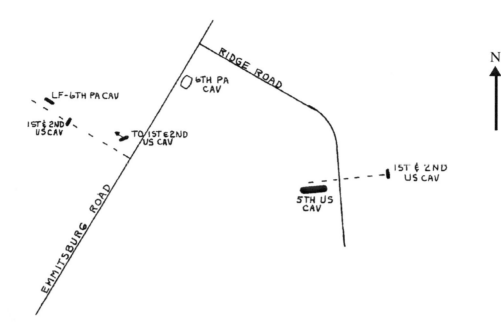

6th Pa* Major James H. Hazeltine
  Cavalry 6th Pennsylvania Cavalry Lancers, Reserve Brigade, 1st Division, Cavalry Corps, Army Of The Potomac.
  Cav-1-Res <u>7-3</u>: Casualties: 3 Killed, 7 Wounded, 2 Missing; Total 12.

6th Pa LF* 6th P C Left
  Cavalry

1st & 2nd To Position Of Detatchments Of The 1st and 2nd Regiments,
  US Cav* US Cavalry, July 3, 1863

1st & 2nd Position occupied by detatchments of the 1st and 2nd Regiments,
  US Cav* United States Cavalry during July 3rd.

1st & 2nd 1st and 2nd Regiments US Cavalry
  US Cav* Casualties: 1st US Killed 1, Wounded 9, Missing 5; Total 15
                 2nd US Killed 3, Wounded 7, Missing 7; Total 17

5th US Capt. Julius W. Mason
  Cavalry Detatchment at Headquarters, Army Of The Potomac.
  Cav-1-Res <u>7-3</u>: Moved with the Brigade at 12 PM under Brig. Gen. Wesley Merritt from Emmitsburg and attacked Confederate right and rear and was engaged for four hours until the action was brought to a close by a heavy rain.
        Casualties: Wounded 4, Missing 1; Total 5.

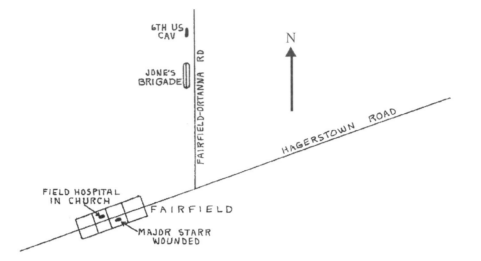

<table>
<tr><td>6th US
Cavalry*
Cav-1-Res</td><td>Major Samuel S. Starr</td></tr>
</table>

6th US Cavalry* Cav-1-Res Major Samuel S. Starr

7-3: The Marshall and Culberson Houses were the temporary field hospitals of the Regiment on July 3rd, 1863. The Regiment, commanded by Major S. S. Starr, was sent to Fairfield to capture a Confederate wagon train guarded by Jones' Brigade of Confederate Cavalry consisting of the 6th, 7th and 11th Regiments of Virginia Cavalry, Clue's Virginia Battery and the 35th Virginia Battalion, were met on this road and after a severe hand-to-hand fight were compelled to retire.

Casualties: 242 of 400 brought into action.

Stuart's Division Jones' Brigade* Brig. Gen. William E. Jones

6th, 7th, 11th, 12th Virginia Cavalry Regiments and 35th Virginia Battalion.

7-1: The 12th Regiment was detached and remained on the south side of the Potomac River. White's 35th Virginia Battalion was also detatched. The remaining regiments crossed the Potomac at Williamsport, Md.

7-2: Marched from near Greencastle, Pa to Chambersburg, Pa.

7-3: The Brigade marched from Chambersburg, Pa via Cashtown to Fairfield, Pa., met the 6th US Cavalry about two miles from Fairfield. The 7th Virginia charged in the advance and was repulsed. The 6th Virginia in support, charged and forced the Union Regiment to retire with heavy losses. The Brigade encamped at Fairfield for the night.

7-4: The Brigade held the mountain passes and picketed the left flank of the Army.

Casualties: Killed 11, Wounded 30, Missing 6; Total 47

Fairfield Church Hospital Wounded of the 6th US Cavalry and 6th Virginia Cavalry, CSA, were cared for in this church building after a severe engagement that took place north of here on July 3rd, 1863.

Major Starr Wounded

Major Samuel S. Starr
And Other Wounded Officers
Of The 6th US Cavalry
Were Cared For Here
July 3, 1863

*see index

~ Gettysburg Battlefield Monuments, Locations & Inscriptions ~

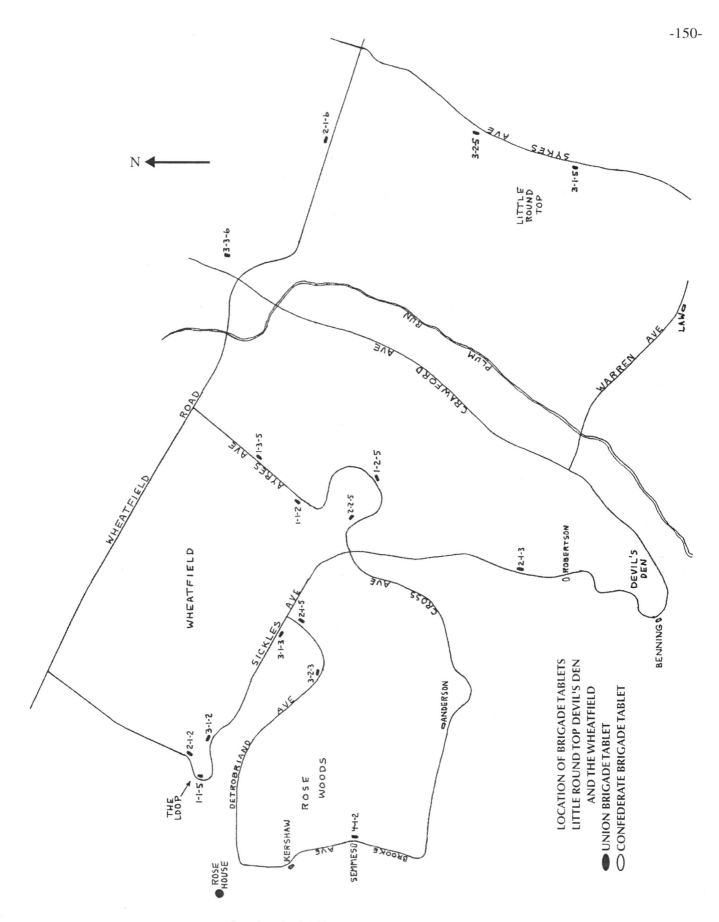

N

WHEATFIELD ROAD

3-3-6

2-1-b

SYKES AVE

3-2-5

3-1-5

LITTLE ROUND TOP

CRAWFORD AVE

PLUM RUN

WARREN AVE

LAWS

AYRES AVE

1-3-5

1-2-5

1-1-1   1-2-1

5-2-2

WHEATFIELD

2-1-3

ROBERTSON

SICKLES AVE

2-1-5

CROSS AVE

DEVIL'S DEN

3-1-3

3-2-3

DETROBRIAND AVE

2-1-2   3-1-2

THE LOOP   1-1-5

BENNING

SANDERSON

ROSE WOODS

KERSHAW

SEMMES   4-1-2

BROOKE AVE

ROSE HOUSE

LOCATION OF BRIGADE TABLETS
LITTLE ROUND TOP, DEVIL'S DEN
AND THE WHEATFIELD
● UNION BRIGADE TABLET
○ CONFEDERATE BRIGADE TABLET

~ Gettysburg Battlefield Monuments, Locations & Inscriptions ~

LOCATION OF BRIGADE AND DIVISION TABLETS
Little Round Top, Devil's Den, Rose Woods and the Wheatfield

ARMY OF THE POTOMAC

	SYMBOL	BRIG	DIV	CORPS	COMMANDER	LOCATION	MAP	MKR
2nd Corps								
Caldwell's Division	1-1-2	1st	1st	2nd	Cross	WF-East	159	160
	2-1-2	2nd	1st	2nd	Kelly	The Loop	164	174
	3-1-2	3rd	1st	2nd	Zook	The Loop	164	172
	4-1-2	4th	1st	2nd	Brooke	Rose Woods	164	165
3rd Corps								
Birney's Division	2-1-3	2nd	1st	3rd	Ward	Devil's Den	152	152
	3-1-3	3rd	1st	3rd	DeTrobriand	WF-South	164	171
	3-2-3	3rd	2nd	3rd	Burling	WF-South	164	167
5th Corps								
Barnes Division	1-1-5	1st	1st	5th	Tilton	The Loop	164	173
	2-1-5	2nd	1st	5th	Schweitzer	WF-South	164	168
	3-1-5	3rd	1st	5th	Vincent	LRT	130	134
Ayres' Division	1-2-5	1st	2nd	5th	Day	Ayres Ave-South	153	156
	2-2-5	2nd	2nd	5th	Burbank	Ayres Ave-South	153	154
	3-2-5	3rd	2nd	5th	Weed	LRT	130	133
Crawford's Division	1-3-5	1st	3rd	5th	McCandless	WF-East	159	161
6th Corps								
Wright's Division	2-1-6	2nd	1st	6th	Bartlett	North of LRT	126	127
Wheaton's Division	3-3-6	3rd	3rd	6th	Nevin	North End of Plum Run Vy	126	128

Army of Northern Virginia

	BRIGADE	LOCATION	MAP	MKR
Longstreet's Corps				
McLaws' Division	Kershaw's	Rose Woods-West	164	166
	Semmes'	Rose Woods-West	164	166
Hood's Division	Anderson's	Rose Woods-South	164	165
	Robertson's	Devil's Den	151	152
	Benning's	Devil's Den	151	151
	Law's	Warren Ave	130	136

WF — Wheatfield
LRT — Little Round Top
Sou — South
Vy — Valley
MKR — Marker Inscription

~ Gettysburg Battlefield Monuments, Locations & Inscriptions ~

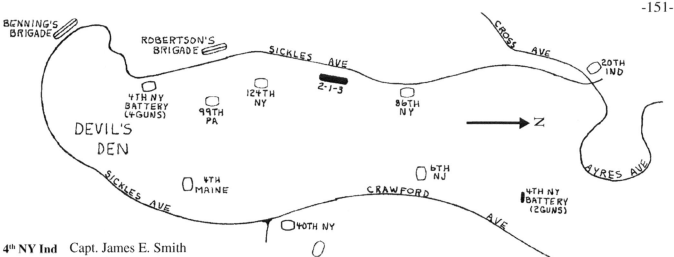

4ᵗʰ NY Ind Battery*
3ʳᵈ Corps Artillery Brigade (2 guns)
Capt. James E. Smith
Two 10 Pounder Parrotts
<u>7-2</u>: Arrived from Emmitsburg at 9 AM. Four guns posted on the height above Devil's Den at 2 PM; two guns in this position. After the capture of three of the guns in the advanced position and the repulse of their supports, this section opened fire with great effect on the Confederate forces advancing up the valley. At 6 PM, this section was moved to the right near Winslow's Battery and subsequently to the rear.
Casualties: Killed 2, Wounded 10, Missing 1; Total 13. 11 horses killed; 240 rounds expended.

6ᵗʰ NJ*
3-2-3
Lt. Col. S. R. Gilkyson
<u>7-2</u>: Engaged here, being detatched from the Brigade.
<u>7-3</u>: Supported batteries on Cemetary Ridge.
Casualties: Killed 5, Wounded 29, Missing 7; Total 41.

40ᵗʰ NY*
3-1-3
Col. Thomas W. Egan. The Mozart Regiment.
July 2, 1863, 4:30 PM.
Casualties: Killed 23, Wounded 120, Missing 7; Total 150.

40ᵗʰ NY*
(Note: Inscription chiseled in rock 8-9 feet from monument.)

4ᵗʰ Maine*
2-1-3
Col. Elijah Walker, Capt. Edwin Libby
<u>7-2</u>: In remembrance of our casualties July 2nd, 1863.
Casualties: Killed and died of wounds 22, Wounded 38, 56 Missing.

Longstreet's Corps Hood's Division Benning's Bridgade*
Brig. Gen. Henry L. Benning
2nd, 15th, 17th, 20th Georgia Infantry
<u>7-2</u>: Formed in line about 4 PM in rear of Law's and Robertson's Brigades and, moving forward in support, took active part in the conflict which resulted in the capture of the Devil's Den, together with a number of prisoners and three guns of Smith's 4th New York Battery.
Casualties: Killed 76, Wounded 299, Missing 122; Total 497 (NY @Gbg)

4ᵗʰ NY Ind Battery*
3ʳᵈ Corps Artillery Brigade (4 guns)
Capt. James E. Smith
Four 10 Pounder Parrotts
<u>7-2</u>: July 2, 1863, 2 to 5 PM.
Casualties: (Note: See 4th New York Independent Battery above.)

*see index

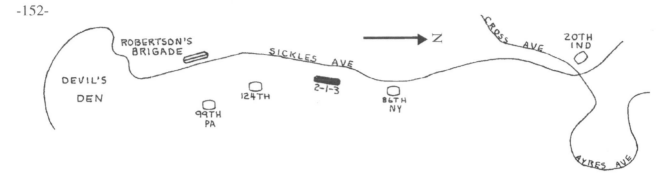

Longstreet's Corps Brig. Gen. J. B. Robertson
Hood's Division 1st, 4th, 5th Texas, 3rd Arkansas Infantry.
Robertson's Brigade 7-2: Arrived on the field about 4 PM. Advanced against the Union positions. The 4th and 5th Texas joined in the attack on Little Round Top which continued until dark. The 1st Texas and 3rd Arkansas attacked and assisted in taking the Devil's Den and Rocky Ridge with a number of prisoners and three guns of Smith's 4th New York Battery.
Casualties: Killed 84, Wounded 393, Missing 120; Total 597 (NY@Gbg)

99th PA
2-1-3 Major John W. Moore
7-2: Fought on this line in the afternoon of July 2nd.
Casualties: Killed 25, Wounded 74, Missing 11; Total 110 of 399 officers and men.

124th NY
2-1-3 Col. A. Van Horne Ellis
The Orange Blossoms
7-2: The Orange Blossoms went into action on this spot with 18 officers, 220 men. Lost in killed and wounded 7 officers, 85 men. Orange County's Tribute To Her Brave Defenders. Our Comrades, They Died For Their Country.

2-1-3 Brig. Gen. J. Hobert Ward, Col. Hiram Berdan
20th Ind, 3rd, 4th Maine, 86th, 124th NY, 99th Pa Infantry
7-1: Arrived after sunset and bivouacked for the night.
7-2: The Corps having relieved the 2nd Division 12th Corps in the morning, the Brigade took position on the left of the Division and extended to Little Round Top. Between 2 and 3 PM advanced with the Division to the line from the Peach Orchard to Devil's Den, occupying the left of the line to the west base of Little Round Top. The 1st US SS and 3rd Maine were engaged in a reconnissance into the woods in front of the Peach Orchard from noon to about 2 PM and then served with 1st Brigade at the Peach Orchard. The 6th NJ and 40th NY were sent to Brig. Gen. Ward and supported his left. Between 4 and 5 PM the Brigade was fiercely attacked by Brig. Gen. Robertson's and Brig. Gen. Benning's Brigades supported on their flanks by Brig. Gen. Law's and Brig. Gen. Anderson's Brigades, Maj. Gen. Hood's Div and after a prolonged conflict was forced back.
Casualties: 129 Killed, 482 Wounded, 170 Missing; Total 781.

86th NY
2-1-3 Lt. Col. Benjamin L. Higgins
7-2: This Regiment held this position the afternoon of July 2, 1863. I Yield Him Unto His Country And His God. .
Casualties: Killed 11, Wounded 51, Missing 4; Total 66.

20th Ind
2-1-3 Col. John Wheeler, Lt. Col. William C. Taylor
7-2: Colonel John Wheeler killed nearby.
Casualties: Killed 32, Wounded 114, Missing 10; Total 156.

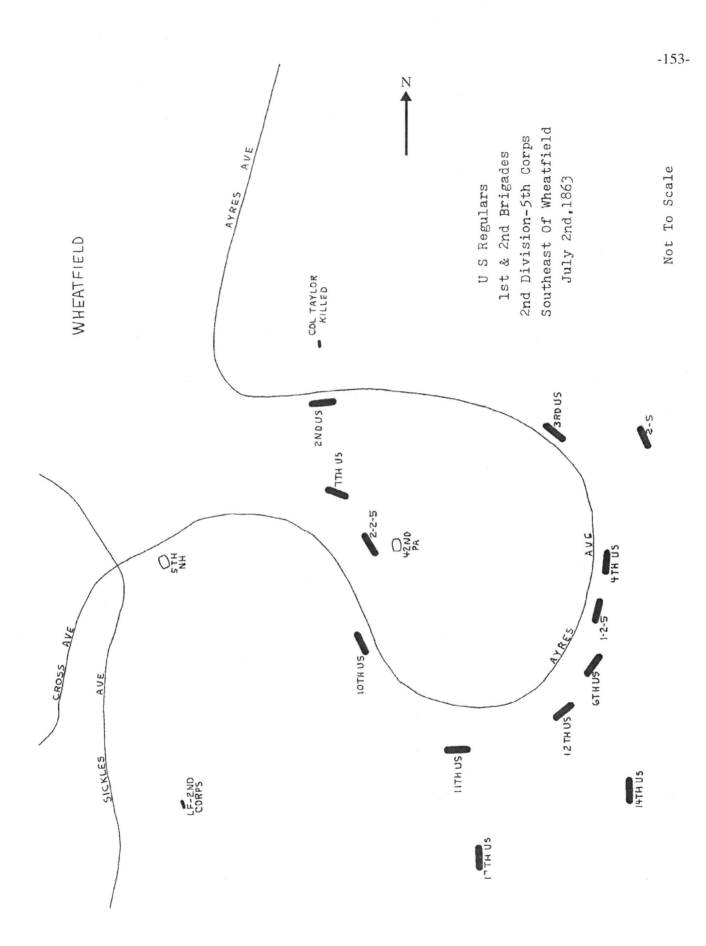

~ Gettysburg Battlefield Monuments, Locations & Inscriptions ~

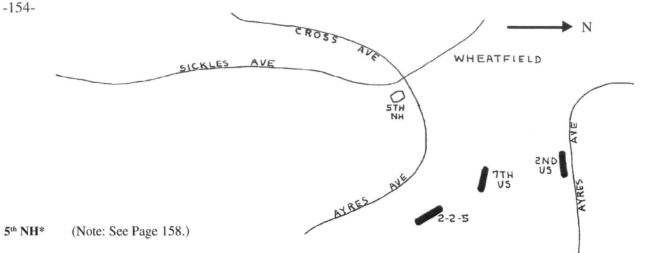

5th NH*   (Note: See Page 158.)

2-2-5   Col. Sidney Burbank
        2nd (6 Cos), 7th (4 Cos), 10th (3 Cos), 11th (6 Cos), 17th (7 Cos) US Infantry.
        <u>7-2</u>: Arrived early in the morning and formed on the right of the 12th Corps. Afterwards, crossed Rock Creek and remained near the Baltimore Pike until late in the day, then moved with the Division to the north slope of Little Round Top and soon advanced across Plum Run Valley supported by the 1st Brigade, and formed line on the hill beyond facing the Wheatfield, through which 1st Division 2nd Corps was forcing the Confederates perpendicular to the line of the Brigade. Later, advanced on the left of 1st Division 2nd Corps and the 1st Brigade in support, when the Union forces on the right and front having been forced back by superior numbers, the two Brigades retired in good order, but with great loss under a heavy fire of musketry on its front and flank to Little Round Top and in the evening to the other side in reserve.
        <u>7-3</u>: Remained in the same position until the close of the battle.
        Casualties: Killed 78, Wounded 342, Missing 27; Total 447 out of a strength of 900 muskets.

2nd US   Major Arthur T. Lee and Capt. Samuel A. McKee
Infantry   <u>7-2</u>: Arrived in the morning and took position with the Brigade on the right of the 12th Corps. Skirmished with
(6 Cos)   the Confederates. Later, moved to the left. At 5 PM formed line with left on north slope of Little Round
2-2-5   Top and the right of Brigade line extending into some woods. Advanced across Plum Run and to the crest of the rocky wooded hill in front near the Wheatfield and facing left, occupied the stone wall on the edge of the woods. The Confederates, having opened fire on the right flank and advanced through the Wheatfield in the rear, the Brigade was withdrawn under a heavy infantry fire on both flanks and from the rear, and of shot and shell from the batteries, and formed line on right of Little Round Top.
        <u>7-3</u>: Remained in same position.
        Casualties: Killed 6, Wounded 55, Missing 6; Total 67.

7th US   Capt. David P. Hancock
Infantry   <u>7-2</u>: Arrived in the morning and took position with the Brigade on the right of 12th Corps. Later, moved with
(4 Cos)   the Brigade to the left and at 5 PM formed line on the right of Little Round Top, advanced across Plum
2-2-5   Run and to the crest of the rocky wooded hill in front near the Wheatfield, and facing to the left occupied the stone wall on the edge of the woods. The Confederates, having opened fire on the right flank and advanced through the Wheatfield in the rear, the Brigade was withdrawn under a deadly fire of musketry on both flanks and on the rear and of shot and shell from the batteries, and formed line on the right of Little Round Top.
        <u>7-3</u>: Remained in same position.
        <u>7-4</u>: Advanced nearly a mile in support of a skirmish line of the 12th and 14th Infantry.
        Casualties: Killed 12, Wounded 45, Missing 2; Total 59.

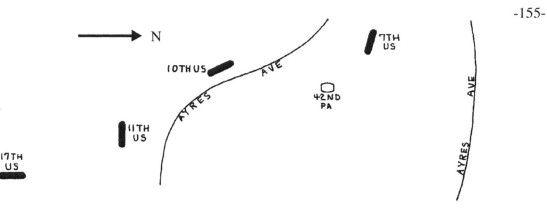

42ⁿᵈ PA   (Note: See Page 160.)

10ᵗʰ US   Capt. William Clinton
Infantry   7-2:   Arrived with the Brigade in the morning and took position on the right of the 12th Corps. Later, moved to
2-2-5   the left and at 5 PM the Brigade formed line with left on north slope of Little Round Top, the right
                       extending into the woods. Advanced across Plum Run and to the crest of the rocky wooded hill in front
                       near the Wheatfield, and facing left, occupied the stone wall on the edge of the woods. The Confederates
                       having opened fire on the right flank and advanced through the Wheatfield in the rear, the Brigade was
                       withdrawn under a heavy infantry fire on both flanks and from the rear and shot and shell from the batter-
                       ies and was formed in line on the right of Little Round Top.
                7-3:   Remained in the same position.
                Casualties: Killed 16, Wounded 32, Missing 3; Total 51.

11ᵗʰ US   Major DeLancey Floyd Jones
Infantry   7-2:   Arrived in the morning with the Brigade and took position on the right of the 12th Corps. Afterwards,
(6 Cos)   moved to the left and at 5 PM formed line on the right of Little Round Top and advanced across Plum Run
2-2-5   and to the crest of the rocky wooded hill in front under a fire of sharpshooters on the left, and faced to the
                       left with the Wheatfield on the right and rear. The Confederates having opened fire on the right flank, and
                       advancing through the Wheatfield in the rear, the Regiment with the Brigade was withdrawn under a
                       heavy fire of musketry and artillery and formed in line at the right of Little Round Top.
                7-3:   Remained in same position.
                Casualties: Killed 19, Wounded 92, Missing 9; Total 120. Present 25 officers and 261 men.

17ᵗʰ US   Lt. Col. J. Durell Green
Infantry   7-2:   Arrived in the morning and took position with the Brigade on the right of the 12th Corps. Later, moved to
(7 Cos)   the left and at 5 PM formed line with the Brigade at the right of Little Round Top and advanced across
2-2-5   Plum Run to the crest of the rocky wooded hill beyond, near the Wheatfield under a severe fire from the
                       Confederate sharpshooters on the left, then facing left the Regiment with the Brigade occupied the stone
                       wall on the edge of the woods. The Confederates, having opened fire on the right, and advanced in the
                       Wheatfield in the rear, the Brigade was withdrawn under a heavy fire on both flanks and from the rear, and
                       formed on the right of Little Round Top having been engaged about two hours.
                7-3:   Remained in same position.
                Casualties: Killed 25, Wounded 118, Missing 7; Total 150.

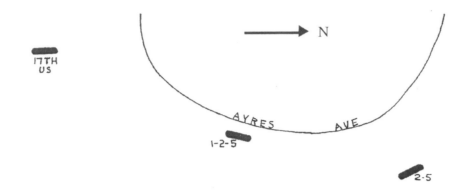

2nd Division Brig. Gen. Romeyn B. Ayres
5th Corps   1st Brigade   Col. Hannibal Day
                      2nd Brigade   Col. Sidney Burbank
                      3rd Brigade   Brig. Gen. S. H. Weed, Col. Kennar Garrard
    <u>7-2</u>: Moved from the Baltimore Pike near Rock Creek about 5 PM, left in front to the support of the 3rd Corps line, preceeded by the 1st Division. The 3rd Brigade halted at Little Round Top and occupied the summit and north slope just in time to repel an attack on the right of the 3rd Brigade 1st Division. Here General Weed fell mortally wounded. The 1st and 2nd Brigades crossed Plum Run to the hill beyond and formed in two lines, the 1st Brigade in rear fronting the Wheatfield, through which the 1st Division 2nd Corps was advancing at right angles. About sunset the troops in front and on the right retired before a fierce assault on their front and flank and these two Brigades were compelled to retire with heavy losses to Little Round Top, pursued by Wofford's Georgia Brigade and portions of Semmes', Kershaw's and Anderson's Brigades. Later, the 1st and 2nd Brigades took positions in the woods in rear of the 3rd Brigade.
    <u>7-3</u>: Remained in same position.
    <u>7-4</u>: The 1st Brigade made a successful reconnaissance to the front.
    Casualties: Killed 164, Wounded 802, Missing 63; Total 1029.

1-2-5   Col. Hannibal Day
            3rd (6 Cos), 4th (4 Cos), 6th (5 Cos), 12th (8 Cos), 14th (8 Cos) US Infantry
    <u>7-2</u>: Moved left in front with the Division late in the day from the Baltimore Pike near Rock Creek, to Little Round Top and 3rd Corps line. Halted on the north slope of Little Round Top. 3rd Brigade in advance went to support of 3rd Brigade 1st Division. The Brigade preceeded by 2nd Brigade, advanced across Plum Run Valley to the hill beyond and formed line in rear of 2nd Brigade facing the Wheatfield through which 1st Division 2nd Corps was advancing perpendicular to the line of the Brigade. Later, advanced supporting 2nd Brigade towards the left, when the Union forces on the right and front having been driven back by superior numbers, the Brigade retired under a heavy musketry fire on its front and flank, to Little Round Top and at night to the woods on the east side.
    <u>7-3</u>: Remained in same place.
    <u>7-4</u>: Made a reconaissance to the front supported by the 2nd Brigade 1st Division 6th Corps, forcing in the Confederate pickets and drawing the fire of artillery.
    Casualties: Killed 46, Wounded 318, Missing 18; Total 382.

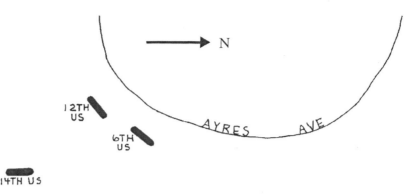

14th US Infantry (8 Cos) 1-2-5	Capt. Grotius R. Giddings
	<u>7-2</u>: Arrived in the morning and took position with the Brigade and Division with the 12th Corps on the right. Moved with the Division from the right to the left of the line and at 5 PM with the Brigade, moved across Plum Run near Little Round Top and supported the 2nd Brigade in its advance to the crest of the rocky wooded hill beyond, and facing left, engaged the Confederates, but retired under a heavy fire on both flanks and from the rear, after the Confederates had possession of the Wheatfield in the rear of the Brigade, and went into position on Little Round Top.
	<u>7-3</u>: Remained in the same position.
	<u>7-4</u>: The Regiment with the 12th supported the 3rd, 4th and 6th US Infantry in a reconnaissance and developed a force of the Confederate infantry and artillery in front.
	Casualties: Killed 18, Wounded 110, Missing 4; Total 132.

12th US Infantry (8 Cos) 1-2-5	Capt. Thomas S. Dunn
	<u>7-2</u>: Arrived in the morning and took position with the Brigade and Division near the 12th Corps on the right. Moved with the Division from the right to the left of the line and at 5 PM, with the Brigade moved across Plum Run near Little Round Top and supported the 2nd Brigade in its advance to the crest of the rocky wooded hill in front, and facing left, engaged the Confederates but retired under a heavy fire on both flanks and from the rear, after the Confederates had obtained possession of the Wheatfield in the rear of the Brigade and went into position on Little Round Top.
	<u>7-3</u>: Regiment with the 14th supported the 3rd, 4th and 6th US Infantry in a reconnaissance and developed a force of the Confederate infantry and artillery in front.
	Casualties: Killed 8, Wounded 71, Missing 13; Total 92.

6th US Infantry (5 Cos) 1-2-5	Capt. Leon C. Bootes
	<u>7-2</u>: Arrived in the morning and took position near the line of the 12th Corps. The Regiment with the Brigade moved from the right to the left of the line and at 5 PM, advanced across Plum Run near Little Round Top and supported 2nd Brigade in its advance to the crest of the rocky wooded hill beyond, and facing to the left, engaged the Confederates, but retired under a deadly fire on both flanks and from the rear after the Confederates got possession of the Wheatfield in the rear of the Brigade, and took position on Little Round Top.
	<u>7-3</u>: Remained in same position.
	<u>7-4</u>: The Regiment with the Brigade made a reconnaissance and developed a force of the Confederate infantry and artillery in front.
	Casualties: Killed 4, Wounded 40; Total 44.

4th US Infantry (4 Cos) 1-2-5 Capt. Julius W. Adams, Jr.

7-2: Arrived in the morning and took position near the line of the 12th Corps. The Regiment with the Brigade moved from the right to the left of the line and at 5 PM advanced across Plum Run near Little Round Top and supported the 2nd Brigade in its advance to the crest of the rocky wooded hill beyond, and facing to the left, engaged the Confederates, but retired under a deadly fire from both flanks and from the rear after the Confederates had gained a position in the Wheatfield in the rear of the Brigade.

7-3: Remained in same position.

7-4: The Regiment with the Brigade made a reconnaissance and developed a force of Confederate infantry and artillery in front and engaged on the skirmish line well to the front.

Casualties: Killed 10, Wounded 30; Total 40.

3rd US Infantry (6 Cos) 1-2-5 Capt. Henry W. Freedly and Capt. Richard G. Gray

7-2: Arrived in the morning and took position near the line of the 12th Corps. The Regiment with the Brigade moved from the right to the left of the line and at 5 PM advanced across Plum Run near Little Round Top and supported 2nd Brigade in its advance to the crest of the rocky wooded hill beyond, and facing to the left, engaged the Confederates, but retired under a deadly fire on the left, right and rear, after the Confederates had gained a position in the Wheatfield in the rear of the Brigade, and took position on east slope of Little Round Top.

7-3: Remained in same position.

7-4: The Regiment with the Brigade, made a reconnaissance and developed a force of Confederate infantry and artillery in front.

Casualties: Killed 6, Wounded 67, 1 Missing; Total 74.

Left Flank 2nd Corps Left Of The 5th New Hampshire Volunteer Infantry
Left Of Cross' Brigade
Left Of Caldwell's Division
Left Of The 2nd Army Corps

5th NH* 1-1-2 7-2: On this spot fell mortally wounded Edward E. Cross, Colonel, 5th New Hampshire Volunteers, Commanding 1st Brigade, 1st Division, 2nd Corps.
Here from 5 PM to 7 PM the 5th New Hampshire Volunteers stood and fought.
The State of New Hampshire erected this monument July 2nd, 1863 to commemorate the valor of her sons.
Casualties: Killed or Mortally Wounded 31, Total Killed and Wounded 81, 182 Total engaged.

*see index

N

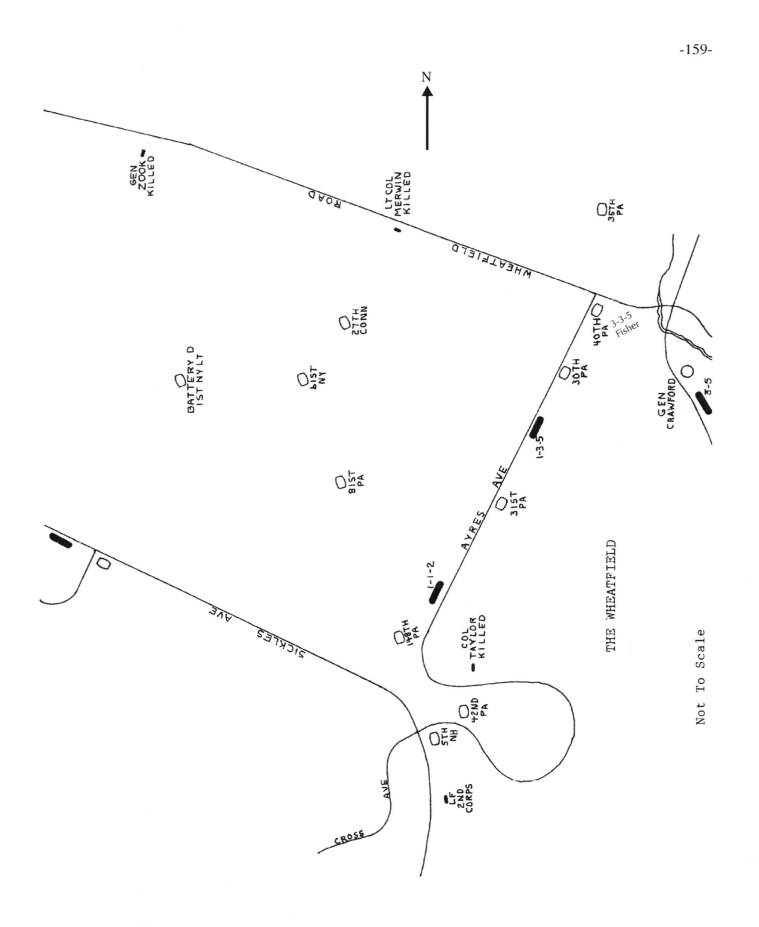

GEN
ZOOK
KILLED

ROAD

LT COL
MERWIN
KILLED

WHEATFIELD

35TH
PA

27TH
CONN

BATTERY D
1ST NY LT

61ST
NY

40TH
PA 3-3-5
Fisher

30TH
PA

GEN
CRAWFORD

3-5

81ST
PA

1-3-5

AYRES   AVE

31ST
PA

1-1-2

THE WHEATFIELD

148TH
PA

SICKLES AVE

COL
TAYLOR
KILLED

42ND
PA

5TH
NH

LF
2ND
CORPS

CROSS

AVE

Not To Scale

*see index

~ Gettysburg Battlefield Monuments, Locations & Inscriptions ~

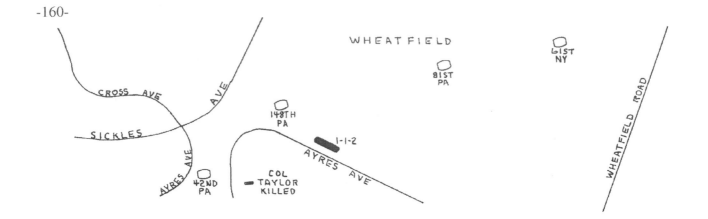

148th PA* Lt. Col. Robert McFarlane
1-1-2 <u>7-2</u>: The Regiment engaged the enemy on this position in the afternoon of July 2nd, 1863.
Killed and Died of Wounds 27, Wounded 93, Captured or Missing 5; Total 125 of 468 officers and men present at Gettysburg.

1-1-2 Col. Edward E Cross, Col. H. Boyd McKeen
5th NH, 61st NY, 81st, 148th Pa Infantry.
<u>7-2</u>: Arrived about 7 AM and was massed in the woods at left and rear of Corps and at 10 AM took position forming the left of Division in column of regiments. Between 5 and 6 PM, moved with Division to the support of 3rd Corps, forming line of battle along a stone wall at the rear and east of the Wheatfield and advanced against the Confederate forces in the Wheatfield and in the woods at the left, forcing them back to the farther end of the Wheatfield and taking many prisoners, when the ammunition being exhausted, the Brigade was relieved by part of the 2nd Division 5th Corps and 2nd Brigade, 1st Division 5th Corps and retired to the stone wall, and finally with Division to former position in line with the Corps. Colonel Cross fell mortally wounded early in the engagement.
<u>7-3</u>: Constructed breastworks early in the morning which gave protection from the cannonade in the afternoon. Remained in position until close of the battle.
Casualties: Killed 57, Wounded 260, Missing 13; Total 330.

81st PA Col. H. Boyd McKeen, Lt. Col. Amos Stroh
1-1-2 <u>7-2</u>: Fought on this line in the afternoon of July 2nd.
Killed and Died of Wounds 9, Wounded 45, Missing 8; Total 62 of 175 present.

61st NY Lt. Col. K. Oscar Broady
1-1-2 <u>7-2</u>: This position held by the 61st NY Infantry on the afternoon of July 2nd, 1863.
Casualties: Killed 6, Wounded 56; Total 62.

42nd PA Col. Charles F. Taylor, Major William R. Hartshorne
1-3-5 The Bucktails.
(13th PA <u>7-2</u>: In the evening, charged from the hill in rear to this position and held it until the afternoon of July 3rd.
Reserves <u>7-3</u>: The Brigade advanced through the woods to the front and left, driving the enemy and capturing many
1st Rifles) prisoners.
Casualties: Killed and Died of Wounds 11, Wounded 35, Missing 2.
Present at Gettysburg 349 officers and men.

Colonel Here fell Charles Frederick Taylor, July 2, 1863, aged 23 years, 4 months and 26 days, Colonel of the Bucktails,
Taylor 1st Rifle Regt, PRV. Charles Frederick Taylor, Born February 6, 1840, enrolled May 15, 1861,
Killed Capt. Co H 13th Pennsylvania Reserves 1st Rifles May 28, 1861, Colonel March 1, 1863; Killed In Action July 2, 1863. Erected By His Comrades And Friends 1905.

*see index

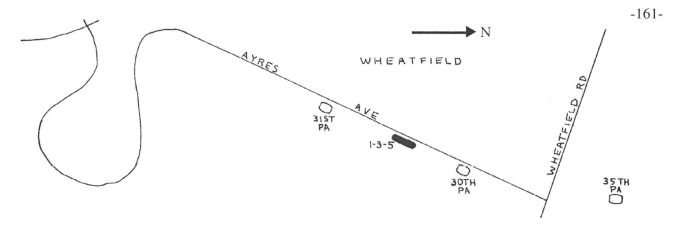

31st PA
(2nd PA
Reserves)
1-3-5

Lt .Col. George A. Woodward

<u>7-2</u>: In the evening charged from the hill in rear to this position and held it until the afternoon of July 3rd.

<u>7-3</u>: Brigade advanced through the woods to the front and left, driving the enemy and capturing many prisoners.

Casualties: Killed and Died of Wounds 9, Wounded 27, Missing 1; Total 37 of 273 present at Gettysburg.

1-3-5

Col. William McCandless

30th, 31st, 35th, 42nd Pa Infantry

1st (9 Cos), 2nd, 6th, 13th Pennsylvania Reserves.

<u>7-2</u>: Moved with Division from Baltimore Pike near Rock Creek late in the day to Little Round Top north of the Wheatfield Road. After sunset formed line to cover the retiring of 1st and 2nd Brigades 2nd Division and supported by 3rd Brigade 3rd Division 6th Corps charged the advancing Confederates and forced them down the hill and across into the Wheatfield. Col. Taylor, commanding 13th Pennsylvania Reserves fell in the advance. The Brigade remained at a stone wall in rear of the Wheatfield.

<u>7-3</u>: Advanced through the Wheatfield into the woods beyond, supported by 3rd Brigade 3rd Division 6th Corps and changing front, swept southward through the woods west and south of the Wheatfield encountering a portion of Brig. Gen. Benning's Brigade and capturing about 200 prisoners and the colors of the 15th Georgia. The Confederates retired to the crest of the ridge from which they advanced the previous day. In this movement one 10 Pounder Parrott was recovered and about 3000 small arms were gathered from the field.

Casualties: Killed 20, Wounded 132, Missing 3; Total 155.

30th PA
(1st PA
Reserves)
1-3-5

Col. William C. Talley

<u>7-2</u>: In the evening charged from the hill in rear to this position and held it until the afternoon of July 3rd.

<u>7-3</u>: The Brigade advanced through the woods to the front and left, driving the enemy and capturing many prisoners.

Casualties: Killed and Died of Wounds 13, Wounded 33; Total 46.

Present at Gettysburg: 26 officers and 418 men.

35th PA
(6th PA
Reserves)
1-3-5

Lt. Col. Wellington H. Ent

<u>7-2</u>: Charged from hill in rear to this position and held it until afternoon of July 3rd.

<u>7-3</u>: The Brigade advanced through the woods to the front and left, driving the enemy and capturing many prisoners.

Casualties: Killed and Died of Wounds 3, Wounded 20; Total 23.

Present at Gettysburg: 25 officers and 355 men.

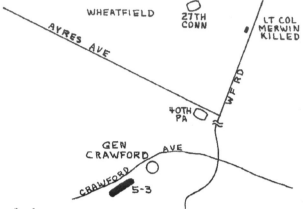

3rd Division
5th Corps   Brig. Gen. Samuel W. Crawford
          1st Brigade   Col. William McCandless
          3rd Brigade   Col. Joseph W Fisher

7-2:   Moved to Little Round Top late in the day and went into position on the right of the Wheatfield Road. On the retreat of the troops from the Wheatfield in front after sunset, the 1st Brigade was advanced against the pursuing forces and drove them across the Plum Run Marsh and beyond the stone wall and into the Wheatfield. The 3rd Brigade was sent to the left to take possession of Round Top.

7-3:   The 1st Brigade remained in position until about 5 PM and then advanced across the Wheatfield and through the woods beyond and on the left, capturing many prisoners. The Confederates retired to the crest of the ridge they originally formed on. These positions were held until the close of the battle.

Casualties: Killed 26, Wounded 181, Missing 3; Total 210.

40th PA   Col. Samuel M. Jackson
(11th PA   7-2:   In the evening charged from the hill in rear to this position and held it until the afternoon of July 3rd.
Reserves)   7-3:   The Brigade advanced through the woods to the front and left, driving the enemy and capturing many
3-3-5   prisoners.

Casualties: Killed 4, Wounded 35; Total 39. Present at Gettysburg: 25 officers and 367 Men.

27th Conn*   Lt. Col. Henry C. Merwin, Major James H. Coburn
4-1-2   7-2:   The 27th Regiment Connecticut Volunteers, Commanded by Lt. Col. Henry C. Merwin and forming a part of the 4th Brigade 1st Division 2nd Corps, charged over this ground the afternoon of July 2nd, 1863. The 4th Brigade forced the enemy from the Wheatfield and beyond the woods in front where the advanced position of the 27th Regiment is indicated by a tablet on the crest of the ledge. On this spot, Lt. Col. Merwin was killed while gallantly leading his command of 75 officers and men, 38 of whom were killed or wounded in the charge. Eight Companies of the Regiment captured at Chancellorsville were still prisoners of war. Capt. Jedediah Chapman, Jr. was also killed in the charge while commanding a company organized from detatched members of the eight companies taken prisoner at Chancellorsville.

Casualties: Killed 10, Wounded 23, Missing 4; Total 37 (NY@Gbg)

Col. Merwin   In memory of Lt. Col. Henry C. Merwin, 27th Conn. Volunteers,
Killed   who fell mortally wounded where the monument of his Regiment stands.

Crawford   Brig. Gen Samuel Wiley Crawford
Statue   Commander of The Pennsylvania Reserves
          1829 - 1892

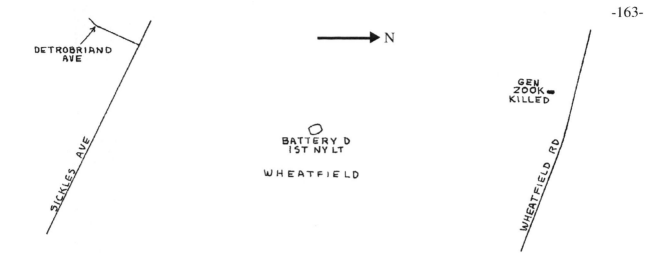

Gen. Zook
Killed
To the memory of Samuel Kosciosko Zook, Brevet Major General United States Volunteers, who fell mortally wounded at or near this spot, while leading his Brigade in battle July 2nd, 1863.
Erected by General Zook Post Number 11 GAR, July 25, 1882.

1st NY LT
Battery D
3rd Corps
Artillery
Brigade
Capt. George B. Winslow
Six 12 Pounders
7-2: This Battery (Winslow's) held this position during the afternoon of July 2nd, 1863.
Casualties: Wounded 10, Missing 8; Total 18.

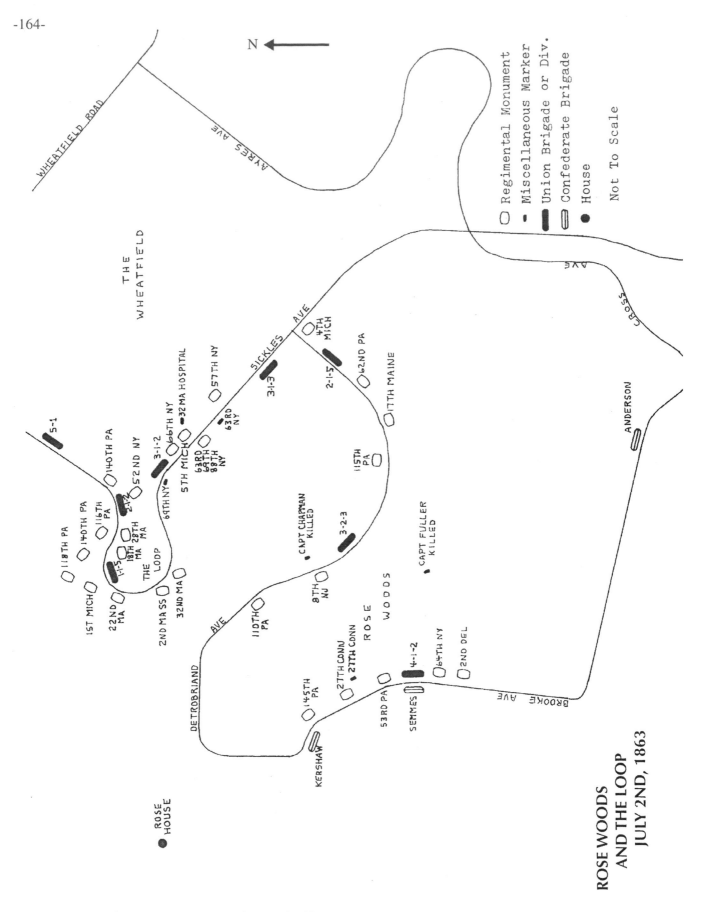

N

Regimental Monument
Miscellaneous Marker
Union Brigade or Div.
Confederate Brigade
House
Not To Scale

WHEATFIELD ROAD

AYRES AVE

THE WHEATFIELD

SICKLES AVE

CROSS AVE

AVE

5-1

140TH PA

52ND NY

3-1-2

5TH MICH

66TH NY

32 MA HOSPITAL

57TH NY

63RD NY

63RD
64TH
68TH
88TH NY

3-1-3

4TH MICH

62ND PA

2-1-5

17TH MAINE

115TH PA

ANDERSON

118TH PA

140TH PA

116TH PA

2-1-2

28TH MA MA

18TH MA MA

1-1-5

THE LOOP

69TH NY

1ST MICH

22ND MA

2ND MASS

32ND MA

CAPT CHAPMAN KILLED

3-2-3

CAPT FULLER KILLED

ROSE WOODS

8TH NJ

110TH PA

DETROBRIAND AVE

145TH PA

27TH CONN

27TH CONN

53RD PA

SEMMES

4-1-2

64TH NY

2ND DEL

BROOKE AVE

KERSHAW

ROSE HOUSE

**ROSE WOODS
AND THE LOOP
JULY 2ND, 1863**

~ Gettysburg Battlefield Monuments, Locations & Inscriptions ~

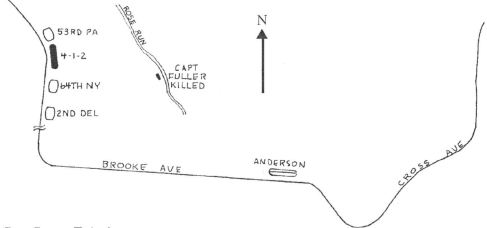

Longstreet's Corps Hood's Division Anderson's Brigade* Advanced Position	Brig. Gen. George T. Anderson 7th, 8th, 9th, 59th Georgia Infantry <u>7-2</u>: Reached the field about 4 PM and formed line. The 7th Regiment was sent southward to watch the Union Cavalry. The others charged into the woods south of the Wheatfield and dislodged the Union line from the stone fence. Being flanked on the left, retired to crest of Rose Hill. Reinforced by parts of other brigades they again advanced. The brigades advanced a third time and after a struggle, occupied the woods to its border in Plum Run Valley.

2nd Del*
4-1-2

Col. William P. Baily

<u>7-2</u>: Position held by the 2nd Regiment Delaware Volunteer Infantry, 4th Brigade, 1st Division, 2nd Army Corps. Erected by the State of Delaware to commemorate the gallantry of her sons. AD 1885.

Casualties: Killed 11, Wounded 61, Missing 12; Total 84.

64th NY
4-1-2

Col. Daniel G. Bingham, Major Leman W. Bradley

<u>7-2</u>: Killed 15, Wounded 64, Missing 19; Total 98

Capt. Fuller
Killed

Capt. Henry V. Fuller, Company F, 64th NY Infantry

Killed July 2, 1863

4-1-2

Col. John R. Brooke

27th Conn (2 Cos), 2nd Del, 64th NY, 53rd and 145th Pa Infantry.

<u>7-2</u>: Arrived early in the morning, took position on the line from Cemetary Hill to Round Top and was the right brigade of Division. Between 5 and 6 PM, went with Division to Wheatfield and advanced in reserve on the left of 3rd Brigade across a marsh to the crest of a wooded hill. The Union line along the Emmitsburg Road having soon thereafter been forced back by Brig. Gen. Semmes, Brig. Gen. Kershaw's, and Brig. Gen. Wofford's Brigades, which advanced in front and on the right flank, Brig. Gen. Anderson's Brigade advancing on the left flank, the Brigade retired with the Division and resumed its former place in Corps line.

Casualties: Killed 54, Wounded 284, Missing 51; Total 389.

53rd PA
4-1-2

Lt. Col. Richards McMichael

<u>7-2</u>: About 5 PM the Regiment deployed with the Brigade on the northerly side of, and charged through, the Wheatfield driving the enemy and continuing the advance to this position, holding it until ordered to retire.

<u>7-3</u>: In position with Division on the left centre. Carried into action 135 officers and men.

Casualties: Killed 7, Wounded 67, Missing 6; Total 80.

*see index

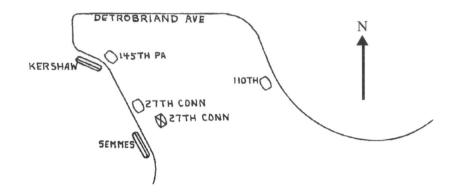

Longstreet's Brig. Gen. Paul J. Semmes, Col. Goode Bryan
Corps 7-2: Arrived on the field about 3:30 PM. Advanced about 5 PM in support of Kershaw's and Anderson's
McLaws' Brigades and took an active part in the conflict on Rose Hill and in the ravine and forest east of there and
Division in the vicinity of the Loop. Participated in the general advance later in the evening by which the Union
Semmes' forces were forced out of the Wheatfield and across Plum Run Valley. General Semmes fell mortally
Brigade* wounded in the ravine near the Loop.

27th Conn* This tablet indicates the advanced position of the 27th Regiment Connecticut Volunteers in its charge the
Advanced afternoon of July 2, 1863.
Position

27th Conn* Lt. Col. Henry C. Merwin, Major James H. Coburn
4-1-2 7-2: Advanced position of this Regiment in the Brigade charge. Erected by the Commomwealth of
Connecticut as a memorial to the valor of her loyal sons.
Casualties: Killed 10, Wounded 23, Missing 4; Total 37.

145th PA Col. Hiram L. Brown, Capt. John W. Reynolds, Capt. Moses W. Oliver
4-1-2 7-2: In the evening about 5 PM the Regiment with the Brigade charged from the northerly side of the Wheatfield,
driving the enemy and capturing many prisoners. This position was held until the command was outflanked, when it retired under orders.
7-3: The Regiment was in position on the left centre with the Divison.
Casualties: Killed 24, Wounded 56, Missing 10; Total 90. Present: 228 officers and men.

Longstreet's Brig. Gen. Joseph B. Kershaw
Corps 2nd, 3rd, 7th, 8th, 15th South Carolina Infantry
McLaws' 7-2: Arrived on the field at 3:30 PM. Formed line and advanced about 4:30 o'clock. The 8th and 2nd Regi-
Division ments and the 3rd Battalion shared in the attack on the Peach Orchard and batteries near there on Wheatfield
Kershaw's Road. The 7th and 3rd Regiments engaged at and around the Loop. The 15th Regiment fought on Rose
Brigade Hill and in the ravine and forest beyond. Late in the evening the Brigade took part in the advance by which
the Union forces were forced from the Wheatfield and across Plum Run Valley. At dark, under orders, the
Brigade retired to and occupied the Peach Orchard.

110th PA Lt. Col. David N. Jones, Major Isaac Rogers
3-1-3 7-2: The Regiment fought on this line from 4 until 6 o'clock.
7-3: Supported batteries on Cemetary Hill.
Casualties: Killed and Died of Wounds 16, Wounded 37; Total 53.

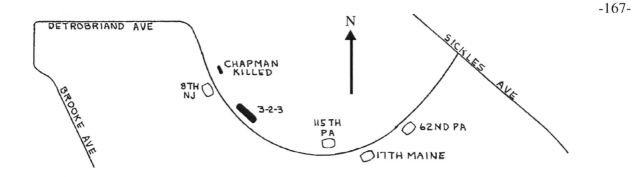

Chapman Killed   Here fell Jedediah Chapman, Capt. Co. H, 27th Connecticut Volunteers.

8ᵗʰ NJ
3-2-3   Col. John Ramsey
7-2: Engaged here July 2nd, being detatched from the Brigade.
7-3: Supported batteries on Cemetary Hill.
Casualties: Killed 7, Wounded 38, Missing 2; Total 47 of 170 taken into action.

3-2-3   Col. George C. Burling
2 NH, 5th, 6th, 7th, 8th NJ, 115th Pa Infantry
7-2: Arrived between 9 and 10 AM and joined Division between 2 and 3 PM. Advanced with Division and was placed in reserve in rear of 2nd Brigade and soon thereafter was ordered to 1st Division except that 5th NJ supported Battery K-4th US on the Emmitsburg Road. The 2nd NH and 7th NJ reported to Brig. Gen. C. K. Graham and supported batteries in the Peach Orchard, the 63rd PA on the left. The 6th NJ went to the support of 2nd Brigade 1st Division. The Regiments of the Brigade were severely engaged where assigned and retired with the organizations they served.
Casualties: Killed 59, Wounded 376, Missing 78; Total 513.

115ᵗʰ PA
3-2-3   Major John P. Dunne
7-2: This Regiment detatched from the Brigade, engaged the enemy here at 4:30 PM.
7-3: In position with Division on left centre of the line.
Casualties: Killed 3, Wounded 18, Missing 3; Total 24 of 182.

17ᵗʰ Maine
3-1-3   Lt. Col. Charles B. Merrill
7-2: Fought here in the Wheatfield 2 1/2 hours and at this position from 4:10 to 5:45 PM, July 2, 1863.
7-3: At time of the enemy's assault, it reinforced the centre and supported artillery.
Casualties: 40 Killed or Mortally Wounded 40, Wounded 92, Total 132.

62ⁿᵈ PA
2-1-5   Lt. Col. James C. Hall
7-2: Position occupied by the Regiment in the evening of July 2nd after the troops on the right had retired, and where the Brigade had a bayonet contest.
Casualties: Killed 28, Wounded 107, Missing 40; Total 175 of 426 carried into action.

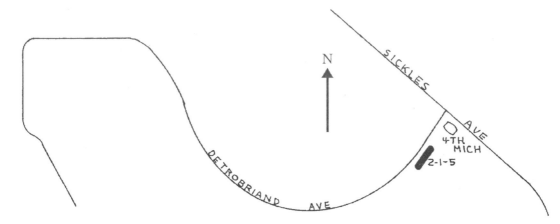

2-1-5   Col. Jacob Sweitzer

9th, 32nd Mass, 4th Mich, 62nd Pa Infantry

7-2: After 4 PM moved from Baltimore Pike near Rock Creek with the Division left in front to support of 3rd Corps line. 3rd Brigade was detatched to occupy Little Round Top and the Brigade crossed Plum Run followed by 1st Brigade and went into position on the edge of the woods west of the Wheatfield facing partly towards the Rose House, 1st Brigade on right. Kershaw's Brigade supported by Brig. Gen. Semmes' Brigade having attacked this position and 1st Brigade having retired, the Brigade retired across the Wheatfield Road and formed on the north side of woods, facing the road, when by order of Brig. Gen. Barnes, the Brigade advanced to the support of 1st Division 2nd Corps and engaged Brig. Gen. Anderson's Brigade at the stone wall at the south end of the Wheatfield, but the supports on the right having given way, the Brigade was attacked on the right and rear and it retired under a heavy fire to a line north of Little Round Top and there remained until the end of the battle.

Casualties: Killed 67, Wounded 239, Missing 121; Total 427.

4th Mich   Col. Harrison H. Jeffords, Lt. George W. Leonard

2-1-5

7-2: This marks the position held by the Regiment July 2, 1863. Col. Harrison H. Jeffords fell mortally wounded at this point, thrust through by a bayonet in recapturing the colors of his Regiment.

"From his bosom that heaved the last torrent was streaming,

And pale was his visage, deep marked with a scar,

And dim was that eye, once expressively beaming,

That melted in love, and that kindled in war."

Casualties: Killed 25, Wounded 64, Missing 76; Total 165 of 403 Present for Duty.

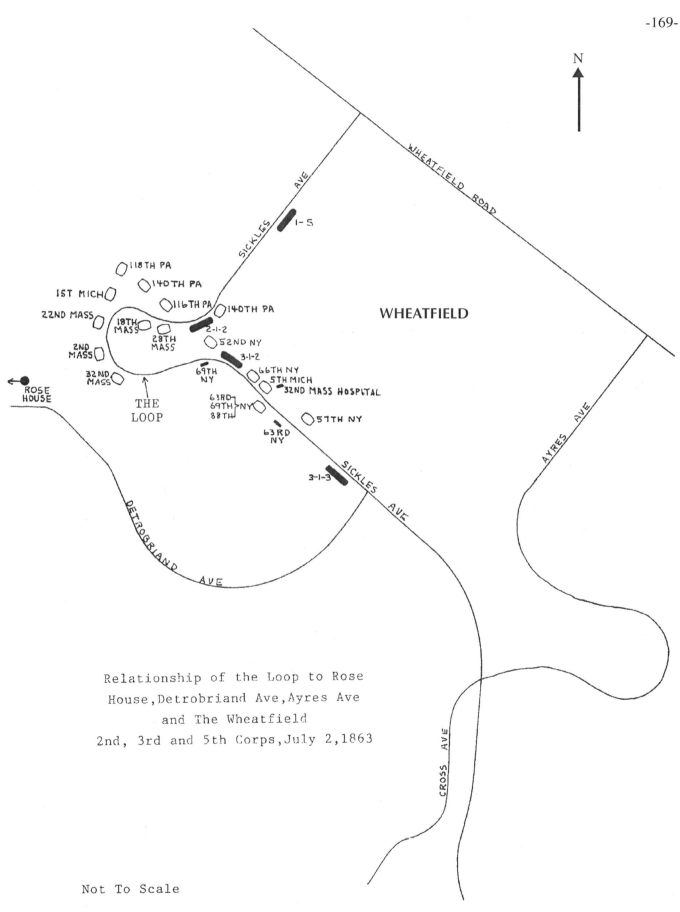

N

WHEATFIELD ROAD

WHEATFIELD

SICKLES AVE

1-5

118TH PA

140TH PA

1ST MICH

116TH PA

140TH PA

22ND MASS

18TH MASS

28TH MASS

2-1-2

52ND NY

2ND MASS

3-1-2

32ND MASS

THE LOOP

69TH NY

66TH NY
5TH MICH
32ND MASS HOSPITAL

ROSE HOUSE

63RD
69TH NY
88TH

57TH NY

63RD NY

3-1-3

SICKLES AVE

AYRES AVE

DETROBRIAND AVE

CROSS AVE

Relationship of the Loop to Rose
House, Detrobriand Ave, Ayres Ave
and The Wheatfield
2nd, 3rd and 5th Corps, July 2, 1863

Not To Scale

~ Gettysburg Battlefield Monuments, Locations & Inscriptions ~

THE SYMBOLS LISTED BELOW ARE USED TO IDENTIFY THE MONUMENTS, MARKERS, TABLETS, STATUES, ETC. WHICH ARE DRAWN ON THE MAPS IN THESE PAGES

SYMBOL	TYPE	REPRESENTING	DESCRIPTION
	Bronze Tablet	Army of The Potomac, Union Corps or Division or Brigade, Regular Army Regiment, Regular Army Artillery Battery, Volunteer Artillery Brigade.	Brigade Tablet Mounted on Square Marble base. All other Tablets are on large vertical Granite Blocks.
	Bronze Tablet	Army of Northern Virginia, Confederate Corps or Division or Brigade or Artillery Battalion	Brigade Tablet and Artillery Battalion Tablet Mounted on Round Marble base. All other Tablets are Mounted on large vertical Granite blocks.
	Iron Tablet	Union Army Battery (other than Regular Army)	Mounted on Black Iron Shaft.
	Iron Tablet	Confederate Artillery Battery	Mounted on Black Iron Shaft.
	Iron Tablet	Confederate Brigade Advanced Position	Mounted on Black Iron Shaft.
	Regimental or Battery Monument	Principal Position of Volunteer Regiment or Volunteer Artillery Battery	Usually Granite or Marble in a Great Variety of Shapes and Sizes.
	Regimental Marker	Other than Principal Position of Regiment or Battery	Usually a Square Granite Marker or tablet or may be another monument.
	Flank Marker or Company Marker	Left and/or Right Flank of Regiment or Battery or Position of a Company.	Usually a Small Square or Rectangular Granite Marker.
	Army Or Corps Headquarters	Site of Headquarters of Army Commander or Corps Commander or Chief of Artillery	Cannon Barrel Mounted Vertically on Stone, Granite or Marble Base.
	State Monument	Monument Erected by Union or Confederate State.	
	Statue	Standing or Equestrian	Bronze Sculpture
	Building	House, Barn or other Structure	Identified by Owner's Name.
	Miscellaneous Marker	Marker or Inscription of a type not listed above	Granite or Metal Marker.

*Asterisk — Used whenever a Division or Brigade or Regiment or Battery has more than one Monument or Marker.

Check the Index for other Monument or Marker.

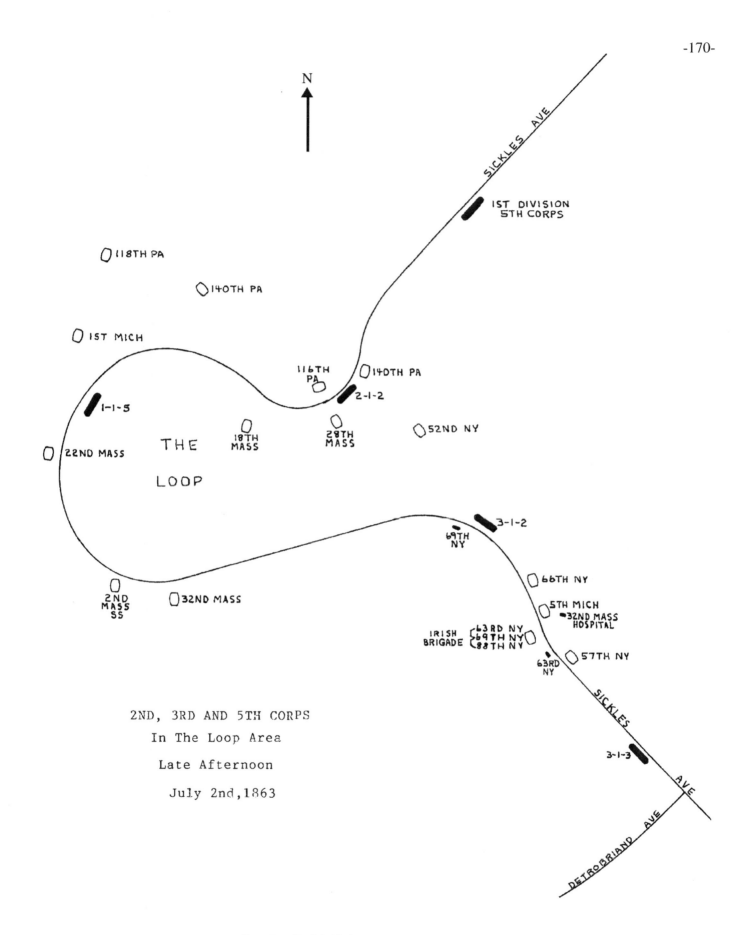

N

SICKLES AVE

1ST DIVISION
5TH CORPS

118TH PA

140TH PA

1ST MICH

116TH PA

140TH PA

1-1-5

2-1-2

THE

18TH
MASS

28TH
MASS

52ND NY

LOOP

22ND MASS

3-1-2

69TH
NY

2ND
MASS
SS

32ND MASS

66TH NY

5TH MICH

32ND MASS
HOSPITAL

IRISH
BRIGADE

63RD NY
69TH NY
88TH NY

57TH NY

63RD
NY

SICKLES

AVE

2ND, 3RD AND 5TH CORPS
In The Loop Area
Late Afternoon
July 2nd, 1863

3-1-3

DETROBRIAND AVE

~ Gettysburg Battlefield Monuments, Locations & Inscriptions ~

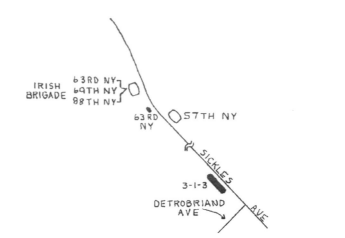

3-1-3   Col. Regis deTrobriand
17th Maine, 3rd, 5th Mich, 40th NY, 110th Pa (6 Cos) Infantry
7-2:   Arrived at 10 AM. On the advance of the Division between 2 and 3 PM, the Brigade took position in column between 1st and 2nd Brigades to support either. The 3rd Mich was sent to support 1st Brigade. The 17th Maine moved across the Wheatfield to the stone wall on the south. The 40th was sent to the gorge between Devil's Den and Little Round Top. The 5th Mich and the 110th Pa held the summit commanding a ravine in front and east of the Rose buildings until relieved by two brigades of the 5th Corps, when they retired through the Wheatfield, where being joined by the 17th Maine, they held back a superior Confederate force until the arrival of the 1st Division, 2nd Corps, when ammunition being exhausted, this portion of the Brigade retired and at night was joined by the other Regiments.
7-3:   In reserve.
Casualties: Killed 75, Wounded 394, Missing 21; Total 490.

57ᵗʰ NY   Lt. Col. Alfred B. Chapman
3-1-2   7-2:   Engaged the enemy here.
7-3:   On Cemetary Ridge resisting Pickett's attack.
Casualties: Killed 4, Wounded 28, Missing 2; Total 34.

63ʳᵈ NY   Lt. Col. Richard C. Bentley, Capt. Thomas Touhy
2-1-2   63rd New York Infantry, Irish Brigade.
Casualties: Killed 5, Wounded 9, Missing 8; Total 23

Irish   63rd NY, Lt. Col. Richard C. Bentley, Capt. Thomas Touhy
Brigade   69th NY, Capt. Richard Maroney, Lt. James E. Smith
2-1-2*   88th NY, Capt. Dennis F. Burke
The Brigade entered the battle under the command of Col. Patrick Kelly, 530 strong, of which this contingent(composing three battalions of two companies each) numbered 240 men. The original strength of these battalions was 3000 men. The Brigade participated with great credit to itself and the race it represented, in every battle of the Army of the Potomac in which the 2nd Corps was engaged from Fair Oaks, June 1, 1862, to Appomattox Court House, April 9, 1865.

14ᵗʰ NY   In memory of Capt. James McK Rorty and four men who fell at the Bloody Angle, July 3, 1863. The Battery
Indepen-   was mustered on December 9, 1861 as part of the Irish Brigade. It was detatched therefrom and at Gettysburg
dent   was consolidated with 1st NY Artillery-Battery B*:
Battery

Irish   This, in the matter of size and structure, truthfully represents the Irish Wolfhound, a dog which has been
Wolfhound extinct for more than 100 years. William Rudolph O'Donovan.
Casualties: 63rd NY: Killed 5, Wounded 10, Missing 8; Total 23
69th NY: Killed 5, Wounded 14, Missing 6; Total 25
88th NY: Killed 7, Wounded 17, Missing 4; Total 28

*see index

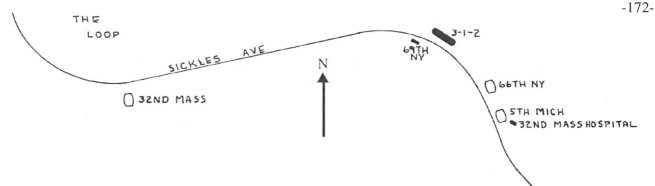

5th Mich
3-1-3
Lt. Col. John Pulford
<u>7-2</u>: This Regiment fought here about 4:30 o'clock, July 2, after it had been assembled from the skirmish line far in advance of this position.
<u>7-3</u>: It moved to the support of the 2nd Corps in resisting Pickett's Charge.
Casualties: Killed 19, Wounded 86, Missing 4; Total 109.

32nd Mass
Hospital
Behind this group of rocks on the afternoon of July 2, 1863, Surgeon Z Boylston Adams placed the Field Hospital of the 32nd Massachusetts Infantry, 2nd Brigade, 1st Division, 5th Army Corps. Established so near the line of battle, many of our wounded escaped capture or death by its timely aid.
Placed By The Veteran Association Of The Regiment.

66th NY
3-1-2
Col. Orlando H. Morris, Lt. Col. John S. Hammell, Maj. Peter Nelson
<u>7-2</u>: 6 PM.
Casualties: Killed 5, Wounded 29, Missing 10; Total 44

3-1-2
Brig. Gen. Samuel K. Zook, Lt. Col. John Fraser
52nd, 57th, 66th NY, 140th Pa Infantry
<u>7-2</u>: Arrived early in the morning and formed on the right of 2nd Brigade on line from Cemetary Hill to Round Top. Between 5 and 6 PM, advanced with Division to left and entered the Wheatfield and the woods on its right in line of battle, forcing the Confederates through the field and the woods to the further end. Brig. Gen. Zook fell mortally wounded in the advance. The Brigade, being on the right of the Division, it extended to an open field on the west. The line of the 3rd Corps on the Emmitsburg Road having been forced back and the Division having been flanked by superior forces on its right and left, the Brigade retired with the Division and resumed position in line with Corps.
<u>7-3</u>: Constructed entrenchments and held the position until the close of battle.
Casualties: Killed 49, Wounded 227, Missing 82; Total 358

52nd NY
3-1-2
Lt. Col. Charles C. Freidenberg, Capt. William Scherrer
<u>7-2</u>: July 2, 1863; 6 to 7 PM.
Casualties: Killed 2, Wounded 26, Missing 10; Total 38

69th NY*
2-1-2
Capt. Richard Maroney, Lt. James E. Smith
69th New York Infantry, Irish Brigade.
Casualties: Killed 5, Wounded 14, Missing 6; Total 25

32nd Mass
2-1-5
Col. George L. Prescott
<u>7-2</u>: Withstood an attack of the enemy about 5 o'clock PM. Withdrew from here; it fought again in the Wheatfield. It lost in both actions 78 killed and wounded out of 227 officers and men.

*see index

~ Gettysburg Battlefield Monuments, Locations & Inscriptions ~

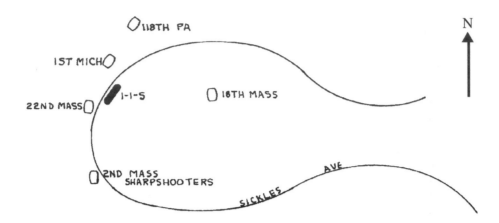

2ⁿᵈ Mass Sharp-shooters 1-1-5
7-2: July 2, 1863; 2nd Company Andrew Sharpshooters, Massachusetts Volunteers. (Note: Attached to 22nd Massachusetts Infantry.)

22ⁿᵈ Mass 1-1-5
Lt. Col. Thomas Sherwin, Jr.
7-2: The 22nd Massachusetts Infantry stood here July 2, 1863.
Casualties: Killed 3, Wounded 27, Missing 1; Total 31 (NY@Gbg)

1ˢᵗ Mich 1-1-5
Col. Ira C. Abbott, Lt. Col. William A. Throop
7-2: This monument marks the position where the Regiment fought July 2,1863.
Casualties: Killed 5, Wounded 33, Missing 4; Total 42.

118ᵗʰ PA* 1-1-5
The Corn Exchange Regiment
Lt. Col. James Gwyn
7-2: First Position.
7-3: On Big Round Top.
Casualties: Killed 3, Wounded 19, Missing 3; Total 25 of 332 present

1-1-5
Col. William S. Tilton
18th, 22nd Mass, 1st Mich, 118th Pa Infantry
7-2: In position in column with the Division and Corps on the Baltimore Pike near Rock Creek until after 4 PM, then moved with Division left in front to the support of 3rd Corps line.The 3rd Brigade, having detatched to occupy Little Round Top, the Brigade preceeded by 2nd Brigade, crossed Plum Run and the Wheatfield and went into position on the high ground on the edge of the woods facing westerly and southerly toward the Rose House, 2nd Brigade on the left. The Brigade was sharply attacked by Brig. Gen. Kershaw's Brigade and in compliance with orders by Brig. Gen. Barnes, it retired to the rear and right to the woods across the Wheatfield Road, and later to a line extending northerly to Little Round Top.
7-3: Relieved 3rd Brigade on Little Round Top.
7-4: Remained in position until close of the battle, except reconnaissance in front.
Casualties: Killed 12, Wounded 102, Missing 11; Total 125.

18ᵗʰ Mass 1-1-5
Col. Joseph Hayes
7-2: "Let Us Have Peace."
7-3: Little Round Top.
Casualties: Killed 1, Wounded 23, Missing 3; Total 27.

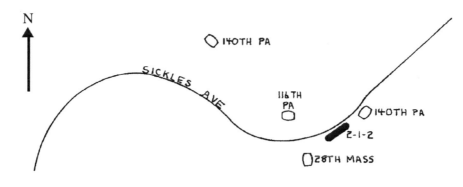

28th Mass   Col. Richard Byrns
2-1-2   Meagher's Irish Brigade, Col. Patrick Kelly, Commanding
     7-2:   This Regiment went into battle July 2, 1863 numbering 220 officers and men of whom 101 were killed and wounded.

"AUGH A BALLAUGH"

140th PA*   Col. Richard P. Roberts, Lt. Col. John Fraser
3-1-2   7-2:   The Regiment engaged the enemy in this position late in the afternoon of July 2, 1863, succeeding 5th Corps troops and holding the right of the 1st Division, 2nd Corps.
     7-3:   Supported battery on left centre July 3.
     Casualties: Killed 53, Wounded 128, Missing 60; Total 241 of 588 present.

116th PA   Major St. Clair A. Mulholland
2-1-2   7-2:   In action.
          37 Killed of 142.

2-1-2   Col. Patrick Kelly
   28th Mass, 63rd (2 Cos), 69th (2 Cos), 88th (2 Cos) NY, 116th Pa (4 Cos)
     7-2:   Arrived at 7 AM and took position on line from Cemetary Hill to Round Top at right of 1st Brigade. Between 5 and 6 PM went with Division to left, 1st Brigade on left, 3rd Brigade on right. Engaged Confederate forces including Brig. Gen. Anderson's Brigade, Major Gen. Hood's Division, in the Wheatfield and forced them through the field southerly into the woods beyond, capturing many prisoners. The 4th Brigade having advanced on the left, this Brigade held its position until the Division having been flanked on the right and left, retired and resumed former position in line of Corps.
     7-3:   Constructed breastworks.
     Casualties: Killed 27, Wounded 109, Missing 62; Total 198.

140th PA*   Col. Richard P. Roberts, Lt. Col. John Fraser
3-1-2   7-2:   Succeeded 5th Corps troops. Carried into action 29 officers and 560 enlisted men. In Memory Of Our Comrades, 1885.
     Casualties: Killed 37, Died of Wounds 17, Wounded 127, Missing 60; Total 241.

*see index

~ *Gettysburg Battlefield Monuments, Locations & Inscriptions* ~

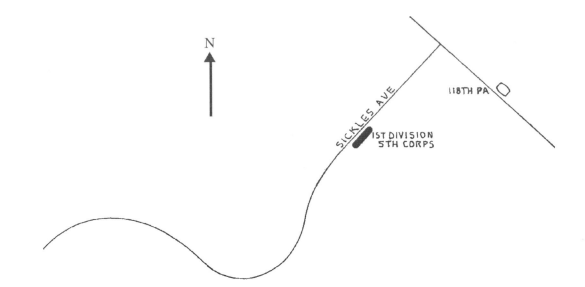

1ˢᵗ Division   Brig. Gen. James Barnes
5ᵗʰ Corps   1st Brigade   Col. William S. Tilton
                2nd Brigade   Col. Jacob B. Sweitzer
                3rd Brigade   Col. Strong Vincent, Col. James C. Rice

     <u>7-2</u>: Crossed Rock Creek in the morning and was massed on Baltimore Pike with the Corps until between 4 and 5 PM and moved to the left by command of General Sykes to the support of 3rd Corps line. The 3rd Brigade in the advance, hastened to take possession of Little Round Top. The 1st and 2nd Brigades crossed Plum Run and the Wheatfield to the further edge of the woods beyond, near the Rose House. The 1st Brigade was formed on the right of the 2nd. These Brigades were more or less engaged until after sunset, when with other troops on the line they were compelled to retire to a line extending north from the summit of Little Round Top.

     <u>7-3</u>: 3rd Brigade was relieved by the 1st Brigade and joined 2nd Brigade north of Little Round Top. Remained in these positions until the close of the battle except reconnaissance in front.

Casualties: Killed 167, Wounded 594, Missing 143; Total 904.

118ᵗʰ PA*   The Corn Exchange Regiment
1-1-5   Lt. Col. James Gwyn
          <u>7-2</u>: 1st Brigade, 1st Division, 5th Corps.
          Casualties: Killed 3, Wounded 19, Missing 3; Total 25 (NY@Gbg)

*see index

~ Gettysburg Battlefield Monuments, Locations & Inscriptions ~

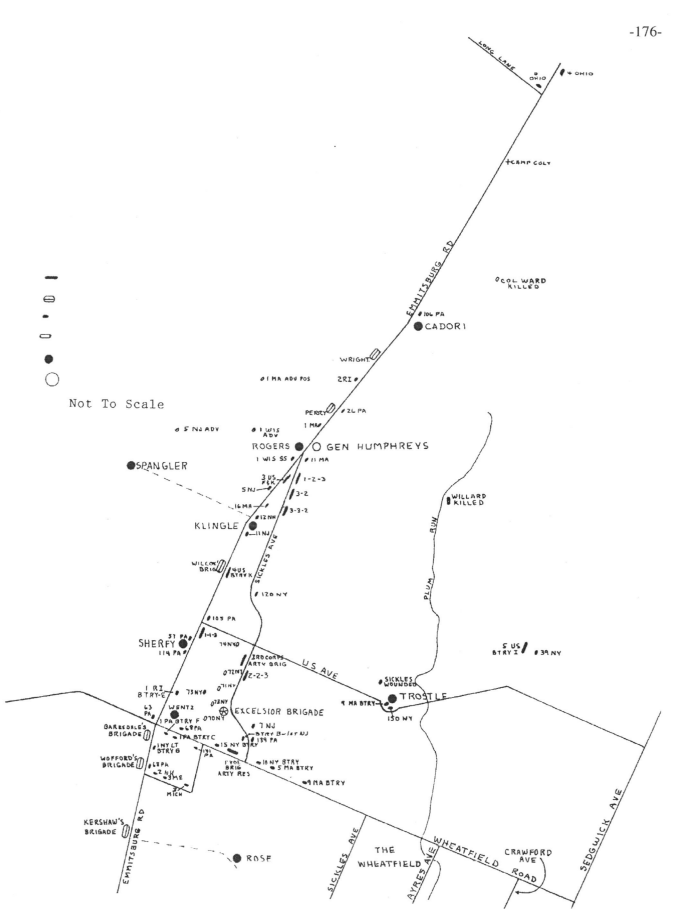

Not To Scale

~ Gettysburg Battlefield Monuments, Locations & Inscriptions ~

THE SYMBOLS LISTED BELOW ARE USED TO IDENTIFY THE MONUMENTS, MARKERS, TABLETS, STATUES, ETC. WHICH ARE DRAWN ON THE MAPS IN THESE PAGES

SYMBOL	TYPE	REPRESENTING	DESCRIPTION
(filled oval)	Bronze Tablet	Army of The Potomac, Union Corps or Division or Brigade, Regular Army Regiment, Regular Army Artillery Battery, Volunteer Artillery Brigade.	Brigade Tablet Mounted on Square Marble base. All other Tablets are on large vertical Granite Blocks.
(open oval)	Bronze Tablet	Army of Northern Virginia, Confederate Corps or Division or Brigade or Artillery Battalion	Brigade Tablet and Artillery Battalion Tablet Mounted on Round Marble base. All other Tablets are Mounted on large vertical Granite blocks.
(small filled oval)	Iron Tablet	Union Army Battery (other than Regular Army)	Mounted on Black Iron Shaft.
(small open oval)	Iron Tablet	Confederate Artillery Battery	Mounted on Black Iron Shaft.
(tall oval)	Iron Tablet	Confederate Brigade Advanced Position	Mounted on Black Iron Shaft.
(small open)	Regimental or Battery Monument	Principal Position of Volunteer Regiment or Volunteer Artillery Battery	Usually Granite or Marble in a Great Variety of Shapes and Sizes.
⊗	Regimental Marker or Battery	Other than Principal Position of Regiment tablet or may be another monument.	Usually a Square Granite Marker or
□	Flank Marker or Company Marker	Left and/or Right Flank of Regiment or Battery or Position of a Company.	Usually a Small Square or Rectangular Granite Marker.
⊕	Army Or Corps Headquarters	Site of Headquarters of Army Commander or Corps Commander or Chief of Artillery	Cannon Barrel Mounted Vertically on Stone, Granite or Marble Base.
(filled shape)	State Monument	Monument Erected by Union or Confederate State.	
○ ○	Statue	Standing or Equestrian	Bronze Sculpture
●	Building	House, Barn or other Structure	Identified by Owner's Name.
•	Miscellaneous Marker	Marker or Inscription of a type not listed above	Granite or Metal Marker.
*Asterisk		Used whenever a Division or Brigade or Regiment or Battery has more than one Monument or Marker.	Check the Index for other Monument or Marker.

~ Gettysburg Battlefield Monuments, Locations & Inscriptions ~

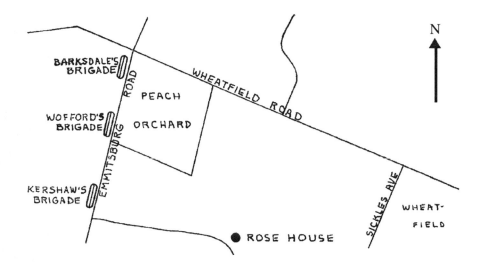

Kershaw's Brigade* Brig. Gen. Joseph B. Kershaw

Brigadier General Joseph B. Kershaw's So. Carolina Brig. of McLaws' Division, ordered on the afternoon of July 2, 1863, to attack the Union battle line north and east of the Rose Farm, 100 yards eastward, crossed the Emmitsburg Road in this area. By nightfall their attack, joined with those of other Confederate Brigades, had forced the Union troops from the Peach Orchard and Wheatfield. Late on July 3, the Brigade withdrew and went into position in the woods a quarter mile west.

Erected By "Project Southland" In Cooperation With

The Gettysburg Battlefield Preservation Association, 1970.

Wofford's Brigade* Brigadier General W. T. Wofford

16th, 18th, 24th Regiments, Cobb's and Phillip's Legions Georgia Infantry.

7-2: Arrived at 4 PM and formed line 500 yards west of here. Ordered to the front about 6 o'clock. Advanced soon afterward along Wheatfield Road, struck the Union line near the Loop and joined Kershaw's Brigade in driving the Union forces through the Wheatfield to the base of Little Round Top. Assailed by reinforcements and receiving orders to withdraw, the Brigade fell back at sunset to the cover of the woods west of the Wheatfield.

7-3: One regiment was left on outpost duty in that grove. The others supported artillery on Peach Orchard Ridge. All withdrew late in the afternoon.

7-4: In line 500 yards west of here all day. At midnight began the march to Hagerstown.

Present about 1355.

Casualties: Killed 36, Wounded 207, Missing 112; Total 355.

Barksdale's Brigade* Brigadier General William Barksdale

13th, 17th, 18th, 21st Mississippi Infantry

7-2: Arrived about 3 PM and formed in line. Advanced at 5 o'clock and took part in the assault on the Peach Orchard and adjacent positions, pursuing the Union forces as they retired. The 21st Regiment pushed beyond the Trostle House and captured, but were unable to bring off, Bigelow's and Watson's Batteries. The other Regiments inclining to the left, pressed forward to Plum Run where they encountered Union troops and a fierce conflict ensued in which Brig. Gen. Barksdale fell mortally wounded.

Casualties: Killed 105, Wounded 550, Missing 92; Total 747 (NY@Gbg)

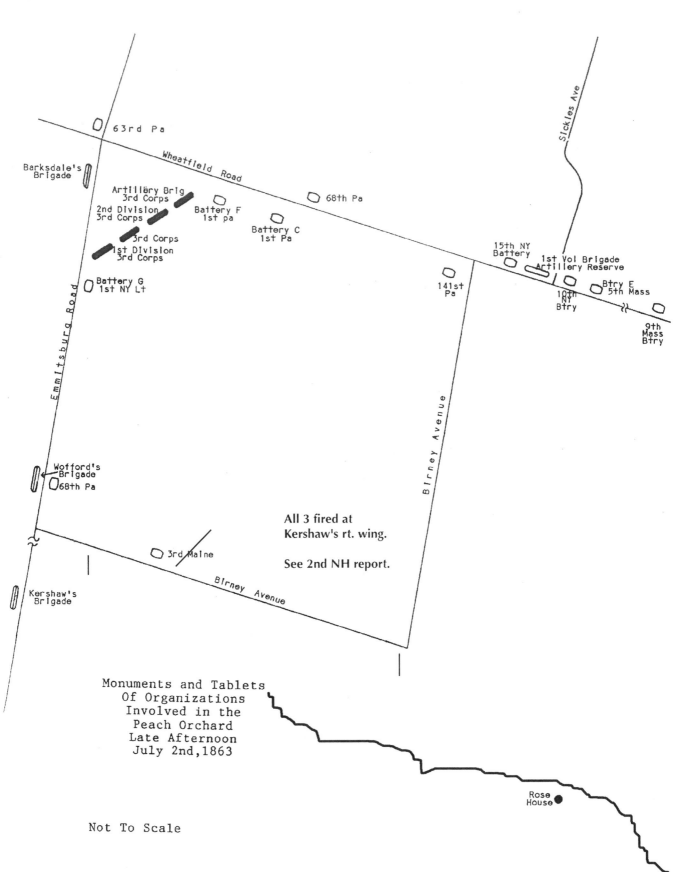

63rd Pa

Wheatfield Road

Barksdale's
Brigade

Artillery Brig
3rd Corps

Battery F
1st pa

68th Pa

2nd Division
3rd Corps

3rd Corps

Battery C
1st Pa

Sickles Ave

1st Division
3rd Corps

15th NY
Battery

1st Vol Brigade
Artillery Reserve

Battery G
1st NY Lt

141st
Pa

Btry E
5th Mass

10th
NY
Btry

9th
Mass
Btry

Emmitsburg Road

Birney Avenue

Wofford's
Brigade

68th Pa

All 3 fired at
Kershaw's rt. wing.

See 2nd NH report.

3rd Maine

Birney Avenue

Kershaw's
Brigade

Monuments and Tablets
Of Organizations
Involved in the
Peach Orchard
Late Afternoon
July 2nd,1863

Rose
House

Not To Scale

~ Gettysburg Battlefield Monuments, Locations & Inscriptions ~

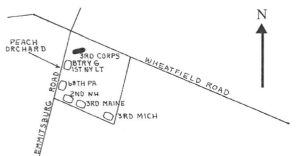

3rd Mich Col. Byron R. Pierce, Lt. Col. Edwin S. Pierce
3-1-3 <u>7-2</u>: This Regiment, deployed as skirmishers 150 yards in advance of this position, held the line extending from the Peach Orchard east to the woods. Was the right of DeTrobriand's Brigade and connected with the left of Graham's. Went into action with 19 officers and 267 men, total 286.
Casualties: Killed 7, Wounded 31, Missing 7; Total 45.

3rd Maine* Col. Moses B. Lakeman
2-1-3 <u>7-2</u>: Detached from the Brigade, fought here in the afternoon of July 2, 1863, having been engaged in the forenoon at point in advance, as indicated by a marker.
<u>7-3</u>: In position on left centre of line until afternoon, when with other Regiments of the Brigade, it moved to support of the centre at the time of the enemy's assault.
Strength of Regiment morning of July 2nd: 14 officers and 196 men.
Casualties: Killed 18, Wounded 59, Missing 45; Total 122.

2nd NH Col. Edward L. Bailey
3-2-3 <u>7-2</u>: Engaged 24 officers, 330 enlisted men.
Casualties: Killed 25, Wounded 133, Missing 35; Total 193.

68th PA* Col. A. H. Tippen
1-1-3 The Scott Legion
<u>7-2</u>: In memory of 183 of our comrades who fell on this field July 2 and 3, 1863.
Erected by the survivors of the 68th Regiment Pennsylvania Vols.

Battery G Capt. Nelson Ames
1st NY Lt* <u>7-2</u>: Engaged here with 3rd Corps, 3 PM to 5:30 PM, July 2, 1863.
4th Vol <u>7-3</u>: On Cemetary Ridge with 1st Division, 2nd Corps. Casualties: 7 Wounded Total.
Brigade
Artillery
Reserve

3rd Corps Major Daniel E. Sickles, Major General David B. Birney
1st Division Major General David B. Birney
2nd Division Brigadier General Andrew A. Humphreys
<u>7-1</u>: This Corps was at Emmitsburg. Complying with General Howard's request received at 3:10 PM, General Sickles marched his Corps, except two brigades and two batteries, to Gettysburg.
<u>7-2</u>: At daybreak these troops rejoined the Corps massed on the left of Cemetary Ridge. During the forenoon the Confederates advanced toward the Union left. A reconnaissance disclosed their formation in three columns. Buford's Cavalry Division on left flank had been withdrawn. About 2 PM this Corps, then the extreme left of the Union line, changed front to check the enemy until the 5th Corps could march from the Union right and occupy the Round Tops. The 3rd Corps, about 9800 men, formed line of battle from Plum Run to the Peach Orchard, thence along the Emmitsburg Road 300 yards past the Rogers House, Birney's Division on left and Humphrey's Division along Emmitsburg Road against three Divisions, about 17,000 strong under Longstreet. The Confederate batteries opened about 3 o'clock, the infantry advancing soon after against the 3rd Corps left centre. Following an oblique order of battle, at 5:45 PM the enemy attacked the 3rd Corps left centre. Reinforcements repulsed this attack and occupied the Round Tops, relieving Birney's Division except at the Peach Orchard. About 6:30 PM, the 3rd Corps center at the Peach Orchard was broken after a stubborn resistance, uncovering the left of Humphrey's

*see index

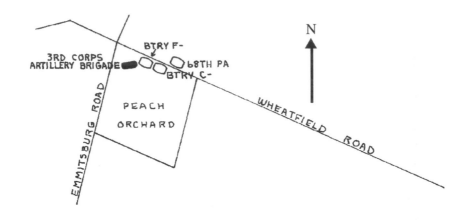

3rd Corps
(con't)
Division, which changed front and slowly retired, following Birney to Cemetary Ridge and again advancing to the Emmitsburg Road, held that line until morning, the battle continuing until 7:30 PM. Gen. Sickles was severely wounded about 6 o'clock, Gen. Birney taking command.

7-3: In support of the left centre on Cemetary Ridge.

Casualties: Killed 593, Wounded 3029, Missing 589; Total 4211.

1st Division Major General David B. Birney, Brig. Gen. J. H. Hobart Ward
3rd Corps 7-1: This Division was at Emmitsburg, Md. covering roads from Fairfield and Gettysburg. Shortly after 3 PM, marched to Gettysburg, leaving DeTrobriand's Brigade.

7-2: This Brigade rejoined. At about **7 AM** Birney relieved Geary's 2nd Division 12th Corps, his left resting near Little Round Top, his right joining Humphrey's on Cemetary Ridge, picket line holding Emmitsburg Road. Shortly after 2 PM, Division wheeled to the left, occupying high ground from Plum Run to the Peach Orchard and thence along Emmitsburg Road to Sherfy House, Ward's Brigade on the left, DeTrobriand's in the centre and Graham's on the right, Burling's Brigade, Humphrey's Division in reserve near Birney's centre. Confederate artillery opened at 3 o'clock. Soon after, three brigades of Hood's Division attacked Ward on Birney's left, extending later to DeTrobriand. These attacks were successfully resisted.

At 5:45 PM two brigades of McLaws' Division attacked Birney's right and center. Two brigades of 5th Corps advanced to the rocky knoll at DeTrobriand's right but withdrew after a brief contest. Here occured the first break in Birney's line. Movement against south face of Peach Orchard checked by batteries on Birney's right centre.

The Confederates renewed their attack on Birney's centre. Caldwell's Division, 2nd Corps now arrived, and, with troops from 5th Corps, relieved Birney except at the Peach Orchard.

About 6:30 PM, Birney's right at the Peach Orchard was attacked on both fronts and broken opposite Sherfy House after stubborn resistance. Through this gap the Confederates swept forward, crushing Birney's right which rejoined its Division.

7-3: The Division was held in reserve and detatchments moved to threatened points.

Casualties: Killed 271, Wounded 1384, Missing 356; Total 2011

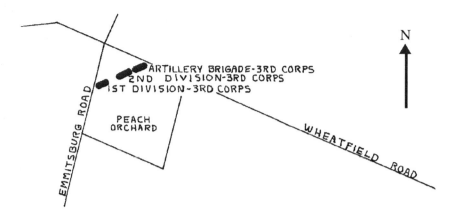

2nd Division* Brig. Gen. Andrew A. Humphreys

3rd Corps

7-1: This Division was at Emmitsburg. Shortly after 3 PM, marched by indirect route about two miles west of main road to Gettysburg, leaving Burling's Brigade.

7-2: Arrived at 1 AM and massed on Cemetary Ridge between Birney on the left and 2nd Corps. Burling's Brigade rejoined. Between 2 and 3 PM, formed line of battle along the Emmitsburg Road to resist attack on Union left, its right opposite left of Caldwell's Division, 2nd Corps, its left joining Birney's Division; Carr's Brigade on the right, Brewster's Brigade massed on the left centre, Burling's Brigade in reserve until sent to General Birney. The Confederates made demonstrations on this Division's front which remained in position after the 5th and 6th Corps had arrived on the Union left, until about 6:30 PM, when McLaws' Division, following the Confederate oblique order of battle, broke Birney's line at the Peach Orchard uncovering the left of Humphrey's, who changed front to connect with the 2nd and 5th Corps troops in the Wheatfield. That line, enfiladed by the enemy, fell back across Plum Run, while Humphreys, outflanked by McLaws' Division and pressed by Anderson's Division Hill's Corps gradually retired to Cemetary Ridge, reformed on 2nd Corps' left and drove the Confederates beyond the Emmitsburg Road, recovering abandoned artillery and holding the advanced position during the night.

7-3: Division moved to different points in the rear of 1st, 2nd, 5th and 6th Corps, supporting threatened positions.

Casualties: Killed 314, Wounded 1562, Missing 216; Total 2092.

3rd Corps Artillery Brigade Capt. George E. Randolph, Capt. A. Judson Clark

Battery B -1st NJ	Six 10 Pounders	Capt. A. Judson Clark, Lt. Robert Sims
Battery D -1st NY	Six 12 Pounders	Capt. George B. Winslow
4th NY Battery	Six 10 Pounders	Capt. James E. Smith
Battery E -1st RI	Six 12 Pounders	Lt. John K. Bucklyn, Lt. Benjamin Freeborn
Battery K - 4th US	Six 12 Pounders	Lt. Francis W. Seeley, Lt. Robert James

7-2: Upon the advance of the 3rd Corps between 2 and 3 PM, the 4th NY Battery was posted near Devil's Den, Battery D-1st NY in the Wheatfield, Battery B-1st NJ in the Peach Orchard north of Wheatfield Road, Battery G-1st NY from the Artillery Reserve, on the Emmitsburg Road in the Peach Orchard, Battery E-1st RI on the same road near the right of the Division and Battery K-4th US near left of 2nd Division.

About 3:30 PM, Lt. Col. McGilvery brought from the Artillery Reserve the 9th Massachusetts Battery which was posted on the Wheatfield Road east of the Peach Orchard, 5th Massachusetts Battery (10th NY attached) within a hundred yards of the 9th Massachusetts and the 15th NY Battery to the east side of the Peach Orchard.

Later, and during the battle, there was brought up Pennsylvania Batteries C and F, which took position at the salient in the Peach Orchard, and Batteries F&K-3rd US posted near the Rogers House, Battery I-5th US was brought from 5th Corps and relieved Battery G-1st NY.

Casualties: Killed 8, Wounded 81, Missing 17; Total 106.

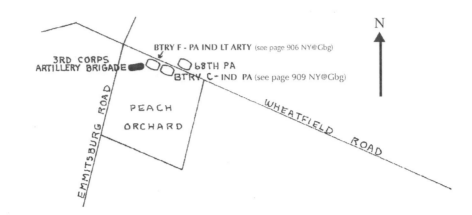

Battery F
PA Ind. Lt*
1ˢᵗ Vol
  Brigade
  Artillery
  Reserve

Hampton's Battery
Capt. James Thompson
7-2: Occupied this position from about 5 to 6 o'clock PM.
7-3: With the left centre on Cemetary Ridge, on left of 1st Volunteer Brigade, Artillery Reserve marked by tablet. 24 men from Battery F were detailed to Battery H-1st Ohio Artillery posted in the cemetary during the battle. (Note: This Battery was combined with Battery C below.)

Battery C
PA Ind.
Lt*
1ˢᵗ Vol
  Brigade
  Artillery
  Reserve

Six 3 Inch Rifles (Batteries C & F combined)
7-2: Occupied this position from about 5 to 6 PM.
7-3: In position on right of 1st Volunteer Brigade, Artillery Reserve and engaged the enemy.
Present at Gettysburg: 105 officers and men (Combined C&F)
Casualties: Killed 2, Wounded 23, Missing 3; Total 28 (NY@Gbg)

68ᵗʰ PA*
1-1-3

The Scott Legion
Col. Andrew H. Tippen
7-2: This monument marks the left of the Regiment while supporting Clark's Battery July 2, 1863, the right resting 150 feet north as indicated by flank marker. In the afternoon, the Regiment advanced southward into the Peach Orchard where its other monument stands and engaged the enemy.
7-3&4. The Regiment was in line with the Division on left center.
Present at Gettysburg: 383 officers and men. Casualties: Killed 13, Wounded 126, Missing 13; Total 152.

*see index

~ Gettysburg Battlefield Monuments, Locations & Inscriptions ~

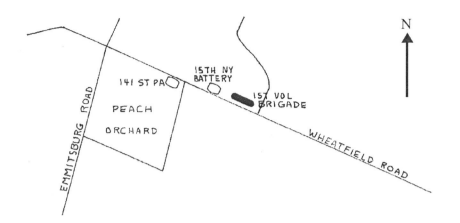

141st PA Col. Henry J. Madill
1-1-3 <u>7-2</u>: Occupied this position from 4 to 6 PM. Advanced and successfully resisted an attack on the 15th NY Light
Artillery by the 2nd and 8th South Carolina Infantry. Afterwards retired. Changed front to the right and
encountered a brigade composed of the 13th, 17th, 18th and 21st Mississippi Infantry. Held them in check
with great gallantry until outflanked. Retired firing by successive formations from the field.
Present at Gettysburg: 9 officers and 200 men. Casualties: Killed 42, Wounded 86, Missing 21; Total 149.

15th NY Ind. Capt. Patrick Hart, Lt. Edward M. Knox
Battery* Four 12 Pounders
1st Vol Formerly Light Battery B-Irish Brigade
Brigade July 2, 1863
Artillery Casualties: Killed 3, Wounded 13; Total 16.
Reserve

1st Vol Lt. Col. Freeman McGilvery
Brigade* 5th Mass Battery E
Artillery (10th NY attached)
Reserve Capt. Charles A. Phillips
9th Mass Battery
Capt. John Bigelow
Lt. Richard S. Martin
15th NY Battery
Capt. Patrick Hart
Batteries C & F Penna
Capt. James Thompson

<u>7-2</u>: Went into action at 3:30 PM on this road. Batteries C & F Penna on the right in the Peach Orchard line
facing west. About 5 PM opened and repulsed a heavy column of infantry charging the Brigade. About 6
PM, the Confederates gained position on the left and the infantry fell back leaving the artillery without
support. Four batteries fell back 250 yards and renewed their fire. Battery B-1st NJ and 15th NY Battery
retired from the field. The advanced line of the 3rd Corps having been abandoned, the Artillery Brigade
took up a new position 400 yards in the rear and opened with cannister and at 8 PM retired to the battle line
of the Army.

*see index

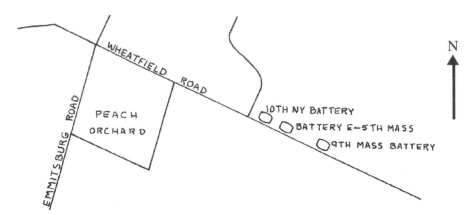

10ᵗʰ NY Ind <u>7-2</u>: Attached to 5th Massachusetts Light Battery E.
Battery   Casualties: Killed 2, Wounded 3; Total 5.
1ˢᵗ Vol
Brigade
Artillery
Reserve

Battery E* Capt. Charles A. Phillips
5ᵗʰ Mass   Six 12 Pounders
1ˢᵗ Vol   <u>7-2</u>: "The Nation Lives"
Brigade   7 Enlisted Men Killed, 1 Officer 12 Enlisted Men wounded. 700 Rounds Fired. July 2, 1863.
Artillery
Reserve

9ᵗʰ Mass   Capt. John Bigelow, Lt. Richard S. Martin
Battery*   Four 12 Pounders
1ˢᵗ Vol   <u>7-2</u>: First position left gun, Wheatfield Road 4:30 to 6 PM July 2, 1863. Shelled Confederate batteries on
Brigade   Emmitsburg Road, also the enemy around Rose Farm buildings. Enfilades with cannister Kershaw's
Artillery   Brigade CSA, moving across field in front from Emitsburg Road to woods on left where battle was
Reserve   raging in front of Round Tops. 6 PM alone on field; Graham's Brigade 3rd Corps forced from Peach
                    Orchard had retired by detatchments. By "prologue firing" retired before Kershaw's skirmishers and
                    Barksdale's Brigade 400 yards.
                    2nd Position: Angle of stone wall near Trostle House where the Battery was halted by Lt. Col.
                    McGilvery and ordered to hold enemy in check until line of artillery could be formed 560 yards in the
                    rear. Was without support and hemmed in by stone wall. Enemy closed in on flanks. Men and horses
                    were shot down. When finally overcome at 6:30 PM, Lt. Col. McGilvery had batteries unsupported in
                    position near the Weikert House covering openings in lines between Round Tops and left of 2nd Corps
                    3/4 of a mile, occassioned by withdrawal of Graham's Brigade.
                    7:15 PM: Willard's Brigade 2nd Corps and later Lockwoods Brigade 12th Corps came to support of
                    artillery.
                    8:00 PM: The enemy finally repulsed.
           Casualties: Killed 10, Wounded 20, Total 30.

*see index

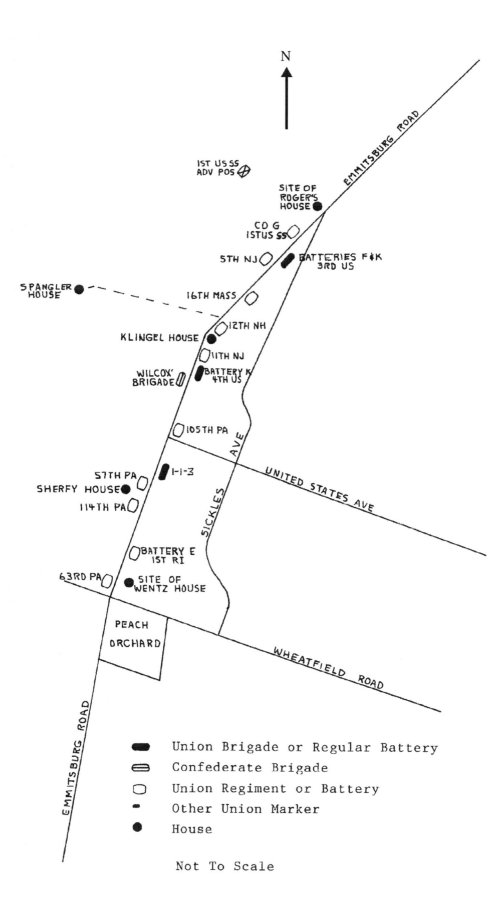

N

IST US SS
ADV POS

SITE OF
ROGER'S
HOUSE

CD G
IST US SS

5TH NJ

BATTERIES F & K
3RD US

EMMITSBURG ROAD

SPANGLER
HOUSE

16TH MASS

12TH NH

KLINGEL HOUSE

IITH NJ

WILCOX'
BRIGADE

BATTERY K
4TH US

105TH PA

AVE

57TH PA

I-I-3

UNITED STATES AVE

SHERFY HOUSE

114TH PA

SICKLES

BATTERY E
IST RI

63RD PA

SITE OF
WENTZ HOUSE

PEACH
ORCHARD

WHEATFIELD ROAD

EMMITSBURG ROAD

███ Union Brigade or Regular Battery
▱ Confederate Brigade
◯ Union Regiment or Battery
▬ Other Union Marker
● House

Not To Scale

~ *Gettysburg Battlefield Monuments, Locations & Inscriptions* ~

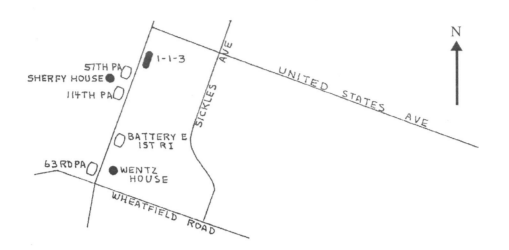

63rd PA
1-1-3
Major John A. Danks
Present at Gettysburg: 296 officers and men.
Casualties: Killed 1, Wounded 29, Missing 4; Total 34.

Battery E
1st RI Lt
3rd Corps
Artillery
Brigade
Randolph's Battery
1st Lt. John K. Bucklyn, Lt. Benjamin Freeborn
Six 12 Pounders
Casualties: 3 Killed, 26 Wounded; Total 29.

114th PA*
1-1-3
Collis Zouaves
Lt. Col. Frederick F. Cavada, Capt. Edward R. Bowen
7-2: Erected by the surviving members of the 114th Pennsylvania Volunteers to mark the position held by that organization on the 2nd day of the memorable battle fought on this field the 1st, 2nd and 3rd days of July, AD 1863, and in memory of the heroic men of that command who here laid down their lives in defence of their country's flag.
Killed and Wounded 95 officers and men.

57th PA
1-1-3
Col. Peter Sides, Capt. Alanson H. Nelson
7-2: This Regiment occupied this position exposed to a heavy artillery fire on the afternoon of July 2 for two hours, when it advanced 170 feet and engaged the enemy.
Killed and Died of Wounds 14, Wounded 43, Missing 58, Total 115.

1-1-3
Brig. Gen. Charles Graham, Col. Andrew H. Tippon
57th (8 Cos), 63rd, 68th, 105th, 114th, 151st Pa Infantry
7-1: Arrived between 5 and 6 PM.
7-2: The Corps having relieved 2nd Division 12th Corps in the morning, the Brigade took position on the right of the Division connecting with 2nd Division on right. Between 2 and 3 PM advanced to the Emmitsburg Road and took position at the Peach Orchard, supported by 3rd Maine, 3rd Michigan, 2nd NH and 7th NJ. About 3 PM, artillery opened on the Confederate columns moving to the left and soon thereafter, the Confederate artillery replied and later the Brigade was attacked by Maj. Gen. McLaws' Division and forced back by superior numbers in front and on the flanks, and at sunset it fell back with the Division. Brig. Gen. Graham was wounded and captured at the Peach Orchard.
7-3: The Brigade was in reserve during the day.
Casualties: Killed 67, Wounded 508, Missing 165; Total 740.

*see index

~ Gettysburg Battlefield Monuments, Locations & Inscriptions ~

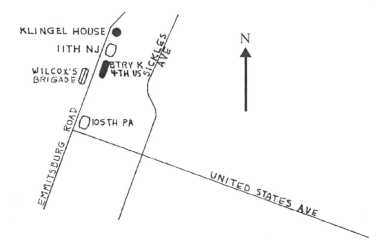

105th PA
1-1-3
Col. Calvin A. Craig
The Wildcat Regiment
7-2: Position from 2 to 4 PM. Moved across the Emmitsburg Road. Being outflanked, the Regiment changed front facing south and formed line along the lane at right angles to the road from which it retired fighting. In retiring, joined 2nd Division 3rd Corps, advancing and recapturing with the aid of other troops three guns of Battery C-5th US Artillery.
Present at Gettysburg: 257
Casualties: Killed and Died of Wounds 15, Wounded 108, Missing 9; Total 132.

Hill's Corps
Anderson's Brig. Gen. Cadmus M. Wilcox
Division 8th, 9th, 10th, 11th; 14th Alabama Infantry
Wilcox's 7-2: Formed line in forenoon, the 10th and 11th Regiments taking position on the right. After a severe skirmish
Brigade* with a Union outpost, advanced at 6 PM and broke the Union line on the Emmitsburg Road, capturing two guns and pursuing rapidly, took many prisoners and six more guns. At Plum Run was met by a heavy fire of artillery and infantry and being unsupported, after severe losses fell back without being able to bring off the captured guns.

Battery K
4th US Lt. Francis W. Seeley, Lt. Robert James
3rd Corps Six 12 - Pounders
Artillery 7-1: Arrived at night and encamped in a field south of the town between the Emmitsburg and Taneytown
Brigade Roads.
7-2: Went into position at 4 PM on the right of Smith's log house on Emmitsburg Road with Brig. Gen. A. A. Humphreys' Division, and soon took position on the left of the log house and at the left of an apple orchard, and opened fire on the Confederate infantry as it began to advance.
Hotly engaged with the Confederate infantry and artillery in front and on the left until about 7 PM, when forced to retire and took position on the line from the Evergreen Cemetary to Little Round Top. Lt. Seeley having been wounded, the command evolved on Lt. Robert James.
7-3: Remained in the position of the previous night.
Casualties: Killed 2, Wounded 19, Missing 4; Total 25.

11th NJ
1-2-3 Col. Robert McAllister, Capt. William H. Lloyd, Capt. Samuel D. Sleeper, Lt. John Schoonover
7-2: This stone marks the spot reached by the right of the Regiment, the left extending toward the southeast. The position was held under a severe fire which killed or disabled nearly three-fifths of the Regiment, including every officer present above the rank of lieutenant.
Number engaged: 276
Casualties: Killed 31, Wounded 109, Missing 12; Total 152. Of the missing, 6 are supposed to have been killed.

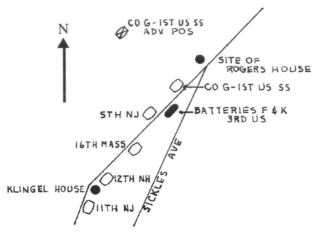

12ᵗʰ NH
1-2-3

Capt. John F. Langley

7-1: This Regiment marched to this field on the night of the first.

7-2: Fought here on the 2nd.

7-3: Supported the centre against Pickett's Charge on the 3rd.
"Our Union Is River, Lake, Ocean And Sky
Man Breaks Not The Medal, When God Cuts The Die."

Casualties: 20 Killed, 6 Died of Wounds, 73 Wounded, Total 99. Number engaged: 224.

16ᵗʰ Mass
1-2-3

Lt. Col. Waldo Merriam, Capt. Matthew Donovan

7-2: On this field, 4 officers and 23 men were killed, to whose memory this monument is erected by the Commonwealth of Massachusetts.

5ᵗʰ NJ
3-2-3

Col. William J. Sewell, Capt. Thomas G. Godfrey, Capt. Henry H. Woolsey.

7-2: The Regiment first held the skirmish line 400 yards to the front and left of this spot and afterward took position in the line of battle here.

Casualties: 18 Killed, 60 Wounded, 16 Missing; Total 94, being one half the number engaged.

Batteries
F & K*
3ʳᵈ US
1ˢᵗ Reg
Brigade
Artillery
Brigade

Lt. John G. Turnbull

Six - 12 Pounders

7-1: Took position on crest of hill near Gen. Meade's Headquarters.

7-2: Moved to a position at the right of a log house on the Emmitsburg Road with Brig. Gen. A. A. Humphrey's Division 3rd Corps. Engaged here but was compelled to retire with a loss of 45 horses killed and four guns which were afterward recaptured.

7-3: Went into position near the Taneytown Road on the left of Cemetary Hill.

Casualties: 9 Killed, 14 Wounded, 1 Missing; Total 24.

Company
G*
1ˢᵗ US
Sharp-
shooters

Company G, 1st United States (Wisconsin) Sharpshooters

7-2: Position held by the Company was 200 yards in advance of this monument.

Company
G*
1st US SS

"1st Wis-Co G".

(Note: This is their advanced position.)

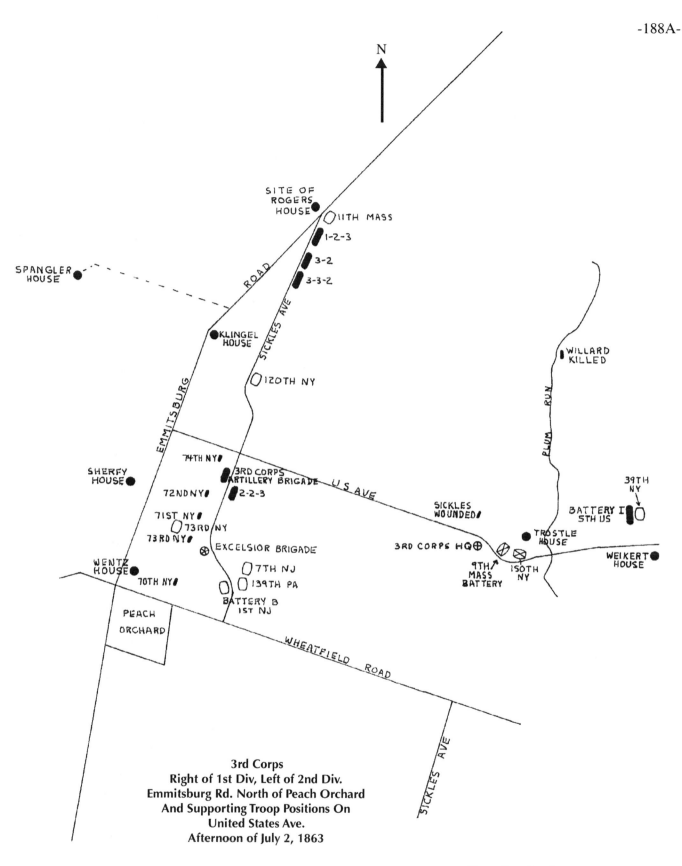

3rd Corps
Right of 1st Div, Left of 2nd Div.
Emmitsburg Rd. North of Peach Orchard
And Supporting Troop Positions On
United States Ave.
Afternoon of July 2, 1863

Not To Scale

~ Gettysburg Battlefield Monuments, Locations & Inscriptions ~

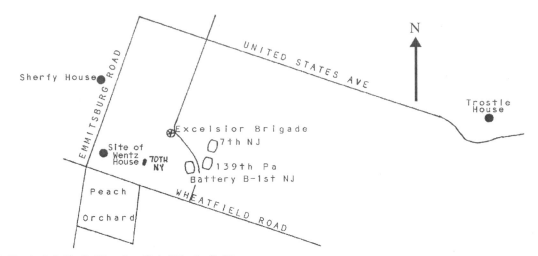

139th PA*
3-3-6

Col. Frederick H. Collier, Lt. Col. Edwin S. Pierce
<u>7-2,3,4</u>: Advanced near this point driving the enemy the evening of July 3rd.
Casualties: Killed 1, Wounded 19; Total 20.

7th NJ
3-2-3

Col. Lewis R. Francine, Major Frederick Cooper
<u>7-2</u>:   1st position 300 yards northeast of this. Heavily engaged there. Moved here to reinforce Graham's
        Brigade.
        Here Col. Francine fell.
Casualties: Killed 29, Wounded 77, Missing 13; Total 119.

70th NY
2-2-3

70th New York Infantry, Sickles Brigade.

Battery B
1st NJ Lt*
3rd Corps
Artillery
Brigade
(2nd Btry)

Capt. A. J. Clark, Lt. Robert Sims
Six 10 Pounder Parrotts
<u>7-2</u>:   Fought here from 2 until 7 o'clock on July 2,1863 firing 1300 rounds of ammunition.
        Erected by the State of New Jersey.
Casualties: Killed 1, Wounded 16, Missing 3; Total 20.

Sickles
Excelsior
Brigade
2-2-3*

Col. W. R. Brewster
70th NY Infantry (1st Excelsior): On the afternoon of the 2nd of July, 1863 the Brigade of which this Regiment formed a part, supported Carr's Brigade in resisting the assault of the enemy along the line of the Emmitsburg Road. On July 3, supported the left centre of the Army.
71st NY Infantry (2nd Excelsior): On the afternoon of the 2nd of July, 1863 the Brigade of which this Regiment formed a part, supported Carr's Brigade in resisting the assault of the enemy along the line of the Emmitsburg Road. On July 3, supported the left centre of the Army.
72nd NY Infantry (3rd Excelsior): Col. John S. Austin, Lt. Col. Leonard. On the afternoon of July 2, 1863 the Brigade of which this Regiment formed a part, supported Carr's Brigade in resisting the assault of the enemy along the line of the Emmitsburg Road. On July 3, supported the left centre of the Army.
73rd NY Infantry (4th Excelsior, 2nd Fire Zouaves): At 5:30 PM, July 2, 1863, this Regiment was detached to support Gen. Graham's Brigade at the Peach Orchard, which was heavily attacked by McLaws' Division of the Confederate Army. On July 3, supported the left centre of the Army.
74th NY Infantry (5th Excelsior): On the afternoon of the 2nd of July, 1863, the Brigade of which this Regiment formed a part, supported Carr's Brigade in resisting the assault of the enemy along the Emmitsburg Road. On July 3, supported the left centre of the Army.

Casualties:	Killed	Wounded	Missing	Total
70th NY	32	81	4	117
71st NY	14	64	13	91
72nd	7	94	15	116
73rd NY	51	103	8	162
74th NY	17	69	3	89

*see index

~ Gettysburg Battlefield Monuments, Locations & Inscriptions ~

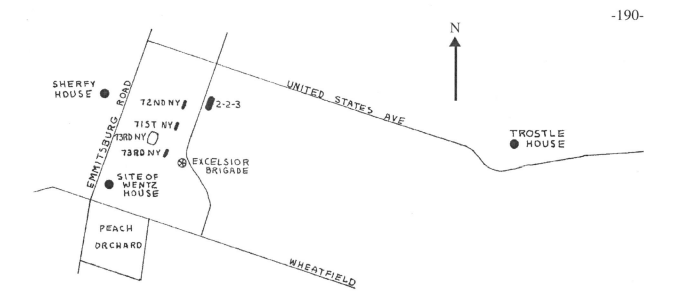

73rd NY*
2-2-3   73rd New York Infantry, Sickles Brigade

73rd NY*   The 2nd Fire Zouaves
2-2-3   Major Michael W. Burns

7-2:   The 4th Excelsior Regiment was conducted to this position by Major H. E. Tremain of 3rd Corps staff
          about 5:30 PM, July 2, 1863. Its loss on this field was 4 officers and 47 enlisted men killed, 11 officers and
          92 enlisted men wounded and 8 missing; Aggregate 162.

71st NY
2-2-3   71st New York Infantry, Sickles Brigade.

72nd NY
2-2-3   72nd New York Infantry, Sickles Brigade.

2-2-3*   Col. William R. Brewster
                   70th, 71st, 72nd, 73rd, 74th, 120th NY Infantry

7-2:   Arrived about 1 AM and bivouacked for the night. Near 1 PM formed in rear of 1st Brigade, the 73rd being
          advanced to the crest of the hill in front. The Brigade advanced between 2 and 3 PM, the 71st and 72nd to
          the left of 1st Brigade, the 70th and 120th in reserve. Later the 73rd was sent to the support of 1st Brigade
          1st Division. Fiercely attacked toward sunset and the forces on the left having fallen back, the Brigade
          retired and after sunset again advanced and captured the colors of the 8th Florida and 30 prisoners, and
          recaptured guns that had been left on the field. Again retired and formed in rear of a brigade of 2nd Corps
          and bivouacked for the night.

7-3:   Moved further to the rear and was supplied with rations and ammunitions. About 3 PM moved forward to
          support batteries in front.

Casualties: Killed 132, Wounded 573, Missing 73; Total 778

*see index

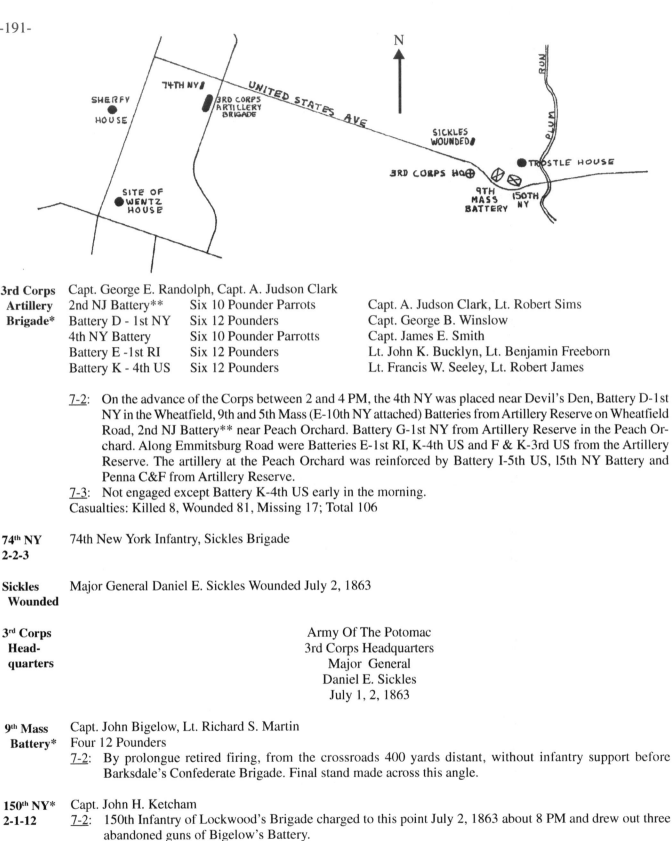

3rd Corps Artillery Brigade* Capt. George E. Randolph, Capt. A. Judson Clark

2nd NJ Battery**	Six 10 Pounder Parrots	Capt. A. Judson Clark, Lt. Robert Sims
Battery D - 1st NY	Six 12 Pounders	Capt. George B. Winslow
4th NY Battery	Six 10 Pounder Parrotts	Capt. James E. Smith
Battery E -1st RI	Six 12 Pounders	Lt. John K. Bucklyn, Lt. Benjamin Freeborn
Battery K - 4th US	Six 12 Pounders	Lt. Francis W. Seeley, Lt. Robert James

7-2: On the advance of the Corps between 2 and 4 PM, the 4th NY was placed near Devil's Den, Battery D-1st NY in the Wheatfield, 9th and 5th Mass (E-10th NY attached) Batteries from Artillery Reserve on Wheatfield Road, 2nd NJ Battery** near Peach Orchard. Battery G-1st NY from Artillery Reserve in the Peach Orchard. Along Emmitsburg Road were Batteries E-1st RI, K-4th US and F & K-3rd US from the Artillery Reserve. The artillery at the Peach Orchard was reinforced by Battery I-5th US, 15th NY Battery and Penna C&F from Artillery Reserve.

7-3: Not engaged except Battery K-4th US early in the morning.

Casualties: Killed 8, Wounded 81, Missing 17; Total 106

74th NY
2-2-3 74th New York Infantry, Sickles Brigade

Sickles Wounded Major General Daniel E. Sickles Wounded July 2, 1863

3rd Corps Head-quarters

Army Of The Potomac
3rd Corps Headquarters
Major General
Daniel E. Sickles
July 1, 2, 1863

9th Mass Battery* Capt. John Bigelow, Lt. Richard S. Martin
Four 12 Pounders
7-2: By prolongue retired firing, from the crossroads 400 yards distant, without infantry support before Barksdale's Confederate Brigade. Final stand made across this angle.

150th NY*
2-1-12 Capt. John H. Ketcham
7-2: 150th Infantry of Lockwood's Brigade charged to this point July 2, 1863 about 8 PM and drew out three abandoned guns of Bigelow's Battery.

**Note: 2nd NJ Battery was also called Battery B-1st New Jersey - See pages 118 and 189.

*see index

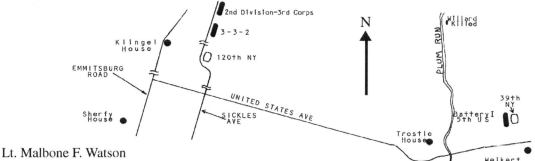

Battery I	Lt. Malbone F. Watson
5th US	Four 3 Inch Rifles.
5th Corps	7-2: About 4:30 PM arrived and took position north of Little Round Top. 5:30 moved to the front at the Peach
Artillery	Orchard. On the advance of the Confederates driving back the Infantry, the Battery was retired across
Brigade	Plum Run near the Trostle House and fired shell and cannister at the approaching Confederates until the

Battery, disabled by the loss of men and horses, was captured by the 21st Mississippi Regiment. It was almost immediately recaptured with the assistance of the 39th NY Infantry and being unservicable went to the Artillery Brigade.

Casualties: Killed 1, Wounded 19, Missing 2; Total 22.

39th NY*   Major Hugo Hildebrandt

3-3-2   7-2: On this spot the 39th NY Infantry recaptured the guns and equipment of Battery I-5th US Artillery.

120th NY*   Lt. Col. George D. Westbrook, Major John R. Tappen

2-2-3   7-2: The 120th NY Infantry held this part of the line on the 2nd day of July, 1863.

Present for duty: 30 officers, 397 men; Total 427.

Casualties: Killed 33, Wounded 154, Missing 17; Total 204.

3-3-2*   Col. George L. Willard, Col. Eliakim Sherrill, Lt. Col. James M. Bull

7-2: The 3rd Brigade of the 3rd Division 2nd Corps was conducted by General Hancock at 7 o'clock PM, July 2, 1863 from near Zeigler's Grove to the rear of a bushy swale along Plum Run. The 39th NY, commanded by Major Hugo Hildebrandt, faced left to guard against a flank and rear attack. The 125th NY, commanded by Col. Leven Crandall, took position on the left. The 126th NY, commanded by Col. Eliakim Sherrill, in the centre and the 111th NY, commanded by Col. C. D. MacDougal, on the right and charged the 13th, 17th and 18th Mississippi Regiments of Barksdale's Brigade in line in the thicket and drove them through the swale and up the slope toward the Emmitsburg Road to within 317 yards due east from this position, when the enemy's artillery fire became very severe and the Brigade retired to the swale where Col. George

Willard*   L. Willard, commanding the Brigade, was killed. After being relieved at dark, the Brigade returned to near

Killed   its former position on Cemetary Ridge.

2nd Division* Brigadier General Andrew A. Humphreys

3rd Corps   1st Brigade   Brig. Gen. Joseph B. Carr

2nd Brigade   Col. William R. Brewster

3rd Brigade   Col. George C. Burling

7-2: Arrived about 1 AM and bivouacked for the night. In the morning took position between Birney's Division on the left and the 2nd Corps facing Emmitsburg Road. Between 2 and 3 PM advanced to the Emmitsburg Road; Carr's Brigade in line along the road, Brewster's Brigade in reserve, Burling's Brigade at first in reserve and then, except the 5th NJ, sent to General Birney. The Division was attacked by McLaws' and Anderson's Divisions and by sunset was compelled to retire to the first position occupied, where it reformed on the left of 2nd Corps and drove back the Confederate forces beyond the Emmitsburg Road and recovered the artillery that had been abandoned, and captured many prisoners and held the position during the night.

7-3: About sunrise, moved to the rear and left, and was supplied with rations and ammunition. Burling's Brigade joined the Division. Moved to different points in rear of the 1st, 2nd, 5th and 6th Corps in support of threatened positions. Suffered some casualties in the afternoon from Confederate artillery.

Casualties: Killed 314, Wounded 1562, Missing 216; Total 2092.

*see index

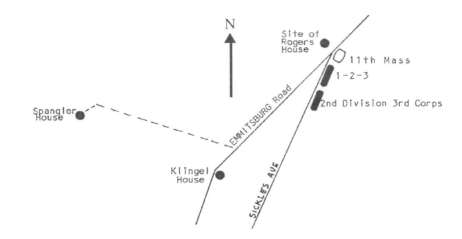

1-2-3 Brig. Gen Joseph B Carr

1st, 11th, 16th Mass, 12th NH, 11th NJ, 26th, 84th Pa Infantry

<u>7-2</u>: Arrived about 1 AM and bivouacked for the night. Early in the afternoon formed line on right of Division connecting with 2nd Corps on the right. Between 3 and 4 PM, advanced 300 yards to the Emmitsburg Road connecting with 1st Division. The Brigade, with the support of the 5th NJ on the left and 15th Mass and 82nd NY on the right, held the front line, 2nd Brigade in reserve, until the line on the left gave way, when the Brigade with the Division, changed front to the left. The Brigade then retired with the Corps by order of Major General D. B. Birney, Commanding, to the main line in the rear where it formed and forced back the pursuing forces, regained the lost ground, capturing many prisoners and held the position until morning.

<u>7-3</u>: The Confederate artillery opened fire at daylight which continued over an hour. At 6 AM, the Brigade was ordered to join the Corps in the rear and then to support the 5th Corps, and at 3 PM to support the 2nd Corps. The Brigade, lying in close column, suffered severely from artillery fire.

Casualties: Killed 121, Wounded 604, Missing 65; Total 790.

11th Mass Lt. Col. Porter D. Tripp

1-2-3 <u>7-2</u>: Upon this spot stood the 11th Massachusetts during the 2nd day's Battle of Gettysburg, July 2nd, 1863.

Casualties: Killed 26, Wounded 93, Missing 10; Total 129.

Assisted by the State and generous friends, the survivors of the Regiment have erected upon this historic field, this monumental tablet in the year 1885. "All's Well That Ends Well"

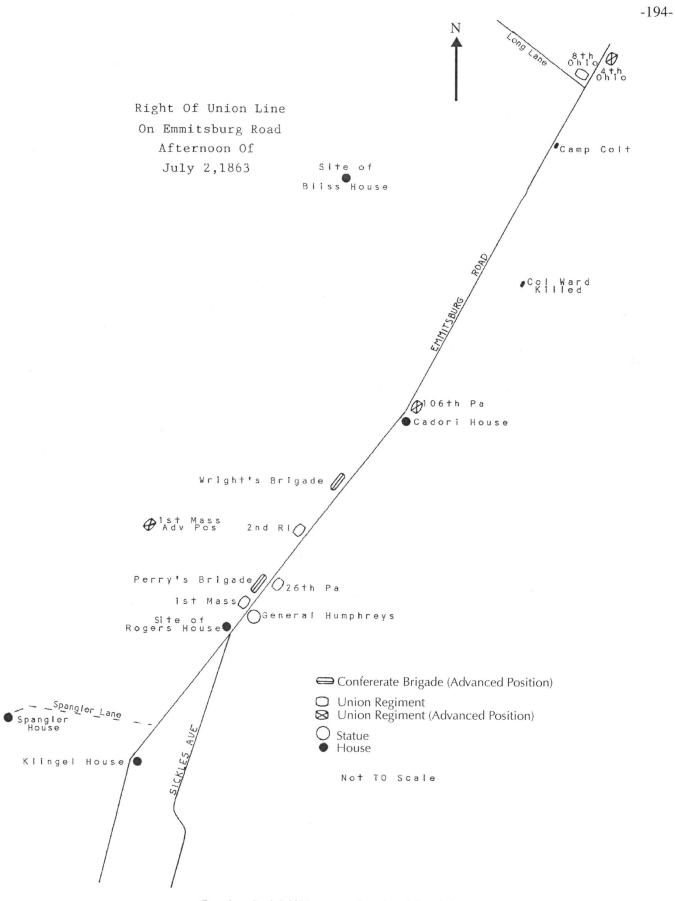

Right Of Union Line
On Emmitsburg Road
Afternoon Of
July 2, 1863

N

Long Lane

8th Ohio

4th Ohio

• Camp Colt

Site of
Bliss House

EMMITSBURG ROAD

• Col Ward
Killed

106th Pa
• Cadori House

Wright's Brigade

1st Mass
Adv Pos   2nd RI

Perry's Brigade   26th Pa
1st Mass
Site of   General Humphreys
Rogers House

⊖ Confererate Brigade (Advanced Position)
▢ Union Regiment
⊠ Union Regiment (Advanced Position)
○ Statue
● House

Not TO Scale

Spangler Lane
Spangler
House

SICKLES AVE

Klingel House

~ Gettysburg Battlefield Monuments, Locations & Inscriptions ~

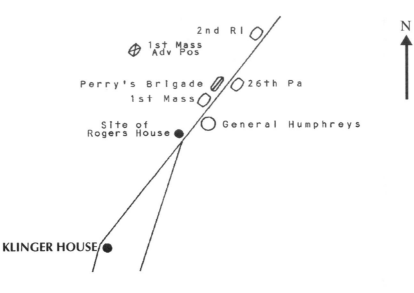

Humphrey's Andrew Atkinson Humphreys
Statue   Cadet USMA 7/1/1827, Brevet 2nd Lt. 2nd US Artillery 7/1/31. 2nd Lt. 7/1/31, 1st Lt. 8/16/36, Resigned
9/30/36. 1st Lt. Topographical Engineers USA 7/7/38, Capt. 5/31/48, Major 8/6/61, Lt. Col. of Engineers
3/3/63, Honorably Mustered Out of Volunteer Service, 9/1/66.
Brevetted Col. USA 12/62 "For gallant and meritorious services at the Battle of Fredericksburg, Va",
Brig. Gen. 3/13/65 "For gallant and meritorious services at the Battle of Gettysburg, Pa",
Maj. Gen. 3/13/65 "For gallant and meritorious services at the Battle of Saylor's Creek, Va".
Born November 2, 1810 at Philadelphia, Pa. Died December 27, 1883 at Washington, DC.

1ˢᵗ Mass*   Lt. Col. Clark B. Baldwin
1-2-3   <u>7-2</u>: From 11 AM until 6:30 PM, the 1st Regiment Massachusetts Volunteer Infantry, Lt. Col. Clark Baldwin
Commanding, occupied this spot in support of its skirmish line 800 feet in advance. The Regiment subsequently took position in the Brigade line and was engaged until the close of the action.
Casualties: Killed 18, Died of Wounds 9, Wounded 80, Missing 15; Total 122.

1ˢᵗ Mass*   <u>7-2</u>: Right of skirmish line of the 1st Massachusetts Infantry, left resting on Spangler Lane 11 AM to
Advanced   6:30 PM.
Position   Loss on skirmish line: Killed 10, Wounded 32, Missing 10; Total 52.

Hill's Corps Col. David Lang
Anderson's 2nd, 5th, 8th Florida Infantry
Division   <u>7-2</u>: Formed line in forenoon in the western border of these woods. Advanced at 6 PM and assisted in driving
Perry's   back the Union lines on Emmitsburg Road, and by rapid pursuit, compelled the temporary abandonment
Brigade   of several guns. At the foot of the slope met Union infantry and the line on the right retiring, it also fell
back. The color bearer of the 8th Florida fell and its flag was lost.

26ᵗʰ PA   Major Robert L. Bodine
1-2-3   <u>7-2</u>: Went into action here with 365 officers and men.
Casualties: Killed 30, Wounded 176, Missing 7; Total 213.

2ⁿᵈ RI*   Col. Horatio Rogers, Jr.
2-3-6   <u>7-4</u>: Skirmish line 2nd Rhode Island Volunteers.
Casualties: Killed 1, Wounded 5, Missing 1; Total 7.

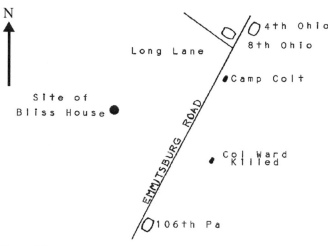

Hill's Corps Brig. Gen. A. R. Wright, Col. William Gibson
Anderson's 3rd, 27th, 48th Regiments and 2nd Battalion Georgia Infantry
Division 7-2: Formed line in forenoon. Advanced at 6 PM and dislodged Union troops posted near the Cadori House,
Wright's capturing several guns and many prisoners. Pursuing on, broke the Union line at the stone wall south of
Brigade* the angle. Reached the crest of the ridge beyond, capturing more guns. The supports on the right being
repulsed and those on the left not coming up, with both flanks assailed and converging columns threaten-
ing its rear, it withdrew fighting its way out with heavy losses and unable to bring off the captured guns.

106ᵗʰ PA* Lt. Col. William L. Curry
2-2-2 7-2: In the morning, Companies A and B on skirmish line. Company B, by order of General Meade, advanced
and uncovered enemy position on Seminary Ridge. In the afternoon, Company B advanced to Bliss House
held by the 16th Mississippi where it was repulsed, losing 12 men. Later, in connection with four companies of the 12th NJ, again advanced and captured the Bliss House and a number of prisoners. In the
evening, the Regiment assisted in repelling the charge of Wright's Georgia Brigade, made a counter-
charge to the Emmitsburg Road, recapturing the guns of Brown's Rhode Island Battery and capturing 250
prisoners, including Col. Gibson wounded, five Captains and 15 Lieutenants of the 48th Georgia. The
Regiment, except Companies A and B and a detail of 50 men and 3 officers, was subsequently ordered to
reinforce the 11th Corps and was assigned position on East Cemetary Hill, supporting a battery, where it
remained during the battle.
7-3: The Regiment with 11th Corps on East Cemetary Hill, except Companies A and B and a detail of 50 men
from the other companies, who remained with the Brigade at this point and assisted to repel Pickett's
Charge.
Casualties: Killed 11, Wounded 59, Missing 2; Total 72.

Col. Ward Col. George H. Ward, Commanding 15th Massachusetts Regiment Volunteers*, here fell mortally wounded.
Killed His comrades and fellow citizens of Worcester raised this memorial of his valor and patriotism.

8ᵗʰ Ohio (Note: see page 78.)

4ᵗʰ Ohio (Note: see page 78.)

CAMP COLT

Although Camp Colt was not a part of the 1863 Battle of Gettysburg, it was within the confines of that battlefield as a training camp in World War 1. A tablet on the Emnitsburg Road commemorates that training camp.

The spot where the tablet stands was crossed by the center of Longstreet's Assaulting Troops at about 3:30 PM on July 3rd, 1863, as they were charging the last few hundred feet up the slope to the High Water Mark of the Southern Confederacy.

The tablet's inscription follows:

United States Army
Tank Corps

This spot marks the site of Camp Colt, the birthplace of the Tank Corps of the United States Army in the spring of 1918. Behind the marker stands a tree planted in soil from each of the 48 States and dedicated in honor of

The Commanding Officer

Captain Dwight D. Eisenhower

who on January 2, 1953 was inaugurated

the 34th President of the United States of America.

This living testimonial is a tribute of the affection

and high esteem of his 1918 Tank Corps comrades

Dedicated
August 28, 1954

World Wars
Tank Corps
Association

THE SYMBOLS LISTED BELOW ARE USED TO IDENTIFY
THE MONUMENTS, MARKERS, TABLETS, STATUES, ETC.
WHICH ARE DRAWN ON THE MAPS IN THESE PAGES

SYMBOL	TYPE	REPRESENTING	DESCRIPTION
(filled oval)	Bronze Tablet	Army of The Potomac, Union Corps or Division or Brigade, Regular Army Regiment, Regular Army Artillery Battery, Volunteer Artillery Brigade.	Brigade Tablet Mounted on Square Marble base. All other Tablets are on large vertical Granite Blocks.
(open oval)	Bronze Tablet	Army of Northern Virginia, Confederate Corps or Division or Brigade or Artillery Battalion	Brigade Tablet and Artillery Battalion Tablet Mounted on Round Marble base. All other Tablets are Mounted on large vertical Granite blocks.
(small filled circle)	Iron Tablet	Union Army Battery (other than Regular Army)	Mounted on Black Iron Shaft.
(small open circle)	Iron Tablet	Confederate Artillery Battery	Mounted on Black Iron Shaft.
(tall filled bar)	Iron Tablet	Confederate Brigade Advanced Position	Mounted on Black Iron Shaft.
(open oval)	Regimental or Battery Monument	Principal Position of Volunteer Regiment or Volunteer Artillery Battery	Usually Granite or Marble in a Great Variety of Shapes and Sizes.
⊗	Regimental Marker	Other than Principal Position of Regiment or Battery	Usually a Square Granite Marker or tablet or may be another monument.
□	Flank Marker or Company Marker	Left and/or Right Flank of Regiment or Battery or Position of a Company.	Usually a Small Square or Rectangular Granite Marker.
⊕	Army Or Corps Headquarters	Site of Headquarters of Army Commander or Corps Commander or Chief of Artillery	Cannon Barrel Mounted Vertically on Stone, Granite or Marble Base.
(filled shape)	State Monument	Monument Erected by Union or Confederate State.	
○	Statue	Standing or Equestrian	Bronze Sculpture
●	Building	House, Barn or other Structure	Identified by Owner's Name.
▪	Miscellaneous Marker	Marker or Inscription of a type not listed above	Granite or Metal Marker.

*Asterisk

Used whenever a Division or Brigade or Regiment or Battery has more than one Monument or Marker.

Check the Index for other Monument or Marker.

~ Gettysburg Battlefield Monuments, Locations & Inscriptions ~

This page left intentionally blank

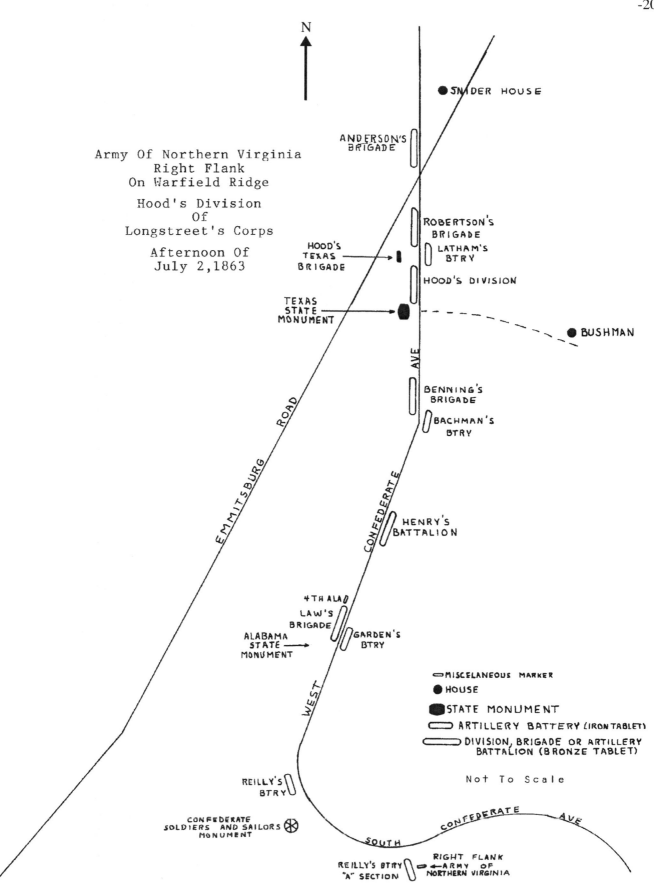

N

Army Of Northern Virginia
Right Flank
On Warfield Ridge

Hood's Division
Of
Longstreet's Corps

Afternoon Of
July 2,1863

SNIDER HOUSE

ANDERSON'S BRIGADE

HOOD'S TEXAS BRIGADE

ROBERTSON'S BRIGADE

LATHAM'S BTRY

HOOD'S DIVISION

TEXAS STATE MONUMENT

BUSHMAN

BENNING'S BRIGADE

BACHMAN'S BTRY

EMMITSBURG ROAD

AVE

CONFEDERATE

HENRY'S BATTALION

4TH ALA

LAW'S BRIGADE

ALABAMA STATE MONUMENT

GARDEN'S BTRY

WEST

⊂⊃ MISCELANEOUS MARKER

● HOUSE

⬢ STATE MONUMENT

▭ ARTILLERY BATTERY (IRON TABLET)

⬭ DIVISION, BRIGADE OR ARTILLERY BATTALION (BRONZE TABLET)

Not To Scale

REILLY'S BTRY

CONFEDERATE SOLDIERS AND SAILORS MONUMENT ⊕

CONFEDERATE AVE

SOUTH

REILLY'S BTRY "A" SECTION

RIGHT FLANK ← ARMY OF NORTHERN VIRGINIA

~ *Gettysburg Battlefield Monuments, Locations & Inscriptions* ~

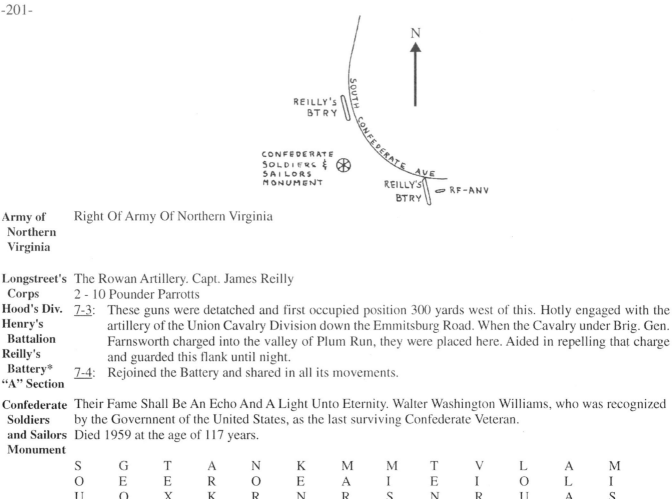

Army of Northern Virginia	Right Of Army Of Northern Virginia	

Longstreet's Corps Hood's Div. Henry's Battalion Reilly's Battery* "A" Section	The Rowan Artillery. Capt. James Reilly	
	2 - 10 Pounder Parrotts	
	7-3:	These guns were detatched and first occupied position 300 yards west of this. Hotly engaged with the artillery of the Union Cavalry Division down the Emmitsburg Road. When the Cavalry under Brig. Gen. Farnsworth charged into the valley of Plum Run, they were placed here. Aided in repelling that charge and guarded this flank until night.
	7-4:	Rejoined the Battery and shared in all its movements.

Confederate Soldiers and Sailors Monument	Their Fame Shall Be An Echo And A Light Unto Eternity. Walter Washington Williams, who was recognized by the Government of the United States, as the last surviving Confederate Veteran. Died 1959 at the age of 117 years.

```
S  G  T  A  N  K  M  M  T  V  L  A  M
O  E  E  R  O  E  A  I  E  I  O  L  I
U  O  X  K  R  N  R  S  N  R  U  A  S
T  R  A  A  T  T  Y  S  N  G  I  B  S
H  G  S  N  H  U  L  O  E  I  S  A  I
   I     S     C  A  U  S  N  I  M  S
C  A     A  C  K  N  R  S  I  A  A  S
A        S  A  Y  D  I  E  A  N  A  I
R        S  R     O  E  E  N     A  P
O           O        S        A     P
L           L              A        I
I           I
N           N
A           A
```

Longstreet's Corps Hood's Division Henry's Battalion Reilly's Battery*	The Rowan Artillery. Capt James Reilly	
	2 - Napoleans, 2 10 Pounder Parrotts, 2 3" Rifles	
	7-2:	Took position here 4 PM and was actively engaged until night. One rifle burst and a captured Parrott was substituted.
	7-3:	Two Parrotts moved to right. The other guns engaged in firing upon the Union lines within range. About 5 PM aided in repelling cavalry charge under Brig. Gen. Farnsworth which had charged into the valley between this point and Round Top.
	7-4:	Occupied position nearby and position west of this until 6 PM, then withdrew from the field.
	Losses not reported in detail.	

*see index

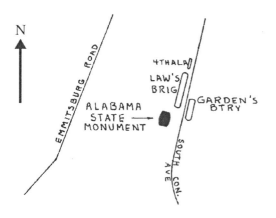

ALABAMIANS
YOUR NAMES ARE INSCRIBED ON FAME'S IMMORTAL SCROLL
By The Alabama Division - United Daughters of The Confederacy

Unveiled November 12, 1933

Alabama State Monument

Longstreet's Corps
Hood's Division
Henry's Battalion
Garden's Battery

The Palmetto Light Artillery. Capt. Hugh R. Garden
2 - Napoleans, 2 10 Pounder Parrotts
7-2: In reserve near here but not engaged.
7-3: In position here and actively engaged in firing upon the Union lines within range. About 5 PM aided in repelling cavalry under Brig. Gen. Farnsworth which had charged into the valley between this point and Round Top.
7-4: Occupied position nearby and west of this until 6 PM, then withdrew from the field.
Losses not reported in detail.

Longstreet's Corps
Hood's Division
Law's Brigade*

Brig. Gen. Evander M. Law, Col. James M. Sheffield
4th, 15th, 44th, 47th, 48th Alabama Infantry
7-2: Left New Guilford, 25 miles distant, at 3 AM. Arrived and formed line 50 yards west of this about 4 PM and advanced against the Union positions. 4th, 15th and 47th Regiments attacked Little Round Top and continued the assault until dark. The 44th and 48th assisted in capturing Devil's Den and 3 guns of the 4th New York Battery.
7-3: Occupied breastworks on the west slope of Round Top. The 4th and 15th Regiments assisted at 5 PM in repulsing cavalry charge led by Brig. Gen. E. J. Farnsworth in Plum Run Valley.
7-5: Began the march to Hagerstown, Md.
Present: about 1500. Losses: about 550.

4ᵗʰ Alabama Infantry
Longstreet's Corps
Hood's Division
Law's Brigade

Lt. Col. L. H. Scruggs
7-2: Left New Guilford, 25 miles distant, at 3 AM. Arrived here and formed line about 4 PM and under fire from Smith's Union Battery on rocky ridge and the sharpshooters in Plum Run Valley. Advanced at once against the Union position on Little Round Top. The Regiment encountered the 83rd Pa and the right wing of the 20th Maine. The conflict lasted until nightfall.
7-3: Occupied breastworks on western slope of Round Top with firing on skirmish line. At 5 PM, intercepted near the Slyder House, and aided in repulsing the Union Calvary under Brig. Gen. Farnsworth and pursued it into the forest south of the valley. About 11 PM, the Regiment, under orders resumed position near here and lay inactive the next day and night
7-5: About 5 AM, began the march to Hagerstown.
Present: Officers and Men about 275, Killed and wounded 87.

*see index

~ Gettysburg Battlefield Monuments, Locations & Inscriptions ~

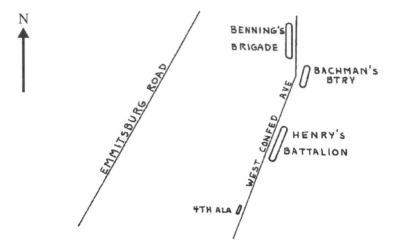

Longstreet's	Rielly's, Bachman's, Garden's and Latham's Batteries
Corps	Major M. W. Henry
Hood's	11 - Napoleans, 4 - 10 Pounder Parrotts, 2 - 3" Rifles, 1 - 12 Pounder Howitzer, 1 - 6 Pounder Bronze Gun.
Division	7-2&3: Occupied this line and took part in battle as described on tablets of the several batteries. The howitzer,
Henry's	the bronze gun and one three inch rifle were disabled and three captured 10 Pounder Parrotts were substi-
Battalion	tuted.
	7-4: On a line a little west of this until 6 PM, then withdrew from the field.
	Losses: Killed 4, Wounded 23; Total 27. Ammunition expended: about 1500 rounds.

Longstreet's	The German Artillery. Capt. William K. Bachman
Corps	4 Napoleans
Hood's	7-2: In reserve near here, but not engaged.
Division	7-3: In position here and actively engaged in firing upon Union Batteries within range. About 5 PM aided in
Henry's	repelling cavalry under Brig. Gen. Farnsworth, which had charged into the valley between this point and
Battalion	Round Top.
Bachman's	7-4: Occupied position nearby and west of this until 6 PM, then withdrew from field.
Battery	Losses not reported in detail.

Longstreet's	2nd, 15th, 17th, 20th Georgia Infantry
Corps	Brig. Gen. Henry L. Benning
Hood's	7-2: Arrived and formed line about 4 PM in rear of Law's and Robertson's Brigades and moving forward in
Division	support of these, took prominent part in the severe conflict which resulted in capture of Devil's Den,
Benning's	together with a number of prisoners and three guns of the 4th New York Battery.
Brigade	7-3: Held Devil's Den and adjacent crest of rocky ridge until late in the evening, when under orders of the
	Brigade retired to position near here. Through mistake of orders, the 15th Ga did not retire directly, but
	moved northward, encountered a superior force and suffered considerable loss.
	7-4: Occupied breastworks near here facing southward until midnight.
	7-5: About 5 AM, began the march to Hagerstown, Md.
	Present: about 1500. Losses: 509.

N ↑

HOOD'S
DIVISION

● TEXAS STATE MONUMENT

BENNING'S
BRIGADE

EMMITSBURG ROAD

Texas State Monument Texas remembers the valor and devotion of her sons who served at Gettysburg July 2-3. From near this spot, the Texas Brigade, at about 4:30 PM on July 2, crossed the Emmitsburg Road and advanced with Hood's Division across Plum Run toward Little Round Top. The Texas Brigade, after severe fighting on the slopes of Little Round Top, retired to a position on the south side of Devil's Den. The Brigade held this position on the night of July 2nd and during July 3rd. The Brigade then fell back to a position near this memorial on the evening of July 3rd. On the field of Gettysburg the Texas Brigade suffered 597 casualties.

Longstreet's Corps Hood's Division Major General J. B. Hood, Brigadier General E. M. Law

Law's Brigade	Brig. Gen. E. M. Law
Robertson's Brigade	Brig. Gen. J. B. Robertson
Anderson's Brigade	Brig. Gen. George T. Anderson, Lt. Col. Luffman
Benning's Brigade	Brig. Gen. Henry L. Benning
Artillery Battalion	Major M. W. Henry - 4 Batteries

7-1: On the march to Gettysburg. Encamped about 4 miles from the field with the exception of Law's Brigade left on picket at New Guilford.

7-2: Law's Brigade joined about noon from New Guilford. About noon, the Division was formed on extreme right of the Army and directed to drive in and envelope the Union left. About 4 PM, the batteries opened and soon after the Division moved forward. After a severe struggle, the Union retired to a ridge in rear. The ground fought over was obstructed by stone fences and very difficult. The movement was partially successful. The battle continued until nearly dark. The advance gained was held.

7-3: Occupied the ground gained and with the exception of resisting a cavalry charge and heavy skirmishing, was not engaged.

7-4: The Division took up the line of march during the night.

Casualties: 343 Killed, 1504 Wounded, 442 Missing; Total 2289.

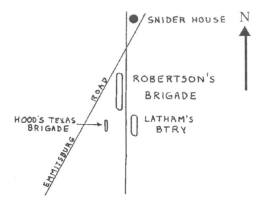

Hood's Texas Brigade

1st, 4th, 5th Texas and 3rd Arkansas Infantry Regiments
July 2nd and 3rd, 1863

Texas Troops At Gettysburg Were:
1st Texas Infantry, Lt. Col. P. A. Work: 4th Texas Infantry, Col. J. C. E. Key, Lt. Col. B. F. Carter, Maj. J. P. Bain; 5th Texas Infantry, Col. R. M. Powell, Lt. Col. K. Bryan, Maj. J. C. Rogers. The Texas Brigade included the 3rd Arkansas Infantry, Col. Van H. Manning. (Brig. Gen. J. B. Robertson's Texas Brigade, Hood's Division, Longstreet's Corps.)

OF ALL THE GALLANT FIGHTS THEY MADE
NONE WAS GREATER THAN GETTYSBURG

A Memorial To Texans Who Served The Confederacy
Erected By The State of Texas 1964

Longstreet's Corps
Hood's Division
Henry's Battalion
Latham's Battery

The Branch Artillery. Capt. A. C. Latham
3 - Napoleans, 1 - 12 Pounder Howitzer, 1 - 6 Pounder Bronze Gun

7-2: Took position here 4 PM and was actively engaged until night. The howitzer and the bronze gun were disabled and two captured 10 Pounder Parrotts substituted.

7-3: Engaged in firing upon Union lines within range. About 5 PM, aided in repelling cavalry under Brig. Gen. Farnsworth which had charged into the valley between this point and Round Top.

7-4: Occupied position nearby and west of this until 6 PM, then withdrew from field.
Losses not reported in detail.

Robertson's Brigade*

Brig. Gen. J. B. Robertson

7-2: Arrived after a march of several miles and formed line 50 yards west of this about 4 PM. Advanced against Union position. The 4th and 5th Texas joined in attack on Little Round Top which continued until dark.
The 1st Texas and 3rd Arkansas attacked and assisted in taking Devil's Den and rocky ridge with a number of prisoners and three guns of the 4th New York Battery.

7-3: At 2 AM, the 1st Texas and 3rd Arkansas were moved to rejoin the 4th and 5th Texas on the northwest spur of Big Round Top. Three Regiments occupied the breastworks there all day, skirmishing hotly with Union sharpshooters. Early in the day the 1st Texas was sent to confront the Union Cavalry threatening the right flank. After dark, the Brigade took position near here.
Present: about 1100. Losses: about 540.

*see index

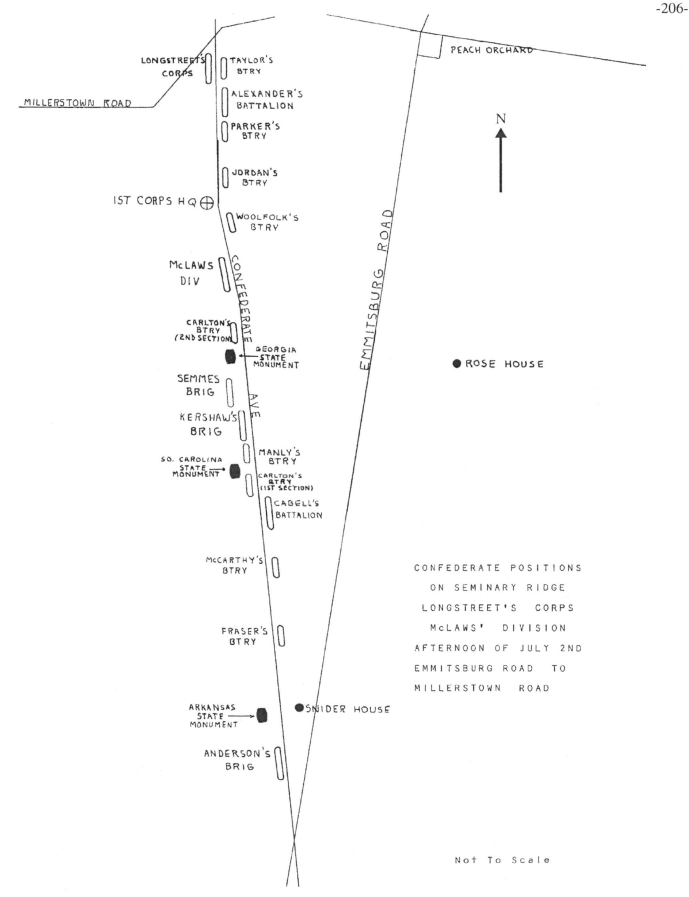

~ Gettysburg Battlefield Monuments, Locations & Inscriptions ~

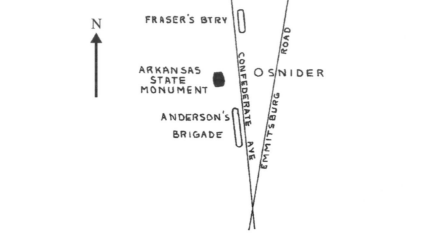

Longstreet's Corps
Hood Division
Anderson's Brigade*

Brig. Gen. George T. Anderson. Lt. Col. William Luffman
7th, 8th, 9th, 11th, 59th Georgia Infantry

7-2: After a march of several miles, about 4 PM formed line 100 yards west of this spot. The 7th Regiment was sent southward to watch Union Cavalry. The others charged into the woods south of the Wheatfield and dislodged the Union line from the stone wall there, but flanked on the left, retired to the crest of Rose Hill. Reinforced by parts of other brigades, they again advanced. The wounding of Gen. G. T. Anderson caused a brief halt and some confusion, but they advanced a third time and after a struggle, occupied the woodland to its border on Plum Run Valley.

7-3: Brigade sent down Emmitsburg Road and assisted in repulsing and holding in check Union Cavalry which sought to flank the Division.

7-4: Assisted in constructing works to protect the flank.

7-5: About 5 AM, began the march to Hagerstown.

Present: about 1800. Losses: 671.

Arkansas State Monument

THE THIRD ARKANSAS INFANTRY,
CONFEDERATE STATES ARMY

The Grateful People Of The State Of Arkansas Erect This Memorial As An Expression Of Their Pride In The Officers And Men Of The 3rd Arkansas Infantry, Confederate States Army Who, By Their Valor And Their Blood, Have Made This Ground Forever Hallowed.

Longstreet's Corps
McLaws' Division
Cabell's Battalion
Fraser's Battery

The Pulaski Artillery. Capt. J. C. Fraser, Lt. W. J. Furlong
2 10 Pounder Parrotts, 2 - 3" Rifles

7-2: Took position here 3:30 PM and opened fire on Peach Orchard and the Union Batteries east of it. At 4 PM, the rifles were silenced by loss of men. The fire of the Parrotts continued until the Peach Orchard was taken.

7-3: The Parrotts moved to crest north of Peach Orchard in main artillery line. Took part in the great cannonade. Aided in checking pursuit after Longetreet's Assault and retired from the front after dark. The rifles were placed under command of Capt. Manly of the North Carolina Artillery, and served by his men in position with his own rifles.

7-4: In position near here. After night withdrew from the field. Their ammunition was nearly expended.

Losses: 6 Killed, 13 Wounded; Total 19. Horses killed or disabled: 18

*see index

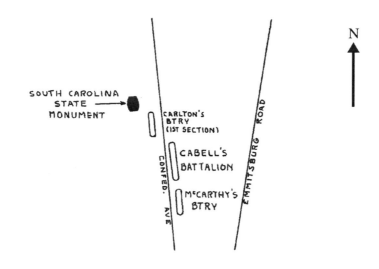

Longstreet's Corps McLaws' Division Cabell's Battalion McCarthy's Battery

1st Richmond Howitzers. Capt. E. S. McCarthy
2 - Napoleans, 2 - 3" Rifles.

<u>7-2</u>: At 3:30, placed in reserve near here. The rifled guns advanced to this position at 4 PM and engaged in severe artillery fight until dark. The men of the Napolean Section sometimes relieved those of the Rifle Section.

<u>7-3</u>: Advanced and formed part of the main artillery line, the rifles near the Emmitsburg Road, the Napoleans further to the left. All hotly engaged sometimes changing positions. Retired from the front after dark.

<u>7-4</u>: In position near here. One Napolean aided in checking a hostile advance. All withdrew from the field at night.

Ammunition expended: about 850 rounds. One rifle was disabled.
Losses: 2 Killed, 8 Wounded; Total 10. Horses killed or disabled: 25.

Longstreet's Corps McLaw's Division Cabell's Battalion

Col. H. C. Cabell
Fraser's, McCarthy's, Carlton's and Manly's Batteries
4 Napoleans, 4 -10 Pounder Parrotts, 6 - 3" Rifles, 2 - 12 Pounder Howitzers.
<u>7-2&3</u>: Took an active part in the battle.
<u>7-4</u>: Remained in position here and withdrew from the field after night.
Ammunition expended: about 3300 rounds.
Losses: 12 Killed, 30 Wounded, 4 Missing; Total 46. Horses killed or disabled, 46.

Longstreet's Corps McLaw's Division Cabell's Battalion Carlton's Battery* (1st Section)

The Troup Artillery. Capt H. H. Carlton, Lt. C. W. Motes
2 10 Pounder Parrotts
<u>7-2</u>: This Section took position here at 3:30 PM and was actively engaged until near dark.
<u>7-3</u>: In position on the main artillery line on the ridge in front of Spangler's Woods. After repulse of Longetreet's Assault, advanced 300 yards and aided in checking pursuit. Retired from the front after dark.
<u>7-4</u>: In position here all day and withdrew from the field after night. Their ammununition was nearly exhausted.
Losses: (Note: See 2nd Section, Page 211)

(Note: see page 209.)

South Carolina State Monument

*see index

SOUTH CAROLINA MONUMENT

SOUTH CAROLINA

That Men Of Honor
Might Forever Know
The Responsibilities
Of Freedom. Dedicated
South Carolinians Stood
And Were Counted For
Their Heritage And
Convictions. Abiding
Faith In The Sacredness
Of States Rights Provided
Their Creed. Here, Many
Earned Eternal Glory.

1st ARMY CORPS

Lieutenant General James Longstreet

McLaws' Division
Kershaw's Brigade
Br. Gen. J B Kershaw
2nd So Carolina Inf
3rd So Carolina Inf
7th So Carolina Inf
8th So Carolina Inf
15th So Carolina Inf
3rd So Carolina Inf Battalion

Hood's Division
Artillery
German Artillery
Palmetto Artillery
Artillery Reserve
Alexander's Battalion
Brook's Artillery

3rd ARMY CORPS

Lt. Gen. A. P. Hill

Pender's Division
1st Brigade
1st So Carolina Rifles
1st So Carolina Inf.
12th So Carolina Inf.
13th So Carolina Inf.
14th So Carolina Inf.
Artillery Reserve
Pegram's Battalion
Pee Dee Artillery

CAVALRY

Stuart's Division

Maj. Gen. J. E. B. Stuart
Hampton's Brigade
Br. Gen. Wade Hampton
1st So Carolina Cav
2nd So Carolina Cav
Stuart's Horse Art'y
Hart's Battery

"There Is No Holier Spot Of
Ground Than Where Defeated
Valor Lies, By Mourning
Beauty Crowned."

—Henry Timrod

(Note: Henry Timrod was the Civil War Poet Laureate of South Carolina)

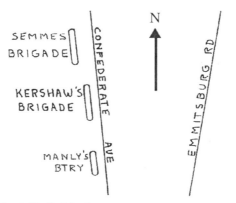

Longstreet's Corps
McLaw's Division
Cabell's Battalion
Manly's Battery

1st Carolina Artillery. Capt. B. C. Manly
2 - Napoleans, 2 - 3" Rifles
7-2: Took position here 3:30 PM and became actively engaged at 5 PM. Advanced to the Peach Orchard and continued firing until dark. Returned here after night.
7-3: The Napoleans remained here. The Rifles, with the two Rifles of Fraser's Battery took position at 5 AM under Capt. Manly on the crest beyond Emmitsburg Road and north of the Peach Orchard. Were engaged in the great cannonade and after Longstreet's Assault, aided in checking pursuit. Continued firing at intervals until 7:30 PM. Then resumed this position.
7-4: At 10 AM aided in checking an advance of three regiments. After night, withdrew from the field.
Ammunition expended: 1146 rounds.
Losses: 3 Killed, 4 Wounded, 4 Missing; Total 11. Horses killed or disabled: 20

Longstreet's Corps
McLaw's Division
Kershaw's Brigade*

Brig. Gen. Joseph B. Kershaw
2nd, 3rd, 7th, 8th, 15th Regiments, 3rd South Carolina Battalion.
7-2: Arrived 3:30 PM and formed line here. Advanced about 4:30 PM to battle. The 8th and 2nd Regiments and 3rd Battalion shared in the attack on the Peach Orchard and batteries near there on Wheatfield Road. The 7th and 3rd Regiments were engaged in the long and severe conflict at and around the Loop. The 15th Regiment fought on Rose Hill and in the ravine and forest beyond. Late in the evening, the Brigade took part in the general advance by which the Union forces were forced from the Wheatfield and across Plum Run Valley. At dark, under orders, it retired to the Peach Orchard.
7-3: At Peach Orchard until noon, then sent farther to front. At 1 PM, under orders, resumed position here extending to right and keeping in touch with Hood's Division.
Present: about 1800. Losses 630
(Note: See Pages 167 and 177 for advanced positions.)

Longstreet's Corps
McLaw's Division
Semmes' Brigade*

Brig. Gen. Paul J. Semmes, Col. Goode Bryan
10th, 50th, 51st, 53rd Georgia Infantry
7-2: Arrived about 3:30 PM, formed line 50 yards west of here. Advanced about 5 PM in support of Kershaw's and Anderson's Brigades and took a prominent part in the severe and protracted conflict on Rose Hill and in the ravine and forest east of there and in the vicinity of the Loop. Participated also in the general advance later in the evening by which the Union were forced out of the Wheatfield and across Plum Run Valley. Brig. Gen. Paul J. Semmes fell mortally wounded in the ravine near the Loop.
7-3: During the forenoon, Anderson's Brigade being withdrawn for duty elsewhere, the Brigade was left in occupancy of the woodland south of the Wheatfield. At 1 PM, under orders, it resumed its original position near here.
Present: about 1200. Losses: 430

*see index

~ Gettysburg Battlefield Monuments, Locations & Inscriptions ~

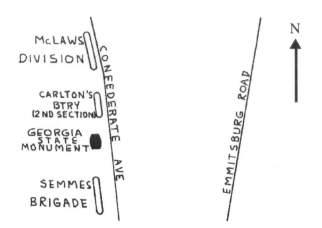

**Georgia
State
Monument**

GEORGIA CONFEDERATE SOLDIERS
We Sleep Here In Obedience To Law;
When Duty Called We Came,
When Country Called We Died.

Longstreet's Capt. H. H. Carlton, Lt. C. W. Motes
Corps 2 - 12 Pounder Howitzers
McLaws' 7-2: This Section took position here at 4 PM and was actively engaged until near dark.
Division 7-3: In position near main artillery line but under cover of hill in front of Spangler's Woods. After repulse of
Cabell's Longstreet's Assault, advanced 300 yards and aided in checking pursuit. Reired from the front after dark.
Battalion 7-4: In position here all day and withdrew from field after night. Their ammunition was nearly exhausted.
Carlton's Losses of both Sections: 1 Killed, 6 Wounded; Total 7. Horses of both Sections killed or disabled: 17.
Battery*
(2nd Section)

Major General Lafayette McLaws
Kershaw's Brigade   Brig. Gen. Joseph B. Kershaw
Barksdale's Brigade   Brig. Gen. William Barksdale, Col. B. G. Humphreys
Longstreet's Semmes Brigade   Brig. Gen. Paul J. Semmes
Corps Wofford's Brigade   Brig. Gen. W. T. Wofford
McLaws' Artillery Battalion   4 Batteries, Col. H. C. Cabell
Division 7-1: Division reached Marsh Creek, 4 miles from Gettysburg.
7-2: The Division was placed in position facing Union line on the Emmitsburg Road. About 4 PM, the batteries
opened on the position, the Division pressing to the front and the Union troops retiring to the hill in the
rear. The battle continued until nearly night, when a strong Union force met the supporting Division which
was cooperating on the left and drove one Brigade back and checked the support of the other Brigade,
exposing the left. It was thought prudent not to push further until other troops of the Corps came up. The
Division was withdrawn to the first position of Union troops, resting at the Peach Orchard, the conflict to
be renewed in the morning when other orders were received.
7-3: With the exception of severe skirmishing, the Division was not engaged and after night, dispositions were
made to withdraw.
7-4: The Division took up the line of march during the night.
Casualties: 313 Killed, 1538 Wounded, 327 Missing; Total 2178

*see index

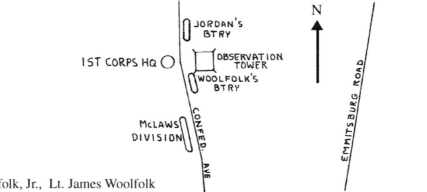

Longstreet's	Capt. P. Woolfolk, Jr., Lt. James Woolfolk
Corps	The Ashland, Va. Artillery
Alexander's	2 - Napoleans, 2 - 20 Pounder Parrotts.

Battalion
Woolfolk's
Battery
Artillery
Reserve

7-2: Took position here 4:30 PM and opened fire. Joined soon in the advance of the infantry. During remainder of day, occupied position on the crest near Peach Orchard and was actively engaged in firing on Union forces' new line.

7-3: In position near northeast corner of Spangler's Woods on left of the artillery line which occupied the ridge from the Peach Orchard to that point. Took part in the cannonade preceeding Longstreet's Assault, followed and supported it, aided then in repelling sharpshooters and withdrew at midnight.

7-4: In position here until 4 PM, then to Marsh Creek on Fairfield Road.

Losses heavy but not reported in detail.

1st Corps
Head-
quarters

ARMY OF NORTHERN VIRGINIA
1ST CORPS HEADQUARTERS
LT. GEN. JAMES LONGSTREET
DIVISIONS
MAJ. GEN. GEORGE MC LAWS'
MAJ. GEN. GEORGE E. PICKETT
MAJ. GEN. JOHN B. HOOD
JULY 1, 2, 3, 4, 5, 1863
(These Headquarters Were Located
At A Schoolhouse 900 Yards Westerly)

Longstreet's The Bedford, Va. Artillery. Capt. T. C. Jordan

Corps 4 - 3" Rifles.

Artillery
Reserve
7-2: Took position here at 4:30 PM. Fired a few rounds at the Peach Orchard. Joined in the infantry charge and afterwards occupied position on the crest near the Peach Orchard and was actively engaged until night.

Alexander's
Battalion
7-3: Remained near the same position which was on main artillery line. Took part in the cannonade preceeding Longstreet's Assault and aided in supporting that assault. Retired from the front after night.

Jordan's
Battery
7-4: In position near here until 4 PM, then to Marsh Creek on Fairfield Road.

Losses serious but not reported in detail.

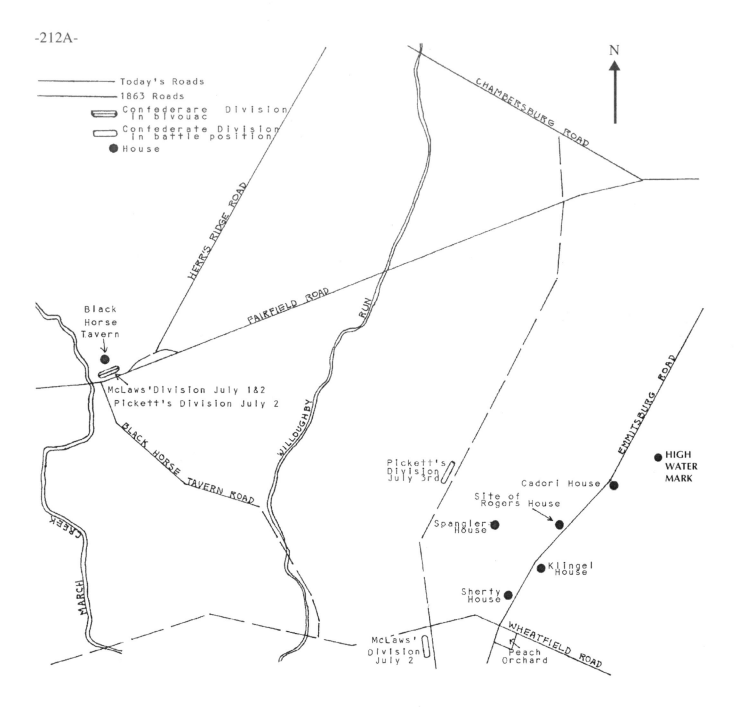

Legend:
- Today's Roads
- 1863 Roads
- Confederate Division in bivouac
- Confederate Division in battle position
- House

Longstreet's 7-1: Mc Laws' Division arrived late in the day and camped in this vicinity.
Corps 7-2: In the morning, McLaws' Division moved on the road towards Gettysburg, but turning to the right one
McLaws' half mile this side of Willoughby Run and crossing that stream lower down, formed line as marked on the
and battlefield.
Pickett's Pickett's Division marched by this place in the afternoon but followed the other road with some deflec-
Divisions tions to avoid being seen by the Union Signal Corps, and crossing Willoughby Run, lay that night on the
west side of Spangler's Woods.

Black Horse At the time of the Battle of Gettysburg, this was the name of the tavern kept in this stone house, which
Tavern was built in 1813, and in a large log house of much older date then adjoining.

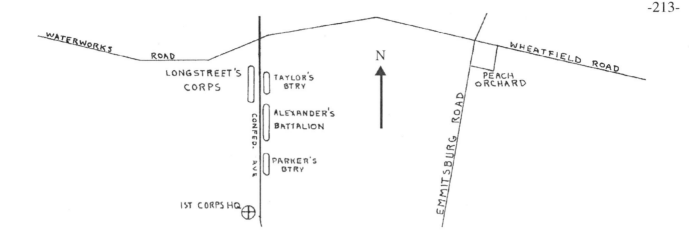

Longstreet's Corps Artillery Reserve Alexander's Battalion Parker's Battery Capt. W. W. Parker

1 - 10 Pounder Parrott, 3 - 3" Rifles

7-2: Took position here and opened fire on Peach Orchard. Joined at 5 PM in the Infantry charge, advancing into position east of the Emmitsburg Road and north of the Peach Orchard, continuing actively engaged until night.

7-3: Remained near the same position which was on the main artillery line. Took part in the cannonade which preceeded Longetreet's Assault and aided in supporting that assault. Retired from the front after midnight.

7-4: In position near here until 4 PM, then withdrew to Marsh Creek on the Fairfield Road.

Losses heavy but not reported in detail.

Longstreet's Corps Artillery Reserve Alexander's Battalion Col. E. Porter Alexander

Woolfolk's, Jordan's, Parker's, Taylor's, Moody's & Rhett's Battery's

7-2: Came into position on this line about 4 PM. Advanced soon after with the infantry and occupied a line on the crest near the Peach Orchard.

7-3: In the line on ridge from Peach Orchard to northeast corner of Spangler's Woods. Aided in the cannonade and supported Longstreet's Assault.

7-4: In position near here until 4 PM, then withdrew to Marsh Creek on the Fairfield Road.

Losses: 19 Killed, 114 Wounded, 6 Missing; Total 139. Horses killed or disabled: 116.

Longstreet's Corps Artillery Reserve Taylor's Battery Capt. O. B. Taylor

4 - Napoleans

7-2: Took position here at 4 PM and opened fire on Peach Orchard. Advanced at 5 PM with the infantry to a position about 400 feet north of Peach Orchard and east of the Emmitsburg Road, continuing actively engaged until night.

7-3: Took position 3 AM in main artillery line near Smith House northeast of Sherfy House on Emmitsburg Road and held it all day. Took part in cannonade preceeding Longstreet's Assault, supported that assault and aided in repelling sharpshooters afterwards. Retired from the front after night.

7-4: In position near here until 4 PM, then withdrew to Marsh Creek on the Fairfield Road.

Losses: 2 Killed, 10 Wounded; Total 12.

Longstreet's Corps (Note: See Page 214)

ARMY OF NORTHERN VIRGINIA
1st ARMY CORPS

Lt. Gen. James Longstreet

McLaws' Division	Maj. Gen. Lafayette McLaws'
Picketts' Division	Maj. Gen. George E. Pickett
Hood's Division	Maj. Gen. John B. Hood
Artillery Reserve	Col. J. B. Walton - 10 Batteries

7-1: McLaws' Division encamped about 4 miles from Gettysburg a little after dark. Hood's Division reached the same distance about 12 PM. Law's Brigade on picket at New Guilford. Pickett's Division guarded trains at Chambersburg.

7-2: Moved that portion of the command which was up to gain the Emmitsburg Road on the Union left. Delayed attack until 3:30 PM when Law's Brigade joined from New Guilford. McLaws' Division facing Union left about 4 PM. Hood's Division moved further to the right and took position enveloping Union left. The batteries opened about 4 PM upon Union troops on Emmitsburg Road. Hood's Division pressing on left and McLaws' in front, the Union troops were dislodged. The engagement lasted until nearly night with heavy losses. The ground gained on the right was held. The left was withdrawn to first Union position at the Peach Orchard.

7-3: Pickett's Division reached the field at 9 AM. Pickett's, Heth's and part of Pender's Divisions were ordered to form column of assault on Union centre on Cemetary Hill. The batteries opened about 1 PM. About 3 PM, Pickett advanced in good order under a severe fire and was repulsed at the stone wall losing heavily. McLaws' and Hood's Divisions were not seriously engaged and after rectifying their lines, remained on the field during the day and night.

7-4: The Corps took up the line of march during the night.
Casualties: 910 Killed, 4339 Wounded, 2290 Missing; Total 7539

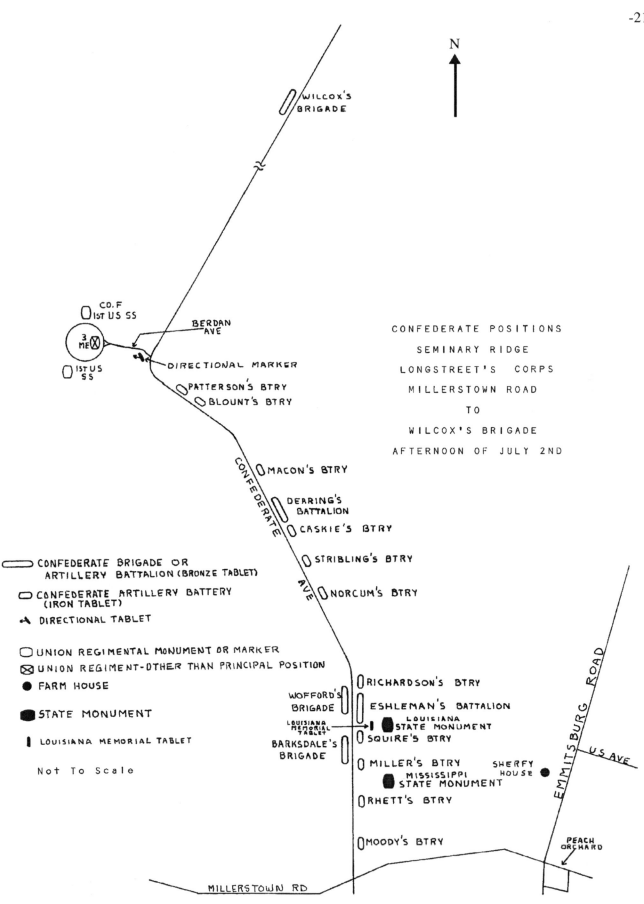

N

WILCOX'S BRIGADE

CO. F
1st US SS

3
ME

1st US
SS

BERDAN
AVE

DIRECTIONAL MARKER

PATTERSON'S BTRY

BLOUNT'S BTRY

CONFEDERATE POSITIONS
SEMINARY RIDGE
LONGSTREET'S CORPS
MILLERSTOWN ROAD
TO
WILCOX'S BRIGADE
AFTERNOON OF JULY 2ND

CONFEDERATE

MACON'S BTRY

DEARING'S
BATTALION

CASKIE'S BTRY

STRIBLING'S BTRY

AVE

NORCUM'S BTRY

CONFEDERATE BRIGADE OR
ARTILLERY BATTALION (BRONZE TABLET)

CONFEDERATE ARTILLERY BATTERY
(IRON TABLET)

DIRECTIONAL TABLET

UNION REGIMENTAL MONUMENT OR MARKER

UNION REGIMENT-OTHER THAN PRINCIPAL POSITION

FARM HOUSE

STATE MONUMENT

LOUISIANA MEMORIAL TABLET

Not To Scale

RICHARDSON'S BTRY

WOFFORD'S
BRIGADE

ESHLEMAN'S BATTALION

LOUISIANA
MEMORIAL
TABLET

LOUISIANA
STATE MONUMENT

SQUIRE'S BTRY

BARKSDALE'S
BRIGADE

MILLER'S BTRY

MISSISSIPPI
STATE MONUMENT

SHERFY
HOUSE

EMMITSBURG ROAD

US AVE

RHETT'S BTRY

MOODY'S BTRY

PEACH
ORCHARD

MILLERSTOWN RD

~ Gettysburg Battlefield Monuments, Locations & Inscriptions ~

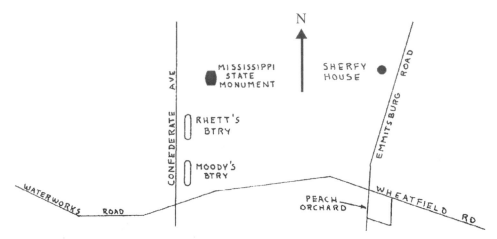

Longstreet's The Madison (Louisiana) Artillery. Capt. George W. Moody

Corps   4 - 24 Pounder Howitzers

Artillery   7-2:   Arrived here and opened fire at 4 PM. Following the infantry charge upon the Peach Orchard, took posi-

Reserve   tion near there and with other batteries, supported the infantry in its further advance. Aided in so harassing

Alexander's   the remaining Union forces as to compel the temporary abandonment of several guns. Kept up a spirited

Battalion   fire until nightfall and prevented pursuit of the Confederate advanced line when they fell back shortly

Moody's   before dark.

Battery   7-3:   In position at dawn on the artillery line on the ridge running north from the Peach Orchard and on duty there all day. Took part in the cannonade preceding Longstreet's Assault and retired from the front after night.

          7-4:   Remained near here until 4 PM and then withdrew to Marsh Creek on the Fairfield Road.

          Losses heavy but not reported in detail.

Longstreet's The Brooks (South Carolina) Artillery. Lt. S. C. Gilbert

Corps   4 - 12 Pounder Howitzers

Artillery   7-2:   Took position here at 4 PM and opened fire. When the charge was made on the Peach Orchard, moved to

Reserve   a point near there and with other batteries supported the infantry in its further advance. Assisted in harass-

Alexander's   ing the retiring Union forces, causing them to temporarily abandon several guns. Continued firing until

Battalion   night and aided in preventing pursuit of the Confederate advanced lines when they fell back shortly before

Rhett's   dark.

Battery   7-3:   In position at dawn in the artillery line on the ridge running north from the Peach Orchard and on duty there all day. Took part in the cannonade preceding Longstreet's Assault and retired from the front after night.

          7-4:   Remained near here until 4 PM and then withdrew to Marsh Creek on the Fairfield Road.

          Losses heavy but not reported in detail.

Mississippi   MISSISSIPPI

State   JULY 1, 2, 3, 1863

Monument   On This Ground Our Brave Sires Fought For Their Righteous Cause;

In Glory They Sleep Who Gave To It Their Lives,

To Valor They Gave New Dimensions Of Courage,

To Duty Its Noblest Fulfillment,

To Posterity The Sacred Heritage Of Honor.

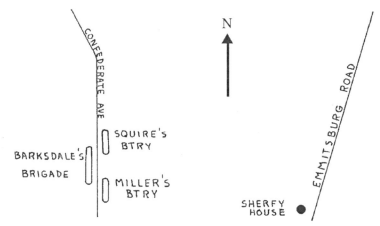

Longstreet's Corps
Artillery Reserve
Eshelman's Battalion
Miller's Battery

The Washington Artillery - 3rd Company. Capt. M. B. Miller.

3 - Napoleans

7-3: Advanced before daylight into position about 100 yards north of the Peach Orchard. This Battery fired the signal guns for the cannonade preceeding Longstreet's Assault, took part therein and supported the charge of the infantry by advancing 450 yards and keeping up a vigorous fire. After the repulse of the assault, moved to the left and west of the Emmitsburg Road, ready to aid in resisting a countercharge if attempted. From loss of horses, but one gun could be used. The others were sent to the rear and that gun was withdrawn after dark.

7-4: At 9 AM marched with the Battalion to Cashtown to reinforce the cavalry escorting the wagon train.
Losses heavy but not reported in detail.

Longstreet's Corps
Artillery Reserve
Eshelman's Battalion
Squire's Battery

The Washington (Louisiana) Artillery - 1st Company. Capt. C. W. Squires

1 - Napolean

7-3: Having but one gun, it cooperated all day with Miller's Battery. Advanced before daylight into position about 100 yards north of the Peach Orchard, assisted in repelling skirmishers and took part in the cannonade preceeding Longetreet's Assault. Moved several hundred yards to the left after the repulse of that assault to aid in resisting a countercharge if attempted. Withdrew soon afterward to the rear.

7-4: At 9 AM marched with the Battalion to Cashtown to reinforce the cavalry escorting the wagon train.
Losses not reported in detail.

Longstreet's Corps
McLaws' Division
Barksdale's Brigade*

Brig. Gen. William Barksdale

13th, 17th, 18th, 21st Mississippi Infantry

7-2: Arrived about 3 PM and formed line here. Advanced at 5 PM and took part in the assault on the Peach Orchard and adjacent positions, vigorously pursuing the Union forces as they retired. The 21st Regiment pushed on past the Trostle House and captured, but were unable to bring off, the 9th Massachusetts Battery and I Battery-5th US. The other Regiments inclining more to the left, pressed forward to Plum Run where they encountered fresh troops and a fierce conflict ensued in which Brigadier General Barksdale fell mortally wounded.

7-3: Supported artillery on Peach Orchard ridge. Withdrew from the front late in the afternoon.

7-4: In position near here all day. About midnight, began the march to Hagerstown.
Present: 1598. Killed 105, Wounded 550, Missing 92, Total 747.

*see index

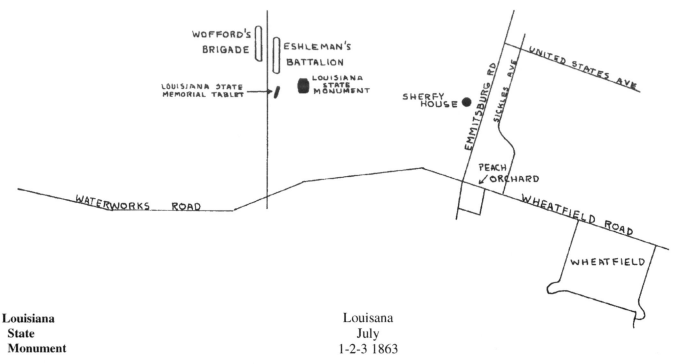

Louisiana State Monument	Louisana July 1-2-3 1863

Louisiana State Monument Tablet

"This Memorial Was Erected By The State Of Louisiana To Honor Her Sons Who Fought And Died At Gettysburg, July 1, 2, 3, 1863. In Particular It Memorializes The 2300 Infantrymen Of Hays and Nicholl's Louisiana Brigades, The Cannoneers In The Washington Artillery Of New Orleans, And Those In The Louisiana Guard, Madison, and Donaldsonville Artillery Batteries."

Longstreet's Corps Artillery Reserve Eshleman's Battalion

The Washington (Louisiana) Artillery. Major B. F. Eshleman. Miller's, Squires's, Richardson's and Norcom's Batteries.

8 - Napoleans, 2 - 12 Pounder Howitzers.

7-3: Arrived on the field before daylight and was engaged all day. Captured 1 - 3" Rifle.

7-4: At 9 AM ordered to Cashtown to reinforce the cavalry escorting the wagon train.

Losses: 3 Killed, 26 Wounded, 16 Missing; Total 45. Horses killed or disabled: 37. Guns disabled: 3.

Longstreet's Corps McLaws' Division Wofford's Brigade*

Brig. Gen. W. T. Wofford

16th, 18th, 24th Regiments, Cobb's and Phillip's Legions Ga. Inf.

7-2: Arrived at 4 PM and formed line 100 yards west of this. Ordered to the front about 6 PM and advancing soon afterward along the Wheatfield Road, flanked the Union forces assailing the Loop and aided the Confederates thereby relieved, in forcing them back through the Wheatfield to the foot of Little Round Top. Assailed there by a strong body of fresh troops and receiving at the same moment an order to withdraw, the Brigade fell back at sunset to the grove west of the Wheatfield.

7-3: One Regiment was left on outpost duty in that grove. The others supported artillery on Peach Orchard ridge. All withdrew late in the afternoon.

7-4: In line here all day. At midnight began the march to Hagerstown.

Present: about 1350. Killed 36, Wounded 207, Missing 112; Total 355.

*see index

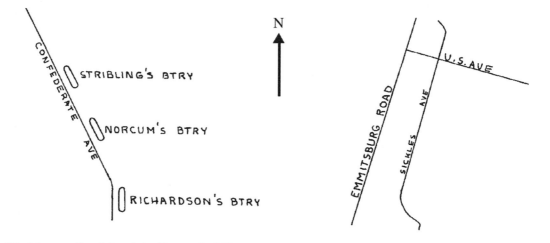

Longstreet's The Washington (Louisiana) Artillery - 2nd Company
Corps Capt. J. B. Richardson
Artillery 2 - Napoleans, 1 - 12 Pounder Howitzer
Reserve 7-3: The Napoleans took position before daylight north of the Peach Orchard but moved at dawn further north
Eshleman's and west of the Emmitsburg Road. A Union 3" rifle left the day before between the lines was brought in
Battalion under a heavy fire of skirmishers and served with this battery which took part in the cannonade preceeding
Richardson's Longstreet's Assault. After the repulse of that assault was joined by the howitzer and made preparations to
Battery assist in repelling a countercharge, if attempted. Withdrew from the front after dark.
7-4: At 9 AM marched with the battalion to Cashtown to reinforce the cavalry escorting the wagon train.
Losses not reported in detail.

Longstreet's The Washington (Louisiana) Artillery - 4th Company
Corps Capt. Joe Norcom, Lt. H. A. Battles
Artillery 2 - Napoleans, 1 - 12 Pounder Howitzer
Reserve 7-3: The Napoleans advanced before daylight into position 150 yards north of the Peach Orchard near the
Eshleman's Emmitsburg Road but their fire was desultory. Took active part in the cannonade preceeding Longstreet's
Battalion Assault and one of the guns supported the infantry attack by pushing forward 450 yards and keeping up a
Norcom's vigorous fire. After the assault was repulsed, the Napoleans were moved several hundred yards to the left
Battery but soon disabled and sent to the rear. The Howitzer was brought forward and did effective service until
withdrawn after dark.
7-4: At 9 AM, marched with the Battalion to Cashtown to reinforce the cavalry escorting the wagon train.
Losses not reported in detail.

Longstreet's The Fauquier (Virginia) Artillery. Capt. R. M. Stribling
Corps 2 - 20 Pounder Parrotts, 4 - Napoleans
Pickett's 7-3: Advanced to the front about daylight. Later in the morning, took position on the crest of ridge west of
Division Emmitsburg Road and near the Rogers House. Drove back with a dozen well-directed rounds, a strong
Deering's line of skirmishers whose fire wounded a few men and horses. Bore a conspicuous part in the cannonade
Battalion preceeding Longstreet's Assault. But, its ammunition being exhausted about the time the assault began
Stribling's and repeated efforts to obtain a fresh supply proving fruitless, the battery was withdrawn.
Battery 7-4: In line of battle all day with the left wing of McLaws' Division. Marched about sunset to Black Horse
Tavern.
Losses not reported in detail.

THE SYMBOLS LISTED BELOW ARE USED TO IDENTIFY
THE MONUMENTS, MARKERS, TABLETS, STATUES, ETC.
WHICH ARE DRAWN ON THE MAPS IN THESE PAGES

SYMBOL	TYPE	REPRESENTING	DESCRIPTION
	Bronze Tablet	Army of The Potomac, Union Corps or Division or Brigade, Regular Army Regiment, Regular Army Artillery Battery, Volunteer Artillery Brigade.	Brigade Tablet Mounted on Square Marble base. All other Tablets are on large vertical Granite Blocks.
	Bronze Tablet	Army of Northern Virginia, Confederate Corps or Division or Brigade of Artillery Battalion	Brigade Tablet and Artillery Battalion Tablet Mounted on Round Marble base. All other Tablets are Mounted on large vertical Granite blocks.
	Iron Tablet	Union Army Battery (other than Regular Army)	Mounted on Black Iron Shaft.
	Iron Tablet	Confederate Artillery Battery	Mounted on Black Iron Shaft.
	Iron Tablet	Confederate Brigade Advanced Position	Mounted on Black Iron Shaft.
	Regimental or Battery Monument	Principal Position of Volunteer Regiment or Volunteer Artillery Battery	Usually Granite or Marble in a Great Variety of Shapes and Sizes.
	Regimental Marker	Other than Principal Position of Regiment or Battery	Usually a Square Granite Marker or tablet or may be another monument.
	Flank Marker or Company Marker	Left and/or Right Flank of Regiment or Battery or Position of a Company.	Usually a Small Square or Rectangular Granite Marker.
	Army Or Corps Headquarters	Site of Headquarters of Army Commander or Corps Commander or Chief of Artillery	Cannon Barrel Mounted Vertically on Stone, Granite or Marble Base.
	State Monument	Monument Erected by Union or Confederate State.	
	Statue	Standing or Equestrian	Bronze Sculpture
	Building	House, Barn or other Structure	Identified by Owner's Name.
	Miscellaneous Marker	Marker or Inscription of a type not listed above	Granite or Metal Marker.
*Asterisk		Used whenever a Division or Brigade or Regiment or Battery has more than one Monument or Marker.	Check the Index for other Monument or Marker.

*see index

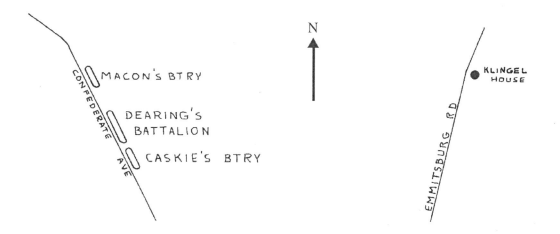

Longstreet's The Hampden (Virginia) Artillery. Capt. W. H. Caskie
Corps 1 -10 Pounder Parrott, 1 - 3" Rifle, 2 - Napoleans
Pickett's 7-3: Advanced to the front about daylight. Later in the morning took position on the ridge west of the
Division Emmitsburg Road near the Rogers' House, remaining for hours unengaged. When the signal guns were
Dearing's fired about 1 PM, moved forward to the crest of the hill and took an active part in the cannonade. Ammu-
Battalion nition was exhausted while Longstreet's column was advancing, the last rounds being fired at the Union
Caskie's infantry which assailed his right flank. Efforts to procure a fresh supply of ammunition proving unsuc-
Battery cessful, the battery was withdrawn.
7-4: In line of battle all day with McLaws' Division. Marched at sunset to Black Horse Tavern.
Losses not reported in detail.

Longstreet's Major James Dearing, Stribling's, Caskie's, Macon's and Blount's Batteries
Corps 2 - 20 Pounder Parrotts, 3 - 10 Pounder Parrotts, 1 - 3" Rifle, 12 - Napoleans
Pickett's 7-3: Advanced to the front about daybreak and took a conspicuous part in the battle. In the cannonade preceeding
Division Longstreet's Assault, it fired by battery and very effectively. Having exhausted its ammunition and being
Dearing's unable to obtain a fresh supply, it was withdrawn from the field about 4 PM.
Battalion 7-4: In line of battle all day with McLaws' Division. Marched at sunset to Black Horse Tavern.
Losses: 8 Killed, 17 Wounded; Total 25.

Longstreet's The Richmond Fayette Artillery. Capt. M. C. Macon
Corps 2 - Napoleans, 2 - 10 Pounder Parrotts
Pickett's 7-3: Advanced to the front about daybreak. Later in the morning took position on the ridge west of the
Division Emmitsburg Road and near the Rogers' House, but remained inactive until the signal guns were fired
Dearing's sometime after noon. Moved forward then to the crest of the hill and took a prominent part in the cannon-
Battalion ade. Ammunition exhausted while Longstreet's column was advancing, the last rounds being fired at the
Macon's Union infantry assailing his flank. Efforts to procure a fresh supply proving unsuccessful, the battery was
Battery withdrawn.
7-4: In line of battle all day with left wing of McLaws' Division. Marched at sunset to Black Horse Tavern.
Losses not reported in detail.

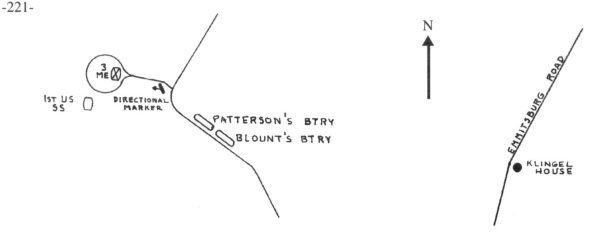

Longstreet's Blount's (Virginia) Battery. Capt. Joseph G. Blount
Corps 4 - Napoleans
Pickett's 7-3: Advanced to the front about daybreak. Later in the morning took position on the ridge west of the
Division Emmitsburg Road 200 yards from the Rogers' House and remained there for hours unengaged. When the
Dearing's signal guns were fired about 1 PM, moved forward to the crest of the hill and took an active part in the
Battalion cannonade. But, its ammunition being exhausted as Longstreet's infantry was advancing and all the ef-
Blount's forts to secure a fresh supply proving fruitless, the battery was withdrawn.
Battery 7-4: In line of battle all day with the left wing of McLaws' Division. Marched at sunset to Black Horse Tavern.
Losses not reported in detail.

The Sumter Battalion - Company B, Capt. George M. Patterson. 2 - Napoleans, 4 - 12 Pounder Howitzers
Hill's Corps 7-2: Was detached from the Battalion in the morning, together with the Howitzer from Ross's Battery, and
Anderson's ordered into position here. In the afternoon opened fire on the Union batteries north of the Peach Orchard.
Division and when the infantry advanced at 6 PM, moved forward with it beyond the Emmitsburg Road and was
Lane's engaged until dark.
Battalion 7-3: Occupied a position near here in reserve and did not take part in the active operations of the day.
Patterson's 7-4: Withdrew about sunset and began the march to Hagerstown.
Battery Losses: 2 Killed, 5 Wounded, 2 Missing; Total 9.
Horses killed or disabled: 7

1ˢᵗ US SS   To The Positions Of
&   3rd Maine Infantry
3ʳᵈ Maine   And 1st United States
                                  Sharpshooters
                                  Co's A, B, D, H, F

1ˢᵗ US SS Col. Hiram Berdan
2-1-3 One hundred sharpshooters reconnoitered to this spot about 12 noon, July 2, 1863, losing 19 men. They first
developed the enemy's threatened attack on our left and rear.
7-3: The Regiment supported the batteries along Cemetary Ridge.
7-4: Picketed and skirmished near the Peach Orchard.
Casualties: 6 Killed, 37 Wounded, 6 Missing; Total 49.
This monument is dedicated to the brave men of this command who fell at Gettysburg.

3ʳᵈ Maine* 7-2: Engaged here forenoon of July 2.
2-1-3 (Note: See Page 180 for principal position.)

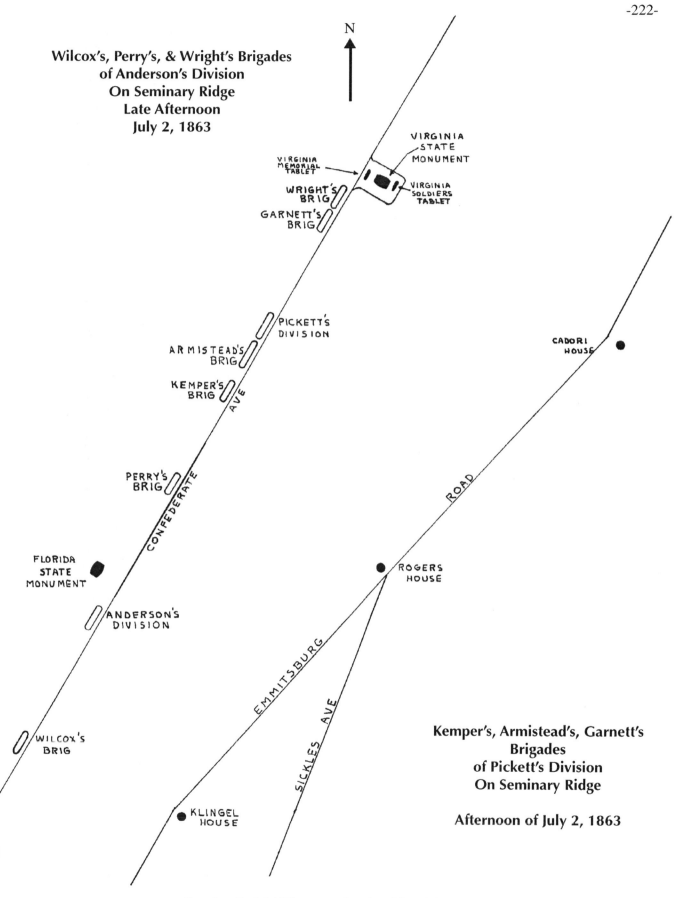

N

Wilcox's, Perry's, & Wright's Brigades
of Anderson's Division
On Seminary Ridge
Late Afternoon
July 2, 1863

VIRGINIA STATE MONUMENT

VIRGINIA MEMORIAL TABLET

WRIGHT'S BRIG

VIRGINIA SOLDIERS TABLET

GARNETT'S BRIG

PICKETT'S DIVISION

ARMISTEAD'S BRIG

KEMPER'S BRIG

CONFEDERATE AVE

PERRY'S BRIG

CADORI HOUSE

FLORIDA STATE MONUMENT

ANDERSON'S DIVISION

ROGERS HOUSE

ROAD

EMMITSBURG

SICKLES AVE

WILCOX'S BRIG

Kemper's, Armistead's, Garnett's
Brigades
of Pickett's Division
On Seminary Ridge

Afternoon of July 2, 1863

KLINGEL HOUSE

~ Gettysburg Battlefield Monuments, Locations & Inscriptions ~

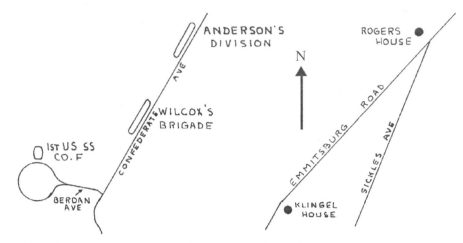

1st US SS   7-2:   Engaged at this point on the morning of July 2nd.
Company F 7-3:   On Cemetary Ridge.
2-1-3   7-4:   On the skirmish line.
           Casualties: 1 Killed, 4 Wounded; Present for duty 44

Hill's Corps Brig. Gen. Cadmus M. Wilcox
Anderson's 8th, 9th, 10th, 11th, 14th Alabama Infantry
 Division   7-2:   Formed line here in forenoon, the 10th and 11th Regiments taking position on the right after a severe
Wilcox's   skirmish with Union outposts. Advanced at 6 PM and broke the Union line on the Emmitsburg Road,
 Brigade*   capturing two guns and pursuing rapidly, took many prisoners and 6 more guns. At Plum Run, was met by
                a heavy force of artillery and fresh infantry and being unsupported, after severe losses fell back without
                being able to bring off the captured guns.
        7-3:   Took position west of Emmitsburg Road in support of artillery. Soon after Longstreet's columns started,
                an order was received to advance and support it but smoke hiding the oblique course of Pickett's Division,
                the Brigade moving straight forward, found itself engaged in a separate and useless conflict and was
                promptly wfthdrawn.
        7-4:   In line here all day and at dark began the march to Hagerstown.
        Present: 1777. Killed 51, Wounded 469, Missing 261; Total 781.

Hill's Corps Major General R. H. Anderson
Anderson's   Wilcox's Brigade   Brig. Gen. Cadmus M. Wilcox
 Division   Mahone's Brigade   Brig. Gen. William Mahone
            Wright's Brigade   Brig. Gen. A. R. Wright
            Perry's Brigade   Col. David Lang
            Posey's Brigade   Brig. Gen. Carnot Posey
            Artillery Battalion 3 Batteries   Major John Lane
        7-1:   Anderson's Division on the march to Gettysburg was directed to occupy the position vacated by Heth's
                Division and to send a brigade and battery a mile or more to the right.
        7-2:   In the morning a new line of battle formed extending further to the right. About noon, Longstreet's Corps,
                placed on the right nearly at right angles to the line, directed to assault the Union left, the Division to
                advance as the attack progressed to keep in touch with Longstreet's left. The Union troops were forced
                from the first line and a portion of the ridge beyond. Union reinforcements pressing on the right flank,
                which had become disconnected from McLaws' left, made the position gained untenable. The brigades
                withdrew to their positions in line.
        7-3:   The Division remained in position until 3:30 PM. Orders were given to support General Longstreet's
                attack on the Union centre. Wilcox and Perry moved forward. The assault failed, the order to advance was
                countermanded.
        7-4:   The Division, after dark, took up the line of march to Hagerstown.
        Casualties: Killed 147, Wounded 1128, Missing 840; Total 2115.

*see index

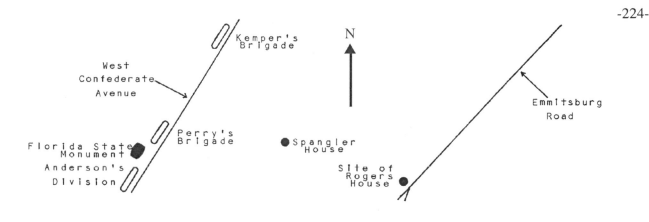

Florida State Monument*

Floridians of Perry's Brigade comprised of the 2nd, 5th and 8th Florida Infantry fought here with great honor as members of Anderson's Division of Hill's Corps and participated in the heaviest fighting of July 2 and 3, 1863. The Brigade suffered 445 casualties of the 700 men present for duty. Like all Floridians who participated in the Civil War, they fought with courage and devotion for the ideals in which they believed. By their noble example of bravery and endurance, they enable us to meet with confidence any sacrifice which confronts us as Americans.

Anderson's Division Hill's Corps Perry's Brigade*

Col. David Lang

7-2: Formed line in forenoon on the eastern border of these woods. Advanced at 6 PM and assisted in forcing the Union line on the Emmitsburg Road, and by rapid pursuit compelled the temporary abandonment of several guns. At the foot of the slope met first Union forces and the line on its right retiring, it also fell back. The color bearer of the 8th Florida fell and his flag was lost.

7-3: Ordered to join Wilcox's Brigade on its left and to conform to its movements. Supported artillery until Longstreet's column started and then advanced in aid of his assault. But dense smoke hiding his oblique course, the Brigade moved directly forward in the gap caused thereby. A strong force struck its left flank capturing about half of the 2nd Florida and its colors.

7-4: In line here and at dark began the march to Hagerstown.

Present: 700. Killed 33, Wounded 217, Missing 205; Total 455

Longstreet's Corps Pickett's Division Kemper's Brigade

Brig. Gen. James L. Kemper, Col. Joseph Mayo, Jr.

7-2: Arrived about sunset and bivouacked on the western border of Spangler's Woods.

7-3: In the forenoon formed line in the field east of the woods with the right flank near Spangler's Barn. At the close of the cannonade, advanced and took part in Longstreet's Assault upon the Union position in the vicinity of the angle. Exposed to severe fire of artillery and, vigorously beyond the Emmitsburg Road, by infantry on the right flank, with ranks thinned and much disorganized by its losses, especially of officers, it pressed on against the Union line at the stone wall where, after a fierce encounter, the struggle ended. General Kemper fell wounded in front of the stone wall.

7-4: Spent the day in reorganization and during the night began the march to Hagerstown.

Present: 1575. Killed 58, Wounded 356, Missing 317; Total 731

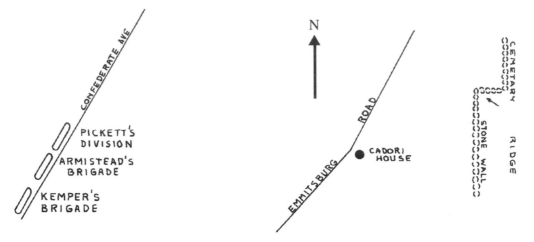

Longstreet's	Brig. Gen. L. A. Armistead
Corps	9th, 14th, 38th, 53rd, 57th Virginia Infantry.

Pickett's 7-2: Arrived about sunset and bivouacked on the western border of Spangler's Woods.

Division 7-3: In the forenoon formed line behind Kemper and Garnett east of the woods. When the cannonade ceased,

Armistead's advanced to support Kemper's and Garnett's Brigades forming the right of Longstreet's column. Its losses

Brigade being less at first than those of the other Brigades, it passed the Emmitsburg Road in compact ranks and as the front line was going to pieces near the stone wall, it pushed forward and many of its men and some from other commands, responding to the call and following General L. A. Armistead, sprang over the wall into the angle and continued the desperate struggle until he fell mortally wounded beyond the stone wall.

7-4: Spent the day in reorganization and during the night began the march to Hagerstown.

Present: 1650. Killed 88, Wounded 460, Missing 643, Total 1191.

Longstreet's Major General George E. Pickett

Corps

Pickett's

Division

Garnett's Brigade	Brig. Gen. R. V. Garnett, Major C. S. Peyton
Armistead's Brigade	Brig. Gen. L. A. Armistead, Lt. Col. Wm. White
Kemper's Brigade	Brig. Gen. J. L. Kemper, Col. Joseph Mayo, Jr.
Artillery Battalion	4 Batteries - Major James Dearing

7-1: Guarding trains at Chambersburg.

7-2: On march to Gettysburg.

7-3: Reached the field about 9 AM. Near 12 PM took position on crest of hill on which the artillery was placed. About 1:30 PM, Division was formed in an open field east of the Spangler's Woods, the right near a barn facing the Union line on Cemetary Ridge. At 3 PM moved forward to assault across the field about three quarters of a mile, under a severe fire losing many officers and men, only a few reaching the salient. The Division being separated from its support on the right and left and the assault having failed, returned to its former position on the ridge.

7-4: The Division took up the line of march during the night.

Casualties: Killed 232, Wounded 1157, Missing 1499, Total 2888

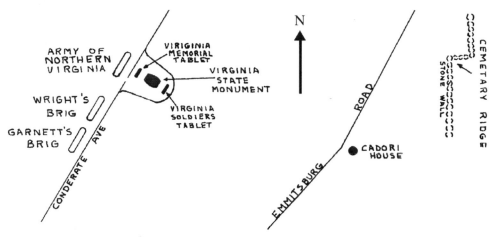

Longstreet's	Brig. Gen. Richard V. Garnett
Corps	8th, 18th, 19th, 28th, 56th Virginia Infantry
Picketts'	7-2: Arrived about sunset, bivouacked on the western border of Spangler's Woods.
Division	7-3: In the forenoon, formed line on Kemper's left in the field east of the woods. At the cessation of the
Garnett's	cannonade, advanced and took part in Longstreet's Assault on the Union position in the vicinity of the
Brigade	Angle. This advance was made in good order under a storm of shells and grape and a deadly fire of

Longstreet's Corps Picketts' Division Garnett's Brigade

Brig. Gen. Richard V. Garnett

8th, 18th, 19th, 28th, 56th Virginia Infantry

7-2: Arrived about sunset, bivouacked on the western border of Spangler's Woods.

7-3: In the forenoon, formed line on Kemper's left in the field east of the woods. At the cessation of the cannonade, advanced and took part in Longstreet's Assault on the Union position in the vicinity of the Angle. This advance was made in good order under a storm of shells and grape and a deadly fire of musketry. After passing the Emmitsburg Road, the lines were much broken in crossing the post and rail fences on both sides of that road, but with shattered ranks the Brigade pushed on and took part in the final struggle at the Angle. General Garnett fell dead from his saddle in front of the stone wall.

7-4: Spent the day in reorganization and during the night began the march to Hagerstown.

Present: 1480. Killed 78, Wounded 324, Missing 539; Total 941

Hill's Corps Anderson's Division Wright's Brigade*

3rd, 22nd, 48th Regiments and 2nd Battalion Georgia Infantry. Brig. Gen. Ambrose Wright

7-2: Formed line here in the forenoon. Advanced at 6 PM and dislodged Union troops posted near the Cadori House, capturing several guns and many prisoners. Pushing on, broke the Union line at the stone wall south of the Angle and reached the crest of the ridge beyond, capturing more guns. The supports on the right being repulsed and those on the left not coming up, with both flanks assailed and converging columns threatening its rear, it withdrew, fighting its way out with heavy losses and unable to bring off the captured guns.

7-3: Advanced 600 yards to cover the retreat of Pickett's Divsion. Afterward was moved to the right to meet a threatened attack.

7-4: In line here all day. At dark began the march to Hagerstown.

Present: 1450. Killed 146, Wounded 394, Missing 333, Total 873

*see index

ARMY OF NORTHERN VIRGINIA

GENERAL ROBERT E LEE, COMMANDING

The Army Consisted of Three Army Corps:

1st Corps	Lt. Gen. James Longstreet
2nd Corps	Lt. Gen. Richard S. Ewell
3rd Corps	Lt. Gen. Ambrose P. Hill
Cavalry Division	Maj. Gen. J. E. B. Stuart

7-1: Heth's and Pender's Divisions, Hill's Corps, and Early's and Rodes' Divisions, Ewell's Corps reached the field about 1 PM and were soon engaged on the north and west of town with the 1st and 11th Corps of the Army of the Potomac. Johnson's Division, Ewell's Corps and Anderson's Division, Hill's Corps reaching the field about dark, were not engaged. Longstreet's Corps on the march. Stuart's Cavalry Division marching from Dover to Carlisle.

7-2: McLaws' and Hood's Divisions, Longstreet's Corps arrived on the field about 3 PM and formed facing the Union left. An assault was made by the two Divisions assisted by Anderson's Division, Hill's Corps. The Union troops were dislodged from Emmitsburg Road and Peach Orchard, engagement lasting until night. Losses heavy. Pickett's Division, Longstreet's Corps on the march. Johnson's Division, Ewell's Corps about dusk advanced to the assault of Culp's Hill in connection with Early's Division, Ewell's Corps. Rodes' Division, Ewell's Corps held position in valley west of town, not engaged. Heth's and Pender's Divisions, Hill's Corps occupied Seminary Ridge facing Union line, not engaged. Stuart's Cavalry on left flank of Confederate Army.

7-3: Pickett's Division, Longstreet's Corps reached the field in the morning, assaulted the Union line on Cemetary Ridge about 3 PM assisted by Hill's Corps. The assault failed with great loss. An attack made on the left by Johnson's Division, Ewell's Corps, reinforced by three brigades of the Corps failed. Stuart's Cavalry Division engaged with 2nd Union Cavalry Division and 2nd Brigade, 3rd Cavalry Division on the Confeasrate left about 1 PM.

7-4: Tne Army took up the line of march during the night.

Virginia State Monument   Virginia To Her Sons at Gettysburg

Virginia Memorial Tablet   Memorial of the State of Virginia to the Virginia troops at Gettysburg

Virginia Soldiers Tablet   The group represents various types who left civil occupations to join the Confederate Army. Left to right, a professional man, a mechanic, an artist, a boy, a business man, a farmer.

Dedicated June 6, 1917   Sculptor F. W. Sievers

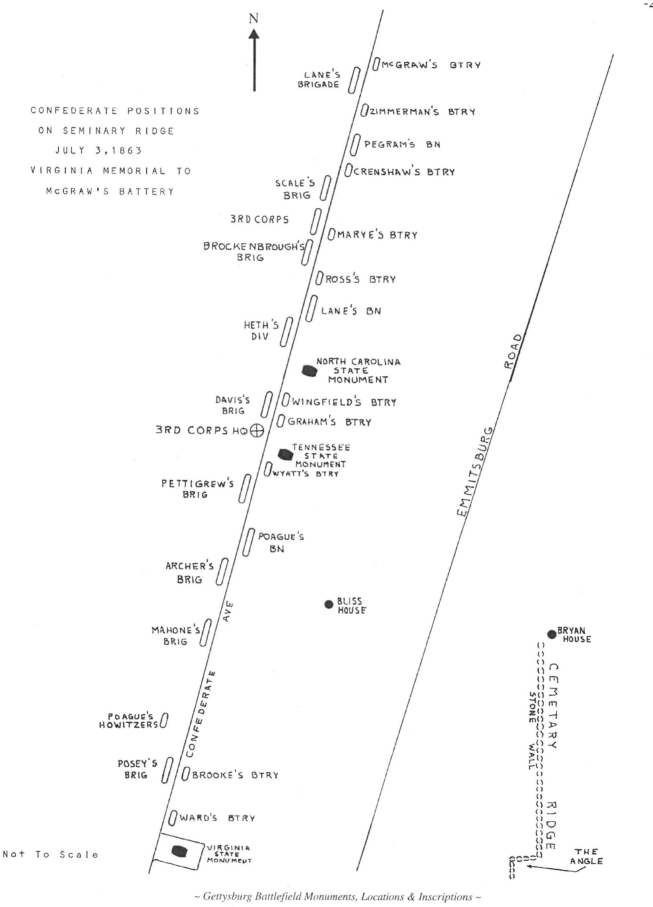

N

CONFEDERATE POSITIONS
ON SEMINARY RIDGE
JULY 3, 1863
VIRGINIA MEMORIAL TO
McGRAW'S BATTERY

McGRAW'S BTRY

LANE'S
BRIGADE

ZIMMERMAN'S BTRY

PEGRAM'S BN

CRENSHAW'S BTRY

SCALE'S
BRIG

3RD CORPS

MARYE'S BTRY

BROCKENBROUGH'S
BRIG

ROSS'S BTRY

LANE'S BN

HETH'S
DIV

NORTH CAROLINA
STATE
MONUMENT

DAVIS'S
BRIG

WINGFIELD'S BTRY

GRAHAM'S BTRY

3RD CORPS HQ ⊕

TENNESSEE
STATE
MONUMENT

WYATT'S BTRY

PETTIGREW'S
BRIG

POAGUE'S
BN

ARCHER'S
BRIG

BLISS
HOUSE

MAHONE'S
BRIG

BRYAN
HOUSE

POAGUE'S
HOWITZERS

POSEY'S
BRIG

BROOKE'S BTRY

WARD'S BTRY

VIRGINIA
STATE
MONUMENT

Not To Scale

CONFEDERATE   AVE

EMMITSBURG   ROAD

CEMETARY   RIDGE   STONE   WALL

THE
ANGLE

~ Gettysburg Battlefield Monuments, Locations & Inscriptions ~

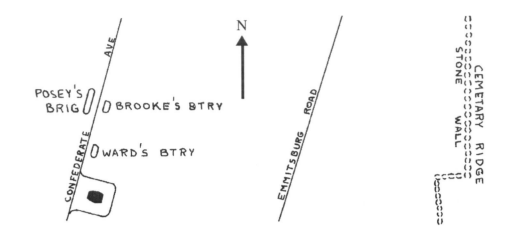

Hill's Corps The Madison (Mississippi) Light Artillery. Capt. George Ward
Fender's 3 - Napoleans, 1 - 12 Pounder Howitzer
Division 7-2: Late in the evening, the Napoleans were placed in position about 400 yards eastward from this point.
Poague's 7-3: The Napoleans participated actively in all operations of the artillery during the day, including the can-
Battalion nonade which preceeded Longstreet's Assault, withdrawing afterward to a position near here. The How-
Ward's itzer was kept in the rear and took no part in the battle, but was held in readiness to resist any advance of
Battery the Union forces.
7-4: In the evening about dusk, began the march to Hagerstown.
Losses not reported in detail.

Hill's Corps Brooke's (Virginia) Battery. Capt. J. V. Brooke
Pender's 2 - Napoleans, 2 - 12 Pounder Howitzers
Division 7-2: Late in the evening, the Napoleans were placed in position about 400 yards eastward from this point.
Poague's 7-3: The Napoleans participated actively in all the operations of the artillery during the day, including the
Battalion cannonade which preceeded Longstreet's Assault, withdrawing afterward to a position near here. The
Brook's Howitzers were kept in the rear and took no part in the battle, but were held in readiness to resist any
Battery advance of the Union forces.
7-4: In the evening about dusk, began the march to Hagerstown.
Losses not reported in detail.

Hill's Corps Brig. Gen. Carnot Posey
Anderson's 12th, 16th, 19th, 48th Mississippi Infantry
Division 7-2: Arrived and took position here in the morning. Through some misunderstanding of orders, instead of the
Posey's Brigade advancing in compact ranks in support of the troops on its right in their assault on the Union
Brigade lines, the Regiments were ordered forward at different times. Deployed as skirmishers and fighting in
detachments, they pushed back the Union outposts and drove some artillerists for awhile from their
guns, but did not join in the attack on the Union positions on Cemetary Ridge.
7-3: Was held in reserve here supporting artillery in its front.
7-4: In line here all day. At dark began the march to Hagerstown.
Present: 1150. Killed 12, Wounded 71; Total 83.

THE SYMBOLS LISTED BELOW ARE USED TO IDENTIFY
THE MONUMENTS, MARKERS, TABLETS, STATUES, ETC.
WHICH ARE DRAWN ON THE MAPS IN THESE PAGES

SYMBOL	TYPE	REPRESENTING	DESCRIPTION
●	Bronze Tablet	Army of The Potomac, Union Corps or Division or Brigade, Regular Army Regiment, Regular Army Artillery Battery, Volunteer Artillery Brigade.	Brigade Tablet Mounted on Square Marble base. All other Tablets are on large vertical Granite Blocks.
▭	Bronze Tablet	Army of Northern Virginia, Confederate Corps or Division or Brigade or Artillery Battalion	Brigade Tablet and Artillery Battalion Tablet Mounted on Round Marble base. All other Tablets are Mounted on large vertical Granite blocks.
●	Iron Tablet	Union Army Battery (other than Regular Army)	Mounted on Black Iron Shaft.
○	Iron Tablet	Confederate Artillery Battery	Mounted on Black Iron Shaft.
▯	Iron Tablet	Confederate Brigade Advanced Position	Mounted on Black Iron Shaft.
▢	Regimental or Battery Monument	Principal Position of Volunteer Regiment or Volunteer Artillery Battery	Usually Granite or Marble in a Great Variety of Shapes and Sizes.
⊗	Regimental Marker	Other than Principal Position of Regiment or Battery	Usually a Square Granite Marker or tablet or may be another monument.
□	Flank Marker or Company Marker	Left and/or Right Flank of Regiment or Battery or Position of a Coppany.	Usually a Small Square or Rectangular Granite Marker.
⊕	Army Or Corps Headquarters	Site of Headquarters of Army Commander or Corps Commander or Chief of Artillery	Cannon Barrel Mounted Vertically on Stone, Granite or Marble Base.
◼	State Monument	Monument Erected by Union or Confederate State.	
○ ○	Statue	Standing or Equestrian	Bronze Sculpture
●	Building	House, Barn or other Structure	Identified by Owner's Name.
•	Miscellaneous Marker	Marker or Inscription of a type not listed above	Granite or Metal Marker.

*Asterisk   Used whenever a Division or Brigade or Regiment or Battery has more than one Monument or Marker.   Check the Index for other Monument or Marker.

Hill's Corps Major William T. Poague
Pender's   5 - 12 Pounder Howitzers
Division   7-2: The Howitzers in the lunettes nearby belonged to the batteries of Poague's Battalion, 1 to Ward's, 1 to
Poague's   Wyatt's, 1 to Graham's, 2 to Brooke's. But on this day they were detached and kept under shelter from
Battalion   the fire of the Union artillery, which they could not return by reason of their short range.
Poague's   7-3: In the morning, the lunettes were constructed and the Howitzers placed in them to meet a possible ad-
Howitzers   vance of the Union forces, but as this did not occur, they took no active part in the battle.
             7-4: At dusk they withdrew from the field with their Battalion and began the march to Hagerstown.

Hill's Corps Brig. Gen. William Mahone
Anderson's 6th, 12th, 16th, 41st, 61st Virginia Infantry
Division   7-2: Arrived and took position here in the forenoon under orders to support the artillery. A strong skirmish line
Mahone's   was sent out, which was constantly engaged, and did effective service.
Brigade   7-3: Remained here in support of the artillery. Took no active part in the battle except by skirmishers.
              7-4: In line here all day. At dark began the march to Hagerstown.
              Present: 1500. Killed 8, Wounded 55, Missing 39; Total 102

Hill's Corps Brig. Gen. James J. Archer, Col. B. D. Fry, Lt. Col. S. G. Shepard
Heth's   5th Battalion and 13th Alabama, 1st, 7th, 14th Tennessee Infantry
Division   7-1: Reached the field in the morning. The Battalion was ordered to watch cavalry on the right. The 4 Regi-
Archer's   ments advancing into Reynold's Woods were met by the 1st Brigade, 1st Division, 1st Corps and fell back
Brigade*   across the Run, losing 75 prisoners, including General Archer.
              7-2: In the evening marched from the woods west of Willoughby Run and took position near here.
              7-3: In Longstreet's Assault was the right brigade of Pettigrew's Division. Advanced to the stone wall at the
                   angle and some of the men leaped over it. Had 13 color bearers shot, 4 of them at the wall. Lost 4 of the
                   5 flags and 5 of the 7 field officers.
              7-4: In line here all day. At dark began the march to Hagerstown.
              Present 1048. Killed and wounded 160, Missing 517; Total 677

*see index

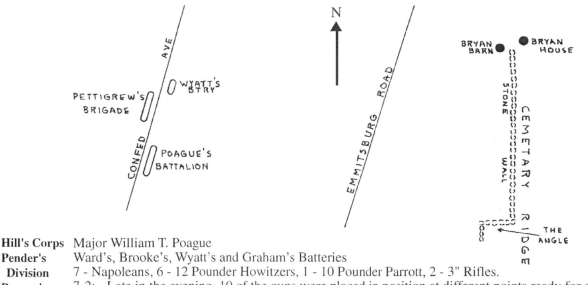

Hill's Corps Major William T. Poague
Pender's Ward's, Brooke's, Wyatt's and Graham's Batteries
Division 7 - Napoleans, 6 - 12 Pounder Howitzers, 1 - 10 Pounder Parrott, 2 - 3" Rifles.
Poague's 7-2: Late in the evening, 10 of the guns were placed in position at different points ready for service the next
Battalion day. The Howitzers were kept in the rear as no place was found from which they could be used with
advantage.
7-3: The 10 guns were actively engaged.
7-4: In the evening about dark, began the march to Hagerstown.
Losses: Killed 2, Wounded 24, Missing 6; Total 32.

Hill's Corps Brig. Gen. Johnston J. Pettigrew, Col. J. K. Marshall
Heth's 11th, 26th, 47th, 52nd North Carolina Infantry
Division 7-1: Crossing Willoughby Run at 2 PM, met the 1st Brigade, 1st Division, 1st Corps in Reynolds Woods and
Pettigrew's drove it back after a bloody struggle. Advancing to the summit of the ridge, encountered and broke a 2nd
Brigade Union line and was then relieved by troops of Pender's Division.
7-2: Lay in the woods west of the Run. In evening took position near here.
7-3: In Longstreet's Assault, the Brigade occupied the right centre of the Division and the course of the charge
brought it in front of the high stone wall north of the angle and 80 yards farther east. It advanced very
nearly to that wall. A few reached it but were captured. The skeleton regiments retired led by lieutenants,
and the Brigade by a major, the only field officer left.
7-4: After night, withdrew and began the march to Hagerstown.
Present on the first day: about 2000.
Casualties: Killed 190, Wounded 915, Missing about 300; Total 1405

Hill's Corps The Albermarle (Virginia) Artillery. Capt. James W. Wyatt
Pender's 1 - 10 Pounder Parrott, 2 - 3" Rifles, 1 - 12 Pounder Howitzer
Division 7-2: Late in the evening, the Parrott and Rifles took position here.
Poague's 7-3: At 7 AM, they opened on the Union positions but were soon ordered to cease firing as they drew the
Battalion concentrated fire of several batteries. They afterward took part in all the operations of the artillery during
Wyatt's the day, including the cannonade which preceeded Longstreet's Assault. The Howitzer remained in the
Battery rear and was not engaged in the battle, but held in readiness to resist any advance of the Union forces.
7-4: In the evening about dusk, began the march to Hagerstown.
Losses not reported in detail.

TENNESSEE
VALOR AND COURAGE WERE
VIRTUES OF THE THREE
TENNESSEE REGIMENTS

THE VOLUNTEER STATE
THIS MEMORIAL IS DEDICATED TO THE MEMORY OF THE MEN
WHO SERVED IN THE 1ST (PACS), 7TH AND 14TH TENNESSEE
INFANTRY REGIMENTS, ARCHER'S BRIGADE, HETH'S DIVISION, 3RD ARMY CORPS,
ARMY OF NORTHERN VIRGINIA.
THEY FOUGIIT AND DIED FOR THEIR CONVICTIONS,
PERFORMING THEIR DUTY AS THEY UNDERSTOOD IT.

	KILLED	WOUNDED	WOUNDED & MISSING	MISSING	
1ST TENNESSEE	6	67	1	104	178
7TH TENNESSEE	5	26	20	60	111
14TH TENNESSEE	5	25	16	81	127
					416

PRESENT JUNE 30, 1863:

1ST TENNESSEE PROVINCIAL	29 OFFICERS,	238 MEN =	267
7TH TENNESSEE	33 OFFICERS,	243 MEN =	276
14TH TENNESSEE	25 OFFICERS,	207 MEN =	232
			775

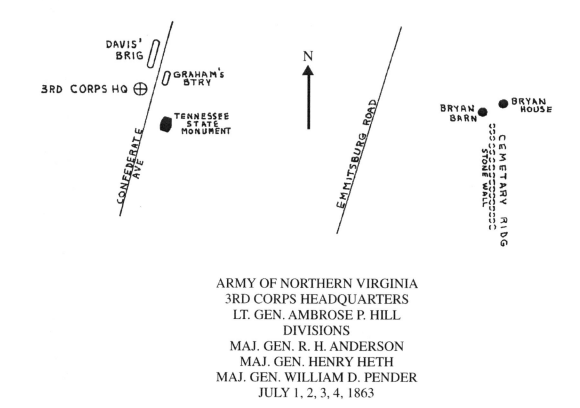

3rd Corps Head-quarters

ARMY OF NORTHERN VIRGINIA
3RD CORPS HEADQUARTERS
LT. GEN. AMBROSE P. HILL
DIVISIONS
MAJ. GEN. R. H. ANDERSON
MAJ. GEN. HENRY HETH
MAJ. GEN. WILLIAM D. PENDER
JULY 1, 2, 3, 4, 1863

(These Headquarters Were Located at a Farmhouse 540 Yards Westerly)

Hill's Corps
Pender's
Division
Poague's
Battalion
Graham's
Battery*

The Charlotte (North Carolina) Artillery. Capt. Joseph Graham
2 - Napoleans, 2 - 12 Pounder Howitzers
7-2: Late in the evening the Napoleans were placed in position here.
7-3: At 7 AM, they opened fire on the Union positions but were soon ordered to cease firing as they drew the concentrated fire of several batteries. They afterward took part in all the operations of the artillery during the day, including the cannonade preceeding Longstreet's Assault. The Howitzers remained in the rear and were not engaged in the battle, but were in readyness to resist any advance of the Union forces.
7-4: In the evening, began the march to Hagerstown.
Losses not reported in detail.

Hill's Corps
Heth's
Division
Davis'
Brigade*

Brig. Gen. Joseph J. Davis
55th North Carolina, 2nd, 11th, 42nd Mississippi Infantry
7-1: Formed line west of Herr's Tavern. Crossing the Run at 10 AM, dislodged 2nd Brigade, 1st Division, 1st Corps. Threatened on the right, it wheeled and occupied railroad cut too deep and steep for defense, whereby it lost many prisoners and a stand of colors. Joined later by the 11th Regiment previously on duty guarding trains. The Brigade fought until the day's contest ended.
7-2: Lay all day west of the Run.
7-3: In Longstreet's Assault this Brigade formed the left centre of Pettigrew's Division and advanced to the stone wall south of the Bryan Barn where, with regiments shrunken to companies and field officers all disabled, further effort was useless.
7-4: After night, withdrew and began the march to Hagerstown.
Present on First Day: about 2000.
Casualities: Killed 180, Wounded 717, Missing about 500; Total 1397

*see index

Hill's Corps	The Sumter Battalion - Company C. Capt. John T. Wingfield
Anderson's	2 - 20 Pounder Parrotts, 3 - 3" Navy Parrotts
Division	7-2: In position here actively engaged and exposed all the while to a heavy fire from the Union artillery.
Lane's	7-3 : Remained here and took part in all the artillery conflicts of the day including that which preceeded
Battalion	Longstreet's Assault.
Wingfield's	7-4: Withdrew about sunset and began the march to Hagerstown.
Battery	Losses: 9 Wounded, 2 Missing; Total 11. Rounds expended: 406 . 20 Horses killed or disabled.

Major General Henry Heth, Brig. Gen. Johnston J. Pettigrew

Hill's Corps

Heth's

Division

1st Brigade	Brig. Gen. J. J. Pettigrew, Col. J. K. Marshall
2nd Brigade	Col. J. M. Brockenbrough
3rd Brigade	Brig. Gen. J. J. Archer, Col. B. D. Fry, Col. S. G. Shepard
4th Brigade	Brig. Gen. Joseph R. Davis
Artillery Battalion 4 Batteries	Lt. Col. John J. Garnett

7-1: Division moved at 5 AM from Cashtown toward Gettysburg. About 3 miles from town, the advance met the Union forces. Archer's and Davis's Brigades moved forward on the right and left of the turnpike and were soon engaged. The brigades were forced to retire with heavy loss. After resting for an hour, the Division was advanced in line of battle to the right of the pike, and met with stubborn resistance. Rodes' Division, 2nd Corps appeared on the left and formed a line at right angles. The Union troops retired to a wooded hill in the rear and finally gave way. The Division bivouacked on the ground won.

7-2: The Division in the morning was relieved by Anderson and held in reserve.

7-3: Division occupied the position of the day before and was ordered to report to Lt. Gen. Longstreet to unite in the attack on the Union centre. The assault was made and failed. The Division returned to its former position.

7-4: At night the Division took up the line of march.

Casualties: Killed 411, Wounded 1905, Missing 534; Total 2850.

North
Carolina
State
Monument

(Note: See Page 235 for North Carolina State Monument)

1863

NORTH CAROLINA

TO THE ETERNAL GLORY OF THE NORTH CAROLINA
SOLDIERS, WHO ON THIS BATTLEFIELD DISPLAYED
HEROISM UNSURPASSED SACRIFICING ALL IN
SUPPORT OF THEIR CAUSE. THEIR VALOROUS DEEDS
WILL BE ENSHRINED IN THE HEARTS OF MEN LONG
AFTER THESE TRANSIENT MEMORIALS HAVE
CRUMBLED INTO DUST.
THIRTY TWO NORTH CAROLINA REGIMENTS WERE IN
ACTION AT GETTYSBURG JULY 1, 2, 3, 1863. ONE
CONFEDERATE SOLDIER IN EVERY FOUR WHO FELL HERE
WAS A NORTH CAROLINIAN.
This Tablet Erected By The North Carolina Division
United Daughters of the Confederacy.

NORTH CAROLINA ORGANIZATIONS IN THE ARMY OF
NORTHERN VIRGINIA AT THE BATTLE OF GETTYSBURG,
JULY 1-3, 1863

6TH, 21ST, 57TH INFANTRY — HOKE'S BRIGADE OF EARLY'S DIVISION
1ST, 3RD INFANTRY — STEUART'S BRIGADE OF JOHNSON'S DIVISION
32ND, 43RD, 45TH, 53RD INFANTRY AND 2ND BATTALION — DANIELS BRIGADE OF RODES' DIVISION
5TH, 12TH, 20TH, 23RD INFANTRY — IVERSON'S BRIGADE OF RODES' DIVISION
2ND, 4TH, 14TH, 30TH INFANTRY — RAMSEUR'S BRIGADE OF RODE'S DIVISION
11TH, 26TH, 47TH, 52ND INFANTRY— PETTIGREW'S BRIGADE OF HETH'S DIVISION
55TH INFANTRY — DAVIS' BRIGADE OF HETH'S DIVISION
7TH, 18TH, 28TH, 33RD, 37TH INFANTRY OF LANE'S BRIGADE OF PENDER'S DIVISION
13TH, 16TH, 22ND, 34TH, 38TH INFANTRY OF SCALES' BRIGADE OF PENDER S DIVISION
1ST NORTH CAROLINA ARTILLERY, BATTERY A - McLAWS' DIVISION
BRANCH (NORTH CAROLINA) ARTILLERY ⎫
⎬ HOOD'S DIVISION
ROWAN (NORTH CAROLINA) ARTILLERY ⎭
CHARLOTTE (NORTH CAROLINA) ARTILLERY - PENDER'S DIVISION
1ST CAVALRY — HAMPTON'S BRIGADE ⎫
2ND, 4TH CAVALRY — ROBERTSON'S BRIGADE ⎬ STUART'S DIVISION OF CAVALRY
5TH CAVALRY — W. H. F. LEE'S BRIGADE ⎭

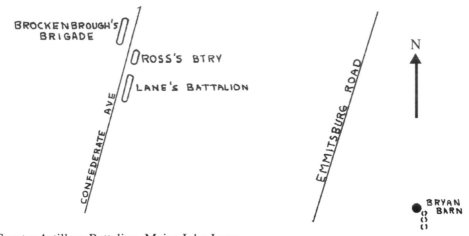

Hill's Corps The Sumter Artillery Battalion. Major John Lane
Anderson's Patterson's, Wingfield's and Ross's Batteries
Division 3 - Napoleans, 2 - 20 Pounder Parrotts, 3 - 10 Pounder Parrotts, 4 - 3" Rifles, 5 - 12 Pounder Howitzers.
Lane's 7-2&3:Took part in the battle.
Battalion 7-4: Remained in position near here and about sunset began the march to Hagerstown.
Losses: 3 Killed, 21 Wounded, 6 Missing; Total 30.
Ammunition expended: 1082 Rounds. Horses killed or disabled: 20

Hill's Corps The Sumter Battalion-Company A. Capt. Hugh M. Ross
Anderson's 3 - 10 Pounder Parrotts, 1 - 3" Navy Parrott, 1 - 12 Pounder Howitzer.
Division 7-2: Five of the guns were engaged here and under a heavy fire of artillery. The Howitzer was detatched and
Lane's served with Patterson's Battery south of Spangler Woods.
Battalion 7-3: Remained here and participated in all the operations of the artillery including the cannonade preceeding
Ross' Longstreet's Assault.
Battery 7-4: Withdrew about sunset and began the march to Hagerstown.
Losses: 3 Killed, 7 Wounded, 2 Missing; Total 10.
Ammunition expended: 506 Rounds. Horses killed or disabled: 36

Hill's Corps Col. J. M. Brockenbrough
Heth's 40th, 47th, 55th Regiments and 22nd Battalion Virginia Infantry
Division 7-1: Crossed Willoughby Run at 2 PM between Chambersburg Pike and Reynold's Woods. Engaged Union
Brocken- forces on McPherson's Ridge, and with other troops on ridge, drove them back to next ridge, capturing
brough two flags and many prisoners with some sharpshooters, in the barn. Soon afterwards, the Brigade was
Brigade relieved by Pender's Division.
7-2: Lay in the woods next to the Run. In the evening took position near here.
7-3 : In Longstreet's Assault this Brigade was on the left flank of the column and as it approached the Union
positions, was exposed to a severe fire of musketry on the left flank and of artillery and musketry in
front. It pushed on beyond the Emmitsburg Road, but was met by a heavy front and flank fire from the
Union lines north of the Bryan Barn and compelled to fall back.
7-4: After night, withdrew and began the march to Hagerstown.
Present: about 1100. 25 Killed, 123 Wounded, 60 Missing; Total 208.

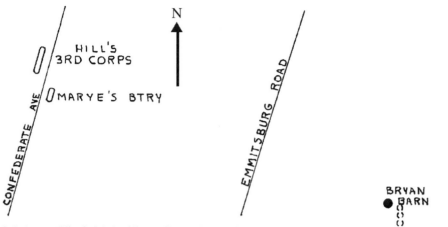

Hill's Corps
Artillery
Reserve
Pegram's
Battalion
Marye's
Battery

The Fredericksburg (Virginia) Artillery. Capt. E. A. Marye
2 - Napoleans, 2 - 10 Pounder Parrotts

7-1: This battery fired the first cannon shot of the battle from a point near the south side of the Chambersburg Pike on the ridge west of Herr's Tavern and was actively engaged until the close of the day's conflict.

7-2: Early in the morning took position here. Opened at intervals upon the Union lines and enfiladed their batteries when they sought to concentrate their fire on the Confederate right.

7-3: Participated actively in all the operations of the artillery which preceeded Longstreet's Assault.

7-4: About sunset, withdrew and began the march to Hagerstown.

Losses not reported in detail.

Hill's
3rd Corps

ARMY OF NORTHERN VIRGINIA
3RD ARMY CORPS

Lt. Gen. Ambrose P. Hill

Anderson's Division	Maj. Gen. R. H. Anderson
Heth's Division	Maj. Gen. Henry Heth, Brig. Gen. J. J. Pettigrew
Pender's Division	Maj. Gen. William D. Pender, Brig. Gen. James H. Lane, Maj. Gen. Isaac R. Trimble
Artillery Reserve	Col. R. Lindsay Walker - 9 Batteries

7-1: The Corps was near Cashtown. Heth's Division, at 5 AM, moved toward Gettysburg. Two Brigades with artillery, advancing across Willoughby Run were soon engaged. Archer's Brigade was driven across the Run. After resting an hour, Heth's Division formed in line west of Willoughby Run and advanced with Fender's Division in reserve. At 2:30 PM the right of Ewell's Corps appeared on the left. Pender's Division was ordered forward. After a severe contest, the Union forces were driven back and through the town. The two Divisions bivouacked on the ground gained. Anderson's Division bivouacked two miles in rear.

7-2: Anderson's Division extended to the right along the crest of hills facing Cemetary Ridge. Pender's Division occupied the crest from the Seminary and joining Anderson's Division with Heth's Division in reserve; the artillery in position on Seminary Ridge. The 1st Corps ordered to attack the left of the Union forces, the 3rd Corps to cooperate. Gen. Anderson moved forward three brigades connecting with left of McLaws' Division and drove the Union forces from their position. Anderson's right, becoming separated from McLaws' left and no support coming to these brigades, they retired to their former line.

7-3: The Corps occupied the same position. Reserve batteries were placed facing the Union lines. The Confederate line was held by Anderson's Division, 1/2 of Pender's, and 1/2 of Heth's. The remainder of Corps ordered to report to Gen. Longstreet as a support in the assault to be made on the Union position on Cemetary Ridge. About 1 PM the artillery along the line opened fire. At 3 PM the assault was made and failed. Anderson's Division was held in reserve and the troops fell back to former position.

7-4: The Corps took up the line of march during the night.

Casualties: Killed 837, Wounded 4407, Missing 1491; Total 6735

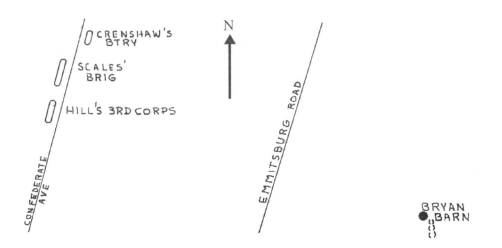

Hill's Corps Brig. Gen. A. M. Scales, Lt .Col. G. T. Gordon
Pender's 13th, 16th, 22nd, 34th, 38th North Carolina Infantry
Division 7-1: Crossed Willoughby Run about 3:30 PM, relieving Heth's line and advancing with left flank on
Scales' Chambersburg Pike, took part in the struggle until it ended. When the Union forces made their final stand
Brigade on Seminary Ridge, the Brigade charged and aided in dislodging them, but suffered heavy losses. General
Scales was wounded and all the field officers but one were killed or wounded.
7-2: In position near here with skirmishers out and on flank.
7-3: In Longstreet's Assault, the Brigade supported the right wing of Pettigrew's Division. With few officers to
lead them, the men advanced in good order through the storm of shot and shell, and when the front line
neared the Union works, they pushed forward to aid in the final struggle and were among the last to retire.
7-4: After night, withdrew and began the march to Hagerstown.
Present: 1250. Killed 102, Wounded 381, Missing 116; Total 599

Hill's Corps Crenshaw's (Virginia) Battery
Artillery 2 - Napoleans, 2 -12 Pounder Howitzers
Reserve 7-1: The Napoleans occupied ridge west of Herr's Tavern and took an active part in the battle. The Howitzers
Pegram's were not engaged.
Battalion 7-2: Early in the morning, took position here and were actively engaged throughout the day, sometimes an-
Crenshaw's noyed by sharpshooters which the Howitzers aided in silencing.
Battery 7-3: Remained here and participated in all the operations of the artillery.
7-4: About sunset, withdrew and began the march to Hagerstown.
Losses not reported in detail.

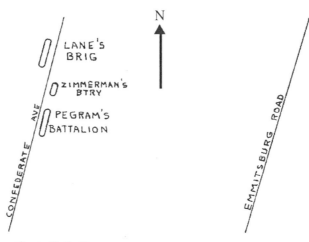

Hill's Corps Major W. J. Pegram, Capt. E. B. Brunson
Artillery Marye's, Crenshaw's, Zimmerman's, McGraws' and Brander's Batteries
Reserve 10 - Napoleans, 4 -10 Pounder Parrotts, 4 - 3" Rifles, 2 - 12 Pounder Howitzers
Pegram's 7-1,2&3: Battalion was actively engaged on each of the three days of the battle. The first cannon shot of the
Battalion battle was fired by one of its batteries from a point near the Chambersburg Pike on the ridge west of Herr's Tavern.
7-4: About sunset, withdrew and began the march to Hagerstown.
Losses: 10 Killed, 37 Wounded; Total 47. Ammunition expended: 3800 Rounds. Horses killed or disabled: 38.

Hill's Corps The Pee Dee Artillery. Lt. William E. Zimmerman
Artillery 4 - 3" Rifles
Reserve 7-1: Three guns were in position on the ridge west of Herr's Tavern. Actively engaged and did effective ser-
Pegram's vice. The other was disabled for the day by accident while hastening into action.
Battalion 7-2: Early in the morning took position here and at intervals was engaged with the Union batteries,
Zimmer- endeavoring especially to enfilade them when they sought to concentrate their fire on the Confederate
man's right.
Battery 7-3: Took an active part in all the operations of the artillery, including the cannonade preceding Longstreet's Assault.
7-4: Withdrew about sunset and began the march to Hagerstown.
Losses not reported in detail.

Hill's Corps Brig. Gen. James H. Lane, Col. C. M. Avery
Artillery 7th, 18th, 28th, 33rd, 37th North Carolina Infantry
Reserve 7-1: Crossed Willoughby Run about 3:30 PM and advanced on the right of the Division in the final and suc-
Pender's cessful movement against the Union forces on Seminary Ridge. Held back Union Cavalry which threat-
Division ened the flank and had a sharp conflict at the stone wall on Seminary Ridge just south of the Fairfield
Lane's Road.
Brigade 7-2: Lay with its right in McMillan's Woods with skirmish line advanced.
7-3: In Longstreet's Assault, the Brigade supported the centre of Pettigrew's Division. Advanced in good order under the storm of shot and shell and when near the Union works north of the angle, pushed forward to the aid of the fragments of the front line in the final struggle and was among the last to retire.
7-4: After night withdrew and began the march to Hagerstown.
Present: 1355. Losses: Killed 41, Wounded 348, Missing 271; Total 660.

THE SYMBOLS LISTED BELOW ARE USED TO IDENTIFY
THE MONUMENTS, MARKERS, TABLETS, STATUES, ETC.
WHICH ARE DRAWN ON THE MAPS IN THESE PAGES

SYMBOL	TYPE	REPRESENTING	DESCRIPTION
	Bronze Tablet	Army of The Potomac, Union Corps or Division or Brigade, Regular Army Regiment, Regular Army Artillery Battery, Volunteer Artillery Brigade.	Brigade Tablet Mounted on Square Marble base. All other Tablets are on large vertical Granite Blocks.
	Bronze Tablet	Army of Northern Virginia, Confederate Corps or Division or Brigade or Artillery Battalion	Brigade Tablet and Artillery Battalion Tablet Mounted on Round Marble base. All other Tablets are Mounted on large vertical Granite blocks.
	Iron Tablet	Union Army Battery (other than Regular Army)	Mounted on Black Iron Shaft.
	Iron Tablet	Confederate Artillery Battery	Mounted on Black Iron Shaft.
	Iron Tablet	Confederate Brigade Advanced Position	Mounted on Black Iron Shaft.
	Regimental or Battery Monument	Principal Position of Volunteer Regiment or Volunteer Artillery Battery	Usually Granite or Marble in a Great Variety of Shapes and Sizes.
	Regimental Marker	Other than Principal Position of Regiment or Battery	Usually a Square Granite Marker or tablet or may be another monument.
	Flank Marker or Company Marker	Left and/or Right Flank of Regiment or Battery or Position of a Company.	Usually a Small Square or Rectangular Granite Marker.
	Army Or Corps Headquarters	Site of Headquarters of Army Commander or Corps Commander or Chief of Artillery	Cannon Barrel Mounted Vertically on Stone, Granite or Marble Base.
	State Monument	Monument Erected by Union or Confederate State.	
	Statue	Standing or Equestrian	Bronze Sculpture
	Building	House, Barn or other Structure	Identified by Owner's Name.
	Miscellaneous Marker	Marker or Inscription of a type not listed above	Granite or Metal Marker.

*Asterisk   Used whenever a Division or Brigade or Regiment or Battery has more than one Monument or Marker.   Check the Index for other Monument or Marker.

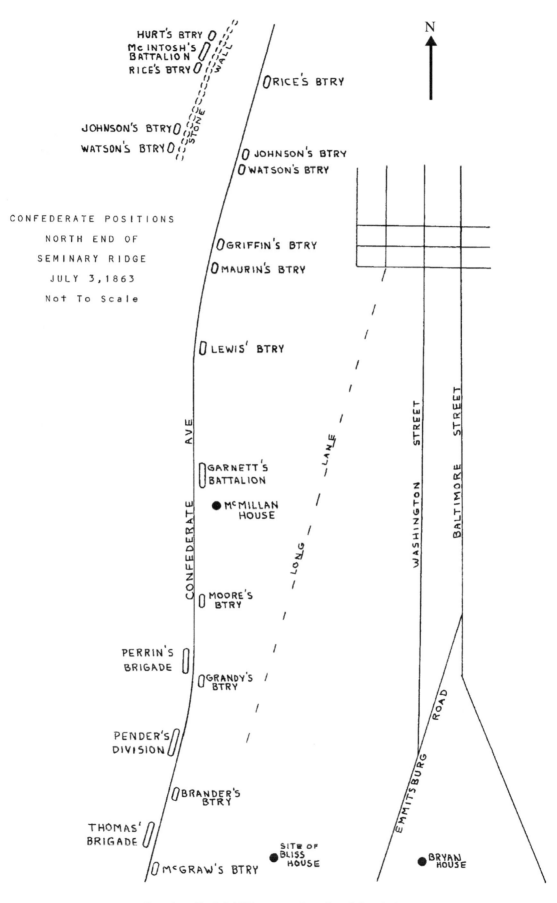

Hill's Corps The Purcell (Virginia) Artillery. Capt. Joseph McGraw
Artillery 4 - Napoleans
Reserve 7-1: In position south of Chambersburg Pike on the ridge west of Herr's Tavern and was actively engaged.
Pegram's 7-2: Early in the morning occupied this position and took part in the day's conflict with the Union batteries and
Battalion now and then dropped a shell among the busy sharpshooters.
McGraw's 7-3: Remained here and actively participated in all the operations of the artillery.
Battery 7-4: Withdrew about sunset and began the march to Hagerstown.
Losses not reported in detail.

Hill's Corps Brig. Gen. Edward L. Thomas
Pender's 14th, 35th, 45th, 49th Georgia Infantry
Division 7-1: In reserve north of Chambersburg Pike on left of Division. At sunset, moved to position in McMillan's
Thomas Woods.
Brigade 7-2: On duty in support of artillery. At 10 AM advancing, took position in Long Lane with the left flank near
the Bliss House and barns.
7-3: Engaged most of the day in severe skirmishing and exposed to a heavy fire of artillery. After dark retired
to this ridge.
7-4: At night, withdrew and began the march to Hagerstown.
Present: about 1200. Killed 34, Wounded 179, Missing 57; Total 270.

Hill's Corps The Letcher (Virginia) Artillery. Capt. T. A. Brander
Artillery 2 - Napoleans, 2 - 10 Pounder Parrotts
Reserve 7-1: In position, at first on the ridge west of Herr's Tavern, but moved later to a hill east of Willoughby's Run
Pegram's about 500 yards from the Union batteries, and from that point fired upon the Union infantry with much
Battalion effect, although exposed itself to a heavy fire of cannister.
Brander's 7-2: Occupied this position early in the morning and was engaged at intervals in firing upon the Union lines
Battery and batteries.
7-3: Actively participated in all the operations of the artillery incuding the cannonade preceeding Longstreet's
Assault.
7-4: Withdrew about sunset and began the march to Hagerstown.
Losses not reported in detail.

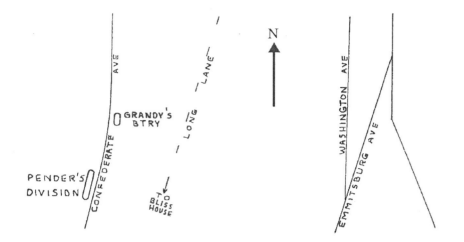

Hill's Corps Maj. Gen. William D. Pender, Brig. Gen. James H. Lane, Maj. Gen. I. R. Trimble

Pender's   1st Brigade   Col. Abner Perrin

Division   2nd Brigade   Brig. Gen. James H. Lane

             3rd Brigade   Brig. Gen. Edward L. Thomas

             4th Brigade   Brig. Gen. A. M. Scales, Lt. Col. G. T. Gordon, Col. W. Lee J. Lowrance

             Artillery Battalion   Maj. William T. Polk - 4 Batteries

7-1: Division moved about 8 AM in the direction of Gettysburg, following Heth's Division. A line of battle was formed on the right and left of the Pike three miles from town. About 3 PM a part of Ewell's Corps appeared on the left and the Union forces, making a strong demonstration, an advance was ordered. Heth became vigorously engaged. The Division moved to support, passing through the lines, forcing the Union troops to Seminary Ridge. Scales' Brigade moved to the left, flanking this position. The Union troops gave way, retiring to Cemetary Ridge. The Division reformed on the ridge, the left resting on Fairfield Road.

7-2: In position on the Ridge, not engaged except heavy skirmshing along the line.

7-3: During the morning, two brigades ordered to report to Lt. Gen. Longstreet as a support to Gen. Pettigrew and were placed in rear of right of Heth's Division, which formed a portion of the column of assault. The line moved forward one mile in view of the fortified position on Cemetary Ridge exposed to a severe fire. The extreme right reached the works but was compelled to fall back. The Division reformed where it rested before making the attack.

7-4: The Division during the night took up the line of march.

Casualties: Killed 262, Wounded 1312, Missing 116; Total 1690.

Hill's Corps The Norfolk (Virginia) Light Artillery Blues. Capt. C. R. Grandy

Heth's   2 - 3" Rifles, 2 -12 Pounder Howitzers

Division   7-1: Arrived on the field in the afternoon but was not engaged.

Garnett's 7-2: The rifles took position here in the morning and participated during the afternoon and evening in the

Battalion   artillery duel with the Union batteries on Cemetary Hill.

Grandy's   7-3: Ordered to the south side of McMillan's Woods and held all day in reserve without firing a shot, though

Battery   sometimes under fire.

            7-4: The Howitzers were never actively engaged in the battle but on this day were placed in position here. At night they rejoined the rifles and with them, began the march to Hagerstown. Losses not reported in detail.

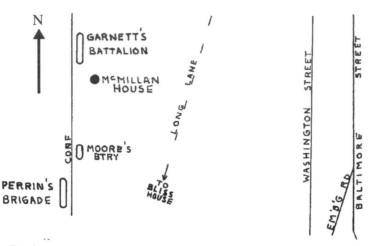

Hill's Corps Col. Abner Perrin

Pender's 1st Rifles, 12th, 13th, 14th Regiments and 1st Provincial S. C. Inf.
Division
Perrin's
Brigade

7-1: Crossed Willoughby Run about 3:30 PM with its left on Reynolds Woods and advancing to relieve Heth's line, took a prominent part in the struggle by which the Union forces were dislodged from Seminary Ridge, and pursuing them into the town, captured many prisoners. The Rifle Regiment was on duty as train guard and not in the battle of this day.

7-2: Supported artillery south of Fairfield Road. At 6 PM, advanced a battalion of sharpshooters which skirmished with the Union outposts until dark. At 10 PM, took position on Ramseur's right in the Long Lane leading from the town to the Bliss House and barn.

7-3: In the same position and constantly engaged in skirmishing.

7-4: After night withdrew and began the march to Hagerstown.

Present about 1600. Casualties: Killed 100, Wounded 477; Total 577.

Hill's Corps The Huger (Virginia) Artillery. Capt. Joseph D. Moore

Heth's 1 - 10 Pounder Parrott, 1 - 3" Rifle, 3 - Napoleans
Division
Garnett's
Battalion
Moore's
Battery

7-1: The Parrott and Rifle about 3:30 PM, relieved some of Pegram's guns on the ridge west of Herr's Tavern, their ammunition being exhausted, and from that time took part in the conflict.

7-2: Opened fire here on East Cemetary Hill at 3:00 PM, and kept it up for some hours. Renewed it at dusk in support of Early's assault.

7-3: Moved under orders to position south of McMillan's Woods and remained inactive all day, though sometimes under fire.

7-4: At 8 AM, marched to Cashtown to reinforce the cavalry escorting the wagon train. The Napoleans took no part in the battle but were in position here on this day, and that evening began the march to Hagerstown.

Losses not reported in detail.

Hill's Corps Lt. Col. John J Garnett

Heth's Grandy's, Moore's, Lewis's and Maurin's Batteries
Division
Garnett's 4 - Napoleans, 2 - 10 Pounder Parrotts, 7 - 3" Rifles, 2 - 12 Pounder Howitzers
Battalion

7-1,2,3&4: The Parrotts and Rifles took part in the battle in a different position on each of the three days, their most active service being on the second day in this position. The Napoleans and Howitzers were in reserve and not actively engaged at any time. All withdrew from the field on the fourth day, but not at the same hour nor by the same route.

Losses: 5 Wounded, 17 Missing; Total 22

Ammunition expended: 1000 Rounds

Horses killed or disabled: 13

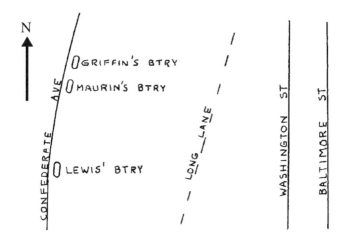

Hill's Corps The Lewis (Virginia) Artillery. Capt. John W. Lewis

Heth's 2 - 3" Rifles, 2 - Napoleans

Division 7-1: One of the rifles at 3:30 PM relieved one of Pegram's guns on the ridge west of Herr's Tavern and was
Garnett's engaged until fight ended.

Battalion 7-2: Both rifles were in position here and took an active part in the artillery duel in the afternoon and evening
Lewis's with the Union batteries on Cemetary Hill.

Brigade 7-3: Moved under orders to a point south of McMillan's Woods but were not engaged at any time, although
from time-to-time under fire.

7-4: The Napoleans were never actively engaged in the battle but on this day were placed in position here. At
night they rejoined the rifles and with them, began the march to Hagerstown.

Losses not reported in detail.

Hill's Corps The Donaldsonville (Louisiana) Artillery. Capt. V. Maurin

Heth's 1 - 10 Pounder Parrott, 2 - 3" Rifles

Division 7-1: About 3:30 PM, relieved some of Pegram's guns, whose ammunition was exhausted, on the ridge west of
Garnett's Herr's Tavern and from that time, took an active part in the conflict.

Battalion 7-2: In position here all day but not actively engaged until 3 PM, when it opened and maintained a steady fire
Maurin's on Cemetary Hill until near sunset, and vigorously renewed it at dusk for the purpose of diverting the fire
Battery of Union artillery from the Confederate infantry then assaulting East Cemetary Hill.

7-3: Ordered to a position south of McMillan's Woods and held in reserve, sometimes fired upon but not
returning the fire.

7-4: Withdrew about 8 AM and marched to Cashtown to reinforce the cavalry escorting the wagon train.

Losses not reported in detail.

Ewell's The Salem (Virginia) Artillery. Lt. C. B. Griffin

Corps 2 - 3" Rifles, 2 - Napoleans

Artillery 7-1: Reached the field too late to take part in the battle.

Reserve 7-2: Remained in reserve on this ridge north of the railroad.

Dance's 7-3: The Rifles were moved to this position early in the morning and took part in the cannonade preceeding

Battalion Longstreet's Assault, and continued firing for sometime afterward. Withdrew at night to camp in rear.

Griffin's 7-4: The Napoleans occupied a position on this ridge south of the railroad cut but did no firing. After nightfall

Battery* they joined the Rifles, and with them began the march to Hagerstown.

No losses reported. Ammunition expended: 154 Rounds.

(Note: See Page 250 for 1st position where the tablet is listed as Hupp's Battery.)

*see index

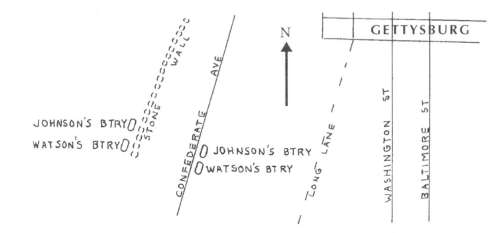

Ewell's
Corps
Artillery
Reserve
Dance's
Battalion
Watson's
Battery
2nd Position

2nd Richmond (Virginia) Howitzers. Capt. David Watson

4 - 10 Pounder Parrotts

7-1: Reached the field in evening too late to take part in the battle.

7-2: Early in the morning, took position on this ridge just north of the Western Maryland RR cut. Opened fire about 4 PM on batteries on Cemetary Hill, continued firing until dark.

7-3: Moved to this position. Took part in the great cannonade preceeding Longstreet's Assault and kept firing for some time afterwards. Withdrew at night to camp in rear.

7-4: After nightfall, began the march to Hagerstown.

Losses not reported in detail. Ammunition expended: 661 Rounds.

(Note: The first position was north of the RR Cut as mentioned for 7-2 above, the 3rd position is described below.)

Ewell's
Corps
Artillery
Reserve
Dance's
Battalion
Watson's
Battery
3rd Position

2nd Richmond (Virginia) Howitzers. Capt. David Watson

4 - 10 Pounder Parrotts

7-3: Moved to this position. Took part in the cannonade preceeding Longstreet's final assault and continued firing for some time afterwards. Moved at night to the rear of this line.

7-4: Withdrew in the night and began the march to Hagerstown.

Losses not reported in detail. Ammunition expended: 661 Rounds.

(Note: This 3rd position is behind the stone wall 100 feet west of the 2nd position.)

Hill's Corps
Artillery
Reserve
McIntosh's
Battalion
Johnson's
Battery
1st Position

Johnson's (Virginia) Battery. Capt. M. Johnson

2 - Napoleans, 2 - 3" Rifles

7-1: In position on hill near Fairfield Road west of Willoughby Run. Not engaged though under fire, losing one man killed.

7-2: In position here and actively engaged under heavy fire of sharpshooters and artillery.

7-3: Remained in this position and was actively engaged.

7-4: Withdrew at evening to Marsh Creek on Fairfield Road.

Losses not reported in detail.

Hill's Corps
Artillery
Reserve
McIntosh's
Battalion
Johnson's
Battery
2nd Position

Johnson's (Virginia) Battery. Capt. M. Johnson

2 - Napoleans, 2 - 3" Rifles.

7-2: In position here and actively engaged under the heavy fire of Union sharpshooters and artillery.

7-3: Remained in this position all day and actively engaged.

7-4: Withdrew in the night to Marsh Creek on the Fairfield Road.

Losses not reported in detail.

(Note: This 2nd position is behind the stone wall 100 feet west of the 1st position.)

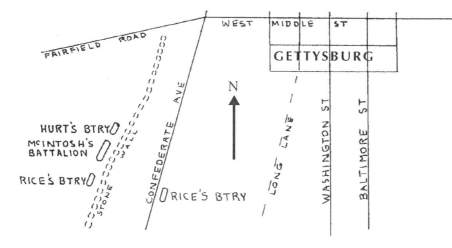

Hill's Corps Danville (Virginia) Battery. Capt. R. S. Rice
  Artillery   4 - Napoleans
  Reserve   7-1:   In position near Chambersburg Pike west of Herr's Tavern and firing when Union forces were visible.
  McIntosh's   Enfiladed their line at one time in and near the railroad cut.
  Battalion   7-2:   Two guns took position here and were actively engaged under heavy fire of sharpshooters and artillery, the
  Rice's   other two guns in reserve.
  Battery   7-3:   All the guns were actively engaged in this position.
  1ˢᵗ Position   7-4:   Withdrew at evening to Marsh Creek on the Fairfield Road.
             Losses not reported in detail.

Hill's Corps Danville (Virginia) Battery. Capt. R. S. Rice
  Artillery   4 - Napoleans
  Reserve   7-2:   Two guns took position here and were actively engaged under the heavy fire of Union sharpshooters and
  McIntosh's   artillery. Two guns of the battery were in reserve.
  Battalion   7-3:   All guns actively engaged in this position.
  Rice's   7-4:   Withdrew in the night to Marsh Creek on Fairfield Road. Losses not reported in detail.
  Battery   (Note: This 2nd position is behind the stone wall 100 feet west of the 1st position.)
  2ⁿᵈ Position

Hill's Corps Major D. G. McIntosh
  Artillery   Johnson's, Rice's, Hurt's and Wallace's Batteries
  Reserve   6 - Napoleans, 2 - Whitworths, 8 - 3" Rifles
  McIntosh's 7-1, 2, 3, 4: The Battalion was actively engaged on each of the three days of the battle and withdrew from the
  Battalion   field under orders on the evening of the fourth day.
             Losses: 7 Killed, 25 Wounded; Total 32. Horses killed or disabled: 38.

Hill's Corps Hardaway (Alabama) Artillery. Capt. W. B. Hurt
  Artillery   2 - Whitworths, 2 - 3" Rifles
  Reserve   7-1:   The Whitworths were in position near the Chambersburg Pike west of Herr's Tavern and actively en-
  Hurt's   gaged. The 3" Rifles occupied the hill near Fairfield Road west of Willoughby Run but did no firing,
  Battery*   though sometimes under fire.
          7-2:   All the guns were in position here and actively engaged under heavy fire of sharpshooters and artillery.
          7-3:   The 3" rifles remained here. The Whitworths were beyond the range of the Union guns, whilst their own
               fire reached all parts of the field.
          7-4:   Withdrew at evening to Marsh Creek on Fairfield Road.
             Losses not reported in detail.
             (Note: See Page 18 for 1st position.)

*see index

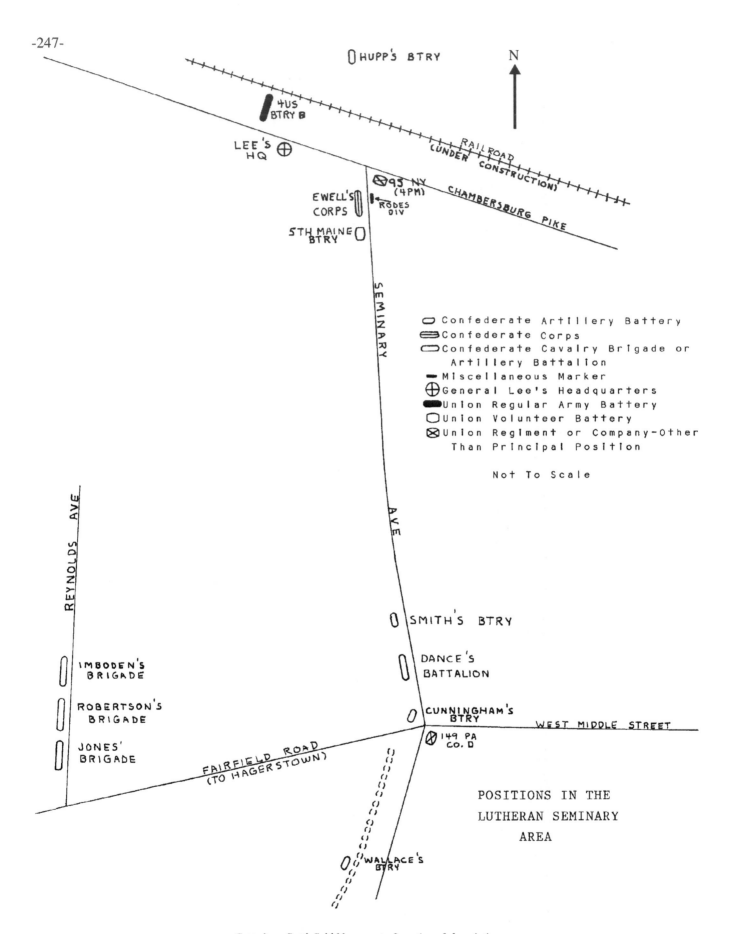

POSITIONS IN THE
LUTHERAN SEMINARY
AREA

~ Gettysburg Battlefield Monuments, Locations & Inscriptions ~

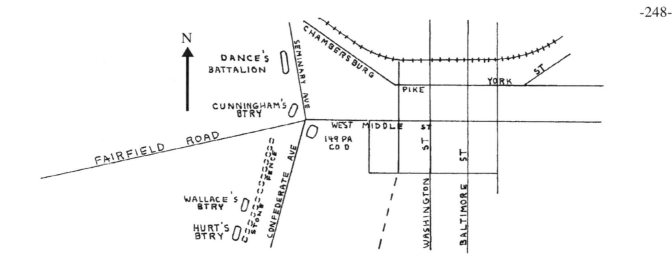

Hill's Corps
Artillery
Reserve
Wallace's
Battery

2nd Rockbridge (Virginia) Artillery. Lt. Samuel Wallace
4 - 3" Rifles
7-1: In position near Chambersburg Pike west of Herr's Tavern and actively engaged, advancing in the evening.
7-2: Occupied this position. Was actively engaged. Had one gun disabled.
7-3: Remained here and was actively engaged.
7-4: Withdrew at evening to Marsh Creek on Fairfield Road.
Losses not reported in detail.

149th PA
Company D
2-3-1

Headquarters Guards
Eected and presented to the Company by George W. Baldwin in memory of his brother, Joseph H. Baldwin, who was killed here July 1st, 1863 and Alex M. Stewart mortally wounded, dying in Gettysburg, July 6, 1863. Company D, 149th Pennsylvania Volunteers held this ground for 20 minutes on the evening of July 1st, 1863, against the right of Scales' Brigade by order of Maj. Gen. Abner Doubleday, Commanding 1st Army Corps.

Ewell's
Corps
Artillery
Reserve
Dance's
Battalion
Cunningham's
Battery

The Powhatan (Virginia) Artillery. Lt. John M. Cunningham
4 - 3" Rifles
7-1: Reached the field in the evening too late to take part in the battle.
7-2: Early in the morning, took position here. Opened fire about 4 PM upon the batteries on Cemetary Hill and continued firing until dark.
7-3: Remained here all day. Took part in the great cannonade preceeding Longstreet's final assault. At night withdrew to camp in rear.
7-4: After nightfall, began the march to Hagerstown.
Losses not reported in detail. Amunition expended: 308 Rounds.

Ewell's
Corps
Artillery
Reserve
Dance's
Battalion

Cunningham's, Smith's, Watson's, Griffin's, Graham's Batteries. Capt. Willis J. Dance
1st Virginia Battalion
4 - 20 Pounder Parrotts, 4 - 10 Pounder Parrotts, 10 - 3" Rifles, 2 - Napoleans.
7-1: Battalion reached the field in the evening too late to take part in the battle.
7-2 & 3: The first four named batteries occupied positions on this ridge. Graham's Battery of 20 Pounder Parrotts served east of Rock Creek. All were actively engaged.
7-4: At nightfall, began march to Hagerstown.
Casualties: 3 Killed, 19 Wounded; Total 22. Ammunition expended: 1886 Rounds.

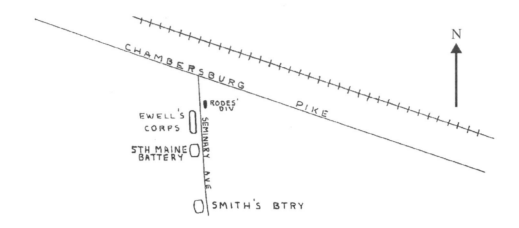

Ewell's **Corps** **Artillery** **Reserve** **Dance's** **Battalion** **Smith's** **Battery**	3rd Richmond (Virginia) Howitzers. Capt. B. H. Smith, Jr. 4 - 3" Rifles 7-1: Reached the field in evening too late to take part in the battle. 7-2: Early in the morning took position here. About 4 PM opened fire upon the batteries on Cemetary Hill and continued firing until dark. 7-3: Moved to position south of Fairfield Road, took part in the great cannonade preceeding Longstreet's final assault and kept firing for sometime afterwards. Withdrew at night to camp in rear. 7-4: After nightfall began the march to Hagerstown. Losses: 1 Killed; Wounded not reported. Ammunition expended: 314 Rounds.

1st Corps **Artillery** **Brigade** **5th Maine** **Battery***	Capt. Greenleaf T. Stevens, Lt. Edward N. Whittier 6 - Napoleans 7-2: Position of July 1, 1863. (Note: See Page 61 for other position of this battery.)

Ewell's **Corps** **Rodes'*** **Early's*** **Johnson's** **Divisions***	7-4: Having withdrawn, under orders, from its previous positions, the Corps formed line about daybreak on this ridge with its right a short distance south of the Hagerstown Road, its left near the Mummasburg Road and its center near here. Rodes was on the right, Johnson on the left early on a supporting line in their rear. The breastworks of stone here and the old earthworks beyond the railroad are remains of defences then thrown up and indicate the positions of the front line. 7-5: The three Divisions left here at different hours but all were on the march to Hagerstown early in the morning of this day. (Note: See Page 17 for 1st position.)

Ewell's **Corps** **Rodes'** **Division***	This breastwork was constructed by Rodes' Division, C S A, July 4, 1863.

THE SYMBOLS LISTED BELOW ARE USED TO IDENTIFY THE MONUMENTS, MARKERS, TABLETS, STATUES, ETC. WHICH ARE DRAWN ON THE MAPS IN THESE PAGES

SYMBOL	TYPE	REPRESENTING	DESCRIPTION
	Bronze Tablet	Army of The Potomac, Union Corps or Division or Brigade, Regular Army Regiment, Regular Army Artillery Battery, Volunteer Artillery Brigade.	Brigade Tablet Mounted on Square Marble base. All other Tablets are on large vertical Granite Blocks.
	Bronze Tablet	Army of Northern Virginia, Confederate Corps or Division or Brigade or Artillery Battalion	Brigade Tablet and Artillery Battalion Tablet Mounted on Round Marble base. All other Tablets are Mounted on large vertical Granite blocks.
	Iron Tablet	Union Army Battery (other than Regular Army)	Mounted on Black Iron Shaft.
	Iron Tablet	Confederate Artillery Battery	Mounted on Black Iron Shaft.
	Iron Tablet	Confederate Brigade Advanced Position	Mounted on Black Iron Shaft.
	Regimental or Battery Monument	Principal Position of Volunteer Regiment or Volunteer Artillery Battery	Usually Granite or Marble in a Great Variety of Shapes and Sizes.
	Regimental Marker	Other than Principal Position of Regiment or Battery	Usually a Square Granite Marker or tablet or may be another monument.
	Flank Marker or Company Marker	Left and/or Right Flank of Regiment or Battery or Position of a Company.	Usually a Small Square or Rectangular Granite Marker.
	Army Or Corps Headquarters	Site of Headquarters of Army Commander or Corps Commander or Chief of Artillery	Cannon Barrel Mounted Vertically on Stone, Granite or Marble Base.
	State Monument	Monument Erected by Union or Confederate State.	
	Statue	Standing or Equestrian	Bronze Sculpture
	Building	House, Barn or other Structure	Identified by Owner's Name.
	Miscellaneous Marker	Marker or Inscription of a type not listed above	Granite or Metal Marker.
*Asterisk		Used whenever a Division or Brigade or Regiment or Battery has more than one Monument or Marker.	Check the Index for other Monument or Marker.

*see index

~ Gettysburg Battlefield Monuments, Locations & Inscriptions ~

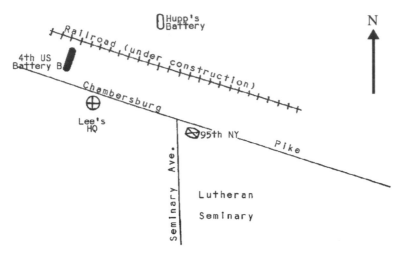

96th NY*   <u>7-1</u>:   4 PM.
2-1-1

Head- **quarters** **Army of** **Northern** **Virginia**	CSA IN THIS FIELD WAS LOCATED HEADQUARTERS OF THE ARMY OF NORTHERN VIRGINIA JULY 1, 2, 3, 4, 1863 "My Headquarters Were In Tents In An Apple Orchard Back Of The Seminary Along The Chambersburg Pike" Robert E. Lee

4th US   (Note: See Page 9 for data on this tablet.)
Battery B*

Ewell's   The Salem (Virginia) Artillery. Lt. C. B. Griffin
Corps   2 - 3" Rifles, 2 - Napoleons.
Artillery   <u>7-1</u>:   The Battery reached the field too late to participate in the engagement of the day.
Reserve   <u>7-2</u>:   Held in reserve near the Western Maryland RR Cut.
Dance's   <u>7-3</u>:   Rifled guns were in position near the Fairfield Road. The Napoleons were placed at the Railroad Cut and
Battalion   remained until night but were not engaged.
Hupp's   <u>7-4</u>:   At midnight began the march to Hagerstown.
Battery*   Casualties not reported. Ammunition expended: 154 rounds.
              (Note: See Page 244 for 2nd position where the tablet is listed as "Griffin's Battery")

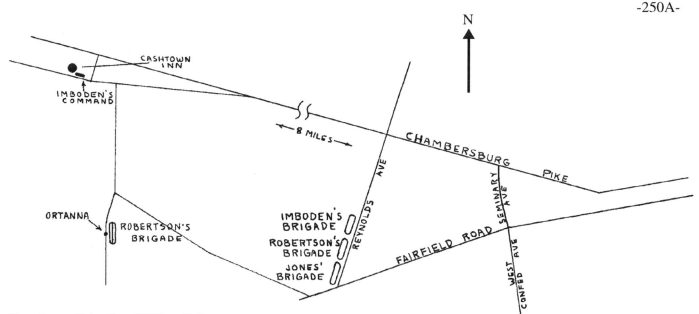

Stuart's   Brig. Gen. William E. Jones
Cavalry   6th, 7th, 11th, 12th Cavalry Regiments and 35th Virginia Battalion.
Division   7-1: The 12th Regiment was detatched and remained on the south side of the Potomac River. White's 35th
Jones'   Virginia Battalion was also detatched. The remaining regiments crossed the Potomac at Williamsport,
Brigade*   Maryland.
          7-2: Marched from near Greencastle, Pa to Chambersburg, Pa.
          7-3: The Brigade marched from Chambersburg, Pa via Cashtown to Fairfield, Pa. Met the 6th US Cavalry
              about two miles from Fairfield. The 7th Va charged in the advance and was repulsed. The 7th Va charged
              and forced the Union Regiment to retire with heavy loss. The Brigade encamped at Fairfield for the night.
          7-4: The Brigade held the mountain passes and picketed the left flank of the Army.
          Casualties: 11 Killed, 30 Wounded, 6 Missing; Total 47.

Stuart's   Brig. Gen. Beverly H. Robertson. 4th and 5th No. Carolina Cavalry.
Cavalry   7-1: The Brigade crossed the Potomac at Williamsport, Md and marched to Greencastle, Pa.
Division   7-2: Marched from Greencastle, Pa to Chambersburg, Pa.
Robertson's 7-3: Marched to Cashtown and in the direction of Fairfield guarding the flank of the Army.
Brigade*   7-4: Held Jack's Mountain and picketed the left flank of the Army of Northern Virginia.
          No report or details of losses made.

Stuart's   Brig. Gen. J. D. Imboden 18th Virginia Cavalry, 62nd Virginia Infantry, Virginia Partisan Rangers,
Cavalry   McClanahan's (Va) Battery.
Division   7-3: Command guarding ammunition and supply trains. Reached the field at noon and retired with the supply
Imboden's   trains at night.
Brigade*   No report nor details of losses made.

Imboden's (Note: A black iron tablet 8 miles west of Gettysburg has the following inscription.
Com-   7-3: Command guarding trains. Reached the field at noon and retired with the trains.
mand*   No report on details of losses.
2nd Position (Note: The tablet is at the Cashtown Inn.)

Robertson's (Note: At Ortanna Methodist Church there is a black iron tablet with the identical report as that listed above for
Brigade* Robertson's Brig.)

*see index

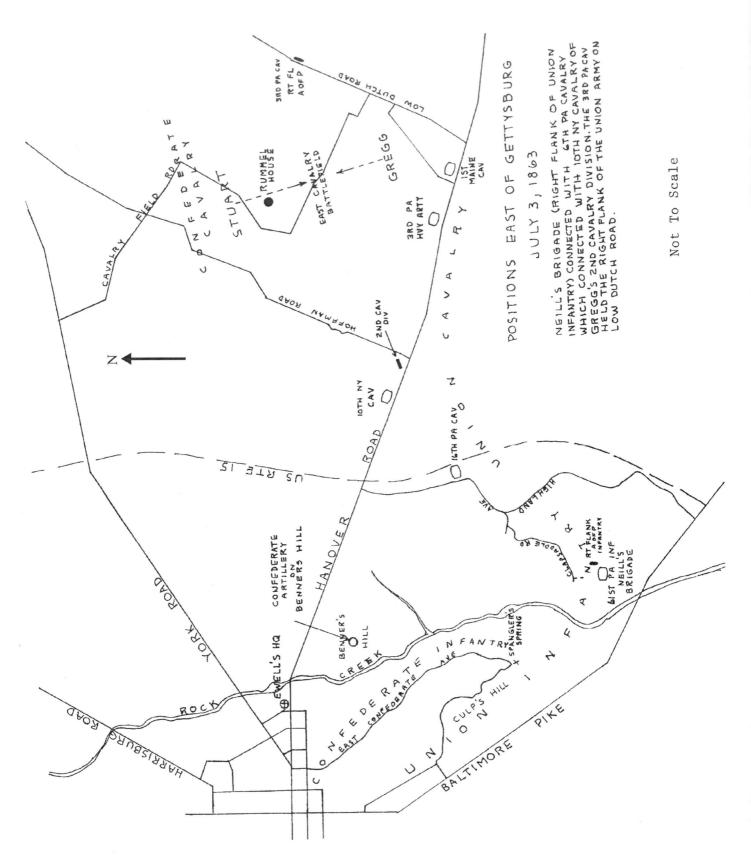

POSITIONS EAST OF GETTYSBURG
JULY 3, 1863

NEILL'S BRIGADE (RIGHT FLANK OF UNION
INFANTRY) CONNECTED WITH 4TH PA CAVALRY
WHICH CONNECTED WITH 10TH NY CAVALRY OF
GREGG'S 2ND CAVALRY DIVISION. THE 3RD PA CAV
HELD THE RIGHT FLANK OF THE UNION ARMY ON
LOW DUTCH ROAD.

Not To Scale

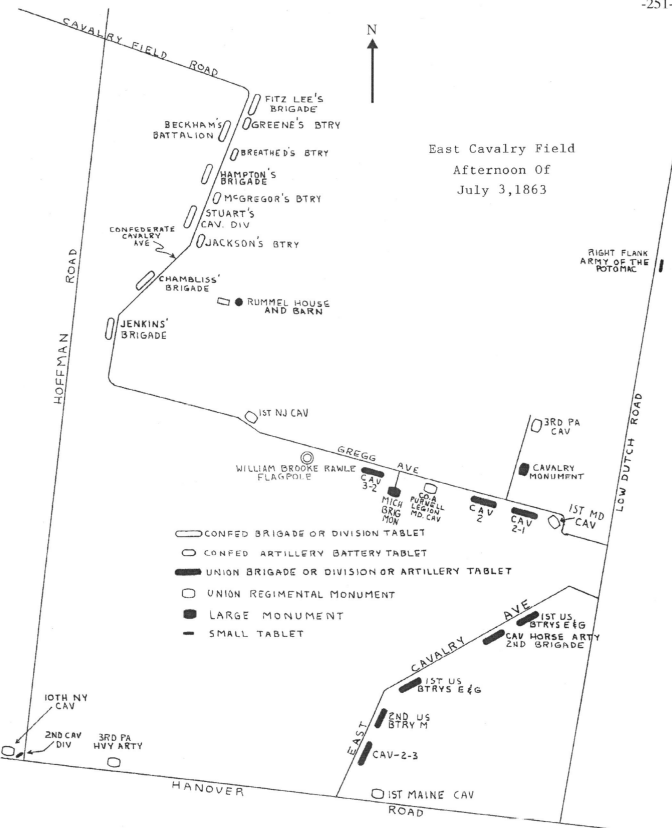

East Cavalry Field
Afternoon Of
July 3,1863

CONFED BRIGADE OR DIVISION TABLET
CONFED ARTILLERY BATTERY TABLET
UNION BRIGADE OR DIVISION OR ARTILLERY TABLET
UNION REGIMENTAL MONUMENT
LARGE MONUMENT
SMALL TABLET

Not To Scale

~ Gettysburg Battlefield Monuments, Locations & Inscriptions ~

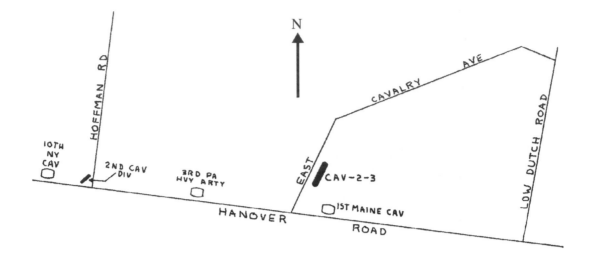

10th NY **Cavalry** **C-2-1**	Major M. H. Avery 7-2: 3 to 8 PM Casualties: 2 Killed, 4 Wounded, 3 Missing; Total 9. (NY@Gbg)

Cavalry
Corps
2nd Division

7-2: Units of the 2nd Cavalry Division commanded by Brig. Gen. D. McM Gregg were engaged here with a portion of the Confederate "Stonewall" Brigade, Johnson's Division, from about 6 to 10 PM. The 3rd Pa Cavalry occupied the ground to the right, the 1st NJ Cavalry and Company A Parnell (Maryland) Legion to the left. The 10th NY Cavalry and a section of Battery H-3rd Pa. Heavy Artillery were in support.

7-3: The 16th Pa Cavalry of Gregg's Division was formed here in a skirmish line which connected on the left with infantry units on Wolf's Hill, and on the right with Brig. Gen. George A. Custer's Cavalry Brigade.

(Note: See Page 37 for 16th Pa Cavalry position, Page 42 for Walker's [Stonewall] Brigade.)

3rd PA
Heavy
Artillery*
C-2-1

Capt. William D. Rank
2nd Section-Battery H serving as light artillery.
7-3: Participated in the battle.
(Note: See Page 117 for other position.)

1st Maine
Cavalry
C-2-3

Lt. Col. Charles H. Smith
7-3: This monument commemorates the services of the 1st Maine Cavalry on this field, July 3, 1863.
Casualties: 1 Killed, 4 Wounded; Total 5. (NY@Gbg)

Cavalry
Corps
2nd Division
3rd Brigade

Col. J. Irvin Gregg
1st Maine (10 Cos), 10th NY, 4th, 16th Pennsylvania Cavalry

7-2: Arrived and took position on Hanover Road two miles from Gettysburg in proximity to Lt. Gen. Ewell's Corps about 11 AM. Two regiments of infantry were in front as skirmishers. They were withdrawn about 3 PM and 10th NY Cavalry deployed in their place. Confederate sharpshooters from hill and woods in front were annoying. 50 dismounted men were ordered to drive them back, but were themselves met by a superior force until checked and forced back by the 1st Brigade.

7-3: Took position in morning on Baltimore Pike and moved to the right near Hanover Road. Not engaged in cavalry fight except one section of Batteries E and G-1st US, Lt. J. Chester, ordered to the left to meet a threatened attack.

7-4: Made reconnaissance to Hunterstown and forced in Confederate pickets.

Casualties: 6 Killed, 12 Wounded, 3 Missing; Total 21.

*see index

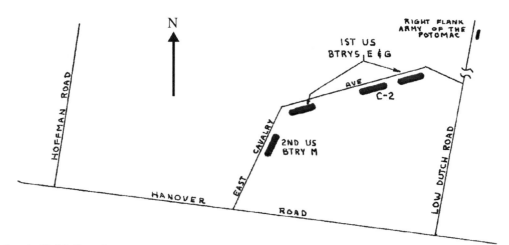

Cavalry 1st Lt. A. C. M. Pennington
Brigade 6 -3" Rifles
Horse 7-2: Engaged with Confederates at Hunterstown.
Artillery 7-3: Engaged in Brig. Gen. Custer's Brigade with Maj. Gen. J. E. B. Stuart's Confederate Cavalry on the right
2nd US of Union Army.
Battery M Casualties: 1 Officer wounded.

Cavalry 2nd Capt. Alanson M. Randol
Brigade 4 - Napoleans
Horse 7-1 & 2: With 1st Brigade, 2nd Cavalry Division, not engaged.
Artillery 7-3: One section under Lt. James Chester was ordered to 2nd Brig., 3rd Cavalry Division and took position
1st US west of Low Dutch Road, and with Brig. Gen. Custer's 2nd Brigade, 3rd Division Cavalry Corps was
Battery's hotly engaged in repelling the attack of Maj. Gen. Stuart's Confederate Cavalry Division. The one section
E & G under Lt. Ernest L. Kinney remained near the Hanover Road.
(One Section)

Cavalry 2nd Capt. John C. Tidball
Brigade 1st US Batteries E & G, Capt. Alanson M. Randol
Horse 7-2 & 3: With Cavalry on right under Brig. Gen. D. McM Gregg
Artillery 1st US Battery K, Capt. William M. Graham
7-3: With Reserve Cavalry Brigade on extreme left.
2nd US Battery A, Lt. John H. Calef
7-1: With 1st Brigade, 1st Division on right and left of Chambersburg Pike.
7-2: In front of Little Round Top.
3rd US Battery C Lt. William D Fuller
With 2nd Brigade, 2nd Division at Manchester; not engaged.
Casualties: 2 Killed, 13 Wounded; Total 15.

Cavalry 2nd Capt. Alanson M. Randol
Brigade 4 - Napoleans
Horse 7-1 & 2: With 1st Brigade, 2nd Cavalry Division, not engaged.
Artillery 7-3: One section under Lt. James Chester was ordered to 2nd Brig., 3rd Cavalry Division and took position
1st US west of Low Dutch Road, and with Brig. Gen. Custer's 2nd Brigade, 3rd Division Cavalry Corps was
Battery's hotly engaged in repelling the attack of Maj. Gen. Stuart's Confederate Cavalry Division. The one section
E & G under Lt. Ernest L. Kinney remained near the Hanover road.
(Note: other
section above)

Right Flank 7-3: The extreme right flank of the Army of the Potomac held by Capt. J. W. Walsh's Squadron, 3rd Pennsyl-
Army of vania Cavalry on the left of which, to the west of the Low Dutch Road, was posted Capt. Frank W. Hess's
the Squadron A, Capt. William E. Miller's Battalion of the Regiment, which charged through the Confederate
Potomac column almost up to their batteries on Cress's Ridge north of the Rummel Farm buildings.

*see index

GREGG AVE

N

3RD PA CAV

UNION—CONFED CAV MONUMENT

CAV 2

CAV 2-1

1ST MD CAV

LOW DUTCH ROAD

EAST CAV AVE

1st Md Cavalry C-2-1
Lt. Col. James M. Deems (11 Companies)
7-3: In the cavalry engagement on this flank.
Casualties: 2 Killed, 1 Missing; Total 3. (NY@Gbg)

Cavalry Corps 2nd Division 1st Brigade
Col. John B. McIntosh
1st Md (11 Cos), Purnell Legion Company A, 1st Mass, 1st NJ, 1st and 3rd Pa Cavalry, Section Battery H 3rd Pa Hvy Artillery
7-2: After an exhausting march, took position about noon on Hanover Road near intersection with Low Dutch Road, 3rd Brigade on left. During the afternoon, there was a skirmish between the 3rd Pa, Purnell Legion, 1st NJ and Section Battery H-3rd Pa Heavy Artillery and 2nd Virginia Infantry for the possession of Brinkerhoff's Ridge. About 10 PM the line was withdrawn and with 3rd Brigade, bivouacked on Baltimore Pike nearly a mile east of Rock Creek Bridge. 1st Mass with 6th Corps.
7-3: Returned in the morning, and finding 2nd Brigade, 3rd Division in position of the day before, the Brigade formed on left of 2nd Brigade, 3rd Division, and soon after noon relieved it. About 2 PM, a large Confederate force having been observed, Brig. Gen. D. McM Gregg ordered 2nd Brig., 3rd Division to return and the Brigade with 2nd Brigade, 3rd Division was soon engaged with Maj. Gen. Stuart's Command. About 3 PM, Brig. Gen. Hampton's and Brig. Gen. Fitzhugh Lee's Brigades, the reserves which had been concealed on the Stallsmith Farm, emerged from the woods in front and charged, but were repulsed with the aid of artillery. ~
Casualties: 26 Wounded, 9 Missing; Total 35.

Union/ Confederate Cavalry Monument
7-3: This Shaft Marks the Field of the Engagement Between Cavalry Commanded by Brigadier General David McM Gregg and the Confederate Cavalry Commanded By Major General J. E. B. Stuart.

3rd PA Cavalry C-2-1
7-2: Reached the field at noon from Hanover. Engaged dismounted a Confederate brigade of infantry on Brinkerhoff's Ridge from 6 to 10 PM.
7-3: Engaged mounted and dismounted with the Condederate Cavalry Division from 2 PM until evening, portions of the Regiment advancing in a mounted charge and driving the enemy beyond the Rummel Farm buildings.
Casualties: 15 Wounded, 6 Missing; Total 21. (NY@Gbg)

Cavalry Corps 2nd Division
Brig. Gen. David McM Gregg
1st Brigade   Col. John B. Mcintosh
2nd Brigade   Col. Pennock Huey
3rd Brigade   Col. J. Irvin Gregg
7-2: General Gregg, with two brigades, left Hanover and took position about noon at the junction of the Hanover Road with the Low Dutch Road. 1st Brigade on the right, 3rd on the left connecting with the infantry pickets, the 2nd Brigade having been sent to Westminster. Took and held Brinkerhoff's Ridge after a sharp skirmish with the 2nd Virginia Infantry. About 10 PM, the two brigades withdrew and bivouacked for the night on the Baltimore Pike a mile east of Rock Creek bridge.

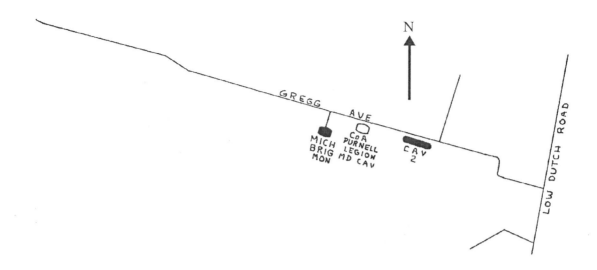

Cavalry Corps 2nd Division (con't) 7-3: Took position with the right on Hanover Road, the 2nd Brigade, 3rd Cavalry Division on the right. General Custer, having received an order from General Pleasanton to rejoin his Division, was relieved about 2 PM by the 1st Brigade. A large force of Confederate Cavalry under General Stuart, screened from view by the woods, having been discovered, General Gregg ordered Custer to remain in support of Mcintosh until the Confederate Cavalry could be driven back. Custer and Mcintosh and the batteries of Randol and Pennington were soon hotly engaged with Confederate Cavalry and Artillery. About 3 PM, Stuart made a charge with his reserves under Hampton and Fitzhugh Lee which was repulsed. This closed operations on the field.

Casualties: 6 Killed, 38 Wounded, 12 Missing; Total 56.

Company A Purnell Legion Maryland Cavalry C-2-1 7-2 & 3: Maryland's Tribute to Her Loyal Sons

This detatched company commanded by Capt. Robert E. Duvall, served in the cavalry engagement on this flank, July 2nd and 3rd, 1863.

Michigan Cavalry Brigade Cav-3-2* MICHIGAN CAVALRY BRIGADE, 2ND BRIGADE, 3RD DIVISION, CAVALRY CORPS. This monument marks the field where the Michigan Cavalry Brigade under its gallant leader, General George A. Custer, rendered signal and distinguished service in assisting to defeat the further advance of a numerically superior force under the Confederate General J. E. B. Stuart, who in conjunction with Pickett's Charge upon the centre, attempted to turn the right flank of the Union Army at that critical hour of conflict upon the afternoon of July 3, 1663.

	Killed	Wounded	Missing
1st Michigan	10	43	20
5th Michigan	8	30	18
6th Michigan	1	26	1
7th Michigan	13	48	39

*see index

CHAMBLISS' BRIGADE

JENKINS' BRIGADE

N

1ST NJ CAV

GREGG

WILLIAM BROOKE RAWLE FLAGPOLE

CAV 3-2

AVE

LOW DUTCH ROAD

Cavalry Corps
3rd Division
2nd Brigade*

Brig. Gen. George A. Custer
1st, 5th, 6th, 7th (10 Cos) Michigan Cavalry
6-30: Skirmished with Stuart's Cavalry at Hanover, supported by Battery M-2nd US.
7-1: Not engaged.
7-2: Engaged with Brig. Gen. Hampton's Brigade of Stuart's Cavalry at Hunterstown and with the aid of Battery M-2nd US, forced it from the field; the 7th Mich dismounted as skirmishers.
7-3: Marched to Two Taverns arriving at daylight, and at 8 AM, moved to the right under orders to report to General Gregg. Took position north of the Hanover Road, and west of the Low Dutch Road, 2nd Division coming up and connecting on the left. Soon after noon, was ordered to join the Division on the extreme left but at 2 PM, Maj. Gen. Stuart's Division and Brig. Gen. Jenkins' Brigade of cavalry, having been discovered on the right and front, Brig. Gen. Custer under orders from General Gregg, turned back his Brigade and with 1st Brigade, 2nd Division was immediately engaged with Confederate forces which were repulsed and forced from the field. Late in the day moved to extreme left and rejoined the Division.
Casualties: 32 Killed, 147 Wounded, 78 Missing; Total 257.

1st NJ Cavalry
C-2-1

Major Myron H. Beaumont
7-3: Fought here both mounted and dismounted holding this position several hours. Assisted in repelling the charges of the enemy's cavalry.
Casualties: 9 Wounded Total. (NY@Gbg)

Stuart's Division Jenkins' Brigade

Col. M. J. Ferguson
14th, 16th, 17th Virginia Cavalry, 34th & 36th Va Cav Battalions
7-3: The Brigade had been with Ewell's Corps but rejoined the Cavalry Division here on this day about noon. It was armed with Enfield rifles, but by an oversight, brought to this field only about 10 rounds of ammunition. While this lasted it was actively engaged, mainly on foot as sharpshooters around and in front of the Rummel barn and outhouses. It was withdrawn from the field at an early hour in the evening.
Losses not reported.

Stuart's Division Chambliss' Brigade

Col. John R. Chambliss, Jr.
2nd No. Carolina and 9th, 10th, 13th Virginia Cavalry
7-3: The Brigade reached here about noon and took an active part in the fight until it ended, some of the men serving as sharpshooters in the vicinity of the Rummel barn, but most of the command participating in the charges made by the cavalry during the afternoon. It left the field after nightfall.
Losses: 8 Killed, 41 Wounded, 25 Missing; Total 74.

* Check Index For Other Position.

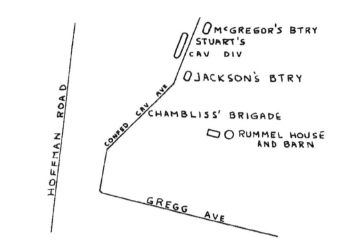

Stuart's Division Jenkins' Brigade Jackson's Battery

Capt. Thomas E. Jackson

2 - 3" Rifles, 2 - Howitzers

7-3: The battery was attached to Jenkins' Cavalry Brigade and took part in the fight here on the right wing of the Confederates, not far from the Rummel barn, but its limited supply of ammunition was soon exhausted and it was withdrawn.

Losses not reported.

Stuart's Cavalry Division

Major General J. E. B. Stuart

Hampton's Brigade	Brig. Gen. Wade Hampton, Col. L. S. Baker
Robertson's Brigade	Brig. Gen. Beverly H. Robertson
Fitz Lee's Brigade	Brig. Gen. Fitzhugh Lee
Jenkins' Brigade	Brig. Gen. A. G. Jenkins
Jones' Brigade	Brig. Gen. William E. Jones
W. H. F. Lee's Brigade	Col. J. R. Chambliss
Stuart's Horse Artillery, 6 Batteries	Major R. F. Beckham

Robertson's and Jones' Brigades, with three batteries, detached operating on the right flank of the Army.

7-1: The Division on the march from Dover to Carlisle received information that the Confederate Army was concentrating at Gettysburg.

7-2: The advance near Gettysburg late in the afternoon, engaged with Custer's Cavalry at Hunterstown on the left and rear of Early's Division.

7-3: Pursuant to order, the Cavalry Division of four Brigades took position on the left in advance of Early on a ridge which controlled the open ground toward Hanover. Gregg's Union Cavalry Division was massed in full view. Sharpshooters were advanced and soon became engaged. The battle continued until near night, being hotly contested. At night the Division withdrew to the York Road.

7-4: The Division was posted on the flanks and rear of the Army.

Casualties: 36 Killed, 140 Wounded, 64 Missing; Total 240.

Stuart's Division Beckham's Battalion McGregor's Battery

Capt. W. M. McGregor

2 - Napoleans, 2 - 3" Rifles

7-3: The Battery took an active part in the fight, arriving about 2 PM and keeping up its fire until the ample supply of ammunition, furnished on its way here, was exhausted. It withdrew from the field under orders.

Losses: 5 Killed, 7 Wounded; Total 12. Horses Killed or Disabled: 11.

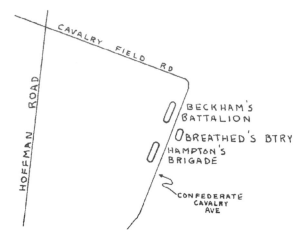

Stuart's Division Hampton's Brigade

Brig. Gen. Wade Hampton, Col. L. S. Baker

1st No. Carolina, 1st & 2nd So. Carolina Cavalry, Jeff Davis (Miss) Legion and Cobb's & Phillip's (Georgia) Legions.

7-2: Engaged in the evening with 3rd Division, Cavalry Corps near Hunterstown. Cobb's Legion led the attack and lost a number of officers and men killed and wounded.

7-3: The Brigade arrived here about noon and skirmished with Union sharpshooters. In the afternoon, the 1st No. Car. and Jeff Davis Legion, advancing in support of Chambliss' Brigade, drove back the Union Cavalry but met their reserve and were in a critical position when the Brigade went to their support, and a hand-to-hand fight ensued in which Brig. Gen. Wade Hampton was severly wounded. The conflict ended in the failure of the Confederates in their purpose to assail the rear of the Union Army.

Losses: 17 Killed, 58 Wounded, 16 Missing; Total 91.

Stuart's Division Beckham's Battalion Breathed's Battery

Capt. James Breathed

4 - 3" Rifles

7-3: The Battery arrived here about 2 PM and took an active part in the fight until its ample supply of ammunition, received in the forenoon on the way here, was exhausted. It was withdrawn from the field about dark.

Losses: 6 Killed, 8 Wounded; Total 14. Horses Killed or Disabled: 10.

Stuart's Division Beckham's Battalion

Major R. F. Beckham

    Breathed's (Virginia) Battery

    Chew's (Virginia) Battery

    Griffin's (Maryland) Battery

    Hart's (South Carolina) Battery

    McGregor's (Virginia) Battery

    Moorman's (Virginia) Battery

7-3: These batteries were not permanently attached to the Cavalry Brigades but were sent to them when needed.

    Breathed's Battery with Brig. Gen. W. H. F. Lee's Brigade

    Chew's Battery with Brig. Gen. W. E. Jones Brigade

    Griffin's Battery with the 2nd Army Corps

    Hart's Battery attached to the Washington Artillery with the Army trains

    McGregor's Battery with Brig. Gen. Wade Hampton's Brigade Moorman's Battery no report

Casualties not reported.

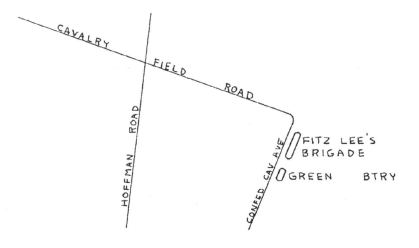

Ewell's Corps Early's Division Green Battery*

Louisiana Guard Artillery. Capt. C. A. Greene
2 - 10 Pounder Parrotts, 2 - 3" Rifles
<u>7-3</u>: After taking part in the fighting on the previous two days at Gettysburg and Hunterstown, this Battery, being detatched from its Battalion, brought its Parrott guns here and rendered important service in the Cavalry Battle, not withdrawing until after dark.
Losses: 2 Killed, 5 Wounded; Total 7. Horses Killed or Disabled: 2

Stuart's Division Fitz Lee's Brigade

Brig. Gen. Fitzhugh Lee
1st Md Battalion and 1st, 2nd, 3rd, 4th, 5th Virginia Cavalry
<u>7-3</u>: The Battalion being on duty with Ewell's Corps, the Brigade brought only the five regiments to this field where it arrived soon after midday and took position on the left of Hampton's Brigade on the edge of the neighboring woods. It participated actively in the conflict which ensued.
Losses: 5 Killed, 16 Wounded, 29 Missing; Total 50

*see index

THE SYMBOLS LISTED BELOW ARE USED TO IDENTIFY
THE MONUMENTS, MARKERS, TABLETS, STATUES, ETC.
WHICH ARE DRAWN ON THE MAPS IN THESE PAGES

SYMBOL	TYPE	REPRESENTING	DESCRIPTION
	Bronze Tablet	Army of The Potomac, Union Corps or Division or Brigade, Regular Army Regiment, Regular Army Artillery Battery, Volunteer Artillery Brigade.	Brigade Tablet Mounted on <u>Square</u> Marble base. All other Tablets are on large vertical Granite Blocks.
	Bronze Tablet	Army of Northern Virginia, Confederate Corps or Division or Brigade or Artillery Battalion	Brigade Tablet and Artillery Battalion Tablet Mounted on <u>Round Marble</u> base. All other Tablets are Mounted on large vertical Granite blocks.
	Iron Tablet	Union Army Battery (other than Regular Army)	Mounted on Black Iron Shaft.
	Iron Tablet	Confederate Artillery Battery	Mounted on Black Iron Shaft.
	Iron Tablet	Confederate Brigade Advanced Position	Mounted on Black Iron Shaft.
	Regimental or Battery Monument	Principal Position of Volunteer Regiment or Volunteer Artillery Battery	Usually Granite or Marble in a Great Variety of Shapes and Sizes.
	Regimental Marker	Other than Principal Position of Regiment or Battery	Usually a Square Granite Marker or tablet or may be another monument.
	Flank Marker or Company Marker	Left and/or Right Flank of Regiment or Battery or Position of a Coppany.	Usually a Small Square or Rectangular Granite Marker.
	Army Or Corps Headquarters	Site of Headquarters of Army Commander or Corps Commander or Chief of Artillery	Cannon Barrel Mounted Vertically on Stone, Granite or Marble Base.
	State Monument	Monument Erected by Union or Confederate State.	
	Statue	Standing or Equestrian	Bronze Sculpture
	Building	House, Barn or other Structure	Identified by Owner's Name.
	Miscellaneous Marker	Marker or Inscription of a type not listed above	Granite or Metal Marker.

*Asterisk — Used whenever a Division or Brigade or Regiment or Battery has more than one Monument or Marker.

Check the Index for other Monument or Marker.

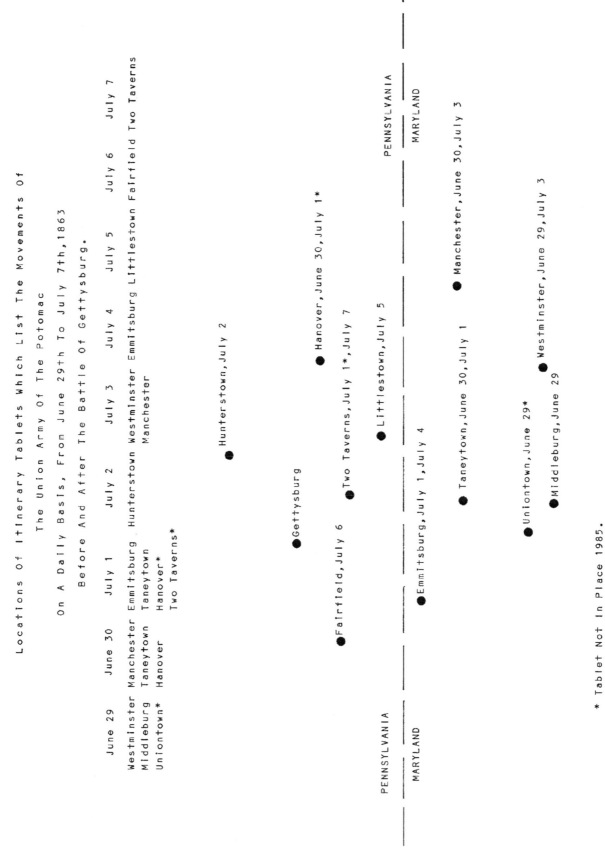

Locations Of Itinerary Tablets Which List The Movements Of

The Union Army Of The Potomac

On A Daily Basis, From June 29th To July 7th, 1863

Before And After The Battle Of Gettysburg.

June 29	June 30	July 1	July 2	July 3	July 4	July 5	July 6	July 7
Westminster	Manchester	Emmitsburg	Hunterstown	Westminster	Emmitsburg	Littlestown	Fairfield	Two Taverns
Middleburg	Taneytown	Taneytown		Manchester				
Uniontown*	Hanover	Hanover*						
		Two Taverns*						

Hunterstown, July 2

Hanover, June 30, July 1*

Gettysburg

Two Taverns, July 1*, July 7

Littlestown, July 5

Fairfield, July 6

PENNSYLVANIA

MARYLAND

Taneytown, June 30, July 1

Manchester, June 30, July 3

Emmitsburg, July 1, July 4

Uniontown, June 29*

Westminster, June 29, July 3

Middleburg, June 29

PENNSYLVANIA

MARYLAND

* Tablet Not In Place 1985.

ITINERARY TABLETS
ARMY OF THE POTOMAC
June 29th to July 7th, 1863

In August of 1901, **Itinerary Tablets** describing the movements of the Union Army Of The Potomac to and from the Battlefield of Gettysburg, were erected in various Maryland and Pennsylvania towns. These towns were selected because Union troops had marched through them between June 29th and July 7th of 1863. The locations of the tablets and their messages follow.

June 29, 1863: Uniontown*, Middleburg and Westminster, Md.

Headquarters Army Of The Potomac moved from Frederick to Middleburg. First and 11th Corps marched from Frederick to Emmitsburg, 2nd Corps from Monocacy Jct. via Liberty and Johnsville to Uniontown, 3rd Corps from near Woodsborough to Taneytown, 5th Corps from Ballinger's Creek via Frederick and Mount Pleasant to Liberty, 6th Corps from Hyattstown via New Market and Ridgeville to New Windsor, 12th Corps from Frederick to Taneytown and Bruceville.

1st and 2nd Brigades 1st Cavalry Division from Middletown via Boonsboro, Cavetown and Monterrey Springs to near Fairfield, Reserve Brigade of the 1st Cavalry Division from Middletown to Mechanicstown, 2nd Cavalry Division from New Market and Ridgeville to New Windsor, 3rd Cavalry Division from Frederick to Littlestown and the Artillery Reserve from Frederick to Bruceville.
Skirmishes at Muddy Branch and Westminster, Md. and at McConnellsburg and at Oyster Point, Pennsylvania.

June 30, 1863: Taneytown and Manchester, Md and Hanover, Pa.

Headquarters Army Of The Potomac moved from Middleburg to Taneytown, 1st Corps marched from Emmitsburg to Marsh Run, 3rd Corps from Taneytown to Bridgeport, 5th Corps from Liberty via Johnsville, Union Bridge and Union to Union Mills, 6th Corps from New Windsor to Manchester, 12th Corps from Taneytown and Bruceville to Littlestown.

First and 2nd Brigades 1st Cavalry Division from near Fairfield via Emmitsburg to Gettysburg, 2nd Cavalry Division from New Windsor to Westminster and thence to Manchester, 3rd Cavalry Division from Littlestown to Hanover and the Artillery Reserve from Bruceville to Taneytown Fight at Hanover, Pa. and skirmishes at Westminster, Md. and at Fairfield and Sporting Hill near Harrisburg, Pa.

July 1,1863: Hanover* and Two Taverns, PA*, and Taneytown & Emmitsburg, Md.

1st Corps marched from Marsh Run, 11th Corps from Emmitsburg to Gettysburg, 2nd Corps from Uniontown via Taneytown to near Gettysburg, 3rd Corps from Bridgeport via Emmitsburg to the field at Gettysburg, 5th Corps from Union Mills via Hanover and McSherrystown to Bonnaughtown, 6th Corps from Manchester en route to Gettysburg, 12th Corps from Littlestown via Two Taverns to the field of Gettysburg.

2nd Cavalry Division marched from Manchester to Hanover Jct., from whence the 1st and 3rd Brigades proceeded to Hanover while the 2nd Brigade returned to Manchester, 3rd Cavalry Division moved from Hanover via Abbottstown to Berlin and the Artillery Reserve 1st Regular and 4th Volunteer Brigades from Taneytown to near Gettysburg. The Vermont Brigade from the defences of Washington joined the 1st Corps on the Battlefield of Gettysburg.

Battle at Gettysburg 1st day and skirmish at Carlisle, Pa.

continued

* Tablet not in place 1985.

~ Gettysburg Battlefield Monuments, Locations & Inscriptions ~

ARMY OF THE POTOMAC
Itinerary Tablets (cont.)

July 2, 1863:   Hunterstown, Pa.

2nd, 5th and 6th Corps, Lockwood's Brigade of the Middle Department, 1st and 3rd Brigades 2nd Cavalry Division, 3rd Cavalry Division and the Artillery Reserve reached the field at Gettysburg. 1st and 2nd Brigades 1st Cavalry Division marched from Gettysburg to Taneytown and Merritt's Reserve Brigade 1st Cavalry Division from Mechanicstown to Emmitsburg.

Battle of Gettysburg 2nd day and skirmishes at Hunterstown and near Chambersburg , Pa.

July 3, 1863:   Manchester and Westminster, Md.

1st and 2nd Brigades 1st Cavalry Division marched from Taneytown to Westminster, Reserve Brigade 1st Cavalry Division from Emmitsburg to the field of Gettysburg and the 2nd Brigade 2nd Cavalry Division from Manchester to Westminster.

Battle of Gettysburg 3rd Day and fight at Fairfield, Pa.

July 4, 1863:   Emmitsburg, Md.

1st and 2nd Brigades 1st Cavalry Division marched from Westminster en route to Frederick, Reserve Brigade 1st Cavalry Division from Gettysburg en route to Frederick, 2nd Brigade 2nd Cavalry Division marched from Westminster via Emmitsburg to Monterey, 3rd Brigade 2nd Cavalry Division marched from Gettysburg to Hunterstown, 3rd Cavalry Division marched from Gettysburg via Emmitsburg to Monterey.

Fight at Monterey Gap, Pa. and skirmishes at Fairfield Gap and near Emmitsburg.

July 5, 1863:   Littlestown, Pa.

2nd Corps marched from Gettysburg to Two Taverns, 5th Corps marched from Gettysburg to Marsh Run, 6th Corps marched from Gettysburg to Fairfield, 11th Corps marched from Gettysburg to Rock Creek, 12th Corps marched from Gettysburg to Littlestown.

1st Brigade 2nd Cavalry Division marched from Gettysburg to Emmitsburg, Artillery Reserve marched from Gettysburg to Littlestown, 1st Cavalry Division reached Frederick, 3rd Brigade 2nd Cavalry Division moved from Hunterstown to Greenwood, 3rd Cavalry Division and 2nd Brigade 2nd Cavalry Division from Monterey via Smithburg to Boonsboro. Skirmishes at or near Smithburg, Md and Green Oak, Mercersburg, Fairfield, Greencastle, Cunningham's Cross Roads and Steven's Furnace (or Caledonia Iron Works), Pa.

July 6, 1863: Fairfield, Pa.

1st Corps marched from Gettysburg to Emmitsburg, 5th Corps marched from Marsh Run to Moritz's Crossroads, 6th Corps marched from Fairfield to Emmitsburg except the 3rd Brigade 2nd Division which, in conjunction with 1st Brigade 2nd Cavalry Division, was left at Fairfield to pursue the enemy, 11th Corps marched from Rock Creek to Emmitsburg.

1st Cavalry Division marched from Frederick to Williamsport and then back to Jones' Crossroads, 3rd Cavalry Division and 2nd Brigade 2nd Cavalry Division from Boonsboro via Hagerstown and Williamsport to Jones' Crossroads, 1st Brigade 2nd Cavalry Division from Emmitsburg to Fairfield, 3rd Brigade 2nd Cavalry Division from Greenwood to Marion.

continued

ARMY OF THE POTOMAC
Itinerary Tablets (cont.)

<u>July 7, 1863</u>:   Two Taverns, Pa.

Headquarters Army Of The Potomac moved from Gettysburg to Frederick, 1st Corps marched from Emmitsburg to Hamburg, 2nd Corps from Two Taverns to Taneytown, 3rd Corps from Gettysburg via Emmitsburg to Mechanicstown, 5th Corps from Moritz's Crossroads via Emmitsburg to Utica, 6th Corps from Emmitsburg to Mountain Pass near Hamburg, 11th Corps from Emmitsburg to Middletown, 12th Corps from Littlestown to Walkersville, Artillery Reserve from Littlestown to Woodsboro. 1st and 3rd Cavalry Divisions and 2nd Brigade 2nd Cavalry Division from Jones' Crossroads to Boonsboro, 3rd Brigade 2nd Cavalry Division en route Chambersburg to Middletown, 1st Brigade 2nd Cavalry Division and 3rd Brigade 2nd Division 6th Corps from Fairfield to Waynesboro.

ITINERARY TABLETS
ARMY OF NORTHERN VIRGINIA
June 26th To July 5th, 1863

Itinerary Tablets describing the movements of the Confederate Army Of Northern Virginia to and from the Battlefield of Gettysburg, were erected on West Confederate Avenue at the site of the North Carolina State Memorial. Although the tablets are no longer on exhibition, the inscriptions on them are listed below.

June 26, 1863:   Headquarters of the Army with Hood's Division Longstreet's Corps crossed the Potomac at Williamsport, Md. and marched to Greencastle, Pa. McLaws' Division Longstreet's Corps crossed the river and encamped near Williamsport. Pickett's Division Longstreet's Corps with the Reserve Artillery marched through Hagerstown to Greencastle. Rodes' and Johnson's Divisions Ewell's Corps with Jenkins' Cavalry Brigade were on the road from Chambersburg to Carlisle, Pa. Early's Division Ewell's Corps with French's 17th Virginia Cavalry marched from Greenwood via Cashtown to Mummasburg. The advance cavalry had a skirmish with the 26th Pennsylvania Militia Infantry. Gordon's Brigade Early's Division marched to Gettysburg, holding a short time in the town. Anderson's Division Hill's Corps marched from Hagerstown and encamped two miles north of Greencastle.

Hampton's, Chambliss's and Fitz Lee's Brigades Stuart's Cavalry Division marched from Buckland via Brentsville to near Wolf Run Shoals on the Occoquan River, Virginia.

Robertson's and Jones' Brigades of Stuart's Cavalry Division guarding gaps in lower Blue Ridge.

June 27, 1863:   Headquarters of the Army moved from Greencastle to Chambersburg, Pa. Rodes' and Johnson's Divisions Ewell's Corps arrived at Carlisle. Early's Division marched from Mummasburg via Hunterstown, New Chester and Hampton to Berlin. Gordon's Brigade Early's Division reached York. McLaws' Division Longstreet's Corps marched from Williamsport via Hagerstown, Middleburg and Greencastle to five miles south of Chambersburg. Hood's Division reached Chambersburg and Pickett's Division marched three miles further north. Anderson's Division Hill's Corps marched via Chambersburg to Fayettesville, Pa; Heth's and Pender's Divisions Hill's Corps to the same place by other routes. Hampton's, Chambliss's and Fitz Lee's Brigades of Stuart's Cavalry Division marched from Wolf Run Shoals on Occoquan River via Fairfax Station, Annandale and Dranesville, Virginia and crossed the Potomac into Maryland below Seneca Creek.

Robertson's and Jones' Brigades Stuart's Cavalry Division remained in Virginia to guard the passes of the Blue Ridge.

June 28, 1863:   Rodes' and Johnson's Divisions Ewell's Corps were at Carlisle. Jenkins' Cavalry Brigade was sent to reconnoiter the defences of Harrisburg. Early's Division Ewell's Corps marched on through York to Wrightsville on the Susquehanna River.

Hill's Corps encamped at Fayetteville, Longstreet's Corps at or near Chambersburg.

Hampton's, Chambliss's and Fitz Lee's Brigades Stuart's Cavalry Division marched via Darnestown and Rockville, Maryland to Brookeville.

June 29, 1863:   Heth's Division Hill's Corps marched from Fayetteville to Cashtown. Pender's and Anderson's Divisions remained at Fayetteville. Johnson's Division Ewell's Corps countermarched from Carlisle to Greenville, Pa. Rodes' Division Ewell's Corps remained at Carlisle and Early's Division at York and Wrightsville.

Longstreet's Corps remained in position near Chambersburg. Three Brigades of Stuart's Cavalry Division marched through Cooksville, Sykesville and Westminster, Md. to Union Mills, Pa.

continued

ARMY OF NORTHERN VIRGINIA
Itinerary Tablets (cont.)

June 30. 1863: Heth's Division Hill's Corps at Cashtown. Pettigrew's Brigade Heth's Division marched to near Gettysburg but was recalled. Pender's Division Hill's Corps marched from Fayettesville to Cashtown. Anderson's Division Hill's Corps remained at Fayettesville.

Rodes' Division Ewell's Corps marched from Carlisle via Petersburg to Heidlersburg. Johnson's Division Ewell's Corps marched from Greenville to Scotland, Pa. Early's Division Ewell's Corps returned from York via Weiglestown and East Berlin and encamped three miles from Heidlersburg. Pickett's Division Longstreet's Corps remained at Chambersburg guarding wagon trains. McLaws' and Hood's Divisions Longstreet's Corps marched from there to Fayettesville except Law's Brigade which was sent to New Guilford.

Stuart's Cavalry Division marched from Union Mills, Md. via Hanover to Jefferson and had a fight at Hanover, Pa. with Kilpatrick's 3rd Division.

July 1, 1863: Heth's and Pender's Divisions Hill's Corps marched from Cashtown to Gettysburg. Anderson's Division Hill's Corps marched from Fayettesville via Cashtown to near Gettysburg.

Rodes' Division Hill's Corps marched from Heidlersburg via Middletown to Gettysburg; Early's Division Ewell's Corps to Heidlersburg, and thence via the direct road to Gettysburg; Johnson's Division Ewell's Corps from Scotland via Cashtown to Gettysburg.

Pickett's Division Longstreet's Corps remained with the wagon train at Chambersburg. McLaws' and Hood's Divisions Longstreet's Corps, except Law's Brigade on outpost duty at New Guilford, marched from Fayetteville to Marsh Creek within four miles of Gettysburg.

Stuart's Cavalry Division marched from Jefferson via Dover and Dillsburg to Carlisle.

Robertson's and Jones' Brigades of Cavalry crossed the Potomac at Williamsport and marched to Greencastle, Pa.

July 2, 1863: McLaws' and Hood's Divisions Longstreet's Corps marched from Marsh Creek to the field of Gettysburg. Law's Brigade Hood's Division marched from New Guilford to Gettysburg, arriving about noon. Pickett's Division Longstreet's Corps marched from Chambersburg and arrived in the vicinity of Gettysburg soon after sunset.

Stuart's Cavalry Division marched from Carlisle via Hunterstown to near Gettysburg. Hampton's Cavalry Brigade, being in front, had an engagement with Union Cavalry in the evening at Hunterstown, Pa. Robertson's and Jones' Brigades Stuart's Cavalry Division marched from Greencastle to Chambersburg.

July 3, 1863: Pickett's Division Longstreet's Corps arrived on the field early in the morning.
Robertson's and Jones' Brigades Stuart's Cavalry Division marched from Chambersburg via Cashtown and Fairfield to a position on the right flank of the Confederate Army. Jones' Brigade had a severe fight with the 6th United States Cavalry near Fairfield, Pa.

Imboden's Brigade of mounted infantry reached the field at noon.

July 4, 1863: Ewell's Corps marched before dawn from the base of Culp's Hill and the streets of Gettysburg to Seminary Ridge and remained in position on that ridge throughout the day. Soon after dark Hill's Corps withdrew and began the march via Fairfield and Waynesboro on the Hagerstown Road.

Pickett's and McLaw's Divisions Longstreet's Corps followed during the night.

continued

~ Gettysburg Battlefield Monuments, Locations & Inscriptions ~

ARMY OF NORTHERN VIRGINIA
Itinerary Tablets (cont.)

July 5, 1863: The Army on the march to the Potomac. Hill's Corps had the advance, Longstreet's the center, Ewell's the rear; Hood's Division Longstreet's Corps started after sunrise. Early's Division Ewell's Corps started near noon and formed the rear guard.

Fitz Lee's and Hampton's Brigades of Cavalry Stuart's Cavalry Division, the latter under Colonel Baker, marched via Cashtown and Greenwood enroute to Williamsport. Chambliss's and Jenkins' Brigades of Cavalry under General Stuart, marched via Emmitsburg. Robertson's and Jones' Brigades of Cavalry held the Jack Mountain passes. Imboden's Brigade of mounted infantry in charge of the wagon train, reached Greencastle in the morning and Williamsport in the afternoon.

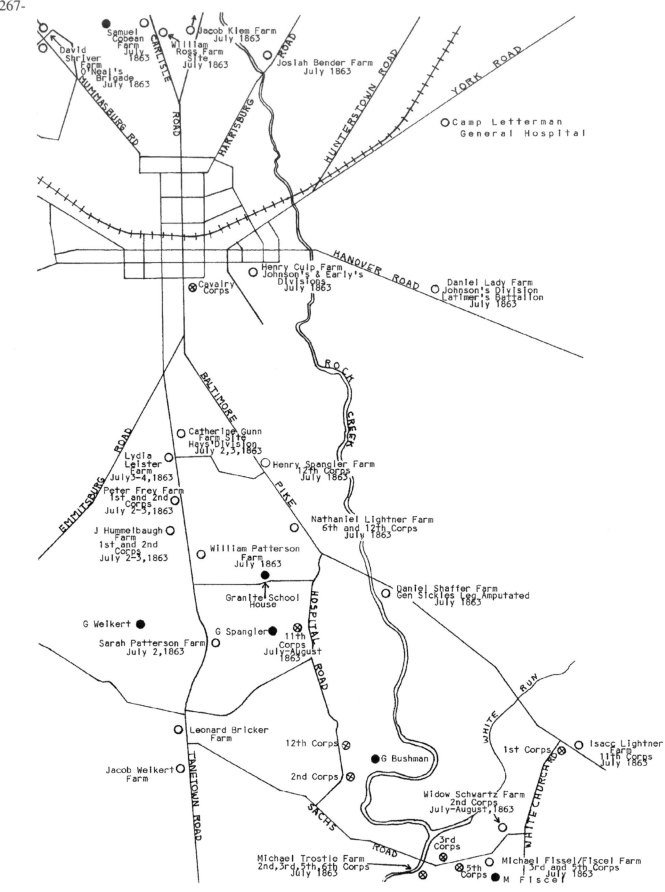

~ Gettysburg Battlefield Monuments, Locations & Inscriptions ~

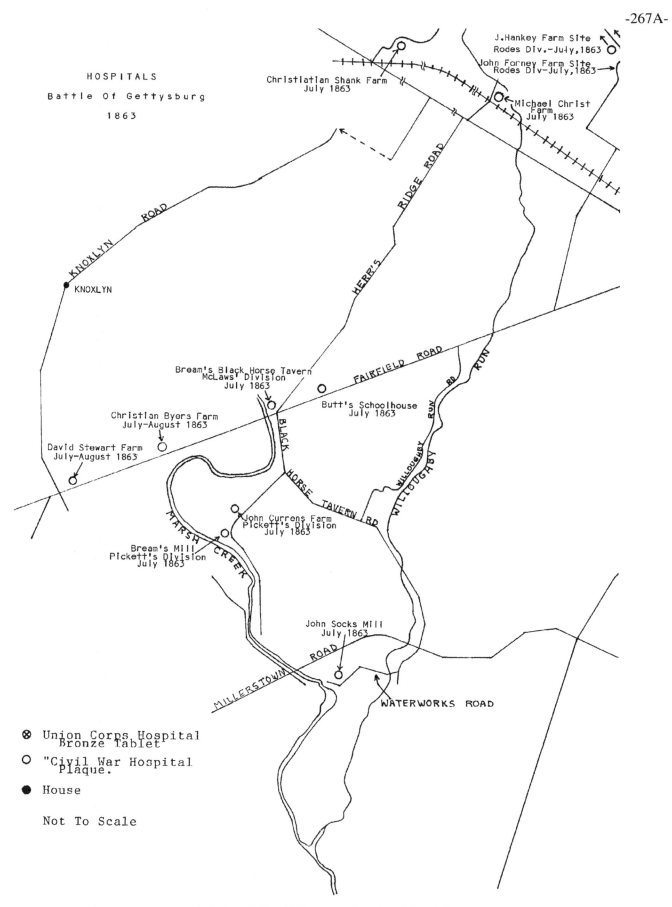

HOSPITALS
Battle Of Gettysburg
1863

J.Hankey Farm Site
Rodes Div.-July,1863
John Forney Farm Site
Rodes Div-July,1863
Michael Christ Farm July 1863
Christiatian Shank Farm
July 1863

KNOXLYN ROAD

KNOXLYN

HERR'S RIDGE ROAD

FAIRFIELD ROAD

Bream's Black Horse Tavern
McLaws' Division
July 1863

Butt's Schoolhouse
July 1863

WILLOUGHBY RUN
RUN RD

Christian Byers Farm
July-August 1863

David Stewart Farm
July-August 1863

BLACK HORSE TAVERN RD

John Currens Farm
Pickett's Division
July 1863

MARSH CREEK

Bream's Mill
Pickett's Division
July 1863

John Socks Mill
July 1863

MILLERSTOWN ROAD

WATERWORKS ROAD

⊗ Union Corps Hospital
   Bronze Tablet

○ "Civil War Hospital
   Plaque.

● House

Not To Scale

~ Gettysburg Battlefield Monuments, Locations & Inscriptions ~

HOSPITALS
BATTLE OF GETTYSBURG

The aftermath of the Battle of Gettysburg was almost as bad as the battle itself, with care of the wounded the major problem. All public buildings were full of wounded men; it would have been unusual to find a building without wounded soldiers in it. After the armies marched away, approximately 14500 Union and 6800 Confederate wounded were left on the field, in private homes, in public buildings, even in tents.

Buildings which sheltered wounded in Gettysburg:

Old Dorm (College)	High Street School
Old Dorm (Seminary)	St. James Lutheran Church
Christ Lutheran Church	St. Francis Xavier Catholic Church
Trinity Reformed Church	Presbyterian Church
Court House	Methodist Church (later became GAR Post Number 9)

The Medical Department of the Army Of The Potomac established large tent field hospitals for the various Union Army Corps east of the Union battleline, to which wounded were being transferred from homes in Gettysburg and the surrounding country before the battle had ended. Eight Corps Hospitals and a General Hospital (Camp Letterman) were established. In 1914, Bronze Tablets were erected at the 1863 locations of these hospitals. The tablets are identified on the map on Page 267A by the symbol Ⓧ.

Army of The Potomac Medical Department

Location of Field Hospitals during The Battle of Gettysburg

1st Corps 7/1: At the Lutheran Theological Seminary and in Gettysburg.
             7/2: Near White Church on the Baltimore Pike.

2nd Corps 7/2: On the east and west sides of Rock Creek east of the Bushman House.

3rd Corps: On the Taneytown Road and soon removed to an angle formed by White Run and Rock Creek.

5th Corps 7/2: On the Taneytown Road east of Round Top.
             7 3: Near Two Taverns.

6th Corps: At the Trostle House east of Rock Creek.

11th Corps: At the G Spangler House southeast of the Granite Schoolhouse.

12th Corps: At the Bushman House near Rock Creek.

Cavalry Corps:
        At Presbyterian Church and other buildings in Gettysburg.

General Hospital:
        Camp Letterman at the Hospital Woods on the York Road.

These hospitals cared for 20,000 wounded, Union and Confederate.

Medical Director of the Army Of The Potomac: Surgeon Jonathon Letterman, US Army

Army of The Potomac Medical Department Field Hospitals 11th Corps

The Division Field Hospitals of the 11th Corps were established July 1st at the Spangler House 230 yards west of this point. Many of the wounded of this Corps were also cared for at the County Alms House, Pennsylvania College and in Gettysburg. The Division Hospitals were consolidated into a Corps Hospital about July 6th, as were all those of all the Corps and the Corps Hospitals continued in operation until the first week of August, 1863. These hospitals cared for 1400 wounded.

continued

Field Hospitals 11th Corps (continued)

Medical Director 11th Corps: Surgeon George Suckley, U S Vols.

1st Division	Surgeon Lewis C. Meyer	25th Ohio Infantry
2nd Division	Surgeon D. G. Brinton	US Volunteers
3rd Division	Surgeon W. H. Thome	US Volunteers

Medical Officer in charge of 11th Corps Hospitals: Surgeon J. A. Armstrong, 75th Pennsylvania Infantry.

Army of the Potomac Medical Department Field Hospitals 12th Corps

The Division Hospitals of the 12th Corps were located July 2nd at the Bushman House 160 yards east. These hospitals cared for about 1200 wounded and were in operation until about August 5th, 1863.

Medical Director 12th Corps: Surgeon John McNulty, U S Vols.

1st Division	Surgeon Artemus Chapel	US Volunteers
2nd Division	Surgeon John E. Herbst	US Volunteers

Medical Officer in charge of 12th Corps Hospitals: Surgeon H. Ernest Goodman, 28th Pennsylvania Infantry.

Army of the Potomac Medical Department Field Hospitals 2nd Corps

The Division Hospitals of the 2nd Corps were located July 2nd at the Granite Schoolhouse but were soon removed to Rock Creek, west of the creek 600 yards southeast of the Bushman House. They remained there until closed August 7th, 1863. These hospitals cared for 2200 Union and 952 Confederate wounded.

Medical Director 2nd Corps: Surgeon A. N. Dougherty, US Vols.

1st Division	Surgeon R. C. Stiles	US Volunteers
2nd Division	Surgeon J. F. Dyer	US Volunteers
3rd Division	Surgeon Isaac Scott	US Volunteers

Medical Officer in charge of 2nd Corps Hospitals: Surgeon J Durnelle, 106th Pennsylvania Infantry.

Army of the Potomac Medical Department Field Hospitals 3rd Corps

The Division Hospitals of the 3rd Corps were located July 2nd in houses and barns along the Taneytown Road from the Schoolhouse Road to the Mill Road. During the night they were removed to the south side of White Run 300 yards from its junction with Rock Creek. These hospitals cared for more than 2500 wounded. They were closed about August 6th, 1863.

Medical Director 3rd Corps: Surgeon Thomas Sim, US Vols.

1st Division	Surgeon J. W. Lyman	US Army
2nd Division	Asst Surgeon J. T. Calhoun	US Volunteers

Medical Officer in charge of the 3rd Corps Hospitals: Surgeon Thaddeus Hildreth, 3rd Maine Infantry.

Army of the Potomac Medical Department Field Hospitals 5th Corps

The Division Hospitals of the 5th Corps were established July 2nd at the Wiekert House and other houses near Little Round Top along the Taneytown Road. During the night they were moved across Rock Creek and located as follows:

1st Division	South of White Run on the Fiscel Farm
2nd Division	100 rods south of White Run near the Clapsaddle House
3rd Division	1/2 mile west of Two Taverns and near the Pike

These hospitals cared for 1400 wounded and remained in operation until August 2nd, 1863.

Medical Director 5th Corps: Surgeon John J. Milhau, US Army.

1st Division	Surgeon Edward Shippen	US Volunteers
2nd Division	Asst. Surgeon Clinton Wagner	US Army
3rd Division	Surgeon Lewis W. Read	US Volunteers

Medical Director in charge of the Corps Hospitals: Surgeon A. M. Clark, US Volunteers

continued

HOSPITALS

BATTLE OF GETTYSBURG (continued)

Army of the Potomac Medical Department Field Hospitals 6th Corps The Division Hospitals of the 6th Corps were established July 2nd near the Trostle House east of Rock Creek and 200 yards southwest of this point. These hospitals cared for 315 wounded.

Medical Director 6th Corps: Surgeon Charles O'Leary, US Volunteers

1st Division	Surgeon E. F. Taylor	1st New Jersey Infantry
2nd Division	Surgeon S. J. Allen	4th Vermont Infantry
3rd Division	Surgeon S. A. Hollman	7th Mass Infantry

Medical Officer in charge of 6th Corps Hospitals: Surgeon C. H. Chamberlain, US Volunteers.

Army of the Potomac Medical Department Field Hospitals 1st Corps The Division Field Hospitals of the 1st Corps were located July 1st at the Lutheran Theological Seminary, the Pennsylvania College, the Courthouse, the Lutheran Church and other churches and buildings in Gettysburg. When these fell into the hands of the Confederates, the Chief Medical Officers remained with the wounded. July 2nd, hospitals were established near White Church on the Baltimore Pike. These hospitals cared for 2379 wounded.

Medical Director 1st Corps: Surgeon J. T. Heard, US Volunteers

1st Division	Surgeon G. W. New	7th Indiana Infantry
2nd Division	Surgeon G. J. Nordquist	83rd New York Infantry
3rd Division	Surgeon W. T. Humphrey	149th Pa. Infantry

Medical Officer in charge of 1st Corps Hospitals: Surgeon A. J. Ward, 2nd Wisconsin Infantry

Army of the Potomac Medical Department Field Hospitals Cavalry Corps The Hospitals of the 1st Division Cavalry Corps were located June 30th in this church and other nearby buildings and fell into the hands of the Confederates on the evening of July 1st. The wounded of the Cavalry Commands were later cared for here and in the hospitals of the Infantry Divisions.

Medical Director Cavalry Corps: Surgeon G. L. Pancoast, US Volunteers

1st Division	Surgeon Abner Hard	6th Illinois Cavalry
2nd Division	Surgeon W. W. Phillips	1st New Jersey Cavalry
3rd Division	Surgeon Henry Capeheart	1st West Va. Cavalry

Medical Officer in charge of the Cavalry Corps Hospitals: Surgeon W. H. Rulison, 9th New York Cavalry

McPherson Barn A bronze tablet on the north wall of the barn carries the following inscription:

This barn was used as a hospital and sheltered
the wounded of the Union and Confederate Armies.

The eight Union Corps hospitals were discontinued during the first week in August and their remaining wounded moved to Camp Letterman General Hospital. By November, all wounded men had been discharged and sent home or to hospitals in other cities with the exception of a very few who remained in Gettysburg homes.

Camp Letterman was closed in November of 1863.

continued

CONFEDERATE WOUNDED

Confederate wounded were cared for in Gettysburg in private homes, in Pennsylvania College and in Lutheran Seminary buildings. Outside Gettysburg, nine Confederate Division hospitals were located on farms west, north and northeast of the town. Their locations were as follows:

Hill's Corps:
Pender's Division	Cashtown
Heth's Division	Old Dorm (Pennsylvania College) and also two miles west where the road leads off to Hereter's Mill.
Anderson's Division	On Fairfield Road two miles west of Gettysburg.

Ewell's Corps:
Early's Division	Shriver Farm 1 1/2 miles out the Mummasburg Road.
Johnson's Division	Hunterstown Road and Fairfield Rd. near Fairfield.
Rodes' Division	On the Newville, Carlisle and Mummasburg Roads north and northeast of Gettysburg.

Longstreet's Corps:
Pickett's Division	Bream's Mill on Marsh Creek.
Hood's Division	South side of Fairfield Road along Willoughby Run.
McLaws' Division	Black Horse Tavern on Fairfield Road.

CIVIL WAR HOSPITAL PLAQUES

The Historic Gettysburg-Adams County Society, a non-profit organization, has identified some 70 local structures as having been used as field hospitals and medical aid stations for soldiers wounded in the Battle of Gettysburg. The Society began erecting commemorative plaques at these structure sites in 1983. Much of the funding was a $5000 grant from the Hospital Association of Pennsylvania whose name and the Historic Gettysburg-Adams County Society initials appear on the plaques, along with the name of the 1863 owner of the site, the name of the Confederate or Union user of the hospital and the date of usage, if known. Plaques for Union sites are blue with white lettering; Confederate plaques are gray. All plaques include the designation "CIVIL WAR HOSPITAL".

Sites on which plaques have been erected through 1985 are identified on the map on Page 267A by the symbol "O".

THE SYMBOLS LISTED BELOW ARE USED TO IDENTIFY
THE MONUMENTS, MARKERS, TABLETS, STATUES, ETC.
WHICH ARE DRAWN ON THE MAPS IN THESE PAGES

SYMBOL	TYPE	REPRESENTING	DESCRIPTION
	Bronze Tablet	Army of The Potomac, Union Corps or Division or Brigade, Regular Army Regiment, Regular Army Artillery Battery, Volunteer Artillery Brigade.	Brigade Tablet Mounted on Square Marble base. All other Tablets are on large vertical Granite Blocks.
	Bronze Tablet	Army of Northern Virginia, Confederate Corps or Division or Brigade or Artillery Battalion	Brigade Tablet and Artillery Battalion Tablet Mounted on Round Marble base. All other Tablets are Mounted on large vertical Granite blocks.
	Iron Tablet	Union Army Battery (other than Regular Army)	Mounted on Black Iron Shaft.
	Iron Tablet	Confederate Artillery Battery	Mounted on Black Iron Shaft.
	Iron Tablet	Confederate Brigade Advanced Position	Mounted on Black Iron Shaft.
	Regimental or Battery Monument	Principal Position of Volunteer Regiment or Volunteer Artillery Battery	Usually Granite or Marble in a Great Variety of Shapes and Sizes.
⊗	Regimental Marker	Other than Principal Position of Regiment or Battery	Usually a Square Granite Marker or tablet or may be another monument.
□	Flank Marker or Company Marker	Left and/or Right Flank of Regiment or Battery or Position of a Company.	Usually a Small Square or Rectangular Granite Marker.
⊕	Army Or Corps Headquarters	Site of Headquarters of Army Commander or Corps Commander or Chief of Artillery	Cannon Barrel Mounted Vertically on Stone, Granite or Marble Base.
	State Monument	Monument Erected by Union or Confederate State.	
○	Statue	Standing or Equestrian	Bronze Sculpture
●	Building	House, Barn or other Structure	Identified by Owner's Name.
•	Miscellaneous Marker	Marker or Inscription of a type not listed above	Granite or Metal Marker.

*Asterisk   Used whenever a Division or Brigade or Regiment or Battery has more than one Monument or Marker.   Check the Index for other Monument or Marker.

GETTYSBURG CAMPAIGN TABLETS

The Pennsylvania Historical and Museum Commission erected 29 iron tablets at roadside points in Adams, Cumberland, Franklin, Fulton and York Counties, which describe important movements of the Union and Confederate Armies during the Confederate invasion of Pennsylvania in June and July of 1863. The tablets are blue with gold lettering.

Tablets A, B, C, D, F and K trace the movements of General Ewell's 2nd Confederate Corps (mainly General Rodes' Divisionand General Jenkins Cavalry Brigade), from Hagerstown, Md. to near Harrisburg. Tablet 0 describes General Jenkins farthest advance position. Tablets R, S and X trace General Rodes' advance to Gettysburg.

Tablets E, H and L trace General Early's Division of Ewell's Corps from Waynesboro via Mummasburg, Hunterstown, Weiglestown and Hampton to York and York Haven. Tablet T describes Early's return via Heidlersburg to Gettysburg.

Tablets l, J, M and N trace General Gordon's Brigade of Early's Division from Gettysburg to Hanover, York and Wrightsville.

Tablets Q and Y trace General Stuart's Confederate Cavalry Division from Hanover to Carlisle via Dover and Dillsburg and then to Gettysburg. Tablet BB explains Stuart's attempt to flank the Army Of The Potomac on the afternoon of July 3rd.

Tablets G, P and V trace General Hill's Corps fromChambersburg through Cashtown to Gettysburg.

Tablets U, W and Z trace the routes of the various Union Army Corps to Gettysburg. Tablet AA describes General Meade's ride to Gettysburg on the night of July 1st.

Tablet CC marks the beginning of the Confederate retreat from Gettysburg to Virginia.

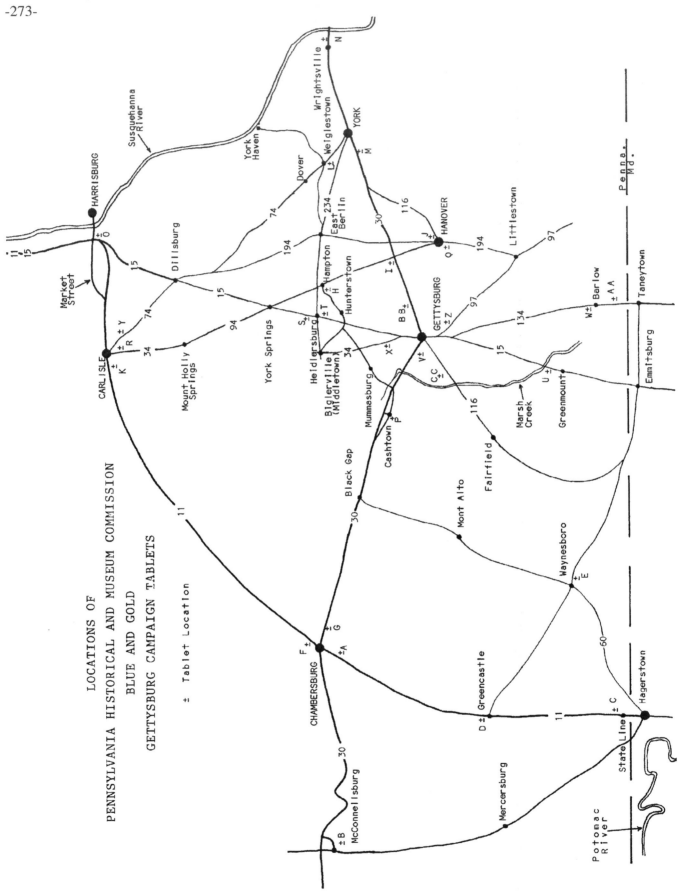

LOCATIONS OF
PENNSYLVANIA HISTORICAL AND MUSEUM COMMISSION
BLUE AND GOLD
GETTYSBURG CAMPAIGN TABLETS

± Tablet Location

~ Gettysburg Battlefield Monuments, Locations & Inscriptions ~

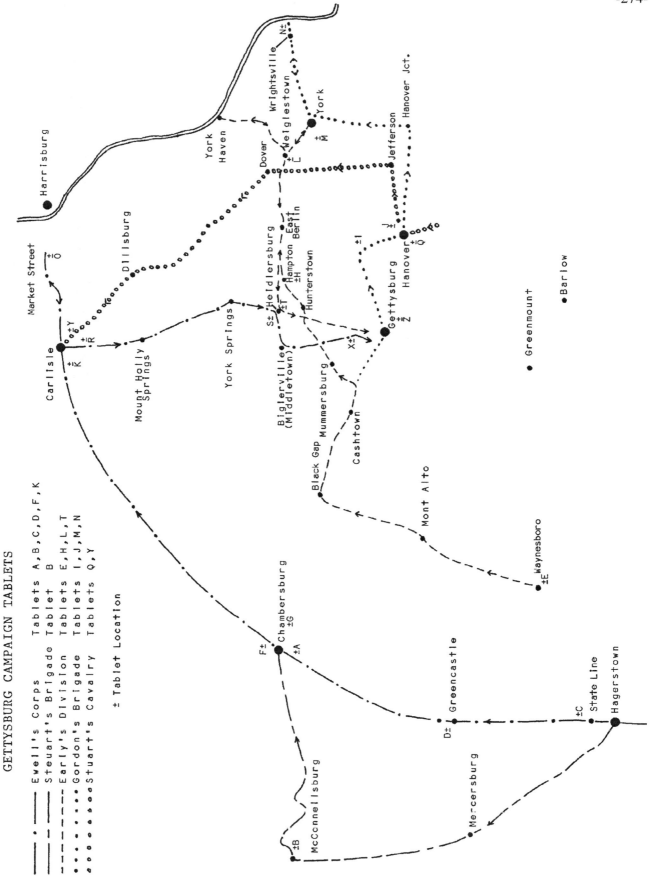

~ Gettysburg Battlefield Monuments, Locations & Inscriptions ~

GETTYSBURG CAMPAIGN TABLETS

The 29 Gettysburg Campaign Tablets are listed below in alphabetical order beginning with Tablet A, which describes General Jenkins' cavalry raid on Chambersburg on June 15th, and ending with Tablet CC, which describes the beginning of the Confederate retreat on July 4th.

Tablet A   Franklin County
U.S. Route 11, south of Chambersburg
General A. G. Jenkins' Southern Cavalry raided Chambersburg June 15-17, 1863, prior to the main invasion, and later led the invading army June 22-24. General R. E. Lee entered Chambersburg on June 26.

Tablet B   Fulton County
Old U.S. Route 30, in McConnellsburg
Three times occupied by Southern invaders, chiefly cavalry: June 19, 1863 by General A. G. Jenkins, June 25-26 by General G. H. Steuart, and June 29 after a brief clash with Union troops by Gen. J. D. Imboden.

Tablet C   Franklin County
U.S. Route 11, one mile north of State Line
Over this route, Confederate General R. S. Ewell's 2nd Army Corps led Lee's invading forces on June 22, 1863. Next day General Jubal Early under Ewell's command entered the State to the east near Waynesboro.

Tablet D   Franklin County
U.S. Route 11, slightly north of Greencastle
Here on June 22, 1863, the 1st New York Cavalry attacked the Southern advance force of cavalry under General A. G. Jenkins. Here died the first Union soldier killed in action in Pennsylvania, Corporal William H. Rihl of Philadelphia, serving in a Pennsylvania unit assigned to the New York Regiment.

Tablet E   Franklin County
Waynesboro, Pa., Route 16, East Shopping Mall
General Jubal Early's Confederate troops occupied Waynesboro June 23, 1863. Next day they marched by Mont Alto to Greenwood (or Black Gap) where, June 25, they were ordered by General Ewell to march to York.

Tablet F   Franklin County
U.S. Route 11, north of Chambersburg
On June 26, 1863 General R. S. Ewell, with orders to take Harrisburg, marched his army by this road toward Carlisle, which he reached next day. On June 29 he was ordered to rejoin Lee's Army at Cashtown.

Tablet G   Franklin County
U.S. Route 30, east of Chambersburg
General Robert E. Lee reached Chambersburg June 26, 1863. Hearing June 28, that Union troops under General Joseph Hooker had crossed the Potomac to Frederick, he decided to unite his forces at Cashtown and left the city by this road.

Tablet H   Adams County
Hampton, PA, Route 394 west of (route) PA 94
General Jubal Early's Confederate Army, marching by Mummasburg and Hunterstown, passed here June 27, 1863 to York. Returning June 30, they passed a little to the north, toward Heidlersburg.
(Note: This tablet was not in place in May 1986)

Tablet I   Adams County
Cross Keys at junction of US 30 and PA 94
Part of General Early's Confederate Army under General John B. Gordon, passed here June 27, 1863 to York. Early's main force followed a parallel route through Hampton and East Berlin. Both entered York the following day. (Note: There are two identical tablets, both on Route 30, one west of PA 94 and the other east of PA 94.)

continued

GETTYSBURG CAMPAIGN TABLETS
(continued)

Tablet J   York County
PA 116 in Hanover (east side of town)
Men of General Early's Confederate Army, detatched by General Gordon to destroy a bridge at Hanover Junction, passed through Hanover by this route June 27, 1863. This work done, the detatchment rejoined General Gordon west of York.

Tablet K   Cumberland County
Walnut Bottom Rd., 1/2 mile SW of Carlisle
June 27, 1863 General Ewell's Confederate Army, marching over this road toward Harrisburg, reached Carlisle. Jenkins' Cavalry went on to reconnoiter. On June 29 Lee ordered Ewell to join the main army at Cashtown.

Tablet L   York County
Weigelstown, off PA 74
June 28, 1863 General Jubal Early's Confederates reached York by this route. Here Early sent Colonel French to York Haven to burn bridges. Ordered next day to rejoin Lee's Army, Early returned over this road June 30.
(Note: Not in place August 1986)

Tablet M   York County
PA Route 462, west of York
June 28, 1863 Confederate General Gordon's Brigade of Early's Division followed this route through York to Wrightsville. Early's main force remained here until June 30, when it left to rejoin Lee's Army.

Tablet N   York County
U.S.Route 30 at Susquehanna River Bridge
Confederate troops sent from York by General Early to cross the river and march on Harrisburg, reached here June 28, 1863. U.S.Militia withdrew, firing the bridge and barring any Southern advance beyond the river.

Tablet O   Cumberland County
Camp Hill, Market Street, east of US 11
Farthest advance of a body of Confederate troops toward Harrisburg. Southern units under General A. G. Jenkins of Ewell's Corps reached Oyster Point on June 28, 1863. On the next day, defending militia faced them here in a skirmish in which both sides suffered casualties.

Tablet P   Adams County
Cashtown Inn
Crossing South Mountain from Chambersburg, General Hill's Corps of Lee's Army assembled here on June 29-30, 1863. On July 1, his advance guard moved up from near Marsh Creek and met Union troops west of Gettysburg.

Tablet Q   York County
PA 194, south of Hanover
On June 30, 1863 General J. Kilpatrick's Union Cavalry, hunting General J. E. B. Stuart's Cavalry, were attacked here by Stuart. Repulsed, Stuart tried to join Early. Finding him gone, he marched to Carlisle, failing to reach Gettysburg until July 2.

Tablet R   Cumberland County
PA 34, south of Carlisle
June 30, 1863, General Ewell's Southern Army, ordered to retire from Carlisle and rejoin Lee's Army, marched over this road to Mount Holly Springs, York Springs and Heidlersburg, where they camped for the night.

continued

GETTYSBURG CAMPAIGN TABLETS
(continued)

Tablet S   Adams County
Old U.S. Route 15, just north of PA Route 234
General Rodes' Confederate troops, returning from Carlisle to join Lee's Army, camped here the night of June 30. The next morning, July 1, they marched west toward Biglerville, then known as Middletown.

Tablet T   Adams County
Old U.S. Route 15, just south of PA Route 234
General Early's Confederate troops marching from York to join Lee's Army, camped June 30 three miles to the east. Arriving here next morning, they turned south toward Gettysburg on orders of General Ewell.

Tablet U   Adams County
Old U.S. Route 30, south of Greenmount & Marsh Creek
The Union Army 1st Corps camped here June 30, 1863 on the way to Gettysburg. Followed by the 11th and 3rd Corps, they marched next morning to relieve Buford's Cavalry, already in action west of the town. (Note: This tablet was not in place in May 1986.)

Tablet V   Adams County
U.S. Route 30, west of Gettysburg
The Battle of Gettysburg began here the morning of July 1, 1863, when Union Cavalry scouts under General Buford met General Hill's Army advancing from the west. Arrival of General Ewell's Army that afternoon drove Union troops to south of the town.

Tablet W   Adams County
PA Route 34, north of Barlow
The Union Army 11th Corps, crossing from the Emmitsburg Road, July 1, 1863, turned north here toward Gettysburg. The Union 2nd Corps camped near here on the night of July 1. (Note: Missing in May 1986.)

Tablet X   Adams County
PA Route 34, three miles north of Gettysburg
General Rodes' Confederate troops marched down this road July 1, 1863 on their way from Carlisle. At this point they turned right along the ridge to Oak Hill to attack the Union flank.

Tablet Y   Cumberland County
PA Route 74 east of Carlisle
General J. E. B. Stuart's Southern Cavalry arrived July 1, 1863, by Dover and Dillsburg. Finding Ewell had left the day before, Stuart burned the U.S. Barracks and left for Gettysburg, where the battle had begun.

Tablet Z   Adams County
U.S. Route 140, two miles southeast of Gettysburg
The Union Army 12th Corps arrived here the afternoon of July 1, 1863, and later moved into battle line on Culp's Hill. On July 2, the 6th Corps arrived by this same road and the 5th Corps by the Hanover Road.

Tablet AA   Adams County
PA Route 13, north of the state line
General George G. Meade, who had replaced Hooker as Union Commander June 28, 1863, traveled this road from Taneytown to Gettysburg the night of July 1. He made his headquarters just south of Gettysburg.

Tablet BB   Adams County
U.S. Route 30, two miles east of Gettysburg
General J. E. B. Stuart's Cavalry moved from north of Gettysburg July 3, 1863, to attack the Union rear in time with Pickett's Charge. Met by Union Cavalry a mile south of here, they were driven back again.

continued

GETTYSBURG CAMPAIGN TABLETS
(continued)

Tablet CC   Adams County
PA Route 116, west of Gettysburg
The Confederate Army the afternoon of July 4, 1863, began an orderly retreat by this road to the Potomac, which they crossed the night of July 13, after delay caused by high water.

MISCELLANEOUS MARKERS IN THE BOROUGH OF GETTYSBURG

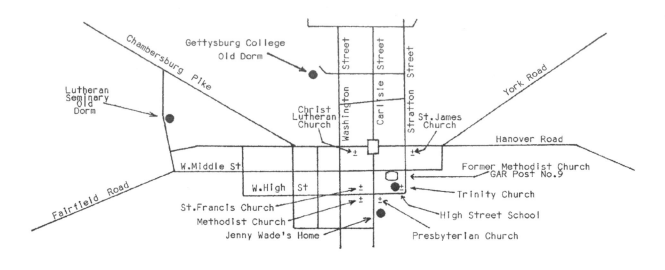

Lutheran Seminary OldDorm Bronze Tablet	This Portico is A Peace Memorial Commemorating The 50th Anniversary of the Battle of Gettysburg A.D. 1913

Sign

Oldest Standing Building
- 1832   In America For Lutheran Theological Education
- 1863   Civil War Hospital And Lookout Station
- 1961   Home of Adams County Historical Society

Gettysburg College Old Dorm Bronze Tablet

This Building Served As A Union Signal Station June 30, July 1 & 4, 1863 And As A Hospital For The Care of Both Union and Confederate July 1st And For Some Weeks Thereafter

St. James Lutheran Church (Founded 1789) Bronze Tablet

The Service Conducted Here When Local Militia Company Independent Blues, Left In Response To Lincoln's Call, April 1861. Mary Virginia Wade, Only Civilian Killed During Rattle Of Gettysburg, Confirmed Here, April 1862. Church Then On This Site Used As A Hospital July 1863. Erected 1963 by the Men's Bible Class

GAR Post No.9 (Formerly Methodist Church)

Erected By The Members Of Corporal Skelly Post No.9, Dep't. PA G.A.R. To The Memory Of Their Fallen Comrades Of Adams Co. PA. From 1861 to 1865.

Trinity United Church Of Christ Bronze Tablet

Congregation Formed	1790
1st Foundation Laid	1812
Present Church Built	1851
Civil War Hospital	1863
WW 1 "Y" Hut, Camp Colt	1918

MISCELLANEOUS MARKERS IN THE BOROUGH OF GETTYSBURG
(continued)

Christ Lutheran Church, Chaplain Howell Memorial

In memorial Reverend Horatio S. Howell, Chaplain 90th Pennsylvania Volunteers,
Was Cruelly Shot Dead On These Church Steps In The Afternoon Of July lst, 1863.
"He Delivereth Me From Mine Enemies; Yea, Thou Liftest Me Up Above
Those That Rise Up Against Me,
18 Psalms 48th Verse
"He Being Dead Yet Speaketh"
Hebrews 11th 4th.

St. Francis Church, Father Corby, Sisters of Charity

SISTERS OF CHARITY TABLET
(Left of entrance)

During The Battle Of Gettysburg
This House Of God
Became
A Hospital For Wounded Soldiers
Within Its Hallowed Walls
Brave Men Of North And South
Foes On The Field Of Battle
Through Weeks Of Pain
Were Nursed with Tender Equal Care
By The
Sisters Of Charity Of Emmitsburg

FATHER CORBY TABLET
(right of entrance)

The Pennsylvania State Council
Knights Of Columbus
In Token Of Ancestral Pride
As
American Catholic Citizens
Renovated
The Facade
Of This Historic Church
MDCCCCXXV

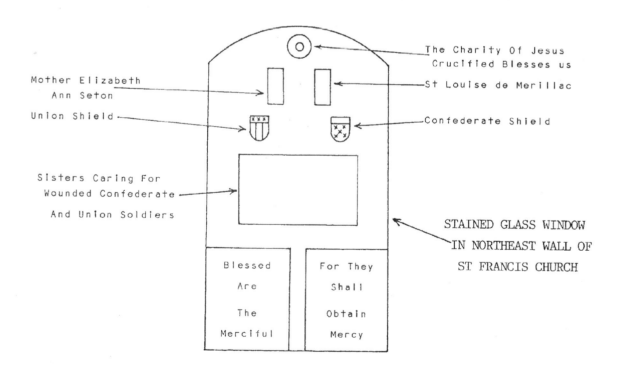

~ Gettysburg Battlefield Monuments, Locations & Inscriptions ~

MISCELLANEOUS MARKERS IN THE BOROUGH OF GETTYSBURG
(continued)

Presbyterian Church
Bronze Tablet

Abraham Lincoln Attended Services
At This Church
On November 19,1863,
The Day He Dedicated The National Cemetary
And Delivered His Gettysburg Address.
The Pew He Occupied Has Been Retained In The Sanctuary.

Dwight D. Eisenhower
Bronze Tablet

Dwight D. Eisenhower
Was A Member Of This Church
February 1, 1961 to March 28,1969.
The Pew He Occupied Has Been Retained In The Sanctuary.

Jenny Wade's Home
Bronze Tablet

Mary Virginia Wade
The Heroine Of The
Battle Of Gettysburg
Born In This House
May 21, 1863
This Tablet Was Unveiled By Her Sister
Georgia Wade McClellen May 21,1922

United Methodist Church
Bronze Tablet

John L. Burns
Citizen Hero
Patriot
Was in the Battle
Of Gettysburg
July 1st, 1863
He Joined This Church
January 28, 1866

THE SYMBOLS LISTED BELOW ARE USED TO IDENTIFY
THE MONUMENTS, MARKERS, TABLETS, STATUES, ETC.
WHICH ARE DRAWN ON THE MAPS IN THESE PAGES

SYMBOL	TYPE	REPRESENTING	DESCRIPTION
▬	Bronze Tablet	Army of The Potomac, Union Corps or Division or Brigade, Regular Army Regiment, Regular Army Artillery Battery, Volunteer Artillery Brigade.	Brigade Tablet Mounted on Square Marble base. All other Tablets are on large vertical Granite Blocks.
▯	Bronze Tablet	Army of Northern Virginia, Confederate Corps or Division or Brigade or Artillery Battalion	Brigade Tablet and Artillery Battalion Tablet Mounted on Round Marble base. All other Tablets are Mounted on large vertical Granite blocks.
●	Iron Tablet	Union Army Battery (other than Regular Army)	Mounted on Black Iron Shaft.
○	Iron Tablet	Confederate Artillery Battery	Mounted on Black Iron Shaft.
‖	Iron Tablet	Confederate Brigade Advanced Position	Mounted on Black Iron Shaft.
▯	Reginmental or Battery Monument	Principal Position of Volunteer Regiment or Volunteer Artillery Battery	Usually Granite or Marble in a Great Variety of Shapes and Sizes.
⊗	Regimental Marker	Other than Principal Position of Regiment or Battery	Usually a Square Granite Marker or tablet or may be another monument.
◻	Flank Marker or Company Marker	Left and/or Right Flank of Regiment or Battery or Position of a Coppany.	Usually a Small Square or Rectangular Granite Marker.
⊕	Army Or Corps Headquarters	Site of Headquarters of Army Commander or Corps Commander or Chief of Artillery	Cannon Barrel Mounted Vertically on Stone, Granite or Marble Base.
▮	State Monument	Monument Erected by Union or Confederate State.	
○	Statue	Standing or Equestrian	Bronze Sculpture
●	Building	House, Barn or other Structure	Identified by Owner's Name.
•	Miscellaneous Marker	Marker or Inscription of a type not listed above	Granite or Metal Marker.

*Asterisk   Used whenever a Division or Brigade or Regiment or Battery has more than one Monument or Marker.   Check the Index for other Monument or Marker.

~ Gettysburg Battlefield Monuments, Locations & Inscriptions ~

INDEX

INDEX

INDEX

INDEX

INDEX

INDEX

INDEX

INDEX

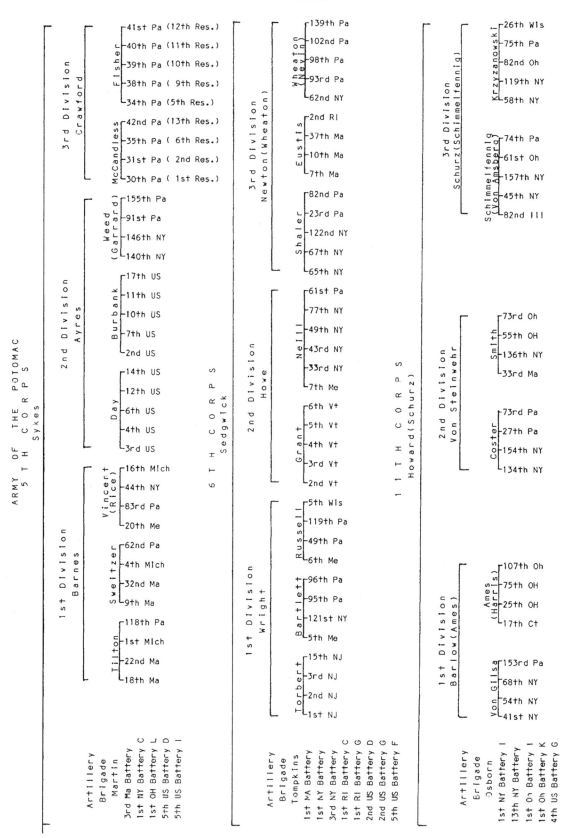

ARMY OF THE POTOMAC

5TH CORPS
Sykes

3rd Division
Crawford

Fisher
- 41st Pa (12th Res.)
- 40th Pa (11th Res.)
- 39th Pa (10th Res.)
- 38th Pa (9th Res.)
- 34th Pa (5th Res.)

McCandless
- 42nd Pa (13th Res.)
- 35th Pa (6th Res.)
- 31st Pa (2nd Res.)
- 30th Pa (1st Res.)

2nd Division
Ayres

Weed
(Garrard)
- 155th Pa
- 91st Pa
- 146th NY
- 140th NY

Burbank
- 17th US
- 11th US
- 10th US
- 7th US
- 2nd US

Day
- 14th US
- 12th US
- 6th US
- 4th US
- 3rd US

1st Division
Barnes

Vincent
(Rice)
- 16th Mich
- 44th NY
- 83rd Pa
- 20th Me

Sweitzer
- 62nd Pa
- 4th Mich
- 32nd Ma
- 9th Ma

Tilton
- 118th Pa
- 1st Mich
- 22nd Ma
- 18th Ma

Artillery Brigade
Martin
3rd Ma Battery
1st NY Battery C
1st OH Battery L
5th US Battery D
5th US Battery I

6TH CORPS
Sedgwick

3rd Division
Newton(Wheaton)

Wheaton
Newton
- 139th Pa
- 102nd Pa
- 98th Pa
- 93rd Pa
- 62nd NY

Eustis
- 2nd RI
- 37th Ma
- 10th Ma
- 7th Ma

Shaler
- 82nd Pa
- 23rd Pa
- 122nd NY
- 67th NY
- 65th NY

2nd Division
Howe

Neill
- 61st Pa
- 77th NY
- 49th NY
- 43rd NY
- 33rd NY
- 7th Me

Grant
- 6th Vt
- 5th Vt
- 4th Vt
- 3rd Vt
- 2nd Vt

1st Division
Wright

Russell
- 5th Wis
- 119th Pa
- 49th Pa
- 6th Me

Bartlett
- 96th Pa
- 95th Pa
- 121st NY
- 5th Me

Torbert
- 15th NJ
- 3rd NJ
- 2nd NJ
- 1st NJ

Artillery Brigade
Tompkins
1st MA Battery
1st NY Battery
3rd NY Battery
1st RI Battery C
1st RI Battery G
2nd US Battery D
2nd US Battery G
5th US Battery F

11TH CORPS
Howard(Schurz)

3rd Division
Schurz(Schimmelfennig)

Krzyzanowski
- 26th Wis
- 75th Pa
- 82nd Oh
- 119th NY
- 58th NY

Schimmelfennig
(Von Amsberg)
- 74th Pa
- 61st Oh
- 157th NY
- 45th NY
- 82nd Ill

2nd Division
Von Steinwehr

Smith
- 73rd Oh
- 55th OH
- 136th NY
- 33rd Ma

Coster
- 73rd Pa
- 27th Pa
- 154th NY
- 134th NY

1st Division
Barlow(Ames)

Ames
(Harris)
- 107th Oh
- 75th OH
- 25th OH
- 17th Ct

Von Gilsa
- 153rd Pa
- 68th NY
- 54th NY
- 41st NY

Artillery Brigade
Osborn
1st NY Battery I
13th NY Battery
1st Oh Battery I
1st Oh Battery K
4th US Battery G

~ Gettysburg Battlefield Monuments, Locations & Inscriptions ~

INDEX

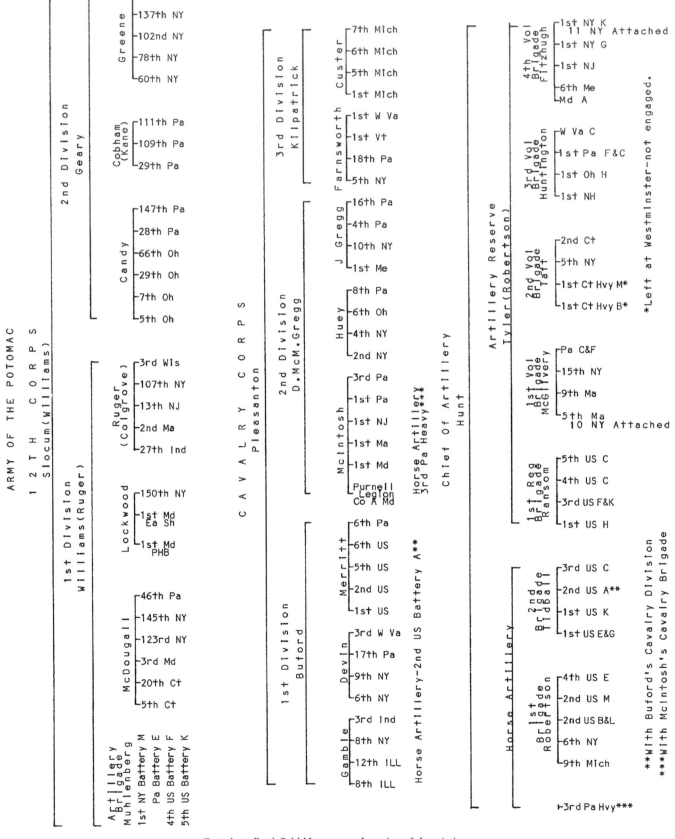

~ Gettysburg Battlefield Monuments, Locations & Inscriptions ~

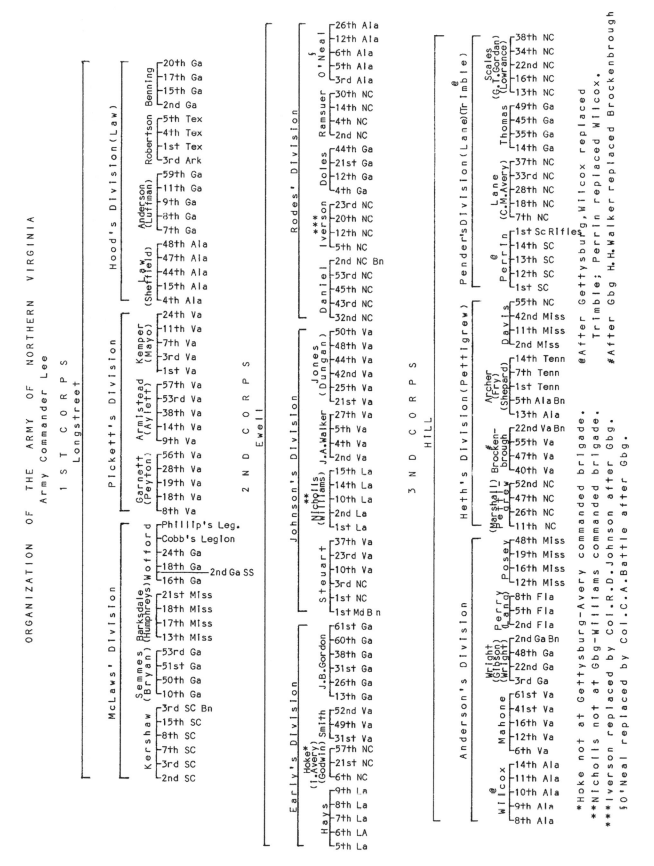

ORGANIZATION OF THE ARMY OF NORTHERN VIRGINIA
Army Commander Lee

1ST CORPS — Longstreet

McLaws' Division
- Kershaw — 2nd SC, 3rd SC, 7th SC, 8th SC, 15th SC, 3rd SC Bn
- Semmes (Bryan) — 10th Ga, 50th Ga, 51st Ga, 53rd Ga
- Barksdale (Humphreys) — 13th Miss, 17th Miss, 18th Miss, 21st Miss
- Wofford — 16th Ga, 18th Ga (2nd Ga SS), 24th Ga, Cobb's Legion, Phillip's Leg.

Pickett's Division
- Garnett (Peyton) — 8th Va, 18th Va, 19th Va, 28th Va, 56th Va
- Armistead (Aylett) — 9th Va, 14th Va, 38th Va, 53rd Va, 57th Va
- Kemper (Mayo) — 1st Va, 3rd Va, 7th Va, 11th Va, 24th Va

Hood's Division (Law)
- Law (Sheffield) — 4th Ala, 15th Ala, 44th Ala, 47th Ala, 48th Ala
- Anderson (Luffman) — 7th Ga, 8th Ga, 9th Ga, 11th Ga, 59th Ga
- Robertson — 3rd Ark, 1st Tex, 4th Tex, 5th Tex
- Benning — 2nd Ga, 15th Ga, 17th Ga, 20th Ga

2ND CORPS — Ewell

Early's Division
- Hays — 5th La, 6th LA, 7th La, 8th La, 9th La
- Hoke* (I. Avery)(Godwin) Smith — 6th NC, 21st NC, 57th NC
- Smith — 31st Va, 49th Va, 52nd Va
- J.B. Gordon — 13th Ga, 26th Ga, 31st Ga, 38th Ga, 60th Ga, 61st Ga

Johnson's Division
- Steuart — 1st Md Bn, 1st NC, 3rd NC, 10th Va, 23rd Va, 37th Va
- Nicholls** (Williams) — 1st La, 2nd La, 10th La, 14th La, 15th La
- J.A. Walker — 2nd Va, 4th Va, 5th Va, 27th Va
- Jones (Dungan) — 21st Va, 25th Va, 42nd Va, 44th Va, 48th Va, 50th Va

Rodes' Division
- Daniel — 32nd NC, 43rd NC, 45th NC, 53rd NC, 2nd NC Bn
- Iverson*** — 5th NC, 12th NC, 20th NC, 23rd NC
- Doles — 4th Ga, 12th Ga, 21st Ga, 44th Ga
- Ramsuer — 2nd NC, 4th NC, 14th NC, 30th NC
- O'Neal§ — 3rd Ala, 5th Ala, 6th Ala, 12th Ala, 26th Ala

3RD CORPS — Hill

Anderson's Division
- Wilcox@ — 8th Ala, 9th Ala, 10th Ala, 11th Ala, 14th Ala
- Mahone — 6th Va, 12th Va, 16th Va, 41st Va, 61st Va
- Wright (Gibson)(Wright) — 3rd Ga, 22nd Ga, 48th Ga, 2nd Ga Bn
- Perry (Lang) — 2nd Fla, 5th Fla, 8th Fla
- Posey — 12th Miss, 16th Miss, 19th Miss, 48th Miss

Heth's Division (Pettigrew)
- Pettigrew (Marshall) — 11th NC, 26th NC, 47th NC, 52nd NC
- Brockenbrough# — 40th Va, 47th Va, 55th Va, 22nd Va Bn
- Archer (Fry)(Shepard) — 13th Ala, 5th Ala Bn, 1st Tenn, 7th Tenn, 14th Tenn
- Davis — 2nd Miss, 11th Miss, 42nd Miss, 55th NC

Pender's Division (Lane)(Trimble)@
- Perrin@ — 1st SC, 12th SC, 13th SC, 14th SC, 1st Sc Rifles
- Lane (C.M. Avery) — 7th NC, 18th NC, 28th NC, 33rd NC, 37th NC
- Thomas — 14th Ga, 35th Ga, 45th Ga, 49th Ga
- Scales (G.T. Gordan)(Lowrance)§ — 13th NC, 16th NC, 22nd NC, 34th NC, 38th NC

*Hoke not at Gettysburg-Avery commanded brigade.
**Nicholls not at Gbg-Williams commanded brigade.
***Iverson replaced by Col. R.D. Johnson after Gbg.
§O'Neal replaced by Col. C.A. Battle after Gbg.
@After Gettysburg, Wilcox replaced Trimble; Perrin replaced Wilcox.
#After Gbg H.H. Walker replaced Brockenbrough.

INDEX

```
ARMY OF NORTHERN VIRGINIA
    CAVALRY DIVISION
        J.E.B. Stuart

            Imboden
                ┌ McClanahan's Va Battery §
                ├ Virginia Rangers
                ├ 62nd Va Infantry #
                └ 18th Va

            W.H.F. Lee (Chambliss)
                ┌ 13th Va
                ├ 10th Va
                ├ 9th Va
                └ 2nd NC

            Jones
                ┌ 11th Va
                ├ 7th Va
                └ 6th Va

            Jenkins (Ferguson)
                ┌ Jackson's Va Battery @
                ├ 36th Va Bn.
                ├ 34th Va Bn.
                ├ 17th Va
                ├ 16th Va
                └ 14th Va

            Fitz Lee
                ┌ 5th Va
                ├ 4th Va
                ├ 3rd Va
                ├ 2nd Va
                ├ 1st Va
                └ 1st Md Bn *

            Robertson
                ┌ 5th NC
                └ 4th NC

            Hampton (Baker)
                ┌ Phillip's Ga Legion
                ├ Cobb's Ga Legion
                ├ Jeff Davis Legion
                ├ 2nd SC
                ├ 1st SC
                └ 1st NC

            Horse Artillery Beckham
                ┌ Moorman's Va Battery
                ├ McGregor's Va Battery
                ├ Hart's SC Battery
                ├ W.H.Griffin's Md Battery
                ├ Chew's Va Battery
                └ Breathed's Va Battery
```

*Served with Ewell's Corps.

@Attached to Jenkins' Cavalry Brigade.

#Mounted Infantry.

§Attached to Imboden's Cavalry Brigade.

~ Gettysburg Battlefield Monuments, Locations & Inscriptions ~

ARMY OF NORTHERN VIRGINIA

Artillery Organization*

(Batteries Listed By Commanders' Names)

Chief Of Artillery Pendleton

1st Corps

Division	Battalion	Battery
McLaws	Cabell's	Manly's
		Fraser's (Furlong's)
		McCarthy's
		Carlton's (Motes)
Pickett's	Dearing's	Stribling's
		Caskie's
		Macon's
		Blount's
Hood's	Henry's	Latham's
		Bachman's
		Garden's
		Reilly's
Artillery Reserve Walton**	Alexander's	Woolfolk's (JWoolfolk)
		Jordan's
		Gilbert's
		Moody's
		Parker's
		Taylor's
	Eshleman's	Squires'
		Richardson's
		Miller's
		Norcom's (Battles)

2nd Corps

Division	Battalion	Battery
Early's	Jones'	Carrington's
		Tanner's
		Green's
		Garber's
Johnson's	Latimer's (Raine)	Dement's
		Carpenter's
		WD Brown's
		Raine's (Hardwicke)
Rodes'	TH Carter's	Reese's
		WP Carter's
		Page's
		Fry's
Artillery Reserve JT Brown	Dance's	Watson's
		Smith's
		Cunningham's
		Graham's
		CB Griffin's
	Nelson's	Kirkpatrick
		Massie's
		Milledge's

3rd Corps

Division	Battalion	Battery
Anderson's	Lane's	Ross's
		Patterson's
		Wingfield's
Heth's	Garnett's	Maurin's
		Moore's
		Lewis's
		Grandy's
Pender's	Poague's	Wyatt's
		Graham's
		Ward's
		Brooke's
Artillery Reserve Walker	McIntosh's	Rice's
		Hurt's
		Wallace's
		M Johnson's
	Pegram's	Crenshaw's***
		Marye's
		Brander's
		Zimmerman's
		McGraw's

* See Cavalry Division (Page HH) for Horse Artillery.

** Walton was officially in command of 1st Corps Artillery Reserve at Gettysburg but Longstreet put Alexander in command on July 3rd preceeding Longstreet's Assault.

*** Commanded at Gettysburg by Lt.A.B.Johnston.

INDEX

ARMY OF NORTHERN VIRGINIA
Artillery Organization*
(Battery Names And Battery Commanders' Names)
Chief Of Artillery Pendleton

3rd Corps

Division	Battalion	Battery Name	Battery Commander
Anderson	Lane Sumter Bn	Company A	Ross
Anderson	Lane Sumter Bn	Company B	Patterson
Anderson	Lane Sumter Bn	Company C	Wingfield
Heth	J.Garnett	Norfolk Lt Arty Blues	Grandy
Heth	J.Garnett	Va Arty	Lewis
Heth	J.Garnett	Huger Va Arty	Moore
Heth	J.Garnett	Donaldsonville La Arty	Grandy
Pender	Poague	Va Arty	Wyatt
Pender	Poague	NC Arty	Graham
Pender	Poague	Miss Lt Arty	Ward
Pender	Poague	Va Btry	Brooke
	McIntosh	Danville Va Arty	Rice
	McIntosh	Hardaway Ala Arty	Hurt
	McIntosh	2nd Rockbridge Va Arty	Wallace
	McIntosh	Va Btry	M Johnson
Pegram	(Brunson)	Richmond Btry	Crenshaw**
Pegram	(Brunson)	Va Arty	Marye
Pegram	(Brunson)	Va Arty	Brander
Pegram	(Brunson)	Va Arty	Zimmerman
Pegram	(Brunson)	Va Arty	McGraw

2nd Corps

Division	Battalion	Battery Name	Battery Commander
Early	Jones	Charlottesville Va Arty	Carrington
Early	Jones	Courtney Va Arty	Tanner
Early	Jones	Louisiana Guard Arty	Green
Early	Jones	Staunton Va Arty	Garber
Johnson	Latimer (Raine)	1st MD Btry	Dement
Johnson	Latimer (Raine)	Allegany Va Arty	Carpenter
Johnson	Latimer (Raine)	Chesapeake Md Arty	WD Brown
Johnson	Latimer (Raine)	Lee Va Btry	Raine
Rodes	TH Carter	Jeff Davis Ala Arty	Reese
Rodes	TH Carter	King Wm Va Arty	WP Carter
Rodes	TH Carter	Morris Va Arty	Page
Rodes	TH Carter	Orange Va Arty	Fry
Artillery Reserve	Dance	2nd Richm'd Howitzers	Watson
Artillery Reserve	Dance	3rd Richm'd Howitzers	Smith
Artillery Reserve	Dance	Powhatan Va Arty	Cunningham
Artillery Reserve	Dance	Rockbridge Va Arty	Graham
Artillery Reserve	Dance	Salem Va Arty	CB Griffin
Artillery Reserve	Nelson	Amherst Va Arty	Kirkpatrick
Artillery Reserve	Nelson	Fluvanna Va Arty	Massie
Artillery Reserve	Nelson	Georgia Btry	Milledge

1st Corps

Division	Battalion	Battery Name	Battery Commander
McLaws	Cabell	1st NC Btry A	Manly
McLaws	Cabell	Pulaski Ga Arty	Fraser
McLaws	Cabell	1st Richm'd Howitzers	McCarthy
McLaws	Cabell	Troup Ga Arty	Carlton
Pickett	Dearing	Fauquier Va Arty	Stribling
Pickett	Dearing	Hampden Va Arty	Caskie
Pickett	Dearing	Richmond Fayette Arty	Macon
Pickett	Dearing	Va Btry	Blount
Hood	Henry	Branch NC Arty	Latham
Hood	Henry	German SC Arty	Bachman
Hood	Henry	Palmetto SC Arty	Garden
Hood	Henry	Rowan NC Arty	Reilly
Artillery Reserve	Alexander	Ashland Va Arty	Woolfolk
Artillery Reserve	Alexander	Bedford Va Arty	Jordan
Artillery Reserve	Alexander	Brooks SC Arty	Gilbert
Artillery Reserve	Alexander	Madison La Lt Arty	Moody
Artillery Reserve	Alexander	Va Btry	Parker
Artillery Reserve	Alexander	Va Btry	Taylor
Artillery Reserve	Eshleman	1st Company	Squires
Artillery Reserve	Eshleman	2nd Company	Richardson
Artillery Reserve	Eshleman	3rd Company	Miller
Artillery Reserve	Eshleman	4th Company	Norcom

* See Page HH for Horse Artillery.

** Commanded at Gettysburg by Lt.A.B.Johnston.

Gettysburg Monuments added since 1997, located in the parking lot near the Visitor's Center.

Maryland
A Final Tribute

More than 3,000 Marylanders served on both sides of the conflict at the Battle of Gettysburg. They could be found in all branches of the Army from the rank of Private to Major General and on all parts of the Battlefield. Brother against brother would be their legacy particularly on the slopes of Culp's Hill. This memorial symbolizes the aftermath of that battle and the War. Brothers again. Marylanders all. The State of Maryland proudly honors its sons who fought at Gettysburg in defense of the causes they held so dear.

Delaware

The first and second Delaware Infantry Regiments arrived on the Battlefield early on July 2 and took position in the federal line along Cemetery Ridge that day. Both units distinguished themselves in fierce fighting. The first defended the Bliss Farm and the second helped to hold the Wheatfield against the Confederate attempt to turn the Federal left flank. On July 3 the two regiments played key roles in repulsing Lee's assault. They each lost nearly a quarter of their men at Gettysburg and were commended for distinguished service. Three soldiers received the Medal of Honor one for heroism under fire and two for the capture of regimental colors. On July 5 the first and second Delaware with the Army of the Potomac, left Gettysburg in pursuit of Lee's Army.

This memorial is dedicated to all Delawareans who fought at Gettysburg both Union and Confederate.

The 11th Mississippi

The 11th Mississippi Infantry Regiment, under the command of Col. Francis M. Green and Major Rueben O. Reynolds, formed west of the tree line on Seminary Ridge behind Major William Pegram's battalion of artillery and immediately south of McMillian's Woods on July 3, 1863. Shortly after 3 PM color Sgt. William O'Brien of Company C, memorialized on this monument, raised the colors and the regiment stepped forward. Although clusters of men reached stone wall near Brian's Barn, the attack was driven back with heavy loss, and the remnants of the regiment reformed in this vicinity.

Lt General James Longstreet
Commanding First Corps, Army of Northern Virginia

Soldiers of Gen. Longstreet's command held and protected the right wing of the Army July 2-4 1863. His first corps attacked and dislodged Union forces at Devils Den, the Wheatfield and the Peach Orchard on July 2. As a portion of his infantry secured the Peach Orchard, Gen. Longstreet advanced on horseback with them.

The following day, Gen. Longstreet was ordered by Gen. Robert E. Lee to coordinate an attack against the Union center on Cemetery Ridge.

On July 3, "Longstreet's assault" was repulsed with great loss after penetrating the enemy's battle line on Cemetery Ridge. During the march back to Virginia, Gen. Longstreet and his first Corps played a prominent role in protecting the retreating army.

By soldiers he is invariably spoken of as "the best fighter in the whole army". Lt. Col. Arthur J Fremantle. Her Majesty's Coldstream Guards (June 27, 1863)

About the Author

Donald William McLaughlin was born in the Bronx, New York in 1917. He spent his childhood on Long Island and eventually moved to upstate New York to work for the General Electric Corporation in the 1940's. He enlisted into WWII serving as a civil engineer in the United States Military along with his 3 brothers, Robert, James and William McLaughlin.

He married Shirley Glaeser of Pittsfield, Massachusetts in 1948 and had seven children. He was a crucial player in changing the railroads from steam to diesel in the 1940's and 50's. He retired from General Electric in 1981 and moved to Gettysburg, Pa. in 1983 to become a Licensed Battlefield Tour Guide, which he continued until 1997.

He was an avid photographer and developed his own photos. He was also an Amateur Cartographer. He published a number of articles from the 1950's - 1980's in history and train magazines. His maps and photographs are in print in *Gettysburg: Stories of Men and Monuments: As Told By Battlefield Guides* by Frederick W. Hawthorne.

He was a member of many Civil War Roundtables in the Gettysburg area for more than a decade. Beginning in 1981 he mapped out the battlefield on foot, spending over 10 years locating every single monument that he could discover and charted them in his maps. Through this work he developed the most extensive record of Gettysburg Battlefield monuments available to the public.

Breinigsville, PA USA
15 June 2010
239978BV00001B/64/P

9 781432 722876